sparks

1-30-62   5-1-123523

ULYSSES S. GRANT

Politician

ULYSSES S. GRANT, PRESIDENT

AMERICAN CLASSICS

ULYSSES S. GRANT

Politician

By
WILLIAM B. HESSELTINE

Illustrated

FREDERICK UNGAR PUBLISHING CO.
NEW YORK

To
GEORGE FORT MILTON

PREFACE

OVER Grant's tomb in New York's Riverside Park is inscribed the phrase—"Let Us Have Peace"—which marked the Civil War General's formal entrance into politics. It might well have been the prayer which accompanied his exit from the White House nine years later. In his two presidential terms, fierce political warfare supplanted and almost surpassed in bitterness the military conflict of the four preceding years. At the center of this political storm stood the hero of the war, but he was a hero no longer. Instead, the cold winds of controversy dissipated his cloud of glory and revealed a man unprepared by the experience and unendowed with the native gifts necessary for a successful political career. Historians and biographers, following closely in the traditions of Grant's political opponents, have kept alive much of the partisan criticism of his enemies and have written him down as the least worthy of the Presidents.

It has been the writer's intention to reëxamine Grant's political career impartially. The task has been rendered difficult by the almost complete lack of Grant manuscripts. Although there are scattered collections of documents relating to his military career, the years of his presidency are singularly barren in documentary remains. Grant himself was a poor writer and had but a limited correspondence with his political associates. Moreover, he kept but few letters, and these he returned to the senders in the years after his Presidency. Three volumes of "White House" letter books in the Library of Congress cover Grant's two administrations, and contain such an assortment of personal, official, and political material as to cause the suspicion that the correspondence from the White House during these years was extremely limited in both volume and scope. In contrast, the collected papers of Grant's opponents are voluminous. Numbering in their ranks the New England literary group and the editors of some of the nation's most widely read newspapers, Grant's enemies were more literate than his friends. Consciously or unconsciously they stuffed the ballot boxes of history against Grant, and the writer has essayed a recount.

Such a recount reveals that many of the more persistent charges of

Grant's stupidity and corruption were born in partisan politics and derive their validity from the political stump. On the other hand, a recount shows Grant peculiarly ignorant of the Constitution and inept in handling men. His mental endowment was not great and he filled his state papers with platitudes rather than thoughts. In his effort to reorient himself in a political world he carried over the hammering techniques which had brought him martial glory. His militant qualities of decisiveness and obstinacy which brought success on the battlefield only insured defeat in politics. Although he grew as a President, his growth was that of a party politician, and he changed from the man who would be the President of all the people in 1869 into the man who could support the Republican party in the theft of the election of 1876. As he acquired the ideology of the politician he lost the vision of the statesman, and became the "safe" representative of the more reactionary economic interests of his day.

The writer's thanks are due to a host of people who have shown an interest in his work and have aided in its completion. Dr. Thomas P. Martin of the Library of Congress, Mrs. N. H. Beauregard of the Missouri Historical Society, Mr. Oliver R. Barrett of Chicago, Col. U. S. Grant, 3rd, of Washington, D. C., and the officials of the Chicago and the Wisconsin Historical Societies' libraries, have aided his work by placing their manuscript materials at his service. President-Emeritus H. A. Garfield of Williams College kindly permitted an examination of his father's papers in the Library of Congress. To Professor Allan Nevins, editor of the series, the writer is especially grateful for many helpful criticisms. At every stage of his research the writer's wife, Katherine Hesseltine, has given valuable assistance as amanuensis, and Miss Isobel Griscom, of Chattanooga, Tennessee, has unsparingly labored to minimize the manuscript's more glaring stylistic crudities. Thanks, too, are due to Mr. George Fort Milton of Chattanooga, and Professor J. D. Hicks of the University of Wisconsin for reading and criticising the manuscript.

Madison, Wisconsin   W. B. HESSELTINE

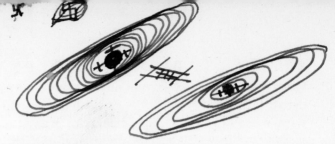

TABLE OF CONTENTS

TABLE OF CONTENTS

ILLUSTRATIONS

THE STORY of the first forty years of Ulysses S. Grant's life is one of dismal failure. Thereafter, the story is one of sudden success, of numerous rewards, and of unexpected honors. However, the forty years of adversity had no uses. They did not give rise to the twenty succeeding years of accomplishment, nor did they serve as an adequate preparation for glory. These two periods—Grant's entire career—were so neatly severed from each other by the Civil War that they might easily have been the careers of two separate individuals. Except for a few idiosyncrasies of manner and habit which Grant the general and Grant the President shared with the ante-bellum Grant, the careers were practically without connection. Had it not been for an occasional ghost of the first, rising to haunt the second, even Grant himself might have forgotten his first four decades of futile existence.

A life thus segmented could have been possible only to a man whose personality was essentially colorless. Strong personalities, possessions of men who roughhew their own destinies, seldom conform to the rules in the copybooks. Their success or failure is absolute and final. In achieving it, they mould themselves. Only a plastic person, following purblindly conventional axioms of his day, could experience both failure and success. Only a person devoid of dramatic characteristics, of dynamic force, and of any definite direction could emerge so calmly from years of adversity and as inertly proceed to years of success. The negative elements in Grant's nature very positively conditioned his career. Ambition was foreign to his makeup. He evinced no desire to hold political office or to rise beyond his appointments. Once having tasted sweets, however, he clung to them with stubborn tenacity. Essentially, Grant's was a submerged personality—an unimaginative, albeit sensitive soul which shrank from contacts with the world, and hid its sensitiveness under an impervious and taciturn shell.

To a large extent this suppressed personality was a result of parental influences. Unfortunate in his parents, neither of whom possessed characteristics which he cared to imitate, Grant inherited no abilities toward adjustment in the world from either his verbose, aggressive, and eccentric father, or his silent, pious, and shrinking mother. Rather, he was temperamentally different from each and attuned to neither.

Jesse Root Grant, the father, is variously described by his contemporaries as a shrewd Yankee and a fool. Actually, he seems to have possessed clear title to both designations. As a child he had been deserted by his ne'er-do-well father and taken into the home of Judge Todd in upper Ohio. Here he learned the trade of a tanner. After working for the father of the famed John Brown, he set up for himself at Ravenna. In a few years, he married and moved to Point Pleasant, in Clermont County, where Ulysses was born.

Although his opportunities for an education were limited, Jesse became a voracious reader. According to his son, his "thirst for education was intense," and he studied all that he read. Certain it is that he possessed an inquisitive mind and made excellent use of the information which he gleaned in disputatious argument with his neighbors. Strongly opinionated and vigorously contentious, he quarreled frequently with his associates, and found himself involved in numerous lawsuits. He was inordinately proud of his erudition and displayed his literary talents by writing letters to the newspapers. One stanza of a poem which he wrote will suffice to illustrate his literary abilities:

> "Dame Fate with me, though need not flirt,
> For I'm not poet enough to hurt!
> The World, 'tis said, owes all a living,
> What can't be bought, then, must be given;
> And though I have not much to spare,
> I can at least supply a pair—
> Or leather for a pair—of shoes,
> That you may sally forth for news.
> And when another pair you want,
> Just drop a note to
>
> J. R. GRANT."

Hannah Simpson, whom Jesse had married in June, 1821, was the antithesis of her husband in every respect. Silent and retiring where he was verbose and aggressive, reticent where he was boastful, amiable where he was contentious, she won and retained the regard of neighbors who would not tolerate Jesse. Contemporaries remembered her even temper, her unselfish kindness, and her modesty; and biographers of her son have been prone to ascribe the reticence of Ulysses to his

GRANT'S PARENTS

mother's influence.[1] Loyal without stint to her Methodist Church, she was earnestly pious. Her only extant letter, written in old age after her son had been President, is a letter of exultation that a grandson, who had long been "under conviction," had at last "been converted." [2]

For the son whom she bore on April 27, 1822, Hannah Grant gave no evidences of affection. Yet, in a formal sense, she was a good mother. She used no rod to keep young Grant from spoiling, but there is evidence that she otherwise admonished him according to the codes of the age. When childhood ailments overcame him, she administered castor oil, put him to bed, and continued about her work, trusting, according to a neighbor, "in the Lord and the boy's constitution." The neighbors could not understand this imperturbability, nor could they understand the quiet confidence in providential protection which she manifested when anxious women of the neighborhood rushed to her with the news that Ulysses was swinging on the tails of the horses in the barnlot. "Oh, 'Lyss will be all right," was her only comment. Throughout his career she maintained her indifference and seemed to take no pride in his successes. When campaign biographers, at a later date, besought her for significant incidents of his babyhood, she remembered nothing; and when fatuous admirers praised him in her presence, she silently left the room. Praise of her children, aver the biographers who knew that the mother of a great man must herself be great, she considered akin to self-praise—a thing she regarded with "unmitigated horror."

But if Ulysses suffered from a lack of solicitous affection from his mother, his father made up the deficiency. From the time of the boy's birth, Jesse enjoyed in him the pride of a self-made man in his possessions. He looked upon this ten and three-quarter pound addition to his household as a superior child, and carried the infant about in his arms to point out his extraordinary qualities to any who would look and listen. The Simpson family in solemn convocation had drawn the names of Hiram and Ulysses out of a hat and given them both to the defenceless baby. However, such an extraordinary child could not be called by the ordinary name of Hiram; so Ulysses he became. This name the neighbors soon converted into "Useless"; and the Hiram, never used, was forgotten and eventually lost in the mazes of governmental red-tape.

[1] Albert D. Richardson, *Personal History of U. S. Grant,* 68; Hamlin Garland, *Life of U. S. Grant,* 56.
[2] MS. Letter in Library of Congress.

Paternal pride, of the variety his father manifested, was only a handicap to Ulysses. In Georgetown, Ohio, where Jesse moved in the fall of 1823,[3] the father's aggressive contentiousness soon turned town ridicule on the son. Biographers of Grant have ascribed Jesse's unpopularity to his abolitionist tendencies, but he would have been obnoxious to his neighbors even if he had not flaunted his whiggery in their democratic and pro-slavery faces. Soon the children of the community, catching the spirit of their elders, transmuted adult dislike into the barbed ridicule of youth. Always they were "laying for" Ulysses, making him the butt of their jokes, and proving, to the smug satisfaction of their parents, that the intelligent boy of whom Jesse had boasted was a surpassing dolt.

With sordid glee the residents of Georgetown rolled under their tongues the story of Ulysses and his purchase of a horse. Told in many versions, the one given by Ulysses himself is probably the most accurate. The story is that, at the age of eight, Ulysses wanted a horse for which a neighbor asked twenty-five dollars. Ever eager to gratify Ulysses' wishes, Jesse told him he might have the horse, but directed him to offer less before paying the amount demanded. Delighted with the prospect, and inexperienced in the ways of the economic world, Ulysses rode to the neighbor, saying, "Papa says I may offer you twenty dollars for the colt, but if you won't take that, I am to offer twenty-two and a half, and if you won't take that to give you twenty-five." The story was of peculiar pungency in a day when the ability to dicker over a horsetrade was a social asset, and it confirmed the suspicions of the community that the lad was stupid.[4]

Not even Jesse's story of how Ulysses, sent into the woods for a load of logs and finding no one there to load his wagon, "snaked" the logs up an inclined tree-trunk and on to his wagon, could overcome the impetus which the legend of Ulysses' stupidity had received. The neighbors continued to scoff, and eventually came to believe that Ulysses was indeed stupid.[5]

Under such a shower of ridicule, many boys would have become belligerent, fighting their way into the respect of their fellows; but Ulysses, despite his sturdy build, was not pugilistically inclined. The

[3] U. S. Grant, *Personal Memoirs of General Ulysses S. Grant*, I, 24.
[4] U. S. Grant, *Memoirs*, I, 29. The story, as told later by campaign biographers, adds the clause, "but since I have seen the horse, I shall not offer more than twenty."
[5] A. D. Richardson, *Personal History of U. S. Grant*, 40–41.

victim of a persecution which he could not comprehend, he adopted a protective coloring. To the disapprobation of the community and the barbed sneers of his contemporaries, he presented a shell of stolid silence. Learning early that his actions and his words would bring mockery upon him, he became a silent and slothful youth. The silence and the sloth, palpable proof of the community opinion, served but to make him the target for more ribaldry. His fear of ridicule soon made him wary, barring him from social games, and excluding him from the play world of make-believe which would have exercised his imagination and laid the foundations of ambition. Throughout his life, Ulysses was to fear ridicule, and when, in his dying days, he wrote his *Memoirs,* the most distinct memories of his childhood were those of the heartaches caused by the jokes played upon him.

The result of public disapprobation was that Ulysses sought compensation in fields other than social. Some compensation was found in the comparative freedom which he enjoyed at home. He grew into an honest and truthful boy, working well at his chores, and causing his parents no trouble. He was seldom scolded and never whipped. Conformity to rules became easier than their violation, especially as that violation would obtain for him no sympathy from his fellows. For thus conforming, he was commended—a welcome change from the scorn he had endured. Another compensation he found in horses. These he learned to control almost as soon as he could sit astride one. Of farm work and teaming, occupations which enabled him to demonstrate his mastery over horses, the boy was fond; and Jesse, proud of his abilities, gave him a team for his own at an age when most boys were not permitted to hold the reins of a plug. Ulysses went into the teaming business for himself, hauling passengers sometimes for long miles, and making occasional trips to visit his maternal grandparents fifteen miles away.[6]

Compensation came, too, in wider travels. In an age and community where the horizon of most boys was limited to a few miles from the homestead, Ulysses soon acquired the distinction of being the best traveled boy in Georgetown. Several times he went to Cincinnati, frequently to Maysville, Kentucky, and once he drove the seventy miles to Chillicothe. Once he went to Louisville on an errand for his father.[7]

These travels, and his ability with horses, served somewhat to avert

[6] Hamlin Garland, *Life of U. S. Grant,* 13–15; U. S. Grant, *Memoirs,* I, 26–29.
[7] U. S. Grant, *Memoirs,* I, 21 ff., 29.

the hated mockery of the village boys; and, so long as he maintained his stolid and silent exterior, Ulysses avoided many heartaches. Colorless mediocrity as well as genius has its rewards, and these rewards Ulysses reaped. In school, the masters of the birch rods refrained from singling out Ulysses for either especial rewards or punishments. And Ulysses, as if to protect himself, gave no opportunity for an embarrassing distinction. He learned readily enough, but he evaded any necessity of demonstrating superior qualities; and, secure among the middle masses, he avoided the extremes of his class, although one teacher did remember him as being *somewhat* above the average in mathematics.

As Ulysses passed into adolescence, his father faced the problem of his son's future. For the work of his father's farm Ulysses showed aptitude, if not liking, but for the tannery, which was Jesse's main source of income, the boy had a positive distaste. With a less ambitious parent than Jesse, Ulysses might have become a farmer, but Jesse's pride and ambition for his son brought about a different destiny. Alert to every possibility, Jesse took advantage of a favorable opportunity to get an appointment for Ulysses at West Point.

A series of fortuitous circumstances brought about Ulysses' appointment. First, after a visit to the neighboring Mrs. Bailey, Mrs. Grant brought home the news that the Baileys' son had just been dismissed from the United States Military Academy. The Baileys, injured in pride, had told no one until Hannah Grant came to call. Realizing the news was not known in Georgetown, Jesse perceived the opportunity for quick action. Unfortunately, Jesse had quarreled with the Congressman from his district, and had to proceed by indirection. Accordingly, he wrote to Senator Thomas Morris, who without sympathy for Jesse's squabbles with Congressman T. L. Hamer, told him to write to the Congressman. Ambitious for Ulysses, Jesse swallowed his pride with what humility he could muster, and wrote to Hamer that "in consequence of a remark from Mr. Morris . . . I was induced to apply to the Department, through him, for a cadet appointment for my son, H. Ulysses. . . . I have thought it advisable to consult you on the subject, and if you have no other person in mind for the appointment, and feel willing to consent to the appointment of Ulysses, you will signify that consent to the department." [8]

Although this was hardly a frank statement of the case, Congressman

[8] Hamlin Garland, *Life of U. S. Grant*, 25–26.

Hamer was too busy with other things to bother with an investigation into the merits of the applicant. Jesse's letter, the only one making application for the place, arrived on March 3, 1839. On the next day, Hamer's term in Congress expired, and, not averse to doing a favor even for a Whig constituent, he immediately sent Ulysses' appointment to the War Department. In his haste, he made a mistake in the name of the appointee, endowing Ulysses with the middle name of Simpson, and consequently with initials of peculiar significance.[9]

In Georgetown, the news of Ulysses' luck was accorded indignation and ridicule. Fathers, whose sons might have had the appointment had they but imitated Jesse's celerity, criticized Hamer; and one, in neighborly congratulations, voiced his astonishment that Hamer "did not appoint someone with intellect enough to do credit to the district." They consoled themselves, however, with the knowledge that Ulysses was too stupid to pass the examinations.

Probably only Jesse believed that Ulysses would make a success at the Academy. Certainly Ulysses, who had a high conception of the standards of West Point, did not share the paternal confidence, but demurred at the idea of taking the examination. However, he bought an algebra, which he could not understand, in order to prepare himself for the ordeal. In the early summer, when he reluctantly departed from Georgetown, he told himself that he was going to visit the cities enroute, and would soon be home. In this way he prepared himself to bear the shock of his failure.

As bitter experience had taught him precaution, he made one other preparation to avoid humiliation. On the trunk he was taking with him, an artistic workman had formed his initials, "H.U.G." with bright tacks. Ulysses could hear himself dubbed "Hug" by his fellow cadets. Such a thought would have been frightful to any adolescent; to the sensitive Ulysses it was harrowing. He persuaded the workman to transpose the letters, and as "U.H.G." he set forth, only to find, when he arrived at the Academy, that Congressman Hamer had already changed his name. With relieved feelings, Ulysses accepted the new appellation.[10]

The career of Ulysses at West Point, as undramatic as his earlier life

---

[9] U. S. Grant, *Memoirs*, I, 32–36; A. D. Richardson, *Personal History of U. S. Grant*, 74–5.
[10] Hamlin Garland, *Life of U. S. Grant*, 31.

had been, sufficed, nevertheless, to give the lie to his Georgetown de-
tractors. More than that, it surprised Ulysses himself. Expecting to fail
the entrance examinations, he was astonished at the announcement that
he had been admitted. At each examination period he expected dismissal,
but while seventy of those who had been admitted with him were dropped
from the rolls in four years, he found himself among the thirty-nine who
remained. And yet he did not study. French he found difficult, mathematics came easily. In later years he remembered that "I never succeeded in getting squarely at either end of my class, in any one study,
during the four years. I came near it in French, artillery, infantry and
cavalry tactics, and conduct." Never reading a lesson more than once,
he found thereby time to enjoy the novels of Scott, Bulwer, and Cooper.
Although this demonstrates that he was more than a dolt, there is no
evidence that he received any intellectual stimuli from his academic
career.

In an atmosphere supercharged with patriotism, the never belligerent
Ulysses gained no enthusiasm for military life. Soon he was watching
with hopeful interest a bill in Congress which bore promise of abolishing
the Academy, and, when that failed, he looked forward to graduation,
with martial glory playing no part in his ambitionless dreams. Instead,
he hoped to be detailed as instructor in mathematics at the Academy, to
be followed by a career as professor in some "respectable" college. The
fear of failure, with its attendant ridicule, was driving him to seek
asylum, and with judgment as shrewd as when he transposed the initials
on his trunk, he perceived that the academic cloister would protect him.
Before he entered the Academy, fear of failure had grown to the
dimensions of an obsession. In his mind any turning back was a symbol
of failure. As Grant told it, he had a "superstition" which made him keep
on with any task he attempted. He relates that even when he was going
to a new place, depending upon inquiries along the road to find it, and
passed his destination, he continued until he came to a road which would
bring him in by another route.[11] This strange obsession, rather than
any military lessons, furnished the dogged determination which opened
the road to Vicksburg and flanked Lee into Richmond.

Ulysses' classmates at West Point remembered him as a quiet and
unassuming lad. Among his intimates he was regarded as frank and
generous, lazy in his studies, careless in drill, but possessed of quick

[11] Grant, *Memoirs*, I, 50.

perception, and a judgment tempered with common sense. "Uncle Sam," or Sam, names inspired by his newly acquired initials, seemed to fit him well. One cadet remembered him as an "uncle-ish" sort of boy. But the circle of his intimates was small. From the Southern society leaders he was excluded by his Western crudities. By the intellectual leaders he was generally ignored. Yet, in 1843, he was President of the Academy's only literary society.[12] Aside from the literary society, Grant was a member of the Twelve in One, a typical adolescent secret society whose mystic name was hidden behind the letters "T.I.O." Among these twelve, Rufus Ingalls, who was to be commissary-general during the war; Simon Buckner, who was to make Grant's initials signify "Unconditional Surrender"; and Fred Dent, who was to become a brother-in-law, were his closest associates. None of these, however, recognized any genius in their friend. W. B. Franklin, who led the class, remembered that Grant "was a good fellow and no dullard," but had no premonition that he would eventually serve under his classmate.[13] Grant's only achievement at West Point was in horsemanship with the record for the high jump.

The class of 1843 was considered by the faculty the poorest ever turned out by the institution. Under the system of making appointments, the best men in a class were commissioned to the engineers, the poorest to the dragoons. Grant, who stood twenty-first in the class of thirty-nine, requested appointment to the dragoons, but received an appointment as brevet second lieutenant in the Fourth Regiment of Infantry. The appointment was a tribute to his mediocrity.

Yet, despite his aspect of mediocrity, he had accomplished something. With no love for the military life and no pronounced mental ability, he had succeeded where many had failed. He returned to Georgetown with a feeling that he had vindicated his father's confidence. However, the neighbors of Jesse Grant did not recognize the success but continued to ridicule the silent son of an unpopular father. Unfortunately Jesse's ebullient pride inspired again the snickers and jeers of the neighborhood, and Hannah Grant's indifference to her offspring raised no bulwark

[12] A certificate of membership in the Dialectic Society, made out to J. A. Hardie, later a General in the Civil War, and signed by Grant as president of the society is in the possession of Col. U. S. Grant, 3d. The certificate is signed "U. H. Grant." Cf., also, Garland, *Grant*, 46. Winfield Scott Hancock was secretary of the society.

[13] For Grant's career at West Point see his *Memoirs*, I, 38–43; Richardson, *Personal History*, 90 ff.; Henry C. Deming, *Life of Ulysses S. Grant*, 34 ff.; Frank A. Burr, *A New Original and Authentic Record of the Life and Deeds of General U. S. Grant*, 185 ff.; Henry Coppée, *Life and Services of General U. S. Grant*, and Adam Badeau, *Military History of Ulysses S. Grant*.

to buffet a rising tide of scorn. Deeply hurt by the community's attitude, the young lieutenant, hoping to impress his neighbors favorably, hastened to order the regalia of an infantry officer. But with this, as with most of his bids for social approbation, the hope of impressing anyone was destined to failure. When the uniform arrived, Grant donned it, and rode proudly to Cincinnati. There a street urchin, shrewdly spotting the newness of both lieutenant and uniform, shrilled out: "Soldier, will you work? No, Sir-ee, I'll sell my shirt first." Crestfallen, he returned home, only to find that the stableman at the village tavern was strutting about with cotton stripes sewed down the seams of his blue pantaloons. "The joke was a huge one in the minds of many people," Grant remembered in later years, "but I did not appreciate it so highly." From that day, the uniform of the army made no appeal to him, and he was eventually to have a reputation for slovenliness in dress. His modesty and simplicity, later to be lauded so highly, were born of disappointment and heartache.

Late in the summer of 1843, Lieutenant Grant reported to his regiment at Jefferson Barracks in St. Louis. The sixteen companies stationed in the barracks made this the largest army post in the country, but the young lieutenant found life little different from that at West Point. There were drills and inspections, but there was no urgency to study and little zeal in discipline. Time hung heavy on the hands of a young lieutenant, and Grant might have been bored had not Fred Dent, his roommate at West Point, invited him to the family estate, "White Haven," where, after meeting his friend's seventeen-year-old sister, he became a frequent visitor. The Dent family were none too well pleased with the colorless youth, who, properly chaperoned by a younger sister, went walking with the eldest daughter.[14]

As the visits became more frequent and the walks longer, young Grant fell into difficulty. Frequently he was late to the officers' mess—a crime involving the fine of a bottle of wine. Captain Robert Buchanan, presiding officer of the mess, and a military martinet of the highest order, enforced the rules with tactless impartiality. Three times in ten days Grant's visits to White Haven brought fines upon him. On a fourth occasion, as he entered the mess hall, Buchanan roared, "Grant, you are late as usual: another bottle of wine, Sir."—The sensitive youth arose. "Mr. President," he said, "I have been fined three bottles of wine within

[14] Grant, *Memoirs*, I, 46–51.

the last ten days, and if I am fined again, I shall be obliged to repudiate."
—"Mr. Grant," roared back the martinet, "young people should be seen
and not heard, Sir." [15] Under ordinary circumstances the incident might
have been merely unpleasant; as it turned out, it was tragic. Eventually,
as a result of it, Grant left the army. Even when dying, Grant remembered the incident and bore sarcastic tribute to the unnamed Buchanan
as he recalled that "it did seem to me, in my early army days, that too
many of the older officers, when they came to command posts, made it
a study to think what orders they should publish to annoy their subordinates and render them uncomfortable. I noticed, however, a few
years later, when the Mexican war broke out, that most of this class
of officers discovered that they were possessed of disabilities which entirely unfitted them for active field service. They had the moral courage
to proclaim it, too. They were right, but they did not always give their
disease the right name."

However, Grant did not intend to remain long in the army. His pro-
fessorial ambitions were still upon him, and he wrote to the professor of
mathematics at West Point with a request for a detail as an instructor.
Awaiting the transfer, he devoted what time he could spare from White
Haven's fair attraction to a course of study. He reviewed mathematics
and read history and an occasional novel as a preparation for an academic life.[16]

/ Yet a nation's needs take precedence over a lieutenant's ambitions.
The Mexican War interfered with a potential professor's career. In May,
1844, Grant obtained leave to visit his home in Ohio. During his absence,
his regiment received orders to go to Louisiana. "I now discovered that
I was exceedingly anxious to get back to Jefferson Barracks," said
Grant; "and I understood the reason without explanation from anyone."
At the end of his furlough, reporting at St. Louis, he received orders to go
to Louisiana. But he got permission to visit White Haven before departing. Although a swollen stream crossed his path, Grant's "superstition"
against turning back stood him in good stead. He plunged through the
stream, borrowed a dry suit from a prospective brother-in-law, and
rode on to offer his hand and heart to Julia Dent. She accepted. They
would be married after the war.[17]

[15] Burr, *Life and Deeds of Grant*, 91–92.
[16] Grant, *Memoirs*, I, 51–52.
[17] *Ibid.*, I, 50–51.

Grant had little knowledge of and less interest in the political events which preceded the Mexican War. In his *Memoirs,* written after he had done much to bring about friendly relations with Mexico, he remembered that he had been "bitterly" opposed to the war, and regarded it as "one of the most unjust ever waged by a stronger against a weaker nation." There is no contemporary evidence, however, that Grant's attitude was other than one of indifference.[18] Certainly there was nothing in his conduct to indicate disapproval. He worked steadily at his assigned task as regimental quartermaster—a job of details involving neither danger nor the opportunity for heroism. Yet he participated in the fighting, riding to the front to do duty as a combatant. At Monterey he volunteered to carry a message through streets lined with snipers, and rode at breakneck speed through the enemy riflemen. At Cerro Gordo, in order to shell the enemy, he mounted a cannon in the spire of a church. For both of these acts he was commended, but in a war that gave military reputations to Lee, Jefferson Davis, and Albert Sidney Johnston, no one recognized ability in Grant. Having been transferred from Taylor's to Scott's army, he was in every battle of the war except Buena Vista. He emerged a full lieutenant—with a beard—who might be trusted with the duties of a quartermaster in charge of the mules.[19]

When the war closed, Grant received a leave of absence, and on August 22, 1848, was married at White Haven to Miss Dent, with "Pete" Longstreet serving at best man. In November, after a visit to Jesse, in Ohio, Grant took his bride to his new post at Detroit.[20] To this bride Grant remained devoted throughout his life. Besides his father, she was the first human being to show him affection. His youth had been one of suppressed emotions, and on Julia, and the four children she bore him in the next decade, Grant lavished the affection of an emotionally starved man. There is not even an intimation, in all the writing about him, that there was ever an unpleasant word between them. Only the most insanely bitter of his partisan opponents would accuse him of infidelity.

Personally, Julia was not especially attractive. A cast in her left eye caused her to squint, and marred one side of her face. Intellectually, she bore the disadvantages of middle-class women of her day. Her letters show her inept in spelling and unfamiliar with the niceties of grammar

[18] Grant, *Memoirs,* I, 53.
[19] *Ibid.,* I, 61–180; Richardson, *Personal History,* 120–127; Garland, *Life of Grant,* 65–92.
[20] Grant, *Memoirs,* I, 193.

—deficiencies she shared with her husband. But she was gifted with intuitive kindliness, and she understood her husband. She returned his affection, bore his children and cared for them devotedly, and sustained him in the dark years of his adversity. Throughout the Civil War she followed him, enduring the hardships and ofttimes the dangers of headquarters camps in order to be near him.

In the spring of 1851, three years after Grant had married, the Fourth Infantry was ordered to the Pacific coast. The order brought consternation to the Grant household, for another baby was expected, and the pay of a lieutenant would not support a family in the golden west. Reluctantly, they parted. Julia took their young son Frederick Dent to Ohio, where Ulysses Simpson, Jr., thereafter known as "Buck," was born. Grant went to the coast, hoping to send for his family as soon he could afford the cost.[21]

Of the three routes to the newly acquired Pacific coast, the one across Panama was shortest, but hardly less difficult than the long journey around the Horn or over the rugged trails of the Rockies. By Panama the troops were sent, arriving on the isthmus in the midst of the rainy season and during an epidemic of cholera. As quartermaster, it was Grant's duty to look after the baggage, and bring up the rear of the march with the sick and with such families as had dared the migration. After his regiment had departed for the rainsoaked march to the Pacific shore, Grant found himself alone with a problem. Unable to procure mules in the cholera-infested region, the contractor, hired to haul regimental supplies, was unable to transport Grant's charges. In the emergency, Grant took the initiative, made a new contract, and personally supervised, amid considerable hardships, the mountainous trip. One third of the people who were with him on the arduous journey were lost, and one seventh of his entire regiment succumbed to disease. The experience had revealed unsuspected reserves of energy and decision in the lieutenant, but no one appreciated him, and he was almost censured for departing from the rules.[22]

Assigned to Fort Vancouver, in Oregon Territory, Grant found himself in another typical army post, even less attractive than the others had been. Prices on the Pacific coast, with flour at twenty-five cents a

[21] Garland, *Grant*, 109–114; Grant, *Memoirs*, I, 193 ff.; Richardson, *Personal History*, 131.
[22] Grant, *Memoirs*, I, 194–199.

pound, potatoes at sixteen, and onions thirty-seven and a half, precluded any possibility of sending for his family. Accordingly, with Rufus Ingalls, friend of West Point days, and two other officers, he ventured into business. The four planted a crop of potatoes, dreaming of success as profiteers, but the Columbia River rose and ruined part of their crop. When they came to sell they found that everyone had been growing potatoes and the bottom had fallen out of the market. The entrepreneurs then chartered a ship and loaded it with ice for San Francisco, but when the ship neared the Golden Gate, an ice-boat from Sitka preceded it into the harbor. The pay of a lieutenant could not stand such losses; and Grant's family was as far away as ever.[23] The life of the post was monotonous. In desperation born of hopeless boredom, Grant took to drink.

Concerning Grant's drinking so much has been said that the truth is almost lost in the maze of legend. That Grant drank, there is no question; to have drunk as much as his enemies allege would have been impossible. There is evidence that Grant drank little, but that that little was of great effect. To a man of Grant's suppressed emotional nature, a little liquor could do a great deal. Under its influence, the silent shell of reticence was temporarily broken, and another personality emerged. Grant drunk was a very different person from Grant sober. To drive three horses tandem at break-neck speed while the three buggies trailed behind—it was local tradition at Fort Humboldt—would have been impossible for Grant in his sober moments. Grant drunk was so much more interesting than Grant sober, that his colorful drunken moments have been remembered while the gray haze of oblivion has obscured his years of sobriety. On the whole, there is authentic evidence for only a few sprees.[24]

In the fall of 1853, Grant was promoted to a captaincy, and ordered to Fort Humboldt in California.[25] As a captain's salary was but little better than a lieutenant's, his family could not yet be brought to the post. His duties at Fort Humboldt, although less onerous than those of a quartermaster, were more strict and distasteful. Grant continued to drink. Under ordinary circumstances the drinking would not have been

---

[23] Grant, *Memoirs*, I, 203.
[24] Richardson, *Personal History*, 148 ff. Richardson says "with his peculiar organization a little did the fatal work of a great deal." Garland collected much similar testimony from Grant's associates; cf., *Life of Grant*, 124 ff.
[25] Grant, *Memoirs*, I, 207.

noticed; but the commander of the fort was Brevet Lieutenant-Colonel Robert Buchanan, erstwhile President of the officers' mess at Jefferson Barracks. That worthy, still a martinet, remembered as clearly as Grant the incident of the fine and its protest. In consequence, when he learned of Grant's departures from sobriety, he demanded that Grant reform or resign. According to some accounts, Buchanan insisted that Grant stand a court martial or hand in his resignation to be used when next he imbibed too freely. Friends urged Grant to stand the trial, assuring him of a lesser penalty, but Grant would not have Julia know that he had been tried on such a charge. He resigned.[26]

Without money, and without definite plans, Grant started home. In San Francisco he stopped in the cheapest of lodging houses. Finally, Major Robert Anderson, the local army quartermaster, obtained money to pay a forty-dollar claim which Grant had against the government, and arranged for the Captain to travel free to Panama. In New York, Grant borrowed money from Simon Buckner for his trip to Ohio.[27]

In Ohio, Jesse received him grimly—the self-made Jesse had small sympathy with failure. With the prescience which had made him a shrewd trader and a successful man, he perceived the bitter truth that Ulysses would be a greater failure in civil life than he had been in the army. When he learned of the resignation, Jesse wrote Jefferson Davis, Secretary of War, pointing out pitifully that "I never wished him to leave the servis," and requesting that the resignation be changed to a six-months' leave to visit his family. But Davis coldly replied that Captain Grant had given no reason for his resignation, and it had been accepted. Mournfully, Jesse turned to his other sons, Orville and Simpson, saying, "West Point has ruined one of my boys for business." [28]

The next six years gave proof to Jesse's forebodings. The fear of failure, which had followed Grant from childhood, became a reality. Never a fighter against circumstances, he sank lower and lower, unable to pull himself from the slough. Colonel Dent, who would not see his daughter suffer, kept him through the first winter, and in the spring gave Julia a farm near St. Louis. During 1855, Grant built a cabin—"Hardscrabble" he called it in bitter humor—on the farm, and for

[26] Grant, *Memoirs*, I, 210; Garland, *Grant*, 127; Richardson, *Personal History*, 149.
[27] Garland, *Grant*, 128; William Henry Barnes, *Grant, A Study*, 9–10.
[28] Garland, *Grant*, 126–8.

three years they lived there. Liking farm work, Grant labored hard in
the fields and in bad weather hauled wood to peddle on the streets of
St. Louis. Again failure attended his efforts. His crops were not good;
money was not available. In 1857, following the death of Mrs. Dent,
Grant managed the larger "White Haven" farm, but he was no more of
a success with better land and equipment. In 1859, he sold his farm and
moved to St. Louis, where a cousin of the Dents had promised him a
job in a real estate house. Here too he failed: he could not collect the
rents. For a month he held a position in the custom house; but the
collector died, and Grant lost his job. He made application for a sur-
veyorship in the county, but failed to receive it because he was nominally
a Democrat. He looked longingly at a vacant mathematics professorship in Washington University, but was too aware of his own unfitness
to apply. His clothes became ragged; his shoulders drooped more than
usual; poverty found him pawning his watch the night before Christmas
in 1858 in order to bring cheer to his family, which now, with the addition of Nellie and Jesse, numbered four.[29]

These dismal days of failure were borne by Captain Grant with
that same silent stolidity which had ever masked his inner feelings.
Doubtless the realization of failure was no worse than fear of it had
been. To his army comrades, whom he occasionally met, he gave the
appearance of having deteriorated to a considerable extent, but he drank
with them, and laughed, albeit hollowly, at his misfortunes. To them
it was evident that he was not fitted to succeed in the world of business.
To his family it was equally evident. In the fall of 1859 he wrote to his
brother a letter which indicated that he could never succeed in a world
of harsh realities. "I have been postponing writing to you," he said,
"hoping to make a return for your horse; but as yet I have received
nothing for him. About two weeks ago a man spoke to me for him and
said that he would try him the next day, and if he suited give me one
hundred dollars for him. I have not seen the man since; but one week
ago Saturday he went to the stable and got the horse, saddle and bri-
dle; since which I have seen neither man nor horse. From this I presume
he must like him. The man, I understand, lives in Florisant, about twelve
miles from the city. . . . The man that has your horse is Captain Covington, owner of a row of six three story brick houses in this city; and
the probabilities are that he intends to give me an order on his agent

[29] Walter Barlow Stevens, *Grant in St. Louis, passim.*

St. Louis,......Dec. 23rd.......185 7

I this day consign to J. S. FRELIGH, at my own risk from loss or damage by thieves or fire, to sell on commission, price not limited, *1 Gold Hunting*

Detached Lever & Gold chain

on which said Freligh has advanced _Twenty two_ Dollars. And I hereby fully authorize and empower said Freligh to sell at public or private sale the above mentioned property to pay said advance—if the same is not paid to said Freligh, or these conditions renewed by paying charges, on or before *Jan 23/58*

U. S. Grant

CHRISTMAS, 1857

for the money on the first of the month, when the rents are paid. At all events, I imagine the horse is perfectly safe." [30]

∨ To brothers Orville and Simpson, managers for Jesse of a leather store in Galena, Illinois, the economic incompetence manifested in this letter must have been pitiful. At Jesse's intercession, they offered their brother a clerkship in their store. The wages were fifty dollars a month. Gratefully accepting it, Grant removed his family to Galena.

During the year in the leather store, Grant exhibited no ability to adjust himself to civil life. Consciousness of failure made him more silent than before. Clad in an army overcoat of faded blue, smoking a clay pipe, silently puttering about a store in which he could not remember the prices, Grant escaped the notice of his fellow townsmen. Scarcely three people in the town knew him. Occasionally he went collecting, spending as much for horse and buggy hire as he collected. Even as a clerk he was a failure.

In those seven years of failure Grant was too busy looking after his family to concern himself with the affairs of the nation. The bitter battles over Kansas and the virulence of the slavery controversy left him a passive spectator. In 1856, because he remembered the army's dislike of Fremont, he voted for Buchanan, and thereby became nominally a Democrat. On slavery he seems to have had no opinions. His father was bitterly anti-slavery, and his father-in-law an equally vehement supporter of the peculiar institution. On the constitutional question of the right of a State to secede, he had definite convictions. He wrote a friend in St. Louis that it would be criminal for Missouri to secede, and he made indignant remarks about Buchanan—"our present granny of an executive." Not until Lincoln had been elected and Fort Sumter fired upon did Grant take more than a passing interest in the national crisis. [31]

When Lincoln, the day after the fall of Fort Sumter, called for volunteers, Galena shared with the country an outburst of military enthusiasm. A meeting was planned to raise a company of troops, and the civic leaders looked about for a man who could tell them something of military affairs. Captain Grant, they learned, was the only citizen of the town who had an intimate acquaintance with such matters. They persuaded him to preside at the meeting, which he did awkwardly enough,

[30] M. J. Cramer, *Ulysses S. Grant, Conversations and Unpublished Letters*, 26–27.
[31] Garland, *Grant*, 152.

but his quiet seriousness impressed the enthusiastic assembly. They asked him to drill the company which was raised, and even offered him the captaincy. He refused, hoping against hope that some better offer would come to him. Perceiving the need for trained men, he hoped for a commission in the regular army. But none came, and Grant decided to apply at Springfield.

When the company he had drilled departed for the State capital to be mustered into the service, Ulysses S. Grant, carpet-bag in hand, swung on to the rear of the train enroute to fame. From the depths of failure began the road to Appomattox.

THE military history of the American Civil War is largely the story of two great leaders, Grant and Lee. Although other generals fought on the side of the Union, and statesmen spent sleepless nights worrying over the struggle, and opposing economic and social forces resisted each other, the war's most interesting and most important military events are focussed in Grant's development, his rise to power, and his success. Where Grant commanded, momentous and dramatic events were in progress; where he did not command, the war took on aspects of fiasco and defeat. Fortune, after she had frowned upon him for forty years, now beamed; and war turned the career which had been marked by hardships and heartache into one of unsurpassed success.

To the host of biographers and historians who have attempted to account for it, the reasons for this meteoric rise have proved an enigma. To many of his contemporaries, Grant's achievements were *prima facie* evidence of martial genius. To many others who came in contact with him, he was a bungler and a butcher whose fame was due to luck, not skill. Protagonists of each of these hypotheses, examining Grant's career in minute detail, have stoutly defended their preconceptions with an unending stream of books, pamphlets, and orations. Discarded generals have written memoirs proving Grant's propensities to secretiveness and malice, while commanders who retained their commands and emolument have been equally conclusive regarding their hero's kindliness and fairness. But despite the plethora of military polemics, whether Grant was the child of genius or the changeling of luck remains an unanswered question.

To look into the years of Grant's failure for an explanation of his success seems quite futile. His repressed boyhood, his lackadaisical acquisition of the rudiments of an education at West Point, his inconspicuous years in the army, and his succeeding seven years of failure apparently contributed nothing which could account for his achievements. By those years his personality was moulded into one adapted to a life of failure. At the end of the war, as at the beginning, Grant was timid, silent, and shy. These, however, were now but the superficial aspects of his personality. In the fires of war he developed aggressiveness, a willingness to take responsibility, clear judgment, and an obstinate will. These were qualities which, in times of peace, he had never tried. Whatsoever of genius shone in Grant's character was a composite of these new qualities. Good fortune placed him where he could opportunely use his abilities.

Merit, rather than luck, gave Grant his first command. Having followed the Galena company to Springfield, he sought an opportunity to enter the army. All about him petty politicians were securing commissions, but Grant lacked the politician's art. While ex-sheriffs were becoming captains, and erstwhile applicants for congressional seats were becoming colonels, Grant, for all his seven years in the "old" army, had to be content with a civilian clerkship in the office of the adjutant-general of Illinois. Here his experiences as a quartermaster were of benefit, and he trained the hastily garnered clerical force in the intricacies of filling out a War Department report. Betimes he exercised his military knowledge by drilling some of the assembling volunteers, and occasionally he mustered regiments into the State service. But though his abilities in these lines were valuable, there was no man in Springfield to recognize that Grant had usefulness beyond such routine. As a "dead-beat military man" he was regarded with suspicion, and he began to fear that the war would be over before he got into the army.

From the time of Lincoln's first call for volunteers, Grant had believed that the war would not last for more than ninety days. A few victories in the South, he was convinced, "will send the secession armies howling, and the leaders in the rebellion will flee the country." The only danger he considered real was a possible revolt of the Southern Negroes, who could "cause more destruction than any Northern man wants to see." A Northern army, he thought, might "be required in the next ninety days to suppress a Negro insurrection." [1]

But despite this idea of the war's brevity, Grant was eager to secure a commission. Losing hope of consideration in Springfield, he made a futile trip to St. Louis to see General J. C. Frémont. Then, with a staff appointment in his dreams, he went to Cincinnati to waste two days in the ante-rooms of General George B. McClellan. Returning to Springfield, he wrote to Secretary of War Cameron that he thought himself capable of handling a regiment, and that he could use a colonel's com-

[1] Cramer, *Conversations and Unpublished Letters*, 31-4.

mission. But the Secretary did not reply, and it seemed that the would-be soldier must serve his country in a paper-work war.[2]

However, the action of one of the regiments which he had mustered in spared Grant such a fate. Having elected a political colonel, the Twenty-first Illinois Volunteers grew weary of their commander's military ignorance and political oratory. When they threatened mutiny, Governor Richard Yates grew desperate. Some time before, Grant had been pointed out to the governor, and in the emergency Yates concluded that a regular army man was needed to take command and exercise army discipline. Grant gratefully accepted the appointment as colonel of the rebellious regiment.

On the day he assumed command, there took place a spectacle typical of the regimental training camps in the first enthusiastic days of the war. Brigadier-Generals John B. McClernand and John A. Logan, both prominent in Illinois politics, appeared before the regiment to induct the new colonel with florid orations. When their rounded sentences and sonorous periods came to the long-awaited close, they presented the Colonel, and the regiment settled itself to hear another verbal excoriation of the rebels. Colonel Grant stepped forward to deliver his inaugural address. "Men, go to your quarters!" was all that he said.[3]

The regiment was soon impressed by the difference between its old and new colonels. Within three weeks Grant had taught it to appreciate properly the meaning of military subordination. In less than a month after taking command, he marched it into Missouri to assist in ridding that State of bands of secessionist insurgents.

Hardly had Grant arrived in the guerilla-infested State when a piece of luck befell him. In Washington, Lincoln called upon the Illinois delegation for nominations of a new set of brigadier-generals, and Congressman Elihu B. Washburne nominated the only colonel among his constituents who had military experience. Experienced in the ways of politicians, Washburne, the oldest member in point of service in the House of Representatives, made himself by this act Grant's congressional sponsor. The situation was to prove beneficial to both.

With the appointment as brigadier-general, Grant was entitled to a staff, and soon selected as assistants a group of "deserving men." [4]

[2] Garland, *Grant*, 154 ff.; Grant, *Memoirs*, I, 222 ff.
[3] Garland, *Grant*, 169–172.
[4] Cramer, *Conversations and Letters*, 44–45.

Most deserving was a rising young lawyer of Galena whom Grant had met while delivering a package from his brother's store. John A. Rawlins had already begun to make a name for himself in politics, and had served as a Douglas elector in the campaign of 1860. He had also spoken at the Galena mass meeting over which Grant had presided. In many respects, Rawlins was a powerful force in Grant's development. His was a volatile personality. He was deep and loud of voice, excitable in manner, and given to swearing in "polysyllabic words and in iambic pentameter verse," and in times of need "his flow of oaths was satisfying to the most avid ear." [5] Understanding Grant better than any of his associates did, Rawlins assumed toward his superior an air of solicitous browbeating. On military matters, about which Rawlins knew little and understood much, he gave sound advice, and in personal affairs he assumed a guardianship which kept his commander from many pitfalls. With two such supporters as Washburne in Washington and Rawlins in the field, Grant's success was assured.

During the two months he served in Missouri, Grant grew in ability. He learned something of the movement of troops, refreshed his memory concerning the details of transportation and supply, and revealed, in his reports to his superiors, a practical common sense and balanced judgment. Acting for the most part without an immediate superior, Grant developed initiative, and obtained, chasing guerillas, a wholesome disrespect for the fighting qualities of Confederates. Although this last quality was eventually to cost him dearly, at the moment it served a good purpose in increasing his aggressiveness. When he was shifted to Cairo, late in August, 1861, Grant was ready to take responsibility. [6]

Almost immediately upon his arrival in Cairo to take command of the district of Southeast Missouri, Grant had an opportunity to exercise his newly revealed aggressiveness. At the time, events of moment were taking place in Kentucky. Proclaiming that Kentucky would be neutral in the struggle between the States, Governor Magoffin had refused to furnish volunteers upon Lincoln's call. After the manner of an experienced politician, Lincoln had bided his time and awaited an opportunity to win over the State. Had the Confederacy been equally shrewd, Kentucky's eventual secession might have resulted. But ex-Bishop

[5] Garland, *Grant*, 156.
[6] A. H. Conger, *The Rise of U. S. Grant*, 4–30; Grant, *Memoirs*, I, 249–250.

Leonidas Polk, commanding the Confederate forces in West Tennessee, was hasty in carrying the gospel of secession into the hesitant State. In his zeal, he moved his troops on to Kentucky soil. Just at that moment Grant arrived in Cairo and immediately saw the opportunity offered by this violation of the State's neutrality. Acting without instructions, he pushed up the Ohio river to Paducah, marched in his troops, and took the town before he could receive orders to delay action. To the people of the city, he announced that he was coming to save them from Polk's invasion. By his quickness of decision and his aggressiveness Kentucky neutrality was overcome and the State was saved for the Union.[7]

This sudden move, bringing some notice in its train, whetted Grant's appetite for action. By the first of November, he had about twenty thousand men in his department, and both men and commander were eager for battle. The nearest Confederates, eighteen miles down the Mississippi at Columbus, Ky., were sending supplies to Price in Missouri. General Frémont, commanding at St. Louis, ordered Grant to patrol the river to prevent such reinforcements from being sent. Consequently, Grant fitted out an expedition of three thousand men to proceed down the river to attack Belmont on the Missouri bank, opposite Columbus. On the morning of November 7, Grant's forces landed above Belmont, and drove the Confederates out of their camp. This done, the enthusiastic victors joined in a round of cheers for the Union, and amid the singing of patriotic songs proceeded to burn and pillage the Confederate camp. No one remembered to pursue the retreating Confederates, who were soon rallied by their officers and returned to drive out the invaders. About the middle of the afternoon, they managed to cut in on Grant's flanks, and the Federals were forced to take refuge, in a pell-mell retreat to their transports. The battle was no victory for the Federals, but in a few days Grant had recovered his composure sufficiently to claim it as a "complete victory." Fundamentally, it was a tribute to his aggressiveness, and from the mistakes of Belmont he was to profit much. Never again did he win a battle without following up his advantage.[8]

For several months before and after Belmont, Grant's attention was mostly devoted to routine problems of military administration over his

[7] Grant, *Memoirs*, I, 265–266; Conger, *op. cit.*, 57–60.
[8] Grant, *Memoirs*, I, 269 ff.; Conger, *op. cit.*, 81–101, and appendix; Cramer, *op. cit.*, 57–61.

division. Most persistent of the problems which he faced was that of trade with the Confederacy, carried on by a host of speculators, who had been attracted to the district by the scent of profits. In retaliation for his attempts to restrict their activities, the traders began to spread stories of Grant's drunkenness. The reasons for his leaving the old army were generally known and furnished a convenient foundation for a crop of new rumors. Newspaper correspondents, short of "copy," intimated these things to their papers. Congressman Washburne, hearing the stories, hastily wrote Rawlins for information. With becoming loyalty, Rawlins replied that Grant had been a "total abstinence man" for years before the war, and that since being in Cairo he had drunk only a few glasses of champagne. His physicians, finding him subject to dyspepsia, had recommended two glasses of beer a day, but Grant had abandoned the remedy. Each day, said Rawlins, the general made out his own reports and was in every respect dutiful and diligent.[9]

According to legend, Grant's drinking was the cause of difficulties with Major-General H. W. Halleck. On November 9, Halleck succeeded to the command of the Department of the Missouri after Lincoln removed Frémont. Himself an ex-army officer and a graduate of West Point, Halleck had followed service in the army with a successful career as a lawyer. Scholarly in his interests, he had written a treatise on military law. As an administrator he was efficient, and there is reason to suspect that much of the credit for military organization which has been given to Secretary of War Stanton should go to Halleck. But the general was blunt in his manner, harsh in his judgments, and dictatorial toward his associates. Few of his contemporaries found praise for his qualities. In his dealings with Grant, Halleck was never tactful, displaying a jealousy unbecoming to his position. Neither general liked the other, but with one exception they maintained an external appearance of cordiality.[10]

During the weeks after Belmont, while Grant was bringing order into his district, Halleck was having troubles of his own. With Missouri in ferment, Lincoln and McClellan in Washington were urging Halleck to make an advance across Kentucky and down the Cumberland river. The command of such an advance would fall upon Grant, and early

[9] Rawlins to Washburne, December 30, 1861. Washburne Mss.
[10] Conger, *Rise of U. S. Grant,* 127–129.

in January Halleck yielded to pressure and sent Grant to make a reconnaissance into Kentucky. When Grant returned to his post it was with the conviction that Fort Henry, on the Tennessee river just below the Kentucky line, could be successfully taken with a slight outlay of effort. Accordingly, he went to St. Louis to present the advantages of such a move to Halleck. Unfortunately, Halleck already knew the advantages—Lincoln had been pointing them out to him for two months —and he received the enthusiastic Grant with coolness. However, uncowed by Halleck's rebuffs, Grant returned to Cairo and persuaded Commodore Foote, commanding the gunboats on the Mississippi, to add his voice in an effort to move Halleck.

Finally, with many misgivings, the harassed commander gave the necessary orders for an expedition, and early in February Grant pushed southward to take the fort. While the muddy roads delayed the land forces, Foote's gunboats pushed on and began to shell the fort. Illequipped and poorly armed, the fort was unable to resist even the naval attack, and its garrison withdrew to Fort Donelson, twelve miles away on the Cumberland river, before Grant's forces could arrive to cut off the escape. The empty fort fell an easy victim to Grant's advancing columns.

Inspired by this easy victory, Grant immediately decided to press on to Fort Donelson. He wired Halleck of his intentions, telling him that he would attack Donelson within two days. But, as he advanced and learned something of the strength of his new objective, Grant delayed his attack until Foote's gunboats could be brought from the Tennessee to the Cumberland river. On the thirteenth of February the gunboats arrived, and Grant invested the fort. Two days of siege convinced the beleaguered Confederates that they could not hold out, and when an attempt to cut through the lines of the besieging forces proved abortive, the Confederate commander determined to surrender the South's strongest battlement. After a night's delay in which Colonel N. B. Forrest, the Confederacy's intrepid cavalryman, led several hundred of his famed "critter company" along the river banks to freedom, Simon Buckner, friend of Grant in the old army, asked his former classmate for an armistice in which to agree on terms of capitulation. "No terms except unconditional and immediate surrender can be accepted," replied Grant. "I propose to move immediately upon your works." Protesting the unchivalrous nature of this reply, Buckner surrendered fort and garrison—11,500 men and forty guns.[11]

The dramatic suddenness of this aggressive campaign appealed to a people who had grown apathetic in watching McClellan's cautious inaction in Virginia. The news of Forts Henry and Donelson was received with joy, and Grant's epigrammatical demand for an "unconditional surrender" gave a new meaning to his mystic initials. Pictures of a burly beef contractor were circulated in the newspapers as that of "Unconditional Surrender Grant," and hundreds of grateful people showered him with boxes of cigars. In Illinois, patriotic citizens proudly recounted that thirty of their State's regiments participated in the victory, and Democratic politicians claimed Grant for their party. In Congress the news of the surrender of Donelson caused Senators to throw their hats, and canes, and dignity into the air; and in the House, Washburne proudly reminded his colleagues that Grant came from Galena. Roscoe Conkling, Senator from New York, climbed aboard the triumphal bandwagon and moved that Congress vote its thanks to Grant and Halleck. For the first time in his life, Grant tasted the sweets of popular approval and acclaim.[12]

But just as Grant was being applauded by the nation, Fate, in the form of General Halleck, rose to snatch his triumph from him. The fall of Donelson and Grant's movements against the fort had not been in accordance with the strategical rules of the textbooks, and Halleck had no very clear idea of the situation. To cover up his ignorance, he engaged in a riot of correspondence. To Washington he wrote demanding that he be given complete command in the West as a reward for Grant's victory, and to Grant he sent a multitude of orders and instructions, some of which miscarried and many of which were impractical. Grant's failure to obey orders he did not receive, together with his popularity and promotion to the rank of major-general, threw Halleck into a fit of jealousy Soon he was writing to McClellan that Grant refused to obey orders and would not report the strength of his command. He reported rumors that "Grant has resumed his former bad habits." To Grant, Halleck wrote demanding that he report the strength of his command, and

[11] Grant, *Memoirs*, I, 284–315; B. H. Liddell Hart, *Sherman: Soldier, Realist, American*, 114; Richardson, *Personal History*, 217 ff.; M. F. Steele, *American Campaigns*, I, 162 ff.
[12] James G. Blaine, *Twenty Years of Congress*, I, 356–357; George Meade, *Life and Letters of George Gordon Meade*, I, 245–248; Horace Porter, *Campaigning with Grant*, 135; Richardson, *Personal History*, 235.

threatening him with arrest. But public commendation had warmed Grant's blood, and he replied to Halleck with a hitherto unsuspected dignity and courage: "I have done my best to obey orders and to carry out the interests of the service. If my course is not satisfactory, remove me at once." For several days there was bitter correspondence between the two, which stopped suddenly when Lincoln learned of the difficulty. Lincoln demanded that Halleck prefer charges against Grant. Without grounds for his accusations, the ingenious jurist proceeded to square himself with both Lincoln and Grant. To Lincoln he stated that the "irregularities" in Grant's command had been remedied, and to Grant he explained that pressure had been brought upon him from Washington. Satisfied with this explanation, Grant accepted his vindication.

New-found confidence, and the sense of social approval, however, soon led Grant into error and showed him the fickleness of public opinion. Less than two months after the victory of Donelson came the defeat at Shiloh. After the fall of Donelson, the Confederates had abandoned Nashville, and concentrated their western forces at Corinth, Mississippi. Preparatory to attacking the Confederates, Grant's forces were placed at Pittsburg Landing on the Tennessee river, about twenty miles from the Confederates, where Grant waited for General Carlos Buell to join him with troops from Nashville. Grant's own headquarters, at Savannah, were seven miles down the river. For two weeks, while waiting for Buell, Grant made daily trips to Pittsburg Landing but returned to Savannah at night, leaving General W. T. Sherman in charge of the camp.

Military critics who have examined the battle of Shiloh have generally agreed that Grant's arrangements at Pittsburg Landing were faulty. Moreover, they criticize his nocturnal absences and his failure to guard against surprise by intrenching. These strictures, justified by the events, are pertinent, but Grant's mistakes were due to his lack of experience. Until that time, Grant had had no experience with charging Confederates, except at Belmont; so, at Shiloh he was confidently awaiting the moment when he could advance. His sources of information concerning the enemy gave him no intimation of a contemplated Confederate attack, and Sherman assured him that such a thing was unlikely. As a result, on the morning of April 6, Grant was astounded at the roar of guns from the direction of the camp.

About six o'clock in the morning, while Grant was at breakfast seven miles away, General Albert Sidney Johnston attacked Grant's encampment. According to the newspaper correspondents, who hastily left the field, the attackers found the Federal troops unprepared, and bayoneted them in their tents. Such reports, widely credited in the country, were vigorously assailed by Sherman, who insisted that the pickets who were driven in gave ample warning of the Confederate approach and that the advancing troops found the defenders before their camp in battle array. However, there is no question that the Union forces were surprised, strategically if not tactically, and that they were psychologically unprepared for such an emergency. Throughout the day they were steadily driven back, and by nightfall their camp was in the hands of the Confederates. During the day Grant, who had rushed to the scene, had been in all parts of the field, but his efforts could not avail to hold back the Confederates.

During the night the long-awaited Buell arrived. These forces bolstered the Union morale, while the Confederate morale had declined with the death of Johnston the day before. By the middle of the afternoon on the second day Grant and Buell had succeeded in recovering their lost position. However, they were unable to press their advantage, and the Confederates fell back in safety on Corinth.[13]

Although the Confederates had lost one fourth of the forty thousand troops they sent into this battle, their successful retreat to their base caused both North and South to regard Shiloh as a Confederate victory Grant's star, which had seemed to be in the ascendant after Donelson, shone now with bedimmed fire. Throughout the country, newspapers which so recently had been praising him, turned now to condemn him. In Ohio, State pride ascribed the success of the second day to Buell, and in Illinois the stunned populace found no reply. In Congress demands for Grant's removal came from men who had just approved his promotion. Only Senator John Sherman, who came to the aid of his brother, and Congressman Washburne tried to justify Grant's failure.

Halleck used Grant's declining popularity as an opportunity to glorify himself. Two days after the battle he wired Grant that he was coming to the front to take command in person. Late in the month, the army

[13] Grant, *Memoirs*, I, 330–367; Garland, *U. S. Grant*, 210 ff.; Steele, *American Campaigns*, I, 175–187; W. T. and John Sherman, *The Sherman Letters*, 143–144; Hart, *Sherman*, 123–131; Richardson, *Personal History*, 245–255; J. F. C. Fuller, *The Generalship of Ulysses S. Grant*, 103–113; Theodore C. Smith, *The Life and Letters of James Abram Garfield*, I, 208; Royal Cortissoz, *The Life of Whitelaw Reid*, 88.

having been increased to number over a hundred thousand, Halleck
began a slow and painful approach, intrenching at every step along the
way to Corinth. His caution was as excessive as Grant's carelessness
had been; and as he approached the city, the Confederate commander,
Beauregard, abandoned it, taking with him all the Confederate supplies.

Although second in command, Grant endured Halleck's complete disregard of him through all of April. Meanwhile the newspapers continued
to flay him for Shiloh. In this situation Grant grew restive, and finally
obtained permission to go to Washington. Just as he was preparing
to leave, General Sherman rode up to Grant's headquarters. "What in
the devil is the meaning of this?" demanded the general. In reply,
Grant explained that he was "in the way" and could endure his position
no longer. "Good God Almighty, Grant, are you crazy?" ejaculated
the general. "Damn it, man, don't you know when you are well off?"
Then, with a liberal allotment of profane expletives, Sherman pointed
out that if Grant left the army he threw away his chances, while if he
remained "some happy accident might restore him to favor and his
true place." Under this presentation of the case Grant decided to remain. Early in June the "happy accident" took place: Halleck was
called to Washington to command the armies in the East, and Grant
was given command of the District of West Tennessee.[14]

The intimate relationship between Grant and Sherman, indicated by
this incident, was of tremendous significance in the history of the Civil
War. Each of them supplied characteristics which the other lacked,
and the combination of the two men was irresistible. In practically every
respect they were opposites. Grant was stocky, slow of movement and
of speech, while Sherman was tall and thin, nervous in temperament,
and prone to give vigorous expression to half-formulated thoughts. Each
of them smoked incessantly; Sherman nervously puffed away on
"stogies" which he quickly discarded, while Grant smoked slowly and
evenly, turning his cigar, and discarding it only when it threatened
to ignite his unkempt beard.[15] In mental processes, the contrast was
equally great. Sherman was keenly alert and quick to perceive the
strategic advantages of a move; Grant was slower in perception and
prone to arrive at his conclusions by intuition. Sherman had a creative
mind, capable of grasping the fundamentals of military problems and

[14] W. T. Sherman, *Memoirs*, I, 282; Garland, *Grant*, 211; Grant, *Memoirs*, I, 272.
[15] George Fort Milton, *The Age of Hate*, 473.

of evolving dramatic solutions. Grant's mind was given to synthesis, able to weigh and mature suggestions and to evolve a plan of action which, although lacking drama, possessed stability. In obstinacy of will, Grant was the superior. Sherman thought Grant was not a brilliant man, but "a good and brave soldier" . . . "sober, very industrious, and kind as a child." In fact, a "good, plain, sensible, kind-hearted fellow" in whom he could place "absolute faith." [16] With two such men in control, the war's outcome is not surprising. It was mere accident that Grant was superior, but it was a happy accident.

Fortunately for Grant's own progress, Halleck had scattered his troops over the department in such a manner that for a time Grant's aggressive tendencies were held in abeyance. Unable to take any sudden action, he had time not only to assimilate the lessons which he had learned from Fort Henry and Corinth, but to understand some of the problems of the war. During the period of inactivity, questions of military administration naturally arose. One problem of a personal nature he handled in an able manner. Newspaper correspondents, remembering Shiloh, freely expressed their lack of confidence in him and took no pains to hide their dissatisfaction at his elevation. As public condemnation always did, this opposition wounded Grant deeply, and he set about to win the friendship of the army correspondents. Halleck, who had suffered from their attacks during his cautious advance on Corinth, had forbidden newspaper men to accompany the army. Grant ignored this order and treated the correspondents with respect. After a time the correspondents changed their tone, and from then on until the end of the war the reporters with the army were for the most part friendly to Grant.[17]

Less satisfactory for Grant's reputation was his handling of the problem of the speculators who sought to bring cotton through his department. Cotton was worth a dollar a pound in the North and the traders used every device to obtain passports to send it through the lines. Believing that the Government should handle the cotton, Grant had vigorous condemnation for men whose "patriotism is measured by dollars and cents," but his posts swarmed with speculators. Even Jesse, always ready to take advantage of a favorable situation, agreed with the deal-

---

[16] Hart, *Sherman*, 149; *Sherman Letters*, 141.
[17] N. Y. *Tribune*, July 28, 1862; Cramer, *Conversations*, 61; Richardson, *Personal History*, 257–258.

ers to obtain passports from his son.[18] Evasions of his regulations became so bad that Grant, who had had much trouble with Jewish traders, ordered "Jews as a class" out of his department. Realizing the injustice of this discrimination, and realizing also the political consequences, Lincoln revoked the order. Unfortunately, the situation was not remedied, and Grant was forced to deal with it as long as he was in the West. The disgruntled traders, however, took ample revenge on Grant by giving wide circulation to new stories of his drunkenness.

With his work as a military administrator adding nothing to his reputation, Grant's rise to success was hampered by many difficulties. Contrary to later legend, Lincoln was slow to preceive Grant's fighting qualities. Press criticisms might well have caused the President to doubt and to hedge against the possibility of Grant's proving a failure. Ben Butler, who had just gained the title of "Beast" by his vigorous administration of New Orleans, alleges that at this time Lincoln offered him Grant's command.[19] However this may be, the President did lend an ear to the seductive promises of General McClernand, erstwhile Democratic politician from Jacksonville, Ill., who proposed to raise a new corps to be used against Vicksburg. He authorized McClernand to approach the governors of the western states with his proposition, but he stated that since the troops were to be used in Grant's department they could be used against Vicksburg only when Grant did not need them. Although Lincoln remarked, "I can't spare this man, he fights," nevertheless he nearly gave McClernand an independent commission for an expedition in Grant's bailiwick. Moreover, the McClernand expedition was kept a secret from Grant, who did not learn of it until Admiral Porter, commanding the Mississippi squadron, told him what was in the air.[20]

The news that McClernand was coming galvanized Grant into action. During the months since he had taken command of the mutinous Twenty-first Illinois, Grant had reverted to his early training and become a professional soldier. Jealous for his own position, and with a West Pointer's distrust for generals whose military preparation had been gained on political stumps, Grant determined to forestall McClernand by himself attacking Vicksburg.

[18] N. Y. *Tribune,* November 26, 1862, September 19, 1872; Nelson Cross, *Life of General Grant: His Political Record,* 76.
[19] Grant MS., Chicago Historical Society; Richardson, *Personal History,* 211, 275.
[20] Louis A. Coolidge, *Ulysses S. Grant,* 109–114; Fuller, *Generalship,* 126.

From the last months of 1862 to July 4, 1863, Grant's whole effort was directed against the last Confederate stronghold on the Mississippi. Strategically, the capture of Vicksburg would give the Union forces control of the great river from St. Louis to New Orleans, and would sever the states west of the river from the heart of the Confederacy. Personally its fall would redound to the glory of the commander who engineered the expedition.

Perseverance, rather than intelligence, characterized Grant's advance on Vicksburg. A more sensitive commander might have hesitated before attacking the well-fortified city protected on two sides by impassable bayous and swamps. But Grant's "superstition" against turning back stood him in good stead. When an overland approach proved infeasible, he turned to a futile attempt to make the city accessible and indefensible by diverting the Mississippi river into a canal. Finally, in April, 1863, the stubborn commander ran the city's batteries with his gunboats, marched his troops overland through Arkansas, crossed the river, and approached the city from the rear. For a month the beleaguered enemy held out. Then, on July 4, the Confederate commander surrendered. Grant's aggressiveness and tenacity had carried the day.

This consummation of a campaign which was heralded as the most brilliant in American military annals, resulted in Grant's complete rehabilitation in popular esteem. In Washington, Congressmen stopped Washburne on the streets to congratulate him on his protégé, and hastened to the White House to admit to the President that they had been wrong in demanding Grant's removal. Crowds serenaded the President, Secretary Stanton, and General Halleck. In the cities of the North, mass meetings celebrated the victory, and speakers vied with the newspapers in praising "the steady purpose, the unshaken fortitude, the fertile talent, and the heroic determination" of General Grant. Democratic newspapers again remembered that Grant was a Democrat, and Republican journals replied that he was obviously a "thorough supporter" of the Administration.[21]

But Grant had learned much since he had entered the army, and he did not permit this new burst of popularity to pass without being capitalized. After Donelson, he had failed to take advantage of the popular acclaim to advance himself, with the result that Halleck had suc-

[21] Gideon Welles, *Diary of Gideon Welles,* I, 364–365; Meade, *Letters,* II, 137; N. Y. *Tribune,* July 8, 9, 25, 1863; Richardson, *Personal History,* 337–341.

ceeded in temporarily discrediting him. Now, Grant took steps to prevent any recurrence of his former humiliation. A few days after
Vicksburg, Lincoln wrote him a note of "grateful acknowledgment for
the almost inestimable service you have done the country," and explained that he had doubted the wisdom of some of Grant's moves. "I
now wish to make the personal acknowledgment that you were right
and I was wrong." In reply, Grant sent Colonel Rawlins to Washington, ostensibly to carry the roll of the prisoners taken at Vicksburg, but
in reality to be Grant's personal agent to Lincoln. Lest this purpose be
suspected, the general wrote that Rawlins "has not a favor to ask for
himself or any other living being. Even in my position it is a great luxury to meet a gentleman who has no ax to grind, and I can appreciate
that it is infinitely more so in yours." [22]

Armed with this ingenious letter of introduction, Rawlins was received with great interest. In a two-hour session with the President and
Cabinet, he gave an "intelligent and interesting" description of the men
and events associated with Vicksburg. Secretary Welles found him
"honest, unpretending, and unassuming," and declared that "his un-
polished and unrefined deportment" pleased him more than that of any
officer whom he had met. But the shrewd naval chieftain, suspecting that
Grant had "sent him here for a purpose," soon found the hidden motive in Rawlins' criticisms of McClernand. According to Rawlins,
McClernand was unfit, insubordinate, and unintelligent. Welles therefore concluded that Grant hated McClernand, but he noted that Rawlins
told his story "with such appearance of candor" that it convinced the
President.[23]

This shrewd capitalization of a nation's gratitude was doubtless due
to Rawlins' political acumen. Certainly at later times Rawlins stood at
his chief's elbow and directed his actions into the channels of greatest
political profit, and this early move smacks of his handiwork. That
Grant himself possessed the imagination to conceive of the situation is
unlikely, but that he had sufficient common sense to follow Rawlins'
suggestions is evident when the relations of the two men are understood.
Only a friend who stood so close that he was a veritable *alter ego* could
have dared, as Rawlins did, to criticize his superior. Less than two

---

[22] *Official Records of the Union and Confederate Armies in the War of the Rebellion,*
CIX, 406, 416.
[23] Welles, *Diary,* I, 386.

months before, while the armies were before Vicksburg, Rawlins wrote Grant a letter that must occupy a unique place in the list of letters from subordinates to their superiors. "The great solicitude I feel for the safety of this army," he began, "leads me to mention what I had hoped never to do again—the subject of your drinking." Then the patriotic aide enumerated several cases where he had reason to suspect his commander had been drunk. "You have full control of your appetite and can let drinking alone," declared this moral mentor. "Had you not pledged me the sincerity of your honor early last March that you would drink no more during the war, and kept that pledge during your recent campaign, you would not today have stood first in the world's history as a successful military leader. Your only salvation depends upon your strict adherence to that pledge. You cannot succeed in any other way." The fact that Grant retained Rawlins after this letter speaks volumes for Grant's essential soundness of judgment.[24]

Upon his return from Washington, Rawlins took up his quarters in a confiscated house. Among the inmates of the house was Miss Mary Emma Hulbut, a native of Danbury, Conn., who had been visiting friends in the city when the siege began. In advancing his own interests Rawlins was as shrewd as when he was advancing those of his chief, and he perceived in the Yankee maiden a fit mother for his own two motherless children. A new siege was laid, and before Rawlins left for Chattanooga, the lady had capitulated to the soldier.

While Rawlins was attending to affairs of the heart, Grant, secure in his position as the leading general of the war, was looking about for more worlds to conquer. As his success had increased and he had gradually become commander of an ever-widening department, his strategical conceptions had grown. Beginning as merely an aggressive fighter, he grew eventually to understand the grand strategy of the conflict. Now, with Vicksburg fallen, he perceived that an advance on Mobile would cut the Confederacy in another place and force Bragg to weaken the defenses of Chattanooga. However, Lincoln was perturbed by the presence of the French in Mexico and forbade Grant's proposed movement against Mobile. Many of Grant's troops were sent to General N. P. Banks in New Orleans, and late in August, Grant himself went thither to consult Banks. In tribute to Grant's reputation for horsemanship,

<hr>

[24] W. F. Smith, *From Chattanooga to Petersburg under Generals Grant and Butler*, 179–180.

General Butler assigned him a spirited horse. At a review, the horse shied at a locomotive, became unmanageable, and fell upon Grant's leg. For two weeks the General was confined to his bed.[25]

While Grant was recuperating from this injury, General Rosecrans in East Tennessee was engaging the Confederate forces under Braxton Bragg. On September 19 and 20, Bragg administered a crushing defeat to the Union arms at Chickamauga, and only the heroic resistance of General George H. Thomas, the "Rock of Chickamauga," who covered the Federal retreat, saved Rosecrans from immediate capture. As it was, Rosecrans was besieged in Chattanooga, cut off from supplies, and faced with the imminent necessity of surrender.

In this situation, Secretary Stanton turned to the only general in the West who had shown the ability to fight. He summoned Grant to Indianapolis, met him there, commissioned him to command all the national troops in the West, and urged him to proceed to Chattanooga to save the army. Despite his injured leg, Grant set out immediately, and arrived in Chattanooga on the evening of October 23, "wet, dirty, and well."

Grant's actions in Chattanooga give an excellent insight into his military ability. The essential elements in that ability were the willingness to make decisions and the will to carry them out. In Chattanooga, the first problem which faced the Union forces was how to get supplies from Bridgeport, Ala., twenty miles down the Tennessee river. The Confederates held Racoon Mountain and Lookout Valley and hence controlled the south bank of the river, thus forcing the Federals to transport their supplies fifty miles over muddy, mountainous roads. As a result, men and horses were starving on half-rations, and the Confederates, occupying Missionary Ridge to the east and Lookout Mountain to the south, were waiting vulture-like to pounce upon the enemy when the inevitable collapse came.

On the night of Grant's arrival, General Thomas, whom Grant had appointed in place of Rosecrans, pointed out the situation and unfolded a plan by which the Confederates could be driven from Lookout Valley, and the "cracker line" to Bridgeport opened. The plan had been devised by Rosecrans and considered by Thomas and his staff, but no action had been taken. As soon as he surveyed the situation and could realize the importance of the movement and the excellence of the plan, Grant

[25] Grant, *Memoirs*, I, 581.

ordered its execution. In the admiring words of Rawlins to his fiancée; "It is decisiveness and energy in action that always accomplishes grand results, and strikes terror to the hearts of the foe. It is this and not the conception of great schemes that makes military genius." [26]

In Rawlins' estimate, one factor of Grant's success was omitted—luck. Hostile critics were prone to exaggerate the part that accident played in Grant's genius, but the Chattanooga campaign gave convincing evidence that Grant was favored by fortune's smiles. Capable plans were awaiting his aggressive orders, and soon the "cracker line" was opened and the danger of starvation averted. Moreover, fortune again played into Grant's hands when dissensions among the Confederates on the encircling mountains caused General Bragg to weaken his forces by sending Longstreet's troops a hundred miles away. Learning of this, Grant gave orders to attack the mountainous slopes which protected the besieging Confederates.

For this move, too, plans had been made, but circumstances prevented their execution. However, luck helped to bring the victory. On the east and west ends of Missionary Ridge Grant's flanks under Hooker and Sherman had failed to make headway. Toward the middle of the afternoon, Grant ordered an advance against the Confederate rifle pits along the four-mile base of Missionary Ridge. The Union soldiers had no orders to advance beyond the first line of pits, but unable to resist the temptation to pursue the retreating Confederates, they charged up the long acclivity. The retreating Confederates formed a shield for the pursuing Federals, and before the Union officers could stop their men the entire line had taken the top of the Ridge and the enemy was flying in confusion. This charge has passed as "one of the greatest miracles in military history." The credit for it redounded to Grant, and Rawlins wrote his beloved that "Grant's 'star' is still in the ascendant, and will continue to be while it lightens the patriot's path." The impetuous troops, however, should have received the credit for the startling victory. [27]

When the news of Chattanooga was received in Washington Congress was just assembling for its long session. On the first day of the session, Washburne rose to introduce a bill to revive the grade of lieutenant-

[26] Rawlins to Mary E. Hulbut, October 27, 1863, Rawlins MSS., Chicago Hist. Society.
[27] Conger, *Rise of Grant,* 293–305; Horace Porter, *Campaigning with Grant,* 1 ff.; Hart, *Sherman,* 222; N. Y. *Tribune,* November 27, 1863; Rawlins to Mary E. Hulbut, December 8, 1863, Rawlins MSS.

general. In a laudatory oration he described the rise of General Grant, and with a clear appreciation of the nation's disgust with commanders who appeared to better advantage on the parade ground than on the battlefield, he made a contribution to the rapidly growing legend of Grant's simple and democratic bearing. "He fared like the commonest soldier in his command, partaking of his rations, and sleeping upon the ground with no covering except the canopy of heaven," said the Congressman.[28] Washburne's bill Congress referred to the Military Committee, but passed a resolution of thanks to Grant and authorized the President to strike a medal to be presented to the hero in the name of the people.[29] Early in January, Lincoln nominated Grant for a major-generalship in the regular army—the appointment to date from Vicksburg—and when, the last of February, Washburne's bill passed, the President nominated Grant to the new office.[30]

During these two months, Grant, in headquarters at Nashville, was exhibiting a modesty and a devotion to duty which comported well with the position he held in the national esteem. He accepted his promotions with mute gratitude for the economic security they gave him, and with the calm exterior of one who deemed them well deserved. Having regained a position in the army, he had no intention of leaving it nor of yielding to many who sought to use it. Jesse Grant urged his son to accept from certain prominent citizens who journeyed to Nashville the offer of a political career. To the delegation, Grant gave a soft answer to the effect that he had never wanted but one office in his life—"I should like to be mayor of Galena . . . to build a new sidewalk from my home to the depot." To his father, Grant's answer was not so soft, and he wrathfully summoned Jesse to Nashville to receive instructions in conduct becoming the parent of a prominent general. Grant had no intention of risking his position in the game of political chance, and he told a solicitous Senator that he would consider such a consummation "as highly unfortunate to myself, if not for the whole country." "All I want," he wrote his father, "is to be left alone to fight this war out, fight all rebel opposition, and restore a happy Union in the shortest possible time." [31]

As soon as Grant's nomination as lieutenant-general was confirmed,

[28] Blaine, Twe: Years of Congress, I, 509–511.
[29] Richardson, M. sages and Papers of the Presidents, VI, 231.
[30] N. Y. Tribune, December 14, 1863, January 11, 14, February 25, 27, 1864.
[31] Cramer, Conversations, 89–90; Richardson, Personal History, 373.

Lincoln called him to Washington. His appearance there made possible
a scene typical of Washington society under the wartime régime of the
Middle Westerners. Arriving in Washington on the evening of March 8,
Grant went unannounced to a White House levée. The President, tower-
ing above the crowd, observed his entrance. "Why, here is General
Grant!" he exclaimed. Eager to see the unknown hero, the crowd pressed
close as Grant mumbled an embarrassed reply to Lincoln's greeting.
He was presented to a few notables and to Mrs. Lincoln, and then
turned over to the crowd. Immediately there formed the most "coat-
tearing, button-bursting jam" that the White House had ever seen.
Secretary Seward persuaded the general to stand on a sofa in order
that the people might see him. It was an hour before the victor of
Vicksburg and Chattanooga could retreat before his cheering admirers.
—"All of which seemed rowdy and unseemly," sighed the bitter Secretary of the Navy.[32]

The next day, before the assembled Cabinet, Lincoln presented Grant
his commission as Lieutenant-General, and the nation settled itself to
see how he would handle the situation. Many were wondering what he
would do with the much maligned and hated Halleck; others wondered
whether he would take the field in person; and in the Army of the
Potomac the sensitive but ambitious George Gordon Meade was wondering if Grant would replace him with some friend from the West.
Predictions were general throughout the country and in the army that
Grant would find Lee a more formidable opponent than Pillow, Johnston, Beauregard, Pemberton, and Bragg had been. But there was a disposition in all parties to "take hold, strengthen his hands for the immense responsibility devolved upon him." [33]

In handling the problems incident to his new position, Grant demonstrated the extent of his growth since the beginning of the war. The
tact he displayed in making his arrangements showed that his two years
of experience in handling men had taught him many lessons. Essentially
kindhearted, he himself had suffered much humiliation, and he sought
to avoid giving offense to the Eastern armies and their commanders.
Halleck, whom Grant admired for his knowledge of military history and
his thorough grasp of textbook strategy, he relieved from duty as

[32] Welles, *Diary*, I, 538–9; Porter, *Campaigning with Grant*, 19–21; N. Y. *Tribune*,
March 9, 1864.
[33] N. Y. *Tribune*, March 8, 1864.

general-in-chief, but appointed him chief-of-staff with headquarters in Washington—a position which made him the principal military adviser to the President.[34] To Meade the new commander displayed a courteous consideration which warmed the cockles of that much-harassed general's heart. Almost daily, Meade wrote his wife of his growing admiration for Grant, who had said nothing about superseding him, and who displayed "much more capacity and character than I had expected." On one occasion he wrote: "I believe Grant is honest and fair, and I have no doubt he will give me full credit for anything I may do." The only Western commander whom Grant transferred to the east was General Phil Sheridan, whom he brought to command the cavalry.[35]

As for himself, Grant quickly rejected the idea that he was to "hire a house at the capital and direct the war from an armchair in a Washington parlor." [36] Rawlins had long before decided that Grant was a man of action whose place was at the front, and Grant readily adopted the idea. Moreover, a fear of politicians oppressed him, and he sought to get away from "Washington and its entourage." Glad to see a fighting general, the people applauded his taking up headquarters with the Army of the Potomac.

For two months after coming East, Grant studied the situation before him. Success, with its attendant responsibility, had forced him to take a larger view of the conflict. Beginning as an aggressive fighter, anxious only to demonstrate an ability to win battles, Grant had learned after Vicksburg to comprehend the strategic problems of the war. Essentially, there was nothing unique in the problems, and no especial genius was needed to perceive the general plans of campaigns. At the beginning of the war, General Winfield Scott had proposed the "Anaconda plan" by which army and navy would coöperate to constrict the Confederacy to a small space. Blockades to isolate the South would, by Scott's plan, prepare the way for a Mississippi campaign which would restrict the rebellion to the Eastern section, where converging Union armies could crush all resistance. In essence, competent military men agreed on this strategy, and, in so far as Lincoln and the politicians left the professional soldiers to their own devices, it was followed out.

Three years of costly war had almost brought Lincoln to the place

[34] Richardson, *Messages,* VI, 234; N. Y. *Tribune,* March 8, 10, 1864.
[35] Meade, *Letters,* II, 162–183.
[36] N. Y. *Tribune,* March 10, 1864.

where he would entrust the conduct of the war to the professional soldiers. The President's insistence on the unnecessary campaign into Eastern Tennessee had eventuated in victory—thanks to Grant—but had
contributed little to winning the war. Moreover, Lincoln's insistence on
the overland approach to Richmond had resulted in three years of futile
campaigning by the Army of the Potomac. McClellan's superior technical training had led him to abandon the idea of marching to Richmond
across the swampy wastelands of Virginia and to determine to approach
the Confederate capital by the slow but effective siege tactics of the
peninsular campaign. It was Grant's good fortune that he came upon
the scene after events had demonstrated to Lincoln his own lack of
military omniscience.

To the solution of the military problems of the war, the new lieutenant-general brought his demonstrated qualities of decisiveness and
aggressiveness. In addition, experience had given him a method of
formulating campaigns which was peculiarly his own. Seemingly, he
gave little study to a problem, but he liked to have the members of his
staff discuss the probabilities of a course of action. The staff members
themselves, sometimes disgusted by the slowness of Grant's mind,
sought opportunities to impress upon their chief their own ideas. In
such discussions, Grant kept silence, but his mind was made for synthesis, and he eventually emerged with a plan to which many men had
contributed. Frequently, this plan was put into words by Rawlins,
who was, according to one staff officer, better able to speak Grant's
thoughts than Grant himself.[37]

In the early campaigns of the war, the obvious defects had been the
failure of the various armies to act in concert. Accordingly, Grant
determined upon a coördinated advance of all the national armies with
the ultimate objective of undermining the economic structure of the
Confederacy. To Sherman, commanding in Chattanooga, was assigned
the task of pressing upon Johnston, taking Atlanta, and destroying the
Confederate connections with the far South. Aiding in this general
plan, Banks was to advance upon Mobile from New Orleans. In
Virginia, Sigel in the Shenandoah Valley and West Virginia was to
advance south and east to destroy the railroads which connected Richmond with East Tennessee, while B. F. Butler was to move from
Fortress Monroe against Petersburg and Richmond. At the same time,

[37] Badeau, *Grant in Peace*, 119. Porter, *Campaigning with Grant*, 250.

Meade, with the Army of the Potomac, was to cross over the Rapidan, strike Lee, and drive him south.

Unfortunately for Grant, three of these movements were carried out in such an indifferent manner that the expected annihilation of Lee could not be executed. Having been defeated in Louisiana, Banks was unable to start against Mobile; and Sigel failed to move promptly. Butler's advance on Richmond, a more important move, was stopped at the battle of Drewey's Bluff, and Butler was "bottled up" at Bermuda Hundred in a position where a handful of Confederates could hold him helpless. Only Meade and Sherman got off at the appointed time.

Grant himself accompanied Meade and the Army of the Potomac. On May 3, the army crossed the Rapidan to press on through the rough country—the Wilderness—before fighting, but Lee elected to give battle in a position where Grant's superior artillery would be ineffective. Within a month Grant and Lee had fought a series of battles from the Rapidan to Cold Harbor, with losses of 54,929 and 19,000 respectively. And at the end, Lee was safe in Richmond.[38]

To many in the North, the long roll of casualties was evidence of Grant's unfitness to conduct a campaign. General Meade, torn between his patriotic exultation that the army had advanced, and his jealousy that his army was "putting laurels" on another's brow, thought that "Grant has had his eyes opened, and is willing to admit now that Virginia and Lee's army is not Tennessee and Bragg's army."[39] To Gideon Welles, the astounding losses were proof that Grant had no regard for human life,[40] and throughout the country newspapers began once more to talk of his drinking. In the ranks of the army there was rejoicing. Grant had met defeats with new advances, flanking Lee after each battle and slowly pushing him back on his base in the Confederate capital. After the first battle Grant had notified Lincoln that he would not turn back, and after the second the General wrote Stanton, "I propose to fight it out on this line if it takes all summer." Under such a determined leader, the morale of the army of the Potomac rose rapidly. In the North morale also rose, and perhaps a majority of the people were overjoyed that Grant had shown no disposition

[38] N. Y. *Tribune*, April to June, 1864; Meade, *Life and Letters*, II, 177–200; Porter, *Campaigning with Grant*, 23–210; Fuller, *Generalship of U. S. Grant*, 207–284.
[39] Meade, *Life and Letters*, II, 201.
[40] Welles, *Diary*, II, 45.

to turn back in admission of defeat. In New York a great mass meeting was held just after Cold Harbor to indorse Grant's course [41] and in Washington, Lincoln, who had kissed the correspondent who brought him the first intimation that Grant would not turn back, now heard from the same source that Grant was a total abstainer. Relieved of his fears, the President sent the general a personal note assuring him of his continued confidence.[42]

The failure to defeat Lee had not caused Grant to despair of eventual success. The same tenacity and force of will which had enabled him to keep on trying at Vicksburg now came into evidence, and, instead of giving up, he merely changed his line of approach. It was perhaps only the fears of the politicians in Washington that had led Grant to attempt the overland route to Richmond. In his original plans he had made provision for transferring his army to the south of the James river should it prove impossible to defeat Lee north of it. Accordingly, he wrote to Halleck that "I find now, after thirty days of trial, that the enemy deems it of first importance to run no risks with the armies they now have. They act purely on the defensive." So, unwilling to risk a "greater sacrifice of life," Grant determined to move his army to join Butler's forces south of Richmond.[43] Under cover of a cavalry raid to the west, Grant slipped out of his trenches before Cold Harbor, and transferred his army to the south side of the Confederate capital. It was three days before Lee knew that Grant had gone.

Once south of Richmond, Grant was on the ground which McClellan had occupied two years before and where he had failed through Lincoln's impatience. Now both Lincoln and Grant profited from early experience; the general carried out McClellan's plans, and Lincoln showed no signs of interfering in the conduct of the war. But there was little drama in the slow siege tactics which Grant now followed. Most of his time was spent in attempting to destroy the railroads which ran into Richmond. Week by week throughout the summer and autumn of 1864 the Union advance, with pick and shovel, brought ever nearer the collapse of the Confederate capital. These lowly instruments were to prove more effective than rifle and cannon.

Drama came in other fields of the war. In the Valley of Virginia

[41] N. Y. *Tribune*, June 6, 1864.
[42] Wing, "Stories of a War Correspondent, II," *Christian Advocate*, Feb. 6, 1913.
[43] *Official Records*, LXVII, 22.

Grant's darling of the cavalry, Phil Sheridan, won victories at Winchester and Fisher's Hill, and plundered the Shenandoah Valley's rich granary. In the far South the nervous genius, Sherman, pushed the Confederates back from Chattanooga to Atlanta, and then, with a masterstroke of ingenuity—which gained Grant's grudging approval—marched his army across Georgia to the sea. The fall of Atlanta, combined with Sheridan's successes in the Valley, proved that the war was no failure. On the crest of these victories, Lincoln was reëlected to the Presidency, and the North settled down with something of Grant's grim determination to win the war.

Throughout these months the Northern people were still unable to decide whether Grant was a butcher or a savior in whom they might put their faith. Gideon Welles, ever critical, early made up his mind that Grant was "dull and heavy" and destitute of strategy or skill. Almost day by day he recorded in his diary an "awakening apprehension that Grant is not equal to the position assigned to him. God grant that I may be mistaken," he exclaimed, "for the slaughtered thousands of my countrymen who have poured out their rich blood for three months on the soil of Virginia from the Wilderness to Petersburg under his generalship can never be atoned for in this world or the next if he . . . prove a failure. . . . A nation's destiny almost has been committed to this man, and if it prove an improper committal, where are we?" [44] Fortunately, others were less critical, and many expressed, like John L. Motley, "a great faith in Grant" even at the time of the Petersburg crater.[45]

In part, at least, these divergent opinions were the result of Grant's relations with his immediate subordinates in the army, Meade and Butler. Meade, a regular army man, was ambitious, and felt keenly the anomalous position in which he was placed by Grant's presence with the Army of the Potomac, but it was inevitable that Grant should have assumed the active direction of the army. The situation was admirably summed up in the *Army Magazine* in the formula—"The Army of the Potomac, directed by Grant, commanded by Meade, and led by Hancock, Sedgwick, and Warren." [46] It was inevitable, too, that Meade should gradually lose his first grateful admiration for the lieutenant-

[44] Welles, *Diary*, II, 78, 90, 92, 94.
[45] Geo. W. Curtis, *The Correspondence of John Lothrop Motley*, 170–171.
[46] Meade, *Life and Letters*, II, 197.

general. Growing restive, he asked to be transferred to another command, and especially desired to be sent against Early in the Shenandoah. But Grant preferred to send Sheridan, for whom he possessed an
admiration as incomprehensible to Meade as it is to the present-day
student. Moreover, in recommending promotions, Grant arranged for
Sherman to outrank Meade. Yet, despite these slights, Meade's patriotism was sufficient for him to make excuses for Grant. "It is the same
old story," he wrote his wife, "an inability to appreciate the sensitiveness of a man of character and honor"; but he still believed Grant a
"good soldier, of great force of character, honest and upright, of pure
purposes." [47]

Meade's willingness to subordinate himself was not shared by Benjamin F. Butler, the Massachusetts politician who commanded the
Army of the James. From the very beginning of the war Butler had
assumed a dramatic rôle. With some bloodshed and much publicity, he
had quelled a secession riot in Baltimore while leading his Massachusetts
troops to answer Lincoln's call for volunteers. With less bloodshed
and vastly more publicity he had so dramatically played the rôle of
military governor of New Orleans that Jefferson Davis placed a price
on his head. But his talents did not lie along the line of martial combat.
Trained military men in general, and Grant's staff of regular army
officers in particular, had small respect for and no confidence in Butler's
military ability, and frequently expressed their wonder that Grant kept
him in command.

An absurd but widely credited explanation of this mystery came
from General W. F. Smith after he had been removed for a fiasco before Petersburg. Going to Washington, he wrote a letter, intended for
Lincoln's eye, in which he alleged that Butler, having seen Grant
drunk, used his knowledge to blackmail Grant into retaining him.
Smith's supporters and Butler's opponents—their names were legion—
accepted this story at face value, and added the theory that Grant obtained his liquor from Butler. Despite Butler's ingenuity in pointing
out the absurdity of this account, Smith's tale was widely believed,
and became the main source for the continued legend of Grant's drunkenness.[48]

[47] Meade, *Life and Letters*, II, 213, 218, 220, 223, 246.
[48] Smith, *From Chattanooga to Petersburg*, 130 *passim;* Benjamin F. Butler, *Autobiography and Personal Reminiscences of Major General Benjamin F. Butler, Butler's Book*,
712 ff. and appendix; B. F. Butler, *Private and Official Correspondence of General Benj. F.*

To Grant, Butler's inefficiency was a source of constant embarrassment. Early in July, he wrote Halleck that Butler's lack of technical knowledge made it desirable to move him to another field. He suggested Kentucky as a proper place for Butler to exercise his proved administrative ability, but Halleck, with unsuspected humor, replied that Butler would drive Kentucky into insurrection. He admitted that it might be desirable to have a "free fight" between Butler and Rosecrans, but he confessed to a fear that Butler would use his "talents in newspaper intrigue to injure Sherman." [49] Political considerations, however, saved Butler from removal. Lincoln's reëlection was none too certain, and to remove so powerful a figure might have endangered it. It even proved impossible to limit his activities to a smaller command, for Butler protested when it was tried, and Grant retracted his orders with apologies.[50] To Butler it was evident that he was being oppressed by a coterie of West Point officers who surrounded Grant, but he was too good a politician not to realize the strength of his position. He decided to hold on until he was ordered out.[51]

When the elections were over, the major reason for retaining Butler was gone. Opportunity for removing him, on defensible grounds, came with his failure to take Fort Fisher, at the entrance to Wilmington harbor—the last seaport of the Confederacy; and early in January, the War Department ordered him to return to Massachusetts. The removal order did not specify a reason, and there was much speculation concerning the summary action. In asking Stanton to issue the order, Grant alleged that the officers lacked confidence in Butler, but to Butler this could only mean that the clique of West Pointers about Grant were jealous of his success. Secretary Welles, who had less respect for Grant than for Butler, was satisfied that "Butler's greater intellect overshadowed Grant, and annoyed and embarrassed the General-in-chief." After Butler's removal, another expedition succeeded without difficulty in taking Fort Fisher and Wilmington.[52]

With the fall of Wilmington began the final campaign of the war.

Butler During the Period of the Civil War, IV, *passim*. The weight of evidence, not all of it as impartial as one might wish, seems to indicate that Grant was a total abstainer during the Virginia campaigns. That he drank at times during the war is likely, but there is no evidence that his drinking injured his military efficiency.

[49] *Butler Correspondence*, IV, 457–9.

[50] *Ibid.*, 481–2.

[51] *Ibid.*, 435.

[52] Welles, *Diary*, II, 128, 133, 146, 150–151, 213, 215, 223; Porter, *Campaigning with Grant*, 336 ff.; *Butler's Book*, 868–871; *Correspondence of Butler*, V, 310 ff., 485–486.

On February 1, 1865, Sherman, having persuaded Grant to allow him to march through the Carolinas to Virginia, left Savannah for the northward trip. From East Tennessee and Southwest Virginia raids eastward, and from Wilmington a westward advance into North Carolina restricted the arena of the war. In Virginia, Grant adopted the plan of extending his line farther south and west along the railroads leading into Petersburg. He thus forced Lee to extend his own lines in opposition. When Lee had sufficiently weakened his line, Sheridan struck at Five Forks and Grant ordered an assault all along the line. The Confederate lines before Petersburg were penetrated by the attack, and Lee evacuated Petersburg and prepared to leave Richmond. On April 3 he concentrated his forces, and struck out into Virginia in hope of joining Johnston, who was retreating before Sherman. The junction of these two armies might give Lee a victory and enable him to sue for better terms of peace. But at Amelia Court House he lost a day waiting for supplies, and Sheridan, with Grant's cavalry, was able to strike the Danville railroad. With escape cut off in this direction, Lee turned toward Lynchburg, but again Sheridan, this time followed by infantry, got ahead of him at Appomattox. Surrounded, Lee could do nothing but ask for the terms upon which he might surrender his army.

At McLean's house in Appomattox, the rival commanders met for the great final scene of the war. Dignified and sorrowing, Lee repulsed Grant's kindly efforts to chat about the course of the war, and insisted in getting the terms which Grant would offer. Knowing full well Lincoln's wish for leniency toward the enemy, and desiring not to humiliate a foeman he had learned to respect, Grant made the terms as generous as possible. Lee and his army were released on parole, rations were issued to them, and the men were allowed to keep their own horses "for the spring plowing." Sadly, Lee signed the capitulation, and the dejection of the great commander hushed the exuberance of the victors. That evening the soldiers of the two armies fraternized, renewing old acquaintances, and exchanging experiences. Before his tent, Grant met James A. Longstreet. "Come on, Pete, let's play another game of brag," he said.

Throughout this final campaign, Grant's resourcefulness, tenacious will, and aggressiveness appeared at their best. As the campaign closed, and Lee surrendered, not even Grant's disgruntled critics could find an ear for their strictures upon him. For the moment, there was nothing but praise for his achievements in the North, and both North and South joined in commending him for the magnanimity of his terms to Lee. Moreover, Grant's personal qualities stood out as distinctly as his military ones, and excited equal approval. His "reticence, modesty, and unostentatious simplicity" adorned the tale of his greatness and pointed the moral that "the qualities by which great things are accomplished . . . have no necessary connection with showy and superficial accomplishments." [53] Stories of his drinking were temporarily forgotten, and the tanner's clerk of Galena was rapidly on the way to becoming a saint.

[53] N. Y. *World,* April 26, 1865.

THE military conflict which ended at Appomattox was but one phase of the American Civil War. Underlying the more dramatic events on the battlefield were a host of problems which could not be resolved by the simple defeat of the Confederate armies. In the background, behind the contending armies, raged a desperate and prolonged conflict between a factory world and a plantation paradise—a struggle for dominance between two opposing economic systems. In 1860, a minority of Southern leaders, foreseeing in the election of Lincoln the passing of their last hope of control, decided to risk their economic order in a desperate effort to separate their section from the North. When their designs for a separate national existence met with catastrophe, many classes in the North planned to secure the fruits of victory. Politicians of the Republican school sought to secure control of the Southern votes, and industrial magnates laid dark plots to preserve the war-created tariff. Eventually, the marriage of the protective tariff and the bloody shirt enabled the industrial areas to dominate and control. Essentially, the outcome of the Civil War was to be a victory of the Captains of Industry over the Lords of the Manor.

Just how this victory was to be secured involved a number of theories. Unfortunately, in the North no very clear-cut understanding of the issues existed, and consequently no definite program for the reconstruction of the South obtained. Old abolitionists, Radical politicians, merchants, bondholders, debtors, and ardent protectionists, each had interests in the question, and each had a solution for the problem. In the realm of constitutional theory, some held the Southern States had committed legal suicide, and their escheated estate should be administered by the nation. Others regarded the South as conquered territory, concerning which Congress might legislate without constitutional scruples. Still others, consistently adhering to the war-time dogma that the States could not secede, contended that since the South had not been out of the Union, it could not be made the victim of discriminatory legislation.

To President Lincoln, the theoretical considerations involved in the question yielded to the problem of how to restore the Southern States to the Union. He regarded constitutional speculation on the status of the South as "a merely pernicious abstraction," and besought his followers to "join in doing the acts necessary to restoring the proper practical relation between these States and the Union." [1] Accordingly, the President established military governments in Tennessee, Louisiana, and Arkansas which would constitue *neuclei* for political governments that would restore the States to their "proper practical" relationships. In a Proclamation of Amnesty and Reconstruction, issued in December, 1863, Lincoln declared that when one-tenth of the legal voters of 1850 should have taken an oath of allegiance and had assumed control of a reorganized government, a State might be restored to the Union.

Immediately there arose opposition from a group of Radical politicians who desired to punish the South for the rebellion. Old abolitionists and Radicals condemned the mild and conciliatory President. Just at the beginning of the presidential campaign of 1864 the violent Henry Winter Davis of Maryland and the crudely belligerent Ben Wade of Ohio sponsored a bill embodying the Radical theory. Essentially, the bill was a congressional protest against the President's assertion of his own power to decide the status of the South. More drastic by far than Lincoln's proclamation, the Wade-Davis bill declared that a state could not be readmitted to the Union until a majority of the white citizens had demonstrated their loyalty by a complete revision of their State Constitutions and the abolition of slavery. In view of what later became the conditions for readmitting the States, it would have been better to have accepted this bill, but Lincoln stated that he was unwilling to be committed to any single program of restoration, and gave it a pocket veto. Incensed, Wade and Davis angrily replied with an immoderate assertion of the right of Congress to determine the conditions upon which a State might be accorded its full rights.

The election of 1864 might have been interpreted as a vindication of Lincoln's plans for the South, but Congress returned in December in a mood to push the fight with the President. Soon there arose the question of recognizing a "reconstructed" government in Louisiana which had been formed at Lincoln's instigation and under the terms of his amnesty proclamation. The embryonic government gave the Radicals an opportunity to air their own theories of congressional control.

[1] John C. Nicolay and John Hay, *Abraham Lincoln's Complete Works*, XI, 85–91.

In the Senate, the theorist Charles Sumner, who had decided that Negro suffrage was necessary to Radical supremacy, declared that the recognition of the new government would be a "national calamity." He began a filibuster which threatened to extend to March 4, and the President's supporters concluded to lay the bill aside.

The moment Lee surrendered, the issue of reconstruction became the leading question before the nation. At the time Grant met Lee at McLean's house the lines of battle between the President and Congress were already being drawn. Lincoln, however, regarded the adjournment of Congress as "providential," and prepared to reorganize the Southern governments before Congress should reassemble in December.[2] At his last Cabinet meeting he had discussed his policy and laid a foundation for a proclamation in regard to North Carolina's reconstruction.

Having arrived in Washington the day before, General Grant was present at this last Cabinet meeting and lent his support to the President's designs. With no clear understanding of the constitutional theories involved in Reconstruction, and with the army's tradition of disregarding political affairs, Grant was nevertheless vitally concerned with the military results of the war. Emotionally, he sympathized with Lincoln's leniency. His own courteous demeanor toward Lee, and his kindly gesture in permitting the paroled Confederates to keep their horses, had indicated that he would have small sympathy with those who desired vengeance upon the conquered.

At the close of this Cabinet meeting, Lincoln invited General and Mrs. Grant to accompany him to the theatre that evening. While the general and the President were in conference, Mrs. Stanton had come to call on Mrs. Grant and to discuss the evening's program. As relations between Mrs. Stanton and Mrs. Lincoln were considerably strained, Mrs. Stanton declared to Julia Grant: "Unless you accept the invitation, I shall refuse. I will not sit in the box with Mrs. Lincoln." Recalling a humiliating scene when the jealous Mrs. Lincoln had accompanied the President to army headquarters, Mrs. Grant decided that she would not go to the theatre. Instead, she would go to see her children's school in New Jersey. Her decision saved Grant from assassination at Ford's Theatre.[3]

[2] Welles, "Lincoln and Johnson," *Galaxy*, XIII, (1872) 526.
[3] Adam Badeau, *Grant in Peace. From Appomattox to Mount McGregor*, 362.

GRANT IN 1865

8

The conspirators who murdered Lincoln had included Grant in their plans for wholesale assassination. Expecting him at the theatre, they neglected to keep a close watch on his movements. In the evening, as General and Mrs. Grant were driving to the station, a dark-visaged man, whom they later thought was Booth, rode close and peered into their carriage. Either the darkness prevented recognition, or the murderer desired bigger game, for there was no attack. In Philadelphia, a wire from Stanton told Grant of the tragedy. A special train rushed the general back to the capital.

For the next two months Grant found himself immersed in the problems of war's aftermath. He frequently attended Cabinet meetings where, as at the last meeting before Lincoln's death, the principal topic of conversation was the condition of the South. In these discussions, Grant appeared as the friend of the South—living up to the rôle he had assumed at Appomattox. In the Cabinet, however, there were few to agree with him. Lincoln's assassination, a diabolical and unnecessary tragedy, caused many in the North to demand vengeance on the Southern leaders and people. The new President, Johnson, long hated by the Southern aristocracy, offered a reward for the capture of Jefferson Davis as an instigator of Booth's crime. Throughout the North, the masses who had been victimized by war propaganda rejoiced in the accession of a President who would show no leniency to the rebellious States.

Just as the body of the martyred President was being carried from the capital, a messenger from General Sherman came to Grant bearing the terms of a convention which Sherman had made with Joseph E. Johnston. Going beyond the mere surrender of the Confederate armies, the convention pledged the President of the United States to recognize the governments of the Southern States, and to guarantee the political privileges of the Southern people. Sherman had acted in accordance with Lincoln's wishes, and his convention practically amounted to a treaty of peace. Had Lincoln lived, he would probably have approved it, but the sentiments of the Northern government and people had suddenly changed. Understanding the change, Grant realized that Sherman's terms could not be accepted, but carried the convention to Secretary Stanton, who discussed the matter with a hastily-called Cabinet which roundly denounced Sherman. Grant, however, was "tender to sensitiveness" of his subordinate's feelings, and "abstained from censure." When the Cabinet decided to reject the convention, Grant hastened to North Carolina to soften the blow.[4] With considerable tact, he persuaded Sherman to substitute the terms under which Lee had surrendered.

Both General Sherman and his Senator brother, John, appreciated Grant's action. "Grant is a jewel," the Senator wrote; "I shall always feel grateful to him." At Stanton, however, General Sherman was intensely angry. The Secretary of War had given an account of the Cabinet meeting to the newspapers, and had criticized the general to the reporters. "Unless Grant interposes from his yielding and good nature, I shall get some . . . good opportunity to insult Stanton," Sherman wrote his wife.[5] At the grand review of the armies on May 23–24, Sherman found his opportunity and refused to shake hands with the offending Secretary.[6]

The grand review was the last concerted action of the Union armies in the Civil War. North and South, soldiers put away their uniforms to resume civilian garb and peace-time duties. In the six months from May to November, 1865, 800,000 returned to their homes.[7] They were to reassemble frequently in commemoration of their services, and stood ready to remind the nation, in Grant's words, that there was "but one debt contracted in the last four years which the people of the United States cannot pay. That is the debt of gratitude to the rank and file of our Army and Navy." [8]

In addition to the duties connected with disbanding the army, Grant concerned himself with two other problems of importance at the moment; the French in Mexico, and the treatment of the Southern generals.

Grant's interest in the French in Mexico led him to pursue a policy which was more creditable to his military aggressiveness than to his appreciation of the tortuous pathways of diplomacy. Throughout the winter of 1864–1865, while still before Richmond, Grant kept an eye on Maximilian's attempt to establish an empire with the support of Napoleon III. Frequently Grant told his staff that as soon as Lee was

[4] Welles, *Diary*, II, 294–297.
[5] *Sherman Letters*, 244–250; James Ford Rhodes, *History of the United States from the Compromise of 1850 to the Final Restoration of Home Rule at the South in 1877*, V, 178.
[6] Porter, *Campaigning with Grant*, 510.
[7] Report of the Secretary of War, 1865; *Official Records*, series 3, V, 517 ff.
[8] Grant to J. J. Talmadge, mayor of Milwaukee, May 25, 1865, MS. Printed in catalogue of Thomas J. Madigan.

defeated they would have to fight the imperalists.[9] On the evening of April 10, after writing Sherman the news of Lee's surrender, Grant rose from his headquarters table and remarked, with the air of one who had found a new world to conquer, "Now for Mexico!"[10] As a military commander, he was willing to lead his veterans to another war, and as a patriot he perceived in Maximilian's attempt an "act of hostility against the Government of the U. S."[11] In Cabinet meetings and in letters to President Johnson, Grant urged intervention, and on the day of the grand review he dispatched Sheridan to command 52,000 troops on the Rio Grande. Furthermore, he planned to send General Schofield into Mexico to recruit discharged Union and paroled Confederate soldiers for the republican armies of President Jaurez. He even urged the War Department to sell arms to the opponents of Mexican Emperor Maximilian. Most of the army officers and many of the people supported Grant in these proposals. The costs of intervention, however, were too great; more peaceful counsels prevailed, and eventually Seward induced France to give up her aggressive intentions.[12]

At the same time Grant was holding a very commendable position on the Southern question. His terms to Lee had been extended to other Confederate forces, and all the erstwhile Southern soldiers were on parole and not to be molested so long as they refrained from taking up arms against the government. Many in the North objected to this protected status, and sought to devise means whereby they might wreak vengeance on the Confederate leaders. Ben Butler hastened from Massachusetts to advise Johnson that Confederate generals were not immune from civil process,[13] and a grand jury at Norfolk indicted Lee for treason. Immediately the Confederate chieftain appealed to Grant for protection, and Grant advised Lee to apply for a pardon. Assured that Grant would endorse his plea, Lee wrote for an interpretation of the terms of his parole and sent an application for a pardon. Intent on having his promises respected by the government, Grant carried the papers to Johnson. "When can these men be tried?" asked the President. "Never, unless they violate their paroles," replied the general.

[9] Badeau, *Grant in Peace*, 180.
[10] Garland, *U. S. Grant*, 314.
[11] Ellis P. Oberholtzer, *A History of the United States since the Civil War*, I, 310.
[12] W. A. Dunning, *Reconstruction, Political and Economic*, 153; Rhodes, VI, 206; Badeau, *Grant in Peace*, 180–189; N. Y. *Tribune*, October 5, 6, 1865; Welles, *Diary*, II, 317, 322, 327, 332–3, 367.
[13] George F. Milton, *Age of Hate*, 170.

On that position Grant remained firm, and no further efforts were made to bring Confederate soldiers to trial.[14]

Except in such matters as Mexico and the Confederate paroles, where politics and military affairs seemed to coincide, Grant paid little attention to the political cauldron boiling around him. So far as the South was concerned, Grant's attitude was one of practical humanity, unclouded by philosophical speculations on constitutional theory. While in North Carolina with Sherman, Grant wrote to Julia that "the suffering that must exist in the South the next year . . . will be beyond conception. People who talk of further retaliation and punishment, except of the political leaders, either do not conceive of the suffering endured already, or they are heartless and unfeeling and wish to stay at home out of danger while the punishment is being inflicted." [15]

How far Grant's attitude influenced President Johnson is impossible to determine. Johnson himself testified that he acted frequently on Grant's advice, and that the general was "the strongest man of all in the support of my policy." [16] Gideon Welles, the indefatigable and irascible diarist, gives no indication that Grant was ever opposed to the President, although he was frequently present at meetings where Johnson's policies were being discussed. Grant and George H. Thomas were Johnson's favorites among the generals.[17]

Upon Johnson's accession, Radical leaders had hailed the new President as a recruit to their cause. Fearful that the return of the Southern States would result in the overthrow of the Republican Party, the Radical leaders were largely agreed on the necessity of imposing Negro suffrage on the South. Almost from the moment of his accession, Senator Sumner, Chief Justice Chase, and other Radicals laid siege to Johnson to convert him to their position. Seemingly to the zealot Sumner, Johnson agreed that Negro suffrage must be the basis of reconstruction. Although it is likely that the doctrinaire Sumner mistook courtesy for agreement, and that the President was withholding his opinion, much in Johnson's own conduct held out hope to the Radicals. Throughout the war, Johnson had fulminated against the Southern leaders, voicing frequently the fiery statement that 'treason must be made

---

[14] Badeau, *Grant in Peace,* 256; Robert E. Lee, Jr., *Recollections and Letters of General Robert E. Lee,* 164.

[15] Badeau, *Grant in Peace,* 31.

[16] Johnson to B. Tremen, *Century Magazine,* LXXXV, (1913) 439.

[17] Welles, *Diary,* II, 367.

odious and traitors punished and impoverished.' [18]

Although Johnson had no respect for the Southern leaders, he was both a strict constructionist in constitutional theory and a Southerner. As a Southerner he realized, as no Northerner could ever do, the social problems involved in emancipation. Slavery had served a useful purpose in adjusting the relations between two different races, and its abolition made necessary new measures of social control. Long devoted to the State Rights dogma of the Democrats, Johnson believed that such matters of internal police should best be left to the States, and could find no warrant in the constitution for dictating the suffrage qualifications in any State. Unable and unwilling to understand the Southern viewpoint, Northern Radicals held to the theory that the Negro was a white man with a black skin, who, freed from bondage, and given political rights, would rapidly adjust himself to a white man's civilization. Moreover, through gratitude to his deliverers he would vote the Republican ticket.

Fundamentally, the issue between Johnson and his Congress was over the treatment of the Negro. In two proclamations on May 29, he made his first declaration of principles—and said nothing about Negro suffrage. In proclaiming amnesty, the President followed closely the model set up by his predecessor, offering pardon to all but a few of the higher civil and military officers of the Confederacy who would take an oath of allegiance. The only difference from Lincoln's proclamation was that Johnson excluded from his general amnesty men who held property worth $20,000. Essentially plebeian, Johnson regarded the rich men of the South with suspicion, and preferred to entrust reconstruction to the submerged white classes.

Johnson's second proclamation related to the reconstruction of North Carolina. A Unionist, W. W. Holden, was appointed provisional governor, and instructed to enroll the loyal people of the State. When that was done, a convention should be elected which should revise the State Constitution. Strangely enough, while both Johnson and his Cabinet thought the President was carrying out Lincoln's program, the procedure provided in the proclamation and in subsequent instructions to the governor was that embodied in the Wade-Davis bill, which Lincoln had vetoed. But the Radicals recognized no similarity. In the year following the Wade-Davis bill the Radicals had moved rapidly

[18] Milton, *Age of Hate,* 178–183.

forward, and had concentrated their attention on Negro suffrage. Constitutionalist and Southerner, Johnson would not force the South's hand on the Negro question.

Johnson's failure to give the Negroes the vote was the signal for the opposition to charge its guns. Immediately upon release of the proclamation, the Radicals began to denounce Johnson in the same way they had denounced Lincoln. Wendell Phillips and Charles Sumner harangued Massachusetts audiences, and before the summer was over Sumner had persuaded the Massachusetts Republicans to condemn the Johnson policy. In Pennsylvania, the bitter Thad Stevens obtained the same result. In other Northern States the Radical element, a vigorous and venomous minority, were on the war path.

At the moment when Johnson was receiving the bitter invectives of the Radicals, General Grant was finding himself the most popular man in the nation. Newspapers had never ceased to praise his military achievements, self-restraint, and simplicity, and the people generally joined in the panegyrics. "I am no admirer of military heroes," Motley wrote the Duchess of Argyll, "but we needed one at this period, and we can never be too thankful that exactly such a one was vouchsafed to us—one . . . so destitute of personal ambition, so modest, so adverse to public notoriety. . . . So long as we produce such a man as Grant, our republic is safe." [19] Grateful citizens heaped gifts upon him. Boxes of cigars, swords, horses, congressional medals, and honorary degrees poured in to express the popular admiration for the man who had saved the Union.

Most valuable of the early tributes to the general was a house in Philadelphia, presented by the Union League Club to Mrs. Grant. The house, generally described as a mansion, was completely furnished, according to the "exquisite taste" of the age, with velvet carpets, lace curtains, and "rich but not gaudy furniture." The parlor, for example, was equipped with a "fine piano, a pair of beautiful vases in an antique style, a handsome clock surmounted by a statuette representing a historian," a "magnificently bound" Bible on a center table, and a bust of General Grant, "resting on a richly carved pedestal." The other rooms were furnished in the same rococo style.

Equally ostentatious—and equally typical of the taste of the age—were the ovations accorded the general wherever he appeared. During

[19] John L. Motley, *The Correspondence of John Lothrop Motley*, II, 202.

the summer of 1865 Grant traveled through the North accompanied by members of his family and military staff. The trip soon took on the appearance of a Roman triumph. Parades, banquets, and public receptions were held in his honor; people congregated at village stations to greet the party and perchance to shake the general's hand. Everywhere as he appeared bands broke into the triumphal notes of "Hail to the Chief," and played it so continuously that the tone-deaf general eventually deluded himself into believing that he recognized the march.

For the many gifts and the public receptions, General Grant was profoundly but mutely grateful. Neither the cheers of the crowds nor the importunities of the "leading citizens" who appeared on, platforms with him availed to break his silence. Occasionally, in low tones, he would speak a sentence of thanks; generally, he asked someone to explain to the audience that he was unaccustomed to speaking. As a result, newspapers throughout the country praised his simplicity; and people weary of oratory enjoyed the novelty of a public man who would not make a speech. But to his children, his taciturnity was a source of embarrassment. Once when the crowds at a station clamored good-naturedly for a speech, Jesse, aged seven, besought his father to comply. Wags in the crowd, hearing the child, called for a speech from Jesse; and to their amusement and the proud embarrassment of the chieftain, the lad bravely sought to retrieve the family honor by reciting "The Boy Stood on the Burning Deck." [20]

At Galena, whence the unknown Grant had departed four years before, the townspeople turned out in full force to welcome home their hero. Remembering Grant's humorous assertion that he would like to be mayor long enough to build a sidewalk from his house to the station, the people strung across the street an immense banner blazoning the news: "General, the Sidewalk is Built." Along that new sidewalk Grant was borne to the humble cottage he had once occupied. Now resplendent with fresh paint and equipped with new furniture, it was presented to its former occupant—a $16,000 gift of residents of Galena to their most distinguished citizen.[21]

The significant feature of these ovations and gifts was the spirit in which they were accorded. "The People," said the New York *World*, "feel that in honoring Grant they are honoring all that is best in them-

[20] Badeau, *Grant in Peace*, 175.
[21] Richardson, *Personal History*, 514.

selves. They endorse no political theory in this frank homage; they
serve no political ambition in paying court. . . ." [22] Although his father
Jesse spoke before the Ohio Republican Convention [23] and Democrats
claimed Grant as a member of their party, no word from him indicated
that he was other than a soldier who eschewed politics. General Badeau,
who constantly attended him as a member of his staff, declared that
Grant had "no political bias, and, I believe, no political ambition." [24]

But if Grant had no political bias, his position in the public esteem
made his support valuable to Johnson. The aged Frank Blair, acutely
observing the political winds, urged Johnson to bind Grant to him
by making him Secretary of War in Stanton's place.[25] Though unwilling to precipitate a struggle with his opponents in this manner, Johnson planned to capitalize Grant's prestige by sending him into the
South to report on conditions there.

While Grant was receiving the nation's praises, the South was under-
going the work of restoration. Following his North Carolina proclamation, Johnson had appointed provisional governors for all the Southern
States. Eagerly turning to the tasks before them, these governors appointed local officials, and called State conventions which would take
the necessary steps to restore the "proper practical relations" with the
Union. Johnson suggested to the State conventions that they repeal
their ordinances of secession, abolish slavery, and extend the franchise
to such Negroes as possessed a reasonable amount of property.

Unfortunately for the President's policy, the conventions ignored his
advice, and revealed an almost criminal ignorance of Northern psychology. Throughout the summer, Radical orators and writers garnered
political capital from the mistakes of the Southern meetings. Chief
Justice Chase, intent on his own political chances in 1868, journeyed
into the South to advance the cause of Negro suffrage. From the various
places he visited he sent back reports on Southern conditions. Although
he found much that was favorable, he remained convinced that Negro
suffrage was a necessity. In the same manner, although in more positive
tone, Carl Schurz wrote reports to a Boston newspaper. Sent south by
the President, Schurz arranged through Senator Sumner to write articles
in support of the Radical position for the Boston *Advertiser*. For this

22 N. Y. *World*, June 8, 1865.
23 N. Y. *Times*, July 2, 1865.
24 Badeau, *Grant in Peace*, 33.
25 Welles, *Diary*, II, 364.

PARLOR OF THE GALENA HOME AS PRESENTED TO GRANT AFTER THE CIVIL WAR

service, the German-American not only received compensation from the newspaper, but had his insurance premiums paid by "friends of the cause." [26]

Although the reports of these men intensified the Radical desire to impose stringent conditions for readmitting the South, a large class in the North nevertheless approved Johnson's actions. To business men it was obvious that the "political adjustments of Southern society are of importance for the material development of the nation." It was widely believed that Johnson's policy, restoring "peace and protection" in the South, would cause a large immigration into the Southern States, open markets, and provide for the profitable expansion of Northern capital.

The widespread approval of the President's course must have been apparent to Grant. General Badeau reported to Washburne that "everywhere I hear warm commendation of Mr. Johnson's policy; in New York as well as St. Louis, at Washington just as at Galena, all the sober, substantial men seemed to support him. The attempt of foolish impractical men has met with no success, so far as I can judge." [27]

After returning from his summer's tour, and before setting out to inspect the South for the President, Grant determined to rent his Philadelphia house and remove to Washington. His original plan to live in the Quaker city and attend to public business by telegraph was obviously impractical.[28] Early in November, he bought, "on excellent terms," a house once occupied by Vice-President Breckenridge, two doors from one once formerly owned by Stephen A. Douglas. To the delight of younger staff officers, Mrs. Grant planned to bring three young ladies from Galena for a winter visit, and the entire family, official and private, looked forward to a winter of festivities.[29]

As soon as he had arranged for his new house, the general and three of his staff started south. Going first to Richmond, they spent an afternoon as the guests of a loyalist who had been a Union refugee. The second day they were in Raleigh, where, invited to seats on the floor of the North Carolina legislature, they were treated to loyal addresses. Both in Virginia and North Carolina they noticed that the Negroes, by refusing to work, were retarding economic recovery. Over execrable

[26] Claude M. Fuess, *Carl Schurz*, 131–132.
[27] Badeau to Washburne, October 20, 1865, Washburne MSS.
[28] U. S. Grant to Jesse Grant, Cramer, *Conversations*, 102–103.
[29] Badeau to Washburne, November 9, 1865, Washburne MSS.

railroads, still showing the ravages of war, they traveled to Charleston, where Colonel Comstock, aide to the general, found that the inhabitants were sullen. "Several who called themselves ladies" made faces at the Yankee officers, and Comstock concluded they were showing openly what their husbands and brothers felt. However, at dinner with a number of notables, among them Governor Aiken, Governor Orr, Dr. Mackey, and Judge Magrath, the conversation was loyal. Magrath, just released from the Federal prison at Port Pulaski, declared the outcome of the war fortunate, and Comstock concluded that his imprisonment had "done him good." From Charleston, the observers went to Savannah and Augusta before returning to Washington.

The trip was hardly extensive enough to furnish valuable information about the South. Information, indeed, was not its purpose. Johnson had sent a number of more competent observers into the South while Grant was receiving Northern ovations; but he was eager to avail himself of the general's prestige. Grant's report supported the President's policy. Comstock, who had seen the same things that Grant saw, believed that for a year or two the government would have to exercise some control over the South to protect the Negro, and concluded that the best way would be to keep Southern members out of Congress until their States had done "everything necessary." [30] But Grant had obtained no such impressions.

Meanwhile Congress assembled in Washington. Having been excluded during the summer from active participation in the work of reconstruction, the Radical leaders hastened to the capital full of schemes for overthrowing Andrew Johnson and all his works. On the eve of the opening session, by shrewd maneuvers Thad Stevens lined up the Republican majority against the President. Intent upon asserting the right of Congress to define the conditions of reconstruction, Stevens instructed the clerk of the House to omit the names of Southern representatives. Without the votes of the excluded Southerners the House was organized, and Stevens immediately pushed through a resolution creating a Joint Committee of Fifteen to which all questions relating to the South would be submitted. Then, having condemned in advance the policies of the President, the Congress settled itself to listen with scorn and bitterness to his first message.

When Grant returned from the South, he was immediately called

[30] Comstock MS. Diary, November 25 to December 12, 1865.

before the Cabinet. To the members he stated that he had found the Southerners more loyal and better disposed than he had expected, and he expressed his conviction that every consideration called for the early reëstablishment of the Union. Gideon Welles urged him to commit these "sensible, patriotic, and wise" views to writing and to communicate them freely to the members of Congress.[31]

While calling on the Naval Secretary the next day, Sumner was forced to listen to Grant's conclusions. "The mass of thinking men of the South accept the present situation in good faith," Welles read to the indignant Senator, and "they are in earnest in wishing to do what is required of them by the government." [32] Unimpressed, Sumner demanded what Grant's opinion was worth as compared with Chase's. "I valued it highly," said Welles, "for it seemed to me practical common sense from a man of no political knowledge or aspiration, while Chase theorized and had great political ambition." [33] A few days later, in the Senate, Sumner branded Grant's report as "whitewashing." [34] Carl Schurz's report was better suited to the Radical taste.

Throughout the session of Congress, which lasted until late in the summer of 1866, Grant remained a supporter of Johnson. Protected by the army tradition of isolation from politics, his support did not incur the open enmity of the President's opponents. Moreover, the General's popularity made any attack on him unwise. Instead, the Radicals began a subterranean campaign to win him over to their cause; and they set themselves to find the weak point in Grant's armor.

Although the Radicals did not recognize it for some time, the weakest point in Grant's armor was the very popularity which made him a valuable addition to any cause. Before it dawned upon the congressional leaders, lesser figures, outside the national legislature, sensed this fact. Grant's willingness to accept gifts and to receive them without suspecting the source from whence they came was early hit upon as a means of approach by men whose motives might be suspected.

The first evidence that Grant had been generally marked as a man of potential political influence came in New York, in November, 1865, before he went into the South. Coming at the end of a summer of almost incessant ovations, the New York celebration surpassed in bril-

---

[31] Welles, *Diary*, II, 396–397.
[32] *Senate Executive Document*, 39th Congress, 1st Session, No. 2, p. 107.
[33] Welles, *Diary*, II, 397–398.
[34] *Cong. Globe*, 39th Congress, 1st session, 78; Welles, *Diary*, II, 400.

liance anything that had gone before. For a week Grant and his family were subjected to a round of festivities which began with public receptions and ended with a banquet of astounding magnificence. Vying with one another for places near his person were a host of minor politicians, and sprinkled among them were many who would not be averse to receiving favors from the government. A. T. Stewart, the merchant prince who owned the largest department store in the city, acted as master of ceremonies. Dancing in attendance were George Wilkes, editor and speculator; General Lew Wallace, who had just presided over the military court which condemned to death the innocent Wirz of Andersonville prison; Moses H. Grinnell, a politician who had long kept his eye on the well-paid offices of the custom house. And though Democrats like General John A. Dix were present, the group which most assiduously pursued Grant was a sinister crew whom a man more versed in the ways of the world would have suspected.

In a final reception that surpassed all others in "grandeur, prestige and brilliancy" and was "remarkably free from ultra-democratic elements," the police were unable to hold back the three thousand people who came without invitations. Gentlemen spilled the refreshments over the dresses of the ladies, or crowded them against the walls, in the rush for tables loaded with salads, champagnes, creams, fruits, and candies.

The sponsors of the reception—although not of the confusion—were A. T. Stewart, Edwards Pierrepont, August Belmont, and Moses Grinnell.[35] These men, most of them figures of importance in the financial life of the metropolis, stood upon the border line between business and politics. To Grant, whose business career had been a succession of failures, the attentions of such men must have been pleasing. It is an interesting psychological speculation whether he did not find in association with these successful men of affairs a compensation for his forty years of repression and failure. Speculation, unfortunately, it must remain, for Grant never analyzed his own mind, and his reticence guarded him against any inadvertent expression of his own emotions. One fact, however, is certain. His complete lack of experience in politics blinded him to the possible uses to which his prestige might be put. Throughout the winter, he continued to be honored by receptions and plied with gifts from his wealthy friends. At Christmas, he received a horse from

35 N. Y. *Tribune*, November 16–21, 1865.

"several gentlemen in New York." [36] In March he was presented with $100,000, raised in New York, to pay the mortgage on his Washington home. Between these two gifts, there came from fifty "solid men of Boston" a library which had cost $75,000.[37]

A revealing incident occurred in connection with this last gift. In order to avoid duplication, the committee raising the money asked the "merchant representative" Samuel B. Hooper, of Boston, to ascertain what military books the General owned. After cautious inquiries, Mr. Hooper reported that Grant owned no military books. In fact, his library consisted largely of patent office reports.[38]

In humorous mood, the New York *Tribune*, whose editor viewed with apprehension Grant's growing political significance, asserted that future generations would read, "as the final evidence of the serene patience, the dogged endurance, the imperturbability which history will attribute to General Grant, that he was the undismayed hero of a thousand receptions." "Since Richmond's capitulation," it declared, "the stern soldier has spent his days, and eke his nights, in conjugating the transitive verb *to receive*, in all its moods and tenses, but always in the first person singular, active or passive." [39] Another paper estimated that Grant had conjugated the verb for a total of $175,000,—a figure obviously too low.[40]

Although Grant may not have realized the significance of these presents, there were many who did. Horace White, editor of the Chicago *Tribune* and vigorous opponent of the protective tariff, hoped to combat the insidious work of the Eastern leaders by educating the general. "I am persuaded that Grant is to be the next President if he gives us half a chance to nominate him," White wrote to Washburne. "Before *his* time is over," the editor prophesied, "the question of high protective tariffs is going to be an overmastering one in politics." Since he believed that the Northwest was "being bled at every pore by the existing tariff for the benefit of New England and Pennsylvania," he sent a copy of the "Catechism on the Corn Laws" to be given Grant in order that "he should read up a little on the question, beforehand." [41]

[36] N. Y. *Tribune*, December 25, 1865.
[37] *Harpers Weekly*, March 25, 1866; Perley's *Reminiscences*, II, 218.
[38] Geo. S. Boutwell, *The Lawyer, the Statesman, and the Soldier*, 173.
[39] N. Y. *Tribune*, February 23, 1866.
[40] Georgetown (D.C.) *Courier*, March 10, 1866.
[41] White to Washburne, March 12, 1866, Washburne Mss.

The book was doubtless shelved among the military volumes in Grant's new library.

During this same winter, Andrew Johnson and the Radicals were locking horns over reconstruction. Just after the Christmas recess debate began on a bill to extend the life of the Freedmen's Bureau and extend the scope of its activities. To the Southerners the operation of the Bureau was particularly obnoxious, and they were anxious to see its end. To the Radicals, however, it was a means of protecting the Negroes from former owners whose legislatures were enacting "black codes" which seemed designed to restore the substance of slavery. Grant reported to Johnson that agents of the Freedmen's Bureau encouraged the Negroes to believe that their masters' property would be divided among them. "This belief is seriously interfering with the willingness of the freedmen to make contracts for the coming year," asserted the general. However, he believed the bureau was an "absolute necessity . . . in some form" until civil law was reëstablished. He recommended that its officials be brought more fully under Army control.[42] While they rejected the remainder, this phase of Grant's report pleased the Radicals.

The new Freedmen's Bureau bill, which attempted to extend civil rights to the Negroes, was sent to the President early in February. On the 19th, Johnson returned the bill with his veto. In his opinion there was no necessity for the measure, which was unconstitutional and ill-adapted to accomplish its avowed purpose. After enumerating his constitutional objections, Johnson echoed Grant's sentiments by pointing out that the bureau would "tend to keep the mind of the freedmen in a state of uncertain expectation and restlessness." Finally, Johnson doubted the validity of any legislation passed when eleven States were unrepresented in Congress.[43]

A holiday crowd of Johnson's supporters gathered at a theatre to indorse his acts. Drawing up resolutions, they proceeded to the White House to present them. Here Johnson, unmindful of promises he had made his friends, addressed them. For the most part, his speech was in good taste and embodied a sound statement of his principles. However, the applause of the enthusiastic audience led him into a denuncia-

[42] *Senate Executive Document*, no. 2, p. 117, 39th Congress, 1st session.
[43] James D. Richardson, *A Compilation of the Messages and Papers of the Presidents*, VI, 398–405.

tion of his enemies, and he even intimated that they would like to assassinate him. Next day these intemperate remarks were pounced upon by the Radical press and presented to the people as the mouthings of a drunken demagogue.[44]

At the moment that Johnson was hurling invectives at his congressional opponents, Grant was being presented a portrait of Winfield Scott at the Union Club in New York. On that same day, Johnson's friends in New York held a meeting to indorse Presidential reconstruction. It was significant that neither donors nor recipient of the picture were present at the Johnson meeting.[45]

On the morning after this presentation, the New York *Herald*, friendly to the Administration, advocated Grant's nomination for President by the Johnsonians. It was the plan of the editor, James Gordon Bennett, to attach Grant to Johnson's policy and bring peace to the country.[46] In veiled opposition to this proposal, Horace Greeley's *Tribune* began to remark that hero-worship was the "besetting sin" of the American people, and to deplore their "pitiable taste" in the selection of heroes. "There is every reason why we should honor those who survived the great battles. . . . But is it this we do when we give gifts and receptions to one man?" [47]

Even before this editorial tilt, the Radicals hit upon the plan of impudently claiming Grant as their own. Grant's reticence in avowing his principles assisted them, and in January the report was current that he had been won over to repudiate his Southern report.[48] Radicals inspired Associated Press stories indicating that Grant was "leaning" toward them. When General Terry suppressed the Richmond *Enquirer*, dispatches asserted that he had acted on Grant's orders. Other items related that Grant had turned a deaf ear to Editor Pollard's plea to have Terry's order revoked, that he planned to "close up" all the disloyal papers in the South, and that he was about to arrest a number of disloyal Kentuckians.[49]

Many of the Radicals, however, were unwilling to resort to such tactics. "If General Grant was really radical this would be well enough,"

---

[44] Milton, *Age of Hate*, 291 ff.
[45] N. Y. *Tribune*, February 22, 23, 1866.
[46] W. B. Phillips to Johnson, Johnson MSS., Cited in Milton, *Age of Hate*, 296.
[47] N. Y. *Tribune*, February 27, 1866.
[48] Milton, *Age of Hate*, 290.
[49] Shaffer to B. F. Butler, February 17, 1866, Butler Mss.

a correspondent wrote Ben Butler; "but I know he has no sympathy with radicals." Some, like Horace Greeley, were unconvinced that Grant would make a satisfactory addition to the cause. Ben Butler, whom Welles suspected of intending to "take an active part in the rising questions," [50] was venomous in his opposition. In December Grant's report of the last year of the war was published. Butler was highly incensed over a statement that he had been "bottled up" at Bermuda Hundred. In February, Butler declined an invitation to one of Grant's receptions in a curt note which was currently quoted as stating: "In no event would I be willing to hold personal intercourse with yourself or any member of your family." [51] Although Butler alleged that he had received overtures to make up, he declared "I never forget nor forgive until reparation is made, and in Grant's case it never can be." "Grant is a rascal," he informed one of his satellites.[52]

Although Greeley intimated that Grant—and Sherman as well—opposed Negro suffrage,[53] the congressional Radicals failed to heed this charge of heresy. Their efforts to claim Grant continued; and, in competition with them, the Johnsonian bids increased. The elder Blair proposed that Johnson should oust Stanton from the Cabinet and give the place to Grant. Johnson's friends repeatedly came to the President charging that Stanton was in league with the Radicals. To these friends, the proposed Cabinet change would serve the double purpose of ridding Johnson of a traitorous adviser, and defeat the Radical bids for Grant.[54] Moreover, the fact that Grant disliked Stanton was well known. In January, friction between them had led Grant to appeal to Johnson. Johnson sustained the general and hinted that Stanton would not stay long.[55] In the spring, "Dick" Taylor, son of "Old Rough and Ready" and brother-in-law of Jefferson Davis, visited Washington. Finding Grant in thorough accord with Johnson's policy, he persuaded him to join in a request for Stanton's removal. Johnson "responded favorably, earnestly, and decidedly."

The next day, Stanton called at Grant's house to discuss the matter with him. To the general's surprise, Stanton proposed that Grant and

[50] Welles, *Diary*, II, 284–289.
[51] N. Y. *Tribune*, February 9, 1866.
[52] Butler to Shaffer, March 12, 1866; Butler to R. Hawkins, May 1, 1866; and to G. Weitzel, May 10, 1866, Butler Mss.
[53] N. Y. *Tribune*, March 7, 1866.
[54] Welles, *Diary*, II, 480.
[55] Comstock MS. Diary, January 15, 1866.

Taylor should join him in an open declaration endorsing Johnson. Unable to fathom the reason for this proposal, Grant went to Taylor, who emphatically refused to have any connection with the Secretary of War. Together, Grant and Taylor set out to inform Johnson of this new development. Because of his characteristic indecision, Johnson seemed confused, and they suspected that the President had been talking to Stanton. Perhaps Johnson had dreamed of holding both Stanton's and Grant's support. [56]

Early in April one of Grant's receptions was made the occasion for another Radical attempt to appropriate the popular general. Led by Thad Stevens and Lyman Trumbull, a number of Radical congressmen planned to attend the reception and to lionize Grant. However, Johnson lacked neither political acumen nor experienced advisers. Grasping the situation, the President and his two daughters appeared at the reception early in the evening. Montgomery Blair, also accompanied by a female contingent, Gideon Welles, and Alexander H. Stephens came to lend a helping hand. When the Radicals, arriving late, saw the President, they were "astonished and amazed"; and Stevens, "though a brave old stager," was so "taken aback" that he plainly showed his discomfiture.[57] In retaliation, at one of Johnson's receptions a month later the Radicals waxed effusive over Grant; but they could not overcome the march that the President had stolen.[58]

These almost comic bids for his favor wrought no outward change in Grant's demeanor. Although John Sherman wrote his brother that "Grant has some political ambitions and can, if he wishes it, easily obtain the presidency," [59] the general gave no indication that he considered himself a potential candidate. To "Dick" Taylor he expressed a distaste for politics and politicians, and averred that he wished to confine himself solely to his duties as commander of the army.[60] Early in June, old Jesse Grant asserted that his son "could not well stand the trial of being a candidate for Republican favors," [61] and General Badeau protested to Washburne against Radical misrepresentations of Grant and his staff. "It is undesirable, especially at this juncture, that

---

[56] Welles, *Diary*, III, 72; Richard Taylor, *Destruction and Reconstruction: Personal Experiences of the Late War*, 242 ff.
[57] Welles, *Diary*, II, 477–478.
[58] N. Y. *Tribune*, May 16, 1866.
[59] *Sherman Letters*, 269.
[60] Taylor, *Destruction*, 242.
[61] J. R. Grant to E. C. Collins, Cited in Cross, *Life of Grant*, 35.

we should be represented as politicians or partisans." [62]

The special "juncture" which made any declaration undesirable can best be understood by another glance at the waxing struggle between Johnson and the Thirty-ninth Congress. In February, the Radicals failed to pass the Freedmen's Bureau bill over Johnson's veto. However, this was the President's last victory. The Radicals immediately began to whip the moderate Republicans into line, and before long presented a "Civil Rights" bill for the executive approval. This measure, which declared that Negroes were citizens of the United States and granted them all the rights of white men, was even more obnoxious to Johnson than the Freedmen's Bureau bill. It received the expected veto. But this time the Radicals were ready; ousting from the Senate a moderate from New Jersey, and forcing another Senator to break a pair, they passed the bill over the veto.[63] Then, with disciplined organization, they set about drafting a second Freedmen's Bureau bill, and when Johnson vetoed it, repassed it over his objections.

However, only in policies relating directly to the South was the Radical discipline effective. Johnson's veto was still potent on non-political measures, and Congress was unable even to override his veto of an act admitting Colorado as a new State. Comprehension of this situation inhibited Grant from making any commitment to either of the opposing forces. Being interested in a bill to create the grade of General of the Armies, he could not afford, at that "juncture" to be known as a "partisan."

In November, 1865, before Congress assembled, William Whiting of Roxbury, Mass., sent Washburne a bill to create the grade of General. "I like the idea of giving to the Savior of the Country every honor we can offer," he wrote in submitting the measure, "and with the honor, some *substantial* recognition of his services by giving him the means of defraying the expenses which must be necessarily incurred in maintaining the dignity of his exalted position." [64] Only Washington had previously held this rank, but so great was the enthusiasm for Grant that the proposal met with general approval. However, Samuel Butterfield of New York asked Washburne to hold it up for a time, as it might interfere with the liberality of the subscriptions he was gather-

---

[62] Badeau to Washburne, July 3, 1866, Washburne Mss.
[63] Ellis P. Oberholtzer, *Jay Cooke, Financier of the Civil War,* I, 177–178.
[64] Whiting to Washburne, November 18, 1865, Washburne MSS.

ing to raise the mortgage on Grant's house.[65]

Another bill in which Grant was interested was the direct outgrowth of his suggestions to the military committees of Congress on the needs of the army. Although he had told them that Negro troops should be removed from the South, he advised the retention of white garrisons there. He did not believe that it would be wise to arm the Southern militia, and he pointed out that western expansion called for additional troops in the regular army.[66]

Grant watched carefully while these two bills went through the legislative mill. The Generalcy bill created the new military grade and provided for salary and emoluments of $20,000 a year. Late in July, a few days before Congress adjourned, these bills received Johnson's approval. Grant was immediately promoted to the higher rank.[67]

His confirmation as General of the Armies was almost the last act of the first session of the Thirty-ninth Congress—a body in which Gideon Welles found "little statesmanship . . . but a vast amount of party depravity." Much of its time had been taken up with granting acts of incorporation, giving bounties and special privileges to favored enterprises, and generally engaging in "profligate legislation of every description." The iron and wool interests were especially active in advancing "schemes" to increase the "enormous taxation" which inured to their profit.[68] The masters of capital were in the saddle, and were using well the whip hand which the exclusion of the South permitted.

The position was so advantageous that the masters of capital attempted to make it permanent. As the most feasible means to this end appeared to be Negro enfranchisement and Rebel disenfranchisement, Congress early in 1866 prepared to force the Fourteenth Amendment on the Southern States. With this amendment as their platform, they adjourned to go before the country in the congressional elections. In opposition to them, President Johnson and his supporters planned a vigorous campaign, and lines were drawn for the conflict. Of the leading men of the country only one had not declared his opinions: everywhere men were asking, "Is Grant a Radical?"

[65] Butterfield to Washburne, December 8, 1865, Washburne MSS.
[66] New York *World*, January 15, 1866; New York *Tribune*, January 15, May 18, 1866.
[67] Badeau, *Grant in Peace*, 47; New York *Tribune*, May 8, 12, 17, July 18, 1866.
[68] Welles, *Diary*, II, 548–549.

"OH, General, horrors upon horrors accumulate," wrote a Louisiana carpetbagger to Ben Butler as he related the gory details of how "the Rebel Mayor John G. Monro armed his Rebel Police with Revolvers and Bowie knives and privately ordered them to go and massacre" the loyal men of New Orleans. "We are determined," he wrote bitterly, "to be avenged as soon as we can procure arms there friend Andrew Johnson can not save them the time has arrived that we must fight it out and God help Andrew Johnson and Seward if we succeed. they must and shall be made responsible for this Whole sale massacre. Oh, for a Butler here now. . . . You must rouse the Northern mind against this massacre. confer with Thadd Stevens, Sumner, Boutwell, Wade, Colfax, Wendall Phillips. . . . Genl Grant must be told not to listen to the cowardly dog Andrew Johnson." [1]

In this letter was forecast much of the Radical program for the fateful summer and fall of 1866. The riot in New Orleans, just at the time Congress was adjourning, and a similar riot in Memphis, in April, served as political capital for Radical orators. Everywhere the Northern people discovered evidence that the South was seething with violence and disloyalty. Northern visitors to the South wrote back letters with harrowing details of the Southerners' bitterness. Loyalists in the South indited strange stories of new rebel plots,[2] and carpetbaggers kept their old neighbors informed on Southern conditions. "Texas is in quite as unsettled and revolutionary a condition as it was in 1861," wrote a Texan who thought that "universal suffrage" presented the only hope for "security and peace." [3] In New Orleans, "Union men" petitioned Congress to protect them from the scorn and villification of the "returned rebels and traitors." "We would prefer to return them their arms and fight them in the open field," said the petitioners, "than thus to permit them under protection of our govt to assume to dictate and govern us." [4] In Virginia, loyalists found the State in the hands of

---

[1] C. C. Morgan to Butler, August 9, 1866, Butler MSS.
[2] Comstock MSS. Diary, Jan. 20, to February 2, 1866.
[3] Wm. Alexander, (Austin) to Geo. Gibbs, (Boston) June 28, 1866, Butler MSS.
[4] "Union Man" to Butler, August 24, 1866, Butler MSS.

Confederate officers, and prayed for relief.[5] From hundreds of platforms, Radical speakers rang the changes on these appeals from the
downtrodden of the South.

Meanwhile heedless of the accumulating horrors, President Johnson's supporters prepared their appeal to the country. Hardly had
Congress adjourned when the Johnson men convened in Philadelphia
to endorse the President's policies. Delegates from all the States were
present. Symbolic of the spirit of loyalty and concord which prevailed,
the Governor of South Carolina—arm in arm with General Couch of
Massachusetts—led the delegates into the huge "Wigwam."

The platform adopted by the enthusiastic convention boldly asserted
that the war had "maintained the authority of the Constitution" with
all its restrictions as well as all its powers. It had preserved the "equal
rights, dignity, and authority of the States perfect and unimpaired."
Among the rights reserved for the States was the right to be represented in Congress, and the Convention called on the people to elect
"none but men who admit this fundamental right." In addition to this
assertion, the Convention accepted the end of slavery, demanded the
payment of the national debt, and favored the settlement of all "just
and rightful" claims of the soldiers. Finally it found in Johnson a
"chief magistrate worthy of the nation." [6]

The Convention appointed a committee of one hundred to present
President Johnson with a copy of its "Declaration of Principles."
Senator Doolittle, who had presided, hastened to the White House to
prepare for the reception of the committee and to tell the President
that the consensus of opinion in the Convention favored the removal
of Stanton. To emphasize the War Secretary's unpopularity Doolittle
asked that the Cabinet, with Grant instead of Stanton, should stand
with Johnson when he received the approaching delegation.

Concurring in this scheme, Johnson invited Grant to attend the
meeting. With no desire to become embroiled, Grant nevertheless felt
constrained to go to the White House. When he arrived, he found the
Cabinet already assembled. Smothering his half-formed intention to
excuse himself, the General found himself placed at Johnson's right
hand before the delegation. Badeau remembered later that Grant was

---

[5] Wm. Thompson, (Richmond) to Butler, September 3, 1866, Butler MSS.
[6] Edward McPherson, *The Political History of the United States During the Period
of Reconstruction*, 241.

disgusted and chagrined at the trick and returned to his office quite angry. Even Gideon Welles, who stood on the President's left, was not sure that the arrangement was proper; but he rejoiced that Grant's presence made the "absence of Stanton . . . the more conspicuous." [7]

The Philadelphia Convention was but a dramatic prelude of a more ambitious effort to convert the Northern people to Johnson's policy. As soon as the Committee of One Hundred had been heard, Secretary Seward began preparations for an extensive presidential speaking tour. In Chicago, a monument had been erected to the memory of Stephen A. Douglas, and Johnson, invited to speak at its unveiling, seized the occasion to present his program to the people.

In arranging for the tour, Seward perceived the desirability of attaching Grant to the party; not only because he wished to demonstrate the general's attachment to Johnson, but also because his presence would deter the Radicals from acts of violence. The Secretary especially dreaded the trip through strongly Radical Philadelphia. Welles suggested that since great danger lurked in the thinly populated rural sections where obstructions might be placed on the tracks, they ought to take Stanton along as a kind of insurance policy. Stanton, however, alleged that his wife was ill, and the Secretaries determined to carry Grant and Farragut as hostages for their own safety.[8]

To Johnson was assigned the task of securing Grant's consent to accompany the party. At the time, the new army bill was under consideration, and Grant found it necessary to see the President frequently. On several occasions Johnson hinted that he would like Grant to accompany him on the trip, but each time Grant evaded the subject. Finally the President saw his opportunity. The list for promotions in the army drawn up by Grant and Stanton, and submitted by Grant, contained many names Johnson would not care to accept. However, the President made objections to but two appointments. Then, having approved the list, he called Grant aside and asked him to go on the "Swing around the Circle." Under the circumstances, the general could not refuse; so it was announced that Grant, with Rawlins and Farragut, would accompany the President.[9]

This announcement astounded the Radicals. Their confident claims

[7] Badeau, *Grant in Peace*, 38–39; Welles, II, 581–582.
[8] Welles, II, 384–387.
[9] Seward, Welles, and Postmaster-General Randall were also members of the party. Badeau, *Op. cit.*, 28–29; Richardson, *Personal History*, 526–527.

that the general secretly sympathized with them were obviously given the lie by Grant's action. Hastily, numbers of them wrote Washburne to find out where Grant really stood. "I am fearful that after all your endeavors to explain the course of Gen. Grant as consistent with loyalty to the Republican Party, you will have to give him up at last," wrote one of Washburne's constituents as he enumerated the evidence that Grant was a Democrat. He had been a Democrat during the war; he had accepted Lee's surrender hastily; he had not opposed Sherman's terms; he had told Southern leaders in Charleston that "he was neither an *extreme* copperhead or a Radical"; he had approved the Philadelphia Convention; and he had always been friendly to Johnson, "your suppositions to the contrary notwithstanding." But whatever his beliefs, this correspondent believed that "Grant owes it to the country to show his hand." [10]

Rumors spread that Washburne himself was going over to Johnson, and many believed that Grant's sponsor had obtained a promise that Johnson would not speak in the Galena district. Rumors also declared that there would be no removals in Washburne's district, and as soon as the election was over Washburne, Grant, and Rawlins would definitely come out in support of the President. Many wrote to protest against this contemplated change of front, and to beseech the Congressman to keep his military protégé in line. "The prayers of the people go up" for Grant, wrote one man, "and he must not fail by the way nor fall into any temptation." If Grant went over to Johnson, declared another, "a long dark and gloomy night of Despotism is before this country, and will result in a struggle for power that may destroy the Government." Others asked Washburne to advise them "how to counteract" the effect of Grant's apostasy. Others insisted that the Congressman make speeches assuring the country that "Grant is all right." [11]

Although some of the Radicals, suspicious of a man who would not definitely commit himself, were inclined to let Grant go, many could see no hope without his support. Desiring to neutralize the effect of his

[10] N. Van Order, (Moline, Ill.) to Washburne, August 24, 1866, Washburne Mss.

[11] Letters of Geo. C. Rice, (Washington) August 24; J. A. McKean, (Mt. Morris, Ill.) August 24; H. Price, (Davenport, Iowa) August 30; L. C. Funk, (Milton, Pa.) September 1; Davis Sankey, (New Castle, Pa.) September 3; A. A. Tinell, (Sterling, Ill.) September 8; B. F. Shaw, (Dixon, Ill.) September 12; C. K. Williams, September 16, to Washburne, Washburne Mss.

presence with Johnson, they organized popular ovations for the general by which they could show their scorn for the President and attract the hero to their cause.

The route of the Presidential party lay through New York, Buffalo, Cleveland, and Detroit. From the very beginning the Radical press alleged that the crowds cheered louder for Grant and Farragut than for the President. At official receptions and at stations along the route the two heroes stood behind the President, lending silent support to his exposition of policies. The Radicals, however, were not to be deterred in their purpose of detaching Grant from Johnson. Cheers for the general interrupted the President's speeches and seemed to prove that the people attended the ceremonies only to catch a glimpse of the victor of Appomattox.

Although he early realized the purpose of these extraordinary attentions, Grant regarded them with indifference. Frequently he grew tired of the crowds, and retired to the baggage car to smoke. Always he was seen smoking his cigar; seldom was he heard to say anything. Occasionally good-natured banter passed between Grant and Farragut. Seward, Farragut, and even Johnson commented humorously on Grant's refusal to make speeches. Grant once explained that ladies always shook his hand while they kissed Farragut because they "didn't mind kissing an old man." Johnson frequently told the crowds that if they tired of the President, Grant would deliver them an "eloquent speech."

Such camaraderie was reserved for the public. On the train between stations the travelers redoubled their efforts to make Grant avow his support of the President. The general, however, remained as quiet in private as in public, merely agreeing that he favored "reëstablishing the Union at once in all its primitive vigor," the immediate representation of the States, and forgiveness for the rebels.[12]

Although their efforts to annex Grant received little encouragement, the Radicals persevered in their course. In order to explain his presence with Johnson, they devised the theory that both Grant and Farragut had been ordered on the tour by their commander-in-chief. Since Grant refused to talk, this thesis went uncontradicted. Radical reporters who accompanied the party took especial pains to mention Grant's apparent boredom.

[12] Welles, *Diary*, II, 591–593.

The ceremonies at Chicago, the ostensible object of the trip, passed without incident, but as Johnson and his companions pressed forward Radical violence increased. In St. Louis a crowd taunted the fighting President beyond endurance, and led him to engage in undignified rejoinders. Calls for Grant indicated clearly that the General was more popular than the President. In Indianapolis, the crowds were inspired by Radical agitators to the point of rowdyism. Calls for Grant interrupted Johnson and turned the meeting into a riot.

In Cincinnati, the Radicals had an opportunity to demonstrate their affection for the General without Johnson's hampering presence. Having hastened ahead of the party to visit his father, Grant gave the Cincinnati Radicals a chance to lay hold on him. Recognizing him in a theatre, the crowds urged him to speak. Conscious of the proprieties, he refused to make a public appearance which would be interpreted as a condemnation of the President. Falling back on the non-committal statement that he was a military man and the President his commander-in-chief, he declined to countenance any display of opposition to his superior. The point gave comfort to the Radicals, while it left the general free to conduct himself as he would.

After the visit to Cincinnati, however, members of the presidential party began to notice a change in Grant's attitude. His father's influence was believed strongly on the side of the Radicals, but Johnson's intemperate speeches, the coarse ballyhoo of the mobs, the especially obnoxious Copperhead support which Johnson received, all doubtless contributed to an alienation between Grant and Johnson. But the most important factor in the change was Grant's belief that the people did not approve of the President. With no knowledge or understanding of the fundamental nature of the American Constitution, Grant shared the erroneous belief that the supreme law of the land was the will of the people, not the Constitution. Accordingly, when he perceived that the elections were certain to go against Johnson, he acquiesced in the decision of the majority and became a supporter of Congress.

Whatever the inward change, Grant did not alter his conduct. At this period his contention that a military man should abstain from politics was almost a personal fetish. Soon after he returned from the "swing," he publicly announced that it was against his convictions of duty to attend any political convention. Moreover, he regretted that "any soldier takes part in questions of the day," and wished it understood that he recognized President Johnson as his commander-in-chief.[13]

Consistently holding to this position, Grant became indignant when a former member of his staff, Colonel Wm. S. Hillyer, declared that Grant supported Johnson. Hillyer was one of Grant's "pets," and at the moment the General was seeking for his appointment as Naval Officer in New York, but this did not deter the general from writing an open letter to Hillyer, scolding him for his presumption. Neither he nor any other man, Grant said, was authorized to speak for him on political questions.[14]

Grant's peculiar theory of his duty perhaps brought him greater comfort than an open declaration of principles would have done, but it gave none to either of the contending parties which sought his influence. Ben Butler, who had wanted him elected President in order that "the people might see if there is any difference between a drunken tailor and a drunken tanner," [15] asked Horace Greeley to "smoke Grant out so that we may know where he is upon the great question of the day." With no sympathy for Grant's idea that a soldier ought not to have political opinions, Butler pointed out that his name had been used against the Republican Party while that party was supporting him. "He feels obliged to obey the orders of his commander-in-chief so strictly," declared Butler, "that he will not even refuse an invitation to be *Hawked* about the country as an appendage to the President's tail."

Far more serious were Butler's fears that Grant could not be counted on to support the Radicals in case of open war between the President and Congress. In the high state of partisan excitement at the moment, Butler believed that either Johnson or Congress might appeal to arms. "Our Republican friends have relied upon Grant in case of a collision with the President, that he would disobey the orders of the President and stand boldly for the right and laws, . . . but can Grant be trusted to disobey positive orders of his chief? When the hour of peril comes, shall we not be leaning on a broken reed?" [16]

[13] New York *Tribune,* September 19, 1866.

[14] Welles, *Diary,* II, 646–647. Senator Doolittle thought this letter was meant as a rebuke to Jesse Grant.

[15] George A. Gordon, (Boston) to Washburne, August 27, 1866, Washburne MSS. I have changed the tense of the verb.

[16] Butler to Greeley, September 20, 1866, Butler MSS.

Butler was not alone in expecting violence at any moment. Wild rumors of war between President and Congress filled the air.[17] Grant, himself, was thoroughly convinced that Johnson planned a Revolution. In October, he wrote to Sheridan that Johnson "becomes more violent with the opposition he meets with, until now but few people who were loyal during the Rebellion seem to have any influence with him. None have unless they join in a crusade against Congress, and declare the body itself illegal, unconstitutional, and revolutionary. Commanders in Southern States will have to take great care to see, if a crisis does come, that no armed headway can be made against the Union. For this reason it will be very desirable that Texas should have no reasonable excuse for calling out the militia authorized by their legislature. Indeed, it should be prevented." As a further precaution, Grant ordered that all arms in the South be removed to Northern arsenals.[18]

Although Grant's non-committal attitude led the Democratic press to insist that he was impartial and therefore his support of Johnson was the more valuable,[19] an inner circle of Republicans knew his real opinions. General James H. Wilson, the captor of Jefferson Davis, gleefully wrote Washburne that Rawlins and Badeau, the staff-officers closest to Grant, had been "completely cured" of sympathy with the President. "There is a God in Israel!" he proclaimed, "and therein rests my hope for a good cause and a glorious country." [20] Another Radical wrote that Grant's reticence delighted the country, although he wondered "how long it may be prudent to keep the nation ignorant of his real position." [21]

To Johnson, however, Grant's changed position was a matter of deep concern. Realizing that an outbreak of violence would cause him to declare for the Radicals, the President sought some means by which he could use the army and still avoid giving Grant an opportunity to declare himself. Faced with this dilemma, he hearkened to Seward's scheme of sending Grant to Mexico.

At the moment, Lewis Campbell, long since appointed minister to Juarez's migratory Republican government, was preparing to depart

<hr/>

[17] Oberholtzer, *History of the U. S.*, I, 416–418; Milton, *Age of Hate*, 374. For an apochryphal story of Johnson asking Grant's support in an effort to overthrow Congress, see Chauncey M. Depew, *My Memories of Eighty Years*, 49–51.
[18] Badeau, *Grant in Peace*, 51.
[19] New York *World*, September 20, 1866.
[20] Wilson to Washburne, October 13, 1866, Washburne MSS.
[21] J. A. Clark (Santa Fe) to Washburne, Washburne MSS.

on his mission. Napoleon's troops were still supporting the desperate Maximilian, and Juarez was hiding in the mountains. In Washington, Grant had continued to insist that more drastic action be taken by the Government, and it was generally known that he had little sympathy with Seward's tortuous diplomacy.[22] To Seward and Johnson, Grant's interest in Mexico constituted a valid reason for attaching him, as military adviser, to Campbell's entourage. Sherman, who was more sympathetic with the President, could be brought to Washington as Secretary of War.

Second in command of the army, Sherman had a far quicker mind than his superior and was strongly on Johnson's side in the basic issues of the Reconstruction quarrel. However, his interests were solely those of the professional soldier, and with a soldier's abhorrence of politics and politicians he consistently refused to be drawn into the conflict.

On October 17, Johnson asked Grant whether he would object to Sherman's coming to Washington for a few days. Showing the general a letter from Sherman, written in February endorsing his policy, the President then inquired whether Sherman would object to its publication. Grant replied that he would gladly order his subordinate to Washington, but he felt sure that Sherman would object to any such use of his letter. However, Grant wrote Sherman, telling him that he was scheduled to succeed Stanton as Secretary of War. "I will not venture in a letter," he cautiously informed his friend, "to say all I think about the matter, or that I would say to you in person." [23]

Before Sherman arrived, Grant attended a Cabinet meeting where Campbell's instructions were read. They contained the statement that Grant would accompany the minister to give him the benefit of his [Grant's] advice in carrying out the instructions of the Secretary of State. Taken aback at the suddenness of this development, Grant hastened to decline the service, stating that he did not believe it to be expedient for him to leave the country at the moment. In a letter to the President, Grant asked to be excused from the duty.

Several days later, Grant attended a second Cabinet meeting where the matter was again discussed. This time, instructions for the general were read. Grant, however, persisted in his refusal to accompany Campbell. Turning to the Attorney-General, Johnson asked if the

[22] Welles, *Diary*, II, 621.
[23] Badeau, *Grant in Peace*, 40–41.

orders were illegal, and if there were any reasons why Grant should not obey them. Indignantly, General Grant arose, "I can answer that question Mr. President, without referring to the Attorney-General. I am an American and eligible to any office to which any American is eligible. I am an officer of the army, and bound to obey your military orders. But this is a civil office, a purely diplomatic duty that you offer me, and I cannot be compelled to undertake it. Any legal military order you give me I will obey; but this is civil and not military; and I decline the duty. No power on earth can compel me to it.[24]

When Sherman arrived in Washington, he went straight to Grant to learn the news. His brother, perturbed by the turn of events, had already written him not to commit himself to Johnson who had "reduced the Presidency to level of a grog house." The general did not need the admonition, for he had an innate distaste for politics and politicians. When Grant informed him of the proposed changes, he immediately declared that he would not accept the War Department or the command of the army.

Going from Grant to Johnson, Sherman listened to Johnson's recital of the situation. When Johnson broached the matter of Sherman's remaining in Washington, Sherman countered with the suggestion that he might accompany Campbell to Mexico instead of Grant. The President, seeing that his scheme for ridding himself of Grant could not succeed, accepted Sherman's proposal. Having averted a crisis, Sherman prepared to aid Campbell in searching for Mexico's fugitive President. "I am determined," he wrote his brother, "to keep out of political, or even quasi-political office, and shall resign before being so placed, though I cannot afford to resign." But, realizing the true situation, he wrote with sly humor: "I have not the remotest idea of riding on mule-back a thousand miles in Mexico to find its chief magistrate." A month later, his real mission over, he was back in New Orleans.[25]

The results of the November elections confirmed Grant's belief that the Northern people would not support Johnson and his suspicion that the next Congress would be more Radical than the last. New men of more extreme opinions were coming to replace the little handful of conservatives who had upheld Johnson and the Constitution. Massa-

[24] Badeau, *Grant in Peace*, 52–55.
[25] Burr, *Life and Deeds of Grant*, 840–842, 852–853; Badeau, *Grant in Peace*, 52–55; Welles, II, 621; Richardson, *Personal History*, 533–534; Comstock MSS. Diary.

chusetts sent Ben Butler from a district in which he was not a resident, and Gideon Welles lamented the "depravity of parties and the times" when he heard the news.[26]

To Grant's practical mind, the people had spoken in favor of the Fourteenth Amendment, and he believed the President should hearken to their voice. To "Dick" Taylor he wrote, "I would like to see one Southern State, excluded State, ratify the amendment to enable us to see the course that would be pursued." However, with no intention of bringing "as a peace offering the conclusive evidence of their self-degradation," the States, with Johnson's approval, had already begun to reject the amendment; for only one of them, Tennessee, was willing to trust Radical promises.

When the Thirty-ninth Congress assembled for its last session, whatever mild program its members once favored was forgotten. Armed with a popular mandate, the violent wing prepared to force the South to compliance. "I was a Conservative in the last session . . ." announced the bitter Thad Stevens, "but I mean to be a Radical henceforth." Other members prepared to follow him in his Radicalism.

The first fruit of this new spirit was a bill granting the suffrage to Negroes in the District of Columbia. Early in January, Grant attended a meeting of the Cabinet to discuss it. The clauses which disfranchised rebels appeared to him acceptable, but he observed that the Northern States did not themselves grant Negro suffrage. Accordingly, he concurred with the Cabinet in endorsing Johnson's veto.[27]

The day following this Cabinet meeting, a delegation from Arkansas, headed by an excluded Senator, called upon Grant. To them, the General expressed his opinions more strongly than he had ever before done in public. His advice was to go home, ratify the Fourteenth Amendment, and grant Negro suffrage. The North was heartily in favor of this program, said the general, and if it were not adopted by the South, Congress would impose more stringent terms.[28]

To those whose opinions on reconstruction were based on constitutional principles, Grant's peculiar viewpoint was incomprehensible. "He has no political principles, no intelligent idea of Constitutional government," lamented Welles as he heard Grant's opinions on the dis-

[26] Welles, *Diary*, II, 620.
[27] *Ibid.*, III, 5–6.
[28] New York *Tribune*, January 4, 8, 1867.

trict bill. "Yet General Grant will very likely be the next President of the United States." When he heard of Grant's advice to the Arkansas delegation, the old democrat snorted: "What nonsense. What business has Congress to impose on the States?" [29] It was all so confusing that he concluded that Grant, "not very intelligent," had been led astray by Stanton and Washburne.

Throughout the session Grant remained in Washington, keeping a close eye on the progress of events. Perhaps no man in the capital was in better position to judge between the two parties. Frequently he attended Cabinet meetings where one or another of the almost unbroken succession of veto messages was being discussed, and at his house on I Street he received a constant stream of visitors—army men, Congressmen, and Senators who called to discuss the progress of the Reconstruction Act.

In December, Thad Stevens introduced a bill to substitute military governments for the existing governments in the Southern States. By the middle of February the bill had passed the House, and went to the Senate. At every stage of its preparation, Grant was consulted by its sponsors.[30]

By the terms of the bill, the military governors were to assemble State conventions which should adopt new Constitutions making provision for Negro suffrage. The delegates to the conventions were to be chosen by loyal men, white and black. On the question of unlimited Negro suffrage, Grant was not in accord with the Radicals. Holding that the Negro would eventually obtain the vote, the General doubted the desirability of conferring it immediately. Gradually, however, he concurred in what seemed to be the consensus of Northern opinion. "It seems almost the only weapon to put into the hands of the blacks for their defense," concluded Comstock, who usually reflected his superior's opinions.[31]

When the reconstruction bill went to the Senate, Grant had still another objection to the measure. Under the House bill, the General of the Army was empowered to appoint and remove the military governors in the South. Since this would bring him into open conflict with Johnson, Grant let it be known that he disapproved of the provision.

[29] Welles, *Diary*, III, 8, 15.
[30] Jesse R. Grant, *In the Days of My Father, General Grant*, 49.
[31] *Ibid.*, 192; Badeau, *Grant in Peace*, 57–58; Comstock MS. Diary, February 14, 1867.

The Senate restored the appointing power to its proper place, and the House ungraciously concurred in the change.[32]

During all this discussion, Grant did not openly move from the impartial position he had chosen for himself. Johnson's friends noticed that the Radicals were "courting" Grant assiduously, but they also noted that there were only a few Congressional leaders who wanted him.[33] So skillfully did Grant withhold his confidence that Johnson's supporters had no idea what he might do in the event of the still-expected crisis.[34]

A description of Grant at this period shows that people generally were seeing in his features physical evidences of his political secretiveness. To one newspaper correspondent, his face was "immobile, heavy, and expressionless," and "lighted by no quick changes of the eyes, by no movement of the short, thin lips." It looked like "the face of the only man in America, perhaps, who could make the calculation of the multitude of lives necessary to blot out a multitude of other lives, and could work out the bloody sum of its accurate terrible results." Moreover, in the features, there was a "free-masonry . . . the square straight brow knows the meaning of the wary, unchanging eyes, and will not tell it. The eyes watch the heavy unquivering nostrils; the nostrils command the locked mouth: when the mouth opens the strong chin keeps the secret of patient brain and tyrannous will." In public, Grant was "the most followed and the least conspicuous person in the room." [35]

Fearful lest Grant's secretiveness should lead the President to make another attempt to replace him with a more communicative commander, the general's friends among the Radicals sought a means by which they could retain him in his place. To Stanton should go the credit for the scheme adopted. At one of Mrs. Grant's receptions, the Secretary edged his way through the "horrid jam" to tell the general that he was "going to get an amendment on some bill requiring that all orders to subordinates in the army should go through the General of the Army.[36] Stanton suggested the idea to George S. Boutwell of Massachusetts, who attached the proposed rider to the army appropri-

[32] Badeau, *Grant in Peace*, 64–65; *Cong. Globe*, 39th Congress, 2nd session, p. 1317.
[33] Welles, *Diary* II, 646–647.
[34] Welles, *Diary*, III, 27.
[35] N. Y. *Tribune*, February 25, 1867.
[36] Comstock MS. Diary, January 23, 1876.

ation bill. Henceforth the headquarters of the army were to be in Washington, and the General of the Army could be assigned to no other post.[37]

The appropriation bill, with its insolent rider, and the Reconstruction bill went to the President at the same time. The latter was returned with a veto, and the appropriation bill carried back to Congress a formal protest. The provision that all orders must go through the General of the Army, said Johnson, "virtually deprives the President of his constitutional functions as Commander in Chief. . . ." In regard to the reconstruction bill, the President's objections were set forth at length. Particularly obnoxious to a State Rights devotee were the powers granted to the military governors in the South. "No master ever had so absolute control over the slaves as this bill gives to the military officers over both white and colored persons." [38]

To Grant, Johnson's message was "one of the most ridiculous . . . that ever emanated from any President," and he rejoiced when Congress immediately overrode the veto. In his opinion, the measure would end all controversy, and would safeguard the results of the Civil War. "The General is getting more and more Radical," Comstock noted in his diary.[39] Publicly, however, the general preserved his reticence. "It is not proper," he wrote to Washburne, "that a subordinate should criticize the acts of his superior in a public manner. I rely upon our personal relations, however to speak to you freely as I feel upon all matters." [40]

Although Grant had expected Johnson to be an obstruction in executing the Reconstruction Act, the President shared with the general a belief that the law should be fairly executed. To the consternation of some of his friends, who were sure that Grant was influenced by Stanton and Judge-Advocate-General Joseph Holt, Johnson consulted the general in selecting the governors for the five military districts into which the South was divided. On Grant's advice, Johnson assigned General Schofield to Virginia, General D. E. Sickles to the Carolinas, General Thomas to Georgia, Florida, and Alabama; and General Ord to Arkansas and Mississippi. All were Radicals, but only Sickles, whose personal character was besmirched by a scandalous past record,

---

[37] *Acts and Resolutions,* 39th Congress, 2nd session, 120.
[38] Richardson, *Messages and Papers of the Presidents,* VI, 472–502.
[39] Comstock MS. Diary, March 1, 1867.
[40] Badeau, *Grant in Peace,* 59–60.

was especially offensive to the Conservatives. But the most objectionable, in the Democratic-Conservative view, was the appointment of
Sheridan to command in Louisiana and Texas. "The slime of the ser-
pent" covered all the appointments, thought Welles, but he concluded
that Grant had borne himself "as well as could be expected." [41]

A few minutes after the Thirty-ninth Congress ended, the more
Radical Fortieth Congress assembled. Almost immediately the members drafted a Supplementary Reconstruction Act giving the military
governors complete control over the registration of voters for the forthcoming constitutional conventions. When the Act was passed, the members settled themselves to await the inevitable veto. It came March 23,
but Congress repassed the bill immediately. Then, ignoring Stanton's
and Grant's plea that it should not leave the country in Johnson's
hands, Congress adjourned until July.[42]

Before it did so, Sheridan had begun to cause trouble in Louisiana.
On March 27, he removed the mayor of New Orleans and the Attor-
ney-General of the State for their parts in the New Orleans massacre.
Early in June he removed the governor, appointing a sycophant of
his own selection. Somewhat later, Sheridan removed the governor of
Texas.

This vigorous action gave general satisfaction to the Radicals. Sheridan "shows himself the same fearless true man he did in the field," declared Grant. "He makes no mistakes." To Sheridan, Grant wrote that
he was supported "by more than party" in the course he had adopted.[43]
In the White House, however, the acts of the young commander were
not so generously commended. Attorney-General Stanbery gave an oral
opinion that he had acted without authority and Johnson asked him
to prepare a written statement. Upon learning of this development,
Grant wrote to Sheridan that, while it was clear that Congress had intended to give full control to the district commanders, it would be best
to wait before removing any more officers. The commanders, Grant declared, were "responsible to the country," but the Attorney-General's
opinion was entitled to respect. As for the threat of removal, Grant assured his subordinates: "Your head is safe above your shoulders, at

[41] Welles, *Diary,* III, 62–65.
[42] *Ibid.,* 74; Comstock MS. Diary, March 26, 1867.
[43] Badeau, *Grant in Peace,* 61–62.

least so that it cannot be removed to produce pain." [44] When late in May the Attorney-General announced that the military governors were required to support the existing governments in the South and interpreted the Supplementary Reconstruction Act in such a way that many ex-Confederates were allowed to register, Sheridan wrote to Grant: "The interpretation is practically . . . opening a broad macadamized road for perjury and fraud to travel on." [45]

The other military governors gave somewhat less trouble, but altogether they kept Grant busy. In Mississippi, Radicals complained that General Ord would not support their efforts to organize the Negro vote.[46] In Alabama, General Pope, imitating Sheridan, removed the mayor of Mobile.[47] In Virginia, General Schofield set about excluding the Confederates from registration so vigorously that Grant cited his work as an example to the other commanders.[48] By June, bayonet rule was working so smoothly that Greeley's *Tribune* declared the congressional policy "glorious." Everything in the South was quiet, and violence and oppression were "almost unknown." [49]

To achieve this result, Grant and Stanton had worked in perfect harmony. The earlier suspicion which existed between them disappeared as they drew close together to thwart the President.[50] Under their combined influence, a majority of the officers of the army went over to the Radical camp.[51]

When Johnson published the Attorney-General's opinion of the Reconstruction acts, Sheridan wrote Grant an "impudent and disrespectful, if not disobedient" letter in which he defied the President. The published letter caused considerable stir in the Conservative ranks. Believing that at last they had a legitimate excuse for dismissing Sheridan, Johnson's intimates in the Cabinet brought the matter up for discussion. Welles thought that Grant would have to recommend a reproof, and that Stanton could not uphold the insubordinate commander. However, Stanton advised the President that the letter was a

[44] Badeau, *Grant in Peace*, 60–61, 65–66.
[45] Rhodes, *Hist. of U. S.*, VI, 62.
[46] R. W. Flournoy, (Pontonoc, Miss.) to Grant, May 7, 1867, Butler MSS.
[47] N. Y. *Tribune*, May 31, 1867.
[48] *Ibid.*, June 6, 1867.
[49] *Ibid.*, June 15, 1867.
[50] Badeau, *Grant in Peace*, 84.
[51] Welles, *Diary*, III, 117–118.

private one that had been stolen for publication, and recommended dropping the matter. Although Welles and Johnson agreed that Stanton and Grant had determined upon such an interpretation, they accepted it.[52]

Less than two weeks after the Attorney-General's opinion, Congress reassembled, and immediately fell to work on a new supplementary bill which would overrule the Attorney's decision. Again the Radical leaders consulted the General of the Army. Some of them were determined to give Grant complete control over the South, but once more the general shrank from the responsibility, and the new bill left power in the hands of the President. "I wish our political troubles were over," wrote Grant to Sherman as he lamented the constant efforts to trap him into some partisan commitment. "No matter how close I keep my tongue each tries to interpret from the little I let drop that I am with them." [53]

The new Supplementary Reconstruction Act provided that the Southern State governments should be subject in every respect to the military commanders. In all their acts, the military governors were responsible only to Grant. Drafted by Stanton, the act completed the President's humiliation.[54] To emphasize its disapproval of Johnson, Congress voted Sheridan its thanks for the manner in which he had performed his duties!

When it became apparent that Stanton had drawn up the new reconstruction measure, Johnson decided to remove him from office. For two years the President's friends had been urging this course, but Johnson's indecision made their admonitions ineffective. Slyly, Stanton had worked against Johnson, and had succeeded, through the Reconstruction acts, in obtaining the complete control of the army. A year earlier, Johnson might have saved something from the wreckage; now, even the President's friends had given up.

On July 31, soon after Congress had again adjourned, the President sent for Grant to inform him that he intended to remove Sheridan from New Orleans and Stanton from the War Department. Astounded, the general tried to stay the President's hand. Stanton, said Grant, had been a loyal man during the war, and his removal would be poor policy. But Johnson's mind was at last made up, and he asked Grant

[52] Welles, *Diary*, III, 125–126.
[53] Badeau, *Grant in Peace*, 73.
[54] Rhodes, *History of the U. S.*, VI, 64; Dunning, *Reconstruction*, 98.

if he would take the war office as an *ad interim* appointee. Without refusing, Grant pointed out that there was much business before the department upon which he could not pass.

The next day, Grant wrote Johnson a formal protest against Stanton's removal. The Secretary of War, he said, was protected by the terms of the Tenure of Office Act, enacted for his especial protection. Grant's letter, thought Welles, was "not discreet, judicious, nor excusable even from his own standpoint." To Johnson, Welles remarked that Grant was "going over"—"Yes," replied the President, "I am aware of it. I have no doubt that most of these offensive measures have emanated from the War Department." [55]

Undeterred by Grant's protest, Johnson discussed the matter fully with his Cabinet and on their advice asked Stanton's resignation. "Public considerations of a high character constrain me," stated the President. But Stanton was not to be ousted by a mere request. "Public considerations of a high character constrain me not to resign . . . before the next meeting of Congress," he replied.[56]

For several days, the President consulted with his friends on the proper procedure. Uppermost in his mind was the proposal to put Grant in Stanton's place. A year before, Grant was "willing and earnest" to accept this plan; now he was "reluctant." [57] On August 11, Johnson again interviewed Grant; the meeting was "pleasant, social, and friendly." Johnson began the conversation by asking whether there was "any alienation, or substantial difference, between them?" Grant replied that he knew of none. In the preceding autumn, as Johnson knew, they had differed on the Fourteenth Amendment, but there was no longer an issue between them. Reassured, Johnson repeated his assertion that Stanton must go. Satisfied that the President was determined on his course, Grant said that he would obey orders to take over the duties of the department; and Johnson concluded that he was secretly pleased with the arrangement.[58]

That evening, Stanton was sitting with Edwards Pierrepont of New York in the wide hallway of his house, when General Grant came to tell his superior of the approaching disaster. After he had gone, the Secretary, "with suppressed agitation which was very marked," up-

[55] Welles, *Diary*, III, 154–156.
[56] Milton, *Age of Hate*, 448–453.
[57] Welles, *Diary*, III, 160.
[58] *Ibid.*, 167.

braided himself for not having resigned. Turning to Pierrepont, he said: "You and Mrs. Stanton are the only ones who gave me good advice, and I ought to have followed it." [59]

The next day, a formal interchange of courtesy and discourtesy brought the matter to an end. In the morning, Johnson wrote a note suspending Stanton, and directing him to turn his office over to General Grant. Grant received an order to take the office. Enclosing a copy of this note, Grant wrote to Stanton: "In notifying you of my acceptance, I cannot let the opportunity pass without expressing to you my appreciation of the zeal, patriotism, firmness and ability with which you have ever discharged . . . your duties." In reply to a letter which he might have thought slightly patronizing, Stanton blusteringly protested against the President's act. But, he concluded, "I have no alternative but to submit, under protest, to the superior force of the President." [60]

To the more extreme Radicals, Grant's acceptance of the War Department seemed to indicate that he was on Johnson's side in the controversy. "I am surprised," wrote one of them, "that General Grant should have consented to succeed Secty Stanton. . . . However, it will dispose of him for President, and consign him to the baffled career of General Scott, and a hasty plate of soup." [61] On the other hand, Grant's friends believed, in the words of Motley, that "the time is fast approaching when Ulysses must cease to do the 'dumb, inarticulate man of genius' business. Thus far it has succeeded . . . !" [62]

[59] Badeau, *Grant in Peace,* 139–140.
[60] N. Y. *Tribune,* August 13, 1867; Welles, *Diary,* III, 168–169.
[61] M. Shankland (Brooklyn) to Joseph Holt, August 13, 1867, Joseph Holt MSS.
[62] Curtis, *Correspondence of Motley,* 282–283, Motley to Mrs. Motley.

FOR months before Stanton's suspension, the Northern people had generally agreed that General Grant should be their next President Publicly, the reticent General had said nothing which would commit him to either party. His popularity was undimmed, and politicians eyed with mixed feelings his obvious availability. Only an intimate group knew of Grant's efforts in behalf of radical legislation, and even the Democrats nursed hopes of making the general their standard bearer. To the rank and file of the politicians, Grant was an enigma: to the people he was still a hero.

From the people, and from the lesser politicians, the demand for Grant was insistent. Interpreting correctly the prevailing sentiment, local partisans hastened to clamber aboard the Grant bandwagon, and wrote fulsome and optimistic letters to Congressman Washburne. "We shall elect Grant," said one of them, "and under Grant we shall have *economy* and *reconstruction*." Another declared that "the *soldiers hold* the balance of power and will make the next President. . . . With Grant at the masthead the combined powers of darkness cannot beat us." [1]

In contrast with the masses of the Republican Party, the Radical leaders did not warm up to the prospect of Grant's candidacy. Horace Greeley in the *Tribune* was openly scornful of Grant's reticence. "Of what use is it," he asked, "to throw away kegs of butter and barrels of apples, hats and boots, and other magnificent specimens of merchandise and manufacture upon a military man who is so extremely afraid of damaging his chances of the Presidency . . . that he never permits himself to go beyond the polite vagueness of 'much obliged'? When . . . is a man to express his opinions . . . if it be not when . . . his stomach is filled with eleemosynary dainties?" [2]

Other Republican leaders shared Greeley's disgust for the noncommittal general. In the spring of 1867, Ben Wade went to Jesse

[1] E. A. Small, (Galena) January 3, 1867, and J. L. Camp, (Dixon, Ill.) January 27, 1867, to Washburne, Washburne MSS.
[2] New York *Tribune,* March 17, 1867.

Grant's house in search of information on Ulysses' opinions. "Father and Mother Grant" were absent when he called, but the Rev. M. J. Cramer, a German Methodist immigrant who had married the general's youngest sister, essayed to enlighten the Senator. Having visited Grant during the previous winter, Cramer could assure Wade that Grant favored the Radical program. According to Cramer, the senator received this news with such vociferous exultation that he threw his hat into the air and broke the parlor chandelier. "That settles the matter," said Wade, "we shall propose Grant as the candidate of the Republican Party." [3] However, Wade lost his enthusiasm rapidly, and said nothing about the interview. Perhaps the Ohio senator believed that his own chances were increased by Grant's silence.

Also bitterly opposed to Grant was the old Abolitionist element of the Republicans. The general's name was hissed at an anti-slavery meeting because the members were convinced that Grant supported Johnson.[4] But the most acrimonious of Grant's enemies was Ben Butler, who lost no opportunity to discredit the popular general. When a correspondent reported that Grant and Butler were developing some mining prospects together, the Massachusetts firebrand indignantly retorted: "I develop nothing . . . neither gold mines or anything else with General Grant." Many of his constituents, apprehensive of the rising tide of Grant sentiment in Massachusetts, urged Butler to enter the lists against the people's hero. "We have been sold enough and don't want to be again," declared one of them. From Indianapolis, Colonel A. D. Streight, who had become a sort of professional prisoner of war after his ignominious surrender to the Confederate General Forrest and a subsequent dramatic escape from Libby Prison, wrote advising Butler to fix upon Grant the blame for the failure to exchange prisoners. Others hoped that the Congressman would expose Grant's butchery and his military incapacity. But Butler had a flair for the dramatic. Rejecting all prosaic means of combat, he set detectives on Grant's trail to prove that the general was "a drunkard, after fast horses, women and whores." [5]

The opposition of such extremists only served to convince the people

[3] Cramer, *Conversations and Unpublished Letters*, 67–68.
[4] New York *Times*, May 9, 1867.
[5] Butler to Wm. G. Butler, June 7, 1867; E. J. Sherman to Butler, June 15; Streight to Butler, July 13, 1867, Butler Mss.; O. E. Babcock to Washburne, August 13, 1867, Washburne MSS.

that Grant was above partisanship. The "vigor and venom" of the Radicals testified to "their fear of him as a candidate, and their conviction they cannot use him." According to the moderate journals, public sentiment was strong for Grant, and there was a general feeling that he was "the man for the crisis." [6] An Atlanta paper declared that Grant was free from all political prejudices and animosities—a "truly national man," and "the nation's only hope in this its dire extremity." [7]

Amid these confusing expressions, Grant maintained his imperturbable silence. Only to his closest intimates did he reveal his opinions on reconstruction; his political aspirations he discussed with no one. To Badeau, who studied him carefully, it seemed that the General felt deeply, but could not express himself in speech. "It seemed to him immodest," said his secretary, "to uncloak himself to the world, or even entirely to his most intimate friend. . . . He had secrets of business from one friend; of politics, from another; of feeling from many, and no one knew all." As for politics, Badeau saw nothing that indicated ambition. Rawlins, most favored of the staff, declared that Grant refused to discuss the possibility of becoming President, and Mrs. Grant said the subject was actually distasteful to her husband.[8] Only General Sherman had any information on the subject: he wrote his brother that Grant had said he would not accept the nomination! [9]

To Gideon Welles Grant's maneuvers offered no mysteries. When Montgomery Blair proposed to reinvigorate the Democratic Party by nominating Grant, the shrewd diarist declared that the general was eager to be a candidate, but not a party candidate. He would prefer to be elected by the army or by a union party. With little intelligence or principle, Grant had "party cunning" and would force the Radicals to nominate him; for they would do so as the only hope of carrying the election.[10]

With the congressional leaders hesitant about committing themselves to a candidate who would not commit himself to their program, the lesser politicians took matters in their own hands. Late in July Thurlow Weed began some characteristic machinations, as a result of which the general was nominated for the presidency by the "Union

[6] N. Y. *Times,* June 11, 1867.
[7] Atlanta *New Era,* cited in N. Y. *Times,* July 8, 1867.
[8] Badeau, *Grant in Peace,* 73–74.
[9] *Sherman Letters,* 292.
[10] Welles, *Diary,* III, 120–121.

Republican General Committee" of New York City.[11] Horace Greeley became indignant. The committee, he declared, was "composed of those kicked out of the Republican party." It was a "Soup Society . . . that does not give soup, but asks for it. The nomination had no significance . . . the hack drivers might as well pass resolutions of thanks to George Washington for his services in the Revolution"— unless it showed that Grant was falling into the hands of Weed, who would lead him in chains "through the land as one of the trophies of the Forlorn Hope." [12] The people, added the Radical editor, were in no mood for "grab-bag experiments." They would insist upon a President who knew his own mind.[13] John Sherman, too, thought that the situation was becoming serious, and wrote his brother that it was "extremely important to know precisely what Grant wants in connection with the presidency." If he wanted the nomination, he could have it, but the senator hoped he would turn it down. His military services would not shield him from the partisan abuse which would follow a nomination. Like Radicals of the Greeley type, Sherman preferred Chief Justice Chase who was "wise, politic, and sane," and would pay the public debt.[14]

After Grant accepted the war portfolio, politicians canvassed his reasons. For once, Greeley's *Tribune* and the Democrats were in accord, both asserting that Grant had now conclusively proved that he supported the President. Both enumerated all his public acts from his Southern report to the day he stepped into Stanton's shoes. Everything he had done showed him to be no Radical. Confronted with this catalogue, moderate Republican papers could only assert that Grant was going to be elected as the candidate of the people and not of a party. Greeley retorted that perhaps Grant could "afford to be a deaf-and-dumb candidate, but this country can't afford to elect a deaf-and-dumb President." Other Generals—Sheridan and Sickles and Thomas and Butler and Logan—had spoken. "They are not uniformed Sphynxes —sashed and girded statues." They had had no word from Grant. "One word from Grant is all we want. If he is not a Radical we will not vote for him. . . ." [15]

[11] N. Y. *World*, July 25, 1867.
[12] N. Y. *Tribune*, July 25, 1867.
[13] *Ibid.*, July 30, 1867.
[14] *Sherman Letters*, 292–294.
[15] N. Y. *Tribune*, August 15–17, 1867; Citations from Democratic papers in *Tribune*, August 14–17, N. Y. *World*, August 14, and N. Y. *Times*, August 15–19.

Whether or not Grant was affected by this fire, evidences of his increasing radicalism rapidly appeared after he entered upon his duties as *ad interim* Secretary of War. At his first Cabinet meeting, he defended the constitutionality of the Reconstruction acts and indicated that he would stand by his military governors. Welles thought the general's "self satisfaction" over his temporary promotion was "very obvious," but he hoped Grant would show common sense in dealing with the South.[16]

Within a few days Johnson sent Grant an order for Sheridan's removal. With Stanton out of the way, the President could see no reason for not proceeding immediately to rid himself of the Radical commanders in the South. Grant was against any such action: on August 1, at the same time that he had objected to Stanton's removal, he had opposed any change in the fifth military district. Since Johnson had not again mentioned Sheridan, but had taken action only against Stanton, Grant had supposed that his favorite was safe. Now, in a desperate effort to save his friend, Grant wrote the President, urging "in the name of a patriotic people who have sacrificed thousands of loyal lives and thousands of millions of treasure to preserve the integrity and union of this country that this order be not insisted on. It is unmistakably the expressed wish of the country that General Sheridan not be removed from his present command. This is a republic where the will of the people is the law of the land. I beg that their voice may be heard." [17]

In this letter Grant expressed the fundamental basis of his own political philosophy. Upon the idea that the executive was commissioned only to execute the will of the people as expressed in Congressional legislation and popular clamor, Grant acted throughout his political career. To Johnson such muddled thinking was odious. Hurriedly seizing his pen, the President proceeded to correct Grant's ignorance of the nature of the American government. He was astonished, he said, that Grant should think that Sheridan's tenure had "ever been submitted to the people themselves." Sheridan had exceeded his authority, had ruled Louisiana with "absolute tyranny," and had made himself generally "obnoxious." It was true, lectured Johnson, that this was a government of the people, but it was one based upon a written Constitu-

[16] Welles, *Diary*, III, 169–170.
[17] *House Executive Documents*, 40th Congress, 2nd session, No. 57, p. 4.

tion. Under that Constitution, the President, who commanded the army and administered the laws, had ordered the removal.[18]

Realizing the hopelessness of trying to thwart the President's will or controvert his argument, Grant sought by an interview to let Sheridan down easily. He immediately agreed that the commander should be sent to Kansas, and Thomas should go to Louisiana. Thomas, however, pleaded illness, and Johnson ordered the moderate Hancock to command at New Orleans. When Hancock arrived in Washington enroute to his new post, Grant sought him out at his hotel and warned him that the President's policies were dangerous to the country. Hancock, however, had decided to support the President, and for a time there was peace in Louisiana.[19]

Grant's failure to prevent Sheridan's removal gave Greeley another excuse for pointing out that he was but an instrument in Johnson's hand. Stanton, who had refused to be so used, had been removed, while Grant enabled the President to defy the people.[20] Rumors that Grant had protested were current, but the *Tribune* challenged anyone to publish documents which would prove Grant's radicalism.[21]

Impelled to action by newspaper assailants, Grant took a bolder tone in his relations with the President. He regarded Johnson's evident purpose to take an active hand in Southern affairs as a threat to his own power. During the preceding winter and spring Grant had been in close touch with the congressional leaders, and he knew that they had determined to take the South out of the President's hands. Since that was the "will of the people," Grant determined to act upon it.

On August 23, Johnson presented to the Cabinet the case of General Sickles, the one-legged commander. He had issued a stay law in North Carolina and prohibited the execution of writs of the Federal court; and, indignant over this action, Johnson asked that he be ordered to retract his commands. Grant sent the required instructions, but almost immediately followed them with a letter authorizing Sickles to pursue whatever course he thought proper. At another Cabinet meeting Grant boldly took Sickles' side, saying that he must have had reasons for his acts and should not be condemned without a hearing; and with

---

[18] *House Executive Documents*, 40th Congress, 2nd session, No. 57, p. 5.
[19] Badeau, *Grant in Peace*, 371.
[20] N. Y. *Tribune*, August 21, 1867.
[21] *Ibid.*, August 23–24, 1867.

a touch of defiance, he added that Congress had placed in his hands the execution of the Reconstruction Acts, and he intended to see them executed. Taken aback by this arrogant assertion, the Cabinet sat aghast. Finally an Assistant Attorney-General broke the silence by expressing the hope that Grant "expected to execute the Acts in subordination to law and authority." [22]

To the constitutionalists of the Cabinet, Grant's assertion of his own powers indicated that the general had no "civil capacity, administrative ability, or general intelligence." Moreover, it was evident that he had been seduced by the Radicals. Welles decided that "Grant is an insincere man . . . very ambitious, has low cunning, and is unreliable, perhaps untruthful." With no knowledge of the Constitution, or "the elementary principles of civil Government," the general was likely to become "an instrument of evil." [23]

About this time, Washburne returned from Europe to visit his protégé.[24] Acting on his advice, Grant appeared at the next Cabinet meeting prepared to reopen the Sheridan case. He protested against sending Hancock to Louisiana, and reiterated his contention that by law he administered Southern military districts. He did not wish a conflict, he assured the President, but he thought that he should be consulted in selecting the military governors.

The President had sat in silence when Grant had made his former claim to executive power, but this time he spoke. With eyes coldly staring at the general, and in a calm voice which portended the approaching storm, Johnson again made reference to the Constitution. He understood, he said, that it was the President's duty to execute the laws! Warned by look and tone, the general asked permission to leave. He was no politician, he said, and he did not like to give advice on political subjects.[25]

Back in his own office, Grant forgot that he was not a politician. Taking his pen, he proceeded to repeat his contentions. Congress, he told Johnson, had imposed on him a duty, and "in the present changes the country sees but one object, no matter whether it interprets the objects of the Executive rightly or not. The object seen is the defeat of

[22] Welles, *Diary*, III, 182–183.
[23] *Ibid.*, 184–185.
[24] N. Y. *Tribune*, August 26, 1867.
[25] Welles, *Diary*, III, 186.

the laws of Congress for restoring peace, union, and representation to the ten States not now represented." The people, said the general, were tired of reconstruction, and looked upon the policy as settled. They wanted peace and quiet in order "to meet the great financial issues before us." [26]

When Johnson received this letter, he summoned Grant to the White House for another lecture on the Constitution. Taking up the letter point by point, Johnson pointed out its weaknesses. Such a letter would ruin its author, said the President, for "he could be annihilated by a reply." Convinced that his action had been unwise, Grant asked permission to withdraw his offending letter. Reaching across the table as he spoke, the general took the letter and put it in his pocket. He would write a note withdrawing the letter, he said, but he would like to take it with him.

Momentarily disciplined, Grant returned to his office to issue the necessary orders for the transfers of Sheridan, Hancock, and Sickles. At the next Cabinet meeting, his "improved" attitude was generally remarked.[27] But in the Republican press he received general commendation for his letters in regard to Stanton and Sheridan, and editors speculated on the imminence of a break between general and President. Greeley alone suspiciously peered beneath the surface and announced that the "President has won. Grant has surrendered his right to control the district commanders." Johnson, said Greeley, had played the game with "resolution, shrewdness, energy," and had succeeded in getting control of the South. "Our champion is only an anxious, earnest, protesting soldier, who at best does not say much, and whose power is limited to signing himself 'by order of the President, General of the army.' " [28]

Although Grant was insisting in the Cabinet on an honest execution of the congressional program, the Radical leaders were still opposed to his nomination. To counteract the Grant movement, the extremists inspired ovations for Sheridan and Sickles which rivaled the receptions for Grant two years before. Even Stanton was lavishly entertained in Boston, where he took pains to deny that there was an "understanding" between him and Grant over the war office.[29] To defeat this

[26] Badeau, *Grant in Peace,* 566–567.
[27] Welles, *Diary,* III, 189–190.
[28] N. Y. *Tribune,* August 27, 30, 31, September 7; N. Y. *Times,* August 29, 1867.
[29] N. Y. *Tribune,* September 13, 14, 1867.

counter-attack, Washburne hastened to New England to assure doubters that Grant was a Radical.[30]

In the administration of the War Department Grant began the practice of economy. Telling Admiral Ammen that he took office to prevent the depletion of the treasury,[31] the general soon announced that a large number of buildings, rented for war purposes, would be given up, and that fifty unnecessary clerks would be dismissed. Extra paymasters were dismissed from the army, and claims for cotton, for soldiers' bounties, and for "everything but honest work" were disallowed. As a result, the "rats" who were trying to drive Secretary McCulloch out of the Treasury turned to Grant to "gnaw, and scratch, and bite and snarl." [32] Aside from this economy, Grant tried to perform the routine duties of the War Department in the same manner that Stanton would have done. To preserve the line between his two offices, he followed the practice of issuing orders as Secretary of War from the War Department. Then, having sent the orders across the street to army headquarters by messenger, he trudged after them to obey the orders as General of the Army. Staff officers who saw him in the Department were addressed by their titles; at army headquarters they were called by name. In every respect, Grant tried to follow the imagined precepts of his predecessor. Even when Edwin Booth requested that the remains of his assassin brother be returned to the family, Grant refused. He did not object, but he felt sure that Stanton would have done so! [33]

While the Radicals were seeking to repudiate the General, Johnson determined to bind him closer to the Administration. Yet, without repeating his theory relative to his own powers, Grant continued to oppose the President. In the Cabinet Grant had supported Sickles, who had requested a court martial, and he had objected to Johnson's proposal that all the Southern elections be held on the same day.[34] Nevertheless, the President still hoped to gain his support, and, seeking an ally, he ordered Sherman to come to Washington.[35] After a week of smoothing over the troubles and advising Grant against politics, Sherman returned to St. Louis.[36]

[30] E. J. Sherman to Butler, September 9, 1867, Butler MSS.
[31] Burr, *Life and Deeds of Grant*, 851.
[32] N. Y. *Tribune*, August 21, 22, 29, 1867.
[33] Badeau, *Grant in Peace*, 106–110.
[34] Welles, *Diary*, III, 207.
[35] *Ibid.*, 221, 222.
[36] *Sherman Letters*, 297; N. Y. *Tribune*, Oct. 7, 8, 11, 1867.

Strangely enough, members of Grant's own staff agreed with Sherman. "I am one of those who hope Genl Grant will not be President," wrote Babcock to Washburne. "I look upon it as a great misfortune to him." And, according to Babcock, Generals Horace Porter and Badeau were of the same opinion! [37]

Early in October, the "off year," elections in some of the Northern States began to bring unexpected results. In Pennsylvania and New York they favored the Democrats, and in Ohio, Massachusetts, and Maine the Republican majorities of 1866 were reduced by many thousands. Negro suffrage was overwhelmingly defeated at the polls in those States where it was an election issue.[38] Taking courage from these returns, Johnson discussed Stanton's successor with the Cabinet. They considered J. D. Cox, of Ohio, and Frank Blair, and canvassed the advantages of appointing Sherman's father-in-law, Thomas Ewing. If Ewing were Secretary of War, he might influence Sherman to influence Grant! [39]

To blunt old Gideon Welles, this indirect pursuit of the elusive general had no appeal. Grant, he decided, had less brains but a stronger will than Sherman, and in a crisis Sherman would bow to his stubborn superior. Although there were many indications that Grant was under the influence of the Radicals, Welles advised Johnson to approach him directly to find out where he stood. The wisdom of the suggestion was evident to the President, and next day he went to the War Department.[40]

At the moment there was much wild talk of arresting the President while his impeachment trial was pending. Johnson began with this, and called to Grant's attention the threats that were being made. What would be the general's attitude if an arrest were attempted? Grant's answer was noncommittal but satisfactory. He assured the President that he would obey the laws. Then Johnson turned to the subject of Stanton, and asked what Grant would do if Stanton sought to take back his office. Grant replied that he had not looked into the Tenure of Office Act, but thought Stanton would first have to appeal to the courts for his office. This accorded with Johnson's idea, and he besought Grant to hold the office and force Stanton into the courts. To

[37] O. E. Babcock to Washburne, October 9, 1867, Washburne MSS.
[38] Oberholtzer, *History of the U. S.*, I, 479–480.
[39] Welles, *Diary*, III, 231–232.
[40] *Ibid.*, 233–234.

this, Grant agreed, unless he should find that the Tenure of Office Act imposed penalties upon him for obstructing its workings. In that case, he would notify the President in time for Johnson to make other arrangements. Satisfied with this position, Johnson returned to the White House.[41]

When Johnson reported to Welles the outcome of his conversation with Grant, the Secretary was delighted and urged the President to increase his intimacy with the general. Grant might yet be won back from the Radicals, who, defeated in the elections, were rallying around him.

Welles was not alone in perceiving the effect which Republican defeats would have on the general's chances. Politicians who read the handwriting on the wall began to call more lustily for the general, and to realize that hard work and much organization were needed to carry the elections. Without Grant at the masthead, the party might well abandon hope. In many Northern cities Grant Clubs were formed, and in Philadelphia the National Union Club resolved to force the party to take the hero of Appomattox.[42]

Washburne frantically reiterated his assurances that Grant was a Radical, and throughout the West, politicians wrote to the Congressman about Grant. "If there had been doubt of the expediency of his nomination before," wrote an office-holder in New Mexico, "it must be dispelled by the election results." The country, thought he, needed some man who would bring out the vote. In Kansas and Illinois, and even in the Eastern States, the politicians perceived the need for organizing behind Grant. "No civilian can carry Pennsylvania, and without Grant our election would go against us," wrote a man from Pittsburgh, who urged that Grant should make no political statements but should be his "own platform." [43]

With true political insight, the politicians everywhere made an effort to give the Grant movement an appearance of spontaneity. In Philadelphia, "political hacks" were ostentatiously excluded from ward meetings [44] and stories were diligently circulated that Grant would ac-

---

[41] Welles, *Diary,* III, 234–235; Richardson, *Messages,* VI, 613–614.
[42] New York *Tribune,* October 18, 1867.
[43] Letters of H. B. Stanton, (N. Y.), October 21; John A. Clark, (Santa Fe), October 28; John M. Read, (Pittsburgh), November 7; D. R. Anthony, November 4; J. L. Berch, (Savannah, Ill.), November 4; N. N. North, (New Mexico), November 5; James Miller, November 6; B. Dornblaser, (Joliet), November 11, to Washburne, Washburne MSS.
[44] N. Y. *Tribune,* October 23, 1867.

cept a conservative but not a radical nomination.[45] A spurious letter, alleged to emanate from Fred Dent, his brother-in-law, was also circulated. "General Grant . . . would prefer to be elected by the people," it stated, and he "will not take the Presidency unless he can enter upon its office unpledged and unembarrassed by party affiliations and platforms." [46] Although this letter was a forgery, it evidently embodied the philosophy upon which Grant was acting. But a silent President, elected by a non-partisan vote, was not at all to the Radical liking. There was more to the Radical program than carrying an election!

To Greeley, it seemed absurd to run a candidate without principles, and the *Tribune* continued to advocate Chase, who was sound on Negro suffrage. Without the Negro vote in the South, "Vallandigham could beat Grant." [47] Desiring to commit the general to the Radical program, the *Tribune* called on him daily to declare himself, and warned the party that it could not afford to nominate a man whose principles were unknown. In Ohio, Ben Wade was equally solicitous about Grant's principles. Forgetting that Cramer had listed Grant as a Radical, Wade declared that he had been trying to learn Grant's opinions. "I would like to know how he stood on the great issues before us— whether for Johnson or for Congress, or what the devil he was for," said the Senator, "but I could get nothing out of him. As quick as I'd talk politics, he'd talk horses. Well . . . in these times a man may be all right on horses and all wrong on politics." [48] If Grant wanted Wade's vote, and the vote of the Western Reserve, he would have to declare himself.

Not all the Republicans, however, agreed on the advisability of Grant's committing himself. In the minds of many, the financial questions before the nation could be solved better if Grant remained silent. Bondholders in the eastern cities were pronounced in their belief that the Government should redeem its War bonds in gold, and were bitterly opposed to any taxes on their bonds. Although divided, Western sentiment largely favored taxation and believed that the bonds should be paid in greenbacks. Payment in gold was a "suicidal policy," wrote one of Washburne's constituents as he begged his Congressman to "let General Grant at this stage not be hampered with such a law." Others

[45] N. Y. *Tribune,* October 28, 1867.
[46] *Ibid.,* December 16; N. Y. *Times,* December 14, 27, 1867.
[47] N. Y. *Tribune,* October 15, 16, 1867.
[48] *Ibid.,* November 9, 1867.

wrote in the same vein, prophesying that it would "do the party no good" to disturb the money question until after the election. Although a Galena banker deplored the "war on the best interests of the business community" he approved Washburne's "cautious commonsense compromise," and predicted that Grant would sweep the country.[49]

The bondholders were anxious to cloud the issue by running Grant. According to one of them, the Democrats were very likely to carry the country for repudiation. "Only Grant can beat this issue," he declared. "If we can run Grant we can generally count upon the soldier's vote—they would vote for him to glorify themselves— . . . that is to say, they will prefer glory to repudiation. But with Chase or any of that school of politicians we will certainly be beaten. . . ."[50]

In New England, Ben Butler came to the conclusion that there was a popular demand for taxing the bonds, and for paying the national debt in greenbacks.[51] For his part, he declared, he was willing to support Grant if the general would come out for manhood suffrage and against the bondholders.[52] On the other hand, the New York *Tribune* bitterly opposed the idea of repudiation, and deprecated the "attempt to carry an election upon the personal strength of a candidate." To beat the Democrats, an appeal should be made to "the holiest impulse and noblest aspiration of the world," and by "commending to every man's judgment the essential righteousness and beneficence" of sound finance. We "cannot win by merely banging away on a drum."[53]

When Congress reassembled in the last days of November, it immediately took up a report of the House Judiciary Committee, which had been diligently gathering information upon which to base an impeachment of Johnson. Politicians eagerly read Grant's testimony before the committee to learn his opinions. Extreme Radicals thought they found in his cautious statements evidence of his sympathy with the President, but even Greeley admitted that his views showed him "an able, sagacious, patriot." Even so, the Radical editor was still of the opinion that the presidency could be better filled by an "eminent

[49] E. B. Warner, (Morrison, Ill.), November 12, 22, December 12, 1867; N. Caruth, (Chicago), November 25; R. H. McClellan, (Galena), November 27, to Washburne, Washburne MSS.

[50] M. B. Brown, (St. Louis), to Washburne, December 9, 1867, Washburne MSS.

[51] Butler to Wm. Hill, (N. Y.) November 26, 1867, Butler MSS.

[52] Butler to E. J. Sherman, (Lawrence), December 10, 26; and to Thomas Russel, December 10, 1867, Butler MSS.

[53] New York *Tribune*, January 11, 1867.

civilian" like Chase.[54] In his report as Secretary of War, transmitted to Congress early in December, Grant took especial pains to indicate that he had taken the office through a feeling of military subordination. However, he avoided any statement to which a political significance might be ascribed, and punctiliously signed the report as General of the Army.[55]

Ignoring the extreme Radicals, the practical politicians of the Republican Party continued their efforts to commit the party to Grant. Early in December Thurlow Weed completed arrangements for a mass-meeting at Cooper Institute to nominate the general. Shrewdly hiding his own handiwork, Weed persuaded A. T. Stewart, Moses Taylor, Cornelius Vanderbilt, and other wealthy and prominent citizens to call the meeting for the avowed purpose of taking Grant's candidacy out of the politicians' hands. To a friend Weed boasted that he had promised Grant to handle his campaign as he had handled Zachary Taylor's. If Grant would make no declarations, and write no letters, Weed would elect him! [56]

The disguised Weed meeting was held December 4th. According to plan, Stewart presided, and there was an impressive list of "Vice-Presidents." William B. and J. J. Astor, Vanderbilt, Peter Cooper, "Uncle Daniel" Drew, Levi P. Morton, George William Curtis, Francis Lieber, George W. Cornell, Frank Moore, Moses Taylor, and Moses H. Grinnell—to mention but a few—were names to be reckoned with in the city's financial life. Their endorsement freed the meeting from the taint of partisanship! Resolutions were hastily but enthusiastically adopted, and a speech by General Sickles declared that Grant's deeds spoke louder than his words.[57]

For six weeks after this "non-partisan" nomination, Grant maintained his imperturbable silence on the issues before the country. The meeting gave some acceleration to the Grant movement, and the work of organizing the party for the national convention proceeded apace. Wendell Phillips took occasion to denounce Grant's reticence, but the only observable result of his vituperation was to drive more conservatives into the Grant ranks.[58] Chase still had aspirations and some

[54] E. J. Sherman to Butler, December 6, 1867, Butler MSS.; New York *Tribune,* November 26, 30; New York *World,* November 26, 1867.
[55] New York *Tribune,* December 4, 1867.
[56] Welles, *Diary,* III, 249–250.
[57] N. Y. *Tribune,* December 5, 1867.
[58] *Ibid.,* December 20, 23, 1867.

support from bankers and capitalists, but the conservative Republicans were united on the general. Grant's eagerness, Welles thought, surpassed Chase's, and his reticence was all a matter of calculation. "Grant may prove a dangerous man," wrote the Secretary of the Navy. "He is devoid of Patriotism, is ignorant but cunning, yet greedy for office and power." [59]

In accordance with the terms of the Tenure of Office Act, Johnson reported to the Senate December 12 his reasons for suspending Stanton. For a month the report was considered by a committee which finally stated, on January 10, that the President's reasons for removing his Secretary were insufficient. When the Senate took up this committee report, the handful of Johnsonites in the Senate bravely began a filibuster. For two days, a Saturday and a Monday, they spoke in defense of the President's right to choose his own advisers. The two days were eventful ones in the War Department and the White House.

As soon as he learned of the committee's report, Grant told Sherman that he would relinquish the office if the Senate upheld Stanton. Sherman had been called East to be on hand for this crisis, and he advised Grant to tell Johnson of his intentions.

Going to the White House, Grant began by recalling to Johnson the conversation they had had shortly after Stanton's suspension. Grant reminded the President that he had then believed that to recover his office Stanton would have to appeal to the courts. At that time Grant had not read the Tenure of Office Act, but had promised to inform Johnson if a reading of the law caused him to change his mind. He had now read the Act and had found that he would be liable to a fine of $10,000 and imprisonment of five years if he persisted in holding the office after the Senate had taken action. Unwilling to subject himself to such risks, he announced that he would surrender the office.

As was his custom when he faced a dilemma, Johnson began to talk about the Constitution. He had removed Stanton, he said, under his constitutional power, and not under the Tenure of Office Act. Since Grant had been appointed under the Constitution, he could not be governed by the Act.

To General Grant this reasoning seemed insufficient. In his mind the law was of considerably more immediate importance than the Presi-

[59] Welles, *Diary*, III, 244–245.

dent's constitutional locutions. Whether constitutional or no, the law was binding upon him until it had been set aside by the proper tribunal. Accordingly, he repeated that he would not be made a party to a political quarrel, and that he could not afford to risk the punishments imposed by the law. An hour passed while the two men sat wrangling over their divergent views. With a bravado that was all too facile, Johnson offered to pay Grant's fine and go to jail in his stead if the general would only stick to the War Department. The magnanimity of this preposterous offer was lost on the general.

With the indecision which characterized his entire Administration, Johnson then sought to delay the issue. Although he might have requested Grant's resignation at the moment and sent a more amenable appointee to take charge of the War Department, the President spent his time in begging Grant to remain. Unwilling to accept Grant's decision as irrevocable, he asked him to reconsider and to return on Monday for a further discussion.

Upon the question whether Grant really agreed to see the President on Monday much discussion ensued in the next few weeks. Johnson repeatedly alleged that Grant had distinctly promised to return. With equal vehemence, Grant declared he had made no such promise. Cabinet officers who heard Johnson accuse Grant concurred with the President that he had admitted the promise. Secretary Seward, however, remembered only that it was agreed the "subsequent conference . . . could reasonably take place on Monday." [60] Members of Grant's staff attested that the general gave no intimation, upon returning to his office, that he expected to see the President again.[61] In view of Johnson's volubility and Grant's inarticulateness, it seems likely that each of the disputants failed to understand the other.

On Sunday, Grant and Sherman consulted Reverdy Johnson on the situation. Neither of them liked Stanton, and both would have been glad to have him permanently displaced. Grant believed that Stanton's power for good was ended, and he saw no reason for impairing the effectiveness of the War Department. Moreover, Stanton's conduct since his suspension had not pleased the general. Sherman's personal quarrel with Stanton inclined him toward a more acceptable superior. As a result of their conversations, Sherman and Reverdy Johnson

[60] Richardson, *Messages and Papers*, VI, 160.
[61] Badeau, *Grant in Peace*, 112.

agreed to recommend Jacob D. Cox for the position.[62]

On Monday, while Grant remained in his office, Sherman and Reverdy Johnson presented their suggestion to the President. Although knowing that they had come from Grant, Johnson asked them nothing about the general. If the President had expected Grant to call on him, he showed small concern over his failure to make an appearance. Meanwhile, in the Senate chamber at the other end of the avenue the Democratic filibuster was coming to an end. Late in the afternoon Johnson's supporters were exhausted, and the Senate approved the committee report. A messenger was immediately dispatched to inform Grant that the Senate had found no sufficient grounds for Stanton's removal.

That evening, Grant went to a White House reception. Although he spoke to the President, he gave Johnson no intimation of his intended action, nor did Johnson mention the general's failure to visit his office. Evidently, the President's assertion that he expected Grant to renew Saturday's conversation was an afterthought.

Early the next morning, Grant went to the office of the Secretary of War. Entering the office, he bolted one door from the inside, and locked the other from the outside. The key he turned over to the Adjutant-General. "I am to be found at my office," he said, "at army headquarters." From his own office, Grant dispatched Comstock to the President with a note stating that in view of the Senate's action, he could no longer act as Secretary of War.[63]

When Comstock delivered Grant's note to the President, Johnson remarked that he "supposed General Grant would be very soon at the Cabinet meeting." Transmitted by Comstock, Grant interpreted this as an invitation to attend and appeared at the regular hour. Before the meeting began, he remarked to Seward that he was present by invitation. Seward expressed surprise, and asked if there "was a change in the War Department?" When Johnson entered, he took his seat without remarking on Grant's presence. The regular order of business was followed until the War Department was reached. When Johnson asked if he had any matters to present, Grant replied that he was no longer Secretary of War.

Immediately Johnson began to upbraid the General and to subject

[62] Badeau, *Grant in Peace,* 111.
[63] *Ibid.,* 125.

him to a rapid fire of questions. Had not Johnson said he expected the Senate's action? Did not Grant agree to return the office to the President rather than surrender it to Stanton? Had not the President declared the Tenure of Office Act unconstitutional? Why had Grant not kept his promise to see the President on Monday?

With the President making positive statements, all of them having a degree of truth, Grant was forced to admit that Johnson was quoting him correctly. It was true that soon after entering the War Department he had said that Stanton would have to appeal to the courts. But he had also said that he had not read the Tenure of Office Act. He had said that he would return the office to Johnson if he found that the law would not permit him to remain. But he had called on Saturday to announce that he would not resist the law. As for Johnson's statement that Grant had promised to call on Monday, the general was taken aback. Without denying that Johnson had said he should call Monday, Grant explained that "many little matters" had kept him busy at the Department all day. However, he had sent Sherman to the President. "Did not General Sherman call on you Monday?" Grant parried. Moreover, in extenuation of his failure to see the President again, he declared that he had not expected the Senate to act so soon.

Grant's obvious confusion in answering these skillfully plied questions contrasted unfavorably with the President's calm pose of offended dignity. Before an audience of friendly supporters, Johnson succeeded in making Grant's course appear a tortuous one. The Cabinet, with the exception of the shrewd Seward, saw before them a humble and hesitating man, and misinterpreted his effort to "soften the evident contradiction (his) statement gave" as a realization that he had been guilty of duplicity. When Grant had gone, Johnson triumphantly remarked that "Grant had been in secret intrigue" with the Radicals.[64]

On the morning after this scene, the *National Intelligencer* carried an account of the dispute between general and President. Obviously inspired from the White House, the article intimated that Grant had deceived Johnson. When Grant read the paper, he became extremely indignant. Taking Sherman with him, he went to the White House to demand a correction. Johnson stated that he had not seen the paper, but he listened to Grant's explanation of his conduct. To Sherman, it

[64] Welles, *Diary*, III, 261.

appeared that Johnson was satisfied with Grant's statements.[65] But Johnson later stated that Grant had "only reaffirmed that he hadn't been true to his understanding and his pledged word." [66] In the course of the conversation, both Grant and Sherman agreed to advise Stanton to resign. Johnson interpreted this agreement as a means of making amends for the general's duplicity.

When the generals were gone, Johnson read the offending editorial and found it correct. At the next Cabinet meeting, he had his secretary read the clipping from his scrap-book; and then, asking the members if it were accurate, he heard them agree that the newspaper account was substantially correct.[67]

For the next two weeks the press was filled with the quarrel. Democratic journals declared that Grant had "acted a part inconsistent with his honor as a gentleman," [68] and Greeley, seeing a means of discrediting Grant, alleged that "it was wrong for General Grant to break his promise." [69] However, even the most extreme Radicals rejoiced that Grant had refused to be a cat's-paw for Johnson. "In a question of veracity between U. S. Grant and Andrew Johnson," said the *Tribune*, "between a soldier whose honor is as untarnished as the sun, and a President who had betrayed every friend, and broken every promise, the country will not hesitate." [70] Johnsonian papers diligently circulated the rumor that Grant was drunk on the much disputed Monday.[71]

[65] *Sherman Letters*, 369.
[66] Welles, *Diary*, III, 262.
[67] *Ibid.*, 262.
[68] New York *World*, January 16, 1868.
[69] New York *Tribune*, January 20, 1868.
[70] *Ibid.*, January 17, 1868.
[71] New York *Tribune*, January 20, 1868. Historians of the Johnson Administration have accepted the assertions of Johnson and his Cabinet that Grant deliberately deceived the President. The sole evidence for the Cabinet meeting when Johnson confronted Grant with duplicity is the statements of the President and the Cabinet members. With the exception of Seward, whose political acumen taught him to avoid issues, these members gave thorough indorsement to Johnson's contentions, and pictured Grant as confused by the evidences of his deception. For a complete acceptance of the evidences of these witnesses, cf. G. F. Milton, *The Age of Hate*. At best such evidence is flimsy. The members present were all enthusiastic Johnson partisans, and their accounts of the meeting were written with the text of Johnson's own account, as it appeared in the *National Intelligencer*, before them. The unanimity of their testimony, therefore, is not convincing. Fundamentally, the whole controversy was occasioned by Johnson's indecision. There is no question but that Grant lived up to his promise to inform Johnson if he changed his mind about Stanton's appeal to the courts. The only point in controversy was whether Grant promised to continue the conversation on Monday. It seems reasonable to suppose that the two men misunderstood each other. Grant's laconic decisiveness contrasted sharply with

Although badly strained, relations between the President and the general were not yet broken. It was only through Grant that Johnson had any connection with the army, for Stanton, although he administered the office, had no communication with the President. Johnson had welcomed Grant's suggestion that he and Sherman would advise Stanton to resign, and had waited patiently for some result. Grant visited Stanton in his office, but the Secretary, suspecting his purpose, flew into such a rage that Grant had no opportunity to speak of the purpose of his visit. However, he gained the impression, which he conveyed to the President, that Stanton would hold on to the office. In the course of the discussion, Johnson suggested that Grant might disobey the orders coming from the War Department—especially such orders as purported to be given "by direction of the President." In this way, Stanton might be circumvented, and Johnson ordered Grant to disobey all such orders in the future.[72]

As Grant thought over this oral order, it appeared to him that Johnson was seeking to entrap him into an insubordinate act. After several days, the general wrote requesting that the President put the order in writing.[73] Four days passed, and Grant received no reply. Then he repeated his request. "I am compelled to ask these instructions in writing," he wrote, "in consequence of the many and gross misrepresentations affecting my personal honor circulated through the press for the last fortnight, purporting to come from the President, of conversations which occurred either with the President privately in his office or in the Cabinet meeting. What is written admits of no misunderstanding."

Having thus led up to his subject, Grant proceeded to "state the facts in the case." He had, he said, fulfilled his promise to inform the President if he could not retain the office. "From the 11th to the

Johnson's loquacious indecision. As the matter eventuated, Johnson's bluster was an attempt to cover his own failure to take prompt action on Saturday. The talk of Grant's resigning was purely a smoke-screen. He was an *ad interim* appointee and an army officer, removable on either ground by the President without explanation.

On the other hand, there can be no question that Grant blundered. His confusion was marked and there was little in his conduct that showed moral stamina. It was his first political controversy and he was doubtless taken aback by the frontal charge, but he never showed courage in battles of words or wars of ideas.

[72] Moore, Johnson's secretary, records that Grant made this suggestion. Cf. Milton, *The Age of Hate*, 488.

[73] Richardson, *Messages and Papers of the Presidents*, VI, 613. The letters which passed between President and Grant on this occasion are the principal source for the account of the entire controversy.

Cabinet meeting on the 14th instant a doubt never entered my mind about the President's fully understanding my position, namely, that if the Senate refused to concur in the suspension of Mr. Stanton my powers as Secretary of War *ad interim* would cease and Mr. Stanton's right to resume at once the functions of his office would under the law be indisputable, and I acted accordingly." Moreover, wrote Grant, "I did not agree to call again on Monday, or at any definite time, nor was I sent for by the President until the following Tuesday." Concerning his admission of a promise, Grant asserted: "I in no wise admitted the correctness of the President's statement of our conversations, though, to soften the evident contradiction my statement gave, I said . . . the President might have understood me the way he said, namely, that I had promised to resign if I did not resist the reinstatement. I made no such promise." [74]

This statement of "fact" gave Johnson an opportunity to enter into a long discussion of the disputed conversations. "My recollection of what . . . transpired is diametrically the reverse of your narration," wrote the President. Moreover, the Cabinet members, hearing Johnson's letter, were again in agreement that the President was telling the truth.

As for the order to disobey Stanton, Johnson endorsed on Grant's letter: "General Grant is instructed in writing not to obey any order from the War Department assumed to be issued by the direction of the President unless such order is known by the General commanding the armies of the United States to have been authorized by the Executive.[75]

When Grant received Johnson's letter of diametrically reverse recollections in regard to the surrender of the War Office, he seated himself to write a reply. Still eager to settle the dispute without a personal rupture, the general sought to elucidate his course rather than believe that Johnson was deliberately attempting to discredit him with the country. Again he explained his actions, and added the further excuse that he had not expected Stanton to act so quickly. He had thought that Stanton would write him, as he had written Stanton when the situation was reversed. Stanton had moved in without formalities.[76]

[74] Richardson, *Messages and Papers,* VI, 613–614.
[75] *Ibid.,* VI., 615.
[76] Comstock MS. Diary; Milton, *The Age of Hate,* 494–5.

Reading this letter before it was sent, General Rawlins immediately perceived that Grant was making a damaging admission. Experienced in the ways of politics, Rawlins saw that the time had come for Grant to take a definite stand against the President. Accordingly, he proceeded to redraft Grant's letter in such a manner as to effect a personal break. The damaging admission was omitted, and in its stead appeared phrases definitely charging Johnson with dishonesty. "I here reassert the correctness of my statements," Rawlins made the general say, "anything in yours to the contrary notwithstanding." As for the War Department, Grant now adopted the explanation which the Republicans had given in August—he had accepted the *ad interim* appointment to prevent the selection of some person who might hamper the work of reconstruction.

"And now, Mr. President," ended the letter, "when my honor as a soldier and integrity as a man have been so violently assailed, pardon me for saying that I can but regard this whole matter, from the beginning to the end, as an attempt to involve me in resistance of law, for which you hesitated to assume the responsibility in orders, and thus to destroy my character before the country." As confirmation of this, there was the order to disobey Stanton.[77]

With the exception of this last statement, the Rawlins-Grant letter had been written with restraint. But Rawlins knew his man, and fully understood the tactics by which the Radicals had tricked Johnson into intemperate denunciations during the ill-fated "Swing around the circle." In reply to Grant's letter Johnson sent a missive whose offensiveness surpassed Rawlins' best efforts. The controversy, said the President, had degenerated on one side "in tone and temper." Grant had accepted the War Department "to circumvent the President," which was a "tacit deception." "In the ethics of some persons such a course is allowable." He had held on to the office "for the very object of preventing an appeal to the courts." This was a "violation of confidence," for Grant had "secretly determined" to surrender the Department to Stanton. Finally, Grant had assumed an "insubordinate attitude" by asserting that he was willing to obey Stanton and disobey the President.[78]

This last remark stung Grant so deeply that he wrote still another letter to the President. It was not his purpose, he assured Johnson, to

[77] Richardson, *Messages and Papers*, VI, 618–619.
[78] *Ibid.*, 603–605.

disobey any order "distinctly given." But he was not able to distinguish which of Stanton's orders might have the Executive approval. Moreover, he presented evidence to show that other members of the Cabinet, by official communications, had recognized Stanton as Secretary of War. The President's order had been ambiguous, and he was simply trying to interpret it. The explanation was an anti-climax after the high-spirited tone of the previous letters.

An hour before the Grant-Rawlins letter was delivered to the President, a resolution in Congress called for the correspondence.[79] The Radicals had hopes of finding therein evidence for impeaching the President: the lesser politicians hoped to prove that Grant was a good Radical. In the latter purpose they were successful. Although Welles thought that Grant was a "fool," who had been deceived by the Radicals,[80] the Republican press and politicians were delighted. When Rawlins took Grant's pen to make the rupture a personal one, he insured Grant's nomination by the Republicans.

When Thad Stevens saw Grant's letter, he exulted: "He is a bolder man than I thought him." "Now we will let him into the Church," declared that High Priest of Radicalism.[81]

[79] Welles, *Diary*, III, 269–270.
[80] *Ibid.*, 267.
[81] Oberholtzer, *History of the United States*, I, 489, citing Philadelphia *Ledger*, February 10, 1868.

THE interchange of recriminations between Grant and Johnson turned the two men into bitter personal enemies. Before the epistolary clash, Grant had sought to preserve an outward appearance of harmonious subordination to his chief, and so skillfully had he maintained an apparent impartiality that even Johnson had been partly deceived as to his real opinions. When their correspondence tore the mask of reticence from Grant's face, he became an open and implacable enemy. Aside from the most formal communications, contact between them entirely ceased. For the Cabinet members who had confirmed Johnson's ingenious statements, Grant developed a rancor which was only surpassed by his hatred of the President. Welles noted that he and the Radicals were even attempting to "establish a Radical *ton* or condition of society, in Washington." Excluded from social contacts with the Administration's cohorts, Grant and Stanton ostentatiously attended only Radical receptions. Cabinet officers replied with open scorn for Grant's "publicly advertised jams." [1]

Not only socially did the general and President seek to damage one another. Already Johnson had made efforts to win Sherman from Grant, dangling before the lieutenant-general's eyes the supposedly tempting lure of the War Department. But Sherman was obsessed by a distrust of politicians, and spurned the offer. Each time that Johnson offered the department, Sherman gave an evasive answer, and turned to Thomas Ewing to save him from the President's designs.[2] Failing to make Sherman Secretary of War, Johnson tried another scheme. With both Stanton and Grant aligned with the Radicals, the President had good reason to fear that his congressional enemies would use the army to seize the government and place him under arrest. In desperate need of an army friend, Johnson planned to give Sherman the brevet rank of general, and place him in command of a new district with headquarters in Washington.[3]

Advisers close to the President warned him that Sherman would

[1] Welles, *Diary*, III, 298.
[2] Milton, *Age of Hate*, 500; Welles, *Diary*, III, 254; Badeau, *Grant in Peace*, 127.
[3] Welles, *Diary*, III, 270–272, 279.

not accept a position which would place him in opposition to Grant, but Johnson persisted in his course, created the new district, ordered Sherman to it, and sent the nomination for the brevet appointment to the Senate.

After refusing the office of Secretary of War, Sherman returned to St. Louis feeling that he had escaped a bad situation. As soon as he learned of Johnson's new plans, he took steps to avoid the assignment. He wrote his brother to vote against confirmation, assuring the Senator that he had no intention of coming East until after Grant's inauguration. Johnson, he was sure, would use him to "beget violence." To the President himself, Sherman wrote a long protest, sending it, according to military usage, through Grant. The blow, he said, was the hardest he had "ever received in a life somewhat checkered with adversity." He would resign his commission if he could support his family elsewhere.

As Grant read this letter, he immediately wrote advising Sherman not to resign. Johnson, he said, had declared that "he intended to have you and me knock our heads together," but Sherman did not owe the President anything, and he was not entitled to such a sacrifice.[4] Against Sherman's opposition, Johnson could do nothing but abandon his plans and retract his orders.[5]

As Johnson's efforts to strike at him met with failure, Grant began to strike back. Hitherto, Grant had been opposed to movements to impeach the President, and the general's supporters, in and out of Congress, had been skeptical of the beneficent results to follow. "Impeachment," a Chicago editor told Washburne, "is an anti-Grant movement, the object being to get Wade into the presidency long enough to give him prestige and patronage to control the next National Convention."[6] Realizing this danger, Washburne did not support the would-be impeachers until after Grant and Johnson had openly quarreled.

On February 21, Johnson appointed General Lorenzo Thomas *ad interim* Secretary of War, and sent him to the War Department to oust Stanton. Just as Stanton seemed ready to obey the President's order to vacate the office, Grant entered the room where Thomas was preparing to assume authority. Sending Thomas out of the room on a

[4] Badeau, *Grant in Peace*, 130–137.

[5] *Ibid.*, 127–131; *Sherman Letters*, 305; Welles, *Diary*, III, 279–282; N. Y. *Tribune*, February 15, 17, 21, 1868.

[6] Horace White to Washburne, August 13, 1868, Washburne MSS.

pretext, he and Stanton hastily consulted on a course of action. When Thomas returned, Stanton asked for time to consider whether he would obey. Fortified by Grant's presence, and by the hastily promised support of the leading Radical Senators, Stanton decided to "stick" to his office.[7]

Next day the House voted to impeach Johnson for this attempt to violate the Tenure of Office Act. Before the vote was taken, "Black Jack" Logan, Representative from Illinois who had inducted Grant into the colonelcy of his first regiment, hastily scribbled a note to Colonel N. P. Chipman in the Judge-Advocate-General's office. Chipman, like Judge-Advocate-General Joseph Holt, was a fanatic whose Radicalism was a direct outgrowth of the psychoses of the Civil War. At the close of the war, he had shown great zeal in persecuting the miserable crowd of Confederate prison officials, and had served as judge-advocate in the trial which had sent Wirz, the Andersonville jailer, to his death.[8] Now, Logan had a comparable service for him. "The House will impeach A. J.," wrote the Congressman, "and . . . I hope you will quietly and secretly organize all our boys that they can assemble at a given signal . . . ready to protect the Congress of the U. S. . . . This must be done quietly. . . ." With willing heart Chipman turned to this task, and prepared the Grand Army posts to "rally at a signal in defense of Secretary Stanton or the Congress." [9] With the G. A. R. organized and ready to act, the Radicals proceeded to impeach the President.

During most of the trial, Grant remained a passive spectator. Members of his staff attended the sessions, and came back hopeful of an early conviction.[10] The Senate debated Grant's correspondence with Johnson, and he was summoned to give testimony as to his conversations. On the stand, the cautious general shrewdly refrained from any show of personal animosity.[11] However, he helped the managers of the House when he could, and even had his servant seduce a White House janitor to send scraps from the President's waste basket to the impeachment counsel.[12] In the press Grant was quoted as saying that

[7] *Impeachment Trial*, 419–429.
[8] William B. Hesseltine, *Civil War Prisons, A Study in War Psychology*, 240–247.
[9] Logan to Chipman, February 22, 1867, and Chipman to Mrs. Logan, June 5, 1907, Logan MSS. See F. M. Thomas to Butler, September 18, 1867, Butler MSS., for other evidence of the organizing of the G. A. R.
[10] Babcock to Washburne, March 31, 1868, Washburne MSS.
[11] Badeau, *Grant in Peace*, 135.
[12] Milton, *Age of Hate*, 552, citing Moore Diary.

"the acquittal of Mr. Johnson would threaten the country, and especially the South, with revolution and bloodshed." [13]

As the trial drew to an end, and it became evident that several Republican Senators were wavering, Grant was galvanized into action. Quietly he moved among his friends, meeting them in the streets and the lobby, and urged them to vote for conviction.[14] Once he went to Frelinghuysen's house to instruct the Senator in his duty, and "returned greatly gratified" with the assurance the New Jersey member gave him.[15] He invited Henderson of Missouri to breakfast with him, and regretfully learned that he would not vote to convict. A week later, on a street car, he again importuned the Senator. "I would impeach him," said the general, ". . . because he is such an infernal liar." [16]

Despite Henderson's defection, the Radical Senators were hopeful of the verdict. On the day before the vote was taken, Ben Wade called at Grant's headquarters. "General," said the President *pro tempore* of the Senate, "I am here to consult with you about my Cabinet in case Mr. Johnson is found guilty." Grant said nothing, and Wade proceeded to explain that he wished to select such men as would meet Grant's approval. Again Grant's superb silence came to his aid, and while Wade talked for half an hour about the various Radicals whom he would appoint, the general sat without mentioning his own preferences. Grant had no objections to Wade's appointees, but he skillfully avoided falling into the trap of agreeing to any of them.[17]

On the morrow, Wade did not appoint his Cabinet. When the vote was taken, the Senate lacked one vote of the necessary two-thirds to convict. For this outcome, Grant bore an inadvertent share of the responsibility. In April, Johnson's counsel had advised him to nominate an acceptable man as Secretary of War. This move would allay the fears that Johnson would renew his war on Congress immediately after acquittal. He agreed to the suggestion, and summoned General John M. Schofield to Washington to offer him the post. Schofield agreed to serve if Grant approved. When he consulted Grant, the latter fulminated against Johnson, alleging that he did "not believe in any

[13] Cross, *Life of Grant*, 37; N. Y. *Tribune*, April 3; N. Y. *Times*, April 4, 1868.
[14] New York *Tribune*, May 15, 1868.
[15] Badeau, *Grant in Peace*, 136.
[16] J. B. Henderson in *Century Magazine*, December, 1912, p. 202 ff.
[17] Badeau, *Grant in Peace*, 136-137.

compromise of the impeachment question. The President ought to be convicted fairly on the facts proved." However, Schofield was acceptable to him as Secretary, and he gave permission to his subordinate to become his superior. After Schofield had accepted the position, Grant attempted to recall his permission, but his change of mind came too late. Schofield became Secretary of War; wavering Senators were convinced that Johnson did not intend violence, and Grant thus contributed to a verdict which he deplored.[18]

During the whole quarrel between Grant and Johnson and the ensuing impeachment trial, the work of organizing the country for the presidential campaign went steadily forward. Chief Justice Chase was actively engaged in a desperate effort to capture the nomination. With considerable support in the South, with the backing of the powerful New York *Tribune,* and with the capitalists and bankers of New England smiling favorably upon his aspirations, his candidacy would in normal times have been formidable. Despite Grant's popularity, Washburne and his friends were disturbed lest Chase should come into the Republican convention with seventy votes from the South, thirty more from New England, and enough money to purchase the nomination.[19] Moreover, they feared the effect of stories, diligently circulated by the Chase cohorts, that Grant was frequently seen drunk on the streets of Washington.[20] However, the Johnson-Grant correspondence demolished the likelihood of Chase's ever securing Republican support, and the Chief Justice's impartial conduct during the impeachment trial alienated the extreme partisans upon whom he had counted. The field was clear for Grant.

Like Chase, Ben Butler saw the handwriting on the political wall, and reluctantly prepared to do obeisance to the popular will. Throughout the session of Congress, Butler's Massachusetts henchmen sent him constant reports that the Republicans of his State were "crazy for Grant." Although many wrote to commend his stand for inflation of the currency, and deprecated the evident intentions of the Republicans to "build up a rich man's party at the expense of the great majority of

[18] John M. Schofield, *Forty-Six Years in the Army,* 413–418.
[19] New York *Tribune,* December 27, 28, 30, 1867, January 4, 18, 1868; U. S. Brisbin, (Lexington, Ky.) to Washburne, January 16, 1868, Washburne MSS.
[20] J. B. Atkinson, (Washington) to Colfax, January 10, 1868, and letters from A. Watson, (Washington) January 19; R. C. White, (New York) February 4; George C. Fogg, (Concord) February 3; Jason March, (Rockford, Ill.) February 3; and Rufus P. Stebbins, (Washington) March 11, 1868, in Washburne MSS.

the people," the weight of evidence convinced Butler that the "bond-holders" would nominate "America's greatest humbug"—the "Galena Tanner's Pup." [21] Accordingly, "for the good of the country," Butler decided to "sacrifice personal feeling" and come out in support of Grant. [22]

But if Butler were to support Grant, it was obviously desirable that their personal enmity should cease. Many of Butler's friends hoped he would make "just and honorable" terms with the general, but one of them reminded him that *"you are Genl Grant's superior in every respect,* and in making terms with him do not forget that fact." [23] Fully cognizant of his own superiority, Butler accepted the good offices of George Wilkes, who offered to negotiate a personal and political truce with Grant. The editor of a Radical weekly, Wilkes was closely associated with Butler in a speculative company to exploit Lower California, and had hopes of being Grant's minister to Mexico. Covering his secret dreams of profit, Wilkes suggested a reconciliation to Grant. Public questions, said the ambitious editor, required the two men to coöperate in a common cause.

Grant made no answer to this overture, and Wilkes understood that the general did not want to discuss the matter. However, the editor was insistent, and proceeded to point out that Butler was offended by two things: the "bottle" phrase in Grant's final report, and a belated invitation to one of Grant's soirées. Perceiving that he could not avoid discussion, Grant assured Wilkes that the simile of the bottle, which had described Butler's position at Bermuda Hundreds, had been used without intention of giving offense. The late invitation had been sent as soon as it was known that Butler was in town. No offense was intended by its lateness. [24]

After pondering the situation for a few weeks, Butler swallowed his pride and laboriously drafted a reply which Wilkes could show to Grant. "I agree with you," said the Congressman, "that General Grant's command of the army; our party relations; his high posi-

[21] Letters from E. J. Sherman, (Lawrence) December 6; Alfred Clapp, (St. Louis) December 20; D. C. Chase, (Clarmont, N. H.) December 21, 1867; E. J. Sherman, January 8; E. W. Whitaker, (Hartford) January 31; and General W. H. Weitzel, February 6, 1868 to Butler in Butler MSS. The "humbug" and "pup" statements are in the latter letter.

[22] Butler to G. Clusett, (France) March 12; to J. R. G. Pitkin, (New Orleans) April 30; and to Simon Stevens, February 28, 1868, Butler MSS.

[23] E. J. Sherman to Butler, December 6, 1867, Butler MSS.

[24] Wilkes to Butler, April 12, 14, 1868, Butler MSS.

tion . . . which almost necessarily must bring us in official contact, would seem to render it convenient, at least, that no impediment should exist to social recognition each of the other . . ." So saying, Butler accepted Grant's explanation of the "bottle." "If other supposed injustices done me in his Report can be as easily elucidated as this, there can be no reason why the most cordial relations should not be resumed." If Grant would signify his willingness to explain, Butler would indicate the other injustices of the *Report*.[25]

But Grant had gone as far as he would go. Although Wilkes wrote him, and even obtained the intercession of Schuyler Colfax, Butler had to be satisfied with the explanations he had received. Butler, however, gave at least one indication of his own desire for peace. Receiving a letter from a woman in San Francisco threatening "much scandal" unless Grant paid her a debt of $4,000, the Massachusetts politician sent the letter to Grant. A note explained that it "looked like a blackmailing scheme." After this, although no formal treaty was made, a tacit truce prevailed between the two men.[26]

With Butler and Chase reconciled to the inevitable, the Grant managers had clear sailing. Greeley definitely came out for Grant [27] and in State after State the Republican conventions instructed delegates to vote for him at Chicago. Long before the convention, it was known that the only contest would be over the Vice-Presidency. For this office, almost every State had a "favorite son" to whom its delegation was pledged. Speaker Colfax, Hannibal Hamlin, Thomas Ewing, Galusha Grow, James G. Blaine, Senators Howard of Michigan, Wilson of Massachusetts, Williams of Oregon, and Wade of Ohio, ex-Governors Buckingham of Connecticut, Fenton of New York, and Newell of New Jersey, were all mentioned. All had local support and high aspirations.[28]

Before the Republican convention met to nominate Grant, an enthusiastic "Soldiers' and Sailors' " convention assembled in Chicago to lend support to the occasion. With a venom surpassing that of the Radical politicians, it denounced the Republican Senators who had voted to acquit Andrew Johnson. As they marched past the offices of

[25] Butler to Wilkes, May 2, 1868, Butler MSS. See draft of the same date.
[26] Wilkes to Grant, May 6; Mrs. Morea B. Fox to Butler, April 14; Grant to Wilkes, June 19; Wilkes to Butler, June 20, 23; Colfax to Wilkes, June 20; Butler to N. H. Upham, July 4, 1868, Butler MSS.
[27] New York *Tribune*, February 7, 15, 1868.
[28] *Ibid.*, January 4, 15, 31, February 10, 14, March 3, 9, 30, April 6, 18, May 6, 8, 11, 1868.

a pro-Johnson newspaper, the parading veterans sang to the ribald strains of "Old Grimes Is Dead." In the convention itself the band played the "Rogues March" in honor of Johnson and his supporters. Generals Hawley, Sickles, and Logan denounced the seven recalcitrant Senators who had deserted the party, and led the prolonged cheers with which the soldiers formally nominated Grant for the Presidency. With the humilty of a Uriah Heep, Jesse Grant addressed the assembly. It astonished him, he said, that he "who had done nothing in particular in the great war for the country, should be called upon by the braves of the nation to speak."

"You had a boy," shouted back the assembled braves. "That is enough!"

Before the convention, Washburne's friends had advised him to keep Grant's father away from Chicago. One of them was certain that "if the fool killer in his rounds should happen to pass by the way of Washington, and by accident catch old Grant, it would go hard with him." Knowing Jesse Grant's peculiar faculty for antagonizing people by his boastful enthusiasms, the Grant managers tried to get Orville Grant to prevail upon his father to stop boosting Ulysses. But nothing could stop the garrulous old man from journeying to Chicago to be lionized by the conventions.[29]

The day after the soldiers' convention, eight thousand people crowded into Crosby's Opera House to watch the Republican delegates nominate Grant. Bishop Matthew Simpson, Radical leader of the Methodists, opened with prayer, and Carl Schurz followed with a ringing appeal for justice to the soldiers, to the Union men and Negroes of the South, and to the "creditor who staked his credit upon the success of the Government." A platform embodying these demands, denouncing the corruption of the Johnson Administration, promising encouragement to immigration, and a strong attitude toward Great Britain, was hastily adopted. Then General Logan, speaking for the soldiers' convention and the Illinois delegation, nominated Grant. No other candidate was offered, and the convention unanimously endorsed the soldiers' nominee. For the Vice-Presidency, Wade, Colfax, and Fenton led in a field of ten favorite sons. On the first four ballots Wade came first with Colfax a close second; on the fifth, the States aban-

---

[29] Chas. L. Stephenson, (Galena) March 26, and Henry M. Smith, (Chicago) May 8, 1868, to Washburne, Washburne Mss.

doned other candidates and nominated Colfax by an overwhelming majority. The nominee, so amiable that he had been nicknamed "Smiler," had a reputation for never having lost a friend or made an enemy. He added little positive strength to the ticket, but the Republicans felt no need for a strong man in the second place. Pointing proudly to the head of the ticket, they called on the Democrats to "Match Him." [30]

In Washington, General Grant went quietly about his duties. Up to the hour of the convention he had spoken no word to indicate his ambitions. While his name was being cheered in Chicago, he was working at Army Headquarters. In the War Department, Secretary Stanton sat beside the telegraph awaiting the convention news. As soon as the General's nomination was confirmed, Johnson's nemesis rushed across the street, and up the steps to Grant's office. "General," he panted as he rushed in, "I have come to tell you that you have been nominated by the Republican Party for President of the United States."

Singularly unable to express his emotions, Grant received the news in silence and stolidly accepted Stanton's congratulations; "there was no shade of exultation or agitation on his face, not a flush on his cheek, nor a flash in his eye." Badeau, who was present, doubted that his chief felt any elation, not "even in those recesses where he concealed his inmost thoughts." [31]

That night there was celebration throughout the country. In Washington a great demonstration was held, and a procession, headed by the Marine band, marched to serenade the nominees. Representative Boutwell of Massachusetts presented Grant as the "next President of the United States" and he delivered his first political address. "Gentlemen," he began, "being entirely unaccustomed to public speaking and without the desire to cultivate the power, it is impossible for me to find appropriate language to thank you for this demonstration. All that I can say is, that in whatever position I may be called by your will, I shall endeavor to discharge its duties with fidelity and honesty of purpose. Of my rectitude in the performance of public duties you will have to judge for yourselves from the record before you." Moving on to Colfax's home, the crowd found the "next Vice-President" eager to dwell on Grant's merits and accomplishments. In

[30] New York *Tribune,* May 18, 20, 21, 22, 1868.
[31] Badeau, *Grant in Peace,* 144.

the enthusiasm of the moment, no one seemed to notice that the Republican nominees voiced no program for a new Administration.[32]

The work of the Chicago convention was at once jubilantly approved by all the "Republican" and "Grant" clubs of the country. Ratification meetings were promptly held, and campaign orators waxed eloquent in extolling Grant. Greeley's long-standing scorn of Grant's reticence was now turned to praise for the General's "calm judgment, sterling sense, accurate estimate of the men whom he selects for executive position, and above all, that sensible habit of confining himself to his own duties . . . and leaving all . . . in complete independence, even of advice, and still more of his control—all these qualities, which have shone so clearly in the character of Gen. Grant, are among the highest qualifications that could be conceived for the presidential office." [33] Although Welles was convinced that there was no spontaneous enthusiasm for the Chicago nominations,[34] and Democratic journals sneered at the use of a military candidate to catch votes,[35] there was no lack of confidence in the Republican ranks.

Nine days after the convention, General Joseph R. Hawley, its presiding officer, came to Washington to make a formal tender of the nomination to Grant and Colfax. The two candidates, their wives, and two hundred friends, received the delegation at Grant's home. Clad in plain black, with only the buttons of his waistcoat to indicate his rank, the general stood at ease while Hawley spoke. Then Grant replied briefly, formulating in a few words his whole political and constitutional philosophy. "You have truly said . . . I shall have no policy to enforce against the will of the people." In a formal letter Grant accepted the nomination, endorsed the Chicago platform, promised to administer the laws in accordance with the popular will, and ended with an almost Lincolnesque epigram: "Let us have peace." [36]

This concise statement of principles delighted the Republican leaders. Fitting nicely into the sentiments of a war-weary nation, "Let Us Have Peace" made an excellent campaign slogan, while the promise of willing submission to the popular will gave hope to the politicians. "This is the true theory of the President's office," said Greeley. The

[32] New York *Tribune,* May 23, 1868.
[33] *Ibid.,* May 23, 1868.
[34] Welles, *Diary,* III, 370.
[35] New York *Tribune,* May 27, 1868.
[36] *Ibid.,* May 30, June 1, 2, 3, 1868.

country needed an executive who would "mind his own business ener-
getically and faithfully, and a Congress who will attend to theirs."
Under such a régime, Congress could restore the Union, and "perfect
sound financial policies." Altogether, Grant's letter was "eminently
judicious, cautious, pertinent, pointed, comprehensive, and satisfactory."

For a month after Grant's acceptance, the country speculated on the
Democratic nominations. Republicans, glorying in their own prospects,
facetiously advised the Democracy to choose Thomas Jefferson. "The
party itself is nothing but a tradition, a myth, a reminiscence, a voice
from the tomb, an ancient and fish-like smell . . . and there is no
reason why it should not nominate a dead man." [37] If not Jefferson,
then Lee would make a good candidate. Lee's principles were the same
as those of the Democracy, except for a lack of contempt for Grant's
military record.[38] But the Democrats had no need to listen to such
sarcastic advice; they had a plethora of candidates who would be
glad of the nomination. Beginning with "Gentleman George" Pendleton of Ohio, who had become enamoured of the "Ohio Idea" to pay the
5–20 bonds in greenbacks, the list ran through such names as Senator
Hendricks of Indiana, General Hancock, and General F. P. Blair, Jr.,
up to the President himself. Each of these, together with the usual
crop of favorite sons, had high hopes, but none was more eager for
the nomination than Chief Justice Salmon P. Chase.

After his chances for the Republican nomination had disappeared,
Chase listened with enchanted reluctance to the beguiling whispers
which came from interested groups in the Eastern cities. Bondholders
and bankers would welcome the candidacy of a man with "sound
money" principles, and political opportunists, with an eye to the party
war chest, came out in his favor. John D. Van Buren assured Chase
that the people were spontaneous in demanding him. The vacillating
New York *Herald* came out for the Chief Justice, and August Belmont,
financier and chairman of the Democratic National Committee, wrote
Chase to ask his views and his ambitions. The day after Grant's letter
of acceptance, Chase replied with a statement that he had formerly
been a Democrat, had left the party on the slavery issue, and had
recently agreed with Johnson on State Rights. He still believed in

[37] New York *Tribune*, April 3, 1868.
[38] *Ibid.*, May 29, 1868.

Negro suffrage. He was not sure, he concluded, whether such a medley of principles made him a fit candidate for any party. "Of that my countrymen must judge." [39] However, as the time for the convention drew near, Chase and Van Buren drew up a platform to circulate among the delegates. If this were adopted, Chase believed that a "new era of Democratic ascendancy" would be inaugurated. When the convention assembled, Kate Chase Sprague, the Chief Justice's politically minded daughter, was on hand to promote the millennium. [40]

In New York, on July 4, August Belmont welcomed the delegates to an ornate new Tammany Hall. Radical Republicans took particular note that General N. B. Forrest, Wade Hampton, Robert Barnwell Rhett, and C. L. Vallandigham, with many a lesser rebel and Copperhead, were seated on the floor. A "Soldiers' and Sailors' " convention, in pale imitation of the Chicago meeting, sat simultaneously. Such military men as Kirby Smith and Grant's classmate, W. B. Franklin, were there, and Blue and Gray were mingled, but the meeting had no candidate to offer to the Democratic convention. [41]

The delegates had several options. In the first place, they might fight the coming campaign on the issue of reconstruction. If they made the Southern question the major issue, their logical candidate was Andrew Johnson. However, if they did not wish to burden themselves with the much-maligned Chief Executive, they could take General Hancock, whose rule in Louisiana had received Presidential commendation and whose military record would attract many a soldier's vote. Again, the party might accept Radical reconstruction and Negro suffrage as accomplished facts, and nominate Chase on a platform of constitutional government and State Rights. Finally, they might ignore reconstruction and give battle on the financial questions before the nation. If this were done, Pendleton was the logical man to carry the party banner.

But the candidate was to be neither of these men. The Ohio financial heresies were written into the platform and the party stood committed to pay the national obligations "strictly according to terms." Taxation of bonds, and "one currency for the producer and for the bondholder" were promised along with the restoration of the States and immediate amnesty. But having gained the platform, the Ohioans failed to get

[39] J. W. Schuckers, *The Life and Public Services of Salmon Portland Chase*, 584 ff.
[40] Oberholtzer, *History of the United States*, II, 171–173; Schucker, *op. cit.*, 567–570; C. H. Coleman, *The Election of 1868*, 102–112.
[41] New York *Tribune*, July 7, 1868.

the nomination. Instead, after twenty-one ballots the Tammany politicians, with more than their usual chicane, snatched the nomination for the Convention's presiding officer, Horatio Seymour.[42] For the second place the convention selected General F. P. Blair.[43]

These nominations took the country by surprise. In every respect, Seymour was an unsuitable candidate with whom to oppose Grant. He had been a Copperhead during the war, and as Governor of New York during the draft riots had laid himself open to Radical charges of treason. As the candidate of the bondholders, his nomination was in itself a repudiation of the party's financial program. Little known outside New York, he was ill fitted to oppose Grant's popular prestige. Equally unwise was Blair's nomination. Before the convention, Blair had written a letter in which he declared: "The issues upon which the contest turns are clear. . . . They all resolve themselves into the old and ever renewing struggle of a few men to absorb the political power of the nation." Adversaries of free government had "trampled under foot" the Constitution and the rights of the States. A barbarism had been created in the South, and "the military leader under whose prestige this usurping Congress has taken refuge . . . has announced his acceptance of the nomination and his willingness to maintain their usurpations over eight millions of people at the South, fixed to the earth with bayonets. He exclaims 'Let us have peace.' . . . The peace to which Grant invites us is the peace of despotism and death." [44]

Although he accepted the platform, Blair's assertion that the Southern military governments should be overthrown enabled the Republicans to charge that he counseled violence. Welles, observing the convention from Washington, thought that the Democrats had put in jeopardy an election they might have won by nominating Hancock or Johnson. Johnson thought Seymour the worst man, next to Pendleton, who could have been nominated.[45] Many Democratic leaders agreed, and the Republicans rejoiced. The Democrats had "set forth their weakest man," and Grant's election was assured. The Republicans themselves, wrote Greeley, could not have selected more satisfactory Democratic candidates.[46]

[42] New York *Tribune,* July 6, 1868; Milton, *Age of Hate,* 639.
[43] Oberholtzer, *History of the United States,* II, 170–180.
[44] *Annual Cyclopedia,* 1868, 752.
[45] Welles, *Diary,* III, 398–401, 404.
[46] New York *Tribune,* July 10, 17, 1868.

Seymour was a man of ability. A student of law and politics, he ran a dairy farm near Utica. Twice Governor of New York, and several times an unsuccessful candidate for the office, he had gained a reputation as a powerful and even eloquent orator. However, his oratorical abilities were in little evidence during the campaign. After a letter of acceptance, and a few speeches in New York, he retired to the seclusion of his estate. Persistent rumors of his sly maneuvers in the convention were circulated, and a silent campaign seemed to become him.

Nor did Grant take part in his campaign. Early in June he attended the graduating exercises at West Point, where his oldest son, Fred, was a cadet. At the exercises, Grant delivered the diplomas to the graduates, and listened to Professor Henry Coppée, his classmate and biographer, deliver the address. Inspired to reminiscence, the orator of the day recalled that when Grant was a cadet, there had been a movement to abolish the academy. Representative Hamilton Fish, "your neighbor . . . dissipated that iniquity and saved the academy." Thus had Grant been given to the nation! [47] Modestly, the general listened to this tribute, and modestly he performed his ceremonial duties, military and social. Mrs. Grant, however, "mortified" some of the Democratic ladies by speaking confidently of occupying the White House.[48]

Immediately after his return to Washington, Grant began to prepare for a Western trip. To the party managers he said that he would take no part in the campaign. His name was enough; he would not engage in a scramble for office. To Badeau, it seemed that Grant wished to be President of the people and not of a party, and meant to keep himself free from pledges about place and about policy. Letters which poured in upon him were turned over to Badeau, and the general saw less than a dozen items of the summer's correspondence.[49]

His decision to refrain from participation in the campaign was eminently wise, and constituted excellent political strategy. Reporters followed his journeyings, and filled the papers with homely accounts of the simple soldier whom the people were calling to the White House. Sherman joined him in St. Louis, and traveled with him to join Sheridan in Kansas. Then the three heroes went together as far as Denver, and turned back to Iowa. From Council Bluffs Grant went to Chicago,

[47] New York *Tribune*, June 10, 12, 13, 15, 16, 1868.
[48] Welles, *Diary*, III, 389.
[49] Badeau, *Grant in Peace*, 145.

and from there to Galena to spend the time before the election.[50]

Before he arrived in Galena, the citizens of his temporary home prepared to welcome him as they had done three years before. Neighbors made ready his house, lent bedding and linen, rented crockery for his use, stocked the larder, and had dinner awaiting him. Even a carriage was placed at his disposal by his proud fellow citizens.[51] Surrounded by these tokens of affection, Grant remained among the Galena townsfolk until after the election. In Washington, Rawlins handled the duties of Army Headquarters, and kept in touch with the party managers. In Galena, Grant refrained from discussing politics, and avoided all politicians except Washburne.[52]

While he rested and waited the Republican chiefs gathered the "sinews of war" in large amounts. Seymour's nomination met the approval of Democratic bondholders and capitalists, and under S. J. Tilden's lead, they prepared to contribute liberally to the campaign funds.[53] The Republicans were not to be outdone by the Democrats. Before the convention A. T. Stewart, Moses Grinnell, and W. E. Dodge had been called upon to aid the Republicans in the New Hampshire spring elections.[54] As the campaign opened, Henry Cooke, younger brother of the famous banker, was adopted as the Republican angel. Under the efficient guardianship of William E. Chandler, Secretary of the National Committee, the bankers, the merchants, and the corporations opened their money chests to the Republicans.[55] Edwards Pierrepont, who had profited greatly from legal business for the War Department, contributed $20,000 to the campaign.[56] So great were the party resources that the Republicans, late in the campaign, undermined their opponents by purchasing Democratic newspapers [57] and bribing press correspondents in Washington with $3,000 or $3,500 a month, payment being contingent on success at the polls.[58]

With the major candidates silent, the campaign got off to a dull start. But as the process of "frying the fat" from the bondholders began to lubricate the machinery, enthusiasm grew. Grant clubs, gen-

[50] New York *Tribune*, July 21, 24, 28, 29, August 3, 4, 15, 22, 24, Sept. 2, 11, 1868.
[51] L. G. Felt to Washburne, July 20, 1868, Washburne MSS.
[52] Badeau, *Grant in Peace*, 146–147.
[53] J. Medill to Washburne, July 10, Washburne MSS.
[54] W. E. Chandler to Washburne, February 12, 1868, Washburne MSS.
[55] Oberholtzer, *Jay Cooke*, II, 354–7.
[56] Welles, *Diary*, III, 452.
[57] Chandler to Washburne, October 19, Washburne MSS.
[58] Coleman, *Election of 1868*, 301.

erally designated as "Tanneries," sprang up as if by magic; hundreds of Republican flags floated in the breezes; the "Boys in Blue," composed of "loyal" veterans, held numerous parades with "Grant uniforms" and "Grant bands." Gentlemen of the pen plied their arts, each after his own kind. Cartoonists, led by the forceful Thomas Nast, drew pictures of the silent general and lampooned the bewhiskered Seymour. Biographers, varying in merit from Grant's secretary, Badeau, to Albert D. Richardson of the New York *Tribune,* wrote campaign lives. Poets, whose merits varied not so much, contributed their mites to the cause. Greeley's *Tribune* headed its political columns each morning with a stanza of Miles O'Reilly's rousing call:—

> So boys! a final bumper
>> While we all in chorus chant—
> "For next President we nominate
>> Our own Ulysses Grant!"
> And if asked what State he hails from
>> This our sole reply shall be,
> "From near Appomattox Court House,
>> With its famous apple tree."
> For 'twas there to our Ulysses
>> That Lee gave up the fight
> Now boys, "To Grant for President
>> And God defend the right!"

While marching enthusiasts were wont to sing a chorus that ran:—

> Oh! God was kind and heaven was true
>> When it gave us a man like U—
>> —lysses Grant
> When it gave us a man like you! [59]

Vote-catching slogans—"Scratch a Democrat and you will find a Rebel under his skin,"—"Grant acts, Seymour talks, Blair blows"— filled the papers.

Combined with such ephemeræ was somewhat more than the usual amount of mud-slinging. Democratic papers searched Grant's military record, and announced that the general was lacking in "real ability or real character." He was a "butcher," a "liar," a "drunkard," a

[59] New York *Tribune,* September 2, 1868.

"weather-cock" and a "puppet." [60] His order removing Jews from his department in 1862 was flaunted before Hebrew citizens,[61] and Jesse Grant's cotton speculations were unearthed for the edification of the populace.[62] On the other side, Seymour's "disloyal" war record and the danger involved in his election constituted the main burden of polemic orations.[63]

More serious speakers and publicists refrained from personalities and obvious claptrap. From platforms everywhere they addressed the voters on the two issues of finances and Reconstruction. Republican Reconstruction policies were explained on the basis of justice to the Negroes, but frequently the orators admitted that the restoration of white government in the South would endanger their own congressional supremacy. Such a result would be calamitous, for once the "rebocracy" were in power, the national debt would be repudiated. Appeals were directed to the bondholders, and it was generally asserted that the Democratic program would raise the price of gold to 500.[64] Adhering to his greenback principles as well as he could, Ben Butler asserted that the Chicago platform did not preclude paying the five-twenty bonds in currency, but his reasoning was little heeded.[65] Many Western politicians feared the power of the "Ohio Idea," and a resolution to tax the bonds received considerable support from the Grant men in Congress. Washburne himself voted for the measure, but his banker, who had just deposited a 7% dividend to the Congressman's account, sounded a note of warning. "Capitalists and holders of Government securities," he said, "felt safe so long as the dominant party professes readiness to uphold the national faith and credit. But as soon as that party joins hands with the Copperheads in repudiating the promises of the government, confidence must fail." [66]

As September 1st approached, all eyes turned to Vermont, where a State election would indicate the direction of the political winds. As was expected, the Republican ticket was elected by a majority twenty-

---

[60] New York *Tribune*, June 13, 1868.
[61] New York *Times*, June 14, 1868; cf. Ph. Van Bort, *Grant and the Jews.*
[62] New York *World*, July 25, 1868.
[63] New York *Tribune*, July 20, 31, August 1, 27, 1868.
[64] *Ibid.*, September 7, 1868.
[65] New York *Commercial and Financial Chronicle*, July 11, 1868.
[66] R. H. McClellan, (Galena) July 17, 1868, to Washburne, Washburne Mss. Also Ed. B. Warner, June 30, and H. Raster, (Chicago) July 3. Raster, editor of the Illinois *Staats Zeitung*, had written the Republican finance plank. "I shall . . . cut loose from any party or men that should aid in destroying that platform," he threatened.

five per cent greater than in 1864.[67] Two weeks later, Maine swept into the Republican line with an increased majority. Always important because of their psychological force, the Maine elections had been vigorously contested. Pendleton—unwisely it appeared—had opened the State campaign, and both sides had spent money freely.[68] The results were a testimonial to Democratic mistakes, and the Republicans went into the "October" States confident of success. Ohio, home of Democratic financial heresies, repudiated the repudiators. In Pennsylvania, the shrewd Simon Cameron distributed a large campaign fund so skillfully that the State was carried, although charges of fraud and minor riots marked election day. Indiana, the home of Colfax, was barely safe, with only a thousand votes to spare.[69]

The elections were not carried without the aid of a new crop of atrocity stories from the South. First used in the elections of 1866, such stories became a part of every campaign for a decade. Before he left Washington for the West, Grant had announced the readmission of seven Southern States. Only Virginia, Mississippi, and Texas were dilatory in ratifying their Constitutions, and did not return to the fold until after election day. Throughout the summer, the Southern States were kept in line. Late in June, the military governor removed Louisiana's Governor and Lieutenant-Governor, and appointed a carpetbagger, H. C. Warmoth, and a Negro politician in their places. In Virginia, General Stoneman removed municipal officers, and on Rawlins' and Grant's advice, filled the vacancies with Negroes.[70]

As was inevitable under such a régime, disorders developed in the South. Northern people were kept informed of the activities of the Ku Klux Klan, of the preachers who pledged Negroes to the Democracy before admitting them to communion, of "open war" in Arkansas, and of universal riots. Although General Longstreet was welcomed to the Radical fold, with no thought that he contaminated the party, the fact that Wade Hampton and B. H. Hill supported Seymour proved that the South was seeking to recoup at the polls its losses on the battlefield.[71]

[67] New York *Tribune*, September 3, 1868.
[68] Welles, *Diary*, III, 439.
[69] Oberholtzer, *History of the U. S.*, II, 192.
[70] New York *Tribune*, June 19, 25, 26, 27, 29, 30, August 3; Grant to Rawlins, August 1, 1868, Bartlett collection.
[71] New York *Tribune*, August 20, 25, 26, September 5, 7, 17, 25, October 2, 1868. Riots between whites and Negroes were frequent, and were magnified in the press. Cf. *Tribune*,

As the meaning of the triumph in the October States was borne home to the Democrats, many of them began to advocate a "change of base." The New York *World*, alleging the suggestion came from Seymour, proposed that Seymour and Blair should resign in favor of Chase. In Washington, the *National Intelligencer* asserted that the Democracy should rally behind Johnson. The Democratic National Committee met, but Seymour did not resign. Instead, at the last moment, he entered the canvass in his own behalf.[72]

That such an unprecedented suggestion should have been made by the leading party organs seems to have been another triumph of the efficient financial work of W. E. Chandler. While the October States voted, Chandler consulted with A. T. Stewart, Morgan, Greeley, Pierrepont, and General Sickles on a scheme to "invest" in the *National Intelligencer*. On October 19, Chandler wrote Washburne that he was about to carry out his plan. "I shall act with caution," he promised, "and get what I bargain for before I pay for it. They are a mercenary, unprincipled set, but the effect produced through the country by such acts as that in the *World* today, which I've telegraphed to Grant, and similar acts in the *Intelligencer* is tremendous, and now is the time to smash the Democratic party in pieces." With remarkable piety, the Radical manager concluded: "I may be mistaken in dealing with such scoundrels—pitch defiles—but I am conscious of the purity of my own motives and I do not want to lose this opportunity of demoralizing the Democracy. I hope you approve, and Grant too, if he finds it out." [73] The *Tribune* attributed the apostacy of the *World* to the influence of a patent medicine advertiser, Humbolt, who had distributed $40,000 in the right manner.[74]

With treason in his own ranks, Seymour could not have expected much success from his own last-minute appeal to the voters. The Democratic Party had thrown away its chances in the convention when it failed to adopt a clear-cut program. With either finance or reconstruction as the issue and with nominees who stood fairly on the plat-

September 23, 25, 26, for the Camilla Georgia riot. See also Sept. 29, October 5, 12, 19, 21, 22, 23, 28 for other riots. It should be noted that the numbers of cases increased greatly in the last days of the campaign. On October 22, for example, the *Tribune* listed seventeen separate riots in the South. Cf. also, Welles, *Diary*, III, 462.

[72] Welles, *Diary*, III, 458; New York *Tribune*, October 16, 17, New York *World*, October 15–20, 1868.

[73] Chandler to Washburne, October 19, 1868, Washburne MSS.

[74] New York *Tribune*, October 20, 1868.

form adopted, they might have won. When the votes were counted, the enormity of their mistakes became apparent. Seymour carried but eight States—New York, New Jersey, Oregon, Illinois, Georgia, Kentucky, Louisiana, and Maryland—with a total of only 80 votes. With twenty-six States behind him, Grant had 214 votes. Yet without Negro suffrage, the general would have been defeated. In the popular vote his majority was a little over 300,000, and more than 400,000 Negroes voted the Republican ticket.[75]

In Galena, Grant received the news of his election with his accustomed calm. He had gone with Badeau to the polls and voted for Washburne and the Republican ticket, but not for presidential electors; in the evening he went to Washburne's house, where telegraph instruments had been installed. A few citizens, several correspondents, and the telegraph operators filled the room. The candidate was the least excited of the group. After listening for several hours to the returns, the general received the congratulations of his friends and walked up the hill to his cottage.

Before the door, fewer than a hundred people had congregated. Standing on his porch, the general addressed them briefly. He thanked them for their support, and promised to perform his duties in accordance with the will of the people. "The responsibilities of the position I feel," said the President-elect, "but accept them without fear." [76]

[75] Coleman, *Election of 1868,* 369–370.
[76] Badeau, *Grant in Peace,* 148–149.

ON the whole, the nation hailed the election results with relieved feelings. Among both Democrats and Republicans, the outcome was considered a triumph for conservative principles. In finance, it was obvious that the "Ohio Idea" had been successfully scotched, and the country was safe for the bondholders. As for the South, Grant's election "finally seal(ed) the restoration of the Union" and plans for upbuilding the section were put under way.[1] In Tennessee, "Parson" Brownlow, the Radical governor, assured his legislature that the election "means peace; it means that carpetbaggers are not to be molested . . . that capital, coming to us from abroad . . . is not to be spurned. . . ."[2] Even such violent Southerners as Wade Hampton and General N. B. Forrest accepted the result "cordially and heartily."[3] Throughout the comment ran the refrain of Grant's epigram—"Let us have peace."

But although the election cleared the atmosphere concerning finances and Reconstruction, it served only to raise political problems of considerable moment. During the four months preceding his inauguration, Grant occupied a unique position. Accepted by the Radicals with considerable reluctance, and only because of his supposed powers as a vote-getter, he was singularly free from political entanglements. While Northern bayonets in the South and Democratic bungling in the North carried him to victory, Grant had remained silent as to the policies he would follow and the persons he would consult. As a result, when the country took stock after the election, there was wide diversity of views as to what had been gained. Grant's belated pronouncement for the Radicals, and his refusal to participate in the campaign, had left Republican leaders in doubt concerning his real opinions. No word favoring the Radical program had escaped the secretive general, and the Democratic papers began to claim that the President-elect was a good Democrat. Moreover, they called upon him to select a Cabinet which

---

[1] New York *Tribune,* November 5, 1868.
[2] Knoxville *Whig and Rebel Ventilator,* November 18, 1868.
[3] New York *Tribune,* November 12, 1868; Wm. R. Moore, (Memphis) to Washburne, November 17, 1868, Washburne MSS.

would not represent "sections, passions, theories, but the broad national spirit of the people." [4] Such moderate Republicans as had no hunger for office agreed with the Democrats. Remembering how Grant drew able generals about him in the army, they hoped he would attract the "best talent in the country" to his administration.[5]

Grant himself adhered to the theory that he was under no obligation to the politicians. Long before the campaign closed he had indicated that he would take a firm stand against those who thirsted for offices. During the summer Badeau had been left in Washington to open mail, and it was generally understood that applications for office would be ignored. Immediately after the election Grant frankly told "certain irrepressible spirits" that he preferred to be left alone. Moreover, the report was current that a note was being made of all visitors who sought favor by personal solicitation. All would be refused.[6] On November 10 it was announced that five hundred written applications had been received by Grant's secretaries, and consigned to the waste basket.[7]

In such a situation, the office-seekers could only resign themselves to the inevitable. To the people, however, the general's decision appeared highly commendable. Confident that Grant would show the same good sense in the White House as on the battlefield, the people chorused approval of his course. "He is a good judge of character," declared the sycophant press, "his method of estimating men leaves little hope for charlatanry and none for notorious unfitness." [8] He had a "contempt for professional politicians" and a "freedom from entangling alliances."

A few days after the election, Grant returned to Washington. Accompanied only by his family and members of the staff, Grant avoided the office-seekers and slipped into the capital unseen. A public hack met him at the station, and his presence was not known until he was seen on the streets near Army Headquarters the next day.[9]

Immediately thereafter, Grant and his family began traveling extensively through the East. Trips to Philadelphia, New York, Boston, and Baltimore occupied much of their time. On these trips, though the politicians were in evidence, it was apparent that the general preferred

[4] New York *Commercial and Financial Chronicle,* November 7, 1868.
[5] E. H. Derby, (Boston) to Washburne, November 10, 1868, Washburne MSS.
[6] New York *Tribune,* November 7, 9, 1868.
[7] *Ibid.,* November 10, 1868.
[8] New York *Times,* November 9, 1868.
[9] New York *Tribune,* November 9, 1868.

the company of such men as A. T. Stewart, Adolph E. Borie, or A. J. Albert to that of party leaders. When not traveling, Grant attended the duties of the army. Resignation as General, which would have deprived him of a needed salary and would have given Johnson the privilege of nominating his successor, he did not consider.

Toward the defeated Johnson and his Cabinet, Grant showed none of that magnanimity which had gained him fame at Appomattox. Since the embarrassing Cabinet meeting in January, he had had no communication with his superior. Moreover, he made no secret of his dislike for those Cabinet members who had corroborated Johnson's perverted story of that meeting. In New York he accepted an invitation to a dinner for Attorney-General Evarts on condition that the other Cabinet members should not attend.[10] Somewhat later he forbade his children to attend a children's party at the White House, and on New Year's Day he and Mrs. Grant hurried to Philadelphia to avoid making a courtesy call on Johnson.[11] Except for Seward, who spoke to Grant on a train and later invited him to dinner, the undesired Cabinet members returned Grant's dislike and dreaded his accession. Welles was positive that he would have no policy. He could not design a course of political action, and had no knowledge of the structure of the Constitution. "He does not intend to labor like a drudge in office, does not propose to study public affairs, has no taste for books or intellectual employment," said the Secretary in prophetic vein. "The appointment of his friends to office is the extent of his ideas of administrative duties." [12] Feeling thus strongly, the grim old Secretary made a point of not inviting Grant to Mrs. Welles' receptions.[13]

In curious contrast with Grant's conduct was the course pursued by Ben Butler. As one of the House managers of the impeachment trial, he had arraigned Johnson before the bar of the Senate with the full force of bitter invective. But despite this he appeared on New Year's Day at the White House, shook hands with the astonished President, and chatted pleasantly with Johnson's friends. During the day, he called upon each of the Cabinet members. Although Butler alleged that he made a distinction between Johnson as President and as a man, the perplexed officials were inclined to read into his actions some politi-

[10] Welles, *Diary*, III, 464–468; New York *Tribune*, November 13–18, 1868.
[11] Welles, *Diary*, III, 491–492, 494, 487–488.
[12] *Ibid.*, 483, 508–509.
[13] *Ibid.*, 512–513.

cal significance. Johnson thought that Butler was taking this means of insulting Grant.[14]

Though such an explanation might have attractions to those who hoped that Grant's Administration would be marked with disaster, the real explanation seems to be that Butler was issuing a challenge to the Grant forces. For a month the Massachusetts Radical had been making a strong but apparently futile bid for Grant's approval. On that same New Year's Day he wrote a friend: "I do not even know my own status with the incoming Administration. . . ."[15]

During the campaign of 1868, Butler had been out of touch and out of sympathy with the leaders of the Republican Party. A candidate for reëlection to Congress, he had stood on a demand for paying the bonds in greenbacks. So strong was he in his own district that few dared to oppose him, but Washburne and Rawlins, with the approval of the National Committee, sent a speaker, one Kilpatrick, into Butler's district to speak for his opponent. Although the National Committee paid Kilpatrick two hundred dollars a night for his services, they carefully concealed the fact of their approval. At the close of the campaign, W. E. Chandler boasted to Washburne that he had skillfully hidden the trail. "Butler only understands that Kilpatrick's raid upon him was a mercenary speculation of his own unauthorized by anyone and countenanced by no friend of General ·Grant. And I mean that he shall continue to think so. Butler is an uncertain man and may make mischief in the future." But though Chandler and Washburne would keep the secret, Kilpatrick boasted that he had Grant's approval for the "raid."[16] With a surprising willingness to sacrifice personal feelings for political ends, Butler seemed no whit perturbed by this deception. Despite a general expectation that he would immediately attack Grant, he hastened to make friendly overtures to the President-elect. When Congress opened in December, he sought means to prove his friendship for the incoming Administration. Within a week he had placed Grant under obligation by moving to repeal the Tenure of Office Act. The new President would not need watching, Butler told his colleagues.[17]

Throughout the Republican Party it was generally understood that

[14] Welles, *Diary*, III, 497; New York *Tribune*, January 2, 1869.
[15] Butler to J. R. G. Pitkin, (New Orleans) January 1, 1869, Butler MSS.
[16] Chandler to Washburne, November 7, 1868, Washburne MSS.; Butler to Editor, *Evening Telegraph*, January 25, 1869, Butler MSS.
[17] Butler to E. J. Sherman, December 5 and 22, Butler MSS.; N. Y. *Tribune*, December 14, 1868.

Grant wished to be freed from the restrictions of the Tenure of Office Act. Just after the election, Republican newspapers announced that the Democrats were planning to "bribe" the new President by repealing the law. Republicans of the Butler stripe became eager to forestall the Democrats and offer the bribe on their own account. Their chief argument for repeal was that Grant desired to reform the Civil Service. Johnsonian appointees were failing to collect the revenues and were wastefully extravagant. Moreover, these officeholders had been nominated by a Conservative President and approved by a Radical Senate —they could only have obtained their offices through duplicity. Such public servants should be ousted at once, but the Tenure of Office Act tied the President's hands.

Despite the logic of such arguments, the Senate showed no inclination to relinquish its strategic position. The law was valuable, alleged the Radicals, and was needed to curb such Presidents as Johnson. As for Grant, if he really wanted to reform the Civil Service he would find no opposition to his removals. Unconvinced, Butler persisted in his efforts, and carried his measure through the House 121 to 47. The Senate, however, secure in its power and fearful of the reform rumors, failed to act on the measure. When Grant was inaugurated, he found the law still in effect.[18]

Though Butler might assure them that the new President would not need watching, politicians who eagerly scanned the horizons could not feel comfortable over the prospects. The popular clamor for a reform administration made them uneasy, and Grant, with characteristic reticence, had said nothing to set them at rest. Instead, on the few occasions when he expressed himself he had promised a vigorous spirit in public affairs.[19] For the most part, Grant limited himself to platitudinous generalizations. He favored economy in government, the appointment of good men to office, and peace at home and abroad. But the vagueness of such generalizations disturbed the politicians' rest, while the expressions which were not vague alarmed them. In his annual report as General of the Army, he recommended that the Indian Bureau be transferred to the War Department. With army officers administering Indian affairs, he said, the costs would be reduced fifty to seventy-

[18] New York *Tribune*, November 12, December 28, 1868, January 11, February 16, 1869; New York *Times*, December 28, 31, 1868, January 4, 12, 16, February 16, 1869; T. C. Smith, *Life of Garfield*, I, 442–443.
[19] Badeau, *Grant in Peace*, 154–155; N. Y. *Tribune*, January 26, 1869.

five per cent.[20] Soon after Congress met, the Pacific Railroad lobby swooped down upon Washington in full force to prevent any investigation of their expenditures and to obtain additional subsidies. Unconvinced that the railroads needed more governmental aid, Grant declared that the national debt should be paid before the Government undertook any further obligations.[21] Somewhat later, he again expressed himself on governmental economy. Approached by Louisiana planters who desired a Federal endorsement of levee bonds, the general stated that he "never knew a Government to endorse bonds that didn't have to pay ultimately." Considering the condition of the national debt, he "refused to discuss any increase of national obligations." [22]

Such indications that Grant would inaugurate a reform era met with hearty approval. Editorials praised his stand, and citizens hastened to write Washburne of their support. John Russell Young, of the *Tribune,* said that Grant's statements had made a marked impression on Greeley. "So long as Grant made general professions of honesty," he stated, "he made no impression on the country . . . but when he singled out the Pacific Ry and the Louisiana corruption and went on record against them, he showed his words were embodied deeds." [23] Others pointed out that the "rings" were "potent in Congress as well as out" and would combine against a reformer. However, Grant had the "confidence and support" of the people.[24]

In addition to these indications of policy, Grant pursued a course in regard to his Cabinet which increased the politicians' suspicion. He showed no inclination to follow the practice which dictated that a President should select his constitutional advisers from among the party leaders. Although politicians were welcomed at Army Headquarters and he listened to their advice, he gave no intimation whom he would select for Cabinet places. As a result, vague rumors spread that there was an impending rupture between the President-elect and the party leaders.[25] Republican papers had difficulty in denying that "the

[20] New York *Tribune,* Nov. 21, 30, 1868.
[21] Welles, *Diary,* III, 474, 485, 490; New York *Tribune,* December 24, 1868; New York *Times,* December 26, 1868; New York *World,* January 3, 1869.
[22] New York *Tribune,* January 4, 1869.
[23] Young to Washburne, January 5, 1869, Washburne MSS.
[24] New York *Tribune,* December 26, 1868; John P. Veree, (Philadelphia) to Washburne, January 7, 1869, Washburne MSS.
[25] New York *Tribune,* February 22; New York *World,* January 16, 1869.

politicians are furious at not being consulted." [26]

Gratuitous advice poured in upon Grant concerning the general nature of his Cabinet. Democratic papers were so impressed with their belief in Grant's conservatism that they urged him to select Seymour and Robert E. Lee as proof of his desire for harmony. Even papers so far apart politically as the *World* and Greeley's *Tribune* united in urging the new President to select statesmen of large civil experience.[27] Military advisers, said the *World,* would be unable to deal with Congress, and the *Tribune* took pains to point out that "no President has ever made his Cabinet merely so many staff officers." [28]

Specific suggestions concerning possible Cabinet members were even more frequent. By the time of the election, speculation had listed the names of over seventy possible Cabinet officers, and the number of aspirants grew daily. According to widespread rumor, Sumner expected to be Secretary of State,[29] and the only question in regard to Washburne was whether he would be Secretary of the Treasury or of the Interior.[30] Generals Rawlins and Schofield, Secretaries Evarts and McCulloch, Admiral Porter, and the tariff reformer David A. Wells each had his supporters, while such merchant princes as A. T. Stewart, George H. Stuart, and A. E. Borie were occasionally mentioned among the possibilities. Even Senator Sherman, who could not accept because the Ohio Legislature would send a Democrat to his place in the Senate, hoped to be offered the Treasury as a "compliment." [31]

To all these suggestions, general as well as specific, Grant remained impassive. Finally, as January rolled past with no hint as to the cabinet, the politicians began to hope for some statement when he was formally notified of his election. On February 12 a committee from Congress appeared at Army Headquarters to hand Grant his certificate of election. Surrounded by his staff and a few friends, he heard Senator Oliver P. Morton praise his "unalloyed patriotism, inflexible integrity" and "great powers of intellect." In reply, Grant turned immediately to

[26] Henry to C. F. Adams, Jr., February 3, 1869, *Letters of Henry Adams,* 152; New York *Times,* December 23, 1868.
[27] New York *World,* November 18, 1868; New York *Tribune,* November 19, 1868.
[28] New York *Tribune,* February 5, 1869.
[29] J. G. Blaine to Washburne, October 24, 1868, Washburne MSS.; Sam Burnham to Butler, January 19, 1869, Butler Mss.
[30] I. B. Gera to Washburne, Dec. 12, 1868, Washburne MSS.; N. Y. *Tribune,* Dec. 14, 1868.
[31] *Sherman Letters,* 324.

E. B. WASHBURNE

BENJAMIN BUTLER

the problem uppermost in the minds of the politicians. "I can promise the committee," he said, "that it will be my endeavor to call around me as assistants such men only as I think will carry out . . . economy, retrenchment, faithful collection of the revenue, and payment of the public debt. If I should fail in my first choice, I shall not at any time hesitate to make a second, or even a third trial. . . ." As for his Cabinet, Grant said that he had felt "it would be rather indelicate" to announce it until he himself had been notified of his election. At the moment not all the men had been selected, and no announcement would be made until the names were sent to the Senate. Till then speculation should cease.[32]

If Grant hoped that this statement would give him relief from office-seekers he was doomed to disappointment. The prospect that he would follow his own dictates confirmed the worst fears of the leaders,[33] and they bent every effort to extract some fuller information from the new President. John Russell Young came from New York to "fathom the mysteries of the inscrutable Ulysses," [34] and even Mrs. Grant became curious to learn her husband's decisions. Humorously Grant alleged that he had to get up several times in the night to examine the pockets of his waistcoat—hidden beneath his pillow—lest Mrs. Grant should discover the list of Cabinet appointees.[35] Less humorously, Henry Adams, in pursuit of an elusive education, but apprehensive of Grant's ability, wrote that he looked for "a reign of Western mediocrity. . . . I swear I feel as though I ought to give my soul a thorough washing." [36]

Meanwhile, ignoring the baffled cries of the politicians, Grant was selecting his Cabinet. Seemingly two theories actuated his choice: the first was the feeling that he was not obligated to the politicians, and the second was the desire to have no Cabinet member who would overshadow him. The latter idea had been impressed upon him by Rawlins, who pointed to the difficulties which Lincoln had with a Cabinet of political rivals.[37] Of the seven Cabinet officers, only three were consulted before the inauguration. A. T. Stewart, owner of New York's largest department store, was selected for Secretary of the Treasury.

[32] New York *Tribune*, February 15, 1869.
[33] New York *Times*, February 15, 1869.
[34] Cortissoz, *Whitelaw Reid*, I, 147.
[35] Badeau, *Grant in Peace*, 410.
[36] Henry Adams, *Letters of Henry Adams*, 152.
[37] Badeau, *Grant in Peace*, 164.

"I thought his genius for business would be the quality required in the Treasury," Grant later explained, "and I wanted the Treasury conducted on strict business principles." [38] A heavy contributor to the campaign fund, Stewart's selection was a tribute both to his party services and to his friendship with the President-elect.

The other two positions filled before March 4 were the War and State Departments. Against his wishes, friendship forced Grant to appoint Rawlins to the War Department. The staff officer suffered from lung trouble, and Grant planned to order him West in order that the climate might benefit him. But Rawlins became ill, and petulantly asked for the War Department. Bound by ties too close to refuse the request, Grant agreed to give his friend the desired office. However, for a week, Schofield should continue to hold the position as a reward for his support during the campaign. [39]

Toward his oldest friend and sponsor, Washburne, Grant maintained the same silence he showed other politicians. In Congress Washburne advocated economy and continued his accustomed attack on the "rings." Though his speeches took on a new significance as his colleagues searched them for evidence of Grant's opinions, Washburne knew nothing of the general's plans. Some weeks before the inauguration, however, Grant offered the Congressman the Interior Department. Washburne was eminently qualified for the post by virtue of his diligence in behalf of the public domain, but he preferred the Treasury. Here, too, his experience and interests would have stood him in good stead, but Grant had already selected Stewart for the place. Finding the Treasury gone, Washburne asked for the French mission, which Grant readily promised. However, in order that Washburne might have added prestige in France it was agreed that he should be Secretary of State for a week. [40]

With the State Department filled only temporarily, Grant looked about for a permanent Secretary. During the campaign he had considered John Lothrop Motley for the place. Dismissed from Vienna by Johnson, Motley had returned to Massachusetts in time to make speeches for Grant. These speeches he carefully sent to Badeau. As an embryonic historian, Badeau had a great admiration for the master of the historian's art and urged Grant to look after Motley. Shortly after

[38] John Russell Young, *Around the World with General Grant*, II, 276.
[39] James Harrison Wilson, *Life of John A. Rawlins*, 350–351.
[40] Badeau, *Grant in Peace*, 161.

the election, Grant met Motley in Boston. "He parts his hair in the middle, and carries a single eyeglass!" said Grant to Badeau on his return.[41]

With Motley's sartorial eccentricities an insuperable barrier, Grant's thoughts turned to Representative James F. Wilson of Iowa for the State Department. Taking the street-car one day, Grant went to the Capitol and spent an hour conferring with Wilson.[42] In the end, Wilson agreed to take the position after Washburne had gone to France.

Late in February, Grant let it be known that he would continue Schofield as Secretary of War. About the same time, a group of Congressmen called on him to urge that Pennsylvania be represented in the Cabinet. To this Grant replied that the State would have a representative. He had already selected a Philadelphian, thoroughly Republican in politics, who "would be as greatly surprised at his appointment as would the Nation."

Immediately speculation broke out afresh. The names of Jay Cooke, Benjamin H. Brewster, George H. Stuart, Horace Binney, and many others came to mind,[43] and Colonel A. K. McClure hastened to Washington to have the place given to ex-Governor Curtin. To this demand Grant returned a peremptory refusal. "Then," said McClure, "select a man who is qualified. . . . The names of George H. Stuart, Borie, Smith, and others have been spoken of, and I must say that not one of them would satisfy the Republican Party of Pennsylvania."

To McClure's surprise, Grant replied: "I cannot understand why any loyal man should object to the appointment of Mr. Stuart, one who has rendered such conspicuous service to the loyal cause. But," he added, "I do not say that he is the man." Then, taking up the other part of McClure's statement, the General went on. "I am not the representative of a political party, though a party voted for me—"

"Then," said McClure, "in my conversation on the subject of your Administration, I have spoken from a mistaken standpoint. . . . I have nothing more to say on the subject." [44]

As McClure immediately reported this conversation, all eyes in Philadelphia turned to Stuart, confident that he would represent them in the Cabinet. Lest Stuart himself should think so, Grant hastened to

[41] Badeau, *Grant in Peace*, 153.
[42] New York *Tribune*, January 29, 1869.
[43] *Ibid.*, February 24, 1869.
[44] New York *Tribune*, February 26, 1869; New York *Times*, February 26, 1869.

write him that McClure had no basis for his conclusion, "except the warmth with which I defended you against the charge of obscurity or lack of acquaintance in the State." However, Grant continued, "I have often thought of you in that connection, and . . . if a place in my Cabinet would be agreeable to you and you will say so to me, I will take the matter into consideration, but without pledge." [45]

In addition to preparing for his Cabinet, Grant made other preparation for his new duties. About the middle of February he called in Badeau and dictated his inaugural address. Unlike Johnson, Grant wrote all of his messages during his Presidency. His speeches, like his Cabinet, were his own handiwork.

Preparations for the inauguration, with its round of ceremonies, interested him not at all. To the consternation of Washington matrons and debutantes, he told the congressional committee on preparations that he cared nothing for an inaugural ball. But the ladies prevailed, and the ball was duly placed on the festal schedule. More important, Grant told the committee he would not ride with Johnson on inauguration day. The committee were deeply concerned until they hit upon the novel scheme of having two parallel columns moving down Pennsylvania Avenue. Grant might head one, and Johnson the other!

The day before the inauguration, Grant made the final preparation for moving into the White House—he sold the house on I Street which he had bought in 1865. Shortly after his return from Galena in November, the general had agreed to sell the house to S. J. Bowen, mayor of Washington, for $40,000. Although Bowen had made a payment of a thousand dollars, Grant changed his mind and began negotiations with A. T. Stewart, who was getting up a subscription to purchase a house for Sherman.[46] Early on March 3 Stewart, accompanied by a committee of the New York donors, called at Army Headquarters to hand Grant a check for $65,000 in return for a deed to the property and a bill of sale for the furniture. Then, crossing the room to the desk where Sherman was seated, Stewart and his committee turned the documents over to the new General of the Army.[47] After Stewart's check was banked, Grant returned Bowen's thousand dollars.

Inauguration day dawned cold and rainy, and Washington streets were a sea of mud. But rain and mud could not dampen the enthusiasm

---

[45] Grant to G. H. Stuart, February 26, 1869. Photostat in Grant MSS., Library of Congress.
[46] New York *Tribune*, August 27, 1872, July 4, 1872.
[47] *Ibid.*, March 3, 1869.

of the cheering crowd assembled to witness the induction of the Soldier-President. Firemen in red shirts and "sheet-iron" hats, committeemen in tall hats and fancy scarfs, Tanners' Clubs, Wide-Awakes, Invincibles, Boys in Blue, and "petted militia companies with waxed mustaches and hands blistered with the friction of the musket stocks" jostled the horde of office-seekers, pickpockets, gamblers, and "soiled doves of fashion, dressed in silks and velvets, glaring in false blushes." Everywhere were Negroes, many of whom came to get muskets for marching in the parade.[48]

As the parade began, and Grant and Rawlins rode in an open carriage to the head of the line, the storm clouds rolled away to let the sun shine upon the glistening uniforms. It was an auspicious omen, and not even the enemy whom Grant was replacing appeared to mar the occasion's glamour. In the White House, Johnson and his despised Cabinet sat finishing the routine business of their offices. Following the precedent set by John Quincy Adams when he refused to ride with Jackson, Johnson and his few friends refrained from honoring Grant. "We," said the President, "know him to be a liar." [49]

At twelve o'clock, Grant, clad in a black dress suit and wearing yellow kid gloves, entered the Senate chamber and seated himself before the clerk's desk. The crowded galleries noticed that not even the excitement of the day had ruffled his wonted composure. When Colfax had been sworn in, the General, with the Chief Justice and the Supreme Court, proceeded to the east portico. There he took the oath of office, and stepped forward to read, in low voice, his inaugural address.[50]

To the eager circle of listeners who awaited some announcement of his policy, the President indicated that he would pursue an independent course. "The responsibilities of the position I feel," he declared again in the words he had used to his Galena neighbors, "but accept them without fear. The office has come to me unsought; I commence its duties untrammeled. . . . On all leading questions . . . I will always express my voice to Congress, and . . . I shall on all subjects have a policy to recommend, but none to enforce against the will of the people."

---

[48] New York *Tribune*, March 5, 1869. But Johnson had vetoed the congressional resolution which would have given $80,000 worth of arms to these vagrants, and the Negroes had nothing but hoots for the retiring President. Welles, *Diary*, III, 542–543.

[49] Welles, *Diary*, III, 498, 536, 540–542.

[50] New York *Tribune*, March 5, 1869.

Less than twelve hundred words in all, the inaugural did not venture far beyond platitudes. A respect for law, which many opponents had alleged a military man would not possess, was avowed and reiterated. "All laws will be faithfully executed"—"Laws are to govern all alike" —"All laws . . . will receive my best efforts for their enforcement" —"It will be my endeavor to execute all laws in good faith" —said the general, and he summed up his philosophy of law by declaring: "I know no method to secure the repeal of bad or obnoxious laws so effective as their stringent execution." In addition to this belief in law, the President urged that problems resulting from the war be "approached calmly, without prejudice, hate, or sectional pride, remembering that the greatest good to the greatest number is the object to be obtained." A faithful collection of the revenues, civilizing the Indians, and respect for the rights of all nations, completed the list of generalizations.

More than half the address was devoted to the debt; the payment of which in gold, "to protect the national honor," was demanded. "Let it be understood," exclaimed the President, "that no repudiator of our public debt will be trusted in public place. . . ." In twenty-five years, he promised, "every dollar" could be paid "with more ease than we now pay for useless luxuries." "Why," continued the orator with a burst of eloquence, "it looks as though Providence had bestowed upon us a strong box in the precious metals locked up in the sterile mountains of the Far West . . . to meet the very contingency that is now upon us." [51]

While Grant was so speaking, a painful scene was being enacted at the other end of the Avenue. Finishing up shreds of business which came to them from the retiring Congress, ex-President Johnson shook hands sorrowfully with his faithful Cabinet, entered a waiting carriage, and drove rapidly away from the house of his tribulations. A few minutes later General Schofield, the only connecting link between the Administrations, welcomed Grant to the Executive Mansion. The new occupant was soon to appreciate some of the difficulties of his predecessor.

[51] Richardson, *Messages and Papers of the Presidents*, VII, 6–8.

ALREADY irate over Grant's assertions of independence, the politicians were lying in wait to discipline the new President. According to the law passed to enable the Radicals to keep an eye on Johnson, the first session of the Forty-first Congress assembled on March 4. The next day, the President sent in the names of his Cabinet. In addition to Washburne and Stewart, the President nominated Judge E. Rockwood Hoar of Massachusetts, to be Attorney-General; General Jacob D. Cox, of Ohio, for Secretary of the Interior; and J. A. J. Creswell, of Maryland, as Postmaster-General. The much-discussed Pennsylvanian turned out to be Adolph E. Borie, appointed Secretary of the Navy. No nomination was made for the War Department.

Only good Republican names appeared on this roster, yet no one of them, with the possible exception of Creswell—who had been a secessionist early in the war, and more recently a violent Radical—would have been chosen by the politicians. Stupefied by the shock, the Senate ratified the list unanimously, while throughout the country the people rejoiced that Grant had "cut himself loose from a set of party hacks" who had been dominating the government.[1] "General Grant will have for his chief assistants only those who are untainted with the trickery and corruption which are the bane of contemporary politics," declared the toadying press,[2] and Greeley's *Tribune* rejoiced that "the new Cabinet means business emphatically." [3]

But though a few sycophants and reformers may have rejoiced in the Cabinet, the politicians of both parties were enraged. "No patriot with right intentions," declared Welles, would have selected such a Cabinet, and the Democratic *World* declared that Grant had made "a terrible blunder . . . in taking no one in his confidence" while making his selections.[4] Especially difficult to swallow were Washburne and Borie. Washburne's consistent fight for economy in government had

---

[1] Emory Washburne, (Cambridge) to Washburne, March 8, 1869, and letters from R. P. Spalding, (Washington) March 6, and Prosper M. Wetmore, (N. Y.) March 9, Washburne MSS.

[2] New York *Times,* March 8, 1869.

[3] New York *Tribune,* March 6, 1869.

[4] Welles, *Diary,* III, 544–545, N. Y. *World,* March 7, 1869.

gained for him the title of "Watchdog of the Treasury," and had won for him the lasting enmity of the predatory interests.[5] Although it had been generally expected that he would occupy a Cabinet place, his nomination was a signal for bitter attacks. He was coarse and illiterate —a demagogue unfit for the position! [6] As for Borie, it was immediately pointed out that he had been a leading contributor to Grant's Philadelphia house. Stewart, too, had been generous in subscribing to Grant's gifts. To the politicians it seemed that Grant regarded the presidency "as a candy cornucopia from which he is to extract a sugar plum for the good little boys who have given him some of their plum cake." [7]

The new Cabinet members who had not been consulted before their appointment were as surprised as Congress and the country. General Cox was teaching a law class in Cincinnati when his appointment was announced to him, and he yielded reluctantly to the advice of his friends. Borie, who had been mentioned only casually in the early speculations, had called at Army Headquarters a couple of days before to introduce two friends to the general. "Well, Mr. Borie," asked Grant, "have you come to learn the name of the man from Pennsylvania?" Denying curiosity, Borie presented his visitors and withdrew. On his way home after the inauguration, he learned that he had been nominated for the Navy Department. He returned immediately to Washington to decline the appointment. Badeau met him at the station, and begged him to hold the position until after Congress had adjourned. Only as a favor to the President did he consent to remain.[8] Hoar, hastening to Washington at the summons of his brother, a Representative, was also persuaded at the station to remain for a time as Grant's legal adviser. His first duty was to advise Grant that Stewart's appointment was illegal.[9]

Although Stewart's appointment had met with wide public approval, the congressional politicians were no more pleased with him than with the rest of the Cabinet. Sumner, especially, was suspicious of the new Administration. Chairman of the Foreign Relations Committee, and a recognized leader of the Senate, his ego was offended because he had

[5] New York *Tribune*, January 11, 1869.
[6] New York *World*, March 7, 1869; Welles, *Diary*, III, 544.
[7] New York *World*, March 9, 1869.
[8] Badeau, *Grant in Peace*, 163, 166.
[9] G. F. Hoar, *Autobiography of Seventy Years*, I, 240-241.

not been offered a place or consulted on appointments! When, on March 6, it was discovered that a law of 1789 prohibited any person "concerned . . . in trade or commerce" from being Secretary of the Treasury, Sumner and the politicians prepared to get a man of their own selection in the position. As Grant heard of this development and learned from Judge Hoar that Stewart came under the prohibition, he sent a message to the Senate asking that Stewart be exempted from the statute.[10] Immediately a Senator arose to grant the request, but Sumner opposed, and the proposal went to committee. Stewart offered to resign, but Grant insisted that he remain; and the New York merchant then proposed that he turn his business over to three trustees to manage during his incumbency. The profits would be given to charity. But even this concession did not satisfy the Radical senators. They generally agreed that George S. Boutwell should be given the place, and Grant's political advisers concurred in the suggestion. On March 9, Grant withdrew his request for Stewart's exemption, and two days later signalized his complete surrender to the politicians by sending in Boutwell's name. Stewart retired to his store to mourn his vanished glory.[11]

Although it marked a clear defeat for the President, Boutwell's appointment was not unacceptable either to Grant or the business interests of the country. In 1862 he had been made commissioner of the new Internal Revenue Bureau, and had organized the work efficiently. Long known as an advocate of conservative financial reform, and personally honest, his nomination caused a rise in Government bonds in New York and London.[12] However, the appointment complicated the political problem, for both Boutwell and Hoar were from Massachusetts. To save Grant embarrassment, Hoar offered his resignation, but the President insisted that he remain.[13]

The change in the Treasury was only the first result of Grant's maladroit handling of his Cabinet. Wilson, who had tentatively accepted the State Department, declined on the ground that he could not afford the expense.[14] The Iowan doubtless saw small hopes for a political

[10] Richardson, *Messages and Papers*, VII, 8–9.
[11] New York *Tribune*, March 2–10, 1869; Horace White to Washburne, March 6, 10, Washburne MSS.; Welles, *Diary*, III, 545–549; Badeau, *Grant in Peace*, 165.
[12] New York *Commercial and Financial Chronicle*, March 13, 1869.
[13] Hoar, *Seventy Years*, I, 241.
[14] Badeau, *Grant in Peace*, 162.

career in Grant's muddled Cabinet.[15] In his stead Hamilton Fish was hastily selected. Formerly Congressman, Senator, and Governor of New York, Fish had been out of politics for two decades. With no intention of reëntering, he was astounded when Grant sent his name to the Senate, and wired that he would not accept the office. When he received this message, Grant sent to withdraw the nomination, but his nominee was already being considered by the Senate. Accordingly, Grant hastily wrote Fish begging him to accept the nomination "for the present, and should you not like the position, you can withdraw after the adjournment of Congress." When private Secretary Babcock hastened to New York and urged Fish to save Grant further embarrassment, he reluctantly yielded.[16]

With the confirmation of Boutwell, Rawlins, and Fish, Grant's Cabinet was complete. Except for Borie, whose appointment was so purely personal that even Grant did not try to defend it, the Cabinet was much better than the disgruntled politicians would admit. Selected without consulting the party leaders, it gave further evidence that Grant considered himself a representative of the people rather than of a party. But whatever its merits, Grant had "made Congress madder than the devil," [17] and had learned that he could not order civilians about in the same manner as army officers.

On March 5, with the list of Cabinet members, Grant sent one of army promotions. As was expected, Sherman was made General of the Army, and Sheridan was raised to the Lieutenant-Generalcy. As senior major general, Meade outranked Sheridan, but his claims were overlooked, as were those of the aged Halleck. To Meade, this was "the crudest and meanest act of injustice," and he assumed command of the division of the Atlantic with heavy heart. Throughout the South, such moderate commanders as Hancock were transferred to other posts, and Radical generals took their places.[18]

As for members of his staff, Grant kept them about him. Early on March 5, he received from Chief Justice Chase a Bible presented by the American Bible Society, and when that ceremony was completed,

[15] Grant to James F. Wilson, April 9, 1869, Grant Letter Books; New York *Tribune*, April 12, 1869.
[16] Grant to Fish, March 11, 1869, Grant Letter Books; Washburne to Fish, March 11, 1869, Grant Letter Book-Telegrams.
[17] *Letters of Henry Adams*, 152–153.
[18] Richardson, *Messages and Papers*, VII, 19–22; Meade, *Life and Letters*, II, 299; New York *Tribune*, March 6, 1869; Cf. *Sherman Letters*, 323, 319, 323–325.

called his staff about him. Generals Porter, Babcock, and Comstock were placed on Sherman's staff and assigned to the White House as private secretaries. Dent was made an aide-de-camp with ceremonial duties at the White House, while Badeau was given a room in the White House, ostensibly as secretary, but in reality to finish a military biography of his superior. That finished, he would receive the Belgian mission.[19] On March 15, in addition, Grant appointed Robert Martin Douglas, son of Stephen A. Douglas, as assistant private secretary.[20]

A visitor to the White House early in the new Administration reported a scene of execrable confusion. Summoned on business to the executive office, he found the room crowded with army officers and miscellaneous visitors. Assistant secretaries of the departments, attending in lieu of their unqualified chiefs, added to the chaos. Washburne was seated at a table writing orders, and popping mysteriously into another room every few minutes. In the midst of the hubbub President Grant, seated at a corner of the fireplace, puffed complacently on his cigar.[21]

As for the minor offices, Grant soon let it be known that he would follow a different policy from that used in selecting his closest advisers. Pennsylvania Republicans in Congress held a caucus and appointed a committee to advise the President that he should consult Congressmen on appointments in their own districts. To the committee, Grant replied that "outside of a few appointments" to be made in their State, he would be glad to consult them.[22] On the same day, the President told a delegation that in general he would follow Lincoln's practice of having a recommendation from a Congressman before making appointments. A few days later, he still further clarified his intended procedure with the announcement that all applications for office would have to come through the Cabinet. He believed, he said, that the Secretaries should have the opportunity to choose their own assistants, and he would hold them responsible for the faithful performance of their duties. In his opinion, the Cabinet would do well to interview Congressmen in

[19] Badeau, *Grant in Peace*, 161.

[20] Porter to Douglas, March 15, 1869, Grant Letter Book. A legend in the Douglas family says that Grant called the young Douglas, then nineteen years of age, to the White House and offered him a diplomatic post. When the young man expressed surprise, Grant declared "your father kept me from entering the Confederate army." Cf. Milton, *The Eve of Conflict*, for a curious story that Grant was offered a Confederate commission.

[21] Welles, *Diary*, III, 547.

[22] New York *Tribune*, March 11, 1869.

their search for the proper assistants. He himself had appointed but a few friends.[23]

This announcement caused the horde of office-seekers who had descended on Washington to turn their attention to the Cabinet officers. Washburne, holding on until Fish should arrive, announced that he would merely file applications for positions, and no foreign missions would be filled before Fish took office. Borie, overwhelmed by potential public servants, hastily posted a notice that there were no vacancies in the Navy Department.[24] In the Treasury, Boutwell took advantage of the situation to weed out unnecessary clerks and reduce expenses. As his move met public commendation, other departments planned to follow his example. Meantime, the office-seekers enlisted the support of their Congressmen in pressing their cause.

At the same time that he indicated he would follow congressional advice in filling offices, President Grant expressed his opposition to the Tenure of Office Act. It was, he said, a "stride toward a revolution in our free system," and he wished it repealed. While it remained, he would enforce it vigorously, and would only fill offices which were vacant.

The repeal of the Act was already before Congress. On March 5, Senator Thayer had introduced a bill for that purpose, but Sumner, who was rapidly putting himself at the head of the opposition to the President, was opposed. Alarmed by the reform agitation which seemed sweeping the country, the Senators were unwilling to give Grant a free hand. John Bigelow, noticing that the Senate was indignant over the Cabinet, concluded that the lawmakers were only "waiting a chance to hamstring" the President. Thayer's resolution was referred to committee, where it remained until Grant announced he would fill only vacant offices.

Since there were few vacant offices, and many aspirants for places, the effect of this announcement was to send the office-seekers to their Congressmen with a demand that the obnoxious law be repealed. Cabinet members advised aspirants that nominations would be made "as soon as the Senate removes the obstacles." In the House, Ben Butler, eager to ingratiate himself with the Administration and willing

[23] New York *Tribune*, March 15, 1869.
[24] *Ibid.*, March 16, 1869.

to shear the Senate of its increased power, again took the lead, and forced a repeal of the Act.

When the House bill came before the Senate, that body found itself torn between a number of desires. While reluctant to give up their power over removals and anxious to discipline the President, the Senators were hesitant to reveal a disagreement with the popular Chief Executive and unable to resist the pressure of their constituents who were besieging them for shares in the victor's spoils. Grant's friends wanted immediate repeal, and the Democrats, seeing in the move a belated vindication of Andrew Johnson, were willing to join them. After a week of wrangling between these conflicting forces, a committee offered an amendment which would suspend the law until the next session of Congress. This would give Grant an opportunity to cleanse the stables of Johnsonian appointees, but would leave the Senate's powers intact. To Grant's friends, this scheme was a trick to put him on probation before the country. "The proposition," said O. P. Morton, "is endorsed upon its back by the words 'distrust,' 'trial,' 'probation.' It is substantially saying to him, 'We will try you until the next session of Congress, and if your conduct does not meet with our approbation, this law will then go into full force and operation again.' " The Senate, said one orator after another, could not afford to start the new Administration with a declaration of distrust. A vote to repeal the law was a vote of confidence in the President.

The debate continued intermittently for ten days, and served to cast some interesting sidelights on the enactment and operation of the Tenure of Office Act. Most Senators were willing to admit that its sole purpose had been to restrict Johnson's abuse of the appointing power, although some theorists were convinced that it embodied a basic constitutional principle. Particularly obnoxious had been Johnson's practices under the law. It was revealed that he removed officers during a recess of Congress and appointed a temporary incumbent whose nomination for the place was delayed as long as possible. Then, if the Senate refused to approve, or failed to act, Johnson gave the temporary appointee another temporary appointment as soon as Congress adjourned. Moreover, the law had brought confusion in its operation. The requirement that the President give reasons for his suspensions had burdened the committees with investigations, and had prevented

the removal of corrupt officials on suspicion. Many Senators were convinced that the law had been of no service either to the people or the
party.

In the course of the discussion, the constitutional theory was evolved
that, whether the power of removal lodged solely with the President or
jointly with the President and Senate, Congress might prescribe by
law the procedure which the President must follow in making removals.
On the basis of this tenuous theory, the Senate finally modified the
existing law by providing that officers might be· removed either with
the consent of the Senate or by the appointment of a successor whom
the Senate would accept. During a recess, the President might suspend
an officer, but within thirty days after the reassembling of Congress he
must notify the Senate by nominating a successor. Should this nominee
not be confirmed, the suspended officer should resume his functions.
The President should have complete control, however, over the selection and removal of his Cabinet. This modification served only to relieve the President of the necessity for reporting the cause of removals.
Grant's friends declared that this was unsatisfactory, but Senatorial
prestige was at stake, and the measure passed.

The amended bill was not voted, however, till after a consultation
with the President. A Republican caucus appointed a committee to
visit the White House and explain the measure to Grant. Just what
arguments were used at this conference are unknown, but Ben Butler
offered a plausible guess that the committee threatened the President
with a party split unless he modified his demands, and that rather than
take the responsibility for a renewed warfare between Executive and
Congress Grant accepted the proposal. "But," said Butler, "I think he
relied on the House to save him."

Acting on the belief that the House should save the President from
the voracious Senators, the Representatives rejected the Senate amendment, and sent the question to a conference committee. From the committee there emerged a new bill which provided that the President
might suspend an officer during a recess, and nominate a successor
within thirty days of a new session. In case this nominee were rejected,
another should be made until an acceptable man was found. No mention
was made of what would happen if the Senate failed to approve any
nominee before the session ended. In the House Butler, speaking for
the conference committee, declared that the office would remain vacant,

or be filled by a temporary appointee. In the Senate Trumbull, also from the conference committee, explained that the suspended officer would resume his duties. Under these contradictory interpretations, the ambiguous law was put through both houses, and on April 6 Grant affixed his signature. Practically, he had gained a modification which removed most of his objections, and with the realism which characterized all his acts he ignored the theoretical fact that the law was not repealed. His explanation was that he did not want to "seem captious" about the matter.

Unfortunately for Grant's reputation, the general was a poor psychologist, and did not realize that his acceptance of a practical victory would be interpreted as a defeat. At the beginning of the discussion, the *National Republican* had prophesied, "If Grant be defeated . . . the combination against his purpose of administering the Government wholly to the end of subserving the public interest will shortly be terrific in its proportions and power for mischief. Corruption, inefficiency, special favors, etc., will marshal an army of professed politicians against Grant's policy. . . ." Legislatures had instructed their Senators to vote for unconditional repeal, and newspapers urged Grant on. The President's failure to fight disappointed his supporters, and discouraged those who had hoped to follow him into an era of reform.[25]

Moreover, in the course of this struggle Grant unconsciously committed some tactical errors. Throughout March he held to his announced policy of appointing only to vacant offices. Such tactics were excellent, but among the nominees were many who were personal friends of the President, and several who claimed relationship with either the Grants or the Dents. To the disgust of belligerent Northerners General James A. Longstreet, best man at Grant's wedding and friend of his old army days, was made surveyor of customs at New Orleans. Moses Grinnell, wealthy merchant and a contributor to the Grant houses and to the campaign fund, was given the collectorship in New York. Although such appointments were few, and for the most part of men eminently fitted for their duties, jealous Senators began to charge Grant with nepotism and favoritism, and were soon parading

[25] *Cong. Globe,* 45th Congress, 1st session, Welles, *Diary,* III, 557–558, 560, 569–571; Hoar, *Seventy Years,* 247–248; New York *Tribune,* March 19, 20, 22, 24, 25, 26–31, April 2–6, 1869; J. Bigelow, *Retrospections of an Active Life,* IV, 285. Cf. B. Corey, (Pittsburgh) to Butler, March 30, 1869, Butler Mss. Horace White to Washburne, March 20, 1869, Washburne MSS.

lists of Grant's relatives in office.

Particularly offensive to the critics of the new Administration were the activities of Jesse Grant, who neglected his Covington, Ky., post-office to spend much of his time with his famous son. Upon leaving the Capitol after the inaugural, Jesse fell down a flight of steps and injured his leg.[26] Although this laid him up for a time, he was soon hobbling about among the office-seekers. Many were successful through his intervention. One woman, whose mother Jesse had known, was appointed postmistress in Garfield's district. The Ohio Congressman made a vigorous protest, but finally acquiesced rather than force Grant to refuse his father's request.[27] Democratic papers declared the first requirement for an office was relationship with the Grants. One critic asserted that the questions in a civil service examination in the new Administration would be: 'Were you a contributor to either of Grant's three houses, in Philadelphia, Washington, or Galena?' and another, 'Are you a member of the Dent family or otherwise connected by blood or marriage with General Grant?' [28]

Though some were inspired to humor, the situation which faced the Congressmen was too serious for levity. After Garfield had seen Jesse Grant's influence dictating postoffice appointments in his own district, he declared, "We are in deep water, and struggling to keep our heads above the surface. General Grant has been making and is making very bad mistakes." His army prejudice against politicians, thought the Congressman, had led him to seek honest men in the limited circle of his own acquaintance. These were men without civil experience, and "some of them very bad." "The wheels of the new government creak," complained the Ohioan, but he hoped that Grant's "native good sense" would show him the error of his course.[29]

Less hopeful were many other observers. The *Commercial and Financial Chronicle* pointed out that Congress had the power to defeat a President, and "we are not disposed to feel sanguine over the Administration's accomplishing all it aims at in the way of cleaning up the public departments." [30] Henry Adams found all the leaders for whom he had any respect—Wells, Evarts, and Sumner—thoroughly disgusted,

[26] Cramer, *Conversations and Unpublished Letters,* 108–109.
[27] Smith, *Garfield,* I, 444–445.
[28] New York *World,* March 23, 1869.
[29] Smith, *Garfield,* I, 445.
[30] New York *Commercial and Financial Chronicle,* March 20, 1869.

and came to the conclusion that Grant was even less capable than Johnson.[31] As John Bigelow summed it up, Grant's "gratitude to his rich and generous friends and his devotion to his family . . . is much like Desdemona's love for Othello"—"No President was ever 'got in the family way' so soon after inauguration. By his secretiveness in regard to his choice of a Cabinet . . . he wounded the pride of Congress incurably. . . . This was a greater indignity than Johnson was ever accused of perpetrating upon Congress and the consequence is that Grant within a month after his inauguration has been obliged to supplicate Congress in vain and is more completely powerless than Johnson was at the end of two years of his reign. He seems to lack tact; has too much confidence in himself, and with the best intentions no doubt, makes the sort of blunder which men always make who undertake to handle tools the use of which they have never learned." [32] Two months earlier, Charles Eliot Norton had written: "Grant grows daily in my respect and confidence." After the President had failed to fight for the repeal of the Tenure of Office Act he found "Grant's surrender to the politicians . . . an unexpected disappointment."

As soon as the Act was modified, Grant sent in nominations to replace Johnsonian incumbents. Although most of these appointments were suggested by the party leaders, the personal nature of the earlier selections continued to rankle in Senatorial minds. To the special session of the Senate, the President sent as many as 150 nominations in a single day, and with few exceptions they were unanimously ratified. A Missouri Methodist ranter named Pile was rejected for the Brazilian mission, while J. Russell Jones, a personal friend appointed to Belgium, and ex-Governor Curtin of Pennsylvania, sent to Russia, were accepted only after wrangling debate; but the overwhelming majority of the nominations passed without question. Nevertheless, Grant's independent course had aroused opposition, and the lines of cleavage between his friends and enemies were already marked. Sumner, Schurz, and an element of the Radicals who had warred against Johnson were prepared to give valiant battle to Grant.

But as these men began to emerge as enemies, others appeared as friends. When the President lost prestige with the reforming elements in the country, the practical politicians—such men as Conkling, Mor-

---

[31] *Letters of Henry Adams*, 153.
[32] John Bigelow, *Retrospections of an Active Life*, V, 284–286.

ton, Cameron, and the shrewdly scheming Butler—perceived that Grant would be amenable to suggestions and prepared to make themselves preëminently the President's friends. So competent an observer as W. E. Chandler found, six weeks after the modification of the Tenure of Office Act, that "matters have settled down very quietly, and the Administration is getting into good working trim. It . . . is true to the principles of the Republican party, and the mistakes it made in appointments are spots on the sun—they do not seriously affect its brightness. I think the Administration will prove a success. The party is full of soreheads, but they alone will never destroy the party." [33]

[33] Chandler to Washburne, May 1869, Washburne MSS.

ALTHOUGH the struggle over the appointments to office occupied much time during this first session of Grant's first Congress, the real significance of the election of 1868 was not lost from sight. On both finance and the South the Republican Party had made pledges, and these the President and Congress were prepared to carry out.

To the delight of the bondholders whose hopes for profits had led them to contribute to Grant's campaign fund, Congress gave immediate attention to the question of the five-twenty bonds. In his last annual message Johnson had surpassed the wildest proposition of the repudiators by suggesting that interest on the bonds should be paid for sixteen and a fraction years and the account closed. To assure the nation's creditors that the Republican Party gave no adherence to such dishonest ideas, Congress passed an "Act to Strengthen the Public Credit" which Johnson tabled to die with his Administration. But the new Congress hastily took up the bill, and on March 18, Grant signed it as the first law of his Administration. By its terms, the act "solemnly pledged" the credit of the United States to pay the bonds in "coin or its equivalent." Moreover, the nation's faith was pledged to redeem the greenbacks in coin "at the earliest practicable period." As soon as Grant had signed the bill, gold on the New York exchange fell to 130—the lowest point since the suspension of specie payments in 1862.[1]

Somewhat more slowly, and with considerable less unity of purpose, the Administration turned its attention to the task of completing reconstruction. At the moment, Virginia, Mississippi and Texas were still unreconstructed. In Virginia a lack of money, and in Texas a factional fight, had prevented the submission of Radical Constitutions to the people, while in Mississippi the Constitution, with stringent disfranchising clauses, had been rejected in the election. Georgia, too, was out of proper relations to the Union as a result of too hasty a zeal for white supremacy. There a white majority in the legislature, deciding that the new Constitution had given Negroes the right to vote but not to hold

---

[1] John Sherman, *Recollections of Forty Years,* 448; New York *Tribune,* March 19, 1869; New York *Commercial and Financial Chronicle,* March 27, 1869.

office, ousted their colored colleagues, and gave their seats to whites whom the Negroes had defeated at the polls.

This flagrant disregard of Northern susceptibilities was the first to receive congressional attention. In February, Butler had attempted to keep Georgia's electoral vote from being counted for Seymour, and although his effort then failed, the Forty-first Congress excluded the State's representatives. In the new Congress Butler's committee took up the matter of a proper discipline, but so many problems of jurisdiction and procedure arose that it was decided to leave Georgia to her guilty conscience until the December session.[2]

The three remaining States received little attention until Grant called on Congress for action. On April 7, after consulting a number of Southerners, the President sent a message upon Virginia which bore evidence of his sincere desire for harmony and peace. Since the Virginia Constitution, completed by a convention in April, 1868, showed that the people were "willing to become peaceful and orderly," Grant urged Congress to provide for a submission of the document for popular ratification. As the Constitution contained proscriptive clauses similar to those in the defeated Mississippi instrument, Grant proposed that a separate vote be taken on those portions which might endanger the success of the whole. "I am led to make this recommendation," asserted the President, "from the confident hope and belief that the people of that State are now ready to coöperate with the National Government . . . and to give to all its people those equal rights . . . which were asserted in the Declaration of Independence. . . ."[3] In conclusion, he suggested that the Mississippi Constitution might be resubmitted to the people with a separation of the obnoxious from the acceptable portions.

This conciliatory and reasonable message was received with hearty approval by a people grown weary of the "Southern Question,"[4] and Congress hastened to carry out Grant's wishes. For the first time in four years Executive and Legislature were in harmony, and in three days Congress had passed and the President signed an act embodying his proposals upon the Constitutions of Virginia, Mississippi, and Texas alike. He was given full power to submit separately any clauses he

[2] New York *Tribune*, March 30, April 2, 1869.
[3] Richardson, *Messages and Papers of the Presidents*, VII, 11–12.
[4] New York *Tribune*, April 8, 10, *National Republican*, April, 9, 10, 15, 1869.

thought advisable, and—significant of a new era in Reconstruction—
the administration of the act was placed in his hands rather than in
those of the General of the Army. The only departure from Grant's
recommendations was contained in a clause providing that the three
legislatures should ratify the pending Fifteenth Amendment. A month
later, the President issued a proclamation setting June 6 for the election
in Virginia, and permitting a separate vote on two disfranchising
clauses.[5]

While Congress was slowly carrying out campaign pledges, and ruefully watching the President's unpopular course with reference to the
patronage, Grant was settling himself comfortably in the Executive
Mansion. Soon there was noticed a change which contrasted strangely
with the hectic days when Andrew Johnson had lived in the White
House. Unlike his predecessor, General Grant interpreted his functions
as Chief Executive in the simplest manner. Untrammeled by constitutional scruples, and free, at least in the beginning, from political or factional alliances, the new President had indeed "no policy to enforce
against the will of the people." It was simply his duty to administer the
government in accordance with the people's wishes as expressed in the
laws of Congress. In mental qualities as well as in governmental con-
cepts, Grant differed from Johnson, and the differences conduced greatly
to his comfort. The two Presidents were equally obstinate, but Grant's
mute persistence often carried him through places where Johnson's
blustering volubility would have united his enemies against him. Johnson was a fighter, quick to resent a slight, and eager for oral combat.
Grant had no aptitude for a war of words and received criticism with
a taciturn silence which puzzled and often disarmed his accusers. Moreover, Johnson, for all his vocal pugnacity, was an indecisive man, while
Grant as President showed the same capacity for sudden decisions that
had marked his military career. Never given to tilting at constitutional
windmills, Grant showed no hesitation when faced with a practical
problem. In both the army and the White House, he manifested long
periods of inactivity, broken by spurts of extraordinary energy.

Since the President refrained from formulating the policies of his
party, it was inevitable that the Cabinet members should be "heads of
departments" rather than "constitutional advisers." Carelessly or ig-
norantly disregarding political factions and the principle of geograph-

[5] Richardson, *Messages and Papers*, VII, 13–15.

ical distribution in selecting his Cabinet, Grant escaped both the jarring personalities and the covert treason that had harrowed the souls of Lincoln and Johnson. In the management of the departments he showed little inclination to interfere, and the public gaze was more often fixed on one of them than on the White House. Most of the achievements of Grant's Administration bear the names of congressional leaders rather than that of the President who gave them a free hand and often made the necessary decisions. Almost from the beginning, Fish and Boutwell overshadowed the President. With commendable self-effacement, he never attempted to "steal" the credit for their accomplishments.

Least capable of the original Cabinet was Secretary Borie, but no one realized his incompetence more than the Secretary himself. Accepting the office only to save the President embarrassment, the Philadelphia millionaire awaited the first favorable moment to resign. Early in June, as a result of newspaper criticism, the President released his friend from his onerous duties. After offering the place to George H. Stuart and Lindley Smith, both of Philadelphia, Grant appointed George M. Robeson of New Jersey to the place.

Secretary Robeson was almost as unknown at the time of his appointment as Borie. A graduate of Princeton, he had practiced law and politics until elected Attorney-General of his State. Radical in doctrine, he was acceptable to the Senate, but his conduct of the Navy Department was the subject of continual criticism. However, he shares with Fish the distinction of having served throughout the eight years of Grant's Administrations.[6]

The other department heads, who could not be charged with incompetence, entered upon their work with zeal. Postmaster-General Creswell, experienced in the way of politicians, distributed the enormous patronage of his office with a minimum of friction. So well did he handle his task that he seemed immune from attack by even the most partisan journals.

In the Interior Department, Secretary Cox early devoted his efforts to economy and to the establishment of a merit system. The most interesting development in the department, however, came in connection

---

[6] George S. Boutwell, *Reminiscences of Sixty Years in Public Affairs*, 212; Blaine, *Twenty Years of Congress*, 427–428; New York *Tribune*, April 3, May 5, June 26, July 3, 1869; Welles, *Diary*, III, 556–560, 563; Oberholtzer, *History of the United States*, III, 220 note.

with Indian affairs. Before Congress adjourned it appropriated two millions for the Indians, but left no instructions as to its expenditure. The situation gave Grant an opportunity to experiment with Indian relations, and, at Cox's suggestion, he appointed a board of philanthropists to advise the government on the Indian policy. In May, another scheme of Secretary and President was revealed when a group of Quakers clothed in the simple garb of their faith, and speaking in unfamiliar "thees" and "thous," appeared at the Interior Department. To test whether their traditional gentleness might soothe the savage breast, two Indian agencies were given to these quiet people. So pacific a program, adopted by a soldier who had recommended, five months before, that the Indian Bureau be transferred to the War Department, bore evidence of Grant's sincere desire for an economical solution of Indian difficulties.[7]

When Fish reluctantly took charge of the State Department, he was immediately faced by two irritating problems of major importance. The one grew out of a Cuban revolt against Spain, which had flared up in September, 1868; the other, arising from the depredations of Confederate cruisers, involved American claim for damages from England.

The Cuban revolution followed what was rapidly becoming the established pattern for such disturbances. Guerilla warfare by the insurgents caused the Spanish officials to conduct a campaign of terrorism. Burnings, secret assassinations, and wholesale massacre marked the fighting on both sides. Traditionally inclined to sympathy with oppressed peoples, Americans were fired to enthusiasm by the propaganda of a Cuban Junta in New York City. Filibustering expeditions left American shores, and in Congress resolutions of sympathy were introduced and debated. In the White House, Secretary Rawlins had the President's ear and was urging him to take action in behalf of Cuban independence.

Fish had hardly been installed in office before he had to give attention to the problem of the Cubans. An American vessel bearing arms for the insurgents was captured by the Spanish, and the Captain-General announced that all persons taken on such vessels would be shot. The Secretary protested to the Spanish minister against the order, and re-

[7] New York *Tribune*, May 8, 13, 22, 27, July 12, 21, 1869; Hugh Lenox Scott, *Some Memories of a Soldier*, 625; Richardson, *Messages and Papers*, VII, 23–24.

ceived in reply a demand that Grant issue a proclamation forbidding American citizens from aiding the revolutionists.[8]

In the meantime, at Rawlins' urgency, Grant freely expressed his sympathy with the Cuban cause. When consulted about Americans held prisoners by the Spanish, he declared it his purpose of "take effective measures to protect the citizens of the United States." Though he wished to avoid being drawn into a hostile attitude, he ordered the American squadron in the West Indies increased.[9] In June, Grant asked Sumner, chairman of the Senate Committee on Foreign Relations, "How would it do to issue a proclamation with regard to Cuba identical with that issued by Spain in regard to us?" Lacking Grant's interest in the Cuban cause, Sumner advised against such a pronouncement.[10]

Despite utterances by Grant and Rawlins, Fish managed to prevent hasty action. Before long, newspapers began to take a more moderate tone, and to appreciate Fish's contention that the insurrection did not justify American recognition.[11] In June, General Daniel E. Sickles was appointed minister to Spain, and Fish instructed him to offer the good offices of the United States in bringing about a settlement. Fish believed that Spain might relinquish the island for a money payment, and thought that Sickles could give impetus to the procrastinating Spanish government by suggestions that American recognition of the insurgents was imminent. Sickles suggested to the Spanish that the Cubans might pay $125,000,000 for their independence. No action was ever taken, and Fish and Sickles continued to worry over Cuban problems.[12]

When on April 12 the Senate met in special session, the Johnson-Clarendon convention on the Alabama claims was presented for approval. Negotiated in the last days of Johnson's Administration, it provided for a commission to which all claims between Great Britain and the United States would be submitted. Although the terms were eminently fair to each nation, neither the Senate nor the American people could accept its sponsors. Reverdy Johnson, minister to England, was a Maryland Democrat who had ardently supported Andrew Johnson's domestic policies. Moreover, in his speeches in England he

[8] *Senate Executive Documents,* 41st Congress, 2nd Session, No. 108; *Ibid.,* No. 7, pp. 12, 16–18.
[9] New York *Tribune,* April 7, 9, 1869.
[10] E. L. Pierce, *Memoirs and Letters of Charles Sumner,* IV, 409.
[11] New York *Tribune,* April 10, 19, 27, May 4; *National Republican,* April 19, 20; New York *Times,* July 1, 1869.
[12] *House Executive Documents,* No. 41, 41st Congress, 2nd session, No. 160.

had mistaken the temper of the Northern people and had vociferously enunciated the doctrine of "hands across the sea" at a moment when a clenched and mailed fist was more symbolic of sentiment at home. He banqueted with Roebuck, the Confederacy's champion in Parliament, and affably shook hands with the Laird who had built the Confederate rams. However popular such acts may have been in England, in America they served only to inflame the minds of the people.

Before his inauguration, Grant had taken pains to let the British minister know his hostility to the Johnson-Clarendon Convention. In so doing, he was in complete harmony with the majority of his party. When the Senate met in executive session, there was no doubt of its course; and Sumner took advantage of the opportunity to express the prevailing American feeling against England. His objection to the treaty was that it proposed to settle only the claims of individuals arising out of the war; the real damage to the United States remained untouched. In addition to the $15,000,000 losses which American shippers had suffered from the depredations of the *Alabama* and other British built Confederate cruisers, the nation had suffered extensive damages. Because the Queen had recognized Confederate belligerency, and admitted Confederate ships to British ports, the war had been prolonged for two years. "England," exclaimed the Senator, "is justly responsible" for half of the money expended in suppressing the rebellion. In addition, she was responsible for $110,000,000 losses to the American merchant marine for "commerce driven from the ocean." [13]

Although this statement of the American case met the approval of neither Grant nor Fish, many newspapers throughout the country commended it. In England the speech was received with consternation, and leading Englishmen began to speculate on American wishes. It was not difficult, however, for them to see that Sumner was making a bid for Canada.

With practical unanimity, the Senate rejected the Johnson-Clarendon Convention, and Grant and Fish took up the work anew. In May, Grant appointed Sumner's friend, John Lothrop Motley, to the English mission. Before receiving his commission, Motley called on Fish to present a "memoir" obviously inspired by Sumner, which he proposed as the basis for his instructions. By the memoir, Motley was to represent that the American claim for "indirect" damages grew out of the

[13] E. L. Pierce, *Sumner's Works*, XIII, 52–59.

Queen's proclamation of belligerency.

To Fish there seemed to be stronger legal arguments than this, and he desired to posit the American contentions on England's persistently unfriendly attitude rather than on a specific act which might be proved to have had some justification. At the moment, Grant was eager to recognize Cuban belligerency on grounds much more flimsy than England had used in 1861. Fish, therefore, rejected Motley's memoir, and proceeded, despite Sumner's violent objection, to instruct the minister to claim that the recognition of belligerency was only the first of a series of acts which revealed England's hostile animus.

Debate with Sumner over the memoir delayed the preparation of the minister's instructions, and Motley read his orders for the first time after he set sail. Once in England, he ignored Fish's orders, and in an interview with Lord Clarendon reiterated Sumner's position. Seeing Motley headstrong, Fish determined to transfer future negotiations from London to Washington. As time went on, Motley found himself ignored by the State Department, and turned more and more to Sumner for advice and inspiration. As the gulf widened between the Secretary of State and the Chairman of the Foreign Affairs Committee, Motley followed his patron in opposing Grant's Administration.

Although Motley was temperamentally unfitted for the conduct of difficult diplomatic negotiations, he would doubtless have succeeded in holding Grant's support longer had it not been for his Assistant-Secretary of the Legation, Adam Badeau. When the New England historian was appointed, Grant offered the Assistant-Secretaryship to his own biographer. Badeau gleefully accepted, and almost immediately began to find fault with his superior. To celebrate his appointment, he planned a breakfast to which Motley, the British Ambassador, Secretary Fish, Sumner and Grant would be invited. When told of the project, Motley informed his subordinate that he thought it improper for a secretary of legation to invite the British Ambassador to meet the President. Badeau, who had entertained hopes of an "agreeable introduction to English society" through the famous historian, perceived that his chances of making social conquests would be limited.

However, there was still a possibility that he might overshadow the minister. Just before sailing, he approached the President for personal instructions. Since he intended to let it be known that he came from Grant's side, he asked his chief "what tone in conversation" he should assume. Ever incautious where his friends were concerned, Grant instructed Badeau to emphasize the President's personal desire to avoid difficulties with England. "Say this in conversation constantly," commended the President. "Make opportunities to say that you know this is my position and that I authorize you to declare it."

Armed with this innocuous message from Grant to the British people, Badeau saw new visions of himself as a social lion. Motley, however, again threw cold water on his dreams. On board ship, Badeau made the mistake of telling his superior of his own verbal instructions, and was informed that he should not presume to "discuss political matters at all, or to speak in any way for the President." The minister did not intend to harbor in his household any rival for social prestige!

Thus checkmated, Badeau immediately became critical of his chief. Using his secretarial position to examine the Legation's files, he read Motley's instructions and a memorandum of his conversation with Lord Clarendon, and hastily reported to Grant that Motley was disobeying his instructions. The letter arrived in Washington before Motley's report, and Grant was prepared to demand Motley's immediate recall. Hoping for some better conduct from the incompetent minister, Fish pointed out to the President that so hasty a removal would be hard to defend, and Grant was constrained to give Motley another chance. In September, with no social conquests behind him, Badeau resigned his post and returned to his room in the White House. His position there gave him ample opportunity to turn the President against the Ambassador to Great Britain.[14]

Although in the first months of Grant's administration, the public gaze was momentarily directed upon broad-brimmed Quakers in the Indian agencies, or to Sumner's claim-making, it remained for the most part fixed upon Secretary Boutwell and his policy. Of all the Cabinet, he stood closest to the business interests of the country. Within the limits of the law, his will could raise or lower prices, and favorably or adversely affect the conditions of credit. Normally, Congress could be expected to legislate upon his advice, and the responsibility of carrying out the legislation devolved upon him.

While business interests watched expectantly for an announcement of policy, Boutwell examined his department's organization. Unnecessary clerks and former members of the "Johnson Club" were promptly

[14] Badeau, *Grant in Peace*, 197–204.

dismissed, and changes were made in the Bureau of Printing and En-
graving which would confuse the most ingenious counterfeiter. The
Secretary inspired the new collectors with a zeal to surpass their predecessors in gathering the internal revenue.[15]

Though his hands were free in changing departmental routine, in the
more significant aspects of his office the new Secretary found himself
limited. At his accession, the bonded debt of the country exceeded two
and a half billion dollars, most of it bearing six per cent interest. By
act of Congress, these bonds could be redeemed only in gold. In addition
to the bonds, and generally regarded as a debt to be redeemed, there
were $356,000,000 outstanding in greenbacks. These had driven gold
coin out of circulation, and fractional paper currency to the extent of
$160,000,000 had replaced subsidiary silver coins. Except on the
Pacific coast and in the ports of entry, gold coins had disappeared.
From customs duties, however, the government obtained large supplies
of gold which it used to pay interest on the bonds.

Boutwell's increased efficiency in collections soon brought a growing
surplus into the treasury. Withdrawn from the channels of trade, such
money tended to increase the price of gold. McCulloch, Johnson's
Secretary of the Treasury, had attempted to reduce his surplus by
selling gold for greenbacks which he retired from circulation. Contractionists had approved his policy, but Congress stopped the practice
after $44,000,000 in treasury notes had been withdrawn. Inflationists
alleged that the policy placed a burden on the debtor classes. Although
the next Congress promised a speedy resumption of specie payments,
it failed to remove the barrier to the necessary contraction. Inhibited
from following his predecessor's policy, Boutwell turned his thoughts
to payment of the debt.

As the merchant classes began to demand that he do something about
the rising surplus, Boutwell went to New York to speak before the
stock exchange. Here he promised the financial world that he would
neither hoard gold in the Treasury, nor use it suddenly to deplete the
channels of trade. Instead, he would follow a steady policy of selling
gold each week, and purchasing bonds with the proceeds. Legal authorization for this program he found in an act of 1862 commanding the
Secretary to purchase annually one per cent of the total indebtedness
of the country as a sinking fund. Chase and McCulloch had failed to

[15] Boutwell, *Sixty Years*, 125–131.

make purchases under this law. To avoid limiting the supply of gold to those who could command bonds, Boutwell planned to sell gold for currency and purchase bonds with the greenbacks.

Although this plan showed little financial statesmanship, it was perhaps the only course the law permitted. In reality, it did little to reduce the debt, but it served the purpose of keeping the gold surplus in the treasury at a minimum. As an assurance to the nation's creditors that the debt would be paid, it could be used to induce them to fund their bonds at a lower interest rate. Despite the feeble potentialities of the scheme, however, the figures on debt reduction were so impressive that Boutwell's policy came in for a goodly measure of popular acclaim. On the first of April, he was able to announce that the debt had been reduced more than $2,500,000, although $3,000,000 in bonds had been issued to the Pacific Railroad. By counting the treasury surplus as debt reduction, the figures for April amounted to $13,000,000. Early in May, Boutwell began to buy bonds and sell gold, and at the end of the month showed a reduction of $12,000,000. For June he reported over $16,000,000; for July, despite interest payments on the Pacific bonds, almost $7,500,000. Since every purchase for the sinking fund saved the interest on the bonds so segregated, the possibilities of speedily paying the debt began to appeal to the popular imagination.[16]

As applause for Boutwell's policy increased, the early criticism of Grant's Administration declined. The President himself allowed Boutwell to control the Treasury, and the Secretary accepted full responsibility. He consulted neither the President nor the Cabinet in forming and administering his policy, and never informed them how much gold he intended to sell. Once, Grant jokingly remarked that Boutwell had cost him money. He had sold some bonds just before the Secretary's order for a purchase had temporarily increased their market value. Yet despite the fact that he was less responsible for Boutwell's success than for that of any other Cabinet member, Grant's financial achievements came in for the highest praise.

By the middle of the summer, when the country had an opportunity to recover from the shock of a President who seemed to ignore the

[16] To a large extent, Boutwell's policy followed the proposals made by the New York *Tribune*. The *Times* and *World* were generally hostile, while the *Commercial and Financial Chronicle* regarded many of the Secretary's actions with suspicion. In addition to the almost daily editorials in these papers, see J. A. Garfield to Jeff. C. Beall (Cleveland) June 8, 1869, Garfield Mss.; Oberholtzer, *Jay Cooke*, II, 1–4, 267–268; *Letters of Henry Adams*, 152–153; John Sherman, *Recollections*, 459.

party leaders, observers were able to survey the scene with better perspective. Although the Democrats continued a partisan criticism, and some impartial critics deplored Grant's seeming surrender to the politicians over the Tenure of Office Act, the general tone of the country was commendatory. The *Times* concluded that there was "no reason to fear that the . . . new Administration . . . will not fully meet the expectations of the country." The reconstruction policy was meeting the "wants and necessities of the Southern States," the payment of the debt and the collection of the revenue was "very gratifying." The War and the Navy Departments had never had greater vigor or success. "In every Department," the journal concluded, "there is decided improvement." [17]

This, too, was Grant's opinion. In the middle of July he planned to go to Long Branch for part of the summer. Although he expected to return to Washington at intervals, he foresaw but little to do. Just before he left, he wrote Badeau his own reflections on conditions. "Public affairs," said the President, "look to me to be progressing very favorably. The revenues of the country are being collected as they have not been before, and expenditures are looked after more carefully. The first thing it seems to me is to establish the credit of the country. This is policy enough for the present." [18]

[17] New York *Times,* June 14, 1869.
Badeau, *Grant in Peace,* 469. I have transposed the last two sentences.

ALTHOUGH Reconstruction occupied a large place in the columns of
the press and the speeches of political orators, Grant was correct in his
estimate that problems of finance demanded the first attention of his
Administration. "Our purchases of bonds," said Secretary Cox, "have
been barely sufficient to keep the money market from being strung up
to the snapping point during the early part of the year. . . . When the
departure of currency to the West for the moving of crops fairly sets
in, it will be strange if we don't hear signs of distress in Wall Street,
and I fear they won't wait for the fall elections." [1] During the summer
Grant held frequent Cabinet meetings to consider the matter, but
agreed on no policy to be followed in the event of a crisis. Boutwell
continued to sell gold and buy bonds for the sinking fund, and Grant,
though much interested in the financial situation, continued his policy
of allowing the Secretary a free hand.

Though Boutwell's policy of purchasing bonds at a premium met the
hearty approval of those who had bonds for sale, and caused Horace
Greeley to point with partisan pride to the mounting figures of debt
reduction, the commendation was by no means universal. Democratic
leaders criticized a policy which enriched bondholders at the expense
of the nation. Jay Cooke, too, opposed the public sales and deplored the
Secretary's lack of aggressiveness, while importers, desiring a lower
premium on gold, wanted the sales of gold increased. On Wall Street,
speculative bulls and bears desired respectively a diminution and an
increase of Treasury sales. Despite these differences, all classes from
gold speculators to Republican politicians were united in one desire—
to know what Boutwell's intentions might be.

Among the Wall Street operators, none were more anxious to determine the government's intentions than James Fisk, Jr., and Jay
Gould. The partnership of these two, men widely different in personal
characteristics, is convincing evidence that economics as well as politics
makes strange bed-fellows. Jim Fisk, a newcomer to Wall Street, had
begun his meteoric career as a pedlar in rural New England. In a

[1] Cox to Garfield, July 26, 1869, Garfield MSS.

gaudily painted wagon, drawn by a pair of fast horses, Fisk developed
an innate knack for showmanship which became more flamboyant as it
proved profitable. From such medicine-show origins, Fisk graduated
into New York financial circles, where his melodramatic audacity soon
gave an agreeable cloak to his rascality. Licentious, litigious, and
utterly unscrupulous, be succeeded in basking in the limelight and gaining a superficial popularity. A veritable demagogue of finance, he had
himself elected colonel of a militia regiment, and strutted in his uniform until he acquired a line of river steamers and conferred the title
and appurtenances of "admiral" upon himself.

In contrast with Fisk's flamboyant personality, Jay Gould's characteristics appear drab indeed. Silent, shrinking from public gaze, and
coldly formal in his contacts with the world, Gould possessed a calculat-
ing shrewdness in business which amounted to financial genius. While
Fisk ostentatiously paraded his immorality, Gould, a devoted husband
and father, adhered to the puritanical moral code of the day. Different
though they were, each was representative of a facet of the Victorian
age, and each a forerunner of a type which was becoming increasingly
prominent in American economic life.

A common unscrupulous acquisitiveness united these two buccaneers
in a partnership which centered in their railway operations, but whose
far-flung frontier comprehended every field where illicit profits might
be made. In 1868 they acquired control of the already overcapitalized
Erie road, and moved its headquarters to an uptown New York opera
house. There, while Fisk amused himself by "commending adultery as
a fine art," [2] Gould seduced politicians, bribed judges, defrauded com-
petitors, and concocted schemes for amassing wealth.[3]

Most grandiose of the schemes which Gould's fertile mind concocted
was one dealing with the influence of gold prices on crop movements.
With Grant's inauguration, gold fell to 130, and Gould noticed a de-
crease in shipments over the Erie Railroad. Primarily interested in
showing an increase of earnings for the Erie which would enable him
to issue more watered stock, Gould surrounded his predatory schemes
with an aura of sanctimony. He would benefit the farmer! Concluding
that the price of gold was too low to move western crops, he entered
the gold market and bid the price up to 142. At that figure, according

[2] New York *Tribune,* April 8, 1869.
[3] Allan Nevins, *The Emergence of Modern American,* 194–199.

HOUSE AT GALENA, ILL., OCCUPIED BY GRANT AND HIS FAMILY IN
1860–61

PRESIDENT GRANT'S COTTAGE AT LONG BRANCH

to his figures, American producers of foodstuffs could compete with Russian and Mediterranean grain in the European markets; western farmers could ship to the seaboard, and the receipts of the Erie would increase. Unfortunately, Boutwell's policy of selling treasury gold tended continually to depreciate the price below this level, and Gould adopted a policy of buying gold when it fell below 140, and selling at above 145. In this way he contrived to keep crops moving—or so he alleged—and incidentally to make a profit on his gold operations.

As was obvious to Gould and to other operators in the gold room, the price of gold depended on the selling policy of the government. Accordingly, Gould proceeded to make an effort to learn the intentions of the government, and to take steps, if possible, to have Boutwell's sales discontinued. To accomplish these objects, he began to improve his acquaintance with Abel R. Corbin, an elderly real-estate operator who had recently married Grant's sister Jenny. Corbin's keen nose scented the possibility of profits from gold speculation, and he began a campaign to convert the President to Gould's theory of the connection between crop movements and the price of gold.

Early in June the President, accompanied by the members of his family and the scheming Corbin, left Washington to attend the examinations at West Point.[4] Dropping Corbin in New York, he enjoyed his annual visit to scenes of his youth. On June 15th he was back in New York, where he met Gould and Fisk at Corbin's house. That night, according to arrangements made through Corbin, the President boarded one of Fisk's boats for Boston to attend the Peace Jubilee. At the nine o'clock supper on the boat, the conversation quickly turned to the gold sales. At considerable length, Gould expounded his theory that the government should not interfere with the natural course of business. With this view the other guests agreed, while Grant sat silent and attentive. Having failed to draw the President into a general discussion, Fisk finally turned to Grant with a request for his opinion.

"There is a certain amount of fictitiousness about the prosperity of the country," he replied, "and the bubble might as well be tapped in one way as another."[5] What Grant thought of his strange companions on this boat is not on record, but this remark is indicative that his suspicions were temporarily aroused. His habit of diffident silence when

[4] New York *Tribune*, June 9, 1869.
[5] Gould Testimony, *"Garfield Report,"* 152–153. I have changed indirect into direct discourse.

he was displeased led many a contemporary to mistake his meaning, but this boatload of schemers felt no doubt that the President was a contractionist who would not interfere with Boutwell's policy. Fisk immediately decided to drop the subject as well as his schemes, but Gould pointed out that Grant's policy would create distress, produce strikes, and close factories. To these arguments the President made no reply, and Gould admitted a temporary defeat.

Gould, however, was not willing to abandon his scheme so quickly, and sought further occasion to impress his ideas on the President. Corbin, too, was unwilling to give up the profitable lure Gould held out to him; and when Grant returned from Boston, Gould, Fisk, and Corbin took the President to the opera. All New York saw and wondered at the President in such company. The meaning, however, remained for some time in doubt.

About the middle of July, the President and his family left Washington. Though he escaped the heat of the capital, he could not divest himself of the cares of office and interviewed a motley host of visitors at his summer residence.

In addition to the problems of Reconstruction and finance, Grant and the Cabinet were faced by a continuance of the Cuban troubles. The rebellion in that island showed no signs of diminution and the friends of the Cubans, notably Secretary Rawlins, were insistent that the United States recognize the rebels. Grant himself was anxious for such action, partly because he thought it a suitable revenge for Spain's recognizing the Confederates. On August 2, he went to New York from Long Branch to confer with Fish about a detention of Spanish gunboats by American officials,[6] and a few days later to Washington for a Cabinet meeting on general Cuban problems.[7] On both occasions, Grant spent much time in conference with the Secretary of State. Leaving Washington, he journeyed to the White Mountains. Enroute, deciding to take matters in his own hands, he suddenly ordered written a proclamation according recognition to the Cuban belligerents. Hastily signing the proclamation, Grant sent it to Fish to be countersigned and published. Knowing full well that the Cuban rebels had no semblance of organized government or effective army, Fish succeeded in obtaining first a delay and then the complete suppression of the curious document.

---

[6] *National Republican,* August 3, 4, New York *Tribune,* August 6, 1869.
[7] New York *Tribune,* August 10, 1869.

Just as this was happening, the pressure on Grant for Cuban recognition was removed by the death of General Rawlins. The Secretary of War, Cuba's most ardent advocate, had continued to suffer from tuberculosis after his elevation to the Cabinet. During the summer his strength steadily declined, although he managed to visit in Connecticut and attend several Cabinet meetings. Late in August, just after returning to Washington, he had a severe hemorrhage and grew rapidly worse. On September 1 he attended a Cabinet meeting, but Grant had hardly left for Saratoga when he again collapsed. On September 6 Grant rushed back to Washington, but his train arrived an hour too late. With Rawlins' death, Grant's interest in Cuba declined, and a year later he thanked Fish for withholding the proclamation.[8]

Stopping in New York on his way to Rawlins' funeral, Grant again met Gould at Corbin's. Since the night on the boat, Gould had not abandoned his dreams of influencing the Government to cease its sales of gold. Late in August, he had formed a pool to raise the price of gold, but had failed to make appreciable headway. At the time, in order to give the impression that the Government would not sell, he had an editorial published in the New York *Times* stating that the Government would not interfere in the gold market. This announcement was so framed that it seemed a semi-official statement, and although a suspicious financial editor modified some of Gould's original statements, the article was taken at face value by the financial public.

In the meantime, Corbin seems to have spent much time in screwing up Gould to stick to his purpose to control the gold market. Neither of these predatory gentlemen was quite frank with the other, and each sought to use the other for his own ends. Corbin assured Gould of his influence over the President, and induced the Erie magnate to carry a considerable amount of gold for him. Gould, on the other hand, purchased gold for Corbin in order to involve a relative of the Chief Executive in his dealings. Somewhat later Gould extended this policy by purchasing a half million of gold for Horace Porter, the President's secretary, and for General Butterfield, assistant treasurer in New York. Porter, however, had the shrewdness and honesty to decline the suspicious offer. Butterfield lacked both qualities and coöperated with the corruptionists. At the same time, Corbin used every opportunity to

---

[8] For Rawlins' death, See the New York *Tribune*, September 6, 7, 9; *National Republican*, September 6, 7, 1869; Richardson, *Messages and Papers*, VII, 24–25.

impress Gould's crop theories upon the President. Once during the summer Fisk carried a letter from Gould to Grant stating that the President's policy would enable American wheat to monopolize the European market. Grant listened to Fisk, and promised to discuss the matter with Boutwell.[9]

The evidence concerning Grant's second meeting with Gould is conflicting. Corbin invited Gould to his house and arranged an interview with the President. According to Corbin's testimony, Grant rebuked his brother-in-law for admitting Gould, and complained to Mrs. Grant that Gould was "always trying to find something out." Gould, on the other hand, declared that Grant met him affably and revealed in a long conversation that he had completely changed his earlier views, stating that the country had a large harvest which must find a market abroad lest it depreciate prices at home. The Government, said the President, would do nothing to "put down the price of gold or make money tight." When questioned how the Government could continue the purchase of bonds without selling gold, Grant pointed out that it might be done with fractional currency!

In the congressional investigation of the Gold Panic, Jay Gould's testimony has a ring of frankness which is completely lacking in Corbin's shifty and evasive statements. But on this matter, the brother-in-law appears more credible. The only evidence from Grant himself is embodied in a note to Boutwell, written September 12. This was just on the eve of Grant's departure—on a special train furnished by Gould—for Washington, Pennsylvania. "Had I known before making arrangement for starting that you would be in this city," the President wrote, ". . . I would have remained to meet you. I am satisfied that on your arrival you will be met by the bulls and bears of Wall Street, and probably by merchants, too, to induce you to sell gold, or pay the November interest in advance, on the one side, and to hold fast on the other. The fact is, a desperate struggle is now taking place, and each party wants the Government to help him out. I write this letter to advise you of what I think you may expect, to put you on your guard. I think, from the lights before me, I would move on without change until the present struggle is over. . . . I would like to hear your experience with the factions . . . if they give you time to write. No doubt you will have a better chance to judge than I, for I have avoided

[9] *Gold Report*, 173.

general discussion on the subject." [10]

From this letter it is evident that Grant had not only divined the nature of Gould's impending conspiracy, but had carefully refrained from committing the Government to any policy. Doubtless Gould, in his conversations with the President, had met either with silence, which he mistook for acquiescence, or with trite generalizations into which he read his own meaning. With Corbin, too, the wish was father to the thought, for he assured Gould that Grant had ordered Boutwell to stop the gold sales—and exhibited the sealed letter, which Grant had left with him for delivery, to prove it!

In New York Boutwell conducted himself with the caution enjoined in Grant's letter, and gave no hint of Governmental policy. Gould, however, decided to act quickly, hoping that Grant's absence would enable him to corner the gold market. In such a rapid movement he needed help, and he approached Fisk to reënlist his old partner. Fisk, however, was wary, and warned Gould that the Government would unload gold if the scheme were attempted. "Oh, this matter is all fixed up," Gould assured him. "Butterfield is all right. Corbin has got Butterfield all right, and Corbin has got Grant all right."

Still unconvinced, Fisk went to Corbin, who whisperingly assured him that Mrs. Grant was in the scheme! Gould had purchased gold for her at 131 and sold it at 137. Corbin himself had about two million in the market. Five hundred thousand of that was Mrs. Grant's, and a like amount belonged to General Porter. Gould confirmed the story by showing that he had recently given Corbin a check for $25,000, and Corbin asserted that he had sent the money to Washington. Actually, the money was Corbin's profits, paid by Gould when Corbin threatened to withdraw from the scheme. But Fisk did not know this, and lured by the possibility of corrupt gain, he entered the bargain.[11]

Some time before, Gould's brokers, Smith, Gould, Martin & Company, together with several other brokerage firms, had acquired control of the Tenth National Bank. This bank played an important part in their proposed coup. At the time there was about $18,000,000 in gold dollars and certificates in New York, an amount sufficient to carry on the busi-

---

[10] Boutwell, *Reminiscences of Sixty Years*, II, 169–170.

[11] At the very time that he was drawing his partner into his net, Gould was writing to Boutwell urging him not to sell gold. Boutwell had, however, ordered Assistant-Secretary Richardson, in Washington, to give Butterfield, in New York, no orders to sell until the Secretary returned. Gould doubtless knew of this through Butterfield.

ness of the city. Importers and others needing gold for commercial transactions obtained it from the Gold Exchange Bank, and receivers of gold were accustomed to sell gold for currency on the Gold Exchange —an institution established soon after greenbacks began to drive gold out of general circulation. Since no one held gold for more than a few days, a comparatively small amount was needed for business. Gould and Fisk and their associates expected, therefore, to corner the market with little difficulty. If the Government would refrain from selling, they could put the price where they pleased.

Everything depended on the Government, and Gould was far less certain of the Government's actions than he represented to his associates. He alone realized the precarious nature of his undertaking, and understood the necessity for acting quickly before Grant could return to Washington. Fortunately for his plans, the President had gone into the remote mountains of Pennsylvania, and was for the moment thirty miles from a railroad or a telegraph station. As soon as Grant was safely in this retreat, Gould and Fisk redoubled their efforts to bid up the price of gold. Fisk appeared in person on the floor of the Gold Exchange, and Gould's agents moved about offering ever higher prices for the precious metal. They soon raised the price, while rumors multiplied that a corner would be obtained, and that high officials of the Government were in the pool. Merchants and others in need of gold hastened to purchase lest they might not have the coin to meet their needs.

Meanwhile, fearful that those short of gold might reach the President before the corner could be obtained, Gould had again sought Corbin. At Gould's insistence, Corbin wrote his brother-in-law urging him not to interfere in the Wall Street furor. Fisk's most trusted flunkey was selected to carry the letter to Grant, and to wire when the letter was delivered.

When the bearer of this important missive reached Grant's retreat, he found the President and General Porter playing croquet, entirely ignorant of the excitement in New York. Waiting until they had finished the game, the agent gave Porter a note from Gould asking that Corbin's letter be given to Grant. Obligingly, but somewhat puzzled, Porter carried Corbin's letter to the President, and returned to tell the messenger that there was no answer. As Fisk's henchman scurried off to wire his master Grant became suspicious. That night Mrs. Grant set herself to the laborious task of penning a letter to Mrs. Corbin.

Arrived at the telegraph station, the messenger wired his chief: "Letter delivered all right." But in transmission, either through error or through the experimentation of a grammarian, the message was changed to read: "Letter delivered. All right." This, thought Fisk and Gould, was a cryptic message from the President! Instantly they redoubled their efforts, assured at last of the Government's complicity.

But whatever comfort Gould might have obtained from the garbled message was dissipated when he again called on Corbin. To Gould's disgust, Corbin was highly agitated over Mrs. Grant's letter to Mrs. Corbin. "Tell your husband," Julia Grant had written, "that my husband is very much annoyed by your speculations. You must close them as quick as you can." Waving this letter wildly, Corbin insisted that he would have to get out of the market in order that he could truthfully tell the President that he had no interest in the gold speculations. Would Mr. Gould, he asked, give him a check for his interest in the pool, and allow him to tell the truth when he wrote the President? With no respect for this sudden conversion to honesty, Gould promised to send a check for $100,000. Corbin would of course not reveal the contents of Mrs. Grant's letter in New York!

The next day, September 23, Gould went as usual to his office. Locking himself in, he summoned his brokers and gave them orders to sell his holdings, but cautioned them against selling to Fisk. To his partner, Gould made no mention of Mrs. Grant's letter, nor of his own change of policy. Throughout the day Fisk bought heavily, but Gould bought "merely enough to make believe I was still a bull." How much Gould sold or Fisk bought is unknown, but Gould estimated that the conspirators held calls for ten million on the night of September 22, and Fisk claimed that by noon of Friday, September 24, he had bought over sixty millions of dollars.

On Friday, the scene at the Gold Exchange was one of indescribable panic. Merchants and speculators who were short of gold were panic-stricken lest the conspirators should call for delivery. Bankers' and brokers' agents milled about the floor, while the hulking form of Showman Fisk towered over them, bellowing that he would put the price of gold to 200. Soon he had raised it to 145, then it was 150; it seemed to the cringing spectators that the Prince of Erie would make good his boast. Bankruptcy stared them in the face, and for decades men remembered this "Black Friday" as the darkest day in Wall Street history.

While bulls were bringing panic to the bears of Wall Street, President Grant and his entourage returned to Washington. Arriving on September 22, Grant consulted with Fish, possibly on Cuban affairs, and talked with Hoar and Cox on routine matters connected with their departments. Boutwell did not call, and Grant made no effort to see him. The Secretary of the Treasury, however, was keeping a close watch on affairs in New York, and was receiving constant reports from Butterfield in the sub-treasury. Merchants and bears importuned him in a flood of telegrams to order a sale of gold. Instead of doing this, he took steps to see that the speculators did not abuse the credit facilities of the Tenth National Bank.

As Gould explained later, it was comparatively simple to transact a large amount of business with a relatively small amount of cash. By having the Tenth National certify checks of his brokers for amounts exceeding their deposits, a large amount of liquid credit was available. On September 22 and 23, the Tenth National certified $18,000,000 worth of checks in excess of the balances due to the conspiring brokers. Realizing that this abuse of the bank's facilities was going on, Boutwell sent the comptroller of the currency and three expert clerks to New York. Armed with commissions as bank examiners, they took charge of the Tenth National early on the morning of the twenty-third. Even this, however, did not stop the illegal practice, for the officers of the bank secretly certified checks all morning.

On Friday morning insistent wires from Wall Street convinced Boutwell that his bank examiners had failed to stop the panic. Accordingly, he called at the White House to suggest that the Treasury sell gold to protect the business of the country. Grant immediately agreed, and asked Boutwell how much he proposed to sell. "Three millions will be enough to break the combination," said Boutwell. "I think," said the President, "you had better make it five million." Boutwell compromised, and returned to his office to wire Butterfield an order to sell four million in gold and buy a like amount of bonds.

A few minutes before the news of this order arrived, Fisk had raised the price of gold to 160, and was offering to buy any part of five millions for 162. Suddenly the news broke that the Government was selling gold, and within fifteen minutes the price had fallen to 133. As Fisk explained, the gold he was buying so vociferously was "phantom gold"; that from the Treasury was the genuine article. Within the sub-treasury vaults there was an estimated eight millions of gold, and while the four millions offered for sale were but a fraction of Fisk's total purchases, both bulls and bears correctly interpreted the Treasury action as an intention to break the conspiracy. The traders rushed to sell the gold which but a minute before they were so anxious to buy. Pandemonium ensued, and to prevent universal bankruptcy and take stock of the situation, the directors closed the gold room.

The aftermath of the panic was a number of failures. Several brokers who were serving the conspirators went bankrupt, while Gould and others escaped with minor losses. Fisk himself was bankrupt, and repudiated a number of the purchases made in his name. Observers suspected that the conspirators had agreed to let some of their number fail. Confirming the suspicion was the continued partnership of Gould and Fisk, with no apparent rift in their predatory alliance.

When Congress assembled, the House Committee on Banking and Currency undertook an investigation of the gold panic. Although Democrats and anti-Grant politicians were eager to prove that the President and other officials had been implicated in the conspiracy, they were unable to convict Grant of anything more than a pardonable indiscretion in accepting hospitality from Gould and Fisk. In Government circles, only Butterfield, who had already been dismissed, was shown to be implicated, while General Porter and Mrs. Grant were exonerated from any connection with the plotters. Corbin's duplicity was fully demonstrated, but only Gould and Fisk seemed to have been duped by the aged scoundrel.[12]

[12] This account is based on the Garfield Report, *House Documents,* 41st Congress, 2nd session, Number 31. Cf. also, Boutwell, *Sixty Years,* II, 164–182.

WHILE bulls and bears bellowed and growled on Wall Street and momentarily attracted popular attention, the perennial problem of the South gave the Administration much anxiety. Just before Grant left Washington for a summer's outing at Long Branch, the Virginians voted to accept a Radical Constitution. In Virginia as in the remainder of the country, the people were beginning to tire of Reconstruction and its problems. Though General Stoneman's sway had been tactful and mild, they were eager to resume their place in the Union. The military governments in other Southern States had taught a vicarious lesson in favor of peaceable acquiescence, and many of them were intrigued by the prospects of the prosperity to follow their submission. Indeed, Horace Greeley and the *Tribune* held out to all the South the lure of industrial development with its attendant riches. With the new Constitution ratified, Greeley assured Virginia, immigrants would hasten into the State to divide up large plantations, and capital from the North would pour in to develop the natural resources.[1]

As soon as Grant proposed to Congress that the Virginia Constitution be submitted with a separate vote on its proscriptive features, political activity had begun throughout the state. Soon there emerged two parties, one of Radicals headed by the civil Governor, H. H. Wells, and one of Conservatives with General Gilbert C. Walker, a native Virginia Unionist, as its candidate.[2]

Both Walker and Wells declared themselves supporters of Grant's Administration, and each hastened to give assurance that he favored the immediate ratification of the Fifteenth Amendment. Each side represented itself as the "true" Republican Party of the State, and each appealed to Grant and the party leaders for endorsement. The Conservatives were particularly insistent, sending numerous delegations to Washington, and writing appealing letters to the leading party journals. But neither President Grant nor the Republican politicians felt justified in making any partisan commitment and the campaign

[1] New York *Tribune*, May 3, 8, 22, 29, June 14, July 8.
[2] New York *Tribune*, July 10; S. S. Cox, *Three Decades of Federal Legislation*.

proceeded without any intimation from the President as to his preferences.

Aside from the fact that the two forces in Virginia were so evenly divided that no one could predict the outcome of the election, Grant was doubtless restrained from interference by realization that the Republican Party was certain to profit from the success of either faction. The fire-eating Democrats were completely disorganized, and former rebels were making a more or less comfortable adjustment to the new order. Robert E. Lee himself visited Washington early in May, and called by invitation upon his former enemy.

This last meeting of the two heroes of the Civil War is as worthy of record as their former encounter at McLean's house in Appomattox. As there, the two men stood in stern contrast. General Lee was coldly formal and correct; Grant attempted with kindly but fumbling graciousness to put his distinguished guest at ease. He presented John Lothrop Motley and the ever-present Badeau, and the Confederate leader bowed stiffly.

But beneath this exterior punctiliousness of the old régime was hidden the bantling of the new South. General Lee was in Washington to look after some railroad business! The Lords of the Manor were seeking an alliance with the Masters of Capital; Virginia had surrendered!

"You and I, General," said the President, "have had more to do with destroying railroads than building them."

But the Southerner ignored the remark, and went on gravely with the conversation. He favored, he said, submitting the Constitution with a separate vote on disfranchisement, and approved alike of the Conservative Party and the Fifteenth Amendment. As for the Negroes, he could see no "prodigious harm" in permitting them to vote. "All the Southern States should be in harmony with the National Government." [3]

With assurances from so high a quarter that Virginia was indeed on the point of acquiescing in Republican principles, Grant could have seen no necessity for interfering in behalf of Wells.[4] General Canby embarrassed the Conservatives by issuing an order that all members of the Legislature would be required to take the test oath. But the Vir-

[3] New York *Tribune*, May 3; Badeau, *Grant In Peace*, 26–27; Robert E. Lee, *Lee*, 349.
[4] Cf. New York *Tribune*, May 5, 8, 1869.

ginians ignored this threat and elected both Walker and a Democratic-Conservative Legislature. The election was held with a minimum of violence or intimidation and the Negro vote was split between the contestants. Walker's majority was about 20,000, and the disfranchising clauses were overwhelmingly defeated.[5]

Strangely enough, the result in Virginia caused considerable agitation in Radical ranks at the North. When Democratic politicians and newspapers hailed Walker's victory as a Republican defeat, Radical leaders took fright and began to propose that the State remain under military government. In the Cabinet Boutwell expressed himself in violent opposition to the Walker Party, and predicted that if Walker were recognized similar movements in Mississippi and Texas would gain strength. From Tennessee came the report that if Grant supported Walker, Radical control of the State would be lost.

To prevent hostile action and obtain a revocation of Canby's order requiring a test oath of legislators, Walker hastened to Washington to assure the President that he supported the Administration and that the legislature would promptly ratify the Fifteenth Amendment. Outside the ranks of the partisans, Northern sentiment favored accepting the Virginians' pledges in good faith. Greeley editorially rebuked Boutwell for thinking more of party advantage than the triumph of principles, and in the Cabinet more moderate sentiments prevailed. As Secretary Cox wrote to Congressman Garfield, "We can't back out of the result of a fair submission, under authority of Congress and the Administration, of the Constitution of Virginia, and we must now hold Walker up to the work of securing the Fifteenth Amendment, so that we may take a last affectionate farewell of the Reconstruction. With the financial problems growing, another session with the gentleman would be the death of us." [6] With some misgivings, the Administration decided to let Virginia alone, and later in the summer Attorney-General Hoar advised that its legislature should not be required to take the test oath.

This success of the Virginia conservatives inspired conflicting emotions in the hearts of observers. To Northern and Southern Democrats it was a lesson in political manipulation which might well be imitated

[5] New York *Tribune,* June 29, July 7, 8, 1869.
[6] New York *Tribune,* July 12, 13, 16, 21, 23, 27, 1869; Garfield to Cox, July 19, and Cox to Garfield, July 26, 1869, Garfield MSS.

in other unreconstructed States. To Radicals the lesson was equally evident, and they took council to forestall its repetition.

To Radical minds, the situation in Georgia was conclusive proof of the unregenerate condition of the Southern Democrats. A vigorous fight, close organization, and considerable intimidation had resulted in giving Georgia's electoral vote to Seymour, and this had been followed by the expulsion of Negro members from the legislature. To show disapproval of this action Grant appointed a number of Negroes to offices in the State,[7] but the real decision on Georgia's punishment was postponed until Congress met in the winter of 1869–1870. Meanwhile, Georgia improved the opportunity to terrorize the Negroes and carpetbaggers. Accounts of assassinations appeared in Northern papers, while a comparison of election statistics with the voting population told a convincing story of fraud at the polls.[8] Senator Henry Wilson appealed to Grant to take action. To his plea, Grant replied that he had ordered the Secretary of War to investigate. He could not, he said, base any action on mere newspaper reports.[9]

To what extent Grant shared the Radical belief that the result in Virginia would produce a repetition of the Georgia situation must be gathered from his action in regard to Mississippi and Texas. In both States there were Radical and Conservative factions—each claiming to represent the "real" Republican Party. In Texas the Radicals nominated E. J. Davis, and the Conservatives selected Andrew J. Hamilton as candidates for Governor. Each faction desired the President's support and the Conservatives besought Grant to set a late date for the election. He made no reply, and seemed determined to pursue the same impartial course he had followed in Virginia. However, the Radical faction had able support from such leaders as Butler, Boutwell, Sumner, Creswell, and the military governor, General Reynolds. Through them, it approached the Republican National Committee; and Chairman William Clafin decided that the Davis faction in Texas was the true party. On learning of this decision, Grant threw aside his

[7] *National Republican,* April 21, 28, 1869.

[8] New York *Tribune,* May 17, 18, 1869. In 27 counties Grant had more votes than Democratic Governor Bullock received in a preceding State election, when he was elected by 7,047 majority. Twelve counties were listed as being "under terror of a white man's Government." In these counties there were 6,774 whites and 9,530 blacks registered. In the State election Bullock received 6,377 to his opponents 6,755; in the national election, Grant had 311 votes in these counties to 8,590 for Seymour.

[9] Grant Letter Book, May 18, 1869.

cloak of impartiality, and announced to party leaders that he was ready
to make the necessary changes among Federal officeholders in Texas.
On July 15, he issued a proclamation setting the Texas election for
November 30—the date already announced for Mississippi. Throughout the summer Grant replaced Conservatives with Radicals in Texan
postoffices. By November, there was little chance of Democratic or
Conservative success.[10]

In Mississippi clever Conservative leaders hit upon a visionary
scheme for securing Grant's support. Remembering the President's
alleged proclivity for appointing relatives to office, the conservatives
prepared to offer the gubernatorial nomination to Mrs. Grant's brother,
"Judge" Lewis Dent. A delegation went to Washington where Judge
Dent, only a temporary resident of Mississippi, eagerly accepted their
offer and assured them that he could count upon Grant's support.[11]

Unfortunately for the dreams of the Mississippi Democrats, this
dodge was too transparent. During the first month of his Administration Grant had appointed a few relatives and friends to office, and had
been so severely criticized for so doing that he was sensitive on the
subject and by no means inclined to back a Democratic brother-in-law.
Moreover, it was no compliment to Grant's intelligence or integrity to
suppose that he would be misled by so artless a scheme. In the Cabinet,
Boutwell gave vigorous expression to the Radical opinion that the
Administration owed a duty to the party that had elected it. On the
same day, Dent called on Boutwell to ask for Treasury Department
support. To this request Boutwell replied that Treasury officials could
not be used to benefit any political organization, but that none were appointed in Mississippi but those loyal to Republican principles, the
Chicago platform, and the Fifteenth Amendment. Bluntly, the Secretary told Dent to "mind his own business." [12]

Although Dent struggled hard to convince leading Republicans that
the Mississippi Conservatives were loyal to the party, his efforts everywhere met with failure. His nomination, instead of being an earnest of
Conservative adherence to Republican precepts, was condemned as a
trap to ensnare unwary voters. Dent entered the campaign condemning
Boutwell and predicting that the Secretary's "folly" would insure

[10] Charles W. Ramsdell, *Reconstruction in Texas*, 275-276.
[11] New York *Tribune*, July 7, 9, 1869.
[12] *Ibid.*, July 15, 1869.

Republican defeat in both Texas and Mississippi. This attitude did nothing to win over the party leaders. When he approached Sherman for an endorsement, the General of the Army wrote him: "Please allow no publication where my name is used to help you or anybody else in a matter of election." [13] The military Governor, General Adelbert Ames, used all his influence against Dent! After studying the situation, Ames concluded "that the success of the men who took this State from the Union will establish a reign of terror which will cause many of the white Union men, especially Northern men, to leave the State at once." Accordingly, he removed conservative officials and filled their places with the supporters of J. L. Alcorn, the Radical candidate.[14]

But the fatal blow to Dent's chances was given in a letter from his high-placed brother-in-law. "I am so thoroughly satisfied in my own mind," wrote Grant to Dent in response to a personal solicitation, "that the success of the so-called Conservative party in Mississippi would result in the defeat of what I believe to be for the best interest of the State and country, that I have decided to say so to you. . . . I would regret to see you run for an office and be defeated by my act; but, as matters now look, I must throw the weight of my influence in favor of the party opposed to you." Although Dent replied that Grant was spurning those who were coming over to the Republican Party in good faith, his protests were of no avail. On November 30, Alcorn won the governorship by a majority of more than two to one.[15]

To the moderate faction of the Republican Party, the Administration's interference in Southern politics seemed to portend certain disaster. Greeley asserted that the time had come for Southern Republicans to stand on their own feet, and declared that the proscriptive policy of the Radicals was but strengthening the Conservative elements. As Greeley saw it, there were two respects in which the Boutwell policy was defeating the results of the war: immigration of men and money to the South was slowing up, and the eventual ratification of the Fifteenth Amendment was endangered. Instead of proscription for rebels, Greeley urged a policy of universal amnesty. Rebels who accepted the Fifteenth Amendment should be welcomed into the fold. Meantime the editor sent correspondents throughout the South to spy out the land. The

---

[13] Sherman to Louis Dent, September 22, 1869, W. T. Sherman MSS.
[14] Ames to Sherman, August 17, W. T. Sherman MSS.
[15] S. S. Cox, *Three Decades of Federal Legislation*, 529–530; New York *Tribune*, July 15 to December 4, for details of the Mississippi and Texas Campaigns.

correspondents duly reported on the agricultural, mineral, manufacturing, and commercial resources of each section of the South. The conclusion was obvious. If there were political peace in the South, its economic progress—under Northern auspices—might be assured. To Butler, Greeley wrote an open letter asserting that it was poor business to continue to support the Southern Radicals, and insisting that the Northern Republicans should be content with ratification of the Amendment by Mississippi, Texas, and Virginia.[16]

Although this advice disturbed the Radicals, and doubtless encouraged Southern resistance, the party leaders continued their support of the Radical elements. W. E. Chandler wrote Butler in a spirit of resignation: "This Southern business must have its run. We are bound to be overwhelmed by the new rebel combinations in every Southern State. With the New York *Tribune* championing Universal amnesty and all the Chase men and disappointed soreheaded Republicans reëchoing the cry, the Negroes deceived coaxed or bullied and the Rebels a solid phalanx in the combination, there can be but one result. We can only look on and see what they do." [17] But Grant's opportunistic policy saved the day for the Radicals and disarmed the Conservatives. In Virginia he accepted Walker, and instructed Hoar that Canby was not to administer the "iron clad" oath to the legislature.[18] In Mississippi and Texas he followed Boutwell's lead in supporting the Radicals. Yet in this apparent inconsistency there was a consistent undercurrent. Grant was eager to have the Southern problem removed from politics. Though sharing none of Greeley's interest in the economic development of the South, he agreed with the editor in a desire to have the Fifteenth Amendment ratified. Had Texas and Mississippi been allowed to follow Virginia's course, they would doubtless have gone the rest of the way with Georgia, and their reconstruction have been further delayed. With the Amendment ratified, the South would no longer be a sore spot in politics.

Late in November, as it became evident that the Radicals would carry Mississippi and Texas, Grant asked the governor of Nebraska to call a special session of his legislature to act on the Amendment. "I

[16] On immigration to the South, and the profits to Northerners, cf., New York *Tribune*, May 15 to October 30; letter to Butler, November 27; on general policy towards the South, May 24 to October 7, 1869.
[17] W. E. Chandler to Butler, August 10, 1869, Butler MSS.
[18] Grant to Hoar, September 25, 1869, Grant Letter Books.

am induced to write you upon this subject," he explained, ". . . in order that it may no longer remain an open issue, and a subject of agitation before the people." [19]

When Congress met in December, 1869, Grant's wish was well on the way to gratification. In his annual message the President announced that Virginia wanted admission. As for Georgia, he recommended that Congress should see the Negro legislators restored and rebels disqualified under the Fourteenth Amendment. Under this stimulus, Congressmen set to work upon the familiar problem of Reconstruction. The Virginia legislature, eager to return to the Union, had a committee in Washington when the session opened. On December 8th the committee called on Grant to thank him for his recommendations, and went to present their case to the Reconstruction Committee. With realistic scorn, Chairman Butler informed them that he was suspicious of Virginia's protestations of reform. Georgia and Tennessee, he bitterly remembered, had "tricked the Republican Party," and the "true Union people" were determined that the Old Dominion should not imitate their treachery. Before he would consent to Virginia's readmission, the legislature would have to promise that the State Constitution should be faithfully carried out and no trickery attempted. The committee solemnly listened to this lecture on morality, and promised to give assurances of good behavior.[20]

On the lines laid down at this meeting, the admission of Virginia was fought out in Congress. Greeley in the *Tribune* wrote open letters to Butler declaring that his policy was responsible for the loss of Tennessee and Georgia, and Moderates took up his demands that the State be readmitted. But Butler was obdurate, and in January the Reconstruction Committee brought in a bill providing that the legislature should meet, take the test oath of the Fourteenth Amendment, and declare that the Constitution should not be changed to deprive Negroes of the franchise, the rights to hold office, to serve on juries, or to share in the school fund. In the House, Bingham opposed Butler with vigor, and brought in a bill to admit Virginia without conditions. After a week of debate, it passed by a vote of 98 to 95, Butler being absent. In the Senate, Sumner succeeded in committing that body by a close vote to require pledges from Virginia. A conference resulted in the adoption of

[19] Grant to David Butler, November 23, 1869, Grant Letter Books.
[20] New York *Tribune,* December 9, 1869.

the House Committee's conditions. On January 27, 1870, military officials in Richmond turned the State over to Governor Walker; [21] and on February 1, Virginia's Congressmen took their seats.

In the same spirit, and under the same conditions, Mississippi and Texas were restored to the Union. Georgia, however, presented other problems. During the summer, the State Supreme Court decided that the legislators had acted illegally in expelling their colored colleagues, and the Conservatives were now ready to restore the ousted Negroes. But Governor Bullock was not satisfied with such a solution, as the Conservatives would still have a majority. Bolstered by General Terry's reports of Ku Klux outrages, Bullock went to Washington to urge a reassembling of the Georgia legislature, with the members who would not take the test oath of the Fourteenth Amendment excluded. A law to this effect passed Congress on December 22, and two days later Grant ordered the State restored to military rule.[22] Under this order, General Terry and Governor Bullock expelled enough Democratic legislators to give a Republican majority, and the remodeled legislature proceeded to reratify the Fourteenth and to approve the previously neglected Fifteenth Amendments.

In Congress, Butler and his Radical cohorts smiled benignant approval on these proceedings, and rallied in support of a bill to impose the Virginia conditions, and to add a provision that the existing legislature should stay in session for an additional two years. In the House, this too obvious device met bitter opposition from Butler's inveterate enemy, Bingham, and despite Butler's violent attacks and Bullock's active lobby, the measure met defeat. In the Senate the Judiciary Committee reported the measure adversely, and despite Sumner's appeal for the Georgia Unionists and Negroes, the Senate disapproved the scheme. July 15, Grant approved an act restoring Georgia.[23]

On March 30, Grant sent a special message to Congress informing them that enough States had ratified and the Fifteenth Amendment was a part of the Constitution. This amendment was of "grander importance than any other one act . . . from the foundation of free government because it gave rights to millions of citizens whom the Supreme Court, a few years before, had declared to have no rights which a 'white man

[21] New York *Tribune*, December 16, 20, 1869, January 1 to 25, 1870.
[22] W. W. Belknap-W. T. Sherman, December 24, 1869, Richardson, *Messages*, VII, 93.
[23] Accounts of the Georgia debates are given in Oberholtzer, *History of the United States*, III, 263–266; C. M. Thompson, *Reconstruction in Georgia*.

was bound to respect.' " The President appealed to the Negroes to make conscious efforts to fit themselves for their new responsibilities; to Congress he recommended legal enactments to protect the Negroes in their rights. At the insistence of George F. Hoar, he added some sentences commending popular education. Both the Negroes and Congress responded to the presidential advice. The former held a series of serenades, parades, and banquets—showing at least that they had learned the externals of white men's government—and the latter made haste to enact a measure to enforce the Amendment. With much debate but with surprising unanimity, Congress refurbished the machinery of the Fugitive Slave Act to do service in securing the Negro the right to vote. The President was authorized to use the military to enforce the law.

With this outcome, congressional Reconstruction come to an end. The Southern problem, however, was not disposed of by this final admission of Southern Congressmen. The problem of keeping the South in the Republican ranks continued to trouble the Administration.

JAMES SCHOULER, visiting Army Headquarters while Grant was still general, has recorded that he gazed upon the hero of the Civil War with a mingled sense of awe, gratitude, and admiration. But, sighed the historian, "Often as I saw him, during the eight eventful years of his Presidency which followed later, that feeling of affectionate reverence towards him on this earliest occasion failed of renewal. Perhaps the military undress suit which he wore when I then saw him . . . enhanced the atmosphere of distinction. . . . Somehow Grant the General, as first beheld in military dress, appeared to me quite a different person from Grant the President, rigged out at a ball in white tie and black suit, or when seen standing alone in early dusk at the White House gate, with glossy top hat, smoking a fragrant cigar." [1] Like the youthful Schouler, many of Grant's contemporaries and later historians have found a marked difference between Grant the General and Grant the President. Deceived by his change of clothing, such commentators have failed to perceive that Grant followed the same course of development and displayed the same tactics in politics as in war. It was the field which changed, and not the man. Proceeding with tenacity, quick decision, and spasmodic outbursts of superhuman energy, Grant had followed the method of trial and error to ultimate military success. In the field of politics, he utilized these methods to gain political power, however much his tenacity and decisiveness might have obscured the process. In his political career there was much of trial and error, and there were battles which were as disastrous and as costly as Belmont, Cold Harbor, and The Wilderness.

Nowhere is this continuity better illustrated than in the selection of the lieutenants whom Grant drew around him. In the army, his subordinates had been practical men, schooled in warfare and willing to give full coöperation. Sherman, and Sheridan, and Thomas, whose ability and loyalty had been tested, Grant drew to his support, while spurning impractical theorists and political generals like McClernand and Butler. So in politics, he selected men schooled in political warfare—Conkling,

---

[1] James Schouler, *History of the United States,* VII, 144–146.

Morton, and Cameron, and even the once-rejected Butler—to command divisions and fight the battles of his Administration, and cast aside the selfish support which might have been obtained from such theorists as Sumner and Schurz.

At the beginning of his Administration, Grant had no real comprehension of the problem before him. Selected by the people, without a campaign pledge, entering an "unsought" office, he was "untrammeled" in beginning its duties. Into this blissful contemplation of his surroundings, the rejection of Stewart, the troubles in forming his Cabinet, and the Senate's refusal to abandon the Tenure of Office Act, came as sudden shocks. By the end of a summer marked by considerable opposition to the Administration's Reconstruction program and by the unsavory Gould-Fisk episode, Grant must have realized that his office would involve something more than mere idyllic repose in the White House, with "no policy to enforce against the will of the people." After this realization, Grant became a politician.

During the eventful summer of 1869, the people, like Schouler, had obtained a somewhat different view of the silent smoker in "glossy top hat" at the White House gate. Democrats remained on the alert to detect the beginnings of the dire calamities they had prophesied during the campaign, and Moderate Republicans were more hopeful than expectant of a brilliant Administration. "I haven't much worship to bestow on General Grant," wrote one of Garfield's correspondents, "and while I hope his Administration may turn out well, I think its commencement has not been very admirable." [2] Gideon Welles perceived a "general demoralization throughout the country," and freely ventured his opinion that Grant's "instincts are low" and he took "greater pleasure in his stable than in the council room." [3] Ben Butler, not yet in the good graces of the Administration, wrote Sumner that Andrew Johnson had spoken against Grant. "One is called the 'drunken tailor,' and the other the 'drunken tanner.' The two high contending parties entertain the same sentiments toward each other that the masses do towards both." [4] In the autumn of 1869, local elections in Ohio, Pennsylvania, New York, and New Jersey, in all of which the President had refused to interfere, indicated that the Republicans had lost ground during the

[2] J. J. Smith of Oakland to Garfield, August 10, 1869, Garfield MSS.
[3] Welles to Bigelow, October 21, 1869, Bigelow, *Retrospections*, IV, 314–315.
[4] Butler to Sumner, July 3, 1869, Butler MSS.

year. Ohio and Pennsylvania remained in the Republican ranks by a small vote. New Jersey stayed Democratic, and minor offices in New York went to the Democrats.

In his first annual message, Grant assumed a tone of optimism. Counting the nation's blessings, the President named the fertile territory, "equal to the abundant support of 500,000,000 people"; minerals, "sufficient to supply the world for generations"; rich crops; mild climate, freedom, revenue in the nation's Treasury, and a host of new manufactures. These blessings, declared the President, were temporarily in the care of Executive and Congress, each of whom would soon return to the people to give an account of his stewardship. "I earnestly desire that neither you nor I," said Grant as he thus served notice that he would again be a candidate, "may be condemned by a free and enlightened constituency nor by our own consciences."

Passing to the situation before them, the President reiterated his devotion to specie, and recommended that Congress enact laws for a gradual return to coin payments and for stabilization of the value of greenbacks. As one step in this process, Congress should authorize Boutwell to redeem the greenbacks and withdraw them from circulation. The public debt should be refunded at a lower rate of interest. Refunding the debt would make possible a reduction of taxes and the tariff. Grant recommended that the funds Boutwell had purchased since March be placed in the sinking fund. On foreign affairs—a section written by Fish—the President asserted that the Cuban insurrection did not justify a recognition of belligerency. He hoped for a renewal of negotiations relative to the Alabama Claims. Finally, he appealed for relief from the "embarrassment of the Tenure of Office Act." "It could not have been the intention of the framers of the Constitution," said the general, to allow the Senate to frustrate the President's will.[5]

With Grant's message went one from the Secretary of the Treasury. Boutwell reported that he had found a national debt of $2,525,963,260, which he had reduced by $71,903,524 in the nine months of his incumbency. In that time he had purchased over $75,000,000 in bonds at an average premium of more than 16 per cent. Twenty millions of these purchased bonds had been placed in the sinking fund, and the Secretary recommended that Congress authorize him to place the remaining $45,000,000 in the same account. As for the future, Boutwell proposed

[5] Richardson, *Messages*, VII, 28–43.

that specie payments be delayed until most of the 5–20 bonds could be refunded by a new loan of $1,200,000,000 to run for fifteen to thirty years. In order to make the loan successful, taxes should be maintained and the system of revenue collection be made more efficient. Every possible step should also be taken to appreciate the value of the greenbacks.[6]

Although many Congressmen kept a critical eye turned upon the Executive Mansion, there was little in these sane, conservative reports with which to quarrel, and Congress lived up to its campaign pledges in a manner satisfying to the Republican magnates. It approved Boutwell's sales of gold, his placing bonds in the sinking fund, and, with modifications, his scheme for refunding the five-twenty bonds at a lower rate of interest. A new bond issue of $1,500,000,000 was authorized for refunding operations.

The insistent demand for tariff reduction which was sweeping the country met slight favor with the Radical Congressmen. Although Garfield, Allison, and other Moderates representing Western sentiment desired to reduce the war rates, the protectionists of Pennsylvania presented an unshakable front. "Pig Iron" Kelley, most vocal of the Pennsylvania politicians whose ideas were inspired by the manufacturers, spoke frequently; Horace Greeley, long enamoured of Clay's "American System," filled the *Tribune* with editorials; and woolen and manufacturing interests maintained hard-working lobbyists at the National Capital. The Special Commissioner of the Revenue, David A. Wells, who had been converted by experience to low-tariff doctrines, recommended a reduction, but Boutwell and Grant opposed his suggestions, and Protectionist Radicals succeeded in ignoring his report. In the tariff law approved July 14, 1870, pig iron and steel rails were given a slight reduction, raw materials were placed on the free list, and coffee, tea, and sugar were lowered. To relieve the demand for tax reduction, internal revenue duties and the hated income-tax were lowered. Wells was marked for vengeance by the Protectionists. His office expired July 1, and Boutwell refused to recommend an appropriation for its continuance.[7]

Though Grant confined himself in financial matters to a silent but

[6] New York *Tribune*, December 7, 1869.

[7] Rhodes, VI, 275–280, New York *Tribune*, December, 1869 to July 14, 1870, *passim;* Garfield MSS., letters of January 15, 1870, November 1, 1869; Boutwell to Washburne, October 16, 1869, Washburne MSS.; Oberholtzer, II, 276–280.

effective support of Secretary Boutwell, neither his supporters nor critics were willing to overlook his ultimate responsibility. In January, Henry L. Dawes, Chairman of the House Ways and Means Committee, discussed the estimates of expenditures presented by the Treasury. Grant was astonished at his assertions and sought to correct his visitor. Unworried by presidential figures, Dawes made a speech, replete with errors, which alleged that the Administration was asking for $29,000,000 more than the extravagant Johnson had spent in his last year. Upon hearing this speech, Ben Butler saw another chance to ingratiate himself with the President. After learning from Grant that Dawes' figures were incorrect, Butler set himself to castigate his colleague. Though Dawes' speech might well have been interpreted as a simple bid for governmental economy, Butler took care that all should know the Administration felt itself unjustly attacked. His friends spread the report that he had spoken at Grant's request. Although many of Grant's supporters denied that he had sought such a defense, they could not avoid the conclusion that Dawes should not have made the speech. "If a division comes in the Republican ranks, then Dawes and not Butler is responsible." [8]

While the House was investigating the Gold Panic, Senatorial critics found an opportunity to vent their disapproval of the Administration. In October, Grant appointed W. W. Belknap, an unknown Iowan, as Secretary of War,[9] and the Senate, largely because General Sherman endorsed him, was constrained to approve the nomination. Shortly after Congress met, Grant sent the Senate a list of some eight or nine new circuit judges. The selections had been made by Attorney-General Hoar without consulting the Senate leaders. Although the nominees were so eminently fit that the Senate dared not reject them, the slighted Senators ventured a vindictive rebuke to Judge Hoar for his discourtesy. By the same law creating the new circuit judges, another justice had been added to the Supreme Court. A second vacancy occurred early in December when the paretic Justice Grier, reluctantly yielding to the insistence of his colleagues, sent in his resignation. To these two places Grant nominated Attorney-General Hoar and Ex-Secretary

[8] Grant to Butler, January 24, 1870, and Haslow Stearns (Boston) to Butler, February 11, 1870, and Frank E. Howe to Butler, February 24, Butler MSS.
[9] Ibid., October 14, 1869.

Stanton. As if to make their disapproval more evident, the Senate promptly ratified Stanton's appointment, and took Hoar's nomination under advisement. Southern Senators were led to believe that they might obtain a Southerner if they would reject Hoar. Extreme Radicals professed a belief that Hoar was a Conservative. Politicians remembered all too well his unwavering policy of appointments for merit only and his persistent disregard of patronage hunters, while Democrats suddenly recalled that Hoar had approved a sentence of a court martial by which a white man had been hanged for killing a Negro. It must be added that the Attorney-General had been outspoken about political hacks and Senatorial demagogues.[10] During the Christmas recess Grant, convinced that Hoar could not be confirmed, offered to withdraw the nomination, but the Attorney-General refused to escape by such a device. In January, the Senate voted to table the nomination.[11]

Though Hoar offered to resign, the President retained him in his Cabinet position. His rejection, however, had a curious result. Within a week of his appointment Stanton died, and Grant had still two Supreme Court vacancies to fill. On February 7, before the vacancies were filled, the Supreme Court decided the case of *Hepburn vs. Griswold,* with Chase and four associate justices holding that greenbacks were not legal tender. Justice Grier's name was signed to the majority report, though his resignation had become effective before the decision was read. Immediately there arose a demand that Grant appoint friends of the "blood-stained" greenback to the vacant places. Already, without knowing the opinions of the court or inquiring into the monetary predilections of the appointees, Grant and Hoar had determined to nominate Joseph P. Bradley of New Jersey, and William Strong of Pennsylvania. Both were Radicals, railroad attorneys, and lawyers of ripe experience. Because of their corporate connections, the Senate forgot the geographical considerations which it had advanced in opposition to Hoar and promptly accepted them. Before the altered court a new greenback case was promptly argued, and the new judges joined with the former minority in overriding the Hepburn decision. But though this result was welcome to the corporations paying interest on heavy bonded indebtedness, the political employees of those same cor-

[10] New York *Tribune,* December 20, 1869.
[11] *Ibid.,* December 9, 1869, January, 1870.

porations found another opportunity to attack the President. They freely accused him of "packing" the Supreme Court! [12]

But such things as Hoar's rejection, the Gold Report, in which Grant luckily escaped condemnation, and the quarrel over appropriations were but petty morsels. Of far greater importance in diminishing the President's prestige was the proposal to annex Santo Domingo which Grant, in early January, sent to the Senate. Because the project was Grant's alone and might be attacked without endangering the complex political structure, and because it gave some of them the opportunity to soar in idealistic orations to humanitarian altitudes, the vultures pounced upon it with obvious relish.

Had Grant been richer in political experience or gifted with an eye more acute to detect the gathering storm, he would have handled the annexation of Santo Domingo with greater finesse. Unfortunately for his peace of mind, his background had not been political, and he had yet to learn that the will of the people was not the supreme law of the land. A boyhood in Ohio and a manhood on the frontier had brought him into contact with the expansionist sentiment of the times. West Point, predominantly Southern and blatantly aggressive, had instilled patriotism but taught nothing of international comity to the youth who, soon after graduation, had marched without compunction to aid in the conquest of Mexico. Though Seward's purchase of Alaska had evoked ridicule from politicians and newspapers whose support had not been purchased, there was no evidence that "Manifest Destiny" had fallen into disrepute. Through the campaign of 1869 marching "Boys in Blue" had made exuberant declarations that the Stars and Stripes should float over Canada and Mexico.

It is not surprising that Grant lent a willing ear to Colonel J. W. Fabens, who appeared at the White House soon after the inauguration as an emissary from President Baez. Fabens had earlier approached the expansionist Seward with propositions for the annexation of Santo Domingo. For years Seward had been casting covetous glances toward the unhappy island, but the opposition to President Johnson was so great that he dared not carry on negotiations for annexation. Though he visited the island unofficially, he confined his ambitions to an effort to purchase the Danish West Indies. A treaty for this was pending in

[12] New York *Tribune*, February 2, 8, 9, 14, 21, March 10; Oberholtzer, II, 284–286; Rhodes, VI, 258–265.

the Senate when Grant was inaugurated.

For almost as many years as Seward had been proclaiming his credo of the manifest destiny of the United States, two American adventurers, Colonel J. W. Fabens and General William Lewis Cazneau, had been fishing in the troubled waters of Santo Domingo. Cazneau, who had won his military title in the Texan revolution, had turned his attention, almost by accident, to Santo Domingo. In 1854 President Pierce had appointed him a Special Commissioner to the black republic; and from that date, though he soon lost his official position, he had resided on the shores of the Samana Bay, seeking his fortune amid the political vicissitudes of his neighbors. Several times he had suggested that the Dominican Government lease the Bay to the United States; he had supported a project to extend French protection over the island, and had welcomed a Spanish invasion during our Civil War. Through all of these changes he had been obtaining valuable concessions from the contending factions which alternately controlled the government.

Early in the Civil War, J. W. Fabens, an adventurous speculator, became associated with Cazneau. Together they launched in New York several companies designed to speculate in land and resources of Santo Domingo. Though Cazneau professed to the Spanish invaders of Santo Domingo his sympathies with the Confederacy, he was not restrained thereby from accepting, in partnership with Fabens, money from the North for the colonization of American freedmen on the island. Recklessly acquisitive, the two men were unscrupulously alert to gather profit wherever it might be found.

No less unscrupulous was Bonaventura Baez, President of the Dominican Republic. In previous terms as President, when his open corruption brought widespread opposition to his rule, Baez had endeavored to obtain both French annexation and British protection. During the Spanish invasion he had welcomed the invaders, and accepted an honorary commission in the Spanish army. When the revolt bore promise of success, he ostentatiously renounced his Spanish honors, and returned to Santo Domingo to intrigue for the Presidency. But his accession brought no peace to the harassed little nation, for Haiti threatened invasion, and Generals Cabral and Luperçon raised the standard of revolt against the adventurer.

Finding himself without money or arms, and with domestic revolt and foreign invasion on his hands, Baez turned in desperation to the

United States. To an application for a loan, Seward returned a proposal for a lease of Samana Bay and its surrounding fortifications. Though Frederick Seward, the Secretary's son, drew up the treaty, there was no hope of putting it through the American Senate. Failing here, the mulatto despot turned to an English firm, Hartmont and Company, and entered into an onerous contract for floating a Dominican loan on the London market. The loan, on its face, called for some £700,000, of which, deducting commissions, interest, and a bonus to the promoter, the Dominican Government might realize approximately £320,000. The mines, lands, and even the customs duties of Samana were hypothecated for the payment. Despite the terms, the loan moved slowly on the London market, and Baez again found himself without funds. At the instance of Cazneau and Fabens, he decided to offer his country to the United States, and Fabens was dispatched to Washington.

Gaining the ear of President Grant, Fabens gave him glowing accounts of the fertility and resources of Santo Domingo. Grant was interested, and, in July, sent Orville E. Babcock, his private secretary, to Santo Domingo. Armed with instructions to report upon the government and finances, Babcock on July 17, 1869, set sail from New York on the *Tybee*. The vessel was owned by a New York firm trading in Santo Domingo, and as fellow passengers, he found Fabens and Senator Cole of California. Naval vessels were ordered into Dominican waters to obey Babcock's instructions. At the capital, Cazneau and Fabens took charge of Babcock, and a treaty for annexation was soon made. Babcock used his naval support in Baez's interest, and hastened back to the United States with his treaty.

On the first cabinet day after his return, Babcock met the Cabinet members as they assembled at the White House. To each he exhibited specimens of Dominican ores, and expatiated on the value of the country. In the Cabinet room President Grant opened the meeting with the remark: "Babcock has returned as you see, and has brought a treaty of annexation. I suppose it is not formal, as he had no diplomatic powers; but we can easily cure that. We can send back the treaty and have Perry, the consular agent sign it; and as he is an officer of the State Department it would make it all right." Though the President was thus opening the matter for discussion, the Cabinet sat silent. Fish, in whose department the matter lay, said nothing. Finally Cox, whom

Fish had told of Babcock's negotiations, asked if it had been decided that the annexation was desirable. As no one replied to this query, Grant turned to other business. Thereafter the President and Secretary of State handled the Dominican question without consulting the Cabinet.[13]

On November 18, Babcock had returned to Santo Domingo, armed this time with official instructions from Fish to negotiate a treaty of annexation, and possessed of a draft on New York for $100,000, besides arms and ammunition valued at half that amount. The arms and money were to constitute the initial payment for the Republic. The total amount to be used in extinguishing the national debt and redeeming the deflated currency was to be ten times that of the down payment. The Hartmont loan was to be canceled. While the treaty, which was to be submitted to a plebiscite in Santo Domingo, was pending, American naval forces would coöperate with Baez in preserving peace.

With Cazneau and Fabens at his side, Babcock soon reached an agreement with Dan Manuel Gautier, the Dominican Commissioner. Just before the treaty was signed, Baez, as a token of his appreciation for the American, made him an extensive grant of land. Babcock, however, refused the offer.[14] November 29, Babcock signed the treaty of annexation and a convention for the lease of the Bay of Samana. The convention was to be ratified in case the treaty failed.

Late in December the news of the negotiation of the convention leaked out to the newspapers. In the midst of editorial comments, mostly non-committal, Grant and Fish began to prepare the way for the acceptance of the treaty of annexation. Fish wrote to the ministers abroad to prepare them for the news, pointing out that the United States was to obtain the forts, arsenals, custom's houses, and public buildings of the Negro republic for the paltry sum of one and a half million.[15] More enthusiastic over his bargain than the Secretary, Grant planned to send the treaties to the Senate soon after the Christmas recess. But before that, as a good politician, the President took steps to marshal support for his projecct. Shortly after the New Year, Grant mounted

[13] Cf. J. D. Cox, *Atlantic Monthly*, August, 1895; Adams, *Lee at Appomattox*, 130 ff., 220 ff.

[14] Welles says "Cagneau and Fabens who had already procured the majority of the concessions and grants authorized by the Dominican Government . . . were in a better position to provide President Grant's agent with satisfactory compensation than the President of the Dominican Republic." Welles, *Naboth's Vineyard*, I, 378–379.

[15] Fish to Washburne, December 24, 1869, Washburne MSS.

the steps of Senator Sumner's Washington home.

Ushered into the presence of the chairman of the Senate's Foreign Relations Committee, Grant found Sumner in conversation with "Dead Duck" Forney, editor of two Radical newspapers, and Ben:Perley Poore, a newspaper correspondent. Depending upon the journalists to maintain secrecy, the President unfolded the annexation scheme. When Sumner asked questions, Grant promised to send Babcock to furnish fuller information. Finally, as he was preparing to leave, Grant asked the Senator's support for annexation.

"Mr. President, I am an administration man," replied Sumner, "and whatever you do will always find in me the most careful and candid consideration."

With this pledge of support from the powerful Senator, Grant left satisfied that the treaty's ratification was assured.[16]

On January 10, after Congress had reassembled, Grant sent the two Dominican treaties to the Senate. But before his message, the newspapers had published the terms and discussed the project for their readers. Without asserting an open opposition, Republican journals had put in suggestive juxtaposition accounts of the Hartmont loan and the protests of the Dominican Generals Lupercon and Cabral. By the time Grant's message reached them, Senators had already obtained much information which made them suspect that Baez and Grant were offering the United States a Trojan horse. Horace Greeley summed up the prevailing attitude by stating, "We have never known a case where it would be more fitting to make haste with extreme slowness."

As the treaties were referred to Sumner's committee, the newspapers continued to expose the secret workings of Dominican politicians and American entrepreneurs, and to publish protests by Dominicans pointing out the selfish designs of Baez, his violations of the Constitution, his meager hold on power, and the machinations of Cazneau and Fabens. Baltimore guano importers with an interest in the island of Alta Vela were alleged to be lobbying for the treaties. Rural inhabitants of the island were convinced that annexation to the United States would restore them to slavery; Haitians were certain that their portion

[16] These are the words as given by Sumner in his later speech attacking annexation. Boutwell, who came in just as Grant was leaving, asserted that Sumner said, "I expect, Mr. President, to support the measures of your administration." Poore and Forney both understood that Sumner had promised to support annexation. Cf. J. C. B. Davis, *Mr. Fish and the Alabama Claims*, 50–51, citing Forney in Philadelphia *Press*, October 31, 1877; and Poore, *Perley's Reminiscences of Sixty Years in the National Metropolis*, II, 280.

of the island would be seized, and foreign powers were jealous of American expansion.[17]

In the midst of the discussion, some remembered the treaty for the purchase of St. Thomas, and sought to use it to defeat the Santo Domingo scheme. This treaty, negotiated by Seward, had been ratified by the Danish Government, and approved by the island's inhabitants. All of the arguments, strategic and economic, which the supporters of Dominican annexation advanced, applied with equal force to the Danish West Indies, and, in addition, there was no doubt of the Danes' right to dispose of the territory, nor any question of trampling upon the independence of a sovereign people. Though Grant had ignored Seward's treaty, opponents demanded that it should be considered by the Senate.[18]

As the discussion waxed in intensity, the press discovered that American warships were supporting Baez by their presence in Samana Bay, and were priming the mulatto President and his armies with new supplies and American arms.[19] Soon the story of Davis Hatch was being told in the newspapers and discussed in the Senate. Hatch, an American resident in Santo Domingo, had obtained some concessions from the government which conflicted with the holdings of Cazneau and Fabens. When he showed a disposition to oppose annexation and support Cabral against Baez, the Dominican President threw him into prison. At the time of Babcock's visits, the American commercial agent, Perry, was attempting to have Hatch released. But though Perry solicited Babcock's influence, Grant's secretary would have nothing to do with the case and Hatch, who opposed annexation, remained in prison, the State Department showing no interest in him.[20]

For two months, while this discussion waged, the Senate Committee on Foreign Affairs held the Dominican treaties. In the meantime neither Fish nor Grant was idle. To still a possible objection in the House, Fish wrote Butler to point out that the treaty, by acquiring Santo Domingo as a Territory, gave Congress full control.[21] The President, at the same time, used his influence to muster recruits for his cause. On March 14, he sent the Senate a message urging haste lest

[17] New York *Tribune* and New York *Times,* January to March, 1870.
[18] New York *Times,* January 27, 1870; New York *Tribune,* February 2, 1870.
[19] New York *Tribune,* January 14, 1870.
[20] *Ibid.,* March 10, 1870.
[21] Fish to Butler, January 1, 1870, Butler MSS.; Babcock to J. C. B. Davis, February 5, 1870, Davis MSS.

the treaty should not be ratified on time. "The people of Santo Domingo," he said, "have already, so far as their action can go, ratified the treaty, and I express the most earnest wish that you will not permit it to expire by limitation." [22] Then, to hasten Senatorial action, Grant summoned Senators for conference. Morton, Conkling, Wilson, Trumbull, Chandler, Cameron, Carpenter, and Schurz went to the White House singly and in groups to discuss the treaty. Senators known to be in opposition received letters asking them to call, and Grant went to the President's room in the Capitol to lobby. [23]

On March 15, the Foreign Affairs Committee reported the treaty to the Senate. Chairman Sumner, with Schurz, Cameron, Casserly, and Patterson, opposed ratification, while only Morton and Harlan favored it. On the 24th, Sumner opened the debate in executive session. Marshaling the figures of the Harmont loan, and estimating the total indebtedness of the Republic, he prophesied that an enormous expense would result from annexation. Annexation could not end with Santo Domingo; Haiti would be next, and following that all the islands of the West Indies would have to be seized. To the Senate this seemed one of Sumner's most powerful speeches, and predictions that it would defeat the treaty were freely made.

Following Sumner, Morton delivered a vigorous defense, and Schurz replied to Morton. Dominicans, said the German-American, "had no interest in common with the United States." They were a lazy, vicious, and immoral people who could not be improved by contact with American citizens! Carpenter, however, was unable to perceive any reason in Schurz's comments for rejecting the treaty. "The general government," said this Radical whose votes were always on the side of strong measures against the South, "has nothing to do with local affairs," and the character of the Dominican people should not be a bar to their annexation! Senator Cole, who had accompanied Babcock in July, spoke feelingly of Santo Domingo's natural resources. [24]

Newspaper criticisms and Senatorial oratory were alike unable to shake Grant from his determination to annex the Black Republic. In fact, opposition served only to call out that tenacity for which he had been noted during the war. Secure in the knowledge of his own up-

[22] Richardson, *Messages*, VII, 52–53.
[23] New York *Tribune*, March 18, 22, 23, 1870.
[24] *Ibid.*, March 25, 26, 29, 1870.

rightness, he discounted as partisan slanders the suspicions cast on his associates in the negotiations with Santo Domingo. Accustomed to upholding his subordinates when he had selected them himself, he read into their conduct his own patriotic zeal, and considered attacks on them merely efforts to strike at him. When opponents of annexation carried their opposition to the point of abusing him and his subordinates, Grant prepared to fight to the end.

Sumner's supposed deception embittered the President, and when the Senator took the leading rôle in opposing the treaty, Grant singled him out for the full force of his counter-attack. Soon after Sumner's speech, Grant gave an interview to a Boston newspaper. The Dominicans, he said, had made the first proposition for annexation, and had pressed the move upon him. Only after sending confidential messengers to report on the Dominican debt, resources, and potentialities, did he consent to listen to the insular agents. The price agreed upon, continued the President, was sufficient to pay the debt; any further claims against the government would have to be settled by selling the public lands. In answer to the assertion that it would cost untold millions to control the people, the President said he anticipated no difficulty in governing a population of less than two hundred thousand, nearly all of whom were eager to be annexed. Dominican soil was rich, and the country needed American enterprise to develop its resources. American citizens would go to the island to open plantations; they would develop the forests and work the mines. Within a decade the exports would exceed $100,000,000 a year, and in two decades Dominican commerce would equal that of Cuba. Strategically, both to protect the Gulf Coast and the proposed Panama Canal, Santo Domingo, and possibly others of the West Indies, should be annexed.[25]

For two months after the debates began, the Dominican Treaty hung fire in the Senate. During that time, Grant continued to solicit Senators and to appeal to public sentiment. Ben Butler, ever willing to be of service, proposed to annex Santo Domingo by joint resolution, but his motions in the House were defeated.[26] Early in May, a mass-meeting in New York attempted to work up enthusiasm for the treaty. Moses Grinnell, Collector of Customs, called it to order, Charles H. Russell, a merchant interested in the West Indies trade, presided, and

[25] New York *Tribune*, April 6, 1870, quoting Boston *Advertiser*.
[26] New York *Tribune*, April 8, 11, 1870.

Fabens was present. Merchants and politicians made speeches setting forth the value of the island, and appealing to the cupidity and
patriotism of the New Yorkers. One speaker, John Fitch of Nevada,
added a new and interesting reason for annexation. "It is a scientific
theory," said the Nevadan, "that the West India islands were formed
out of the wash of the Mississippi Valley, carried out by the Gulf
Stream and deposited into the reefs of the Bahamas. If this is correct
that soil must have been torn out of the heart of the American Continent, and why should we not follow our property?" Impressed by
such scientific erudition, the meeting adopted resolutions demanding
immediate ratification.[27]

On May 31, Grant sent the Senate a message urging immediate action. The Babcock treaty, despite Grant's former appeal, had expired
by limitation on March 29, but Fish had signed, May 14, a new
agreement with Dominican Commissioners, providing for an extension
of time. That the various objections raised during the discussion had
not been without effect on Grant was shown by the President's willingness to compromise. To the Senators he suggested that they amend
the treaty to limit the obligations of the United States to $1,500,000, to
provide for agents to disburse the money, and to determine the class of
creditors who should be preferred. Such other amendments as the
Senate might wish could also be made. Grant assured the Senators that
the $1,500,000 would pay all claims and leave enough to carry on a
Territorial government until a revenue could be collected. Ratification
of the treaty, continued the President, would redown "to the glory of
the two countries," and would help extirpate slavery. The country was
rich—"capable of supporting a population of 10,000,000 in luxury,"—
and the people "yearn[ed] for the protection of our free institutions
and laws, our progress and civilization. Shall we refuse them?" A
European power stood ready to offer $2,000,000 for Samana Bay alone.
"If refused by us, with what grace can we prevent a foreign power
from attempting to secure the prize?" And concluding, Grant reached
the highest peak of literary eloquence in his inarticulate career:

The acquisition of San Domingo is an adherence to the Monroe "Doctrine"; it is a measure of national protection; it is asserting our just claim to
a controlling influence over the great commercial traffic soon to flow from
east to west by way of the Isthmus of Darien; it is to build up our merchant

[27] New York *Tribune*, May 13, 1870.

marine; it is to furnish new markets for the products of our farms, shops, and manufactories; it is to make slavery insupportable in Cuba and Porto Rico at once and ultimately so in Brazil; it is to settle the unhappy condition of Cuba and end an exterminating conflict; it is to provide honest means of paying our honest debts; without overtaxing the people; it is to furnish our citizens with the necessaries of everyday life at cheaper rates than ever before; and it is, in fine, a rapid stride toward that greatness which the intelligence, industry, and enterprise of the citizens of the United States entitle this country to assume among Nations.

To Fabens, Babcock sent assurances that Grant was willing to secure Santo Domingo under any terms so long as the object was obtained.[28] Grant, himself, wrote letters calculated to help his cause. To Senator Zachariah Chandler he confirmed Sumner's reputed duplicity,[29] and to Senator Nye, who asked how far Babcock had exceeded his instructions, the President replied: ". . . General Babcock did no more than was his duty. . . . [His] conduct throughout meets my entire approval." But Senators in opposition harped upon the Hatch case; and though an investigating committee found Hatch properly confined and exonerated Babcock, the report influenced no one, and served only to deepen popular suspicions of the entire project.[30]

Finally, on the last day of June, as the mounting mercury made Senators anxious to leave the stifling capital, the treaty was brought to a vote. The Senators divided equally, twenty-eight members voting for annexation, and twenty-eight against, while sixteen were either paired or non-committally absent. Of those in favor all were Republicans, and the seven paired for the treaty were of the same party. Nineteen Republicans and nine Democrats were in opposition. Senator Cameron, deserting the majority of the Foreign Affairs Committee, voted for the treaty; the others followed Sumner.[31]

The result was not a surprise to Grant. Two days before, Governor Rutherford B. Hayes, calling at the White House, had found the President in a disappointed and bitter mood. The heat had driven the Grant family to the portico facing the Washington monument. Anxious to get to the coolness of Long Branch, Grant offered the pious hope that the Senate Chamber would prove so hot the Senate would adjourn. The President could not keep from talking of Santo Domingo.

[28] Babcock to Fabens, June 2, 1870, Grant Letter Books.
[29] June 8, Grant Letter Book.
[30] New York *Tribune*, June 9, 14, 27, 1870.
[31] *Ibid.*, July 1, 1870.

Member after member of the Foreign Relations Committee was passed in review in the course of the afternoon. Sumner was a man of "very little practical sense," "puffed up" and "unsound"; Carl Schurz was an "infidel and atheist"—a rebel in Germany, and as bad as Jeff Davis; Casserly was a "bigoted Catholic" whose prejudices made him "unsafe." When Hayes expressed surprise that the Administration wanted annexation, Grant furnished him a glowing description of Santo Domingo's resources. Then, his eyes flashing, the President turned once more to Sumner. Sumner had unjustly attacked Babcock, who had only acted upon orders. The secretary had no opportunity to defend himself against a Senator. "But," said the President, "I can defend myself!" [32]

[32] Rutherford B. Hayes, *Diary and Letters,* V, 111–112, July 1, 1870.

As THE turmoil over Santo Domingo revealed a deep-seated opposition to the Administration, the soldier-President found himself confronted with a situation which called for his best political generalship. By 1870, it was obvious that Democrats would not support the nonpartisan Administration of which Grant had dreamed, and the disaffection in the Republican ranks indicated a need for a thorough political house-cleaning. Friends of the Administration must be drawn together in a cohesive group, and marshaled for attack upon the President's enemies. With characteristic realism—a realism which frequently lost sight of the moral character of his agents—Grant set himself to advance the Republican Party on all fronts. The objective of the campaign was the election of 1872!

As early as February, 1870, Grant had begun to worry over the situation which was developing in Missouri. In 1865 a Constitutional Convention under Radical auspices had remodeled the Constitution to disfranchise rebel sympathizers. Opposition to the test clauses was widespread, and a movement of protest developed. Under the leadership of ex-Senator B. Gratz Brown, and with the powerful support of Senator Carl Schurz, this movement gave promise of splitting the Republicans and giving the State to the Democrats.

Meanwhile, as the reform faction of Missouri Republicans grew in strength, Schurz became more hostile to Grant. At a White House conference, he frankly told Grant that he would not vote for the Santo Domingo treaty, and soon after came out in open opposition to the scheme. At this juncture, Grant looked about for a means of saving Missouri for the Republicans.

An agent lay close at hand in the person of General John McDonald. A resident of Missouri, McDonald had served without credit in the war, and had become a speculator in claims against the Government after its close. In 1869 an Erie train wreck had cost him considerable money, and the speculating general journeyed to Washington to get the President to give him a letter to Fisk and Gould. At the time of McDonald's visit, "Black Friday" had just convulsed the nation, and Grant refused to use his influence with his former friends. However, in the course of the conversation McDonald remarked that he would like a job as supervisor of the revenue. "Well, McDonald," said the President, "I would like to give you one of those places, and if you will accept, all you have to do is to return to St. Louis and procure some recommendations, make your application, and file your papers." The general hastened to follow the President's directions, and received an appointment as Supervisor of Internal Revenue for Arkansas and Missouri.

As the Missouri pot began to boil, Grant summoned McDonald to Washington to discuss the situation. After canvassing the situation, the President, on February 14, 1870, decided to add Missouri to McDonald's territory. McDonald was to move his headquarters to St. Louis, and endeavor to restore order and pacify the Republican factions. Immediately upon the announcement of his appointment, Schurz, Congressman D. P. Dyer, the United States Attorney, and the Federal Marshal at St. Louis wired a protest to Boutwell. "The reputation of this man, and his associates, are such that he can bring no moral support to the Government," said the protesters, who added that McDonald's "qualifications, natural and acquired, are such as render the appointment an unfit one. . . ." But Grant was more interested in political than moral support for the Government, and gave McDonald a free hand. Soon he was unearthing a new source of revenue for Republican campaigns.[1]

With the campaign against Schurz under way, Grant turned to defend himself against Sumner. Though angered to the point where he would have relished a direct attack, the President had sufficient respect for Sumner's strength to prefer a series of flanking movements. Both in Massachusetts and the South the fiery Senator had extensive support, while his long service in the Senate, his important committee assignments, and his pose of exalted idealism had given his opinions undue weight with the country. In Massachusetts the old Abolitionist and Radical elements combined with the cultured society of Back Bay to keep him on a pedestal.

Representing an entirely different element in Massachusetts was Ben Butler. His support came from the masses, an element as Radical in regard to slavery and the South as Sumner's bondholding constitu-

---

[1] John McDonald, *Secrets of the Great Whiskey Ring*, 18–24.

ents, but inclined as well to look with favor on radical economic ideas. Though each element regarded the other with well-founded suspicion, the exigencies of politics had made strange bedfellows of the idealistic and cultured Senator and the demagogic Congressman.

As Sumner's opposition to Santo Domingo alienated the cultured element of Massachusetts, including the powerful Springfield *Republican,* from the Administration, Grant turned to Butler for support. With no personal liking for the blatant Congressman and no sympathy for his economic ideas, the President recognized that Butler possessed an ability in political battles which had been lacking in military campaigns. Aiding the President in this recognition was Butler's consistent record of support from the Tenure of Office bill to the Santo Domingo treaty. For this support, the "hero of Fort Fisher" was about to reap his reward.

Especially obnoxious to Butler and his Massachusetts cohorts was the cultured and genial Attorney-General. Coming from the same social stratum as Sumner, Hoar represented in the Cabinet those elements hostile to Butler's control in Massachusetts. Hoar's relations with the President were particularly pleasant, and he used his influence to secure appointments in Massachusetts for Republicans of the Sumner rather than the Butler contingent. Butler's supporters had no hesitancy in reminding him that "it is important that . . . Hoar should be cleaned out." As one of them wrote, it was "no small matter to get rid of Hoar, but in looking around, it seems to me you can secure such tools, as would give him a devil of a lift, even if he should hit his old seat in falling." [2]

There were ample reasons for displacing Hoar in addition to the opposition which Butler was raising. Two members of the Cabinet, the Minister to England, and the chairman of the powerful Senate Committee on Foreign Relations were all from Massachusetts. Realizing that this fact might possibly embarrass the President, Hoar had frequently offered to resign, but Grant had insisted on his remaining. In the spring of 1870, Butler's cohorts began a concerted movement. A number of Senators protested to the President that Hoar was not treating them with proper consideration in the distribution of patronage, but was making appointments of which they could not approve. Until he was removed, they said, they would not visit the Department

[2] R. G. Usher (Boston) to Butler, April 8, 1870, Butler MSS.

of Justice. Shortly after, Grant solicited a group of Southern leaders to support the Santo Domingo treaty, and these men demanded a place in the Cabinet for a Southerner. Already Grant had determined to fill vacancies "from those States that have been so long without representation," and the demand of the Southerners for Cabinet recognition impelled him to action.[3]

According to Hoar's own account, he had no intimation of his impending dismissal. In almost daily visits to the White House, he had heard nothing whatever of the increasing criticism, and when, on the morning of June 15, a messenger arrived from the President curtly asking for his resignation, the Attorney General was thunderstruck. "I sat for a while wondering what it could mean," said Hoar, "why there had been no warning, no reference to the subject. . . . The impulse was to go at once and ask the reasons for the demand; but self-respect would not permit this, and I said to myself that I must let the matter take its own course, and not even seem disturbed about it." Accordingly, he sent in a resignation "as simple and unvarnished as the request for it had been," and sat contemplating the strange mutations of politics.[4]

Later that day another messenger came from the White House, bearing a note from Grant accepting the resignation and expressing a "high appreciation of the able, patriotic, and devoted manner" in which Hoar had conducted his office. "In no less a degree," declared the President, "do I appreciate the pleasant personal relations which have existed from the beginning of our association." With no comprehension of the depth of the wound he had inflicted upon a personal friend, Grant ended his cordial letter with the hope "that you will carry with you nothing but pleasant recollections of your connection with the present Administration!"[5]

For Hoar's place, Grant sent the Senate the name of Amos T. Akerman, a native of New Hampshire who had lived in Georgia since 1854. An opponent of secession, Akerman had served in the Confederate army, but had joined the Republicans in reconstructing the State. Unknown outside Georgia, and little known inside it, he was a "politi-

[3] Babcock to Thomas L. Kane, (Harrisburg, Pa.) Feb. 10, 1870, Grant Letter Book; Boutwell, Sixty Years, II, 210–211; J. D. Cox, "How Judge Hoar ceased to be Attorney-General," in Atlantic Monthly, August, 1895.
[4] Cox, loc cit.
[5] New York Tribune, June 17, 1870.

cal nobody." Perhaps because he had no enemies, or perhaps because Hoar had so many, Akerman, in Sumner's absence, was promptly and unanimously confirmed.[6]

Everywhere the Cabinet change was received with surprise. Speculations concerning the reasons were rife. Republican newspapers found some explanation in the fact that Boutwell and Hoar came from the same State, but Democratic journals were sure that Grant "wants to reëlected and is determined that there shall be no member of the Cabinet who can become important enough to be thought of as a rival candidate. So the dignity, respectability, and usefulness of the government are sacrificed to a small and ignoble ambition." [7] Butler's constituents smacked their lips at the news, while Sumner's friends were sure Grant had "failed terribly . . . from want of tact and great ignorance." [8] A Federal Judge in Alabama facetiously wrote the Secretary of the Republican National Committee: "Who is Ackerman? Where is Santo Domingo? . . . Are there any more dents to be made in the best government the world ever saw? What is the mean depth of the waters of the bay of Samana?—Let us have peace, and a second term all around." [9]

Before the popular excitement over Hoar's dismissal had died away, President Grant made another shift in his political battalions. In New York the Federal patronage had been fairly well divided between Senators Conkling and Fenton, and the President had made some effort to maintain impartiality between their clashing followers. But as the events of the winter of 1869–70 revealed the division within the party, it was apparent that Conkling was more inclined than Fenton to support the Administration.

The New York Custom House was the richest single bit of patronage in the country. To the horror of the politicians, Collector Grinnell administered it with an eye singly to the revenue. Office-seekers complained that Grinnell appointed men from outside the State to desirable posts; politicians complained over the economy which turned many useless employees out of their sinecure positions; and Congressmen found fault with him when he ignored the recommendations they gave their henchmen. The opposition was brought to a focus in the candi-

[6] Thompson, *Reconstruction in Georgia*, 142; New York *Tribune*, June 17–24.
[7] New York *World*, June 18, 1870.
[8] Edward Cary, *G. W. Curtis*, 213–214.
[9] Rob. Busteed to W. E. Chandler, June 20, 1870, Chandler MSS.

dacy of Thomas Murphy, a "shoddy contractor" during the war, and a skillful politician. Supporting Murphy was Ben Butler, whose restless mind could envision advantages to accrue from meddling in politics outside his own State. Having close political and personal connections with Conkling, Butler soon took "stock in the Murphy movement," and began to call Boutwell's attention to the continuous newspaper criticism of the New York Collector. Employees of the Custom House believed Butler had a spy among them who kept him posted on seizures. "Whether they are released or held, it's an equal subject of complaint. If they are held, it's an outrage; if released, it's a connivance at frauds upon the Revenue." [10]

Soon Grant, anxious about the situation in New York, learned of the complaints against Grinnell, and made up his mind to appoint Murphy in his place. But Fenton, equally anxious, told Boutwell that Murphy could not get four votes in the Senate, and Grant hesitated.[11] To the Fentonites, Murphy's appointment would be a transfer of the Custom House to Tammany control, for Murphy was alleged to be in close connection with the notorious "Boss" Tweed.[12] But Butler and Conkling met to refute Fenton's statements; Conkling, Colonel Frank Howe, and Alonzo B. Cornell dined with the President; [13] and a compromise was agreed upon. Grinnell was to be made Naval Officer, and General Merritt, a Fentonite who held that place, was to be dismissed. On July 1, Grant nominated Murphy for Collector and Grinnell for Naval Officer of the Port of New York.[14]

Immediately a storm of denunciation broke out in New York and in the Senate. A multitude of voices declared that Grant was wrecking the Republican Party in the State, that the nomination was a "fatal mistake," that it would produce a "fight and a general hullabaloo." Murphy was a Tammany Republican, a "bigoted Roman Catholic," and entirely "unworthy of confidence." Fenton and Conkling clashed in the Senate, with Fenton declaring the party doomed unless the nomination were rejected. Conkling, denying that Murphy was his own choice, appealed to the Senate to support the President. Unwilling to offend Grant on an issue of local politics, the Senate, by a vote of 48 to

[10] S. G. Clark to W. E. Chandler, April 25, 1870, Chandler MSS.
[11] E. D. Webster to Butler, May 12, 1870, Butler MSS.
[12] Clark to Chandler, May 28, 1870, Chandler MSS.
[13] New York *Tribune*, May 30, 1870.
[14] *Ibid.*, July 2, 1870; Clark to Chandler, June 7, 1870, Chandler MSS.

3, confirmed the nominations.[15]

Murphy immediately entered on his duties in the Custom House. As he began his work, General Porter wrote him at Grant's direction that "many persons in seeking office may use the President's or my name in urging their claims. I wish to state to you distinctly, at the outset, that no one is authorized to do so. . . . I only hope you will distribute the patronage in such a manner as will help the Administration." [16] Murphy took the hint, and in the next eighteen months replaced 338 employees with political jobseekers who would vote and work for Grant.[17]

With the New York and Massachusetts corps under new commanders, Grant continued his flanking movements against Sumner by dismissing Sumner's friend Motley from the English mission. In England, Motley had made something of a social success, but had gained the enmity of many Americans who received cool receptions at the Embassy. In conducting negotiations with the British ministry, he ignored his instructions from Fish and relied upon the wishes and advice of Senator Sumner. To these causes of dissatisfaction the Minister added a personal affront when he refused to follow Grant's suggestion that he name Secretary Fish's son as a Secretary of Legation. In May, Grant walked about the White House grounds listening to the complaints which Badeau, just returned from London, made of Motley's actions. Finally he told Badeau that Motley's removal had long since been decided on. Only Fish's desire to avoid changes had kept the Minister at his post.[18]

Motley was allowed to retain his position until the day following the rejection of the Santo Domingo treaty. After that, respect for Fish's peace of mind could no longer restrain the irate President. The Secretary was instructed to recall the Minister, and Grant nominated Senator Frelinghuysen for the place. To the surprise of all, the Senate promptly confirmed the new nominee. But Grant's troubles had just begun; Frelinghuysen refused the mission, and Motley, seeking refuge in the Tenure of Office Act, refused to resign. Throughout the summer, the President sought for a suitable Minister to England.

---

[15] New York *Tribune*, July 2–12, 1870; Clark to Chandler, May 31, June 7, 22, 1870, Chandler MSS.

[16] Porter to Murphy, July 13, 1870, Grant Letter Book.

[17] Rhodes, VI, 383, citing D. B. Eaton's Civil Service Report, p. 23.

[18] Badeau, *Grant in Peace*, 205–208, 469–470.

As Grant's second year in the White House began, with the Dominican Treaty doomed to defeat, criticism of appointments growing in
intensity, and party factionalism rampant, the Democrats hastened,
with ill-concealed glee, to point out that the soldier-President was a
failure; while there was a steadily-rising undercurrent of opposition
among independent voters and in the independent press. But Republican observers were not yet convinced that the Administration was declining. "Grant is gaining strength with the country so far as I can
judge," Boutwell wrote to Washburne in April. "This fact may not be
shown by the elections that are now taking place, but I am certain that
were he personally before the people of the country his strength would
be greater than in 1868." [19] Similar opinions were held by the New
York *Tribune*. "General Grant from the beginning of his career has
been persistently assailed in the most shameful manner, and after each
assault his character has shone forth not only untarnished but brighter
than ever," said Greeley, as he recalled how the President had emerged
triumphant from the Gold Panic, and from a current story that General Porter was soliciting subscriptions for a life insurance policy for
his chief. "Judging from the past," the editor concluded, "we should
say that General Grant's enemies are taking the best course to insure
his election for another term." [20] Returning to the theme somewhat
later, Greeley declared the Administration "safe and substantial," for
Grant had kept us out of war with Spain over Cuba, kept peace with
the Indians on the frontier, and pacified the South. "The plain people
believe in him as they believed in Lincoln." [21]

On the Fourth of July the *Tribune* went into patriotic ecstasies over
Boutwell's announcement that in the sixteen months of Grant's Administration the national debt had been reduced $138,104,590, and
the Treasury had a coin balance of more than $78,000,000. Viewing
such evidences of prosperity, Greeley was willing to permit the President to juggle the patronage in an eccentric manner. "There was never
a President who submitted more cheerfully to the adverse action of
Congress," said Greeley half-hopefully; "never was a President more
unpretending, less exacting, more sincerely anxious to execute the laws,
preserve public tranquillity, and discharge fairly and impartially all

[19] Boutwell to Washburne, April 3, 1870, Washburne MSS.
[20] New York *Tribune,* June 30, 1870.
[21] *Ibid.,* June 21, 1870.

the duties of his office. He thinks, as a great many others . . . that a certain set of appointments for New York City will strengthen the public service and promote the triumph of sound political principles. The Senate may possibly disagree with him again; and if it should, the whole matter will pass out of sight as quietly as the Baez treaty. Thank Heaven! We have a President who has no policy to enforce against the will of the people." [22]

With such sentiments ringing in his ears as he left Washington for a summer at Long Branch, the President felt he could ignore the clamor of captious Democrats and the disgruntled warnings of Republicans. Shortly after reaching Long Branch he wrote Badeau that "the winding up of Congress was much more harmonious and satisfactory than the beginning. I think the Republican party stands well before the people. We will lose members of Congress in the Fall elections, no doubt, because it always happens that the party in power are less active at the election intervening between two presidential elections than the party out." [23]

The parvenu society of Long Branch saw but little of the President during the two short months of his retreat from Washington. A trip to St. Louis to look after personal business, several hurried Cabinet meetings in Washington, and frequent excursions into New York and New England gave him little time for leisure. Congressional and State campaigns were under way, and politicians boarded the President's train for consultations, or sought him out in Long Branch to discuss the situation in their bailiwicks. The congressional elections turned largely on the policies of the Administration, and while serious orators of both parties juggled Boutwell's financial figures, mud-slingers furnished a new crop of scandals. The Ku Klux became a staple of Republican oratory, while ingenious Democrats assailed Grant's political appointees, his drunkenness, and his gift-taking proclivities. A new story of how Gould and Fisk had paid the President's subscription to the fund raised for Rawlins' widow went the rounds of press and stump. From Long Branch Grant inspired denials of the charges,[24] and imparted to his visitors some of his own quiet confidence in Republican success.

Much time and thought were given to the selection of a man for the

[22] New York *Tribune*, July 2, 8, 1870.
[23] Badeau, *Grant in Peace*, 470.
[24] J. Russell Young to Butler, September 20, 1870, Butler MSS.

English mission. In July, rumors were current that Fish would resign from the State Department to take Motley's place, but Fish was indispensable. Rumor also named Horace Greeley, and it seems that Grant actually contemplated sending him, but Greeley's own request that the appointment be delayed until after the New York campaign caused Grant to turn elsewhere.[25] Finally, he called Senator Morton of Indiana to Long Branch and offered him the mission. Morton tentatively accepted, pending the outcome of the election in Indiana.[26]

Early in October, before the first State elections, Grant returned to Washington, where he could better feel the pulse of the nation. His arrival brought an increase in the stream of politicians, who sought to explain their local troubles to him. From New York came reports of the State Convention on September 7, where Fenton and Conkling supporters had clashed and Murphy's Custom House contingent had carried the day for the Administration Senator. It was openly proclaimed that Fenton was the President's enemy.[27] From Missouri came McDonald to report that he had begun to bring order out of chaos, and to get claims against the government settled for certain prominent Missourians. To Babcock, but not to Grant, McDonald explained how a ring of Federal officials and local politicians connived at illicit distilling to the profit of all, and to the benefit of the party.[28] From all sides came optimistic promises of success in the elections.

But though Grant and such sycophants as sought his ear were convinced of success, the Republican political managers were not so sure. The Democrats were showing more than the usual energy, funds were coming in slowly, and criticisms of Grant were turning voters from the party. Grant's course on appointments was becoming increasingly hard for Republicans to explain. "We are in the Slough of Despond," wrote the Governor of Massachusetts. "A general in the field makes and unmakes men and everybody submits, but in civil life such a course cannot be successful, and General Grant will soon reach that conclusion. Early in 1869 the cry was for 'no politicians' but the country did not mean 'no brains'!" [29]

As a symptom of the opposition to Grant's venture into political

[25] Whitelaw Reid to J. C. B. Davis, August 26, 1870, Davis MSS.
[26] W. D. Foulke, *Life of Oliver P. Morton*, p. 143 ff.
[27] A. R. Conkling, *Life and Letters of Roscoe Conkling*, 329 ff.
[28] McDonald, *Secrets of the Great Whiskey Ring*, 30–37, 52–54.
[29] Wm. Claflin to W. E. Chandler, Aug. 22, 1870, Chandler MSS.; See also letters from H. D. Cooke, August 30, September 26, and Jay Cooke September 14, to Chandler.

manipulations came the resignation of J. D. Cox from the Interior Department. The day that the President returned from Long Branch the Secretary wrote him—as Cox himself condensed the letter—"My committal to civil service reform seems to be a load you do not wish to carry, so here's my resignation." Astonished by this precipitate action, Grant sent a brief acceptance, following the general lines of his letter to Hoar, but lacking the personal warmth with which he parted company with his Attorney-General.[30]

As soon as news of this resignation was known, speculation about the reasons became epidemic. Reporters hastened to the White House, but Grant refused to divulge the contents of Cox's letter. Cox was equally reticent, and the newspapers were forced to find reasons for themselves. Each solved the mystery in accordance with its own political opinions. Grant hinted that Cox had alleged personal and family reasons for his resignation, while Cox dropped some remarks that led critics to announce that the Secretary had resigned because of civil service reform. Before the discussion was over, both friends and critics of the Administration had decided that Cox had resigned over the infamous McGarrahan claim, a notorious scheme which had been before the government for years. Grant had wanted Congress to pass the McGarrahan claim before he signed the patent, while Cox had wanted to hold hearings in the Department in order to quash the proceedings.

Despite the newspapers, the McGarrahan claim had nothing to do with the resignation. According to Cox, as he confidentially wrote to his friend Garfield, he resigned as a test of Grant's purposes:

I learned immediately after the adjournment of Congress that my Department was to be the object of an attack and was not disappointed when it came. I had made up my mind to fight without flinching, and when I saw symptoms of lack of backing at headquarters to tender my resignation. When I went off on my vacation in September, the pack opened in full cry. Washington dispatches were full of my removal, of the action of the intriguers, &c. I kept quiet until Chandler had been in my Department boasting that I was to be removed, and the President had without consulting me peremptorily revoked my order in regard to clerks' absences, besides doing other things which looked like giving way.[31]

Unfortunately for the credibility of this account, the revocation of Cox's order, which denied clerks time to go home to vote, did not

[30] Cox to Garfield, October 24, 1870, Garfield MSS.; Grant to Cox, October 5, Grant Letter Book.
[31] Cox to Garfield, October 24, 1870, Garfield MSS.

occur until after the Secretary's resignation.[32] But neither Garfield nor the public knew of this discrepancy in dates, and Cox reveled in the martyr's rôle. Garfield wrote his indignant sympathies: "So the worst fears of the country are realized in reference to your resignation. It is a clear case of surrender on the part of the President to the political vermin which infest the government and keep it in a state of perpetual lousiness." The whole affair gave significance to a story that Garfield had heard some months before. According to the Congressman, a treasury agent had told an Ohio editor that "Grant was going to be more of a politician, and that to render his Administration more popular three members of his Cabinet, Cox, Fish, and Akerman, would go before the end of October." Slowly it dawned on Garfield that Grant was playing a hand in the game of politics!

Under Garfield's urgings, Cox published the correspondence relating to his resignation. The publication added little to the public knowledge, but served as more fuel for those critics who were advocating civil service reform. As the discussion continued, Cox came to rationalize his actions still further. By December he had become intensely angry at Grant, had decided that the "real trouble was a lack of understanding of the nature of a Cabinet officer," and was freely speaking of the President's "stolid folly," and accusing him of hypocritical duplicity.[33] Meanwhile, Grant denied to the press that the McGarrahan claim had anything to do with Cox's retirement, and asserted that he had always been a friend of civil service reform. Friends of the President explained that Cox wanted a quarrel and hit upon the civil service as an issue. Perhaps General Sherman estimated the situation more correctly than anyone. Political busybodies, said the General, had wanted trouble and had misrepresented Cox and the President to each other.[34]

In Cox's place Grant put Columbus Delano, a shrewd Ohio politician who would take orders without question and handle the details of his Department in a manner to advance the Administration's interests.

Cox's resignation was timed exactly to have the greatest effect on the congressional elections. The October States voted within less than a week, and the rest of the country within a month of his retirement.

[32] Porter to G. Metcalf (chief clerk, Interior Department), October 19, and Porter to Cox, October 20, 1870, Grant Letter Book; *National Republican*, Nov. 10, 1870.
[33] Cox to Garfield, December 6, Garfield MSS.; cf. also T. C. Smith, *Garfield*, I, 462–465; *National Republican*, November 2, 5, 10; New York *Tribune*, October 6, November 2, 3, 8, 12, 17, December 5; New York *Times*, November 22, 1870.
[34] Garfield to Cox, December 7, 1870, Garfield MSS.

Cox himself realized the significance of his action, and wrote Garfield that "the tremendous uprising of public sentiment proves that my downfall will be the gain of the cause of reform, and when I am free from the trammels of office, of course the truth must be fully known. I wonder if I should keep quiet until after the New York elections?" [35] Garfield advised publication, and Cox gave out his story in time to influence the elections.

When the votes were counted, Republicans found that the criticisms of the Administration had been effective in more than thirty congressional districts. Their two-thirds majority in the House had disappeared, never to return, and while the party still had a working majority of thirty-five, the Administration could no longer count on a majority to support the President's policies. Surveying the evidence of disapproval for his own political appointments, Grant decided to modify his plan of campaign. Turning to his annual message, he incorporated passages recommending civil service examinations!

"The present system does not secure the best men, and often not even fit men for public office," wrote the President as he urged Congress to regulate the selection of Federal employees. "There is no job so embarrassing to the executive departments . . . as finding jobs for constituents." [36]

[35] Cox to Garfield, October 4, 1870, Garfield MSS.
[36] Richardson, *Messages*, VII, 109.

THE elections of 1870, with their disastrous effect on the Republican majorities in Senate and House, were unmistakable evidence that the country disapproved of Grant's Administration. Cox's resignation was but a straw in the gale which Grant's appointments had raised. In New York and Missouri, defections from the Administration assumed threatening proportions. Murphy in New York had been able to control the Republican machine, but had lost the support of Fenton and the reformers. The Democrats carried the State, and Greeley marshaled evidence that there were "Republicans enough in New York for one successful party but not for two." Grant, thought the editor, should not recognize any divisions in the ranks of the party, and should remove no worthy Republican from office simply because he supported Fenton.[1]

In Missouri, the opposition to the Administration took the form of a protest against the Radicals' Southern policy. Fundamentally, the Missouri defection was based upon a dislike for the tariff, which Eastern Republicans regarded as inviolate and Western Democrats were pledging themselves to destroy. Within the State, the weak Democratic party set up an outcry against the disabilities which a Radical Constitution had imposed on ex-Confederates. With this proscription removed, Democrats might carry Missouri and send tariff reformers to Washington. Among Missouri Republicans were many who sympathized with their Democratic neighbors on tariff reform, and many who were emotionally sympathetic with the Democratic demand for "universal amnesty and universal suffrage." Moreover, factionalism beset Missouri's erstwhile Radicals. Schurz had done nothing to endear himself to the Administration, and McDonald was expending the money he mysteriously raised for party services in an effort to defeat the Senator. Perceiving the signs, Schurz headed a schism in the party, and led his "Liberal Republican" cohorts out of McDonald's party and into cooperation with the Democrats. Democrats amended the Constitution to

[1] New York *Tribune*, November 10, 1870.

enfranchise former rebels and a Liberal-Democratic coalition carried the fall elections.

Schurz himself had traveled a long way since he had told Andrew Johnson that Southern white men could not be trusted with the ballot, but his tortuous course was marked by some consistencies: He never for a moment lost sight of the prevailing political winds, and he re- mained loyal to Charles Sumner! From the day when Sumner paid Schurz's insurance premium until the Massachusetts zealot retired from politics, Schurz was his ardent admirer and devoted disciple.

To Eastern Republicans, Schurz's conduct in Missouri savored strongly of treason. Talk of removing him from his committees circu- lated in the press,[2] and Grant, incensed by the course of affairs in Missouri, excoriated his attempt to break up the party. These facts brought Schurz scurrying to Washington, where he told reporters that he was not hostile either to the President or the party. He differed with Grant, who was humanly liable to error, and the people of Missouri had rendered their verdict in his favor, but this should not constitute a reason for reading him out of the party.[3]

So saying, the frightened Senator hastened to the White House to lay his rationalizations before the President. But when he arrived Grant was busily talking Indian affairs with a delegation of Quakers and was unable to see the Missouri renegade.[4] Schurz left the White House, and again sought the reporters to tell them that while the West wanted tariff reform, it would not go into a new party.[5] When this brought no response from the White House, he sent a delegation of Missourians to call on the President. To them, Grant declared that Schurz's actions had lost their State to the Republicans for two years. Evidently unable to draw the nice distinction between disloyalty to the party and disagreement with its chief that Schurz had made, Grant rejected the offers to heal the feud. When Congress opened, Schurz was still busily explaining his apostasy.[6]

That tariff and revenue reform had played a large part in the con- gressional elections must have been evident to the political leaders. In Ohio the greenback heresy was still smouldering, and throughout the

[2] New York *Tribune*, November 12, 1870.
[3] *Ibid.*, November 18, 1870.
[4] *Ibid.*, November 18, 1870.
[5] *Ibid.*, November 21, 1870.
[6] *Ibid.*, November 22, December 1, 8, 16, 21, 1870.

West opposition to Eastern bondholders, national banks, and the high tariff was flaming. All of these were a "swindle in the interest of capital to the injury of labor," [7] wrote one of Butler's correspondents, and everywhere "Labor," looking for more votes in the struggle with "Capital"—the terms were loosely applied—was subscribing to the slogan "Universal Amnesty and Universal Suffrage."

Butler declared that both parties were divided along sectional lines on taxation and tariff, but held out no hopes to the reformers. As Congressmen began to assemble in Washington before the session opened, he saw that the stand-pat Republicans had little sympathy with revenue reform. In public statements, the leaders expressed their belief that there were no pressing questions before the country, and promised a dull session. Senator Sherman thought the government's finances "healthful and prosperous," and dismissed reform with a platitudinous remark that "every person is a reformer, but we must find two that agree on revenue reform." [8] As a matter of party safety, neither the Republican leaders who were satisfied with the finances, nor the President who was feeling his way toward a reëlection, could permit the Congress to discuss financial matters lest the reforming winds should tear them from their political moorings, and make possible a Democratic victory in 1872. Grant and the Conservative leaders drew closer together. "Grant finds himself upon unfamiliar ground without high tone or conscientious aspirations," wrote an unsympathetic observer, "and the determination to be reëlected, solely for his own comfort, leads him to rely upon Cameron, Butler and Forney. . . ." More and more, he came to depend on these practical politicians and to despise the cant of the Schurz type of reformer.[9]

With the solid backing of such practical politicians as Conkling, Morton, Chandler, Carpenter, and Butler, Grant adopted the oldest and most effective subterfuge known to politicians—he turned to foreign affairs in the hope of distracting attention from domestic issues. Throughout the winter of 1870–71 and far into the next summer, the Administration labored to extract prestige from Santo Domingo and the settlement of the Alabama Claims.

Appropriately enough, the first evidence of the Administration's

[7] A. Haines (Eaton, Ohio) to Butler, November 19, 1870, Butler MSS.
[8] New York *Tribune,* November 23, 24, December 1, 2, 4, 1870.
[9] Gustavus Vasa Fox (Lowell) to Welles, December 1, 1870, Welles MSS.

change of emphasis came from Ben Butler. Hardly had the votes of 1870 been counted when he demanded that the government take a bold stand with Great Britain. Frankly avowing his purpose of constructing a popular platform for 1872, Butler went the full length of Anglophobia in defending the rights of New England fishermen and demanding a portion of Canada in settlement of the Alabama Claims.[10]

After this, rumors regarding the policy of the Administration flew thick and fast about Washington. The Democratic victory in Indiana had made it impossible for Morton to take Motley's office. "A bitter copperhead would take Morton's place in the Senate if he went to London," moaned Grant as he sought for a new Minister.[11] Newspapers nominated Creswell, Conkling, Orth of Indiana, and others in succession, but none seemed to meet presidential approval.[12] Meantime, the Washington *National Republican*, the Administration's local organ, expressed the opinion that England should give satisfaction for the "grave wrongs" she had done in "deliberately" inflicting injuries on American commerce and prolonging the rebellion. "The President," declared an inspired editorial, "relies upon the sense of justice of the English Ministry and English masses, believing they will seize the first opportunity to close the matter." [13] Simultaneously, Grant summoned Butler to the White House to confer with him on his annual message.[14] Evidently, the President was going to follow Butler's advice to save the party by foreign affairs!

In his message to Congress, Grant gave ample evidence that he was aware of the rising tide of "reform" agitation, and that he preferred to settle other and less dangerous questions. As for the South, the President ignored the movement for universal amnesty and called attention to the denial of a "free exercise of the franchise" in some of the lately rebellious States. Only Georgia remained without congressional representation, and she would be ready for restoration by the beginning of the year. On currency, the President pointed with pride to the decline in the price of gold to an average for the year of 115, and urged legislation which would put the greenbacks at par.

[10] New York *Tribune*, November 10, 1870; *National Republican*, November 11, 1870.
[11] Badeau, *Grant in Peace*, 472.
[12] New York *Tribune*, October 24, November 11, 30, 1870.
[13] *National Republican*, November 22, 1870.
[14] Grant to Butler, November 21, 1870, Butler MSS.; New York *Tribune*, November 22, 1870.

The center of interest to the President, however, was not in past achievements or future reforms. Hastening through them, Grant took up the failure of Dominican annexation in the previous session. "I was thoroughly convinced then that the best interests of this country, commercially and materially, demanded its ratification," he asserted. "Time has only confirmed me in this view." Moreover, he had now come to believe that "the moment it is known that the United States have entirely abandoned the project . . . a free port will be negotiated for by European nations . . . and a large commercial city will spring up to which we will be tributary. . . . Then will be seen the folly of rejecting so great a prize. . . ." As in his message of the previous session, Grant was still sure that ten million people might find sustenance on the island. "So convinced am I of the advantages to flow from the acquisition of Santo Domingo, and of the disadvantages—I might almost say calamities—to flow from non-acquisition, that I believe the subject has only to be investigated to be approved." Since he saw no chance of getting annexation by treaty, the President cited Texas and proposed annexation by joint resolution.

Turning from Santo Domingo, the President regretted that "no conclusion has been reached for the adjustment of the claims against Great Britain." Bearing the unmistakable hand of the moderate Fish, this portion of the message had less bombast than the Santo Domingo paragraphs, but presented the issue with clarity. "The Cabinet of London," said Fish through Grant, ". . . does not appear to be willing to concede that Her Majesty's Government was guilty of any negligence, or did or permitted any act during the war by which the United States has just cause of complaint. Our firm and unalterable convictions are directly the reverse." Accordingly, the President recommended that Congress appoint a claims commission to gather data in proof of the American contentions. To balance this veiled threat, the President declared that the United States would "welcome a change of attitude by Great Britain." [15]

As the clerk read the paragraphs on Santo Domingo, a scowl spread over the harsh features of Charles Sumner, and the galleries noted a vigorous gesture of dissent at the President's proposal for annexation by joint resolution. The sable Haitian Minister read Grant's remarks on acquiring the "island" of Santo Domingo, and made a choleric rush

[15] New York *Tribune*, December 6, 1870; *National Republican*, December 6, 8, 1870.

first to the State Department, and thence to the library of Senator Sumner. In the House Ben Butler announced his intention of sponsoring the scheme, but before he got an opportunity, Sumner. leaped into the limelight by asking the Senate to call on Grant for all information in his possession relating to the annexation treaty and political conditions in the black republic.[16]

As Sumner thus signified his intention of taking up his opposition where he had left off in the previous session, Grant and Fish counseled together to force action in the proper direction. As a result, Grant wrote N. P. Banks to have resolutions looking to the appointment of a commission introduced simultaneously in both Houses of Congress. "I shall be glad to learn this evening," read the President's peremptory command, "that resolutions have been introduced. . . ." [17] That evening he learned that Morton in the Senate and Butler in the House had proposed identical bills to create a commission to investigate the Dominican question.

With these bills before it, the Senate went into executive session, and for a week the curious could only weigh the rumors which emanated from the chamber. They told how Sumner, marshaling his forces, and supported for almost the only time in his career by the Democrats, had attacked Babcock and exposed the gigantic frauds back of the annexation scheme. Against Sumner and his reform and Democratic allies, Senator Morton led the cohorts of the Administration. Nor was there any lack of tale-bearing Senators who carried reports to the White House, where they refueled Grant's hatred of Sumner. To groups of visitors the President loudly denounced his adversary, and was soon telling how Sumner had vilified him in executive session, had abused him in street cars, and had attacked him in interviews.

As busybodies carried these stories back and forth between the White House and Sumner's office, the Senator carried his fight to the floor of the Senate. On the night of December 21, as the first storm of winter blew about the lighted Capitol dome, he rose to launch an attack which for bitter personalities has been surpassed only once in the annals of Senatorial forensics. That once was in the "Crime against Kansas" speech which won for its author a brutal caning from an outraged Congressman. This speech was to win for the same author the

[16] New York *Tribune*, December 9, 10, 1870.
[17] Grant to Banks, December 12, 1870, Grant Letter Books.

loss of both political power and the political prestige which was the substance of his life.

Beginning by reading a clipping from the Washington *Patriot*, Sumner asserted that he wished to make a personal statement. The *Patriot* had referred to an effort which had been made to effect a reconciliation between Sumner and the President. Grant had rejected the overture because of Sumner's attacks, and was reported as saying that were it not for his office he would demand personal satisfaction from the vituperative Senator. To the astonishment of floor and galleries, Sumner denied that he had ever alluded to the President in executive session in any but a respectful manner. He challenged any person to say that he had ever charged Grant with personal dishonesty.

Having thus cleared the ground of false representations, Sumner proceeded to repeat his objections to Dominican annexation. The whole course of the Administration was wrong. The Government of the United States had been deceived by Baez and other "political jockeys" into a dance of death. Were the United States to annex Santo Domingo, it would be committed to the annexation of all the West Indies. Baez himself was using the naval forces of the United States to maintain himself in a position where he might betray his people. The sale of the country would be Baez' personal sale, and the black Iscariot himself planned to slip off to Europe to enjoy the proceeds of his duplicity. None of this would be possible were it not for the illegal use of the American navy.

Turning at last to Vice President Colfax, Sumner begged him to go to the White House and tell Grant "not to follow in the footsteps of Pierce, Buchanan, and Andrew Johnson . . . not to oppress a humble and weak people, not to exercise war powers without the consent of Congress, not to forget there is a grandeur in justice and a peace beyond anything in war!"

Immediately, Morton arose to answer Sumner. "A series of assaults," began the Administration's handy-man, "have been made on the President from time to time since his inauguration. Scarcely one has subsided before another begins. . . . But, sir, one by one those assaults have failed, utterly failed; they have been exposed, and have become contemptible to the people of this country. The arrows of calumny have fallen harmless at his feet. He has always managed to fall on his feet." With that, Morton took up Sumner's attack point by point.

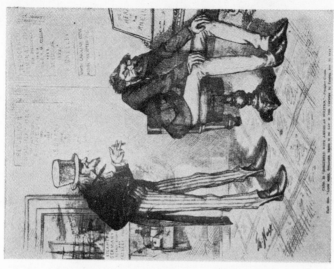

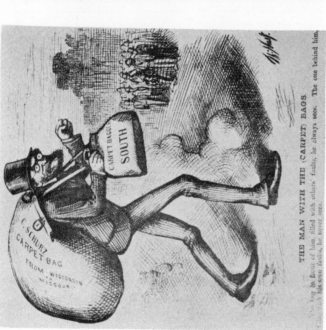

THE MAN WITH THE CARPET BAGS

... long in front of him, filled with others faults, he always sees. The one behind him,
... his own faults, he never sees.

NAST SATIRIZES SCHURZ, 1872

Sumner's assault was "unprovoked and indefensible." Answering Sumner's charge that Grant had tried to remove the Massachusetts Senator from his Chairmanship of the Committee on Foreign Affairs, Morton denied that any such move had been made. As for Santo Domingo, Morton declared that acquisition was inevitable. "Mr. President, the annexation of Santo Domingo will come. I prophesy here tonight that it will come. It may not come in the time of General Grant, or in my time, but I believe it is destined to come, and with it, too, the annexation of Cuba and Porto Rico." John Quincy Adams, said Morton, had advocated Cuban annexation as early as 1823. It was the manifest destiny of the United States to control the West Indies.[18]

For sixteen hours, while the storm raged outside, another storm raged inside the Senate chamber. To the delight of the Democrats, Republicans forgot both dignity and party loyalty as they assailed each other. Schurz allied himself with Sumner, and Conkling and Nye took up the cudgels on Morton's side. All through the night the battle raged—"Santo Domingo will cost us dearly in gas," observed a woman in the galleries—and in the morning, Morton's resolutions were passed and the Senators sought their beds. Schuyler Colfax, however, stopped at the White House to report on the night's struggle and congratulate his chief on the victory.

All eyes now turned to the discussions in the House. Grant hoped for a two-thirds' majority for his measure, and preliminary canvasses showed that the Administration's opponents could not stop the proposal. Yet despite the certainty of defeat, Generals Logan and Farnsworth announced their opposition and their intention to delay action until the session was over. Together with the Democratic minority, these men attempted to delay action by desultory motions and amendments. The Administration's strength, marshaled by Banks and Butler, however, beat down all opposition. On January 9, the resolution passed 121 to 62—one short of the desired two-thirds.

Even before the resolutions were discussed in the House, the Navy Department made ready the frigate *Tennessee* to transport the Commissioners from New York to Santo Domingo. As soon as the House acted, Grant appointed three men under the chairmanship of ex-Senator Ben Wade. In addition, the President invited several unofficial

---

[18] New York *Tribune*, December 21, 22, 23, 1870; Foulke, *Morton*, 157–161; *National Republican*, December 21–23, 1870.

observers, and these, with secretaries, stenographers, and newspaper reporters brought the total to twenty-four members.[19] The respectability of the Commission, thought Hamilton Fish, would "disarm criticism & inspire everyone with confidence, & present the most emphatic rebuke to those who attempted to question the sincerity of the President's motive or the integrity of those who were entrusted with his confidence." [20] Armed with letters from Grant to Baez, the Commission sailed from New York in January 17, 1871.

How much of real zeal for annexation was back of the Administration's insistence on this Commission is impossible to determine. Grant himself was doubtless stung to greater earnestness by Sumner's opposition than he would have been had the Massachusetts Senator forgone his personal attacks. No especial warmth for the project, however, can be detected in the ranks of the Administration's supporters. Men voted for it to escape the President's ire and the weight of his power against them. Yet the debate upon the Dominican Commission served two purposes which could not have escaped the party leaders; it directed popular interest from questions of revenue reform, and it cemented the ranks of the thick-and-thin supporters of the party. Dozens of Senators voted for investigation who would have opposed annexation, and the Administration had shown a strength more apparent than real. Cautious men marveled at Grant's intrepidity— "The President must feel himself possessed of vast reserves of strength if he thinks he can stand many more such quarrels"; but on the whole, the party leaders must have thought the game was worth the candle. "We are getting on pretty well," wrote Fish,—"The President has been wonderfully fortunate. . . ." [21]

In the meantime, other and vastly more important negotiations were progressing secretly in London and Washington. The veiled threats of

[19] Bishop Mathew Simpson of the Methodist Church, and ex-Congressman William E. Dodge of New York were first selected. Both declined—not through any lack of sympathy with the cause—and the President selected President Andrew D. White of Cornell, and Dr. S. G. Howe in their stead. Allan G. Burton of Kentucky was Secretary, and, at the instigation of Fabens, who had watched the proceedings from behind the scenes, Professor William P. Blake, a Fabens employee, was named Geologist. Franz Sigel and Frederick Douglas were the leading unofficial observers.

[20] New York *Tribune*, January 1–17, 1871; Fish to Washburne, January 17, 1871, Washburne MSS.; Grant to Sigel, January 10, 14, Grant to Douglas, January 11, Grant to Baez, January 15, 1871, Grant Letter Books.

[21] Garfield to Cox, December 23, 1870, and to D. A. Wells, January 9, 1871, Garfield MSS.; Sumner to Whitelaw Reid, Royal Cortissoz, the *Life of Whitelaw Reid*, I, 191; *Tribune*, January 2, 1871; Fish to Washburne, January 17, 1871, Washburne MSS.

Grant's message, appearing in the London newspapers on December 6, occasioned indignation in Britain. The London *Times* declared Grant's tone "menacing" and asserted that his words held out no hope for a friendly settlement. The *News* agreed that unless he changed his tone he would bequeath the question to his successor. But British papers were accustomed to the American sport of twisting the lion's tail, and assured Her Majesty's subjects that Grant's words were primarily designed for political effect at home. However, the message came at the psychological moment to induce action from the British Government. For two years, ever since the rejection of the Johnson-Clarendon agreement, it had realized that the Grant Administration had no especial desire to push the settlement of the Alabama question. In July, 1869, Grant wrote Badeau that "it is not half so important that the Alabama Claims should be settled as it is that when they are settled it should be in terms creditable to this nation. I do not see that any harm is to arise from the matter standing in an unsettled state." [22] Englishmen realized, as an American in close touch with them declared, that Grant "would not care if nothing more were ever heard or said of the Alabama Claims, if he were sure of not being called to account by his neglect of them by the Hybernian patriots. . . . We have financial and political troubles enough at home to keep our rulers well occupied for a few years without going abroad to borrow trouble." [23] But that was in 1869, and before political troubles took such a turn that a foreign diversion was necessary.

When Grant's message came, the English were watching with interest the siege of Paris by the Prussian troops, and were affected by a war-scare resulting from Russian abrogation of the Black Sea clauses of the treaty of 1856. The international situation was complicated and the future uncertain. Realizing that times were right for fishing in troubled seas, the Russian Minister had suggested that circumstances were propitious for pressing the Alabama Claims. Without paying any attention to him, Fish reopened the question with Sir Edward Thornton.

Complicating the situation between England and the United States were the problems of the Fenians and the Newfoundland fisheries. Both were of as long standing as the Alabama Claims, and since they

---

[22] Badeau, *Grant in Peace*, 468.
[23] Bigelow, *Retrospections*, IV, 321–323.

affected relations with Canada, were considerably more irritating. Fenian movements against Canada were constantly plotted from Irish centers near the international border, and clashes between rival fishermen along the coast contributed to mutual suspicion. Moreover, the American people and the Administration entertained the idea of the eventual annexation of Canada. Grant expected it, and Fish suggested that a plebiscite be held in portions of the Dominion. This, both Englishmen and Canadians agreed, was "simply a blackguard business," [24] and Thornton eventually told the American Secretary that his government could not associate the Alabama Claims and annexation. Finally Fish ceased to mention his expansionist hopes, and began to discuss with Thornton the other matters at issue between the two countries. Thornton frankly inquired what the United States wanted. Fish replied that an expression of regret, and a declaration of principles of international law to govern the future, would satisfy the American people. It was agreed that the British Government should pay the claims arising out of the actual damage done by the Confederate cruisers, and Fish intimated that the Administration had no intention of pressing Sumner's "indirect damages" claims. Thornton immediately wired this suggestion to London, where, even before Grant's message, the Cabinet had considered the newest development.

Despite this mutual willingness to reach some agreement, the Governments could probably not have arrived at an accord without the activity of Sir John Rose, the Canadian agent in London. Long interested in Canadian-American relations, Rose had risen in Canadian politics while he combined a financial with a semi-diplomatic career in a manner that made him especially concerned with the settlement of the disputed questions. As Her Majesty's Commissioner to settle claims growing out of the Oregon treaty of 1846, he had met Caleb Cushing, exercising a similar function for the United States. Cushing, intimate friend and adviser of Fish, had introduced Rose to the Secretary, and the two had had many conversations over the fisheries and reciprocal trade relations. Moreover, Rose's interest in the Canadian Pacific Railroad and connection with Baring Brothers had brought him into contact with Jay Cooke and Company, and given him wide acquaintance

---

[24] Sir John McDonald to John Rose, December 18, 1869. Cited in "Sir John Rose and the Beginnings of the Canadian High Commissionership," *Canadian Historical Review*, March 1931, p. 31.

in New York financial circles. At the moment, the Canadian agent was interested in a syndicate to float Boutwell's last issue of bonds on the English market.

In England it was generally understood that Rose represented Fish's opinions better than did Motley, and the Ministry were accustomed to look to him for advice on both Canadian and American affairs. When Thornton reported Fish's conversations, and when Grant's message had been read, Lord Granville, with Gladstone's consent, determined to send Rose to Washington to prepare for a settlement. Rose immediately wrote Fish that the "Cabinet is disposed to enter on negotiations," and prepared to follow his letter to Washington immediately.

Meanwhile, in Washington, plans were being pushed to add a diplomatic star to the Administration's crown. Less than a week after the meeting of Congress, Grant nominated General Robert C. Schenck, a "lame-duck" Congressman from Ohio, as Minister to England. Oldest member of the House in point of service, Schenck had long been on the Ways and Means committee. As a strong tariff supporter, he had drawn the fire of Brinkerhoff and the American Free Trade League in the 1870 campaign, and his resultant defeat had given him claims on the pro-tariff Administration.[25] In contrast with Motley and the other authors who had served in the past, Schenck was a practical politician who could be expected to represent a "more American" point of view. Schenck's activities as a poker player constitute his greatest claim to fame. He introduced the game to English society, and eventually wrote a manual which caused him to be referred to as "our literary ambassador." Perhaps Grant, himself no mean poker player and at the time engaged in a stupendous game of bluff, recognized in the Ohio Congressman the essential attributes of a diplomat!

Before accepting the appointment, Schenck consulted Henry Cooke, manager of Jay Cooke's Washington branch. The General had already accepted a position on Jay Cooke's Northern Pacific legal staff, and Henry promised to hold the place open until his return from England. "Now I need not enter into an argument with you," wrote Henry to Jay, "to show how desirable it would be to us, to our railroad enterprises and to our London house to have a personal friend representing the

[25] New York *Tribune*, September 7, 1870; R. Brinkerhoff, *Recollections of a Life Time*, 196–197.

government at London." [26] Thus confirmed by the financial powers, Schenck allowed his nomination to be sent to the Senate.

On January 9th, before Schenck had left for London, Rose arrived in Washington. That night he dined with Fish, and though technically authorized to deal only with the fisheries, the two men mutually took up all questions. Next day Rose communicated with the British Foreign office, and by the 11th, his conversations had progressed to such a point that he handed the Secretary a "Confidential Memorandum" embodying the principles upon which the British Government would negotiate. These principles were acceptable not only to Fish but also to Grant, Conkling, and Schenck. The latter two, however, advised Fish to appeal for Sumner's good will.

At the moment, Sumner had no good will. Despite his most strenuous opposition, he had seen Grant's Santo Domingo Commission approved, and the annexation plan supposed to have scored a success. Moreover, while Rose and Fish were secretly reaching an agreement, Congress and the country were reading the final correspondence between the deposed Motley and the Secretary of State. In the last days of December, Motley sent a letter to the State Department. This dispatch, Sumner told the newspaper correspondents, would be an official insult to Grant's secretary. To make the insult public, the irate Senator introduced resolutions calling upon Grant to furnish the correspondence.[27] The letter, duly sent to the Senate on the day Rose arrived in Washington, did nothing to advance Sumner's cause. Stung by the charges against him, Motley forgot both a historian's objectivity and a diplomat's tact in writing to his chief. On the other hand, Fish, completely master of the situation, coldly answered the minister's charges with logical argument. "As a fencer in words the rather warm-tempered historian is hardly a match for the cool Secretary," observed the New York *Times* editorially,[28] and Whitelaw Reid in the *Tribune* agreed that "the controversy is decidedly with Fish." Moreover, Reid read between the lines and concluded that Motley's appointment was "pushed upon" Grant. "Those who seek appointments at the President's hands," he thought, "are very likely to damage their prospects by undue solicitation." [29] Next day Sumner, again driven upon the de-

[26] Oberholtzer, *Jay Cooke*, II, 229.
[27] New York *Tribune*, December 29, 1870.
[28] N. Y. *Times*, January 11, 1871.
[29] N. Y. *Tribune*, January 11, 1871.

fensive, wrote Reid denying that he had brought excessive pressure upon Grant. "I never spoke to the President on the subject but twice . . ." declared the Senator.[30] But such private explanations failed to persuade the country that either Sumner or Motley was right. Garfield, who was certainly not in sympathy with the Administration, was "reluctantly forced to the conclusion that Motley was a failure as a diplomatic officer. He . . . had Sumner's form of the Alabama Claims so fully fixed in his mind that he could not act consistently in the Administration's view of the case." [31]

On Sunday, January 15, when Fish called on Sumner to consult with him on Rose's memorandum, the Senator was in no mood to receive any Administration proposal calmly. As the Secretary read Rose's suggestions, Sumner's wrath arose, and, he began to declaim against Great Britain. In the midst of the oration, Boutwell, who regularly visited the Senator on Sunday mornings, entered to double the audience. When Sumner demanded that the British should agree, in advance of a treaty, upon what concessions they would make, Boutwell volunteered the information that they would concede the American demands on the fisheries. This the Secretary had learned from the New York bankers; but the concession would be made only if the island of San Juan, at the far western boundary of the Oregon country, be permitted to remain in English hands. But Republicans on the Pacific Coast were interested in the island, and Fish informed Boutwell that this could not be granted. After this interruption, Sumner resumed his monologue, with Fish attempting to bring him to a definite statement of his opinion on the Rose Memorandum. Finally, the Secretary, failing to elicit a rational response, demanded to know, in his official capacity, what were the opinions and the advice of the Chairman of the Senate Committee on Foreign Relations? Thus forced to answer, the Senator sought delay. It was a matter that required much reflection, and he would have to consider it for a few days.

Fish went in the evening to consult Morton at the National Hotel. Again the Secretary read Rose's memorandum, this time to a willing and coöperative auditor, and the two men canvassed the situation. Morton believed that the Alabama question should be settled "and the sooner the better." He believed that the country would accept the

[30] Cortissoz, *Reid*, I, 193.
[31] Garfield to Hinsdale, January 16, 1871, Garfield MSS.

British offer, and that a verbal circumlocution would satisfy the people on Sumner's "consequential damages." The Senate, moreover, would accept such a treaty. The only hitch that Morton saw was in the Foreign Relations Committee. There Sumner would oppose, and Casserly, Schurz, and Patterson would follow him. But Fish had already been to Patterson and secured his approval. Then, said Morton, "that gives a majority of the committee, and there can be no doubt of the Senate."

By Tuesday, Sumner had formulated his pontifical opinion on the Rose Memorandum and sent it to Fish. In two short paragraphs, the Senator served warning that he would not coöperate with the Administration. "The idea of Sir John Rose is that all questions and causes of irritation between England and the United States should be removed absolutely and forever . . ." said the Senator. "Nothing could be better than this initial idea. It should be the starting point. . . . The greatest trouble, if not peril, being a constant source of anxiety and disturbance, is from Fenianism, which is excited by the British flag in Canada. Therefore the withdrawal of the British flag cannot be abandoned as a condition or a preliminary of such settlement as is now proposed. To make the settlement complete, the withdrawal should be from this hemisphere, including provinces and islands." [32]

For a week after he received Sumner's uncompromising statement, the Secretary of State busied himself in circumventing the Foreign Relations Chairman. First he carried Sumner's note to the White House, where Grant, his whole military nature aroused by this insubordination, agreed that Sumner must be removed from his chairmanship both to assure the success of the negotiations and to secure party discipline. Then the Secretary made the rounds of the Senate, interviewing Democrat and Republican alike, for their coöperation. Bayard and Thurman, Democratic leaders, promised their support—possibly as much because they wished to humble the arrogant Sumner as because they had a patriotic desire to settle disputes with England. Among the Republicans, Sumner had few friends; his power in the past had been based upon his bitter tongue and his imperious manner. Few would regret his defeat at the President's hands, and many would welcome an opportunity to abandon a never too comfortable alliance. When Sumner sensed this secret movement against him he gave himself over to

[32] Charles Francis Adams, *Lee at Appomattox and other Papers*, 144–147.

a hopeless and incoherent fury. In private and in public, he consistently denounced Grant and his supporters. "No wild bull ever dashed more violently at a red rag than he does at anything that he thinks the President is interested in," said Fish. To Henry Wilson, Sumner solemnly declared that Grant had threatened personal violence, and to others stated that Babcock was seeking an opportunity to assault him. Wilson called on Babcock to reassure his colleague, but in a few days Sumner was again harping on the same theme. "Vanity, conceit, & ambition have disturbed the equilibrium of his mind," concluded the sage Secretary of State.[33]

Unfortunately for Sumner's case, his conduct again played into the Administration's hands. Fish lost no opportunity to point out how "irrational and illogical" were the actions of the Senator. On January 24, when he again met Sir John Rose, the Secretary of State was prepared to promise success in the negotiations; however, too good a diplomat to fail to show Rose how great a concession he was making, he confidentially handed Rose Sumner's note. When Rose had read it, Fish told him of the Administration's intention to negotiate on the basis of the "Confidential Memorandum." Informally, they agreed that Grant and Queen Victoria should each appoint five commissioners to settle formally the questions between the two governments.

During another week, Rose and Gladstone kept the cables busy, but by the end of that time the arrangements were complete. The continental situation was pressing, London and New York bankers were earnest in urging a settlement, and the American political situation promised to be immensely clarified by the agreement. On February 1, Thornton informed Fish that his government was ready to send the proposed mission, and on February 9, Grant sent the Senate the nominations of the American Commissioners. In addition to Fish, who would head the American Commissioners, the men appointed were Schenck, former Attorney-General E. R. Hoar, George H. Williams of Oregon, and Justice Samuel Nelson of the Supreme Court. Together with the nominations, Grant sent the formal correspondence between Fish and Thornton. The vastly more important correspondence between Fish and Rose was not submitted.[34] The nominations were

[33] Fish to Washburne, February 20, 1871, Washburne MSS.
[34] Richardson, *Messages*, VII, 121–122; For the whole negotiation, see C. F. Adams, *Lee At Appomattox*, and the forthcoming life of Hamilton Fish by Allan Nevins.

promptly confirmed, even Sumner voting with the majority.

On the same day, the Queen sent Parliament the names of five "High Commissioners" to go to Washington to meet Grant's appointees. Like the American delegation, the British members were more distinguished for political acumen than for their statesmanship. No important interest, however, was unrepresented. Sir John Rose was not selected; for when the Colonial office suggested his name as Canada's representative, the Canadian Prime Minister, Sir John MacDonald, replied that he would not be a suitable person.[35] On February 27, the British delegates arrived in Washington, and the sessions of the Commission began. Rose's preliminary work had smoothed the way, and Washington society entertained the "Joint Highs" with its customary lavishness. Proceeding leisurely, it was May before they had completed the treaty of Washington. Meanwhile, less than a week after the Commission had begun its work, the last obstacle to the success of the treaty was removed—Sumner was deposed from the chairmanship of the Senate Committee on Foreign Relations.

When the Forty-Second Congress began its first session on March 4, 1871, it was obvious to all its members that Sumner's relations with the Administration had become unendurable. The spectacle of a chairman of a Foreign Relations Committee completely out of accord with the Administration of his own party was sufficiently anomalous to demand correction even had personal considerations not been involved. But personal considerations were important, and Sumner's final removal was made on the basis of partisanship rather than statesmanship. Fish informed the Senators that he and Sumner were no longer on speaking terms, and all the Senators knew that Sumner was unsparing in denunciation of both the President and the Secretary of State. Moreover, word spread secretly that Grant demanded Sumner's head. Accordingly, when the Republican Senators met in caucus on March 8 there was hardly a dissenting voice against Sumner's removal. Schurz protested, and even carried his opposition to the floor of the Senate, but to no avail. Sumner was made chairman of the innocuous Committee on Privileges and Elections—which he refused—and Simon Cameron, ardent supporter of the Administration, became head of the Foreign Relations Committee. Though reformers were disgusted, Fish

[35] Morden Long, "Sir John Rose and the Informal Beginnings of the Canadian High Commissionership," *Canadian Historical Review*, March, 1931.

was pleased to have a man with whom he could work. It had been a long campaign, but the General in the White House, combining the tactics of flank movements, siege, and direct assault, had emerged the victor.[36]

Magnanimity to the vanquished, a characteristic of General Grant's military campaigns, found no place in his political contests. Visitors to the White House found that Grant had become "suddenly talkative," and his "whole conversation was a denunciation of Sumner." [37] George F. Hoar, walking with Grant past Sumner's house some time later, was astounded to see the President of the United States stop, shake his fist at the Senator's windows, and declare, "The man who lives up there has abused me in a way I have never suffered from any other man living!" [38] The President's abuse was repaid in kind. Sumner continued his splenetic denunciations of the President until his death. Often he followed his visitors to his door, roaring until his friends feared that he must be heard in the White House itself.

[36] Blaine, *Twenty Years,* II, 502–6; New York *Tribune,* March 9, 10, 11, 13, 20; Foulke, *Morton,* 169–173; New York *World,* March 10, 1871.
[37] John A. C. Gray to Bigelow, Bigelow, *Retrospections,* IV, 485.
[38] Adams, *Lee,* 247.

THROUGHOUT this last session of the Forty-First Congress, while the quarrel with Sumner occupied the public eye and the Administration labored to build political capital out of foreign affairs, the perennial questions of finance and Reconstruction were not lost from sight. In the Treasury, Boutwell pursued his methodical reduction of the debt by the application of surplus revenue to outstanding obligations, and the impressive figures of payments mounted each month until partisans and bondholders could rejoice in the tangible evidences of national honesty. By December, 1870, $190,000,000 had been lopped off the debt—easily $100,000,000 more than would have been saved "had a President as lenient to whiskey thieves and other revenue defrauders as Andrew Johnson ruled. . . ." [1] Not only was the debt being reduced by payment but, under an act of July, 1870, the five-twenty bonds were being funded into new bonds with lower interest rates. Boutwell's recommendations for funding the debt had borne fruit in congressional authorization of new issues of $200,000,000 five per cent ten-year bonds, $300,000,000 at four and one-half per cent to run for fifteen years, and $1,000,000,000 four per cents payable in thirty years.

For a year after this law, the Secretary strove against obstacles to exchange the five-twenties for the new bonds. Impetus was given to Boutwell's eagerness by the reduced revenue which resulted from another law of July, 1870, but the outbreak of war in Europe prevented the sale of bonds on foreign exchanges. Finding only the five per cent bonds readily marketable, Boutwell in December, 1870, recommended an increase in the number. By March, he was able to accept subscriptions for the bonds, but by the end of the summer of 1871, he had been able to dispose of but $66,000,000, all but $2,000,000 of which had been taken by national banks. [2] The failure, however, was attributed to European troubles rather than to the absurdity of offering bonds of three different interest rates simultaneously, and as the reduction of the debt went steadily on, the Administration was still able to catalogue a triumph in its financial status.

[1] New York *Tribune,* December 7, 1870.
[2] *Ibid.,* December 21, 1870; March 1, 1871; Boutwell, *Reminiscences,* II, 186.

But while payment of the debt might please the captains of industry, and induce them to furnish the sinews for political campaigns, finances could not make a psychological appeal which would keep the masses of the people loyal to the Republican Party. For that purpose the party kept alive the issues of the Civil War and Reconstruction, and, as usual, conditions in the lately rebellious States played into the Radical hands.

At the opening of Congress in December, 1870, Butler's Reconstruction Committee reported a bill to grant "full and general grace, amnesty, and oblivion of all wrongful acts . . . of all persons engaged in the war of the late Rebellion." [3] The bill, identical with the one killed in the preceding June, was doubtless intended to counteract the agitation of the reformers. The bill, however, was but a gesture, for its consideration was immediately suspended until an examination could be made of Southern conditions. A renewed outburst of Ku Klux activities in parts of the South furnished both excuse and justification for postponing it. Partial amnesty was not thought of for the paradoxical reason that "the class to whom amnesty is given will feel offended—for they will consider that they are thought of as of no importance." [4]

The admission of all of the Southern States to representation in Congress, and the withdrawal of the military governments, inspired leaders of the Southern whites to new efforts to obtain political control. The elections of 1870 witnessed a vigorous campaign by Democratic, Conservative, or "Union Reform" candidates to displace Radical Republican office holders. In South Carolina, where the struggle was especially bitter, the Conservatives joined with moderate Republicans and "Reformers" and even appealed to the Negroes to help save the State. While Radicals organized the Negroes into militia companies, the reformers created "Union Reform" clubs to entice the Negro from his new-found friends. The election was marked by much intimidation and some violence on the part of the Reformers, but Radical frauds when the votes were counted overcame them. A Radical delegation was returned to Congress, and Radicals continued to govern the State.

But even allowing for frauds, it was obvious that the Radicals had an overwhelming majority of the South Carolina voters. The Reform Party disappeared from local politics, its Republican members made

[3] New York *Tribune*, December 9, 1870.
[4] *Ibid.*, December 16, 1870.

peace with the dominant faction, and the Democrats sought new methods of "redeeming" the State. The work of intimidating the Negroes did not cease. In the white counties "up-country" gangs of masked men terrorized their neighborhoods according to the formalities of the Ku Klux Klan. From the elections until the summer of 1871 their outrages continued. Accurate figures on their depredations were obviously impossible, but observers listed 227 outrages in one county, 118 in another, and more than 300 in a third. The outrages, varying in nature from fright to murder, were directed as much against social and economic offenders as against political opponents. The Klansmen represented the least cultured members of the community, but their activities had the silent consent of the better classes, whose political fortunes would advance as the Negro was frightened from the polls.[5]

In other Southern States conditions were as bad as in South Carolina. In Louisiana the campaign had revealed a split in the Republican ranks between the faction of the Carpetbag Governor, Henry Clay Warmoth, and the "Custom House gang" headed by Grant's brother-in-law, James F. Casey, Collector of the Port. In Georgia and North Carolina bands of Klansmen murdered and whipped Republicans with impunity, and in North Carolina and Arkansas Republican factions joined with the Democrats to impeach their Radical Governors. In North Carolina the opposition elements, acting through both legal and extra-legal methods, were most successful. In the elections Klan terrorism and an efficient Democratic organization carried the State by 4,000 majority, and elected five of seven Congressmen. War-Governor Z. B. Vance, still under the disabilities of the Fourteenth Amendment, was elected to the Senate.

The loss of North Carolina was especially distasteful to the Republicans, who were unwilling to relinquish political control without a struggle. On December 16, Oliver P. Morton sponsored a call upon President Grant for information concerning murders and other outrages in the State. On January 13, Grant responded with a number of documents concerning Klan organizations and activities. In addition, the President sent reports on the other Southern States. Five days later Morton moved to appoint a committee to investigate these disorders. Though Democrats protested that there was no evidence to warrant

[5] Francis Butler Simkins and Robert Hilliard Woody, *South Carolina During Reconstruction*, 446 ff.

an investigation, that the purpose was to make political capital, and that the resulting outburst of sectional hatred would serve as a pretext for establishing martial law, the Republicans carried the resolution and appointed sufficient Radicals to insure a report in accordance with party interests. The committee, centering its attention on North Carolina, summoned before it the customary delegations of army officers, Carpetbaggers, and Skalawags, who testified with varying degrees of reliability to a gory set of atrocities.[6]

For six weeks, while Grant and Fish quarreled with Sumner and set the machinery for the Treaty of Washington in operation, and Dominican Commissioners surveyed the natural beauties of the island, the Ku Klux investigation proceeded to catalogue the South's museum of horrors. Its work was soon to bear fruits. When the Forty-Second Congress assembled in March, many members were intent upon affecting their cherished reform of the tariff. Westerners like Garfield of Ohio, reformers who followed Schurz, and Democrats generally were anxious to rid the country of the high protective tariff which had yielded indispensable revenue during the war, but which was now serving only to enrich a favored class of Eastern manufacturers. Even Ben Butler, whose Irish and fishermen constituents had no tariff axes to grind, flirted with the rising revenue reformers. As the time drew near for the Forty-Second Congress, Butler, ever alert to advance himself politically, approached his colleague George F. Hoar to show a call he had prepared for the low tariff men to assemble in caucus to nominate a speaker. "How do you think something like this would answer?" asked the wily Butler.

One look at the call was sufficient for Hoar, and he hastened off, as Butler had intended, to see Speaker Blaine. Realizing that Butler was an excellent political weathercock, Blaine began to consult the tariff reformers and soon made a bargain that in return for their votes on the Speakership he would give them a majority of the Ways and Means Committee. The Chairman, however, General Dawes, and the second ranking member, "Pig Iron" Kelley, were both high protectionists.[7]

As news of these negotiations reached the White House, Grant and his advisers became disturbed. Men interested in the South and politicians interested in their party streamed into the White House to urge

[6] Richardson, *Messages and Papers*, VII, 117; Foulke, *O. P. Morton*, 189.
[7] Hoar, *Seventy Years*, I, 202.

the President to keep Congress in session long enough to pass legislation for suppressing rebellious disorders. But among these callers came others, headed by Don Cameron, who feared lest a March session should disturb the tariff. Torn between these advisers, Grant wrote Blaine an unofficial letter "to express exactly what I do think." In the first place, said the President, "there is a deplorable state of affairs in some parts of the South demanding the immediate attention of Congress. If Congress can be confined to the single subject of providing for the protection of life and property in those Sections . . . I feel we should have such legislation. But if committees are to be appointed and general legislation entered upon, then I fear the object of continuing the present session will be lost." [8]

With this presidential injunction in his hands, Blaine set about holding Congress to a consideration of Southern problems. The Ku Klux Committee was ready to report its findings, and the party press was declaring that a government which neglected to protect its citizens "ought to be hissed off the earth." [9] In the Capitol a joint Republican caucus discussed the Southern question and agreed to support a bill drawn by Butler. The bill gave the President the right to call out the army and suspend the writs of habeas corpus, and conferred on Federal marshals the power to exclude disloyal veniremen from juries. State officers might even be removed by the President were there doubts regarding the validity of their election. Though the Senate supported this measure, the moderates in the House, led by Garfield, and even assisted by Blaine and Dawes, succeeded in defeating the bill. Instead, a combination of high tariff men, Democrats, and moderate Republicans proposed another investigating committee. At its head would be none other than General Benjamin F. Butler, but the members would be men with no sympathy for the Radical program.

Boiling with indignation over this reception of his pet measure, and incensed at the apparent trickery of the proposed committee assignment, Butler rose to repudiate the scheme. After the manner of Thad Stephens, whose mantle he wore, Butler hurled invective upon Blaine, the high tariff men, and the Democrats indiscriminately. Stung by the charges, Blaine deserted both the Speaker's desk and his dignity to take the floor and castigate his accuser. The episode, thought Garfield, was

[8] Grant to Blaine, March 9, 1871, Grant Letter Books.
[9] New York *Tribune*, March 4, 1871.

a worse defeat for Butler than Fort Fisher, but Butler continued the fight and eventually carried the day.

In the midst of this wrangling no one lost sight of the political consequences. Garfield noticed that "public affairs here are hastening from bad to worse very rapidly. We have now been in session three weeks and have received not a word from the President in regard to public affairs and yet the South is crying out for protection against murder and outrage. The President, it is said, greatly desires legislation but hesitates to recommend it for fear the session will be prolonged and the high tariff men will be offended by assaults on some of their pet interests. . . . His [Grant's] power is waning very rapidly and many of the best men here think his reëlection is impossible. It is feared, however, that his renomination is inevitable. There are many ugly signs of disintegration in our party."[10] Such sentiments were widely reflected in Washington. The *Tribune* correspondent hopefully noted that there was a growing opposition to Grant's renomination, and men were pointing out that since Van Buren's renomination in 1840, only Lincoln had been put up for reëlection by a political party. Sherman, Schenck, Colfax, Blaine, Wilson, and even Logan were being mentioned and were pluming themselves for the succession.[11]

But Congressmen in Washington who had been out of contact with their constituencies for months were likely to have a poor comprehension of public opinion. In Ohio, Hayes was living closer to the people, and was beginning to view the political scene from the watch-tower of one about to foreswear politics.[12] "U. S. Grant played out again!" he ejaculated to a correspondent. "Funny, isn't it? A year ago, you remember, you told me the Republicans couldn't reëlect in New York more than six, and none in the West to the Forty-Second Congress. In the natural course of things, the ins grow weaker and the outs stronger with time, until they change places. But how stands the great body of the Republican people? What do they care about public affairs? The questions in the order of their importance, are they not these? 1—The South, 2—The debt, 3—The British question, 4—Santo Domingo, 5—Appointments and personal matters generally. Until 'the South' is

[10] Garfield to A. B. Hinsdale, March 23, 1871, Garfield MSS.
[11] New York *Tribune,* March 24, 1871.
[12] "The old questions interested me so much that the new ones seem small," declared the man who was seven years later to become forever identified with these "new questions."

settled, all other questions are subordinate with the mass of the people who have fought the anti-slavery and the Union battle. 'The debt' overshadows the remaining three—the people believe in the Administration decidedly on the first two questions. A great majority are with it on the British question, a great majority regret the Santo Domingo business and differ from U. S. Grant but will accept it: and as to the fifth, a majority, a vast majority were vexed about the A. T. Stewart, the Sickles, the Cox, the Sumner, the Cameron and the Relations affairs. But each and all of these are merely sensations of the day and do not and will not materially affect the public judgment as long as the Administration is right on the South and the Democracy wrong." [13] In his diary Hayes solemnly recorded that Grant had "been faithful" on the rights of the Negroes, and "successful" with the debt. Santo Domingo was a "blunder" and the personal affairs were "badly managed." However, the Administration could "yet save itself" if it could only get "rid of Santo Domingo."

Fully aware of the necessity of keeping faith on the Southern question, Grant watched uneasily as the Butler Bill met opposition from within the party. Finally, on March 23 the President took Boutwell in his dogcart and drove to the Capitol. Within a few minutes he summoned Edmunds of Vermont, Howe of Wisconsin, Conkling, Henry Wilson, Shellenbarger, Pomeroy, Morton, Chandler, Horace Maynard, and G. F. Hoar to the President's room. When the men assembled, Grant informed them that he had been importuned for weeks to send a message asking larger powers for suppressing disorders. He was, he said, unable to comply with the request. From many sources he had been attacked for the military clique which allegedly influenced his actions, and he feared the country would not approve a request to enlarge his powers and permit him to suspend the writ of habeas corpus.

But if Grant expected that these party leaders could discipline their followers and put through the measure without his interference, he was disappointed. Each Congressman had a constituency to consider, and prevailing Washington opinion would have it that these constituencies were lukewarm on the measure. Before the congressional leaders could act, they would need presidential support. Howe and Shellenbarger put their heads together, and soon drew Hoar off to a corner. After consultation Hoar approached Grant to point out that "there

[13] Hayes to Charles Nordhoff, March 13, 1871, Hayes, *Diary and Letters*, V, 133–134.

was no question of the existence of these disorders and crimes" in the South, and that as the elections approached they would be increased. The situation would then become so bad that Grant would have to take action. It would be better, Hoar implied, to be criticized for asking more power now, than to be criticized for exercising an illegal power then.[14]

Under this presentation of the case, and realizing that legislation would not be passed without his request, Grant called for pen and paper and began to write a message to Congress. Pointing to the condition of the South—"The proof . . . is now before the Senate"—the President declared that the State officers were incapable of suppressing disorder, and he himself without legal authority. "Therefore I urgently recommend such legislation as . . . shall effectually secure life, liberty, and property and the enforcement of law in all parts of the United States."

The dread threat of the tariff reformers, however, bore heavily upon the political allies of the industrialists. Surrounded by men whose whole political careers were bound up with the preservation of the existing tariff, Grant penned the final sentence of his message. "There is no other subject upon which I would recommend legislation during the present session." [15]

Two weeks earlier Governor Scott of South Carolina had asked Grant for troops to suppress disorders in two of his counties. The President complied with this request and sent twelve companies of infantry and four of cavalry. But while these troops were en route the newspapers reported fresh outbreaks, and on the day before Grant's message, South Carolina's Radical Attorney-General, D. H. Chamberlain, arrived in Washington to solicit further support. Talking with Chamberlain, Grant declared that there was more disorder in South Carolina than in any other State, but he would use all his power to put down the disturbers. If two regiments would not suffice, ten should be sent and kept as long as the Administration was in power. And if the Democrats, said the President with an eye on the future, should elect a President in 1872, the first act of the new Administration would be to withdraw the troops. "And I would advise the Democrats to follow the troops out of the State!" [16]

In fulfilment of this pledge to South Carolina Republicans, and with-

---

[14] Hoar, *Seventy Years*, I, 204–206.
[15] Richardson, *Messages*, VII, 127–128.
[16] New York *Tribune*, March 7, 22, 1871. I have changed the quotation from indirect to direct discourse.

out ignoring the possible effect on congressional action, Grant issued a proclamation describing conditions in the State and threatening the "use of military force" unless the "insurgents" dispersed within twenty days.[17] The proclamation was an unnecessary gesture, but it served its purpose in stimulating Congress to action.

Within a few days, the committees on the President's message reported a new bill, drafted by Shellenbarger, and as objectionable to the moderates as Butler's defeated proposals. Democrats were "fully aware of the President's purpose to turn the South into a military camp to control the States in his own interest for the succession in 1872," [18] and anti-Grant Republicans were convinced there could be "no more fatal policy than for us to give the President the enormous and irresponsible powers" contemplated in the act.[19] In the debates constitutional arguments abounded—"we are working on the very verge of the Constitution," said Garfield [20]—and men found various interpretations in the Fourteenth Amendment. The Federal Government should be brought home to the citizens, said the Radicals, while Blaine, Garfield, Poland, and other moderates took strange refuge in the doctrines of State Rights.[21]

As the debate proceeded, the Moderates were gradually whipped into line. Garfield, who exhausted his vocabulary in an unwonted defense of State Rights, "found a kind of party terrorism pervading and oppressing the minds of our best men" and resigned himself to defeat.[22] On April 20, under this "terrorism," the bill passed, and Congress adjourned. Before they separated, the Democrats united in signing an address to the people. The law, they told the people, constituted a dangerous concentration of power in the hands of the President, and was designed solely to stir up strife in the land and hide the fact that the cost of Government was arising at an alarming rate and the revenues were not properly collected.[23] The Moderates made no address, but many agreed with J. D. Cox that the "great grief of the whole Southern business is, that we are getting further and further away from any hope or chance of making a Union with . . . the thinking and influential

17 Richardson, *Messages*, VII, 133.
18 New York *World*, March 27, 1871.
19 Cox to Garfield, March 27, 1871, Garfield MSS.
20 Garfield to Hinsdale, March 30, 1871, Garfield MSS.
21 N. Y. *Tribune*, April 3, 1871.
22 Garfield to Cox, April 8, 1871, Garfield MSS.
23 New York *Tribune*, April 21, 1871.

native Southerners. . . ." According to Cox, there was no hope for the party except by alliance with "the intelligent, well-to-do, and controlling class of white [natives] in the South." [24] But that class would doubtless not have supported the Radicals, and the Administration had no desire to conciliate them. The South, for the moment, was as safe for the party as Congress could make it.

Into the midst of this discussion, the Santo Domingo question was suddenly catapulted by the return of the investigating Commission. The Commissioners had been enjoying the tropical hospitality of President Baez, General Fabens, and Colonel Cazneau. With captivating courtesy, Government officials instructed them in the mysteries of island politics and told of the eagerness of the people for annexation. Fabens and Cazneau entertained lavishly, and Fabens turned the inspectors over to an American geologist, who lectured to them on the mineral resources, scenic beauties, and economic advantages of the land. Carefully planned trips, inspired interviews, and watchful vigilance lest some of the visitors stray from the fold, sufficed to convince the commissioners. Late in March, they returned to Washington with a report endorsing all that Grant had said of the island's potentialities, and assuring the country that the Dominican people hungered to be annexed.

Their appearance at this juncture, despite their favorable report, was politically inopportune. With Sumner's removal still causing its nine-day sensation, with the Congress torn over the South, and with the South itself in the grip of the Ku Klux, the Administration was in no condition to renew the annexation struggle. Moreover, the President's most ardent supporters, never more than lukewarm on Santo Domingo, were beginning to feel with Hayes that it would be well to be rid of the question. Butler was unwilling at the moment to undertake the defense of so dangerous a project, and advised Grant to send the report to Congress but not to press the matter. After December, said Butler, public sentiment would change, and it would be well to give the people time to think over the Commissioners' findings. Moreover, Sumner's personal influence was still too great to be successfully attacked. Visitors to the White House found Grant calm on annexation; he hoped that it would take place, and had sent his Commissioners without knowing their opinions, but he was going to allow the case to rest on its merits.[25]

[24] Cox to Garfield, April 11, 1871, Garfield MSS.
[25] Hayes, *Diary and Letters*, V, 131, February 17, 1871.

"My views on San Domingo were founded upon the reports of able men," wrote the President to a friend. "They were honestly laid before the Senate in December. I do not wish to make annexation a party question." [26]

Fully realizing how the question might embarrass the Administration, Sumner arose once more in the Senate to make what political capital he could out of the situation. At the moment, he was enjoying the notoriety the Grant raid on him gave. Whatever popularity he had ever enjoyed had come as he played the rôle of martyr,[27] so he slipped into his former part with full appreciation of its possibilities. On March 27, the martyr rose to speak to the packed galleries of the Senate chamber. For three hours he declaimed on the iniquities of Grant and Baez, of Cazneau and Fabens, of Babcock and the White House military clique. It was a threadbare recitation, but the actor was a master of his art. The galleries cheered the performance. Next day, as an encore, Schurz took the floor to denounce Grant even more bitterly. But the Senate paid little attention. After the interlude, the discussion of the Ku Klux Act was resumed.

But if Sumner and Schurz seemed to fail, their efforts were not unnoticed in the White House where Grant sat thumbing the pages of the Commissioners' report. The incident confirmed Butler's prophecy that Sumner, though politically dying, still had the power to wound. But if annexation was hopeless, Grant would save what he could from the wreckage. April 5, he handed the report to a messenger to be carried to the Congress. With it went the "most extraordinary document ever signed by an American President." [28]

If some political genius in the White House inspired Grant to write this last message on Santo Domingo, his name has been lost to history and the document stands as the work of the President alone. In truth, the message bears unmistakable evidences of being Grant's own handiwork, and in the light of attendant circumstances should entitle the Hero of Appomattox to admission to the ranks of politicians. By it Grant put the Santo Domingo question outside the pale of politics, and injected a personal issue into the campaign of 1872.

"It will be observed that this report," wrote the President, "more

---

[26] Grant to A. G. Cattell, March 21, 1871, Grant Letter Books.
[27] Bigelow, *Retrospections*, IV, 485.
[28] New York *World*, April 6, 1871.

than sustains all that I have said in regard to the productivity and healthfulness of the Republic of San Domingo. . . ." With this remark he dropped annexation, and entered into a discussion of his own connection with the problem. "When I accepted the arduous and responsible position which I now hold," he said, "I did not dream of instituting any steps for the acquisition of insular possessions." But, if not an expansionist, the President "believed that our institutions were broad enough to extend over the entire continent." So believing, he was interested when agents of Baez appeared with proposals of annexation, and soon came to feel that "if I turned a deaf ear to this appeal I might in the future be justly charged with a flagrant neglect of the public interests. . . . Those opponents of annexation who have heretofore professed to be preëminently the friends of the rights of man I believed would be my most violent assailants if I neglected so clear a duty."

With this statement of his own position, Grant proceeded to trace the rejection of his treaty and the appointment of the Commission. "The mere rejection by the Senate . . . only indicates a difference of opinion between two coördinate departments of the Government, without touching the character or wounding the pride of either. But when such rejection takes place simultaneously with charges openly made of corruption on the part of the President . . . the case is different. Indeed, in such case the honor of the nation demands investigation." The Commissioners' report "fully vindicates the purity of the motives" with which he had acted. "And now my task is finished, and with it ends all personal solicitude upon the subject. My duty being done, yours begins. . . ." But there was still one personal remark he would like to make. No man could "perform duties so delicate and responsible" as those of the Presidency "without sometimes incurring the hostility of those who deem their opinions and wishes treated with insufficent consideration." But a man with a clear conscience could "hear with patience the censure of disappointed men." [29]

Truly, this was a strange document, but it had its effect. Senators took the floor to deny that they had attacked the President,[30] and, in Ohio, Hayes gleefully recorded that "Grant's message . . . put[s] the Republican party again in the front with a future by no means dark."

[29] Richardson, *Messages*, VII, 129–131.
[30] New York *Tribune*, April 8, 1871.

"He who lives a great truth is incomparably greater than he who speaks it," sententiously remarked the Ohio diarist.[31]

Santo Domingo, in accordance with Butler's suggestion, was left for the mature consideration of the people, and Congress continued its discussions until the Ku Klux Act was passed. That done, and with no mention of a new tariff, it adjourned. But there was still another iron in the Administration's fire, and Grant called the Senate into special session to consider the Treaty of Washington.

Late in April the Joint High Commission finished its labors and reported a completed treaty to the two Governments. In few respects were their labors arduous, for they did little more than put into formal terms the agreements which Rose and Fish had made. The claims of the two powers were to be submitted to an arbitral board to meet at Geneva, who were to apply the principles of neutral conduct which were incorporated into the treaty to the cases of the *Alabama* and other Confederate cruisers. Other points in dispute were referred to arbiters, while some minor matters were settled by the Joint High Commissioners themselves.

Although critics alleged that this treaty marked no especial victory for the nation, its political significance was great. The principle of arbitration established a sufficient denial that Grant was a bloodthirsty and martial President, and showed that the "Greatest Soldier of the Age" was essentially a man of peace. The Administration forces, relieved from battle in behalf of San Dominican annexation, were whipped into line for the treaty. All eyes were fixed upon Sumner, and men speculated on his course. "If he resists and the treaty fails, he is done for. If he resists and succeeds, he will break himself down here. . . . If he accedes and votes for the treaty, Grant drags him in triumph at his chariot wheels," thought Henry Adams.[32] But Sumner shrugged his shoulders with the remark that "I never expected much from the High Commission," and voted with the majority to ratify.[33]

Superficial observers, hailing the treaty as a great diplomatic accomplishment, took a curious pride in their antiquarian information as they pointed out that the treaty was approved by the Senate on the birthday of the Queen, ratifications were exchanged in London on the anniversary of Bunker Hill, and Grant proclaimed the treaty on the Fourth of

---

[31] Hayes, *Diary and Letters*, V, 138, April 10, 1871.
[32] Henry Adams to Carl Schurz, May 16, 1871, *Letters of Henry Adams*, 208.
[33] New York *Tribune*, May 10, 1871.

THE LAST SHOT OF THE HONORABLE SENATOR FROM
MASSACHUSETTS—HE PULLED THE LONG BOW ONCE
TOO OFTEN

AS NAST SAW SUMNER

July.[34] But the treaty had a deeper significance which was not lost on the politicians. "If Grant settles the English question satisfactorily it will save his foreign policy," observed the American Ambassador to Spain. "And if he wipes out the Ku Klux his record, including the excellent treasury exhibit, will carry him through safely." [35]

Grant himself was of the same opinion. "My trials here have been considerable," he wrote to Washburne, "but, I believe, so far every tempest that has been aroused has recoiled on them who got it up. First, San Domingo; but you have read all that has been said about that matter in Congress and out of Congress. . . . I will only add that a great many professedly staunch republicans acted very much as if the[y] wanted to outdo the democracy in breaking up the republican party. Everything looks more favorably now though, for the party, than it did in '63, when the war was raging. Sumner and Schurtz [sic] have acted worse than any other two men . . . John Logan is paving the way to be just as bad as he knows how to be; but out of full fellowship with the rep. party he will amount to but little." [36]

[34] New York *Tribune,* July 10, 1871.
[35] Daniel Sickles to W. E. Chandler, May 5, 1871, Chandler MSS.
[36] Grant to Washburne, May 17, 1871, Grant MSS., Chicago Historical Society.

THROUGHOUT the congressional session, the thought uppermost in the minds of the nation's leaders was the approaching election of 1872. Men with presidential ambitions and politicians who fattened on the spoils of office came to the last session of the Forty-First and the first session of the Forty-Second Congress prepared to keep an eye on the political barometer. As the Administration marshalled its followers, dividing submissive sheep from recalcitrant goats—and sedulously built up the Treaty of Washington, the receding debt, and the Ku Klux legislation into a "record of achievement"—the Democrats, the politically ambitious, and those malcontents who had been driven from the public trough sought devices by which they might embarrass the party in power. Though they seldom took a position which concealed the partisan nature of their opposition, they voiced their concerted objections to each Administration project, and sought diligently to discredit it before the people.

When the Forty-First Congress reassembled after the elections of 1870, the enemies of the Administration hoped to make political capital out of the rising demand for civil service reform. The defects in the existing system were so evident that only such arrant spoilsmen as Conkling, Carpenter, Chandler, and Morton could look at them without blushing. Long agitation for civil service reform had made the people sensitive to the situation and even clamorous for a change. But Grant and his advisers were fully aware of the popular will, and in his message of 1870 the President aligned himself with the reformers. J. D. Cox, who in resigning from the Cabinet had sought to identify himself with the reformers, doubted Grant's sincerity. "We ought to force this lip service into real action," he wrote Garfield.[1] Schurz, too, charged Grant with hypocrisy, and introduced a Civil Service Bill in the Senate. But Grant gave his blessing to the measure, and it was his approval, rather than Schurz's activity, which finally put it through as a rider to an appropriation. As further proof of his sympathy with

[1] Cox to Garfield, December 6, 1870, Garfield MSS.

reform, Grant appointed an able commission to devise rules for civil service examinations. At its head was George William Curtis, editor of *Harper's Weekly,* and the ranking member was Joseph Medill, owner of the Chicago *Tribune.* The appointments not only disarmed suspicion but rendered secure the support of two powerful journals![2] Evidently Grant had ample reason for thinking that every "tempest" had "recoiled on them that got it up."

While fumbling for some tangible objection to the Administration and looking about for a positive program of reform, the heterogeneous opposition diligently circulated rumors of dissension in the Republican ranks. Washington correspondents were always able to enliven a dull column with some new rumors of Cabinet changes. Fish's resignation was reported so often that readers would have been bored had it not been for the variety of speculations concerning his successor. Butler and Morton were generally rumored the heirs apparent. Boutwell, who differed with Grant on the income tax, was often on the verge of dismissal, and it was understood that General Pleasanton, Commissioner of Internal Revenue, had Grant's favor. When, in the summer of 1871, Pleasanton tested his position by taking issue with Boutwell, Grant abruptly dismissed him, but this brought no cessation of journalistic prophecies. Creswell was retiring, then Ackerman, and then Fish again. It was all, said Fish, a "system which has for nearly two years been fabricating stories of dissensions in the Cabinet and between its members and the President and of continual coming changes—all designed to weaken the confidence of the country in the President and his administration."[3]

Another phase of the "system" was to deplore Grant's quarrelsome disposition. "Since the beginning of the government," said the contentious *World,* "we have had no elected President who has raised up such hosts of bitter enemies in his own political party as Grant. . . . The bitter enmities incurred are all personal, and they show that his temper incapacitates him for success in a political position. His intellect is so narrow that nobody can respect him and his jealous temper causes him to regard every Republican statesman who can possibly become a rival as his personal enemy." In this way was the hostility of

[2] N. Y. *Tribune,* January 14, 17, 28, June 9, 1871; N. Y. *Times,* March 11, 1871; Cary, *George W. Curtis,* 215–218; Rhodes, VI, 385–390; Smith, *Garfield,* 465–466.

[3] Fish to General C. C. Washburne, February 6, 1871, E. B. Washburne MSS. Cf., for example of rumors, New York *Tribune,* February 3, 1871.

Sumner, Schurz, Cox, Motley, Logan, Fenton, and Greeley to be explained.[4]

As a corollary of this criticism of the President for the enemies he had made, critics condemned his friends. The presence of army officers as secretaries at the White House lent superficial color to Sumner's charges that a military clique ruled the President. In addition, "low coarse men" like Chandler, Conkling, and Morton surrounded Grant to do his bidding.[5] "I fear that such advisors as Chandler, Cameron and Conkling are too influential with Grant," sighed Hayes. "They are not safe counsellors." [6] To Garfield's mind it was "unspeakable folly" for the President to "drive out" of his Cabinet men like Hoar and Cox, and when Sumner was replaced by Cameron, the Ohio reformer diligently circulated the remark of a Philadelphia paper that it could "now understand how Caligua made a consul of his horse." [7]

But despite these criticisms, Grant continued to use the men who represented the Administration on the floors of Congress for his purposes and to reward them with the Federal patronage. Political rather than personal friends, these men had endeared themselves to the President by their constant support of his measures, and had recommended themselves to him by their political success. As representatives and friends of corporate wealth, standing for an "honest" payment of the debt, high tariffs, and aids to big business, these counsellors were eminently "safe" men whose economic theories corresponded with Grant's own. Moreover, they demonstrated an ability in their States to control votes for their own purposes. To Grant, whose sense of the practical exceeded his appreciation of esoteric ethics, and who hoped for reëlection, this was a highly desirable attribute. In the army, Grant had turned from military theorists and political generals to practical soldiers. In the White House he ignored theorists and reformers and put confidence in practical politicians. In both war and politics, though he occasionally trusted a dishonest man, he never trusted an inefficient one!

Thoroughly illustrative of Grant's preference for practical politicians over theorists was his support of the Conkling faction in New York. In January, 1871, the Fenton and Conkling wings came to an

[4] New York World, March 14, 1871.
[5] Bigelow, Retrospections, IV, 485.
[6] Hayes Diary, March 16, 1871.
[7] Garfield to J. H. Rhodes and to A. B. Hinsdale, March 18, 1871; Garfield MSS.

open breach when Conklingites attempted to form a New York City
Committee which would exclude the "Tammany Republicans." Align-
ing himself with Fenton, Horace Greeley used the columns of his paper
to warn Grant of the dangers of factionalism. When this brought no
response from the White House, the indignant editor had recourse to
veiled threats that he would not support the President for another
term.[8] Instead of heeding him, Grant removed Moses Grinnell, the
Naval Officer, and two other officials of the New York Custom House,
and appointed in their stead three of Conkling's henchmen. Greeley
wrote that the new men were "all men of ability, yet we doubt that
the public service can be served by dispensing with" the former officials.[9]

From this time on, Greeley alternately approved and held out the
olive branch to President Grant,[10] rationalizing his course by proclaiming: "To support the Administration is one thing. To advocate
the renomination of its head is another." He supported the Administration even though its record was "not so brilliant as we might desire." Greeley was willing to admit that the inexperienced Grant might
have been "expected to make mistakes on details"; but, asked the
editor, "on what great question has General Grant disappointed the
just hopes of the people?" [11]

Essentially, Greeley's objections to the Administration were based
upon Grant's failure to distribute some of the spoils to Fentonites.
But Fenton had not supported Grant's measures while Conkling had
rendered yeoman service in the cause. Consequently Grant called
Conkling to his cottage at Long Branch and discussed with that master
of politics the forthcoming State campaign.[12]

At the same moment that the *Tribune* was hurling epithets at Roscoe Conkling, its editor was making a trip through the South. His ostensible purpose was to deliver an address at the Texas State Fair, but
he swung on a wide circle to visit most of the Southern States.[13] As a
result of his tour the *Tribune* returned to its ancient refrain that the
South should encourage industry. "The industrial doctrines of Greeley

[8] Conkling, *Life and Letters of Conkling*, 334–335; *National Republican*, January 7,
1871.
[9] New York *Tribune*, April 4, 1871.
[10] Cf. *Ibid.*, March 23, 24, for example.
[11] *Ibid.*, January 2, 1871.
[12] *Ibid.*, May 25, 1871; Conkling, *Life and Letters of Conkling*, 335–336.
[13] New York *Tribune*, January 2, 1871.

have subjugated the South," said a New Orleans paper; "it is the true duty of the South to cultivate all those industries, the want of which enslaved her." [14] A roaming *Tribune* correspondent interviewed various Southern leaders who subscribed to this dream of Southern industrialization. Thus Greeley, long an advocate of amnesty, added prosperity to his program for the South.

While redefining his Southern program, Greeley continued to disclaim any intention of discussing presidential candidates. The prospect for the party was gloomy enough in New York, and he planned to devote his efforts to saving the State.[15] But when it became evident that Federal officeholders would support Conkling in State affairs, with Grant's hearty approval, Greeley remembered that he had always been opposed to the reëlection of a President. He was not for Grant, he definitely announced in August; he was for the "One Term Principle." Grant, he believed, could not be elected, though he should prefer his reëlection to the triumph of any Democrat.[16]

In the State Convention, dominated by Conkling, Murphy, and the Customs House officials, Greeley was discredited, and throughout the campaign the editor attacked his opponents. Conkling had supported a Democratic major; Murphy was a "shoddy contractor" who had been leagued with Tammany! But in November, when the Republican ticket triumphed, Greeley proclaimed that the State was redeemed, Tammany was beaten, and the people had turned against the thieves. Despite his insurgency, he seemed to believe that he had carried New York for "reform." [17]

Immediately following the election, Murphy sent his resignation to Grant. In doing so he pointed out that he had been successful as collector of the customs, and claimed the Republican victory as his own handiwork. Truly appreciative of Murphy's services, Grant thanked him with assurances of confidence. That Greeley's attacks had had no effect on Grant was indicated by the appointment of Chester A. Arthur to the vacant place. Arthur belonged to the Conkling machine, and Greeley remarked in disgust that the "collector is Tom Murphy under another name." [18]

[14] New York *Tribune*, January 12, 1871, quoting New Orleans *Price Current*.
[15] New York *Tribune*, January 26, 1871.
[16] *Ibid.*, August 18, 1871.
[17] Conkling, *Life and Letters of Conkling*, 228–229; New York *Tribune*, September 2 ff.
[18] New York *Tribune*, November 1, 22, 1871.

With discordant factions in the Republican Party quarreling over the spoils of office, and seeking for formulas which would rationalize their insurgency, the Democrats were carefully surveying the situation. There were few Democrats of national reputation whose war record was sufficiently sound to justify the party in offering them to the people. Hancock, whose claims for promotion and preferment Grant had ignored in favor of Sherman and Sheridan, was frequently mentioned in the Democratic press as a possible candidate. The general himself was so pleased with such notice that he blew upon the embers of his wrath against the President to furnish an occasional flame for the papers. Although some talked of Hancock, few had any real enthusiasm for him. Other Democrats whose names were occasionally mentioned were Charles O'Conor and Samuel J. Tilden of New York, and Judge Jeremiah Black. None of these men was a favorite in the party, and Democratic speculation was more likely to dwell on the possibility of uniting with a disgruntled faction of the Republicans in support of some such man as Lyman Trumbull, David Davis, or Gratz Brown.

Although the Democrats could not agree on a likely candidate, they did have a general feeling that a platform in opposition to the Administration might attract many independent votes. Amnesty for the South, civil service reform, tax and tariff reductions, were obvious standards which Democrats might raise and around which they might rally support. But attractive as this program appeared, the Democracy harbored many who were still intent upon the issues which had furnished their stock in trade for two decades. With many members clinging to the old traditions, the party might lose the support of life-long Democrats.

Considering this dilemma, it was not without significance that Clement L. Vallandigham, the man most completely identified with the old issues, should first call for a new Democratic platform. For some time Vallandigham, a thoroughly intelligent politician, had been studying the situation. Rumors had gradually spread among Ohio politicians that he was prepared to announce a new program for the party, and in May all eyes turned to Dayton, where he was a delegate to a county convention. Before the assembled representatives of Montgomery County, the man who had suffered most for the old principles rose to urge Democrats everywhere to forsake old tenets and adopt new ones.

Embodied in resolutions, this "New Departure" declared that, though there were wide differences of opinion among Democrats concerning past issues, the members of the party should exercise a "rational toleration" toward one another in regard to them. "Agreeing to disagree in all respects as to the past," read the resolutions, "we cordially unite upon the living issues of the day, and hereby invite all men of the Republican Party, who believe now upon present *issues* as we believe." Moreover, Vallandigham would accept the "natural and legitimate results of the war," "waiving all differences of opinion as to the extraordinary means by which they were brought about." "Thus burying out of sight all that is of the dead past," Vallandigham proposed that the Democracy declare itself still an adherent of the "vital and long established rule of strict construction," still the defender of State Rights, and still an opponent of centralization. The three war amendments, which he would accept, should "not be held to have in any respect altered or modified the original theory and character of the Federal Government." To these negative principles, Vallandigham added positive ones: universal amnesty, payment of the debt with a "moderate taxation," revenue reform, civil service reform, tariff for revenue only, the taxation of wealth rather than the people, speedy return to specie payments, and no grants of public lands to corporations. Embodied also in the "New Departure" were attacks on Santo Domingo, the Ku Klux Acts, and the corruption of the Grant régime.[19]

Enthusiastically the Montgomery County convention adopted these resolutions, and appealed to Democrats of State and nation to embark upon a new program. While Republican editors found in the vague proposal to pay the national debts "honestly" a repetition of the old "Ohio Idea," the Democratic press seized upon the new scheme with fond expectations that it would restore the party to power.[20] Hopefully, Democrats speculated on whether the Republicans would "make a progress, and eschew class legislation" and the Democracy "fall back on its ancient platform against monopoly." "Or," inquired one of them, "must earnest true Democrats resort to a new political organization to secure immunity from partial and oppressive legislation?" [21]

But it quickly became evident that Grant and the Republicans were

[19] *American Annual Cyclopaedia*, 1871, pp. 609 ff.
[20] New York *Tribune*, June 5, 1871.
[21] J. J. Winans, (Tenia, Ohio) to Butler, July 6, 1871, Butler MSS.

not yet willing to abandon the issues of the War and Reconstruction. While Vallandigham was condemning the Ku Klux Acts and advocating universal amnesty, and Greeley was holding out the lure of industrial development to the South, Grant continued unmodified the Southern policy which had received Radical endorsement. On May 3, the President issued a proclamation "calling the attention of the people of the United States" to the recent Ku Klux law. "This law," said the President, "applies to all parts of the United States and will be enforced everywhere to the extent of the powers vested in the Executive." However, since it was well known that the act was intended for the South, the President "particularly exhorted" Southerners to suppress disorders. Reluctant to exercise these duties, Grant nevertheless warned the South that he would not "hesitate to exhaust" his powers in securing safety to all citizens.[22] So saying, Grant left Washington for Long Branch, but during the summer he kept watch on Southern developments. While Democratic newspapers condemned his proclamation as an "insolent, abusive manifesto," indicating that "Kaiser Ulysses" was "puffed up with a sense of his despotic authority," [23] Grant sent detectives into the South to ferret out the leading Klansmen.[24]

Since the Ku Klux disorders showed no signs of decreasing [25] during the summer, the President decided to make an example of certain counties in South Carolina. October 12, soon after his return from Long Branch, Grant issued a proclamation calling upon armed combinations in nine South Carolina counties to disperse within five days. When there was no evidence of improved conditions, he suspended the writ of habeas corpus and declared martial law in those counties. Immediately the army marched in, and arrests, directed by Federal detectives, began. For the next few weeks the press was filled with accounts of prominent men leaving town, of refugees seeking asylum across the line in Georgia, of dens of Klansmen being broken up by Federal marshals.[26] Two hundred came in to surrender themselves in one county, one hundred and two were in jail in another, and everywhere the officials were busy. Before martial law was withdrawn hundreds of arrests had been made in these counties.

[22] Richardson, *Messages*, VII, 134–135.
[23] New York *World*, May 5, 1871.
[24] Babcock to Ackerman, June 15, 1871, Grant Letter Book.
[25] Cf. New York *Tribune*, Sept. 2, 1871.
[26] *Ibid.*, October 23, November 4, 1871.

In the confused political situation produced by Democratic New Departures, "liberal" programs of reform, and factions within the party, many Republicans began seriously to count the costs of running Grant for reëlection. William E. Chandler, whose services as secretary of the Republican National Committee had gone unrecognized by the President, took counsel with his friends concerning his proper course. But they pointed out that Grant was the only Republican who could be elected in 1872, and that, with the local Republican machines in the hands of the President's friends, no other could be nominated.[27] General Sherman, often mentioned as a candidate by Grant's opponents, declared that he would not accept a nomination from either party, but took occasion to warn Grant against overconfidence. He believed that the South would completely repudiate the Administration, but Grant, with a better insight into Southern conditions, assured his friend that Republicans would carry South Carolina, Louisiana, and Arkansas. Though unconvinced, Sherman conceded that Grant would "be renominated and reëlected unless by personally doing small things to alienate his party adherents of the North." John Sherman, looking after his political fences in Ohio with the eye of a master politician, agreed that Grant would be reëlected. "And so shall I," he declared as he placed himself on the bandwagon.[28]

By midsummer of 1871, it was obvious that Grant's renomination was inevitable. One Democratic paper summed up the situation by saying that he had no opposition, could control all the Southern delegates, and could pack the nominating convention with officeholders.[29] A few disgruntled Republicans hoped that, since he was more talked of than any other candidate, he might draw all the fire. If his antagonists could only keep State Conventions from instructing delegates for the President, there might be a chance of defeating him. Whitelaw Reid, Greeley's editorial and political assistant, thought that "if the delegates can only come to the convention of '72 as they went to that of '60, Grant will have his throat cut as dexterously as was Seward's." [30] But this was absurd. Apart from his control of the party Grant held the support of enthusiastic regulars within the ranks because he stood for a set of principles which must be perpetuated. In

27 Badeau to Chandler, April 4, 1871, Chandler MSS.
28 *Sherman Letters*, 331–333.
29 New York *World*, August 19, 1871.
30 Cortissoz, *Reid*, I, 203.

Conkling's eyes, he had "made a better President than . . . we . . . had any right to expect, and he is a better President every day than he was the day before." "Those who hold the securities of the country, and property holders in general," said the Senator, "dare not risk a Democratic President now." [31]

By October, when Grant returned from Long Branch, the situation had cleared sufficiently to show that the President would be renominated, and could count on the support of the successful politicians in the party. Fish noted the President's cheerfulness at the first Cabinet meeting after the vacation, and attributed it to the "tide . . . setting strongly in our direction." "Everything in this country looks politically well at present," declared the optimistic President.[32]

With the political horizon clear, Grant turned to his annual message. The completed document was a smug elaboration of the thesis that "the past year, under a wise Providence, has been one of general prosperity to the nation," combined with occasional shrewd suggestions for reform which might weaken the "Liberal" opposition. Almost half the message was devoted to a catalogue of the foreign affairs of the United States. Only with Russia, whose minister had been *persona non grata;* Venezuela, which had not paid her debts; and Korea, whose soldiers had fired on a landing party of marines, were relations other than friendly. In domestic affairs the President enumerated the declining debt, the lower cost of the Navy, the "enlarged receipts" of the Post Office, the Indian Peace policy, and the activity of the Agricultural Bureau as worthy of commendation. Marring this perfect picture were the Ku Klux in the South, polygamy in Utah, and the great Chicago fire. In the field of reform, Grant suggested the removal of disabilities from the leaders of the South—except the "great criminals"—the restriction of land grants to actual settlers or to the aid of education, abolition of the fee system for collectors of customs, and Governmental acquisition of the telegraph system. As for Civil Service, he reported that his commissioners had not yet drafted a set of rules, but promised that "at all events, the experiment shall have a fair trial." In the meantime, he pointed out that the Administration had attempted "to enforce honesty and efficiency in all public offices." Due

[31] Conkling, *Life and Letters of Conkling,* 336–337.
[32] Badeau, *Grant in Peace,* 473; Fish to E. B. Washburne, October 7, 1871, Washburne MSS.

to the system of making appointments on congressional recommendations, dishonest men had obtained offices, but these had "been proceeded against with all the rigor of the law." In business, said the
President, a man giving a letter of recommendation enabling the
bearer to obtain credit was morally responsible and a "law which
would enforce this principle against all endorsers of persons for public
place would insure great caution in making recommendations." [33]

Upon the heels of this message came a change in the Cabinet.
Attorney-General Akerman, whose appointment had not saved Georgia from passing into the Democratic column, gave place to Senator
George H. Williams of Oregon. The change was purely a political move
to satisfy the Pacific Coast demand for Cabinet representation though
the particular selection of Williams was partly the result of his being
the legal representative of the Alaska Improvement Company, in
which the President was a stockholder.[34] Akerman became special
government counsel in the pending South Carolina Ku Klux cases.[35]

The Congress which assembled in December was by no means inclined to give up its search for campaign material. "Many good men
are in hopes that something may yet occur to make the choice of some
other than Grant possible," wrote Garfield,[36] and this hope set the
tone for the entire session. From the first day to the closing session,
the work of compiling the mistakes of the Administration went steadily on, while legislation became a secondary consideration. When the
Republican caucus met to consider the needs of the country and the
party, Senator Trumbull arose to demand an investigation of corruption in the public service. For some time Trumbull had been hearing
from friends that "the old issues are lined out, and it's narrowed down
to Grant or anti-Grant. . . . The people are tired of a man who has
not an idea above a horse or a cigar. . . ." [37] With this information,
he declared that men faced "an age of reform" and the abuses of
government should be investigated and eliminated. His proposal met
Conkling's immediate opposition. The Administration, said Conkling,

[33] Richardson, *Messages*, VII, 142–155.
[34] New York *Tribune*, January 6, 1871, December 6, 15, 1871; Louis Goldstine to
J. S. Black, January 6, 1871, Black MSS.
[35] New York *Tribune*, January 1, 1872; Grant to Ackerman, December 14, 1871, Grant
Letter Books.
[36] Garfield to Halsey R. W. Hall, (Ravinna), December 26, 1871, Garfield MSS.
[37] Joseph Brown, (St. Louis) to Trumbull, December 12, 1871. Cf. also letters of D.
W. Wood, December 12, and F. M. Pixley, (San Francisco), December 22, to Trumbull,
Trumbull MSS.

was Republican, and even though it had made mistakes, he was not "going to have every little fault and shortcoming dragged out in the light." [38] Eventually Trumbull's motion carried, but the investigating committee was given little power and its membership was selected from those unlikely to find fault with the ruling party.[39]

Watching this debate between Grant's friends and his enemies, the enemy were convinced that the Administration was making a concerted effort to keep its deeds hidden. Garfield's indignation was aroused by the "superserviceable lackeys" who were afraid of offending "their master," [40] and Greeley, declaring that Conkling's obstructive tactics were bringing the Administration into disrepute, besought Grant to clear his own skirts.[41]

Circumstances caused Grant to take a position which seemingly placed him on a higher plane than that of his followers. Just as the debates over investigations were dying out, the President sent to Congress the report of his Civil Service Commission. It recommended that the Civil Service be classified, and each class divided into grades. Positions were to be filled from applicants who had passed examinations, and promotion was to be based upon like tests. Each department should have its own board of examiners, and no assessments were to be levied upon jobholders. These rules, said Grant, would go into effect on the first of the year, and he asked Congress to appropriate money and pass legislation making the system binding upon his successors.[42]

The coincidence of this announcement with the investigation debates was interpreted to mean that Grant was rebuking the Senators. Greeley continued to point out that the rules simply made every officeholder dependent on Grant, and charged that he was "promoting a vigorous factional proscription in his own party." [43] Garfield, however, noted that Grant's friends were "furious" against the report, and believed the President "must back down or offend his defenders." [44] However, both Grant and his friends were too clever to quarrel over so popular a measure. Though Conkling was silent on

[38] New York *Tribune,* Dec. 13, 1871.
[39] *Ibid.,* December 16, 1871.
[40] Garfield to Whitelaw Reid, December 16, 1871, Garfield MSS.
[41] New York *Tribune,* December 16, 18, 1871.
[42] Richardson, *Messages,* VII, 156–159.
[43] New York *Tribune,* December 19, 20, 1871.
[44] Garfield to Cox., n. d., Garfield MSS.

the proposal and Carpenter declared it the "latest popular delusion," there was tacit agreement to let the Administration take credit for the reform and withhold opposition until after the election.[45] Meanwhile, Grant ousted from office 192 officials whom departmental investigations had shown to be corrupt or inefficient. Though these cases furnished proof to "Liberals" that the administration was corrupt, a majority of the people believed that the President was sincere in demanding honesty and efficiency in the public service.[46]

The appearance of the President in the rôle of a reformer was no deterrent to the faultfinding majority of Congress. A committee had been appointed to investigate alleged corruption in connection with the "general order" business in New York. For months Greeley had been using the *Tribune* to voice the protests of New York merchants against the Custom House's method of handling importations. By long established practice, goods which could not be cleared through the Custom House on the day of their arrival were consigned to privately owned warehouses known as "general order stores." Merchants were accustomed to allow them to remain in these warehouses until needed. The system, which gave warehouse facilities to importers until they needed the goods, and enabled the collectors to distribute their work evenly, worked to the advantage of both government and merchant, and no complaint was heard until shortly after Murphy's appointment as collector.

Congressional investigation men brought to light the fact that the beginning of complaints coincided with the grant of a monopoly of the general order business to the firm of Leet, Stocking & Co. The directing genius of this company, George K. Leet, a minor member of Grant's staff in the last days of the war, had used a formal letter of introduction from Grant to Grinnell as a means of obtaining a portion of the general order business. Then, heading a combination of draymen, he had forced competing warehouses out of business. By the time Murphy became collector, Leet was in a position to demand a practical monopoly of the general order business. Since his organiza-

<hr />

[45] New York *Tribune,* January 11, 1872.

[46] New York *Times,* January 22, 23, 1872. Early in February, Grant wrote to Joseph Medill, "It is my intention that Civil Service shall have a fair trial. The great defect in the past custom is that executive patronage had come to be regarded as the property of the party in power. The choice of Federal officers has been limited to those seeking office. A true reform will leave the office to seek the man." Grant to Medill, February 1, 1872, Grant Letter Book.

tion would coöperate with the Custom House "crowd" in New York politics, Murphy gave him what he demanded.

With a monopoly of the business. Leet and Stocking raised their rates. A month's storage was charged upon all packages consigned to them, and was estimated to have brought Leet a profit of $260,000 a year. Merchants immediately protested, and at least twice A. T. Stewart personally complained to Grant. As the protests became louder, Grant sought out Murphy to tell him that "there is so much noise . . . about the young man Leet, . . . on account of his having been connected with me during the war, that I have come to the conclusion that the young man had better leave." But Murphy, who appreciated the efficiency which Leet had shown both in organizing the business and assisting in politics, refused to dismiss him.

Although these facts were easily ascertained, and it was obvious that Leet had made good use of Grant's letter to Grinnell, the investigators were disappointed in their findings. Greeley, who had proposed the investigation, and A. T. Stewart, who had found the high storage rates oppressive, appeared before the committee to air both their grievances and suspicions, but neither they nor the investigators were able to prove that the President had an interest in the general order business. Babcock and Porter, who had once messed with Leet, were alike innocent, and politically the investigation was a failure. Politicians watched developments carefully, and were pleased when they found no especial popular interest in the case. However, they advised Grant that Leet should go, and the President ordered the general order system abandoned. Although Greeley attempted to criticize the President for his "tardy reform," the effect of the investigation was to add proof that Grant would correct abuses as soon as they were shown to exist.[47]

While the politico-economic aspects of the New York Custom House were being passed in review, Carl Schurz made a contribution to the charges against the Administration. With full appreciation of the effect upon the German vote, Schurz charged that Secretary Belknap had violated the neutrality laws by selling government arms to agents of the French. Ably assisted by Sumner, Schurz showed that Belknap

[47] New York *Tribune,* January 3, 5, 6, 8, 11, 12, 15, 16, 20, 23, 24, February 2, 7, 10, 12, March 5, 7, 18, 22; New York *Times,* January 12, 13, 16, February 13; New York *World,* February 2, *National Republican,* March 7; William Claflin to Chandler, February 16, and Rufas Ingalls to Chandler, January 24, 1872, Chandler MSS.

had accepted bids from Remington & Sons for obsolete American guns, and that after the Secretary had learned that the Remingtons were French agents, he sold arms to one Richardson who was a neighbor of the Remington family. Moreover, the War Department agreed to manufacture cartridges to fit the guns. An investigating committee, composed of friends of the Administration, substantiated these charges, but found no violations of domestic or international law. There was, however, ample evidence of carelessness if not corruption in the War Department, and leading politicians were fearful that General Rufus Ingalls, Grant's friend of old army days, might be closely investigated. However, despite the good grounds for suspicion, the whole matter added nothing to the anti-Grant movement. The sponsors were too obviously seeking for political capital to arouse much popular disapprobation. One observer concluded Sumner was "simply damnably unpatriotic." Even Garfield complained that the Senate had resolved itself into a political caucus.[48]

While Greeley was stimulating New York investigations, and Schurz was charging the Administration with unneutral acts, Charles Sumner was making a characteristic contribution to the cause. Soon after Congress met, Sumner adopted Greeley's newest thesis and proposed a constitutional amendment to limit the presidency to one term. The amendment, if ratified, was to go into effect after March 4, 1873. Although the proposal was obviously intended to embarrass the Administration, and failed to have any real effect, it gave both enemies and friends of the President an opportunity to harangue their opponents. Conkling, ably supported by Morton, took up the cudgels against Sumner. The recent changes in the civil service had ushered in an era of reform, said the Senator. Sumner had charged that Grant had used the patronage to insure reëlection, but the President had given up his patronage. Now that the great objections to the President had been removed, Sumner was trying to keep Grant from succeeding himself. To Conkling it was obvious that Sumner's amendment was merely an electioneering document, designed to injure Grant.

With the Senate wrangling over topics like these, there was little

[48] Foulke, O. P. Morton, 227–228, 242–243; New York Times, February 15, 22, March 2; National Republican, March 7, 1872; New York Tribune, February 15, 17, 23, 26, 29, March 1, 2, 6, 8; Garfield MSS. Diary, May 31; Garfield to Hinsdale, February 22, 1872, Garfield MSS.; William Claflin to Chandler, February 16, 1872, Chandler MSS.; Fairchild to "Dear Doctor," April 4, 1872, Fairchild MSS.; M. H. Carpenter to Geo. B. Smith, March 4, 1872, Smith MSS.

time for serious legislation. Tariff reform, a major issue in 1870, had been forgotten in the welter of charges and countercharges between Grant and anti-Grant men. The President's opponents were by no means united on the tariff, and partisan politics bade Grant's supporters to obscure the issue. Blaine, according to agreement, made Dawes Chairman of the House Ways and Means Committee, and Dawes effectively prevented the reform majority of that body from recommending any substantial reduction in the duties. In February, Grant told a delegation of manufacturers that reduction would hurt the laboring classes, but that he thought the free list ought to be extended to cover non-competitive materials.[49] The changes in the tariff conformed to the President's ideas: tea, and coffee, and hides were placed on the free list and a few items of raw materials were reduced. The income tax was omitted from the new revenue measure. "American industry is safe for another year," exulted Greeley.[50]

In addition to guaranteeing a "free breakfast table," Congress spent much time debating a proposal for general amnesty. On this Sumner blocked action by amending the bill to include the grant of full civil rights to the Negroes. Instead of amnesty, the dominant group were more interested in extending the Ku Klux Act. Though they met defeat in the Senate, a measure permitting troops to police Federal elections was attached to the general appropriation bill in the last days of Congress.

The session did not close, however, without further evidence that Grant was going to support reform—at least until after the election. In April the appropriation for a Civil Service Commission was under debate, and Garfield made an appeal to Grant to save it. Grant sent a message to Congress setting forth the rules he had adopted, and declaring that henceforth "honesty and efficiency, not political activity, will determine the tenure of office." A month later, as further proof of his reforming zeal, he sent a long message calling attention to the exploitation of newly-arrived immigrants. Though nothing was done to improve the sanitary condition of ships or save the immigrant from being swindled upon arrival, the President had made a bid for the "foreign" vote.

By the time Congress adjourned in June the President's opponents

49 New York *Tribune,* February 2, 1872.
50 *Ibid.,* March 23, 1872.

had amassed a valuable collection of insinuations, suspicions, and half-truths for campaign use. Though the investigations had produced few facts, the character of the investigating committees afforded ample grounds for charges of "whitewashing," and furnished the basis for numerous innuendos. The principal function of this abortive congressional session had been to give the members a forum for delivering political stump speeches, and none had neglected his opportunities. But by June those speeches were needed on the hustings, for the campaign of 1872 was already well under way.

IN JANUARY, 1872, the Republican National Committee met in Washington and decided to hold the National Convention at Philadelphia on June 5. In the call, the Committee reminded the people that all the promises of the 1868 campaign had been fulfilled. The States of the South had been restored, the laws had been enforced, and equal suffrage guaranteed to all citizens. A liberal policy had been adopted toward the rebels, and foreign complications had been solved.[1]

Coincident with this call, fresh expressions of loyalty appeared in the Republican press. "There has never been a President in the White House who has been more uniformly fair to all races and classes of men," declared the *National Republican*,[2] while the New York *Times* took up the cry for Grant by asking if the Republicans were ready to trust the Democrats with power? [3] Boston and Philadelphia papers joined in with declarations that Grant was honest, true to the party, a friend of the Negro, and restorer of industry and peace in the South. Throughout the nation, said one paper, "there is work and pay for the laborer, and the capitalist has confidence." [4] Though blunders had been made, admitted the obsequious journals, they had been promptly adjusted, and Grant's policy had been "eminently judicious and patriotic. The Republican Party demands his renomination because he has been its truest and best servant and minister." [5]

In the midst of this inspired demand for Grant the President's opponents continued to insist that he was not popular with the country. The enthusiasm, said the Indianapolis *Journal,* was limited to officeholders who failed to see the depth of public resentment.[6] Garfield thought that Grant was "the second choice of most of our people, and they are not agreed on a first." [7] Whitelaw Reid, who admitted an "instinctive dislike of men of General Grant's calibre

---

[1] New York *Tribune,* January 12, 1872.
[2] *National Republican,* January 19, 1872.
[3] New York *Times,* January 20, 1872.
[4] Philadelphia *City Item* and Boston *Journal,* quoted in *National Republican,* February 14, 17, 1872.
[5] *National Republican,* February 24, 1872.
[6] Quoted in New York *Tribune,* January 16, 1872.
[7] Garfield to R. C. Schenck, March 14, 1872, Garfield MSS.

and character," assisted Greeley in turning the columns of the New York *Tribune* into a clearing house for anti-Grant information.[8]

But while the opposition press was declaring Grant unpopular, the practical politicians began to amass evidence that the dissatisfaction was limited to a few exceptionally articulate soreheads. After the meeting of the National Committee, William E. Chandler, its secretary and the most practical of the practical men who supported Grant, turned to his native New Hampshire, where the first test of the prevailing winds would be taken. Through Chandler's deft hands money from Jay Cooke passed into the purses of political speakers and party workers, and in the spring elections New Hampshire went overwhelmingly for the regular Republicans.[9] This contest over, Chandler turned to national affairs and addressed a series of letters to party chieftains in the several States. From them he soon learned the sentiment of the party.

From one end of the country to the other the politicians reported in favor of Grant. From California came word that "if Grant is the nominee we will carry the state by a hard fight. With any other we lose." From South Corolina came the assurance that Grant could carry the State by 25,000. Kansas promised 20,000 for Grant, but opposed further reduction of the debt and contraction of the currency. Pennsylvania was in chaos, but Grant could carry the State. In New Jersey and Delaware there was no "Liberal" movement, and in Iowa party harmony would insure 60,000 for the President. In Maine, Vermont, Nebraska, Rhode Island, there were likewise no dissensions. Indiana alone reported that it would take real work to carry the election, though North Carolina, West Virginia, and New Jersey echoed the warning that only Grant could lead the party to victory. Alabama, Georgia, and Tennessee politicians hoped to "redeem" their States from the Democrats.[10]

Confirming these reports came the action of various State and

---

[8] Cortissoz, *Reid*, I, 203–204.

[9] Cooke to Chandler, February 26, 29, March 2, 1872, Chandler MSS.

[10] Letters to W. E. Chandler from Horace Harrison, (Tenn.), March 9, E. L. Sullivan, (Calif.), A. J. Ransier, (S. C.), March 16, S. F. Philips, (N. C.), March 23, D. R. Anthony, (Kan.), M. M. Hale, (Georgia), March 25, Russel Scott, (Pa.), March 26, S. S. Olds, (Mich.), March 27, T. B. Van Buren, (N. J.), March 29, James Lewis, (Dela.), Geo. Tichener, (Iowa), March 30, R. Erret, (Pa.), April 1, C. W. B. Allison, (W. Va.), J. W. Foster, (Ind.), April 3, G. G. Benedict, (Vt.), April 5, J. W. Finnel, (Ky.), T. A. Piper, (Maine), April 8, S. B. Packard, (La.), J. L. Pennington, (Ala.), and W. A. Pierce, (R. I.), April 9, 1872, Chandler MSS.

local conventions endorsing Grant for the renomination. Though the State Conventions were controlled by the politicians, officeholders were carefully excluded from the delegates to Philadelphia. No effort was spared to give an appearance of spontaneity to the Grant movement. In April, mass-meetings were held in Brooklyn and at Cooper Institute where resolutions reciting Grant's achievements were enthusiastically adopted. In Brooklyn, Henry Ward Beecher told the assemblage that there "had never been a President more sensitive to the wants of the people." At the Cooper Institute, Morton, Conkling, and Henry Wilson appealed to the voters to "let well enough alone" and continue Grant in office. Conkling praised Grant's ·intelligence, and his willingness to "revise his own judgments and weigh the suggestions of others." To the merchants and bankers of New York he exclaimed: "if the name and character of the administration of U. S. Grant have been of value to the Nation, no one knows it so well as the men who represent the property, the credits, the public securities, and the enterprise of the country. . . ." [11]

Despite these evidences of Grant's popularity, the "Liberals" insisted that he was supported only by the officeholders. Ignoring the regular organizations, they prepared to hold a great Liberal Republican convention. From Missouri, where Carl Schurz reigned supreme, came the call naming Cincinnati as the place where all favoring a change should assemble. J. D. Cox and his group of Ohio tariff reformers made arrangements for the meeting, while endorsements of Missouri's call came from other reformers throughout the country. In New York, tariff revisionists issued a manifesto, and Horace Greeley, ardent protectionist that he was, put his signature on the document! Evidently the Cincinnati Convention would represent every shade of anti-Grant opinion.

As the time set approached, its sponsors looked about for a candidate. With Grant backed by the regular machine, it was obvious that the only chance of defeating the President lay in the nomination of a man who could get Democratic support. Everywhere Democrats now endorsed Vallandigham's "New Departure," and looked to the Liberal Republicans to furnish them a candidate. Early in the canvass

[11] New York *Tribune*, March, *passim* for conventions endorsing Grant. *Ibid.*, April 11, 18, 20, 1872, for N. Y. mass meetings. Cf. also *National Republican*, April 18; New York *Times*, April 11, 17, 21, 1872; Conkling, *Conkling*, 429–430, Foulke, *Morton*, 255–256.

Judge David Davis loomed up as a possibility, but he accepted the nomination of a Labor Convention and thus excluded himself from consideration by a group which, however much they might wish to reform politics, were not intending to disturb the economic order. Lyman Trumbull and Charles Francis Adams were most often mentioned as the candidates who would receive Democratic endorsement.[12] Greeley's enthusiastic support, however, worried the tariff reformers, who feared that he would force the new party to accept a candidate who would favor the protectionists.[13]

When the Cincinnati Convention assembled, the leaders found their worst fears confirmed. Greeley's adherence precipitated the tariff issue in the Convention itself, and the leaders, desiring the support of the powerful *Tribune,* sought some formula which would antagonize neither reformers nor protectionists. The day before the Convention organized some revenue reformers held a caucus and weakly agreed to adopt a plank which would not offend the protectionists.[14] At this juncture, Greeley came out in an editorial announcing that the *Tribune* would support the Liberal nominees if the Convention favored the protection of home industry; [15] and this added to the readiness of the reform element to yield. When the Convention acted, it agreed on a platform which "remanded to the people in their congressional districts" the question of the tariff. By thus surrendering their convictions to political expediency, the reformers not only stultified themselves, but took the first of the steps which led to overwhelming defeat in November.

Still more unfortunate was the Convention's choice of a candidate. At the outset, observers noted that while Trumbull, Cox, Adams, and B. Gratz Brown each had his following, there was a general agreement to support anyone but Judge Davis. Of the leading candidates, only Cox was in attendance. Trumbull's friends worked for him, but the Senator himself gave them little encouragement. Since Davis was also from Illinois, it seemed obvious that Trumbull would not be nominated. A majority of delegates favored Adams, although loyalty to "favorite sons" kept them from naming him on the first ballot. Adams

---

[12] *Cincinnati Enquirer,* quoted in *Tribune,* May 1, 1872.
[13] Cox to Garfield, February 26, March 22, Garfield to Cox, March 3, 1872, Garfield MSS.
[14] New York *Tribune,* April 30, 1872.
[15] *Ibid.,* May 1, 1872.

himself had given the Convention little encouragement, and just before the Convention he had left for Europe to serve as American arbitrator at the Geneva tribunal. His appointment to this position was obviously fitting, but at the moment it was also political wisdom on Grant's part. After this Adams could hardly have expected the nomination, and his supporters suffered no pangs of conscience in deserting him.

Before the meeting, three men behind the scenes had laid plans to control the nomination. "Marse Henry" Watterson, editor of the Louisville *Courier-Journal,* Samuel Bowles, of the Springfield *Republican,* and Horace White, editor of the Chicago *Tribune,* formed a triumvirate which planned to pull the strings while the Convention danced. In conjunction with Schurz, these conspirators prepared to nominate Adams. But in their calculations they had neglected Whitelaw Reid, assistant editor of Greeley's *Tribune.* When Reid arrived with the New York delegation, he soon learned the triumvirate's plans and demanded admission to the secret councils. Unable to exclude the representative of so powerful a journal, the triumvirate turned itself into a quadrumvirate and soon were yielding to Reid's demands.

On the first ballot, Adams led the field with 205 votes. Greeley came second with 147, Trumbull had 110, Brown 95, Davis 92½, Curtin 62, and Chase 2½. The next ballot showed increases to 249, 239, and 148 for Adams, Greeley, and Trumbull respectively, with losses for the other candidates. By the third ballot Greeley had decreased Adams' lead, and on the fourth Trumbull's vote began to decline. Another ballot put Greeley ahead of Adams with 318 to 293, without Illinois, whose delegation had withdrawn for consultation. When the delegation returned with 27 votes for Adams and 15 for Greeley, the landslide to the editor began. First Pennsylvania changed her 50 votes to Greeley; then Indiana, Kentucky, Minnesota, Kansas and Vermont fell into line. Frantic free traders rushed about the hall to stop the stampede, but the Convention was uncontrollable. While State after State changed to the Greeley column, Schurz sat dumfounded on the platform. Not until the frenzied crowd forced him to speak would he announce the astounding result. To run with Greeley the Convention hastily named B. Gratz Brown.[16] Five hours after organizing the Convention adjourned. The nuptials of reform and

[16] New York *Tribune,* May 4, 1872.

protection had been hastily made; repentance was to come with leisure.

The news of Greeley's nomination reached the House of Representatives while Chairman Dawes was presenting the Ways and Means Committee's proposed tariff schedules, and making an impassioned plea for protection. Members rushed in from the lobby to announce the result, and George F. Hoar interrupted to ask if it would be out of order to congratulate the House on the triumph of protection. Dawes replied that it was obviously unnecessary for him to continue—the man who had been most ardent in teaching protection was now leading protection's opponents. Democratic members sat aghast at the news, but several arose to bid farewell to all their principles. Reluctantly one of them admitted that Greeley's strength would force his party to accept the "Liberal" offering. In the Senate, Democrats bemoaned Davis' defeat, and few ventured a half-hearted word for the "reform" nominee.[17]

The first response of the country at large to Greeley's nomination was one of amusement. "No two men could look each other in the face and say 'Greeley' without laughing," said one newspaper. "A ridiculous political mouse" brought forth by the Cincinnati Mountain, said another. "Absurd" was the refrain of the editorials of the day. The second response was to point out, in more serious vein, the candidate's unfitness. He was "an eccentric philosopher," "chimerical and vacillating, visionary and indiscreet, malignant and crochety," "a Grandmother and a trickster," "totally destitute of sound judgment."[18] Among the reformers who had backed the Cincinnati movement nothing was felt but chagrin. "Was such a condition of things ever seen?" asked Cox, who saw his dream of forming the "new party of the future" fading away. "I have only to complain that we have fallen among thieves. The Cincinnati Convention that was to have been the beginning of great and good things is now the most powerful force opposing . . . the friends of true reform."[19]

Rutherford B. Hayes summed up the thoughts in everyone's mind: "A queer result it is. Free traders nominate their bitterest and most formidable foe. A party whose strength is mainly in the German element which is clamorous against temperance fanaticism nominates

[17] New York *Tribune*, May 4, 1872.
[18] Cf. extracts in New York *Tribune*, May 7, 8, 9, 1872.
[19] Cox to Garfield, May 10, 1872, Garfield MSS.

the author of that fanaticism. Democrats are required to support a man who said that he would go for Grant in preference to any Democrat!" Yet despite the absurdity of the situation, Hayes confessed, "I am not confident of results." The Democrats might accept Greeley, and "the people are sick of politics!" [20]

Indeed, the queerest paradox of Greeley's nomination was the fact that there was strength in it. "Pennsylvania pig-iron capitalists" might vote for him, and New York Irish papers promised that the Hibernians would make good any losses from the Germans.[21] Southern Democrats, either lured by his promises of industrial affluence or willing to embrace anyone who promised them the spoils of office, began to hold conventions to demand that their party accept him. "If the nomination were as weak as it is ridiculous," sighed Garfield, "it might be laughed at and passed by, but unfortunately it has much strength." [22] Carl Schurz, ruefully regarding the evidences of his own political ineptitude, declared that "we have not regained one-half the support the movement had before [the Convention], and lost by the nomination;" [23] yet when he took tentative steps to call another meeting he found that the only choice was "Greeley or Grant." Another nominee would insure Grant's election, and reformers must make the best of their bargain.[24]

Late in May, Greeley announced his acceptance of the nomination. Expressing confidence of success, the delighted editor declared that he endorsed the Cincinnati platform, stood for universal political rights and universal amnesty, opposed the granting of more public lands to railroads, and favored the preservation of the National credit. He promised the "full enjoyment of liberty to all," and repeated the platform's weasel words about leaving the tariff to the people. Altogether, the letter of acceptance fell far short of a great State paper.[25] Following this manifesto, the Liberal candidate gave up the active management of the *Tribune* and retired to his estate at Chappaqua, where he affected the garb and habits of a substantial farmer. Visiting delegations found him chopping wood and playing the rôle of homely philosopher. The pose was studied, and the "Farmer of

[20] Hayes *Diary and Letters,* V, 204, May 6, 1872.
[21] New York *Tribune,* May 7, 1872.
[22] Smith, *Garfield,* I, 494–495.
[23] Cortissoz, *Reid,* I, 217.
[24] *Ibid.,* 218.
[25] New York *Tribune,* May 22, 1872.

Chappaqua" was soon the butt of barbed ridicule. When Greeley retired, Whitelaw Reid took over the dual task of managing both the *Tribune* and the Liberal Republican candidate.[26]

Meanwhile, within the Republican ranks all was moving smoothly. The practical politicians who managed the Grant campaign breathed a sigh of relief as Greeley was nominated, and read his acceptance speech without fear. On every hand the politicians organized local meetings for Grant and prepared to send enthusiastic delegations to Philadelphia. Of Republicans who wanted to remain in the party but reject Grant only one was heard. To the last, Charles Sumner hoped for a bolt in the convention.

On May 31, just before the Philadelphia Convention met, Sumner took the Senate floor to catalogue Grant's iniquities again. Before a crowded chamber and packed galleries, he pleaded with his party to abandon the President. Grant was "self-seeking," "indolent," "neglectful of his duties"; he appointed relatives to office—and the Senator called the roll of the President's kindred who fattened at the public trough; he was a "Cæsar," ignoring civil restraints, and surrounding himself with a military clique eager for power. He had quarreled with everyone since his entrance into the White House. He took gifts— bribes from those who sought favors—and had grown rich by toadying to men of great wealth. In fact, there were few political crimes which Sumner did not charge against the President. He reviewed the Administration from the first Cabinet to the packing of the forthcoming convention, and found everywhere evidences of Grant's greed for power. It was Sumner's last major philippic, and he packed into it the venom of a lifetime devoted to castigating his enemies.[27] "Grant," said Greeley's *Tribune*, "is now forever fixed, painted."

But though they listened attentively, neither galleries nor Senate were moved by Sumner's impassioned diatribe. Carpenter and Conkling made replies, denying Sumner's charges *seriatim;* and the National Convention assembled with no change of heart. In fact, one observer in Philadelphia found that the vindictive attacks had caused a reaction in the President's favor.[28] But the Convention was not unaware of the necessity of doing something to counteract Sumner's in-

[26] Cortissoz, *Reid*, I, 212–213.
[27] New York *Tribune*, N. Y. *Times*, and N. Y. *World*, June 1, 1872.
[28] Hayes *Diary and Letters*, V, 204.

fluence. Accordingly, with little hesitation, it nominated Henry Wilson, Sumner's colleague from Massachusetts, for Vice-President. This "flank movement" not only injured Sumner, but helped Grant, especially with the laboring classes and the "old anti-slavery guard"— places where Grant was growing weak.[29]

There was little real fervor among the delegates. In contrast with the Chicago Convention of 1868, the Philadelphia meeting lacked the crowds of cheering soldiers who had given the appearance of spontaneous enthusiasm to Grant's first nomination. Yet the delegates were not officeholders, and the unanimity of the nomination was meant to show that the President's popularity was undimmed. Officeholders who were not delegates kept behind the scenes, and the spirit of the meeting was summed up by one delegate who was told that another was not for Grant. "What's he doing here then?" asked the astonished man.[30]

Speeches were made—speeches that recited the glamorous triumphs of their chieftain from Donelson to Appomattox; speeches which catalogued the achievements of the Administration in the South, in finance, and in foreign affairs. And through them ran the constant refrain that Grant's reëlection was essential to preserve the "results of the war." Gerrit Smith, the veteran Abolitionist, demanded Grant in order that Ku Klux Acts might be enforced and the Negro saved. Logan, who had come perilously near putting himself outside the pale, redeemed himself by hastening to Philadelphia to declare that Grant had been "faithful over a few things, we will make him ruler over many." Another speaker, challenging the statement that Grant neglected his duties, rhapsodized on the General's privations during the war, and declared his willingness to permit the hero of Appomattox to enjoy his horses, his cigars, and his seaside loiterings now.[31]

The platform adopted was as insignificant as the speeches. It, too, declared that the results of the war demanded a continuation of the Republicans in power, enumerated the achievements of the Administration, and pointed with pride to the candidates. On the tariff it asserted the now triumphant doctrines of protection, and on taxation

[29] James Redpath and Geo. L. Fall to Washburne, June 7, 1872, Washburne MSS. Colfax, who had voluntarily retired, receive 321½ votes to Wilson's 368½ on the first ballot. As Wilson needed but 8, a change of Virginia's vote gave him the nomination. Horace Maynard and Governor Davis of Texas were also candidates.
[30] New York *Tribune*, June 4, 1872.
[31] *Ibid.*, June 6, 1872.

and civil service it reiterated the platitudinous promises formerly made. In no wise was it a remarkable document; but personalities and not issues were to dominate the campaign.

Accepting the nomination, Grant spoke with his characteristic brevity. He hoped, he said, to leave to his successor a "country at peace . . . with credit at home and abroad, and without embarrassing questions to threaten the future." The people could judge of his future intentions by his past performance. So saying, he retired to Long Branch for the summer, while the politicians took over the campaign.[32]

The unity and energy of the regular Republicans accentuated the disheartenment of most Liberals. Though Schurz was being forced to accept the inevitable, he continued to deplore Greeley's nomination. On June 6, he united with Cox, William Cullen Bryant, David A. Wells, Jacob Brinkerhoff, and others in letters to a selected list of "gentlemen who are opposed to the present Administration . . . and think all elements should be united," asking them to attend a conference in the Fifth Avenue Hotel on June 20. But the conferees were unable to accomplish anything. The Baltimore Convention of the Democrats was expected to endorse Greeley and Brown, and there was a general feeling that the nominee was strong with the country. It was thought that about one-half the free traders would stick to the reform party, while the others would go for Grant. The conclusion of the meeting was that it was too late to change candidates; that while "there's not much good expected of Greeley," there was little harm; and that "his term will be a sort of bridge over which we can go into the promised land of reform."[33]

Meanwhile, the Democratic Party was swallowing its pride as a preliminary to nominating a man who had been one of its most consistent opponents. State conventions endorsed Greeley, and party newspapers, justifying their apostasy by declaring they would do "anything to beat Grant," came out in favor of the Editor. Republicans had difficulty believing that the Democrats would really fall into line,[34] and in both parties there were prophecies that many would stay away from the polls. As many saw it, the acceptance of Greeley

---

[32] New York *Times,* June 11, 1872; New York *Tribune,* June 12, 1872.

[33] Cortissoz, *Reid,* I, 218; New York *Tribune,* May 31, June 19, 1872; Schurz, Cox, *et al.,* to J. S. Black, June 6, 1872, Black MSS.; Theo. F. Randolph (Morristown, N. J.) to Black, June 9, Black MSS.; Hiram Barney (N. Y.) to Gideon Welles, June 21, Welles MSS.

[34] D. C. Sickles to Chandler, June 7, Chandler MSS.

would "be proof positive that they, as well as the Greeley Republicans, have surrendered all principles, and are simply running for luck, upon the theory that having nothing to lose, they may possibly win something." [35] Some Democrats feared that if the party "sold out" in Baltimore they would lose their organization,[36] but others felt that since the next President was certain to be a Republican, they might as well have a "hand in saying which one." [37] Watching the situation from Long Branch, Grant was moved to one of his rare efforts at metaphor. "The Baltimore Convention is now in incubation," he wrote to Conkling. "Before she hatches and we see [how] the offspring . . . is received by its parents, it is hard to judge how much fondling it will receive. Whether it will be caressed as much after hatching as during incubation, I doubt much." [38]

Whatever doubts Grant may have had, Greeley's supporters ardently counted chickens before they were hatched. The Democrats, declared the *Tribune,* could carry 15 States with 135 votes; the Republicans had 22 states with 231. If the Democrats could hold their fifteen, New York and Pennsylvania would make the balance in their favor 199 to 167. If the Democrats endorsed Greeley, Grant's defeat was certain.[39] Inspired by these calculations, the Democratic Convention accepted Greeley and Brown. There was some opposition to the Cincinnati platform, but this, too, was swallowed. The action was the "most nearly unanimous of any nomination ever made by the Democratic Party," exulted the *Tribune.*[40]

With nominations over, the campaign got under way. The Republicans were fortunate in having no active dissenters, except the eternal Sumner, within their ranks. Men like Blaine and Garfield, whose dislike of Grant was almost as great as Greeley's, bowed their necks to the yoke and campaigned with vigor and the appearance of enthusiasm. At the head of the Republican organization stood E. D. Morgan and W. E. Chandler, Chairman and Secretary of the National Committee. Through Chandler's indefatigable energy the party kept in touch with every locality and every party worker.

[35] Providence *Journal* quoted in New York *Tribune,* June 15, 1872.
[36] Geo. Clark Patterson to Black, June 3, 1872, Black MSS.
[37] Robert Flint, (Fond du Lac, Wis.) to Doolittle, May 10, 1872, Doolittle MSS.
[38] Conkling, *Conkling,* 434–435.
[39] New York *Tribune,* July 9, 1872.
[40] *Ibid.,* July 11, 1872.

By far the most important service rendered by Morgan and Chandler was in gathering the sinews of war for the campaign. According to custom, the campaign committee levied assessments upon the office-holders. Business men with Government contracts were forced to disgorge some of their profits. National banks, the "most compact and powerful interest in the country," were whipped into line without difficulty, while the iron manufacturers of Pennsylvania, who favored protection, were forced to contribute. Business men were told that Greeley's election would precipitate financial catastrophe, and were solicited for aid in preventing a panic. From these sources came the bulk of the money which carried the election.

The largest single contributor was Jay Cooke, "Financier of the Civil War," whose aid in the elections of 1868 and 1872 should give him the additional title of "Financier of the Republican Party." Beginning in February with $5,000 for the New Hampshire campaign, and continuing till after the November elections, he poured money into Republican headquarters as fast as it was necessary. When funds ran low or more effort was required in some doubtful state, Chandler would "spend Sunday with Jay Cooke." Despite his aversion to working on the Sabbath, Cooke usually rewarded these visitations with cash. However, he did not contribute without protest. He told Chandler that "New Hampshire isn't bigger than one of our wards, and I could carry a ward for $1,000," and complained that the secretary should not "ride a free horse to death." He thought that "you ought to make some of the other brethren follow our example. We are very fond of setting a good example, and, like all good fellows, like to have our example followed." On another occasion, he told Chandler that "unless you Republicans stop old Wilson from pirating upon our Northern Pacific and stop the efforts to injure our Railroad interests in the N. W. by passing the St. Croix bill, we'll feel we have been wounded by our friends." But despite these complaints, Cooke continued to play Santa Claus to the party. Henry Cooke, recently appointed Governor of the District of Columbia, ably assisted Chandler in extracting money. "I hope Jay is not giving you too much trouble," wrote Henry, whose liberality with his brother's funds was Chandler's most valuable asset.[41]

[41] Next to Cooke, perhaps the largest contributor was the Philadelphia firm of Drexel & Childs. General McDonald in St. Louis collected money from Indian traders and

The collection of funds was the easier part of Chandler's task; the machinery for this was so well organized that it gave him comparatively little difficulty. More troublesome was the duty of expending the money carefully. Each local committee looked upon the National Committee as a source of revenue, and petty politicians were prone to exaggerate the difficulties before them in order to wheedle money from National headquarters. Newspaper editors expected generous recognition of their support, "Grant and Wilson" clubs needed uniforms, and orators offered their services if expenses were paid. But however besieged, Chandler refused to be swept from his feet, and expended the funds with a skill that bore silent tribute to his astuteness as a politician.

In bringing the press behind Grant, Chandler ignored the appeals of individual journals, but listened attentively to a plan of advertising agents who had "spent hundreds of thousands in newspapers" to control "nearly the entire newspaper press of the country . . . in the interest of the Administration." [42] In addition to lining up the advertisers, Chandler negotiated with the "Southern Newspaper Union" which furnished the "insides" of a hundred Southern Newspapers.[43] Though many proposals came to him to buy newspapers, he resisted the temptation. But Jay Cooke rendered aid personally to a Chattanooga paper which had considerable influence in Tennessee, Georgia, and Alabama.[44] Moreover, Chandler set up in Washington a "correspondent's association" which furnished editorials to Grant papers on request. The head of this enterprise was Grant's secretary, Robert Douglas, son of "the Little Giant." "Secession with its hydra-head would crawl forth and rend the Union in fragments. Infidelity, free-

contractors, as well as from the "Whiskey Ring," which was now in full operation. Among officeholders, the most liberal was J. Russell Jones, old friend of the President and minister to Brussels, whose appreciation of the "good thing" he had in his foreign post led him to be especially generous. "He's a brick," wrote a colleague of the Belgian minister. There is no mention that General Grant made any monetary contribution to his own reëlection.

From the evidence it is difficult to determine the amount of any contribution. Cooke is said to have contributed $50,000, but from the frequent mention of his name in Chandler's correspondence, it would seem that his total contributions to State, local, congressional, and national Committees must far exceed this figure.

These generalizations concerning finances are based on the Chandler MSS. in the Library of Congress, where the author has used letters of February to October, 1872, too numerous to list.

[42] H. A. Wetherill to Chandler, June 17, 1872, Chandler MSS.
[43] R. S. Saunders, (Nashville) to Chandler, June 28, Chandler MSS.
[44] Sam Bard, (Chattanooga) to Chandler, July 10, 1872, Chandler MSS.

love, and Mormonism would run riot . . . and blight over all this fair, happy, prosperous, and peaceful country" if Greeley were elected, stated one editorial by the son of the man who had first wrecked the Democratic Party.[45]

Of far more importance than newspaper publicity was the detailed work of organizing the campaign in the States. For the first time the center of interest shifted from the "October States" to North Carolina, which would hold both State and presidential elections in August. Late in June Chandler decided North Carolina needed help, called on the Congressional Committee for half the expenses, and hastened to see Cooke.[46] Boutwell headed the delegation of visiting speakers sent to North Carolina, and Professor John Langston and a group of his Negro students from Howard University were paid $250 each for their services. The Democrats also used Negro students, but paid $500 for their oratory.[47] Boutwell opened the campaign at Greensborough by asking "What does North Carolina want?" and answered more people, and schools. On immigration alone could the South depend for prosperity, and immigrants as well as natives needed schools. The Democratic Party, said the Secretary, did not want either, and neither immigration, industry, nor schools could exist in Democratic districts.[48]

But the Republicans were not content with a mere appeal to North Carolinians to vote themselves into prosperity. Before Boutwell left Washington, the Federal Marshal for North Carolina carried $200,000 into the State to pay the expenses of the Federal Courts. Some 500 people were already under indictment there, and officers expected to serve papers on hundreds of others suspected of Ku Klux activities. New deputies would receive fees, the power of the government would be upheld, and Democrats would be intimidated so that Negroes could vote for Grant.[49]

That all these tactics had been necessary was evident after the election. First returns from the eastern counties indicated a Democratic victory, and the Liberals rejoiced. The Associated Press estimated a Democratic majority of four to six thousand. But as the western coun-

45 New York *Tribune*, July 18, 1872.
46 Chandler to Morgan, June 22, 1872, Chandler MSS.
47 Frank E. Howe to Morgan, July 14, 1872, P. F. Morris to Chandler, July 16, and Isaac Myers to Chandler, July 16, Chandler MSS.
48 New York *Tribune*, July 18, 1872.
49 *Ibid.*, July 10, 13, 1872.

ties began to total their votes the election was put in doubt. At the end of a week the returns were all in; and while the Democrats had carried both the Legislature and the congressional districts, the electoral vote was given to Grant by 1,000 majority. Greeleyites were loud in their charges of fraud, but as the election was never investigated the count stood.[50]

Throughout the South similar methods were used. The Union League was put to work to rally the Negroes to Grant.[51] Speakers and political writers urged the South to make a definite break with her past, and accept Republican assurances of industrial achievement and prosperity.[52]

Playing definitely into the Republican hands was the opposition to Greeley displayed by the more bitter Confederate leaders. Generals Pillow and Forrest announced their preference for Grant.[53] To one of Jefferson Davis' correspondents, Greeley appeared as the "most absurd ismatic in the world, the most bitter enemy of the South and the Democratic Party." He had called upon Northern soldiers to plunder Southern homes until one could "see privations in the anxious eyes of mother's and the rags of children." Grant, it was true, had fought the war "and by the aid of foreign levies conquered the South and suppressed the Constitution, yet, he did not, like Greeley, labor for 20 years to get it up . . ."[54]

Chandler was of course eager to capitalize the "Bourbon" refusal to support Greeley. Ready to his hand lay one Blanton Duncan, nominally a Democrat, but close to Butler and Dawes, and "smiled upon by Grant." Just what inducements Chandler held out to him is not known, but Liberals alleged that a claim against the Government was hastened through the Interior Department when Duncan stated that he could get 800,000 Democrats to vote against Greeley.[55] Soon Duncan was in conversation with the leading anti-Greeley Democrats, asking them if they agreed with Charles O'Conor "that the present coalition is 'the most infamous phase in American politics.'"[56] By early August,

[50] New York *Tribune*, August 2–9; Geo. M. Robinson, Aug. 2, J. J. Young, Aug. 3, C. E. Doolittle, Aug. 3, J. C. Abbot, Aug. 6, 1872, to Chandler, Chandler MSS.
[51] T. A. Baker to Chandler, May 17, 1872, Chandler MSS.
[52] N. Y. *Times*, May 24, 28, 1872.
[53] Barbour Lewis to Chandler, Sept. 11, 1872, Chandler MSS.
[54] James Lyons to Davis, in Rowland, *Jefferson Davis, Constitutionalist*, VII, 314–7.
[55] N. Y. *Tribune*, Aug. 3, 24.
[56] Cf. Duncan to J. S. Black, July 19, 1872, Black MSS.

he had aligned enough of the "fogy Democracy" to justify a call for a convention at Louisville to nominate a ticket. Leading Republican workers suggested to Chandler that he select good men, give them funds, and send them into the States to work up delegations for the Louisville Convention.[57] The men available were characterized by Chandler as "blowers and adventurers," but he hoped to use them to create disaffection in the South, and especially in Texas, Georgia, and Kentucky, where Republican prospects were poor.[58] Soon agents were reporting to him on their work for the "straight out" movement, and Democrats were soliciting funds to attend the Convention.[59] Many such expenses were paid by the Republicans. In Pennsylvania, for example, Chandler gave $1,000 to send a delegation to Louisville, the State Committee expended $1,800 and J. D. Cameron gave $1,000. From Philadelphia a Democratic band was sent to the Convention at a cost of $500.[60]

Before the Bourbon Democracy assembled Charles O'Conor's name was most often mentioned as the candidate. But on the eve of the meeting, O'Conor announced that he would not accept the nomination. Explaining his action to a friend, O'Conor hoped that posterity would understand that he "was not a visionary enthusiast alike destitute of knowledge and common sense." [61] This renunciation dampened the spirits of the motley crew that assembled in Louisville. However, they could agree on no one else, and adjourned after naming O'Conor and John Quincy Adams on a platform denouncing Greeley and asserting ancient Democratic principles. Though O'Conor refused the nomination again [62] and no effort was made to conduct a campaign, many Democrats on election day cast a protest vote for the Louisville nominees.

Causing considerably more anxiety in Republican councils than the South was the situation in Maine, with her September election, and the October States of Indiana, Ohio, and Pennsylvania. Speaker

[57] B. M. Dodge to Chandler, August, 1872, Chandler MSS.
[58] Chandler to Washburne, August 16, 1872, Washburne MSS.
[59] John Pool to Chandler, August 20, and C. A. Rose to *id.*, Aug. 22, 1872, Chandler MSS.
[60] H. H. Bingham to Chandler, Sept. 26, 1872; cf. also, W. L. Scroggs to Chandler, September 26, Chandler MSS. Local politicians in Wisconsin contributed to a fund to send "straight out" delegates to Louisville. See letters of O. B. Thomas, August 28, Samuel W. Reese, September 12, J. H. Howe, August 23, 1872 to E. W. Keyes, Keyes MSS.
[61] O'Connor to Black, Sept. 3, 1872, Black MSS.
[62] New York *Tribune*, September 4, 5, 6, 1872.

Blaine was active in his own State, and enlisted many speakers.[63] Though normally Republican, Maine was troubled by the perennial temperance question, which kept the Republican leaders anxious. In Ohio the outlook was hopeful, for there Secretary Delano, whose management of his department gained the unqualified endorsement of the politicians, was strong,[64] and the Greeley forces were weak. Even such ardent reformers as Cox could not show enthusiasm over Greeley.[65] In Indiana the Democrats intrusted their campaign to Thomas A. Hendricks, an able man, who rendered the outcome doubtful. Chandler, who had long experience with the pleas of Indiana politicians for money, must have groaned in advance over the cost of carrying the State. "They ought to be aided immediately," he told Morgan, "but I know if we begin liberally now there will be no end to the pressure by and by." However, he hastened off to Jay Cooke to raise the necessary money.[66] Despite the cries of the local politicians, Chandler never took the Indiana situation as seriously as he did those in other States. Knowing it would require a fight to win, he sent in speakers and money, but he was more anxious about the situation in Pennsylvania.[67]

In Pennsylvania the Republicans felt that their prospects were poor. Their candidate for Governor, Hartranft, had been Auditor-General of the State, and was accused of misusing State funds. Chandler spent money lavishly, and speakers from all over the country—even from Tennessee—hastened into the State. Grant himself urged Chandler to spare no effort. Prophecies were made that the State would go Democratic in October and Republican in November, but everybody knew that an October victory would give hope to the Democrats and endanger Republican success. The State was thoroughly canvassed, manufacturers were forced to contribute, Grant made changes in the offices, Negroes from Maryland and Virginia were imported to "work for Massa Cameron and vote for Massa Grant," a "Soldiers' Convention" was held in Pittsburgh, and "there was nothing in Pennsylvania which was not bought." The result was satisfactory. Hartranft carried

---

[63] Blaine to Logan, July 15, 1872, Horace Porter to Logan, July 24, 1872, Logan MSS.
[64] G. M. Dodge to Morgan, August, 1872, Delano to Chandler, September 16, 1872, Chandler MSS.
[65] Cox to Garfield, August 14, 1872, Garfield MSS.
[66] Chandler to Morgan, June 22, 1872, Chandler MSS.
[67] Chandler to Washburne, July 19, 1872, September 22, 1872, W. W. Belknap to Washburne, August 28, 1872, Washburne MSS; Washburne to Chandler, August 9, J. R. Jones to Chandler, September 3, Chandler to Morgan, July 11, O. P. Morton to Chandler, August 11, J. H. Warwick to Chandler, September 26, 1872, Chandler MSS.

the State by 35,000 majority, and with this result Grant's success in the nation was assured.[68]

It was the efficient organization of the national Republican campaign, the lavish use of money, and the constant contact with every locality, rather than the direct appeal to the intelligence or prejudices of the voters, that brought success to the Republican cause. Yet the customary ephemeræ of an American presidential election were not lacking. On both sides, campaign orators devoted far more time to attacking the records of the opposition candidate than to praising their own. Greeley's inconsistent career, his personal eccentricities, and his anomalous position furnished excellent material for Republican campaigners. Ridicule of his long linen duster, his vegetarianism, his spiritualism, his temperance position, his agricultural and financial absurdities, was easy. On the other hand, Democrats and Liberal Republicans attacked Grant's Administration. Charges of corruption, nepotism, favoritism, filled the Democratic speeches.[69] Grant was the "Jockey General" who neglected his office. Yet amid these counter-charges, the Republicans had an advantage over their opponents. They could point with pride to solid achievements, while Greeley's followers were constrained from dwelling on Greeley's record. Many of them, too, found it necessary to admit that Grant's war record was unexceptional. On the whole, while multitudes were disgusted with both candidates, the general feeling was that Grant was the safer of the two. "I prefer the ills we have rather than those threatening us," said General Sherman.[70]

Throughout the campaign efforts were made to appeal to various special classes. Business men were told that they could not afford to vote for Greeley, while Greeleyites, citing the support of A. T. Stewart, who had been estranged from Grant by the general order affair, asked if business could afford to take Grant with "plunder, waste, and corruption." [71] Sumner advised the Negroes that Greeley had long been their friend, while Grant had never had abolition sympathies;[72] but Frederick Douglass and other Negro leaders worked for Grant,[73] and in

---

[68] These statements are based on numerous letters in the Chandler and Logan MSS. for 1872.

[69] Cf. Cross, *Life of Grant*, 160 ff., New York *Tribune*, June 22, 1872.

[70] W. T. Sherman, *Home Letters of General Sherman*, 381–382.

[71] New York *Tribune*, August 19, October 5, 8, 1872.

[72] *Ibid.*, July 31, August 16, 1872.

[73] H. T. Johns to Claflin, June 6, 1872, Chandler MSS.

September Sumner abandoned the campaign and sought rest and for-getfulness in Europe.[74] Farmers were told that Greeley's book *What I Know About Farming* showed him an impossible theorist, while Grant was a man of enormous "common sense."[75] Both sides appealed to the German vote, which showed a tendency to split along sectional lines. Germans in the East reacted against Greeley's temperance doctrines,[76] while those in the West reluctantly followed Carl Schurz. Much was made of the alleged favoritism to France in the Franco-Prussian War.[77] Methodists were appealed to on the ground that the President attended their church—even going to camp meetings at Long Branch—[78] while Democrats reminded Jews of Grant's "infamous Jew Order" at Memphis.[79] Even the women were solicited for their support. Anna Dickinson was reputedly offered $10,000 to speak for Greeley, but Republican friends of Women's Rights prevailed upon her to remain silent.[80]

Two products of the campaign are worth passing notice. One was the purchase by the Government of General George Pickett's "Rebel Archives," which contained a record of Greeley's efforts to negotiate peace in 1864. The publication of documents showing that Confederate agents used Greeley as a cat's-paw was expected to discredit the Democratic nominee's intelligence and patriotism.[81] The papers constituted a valuable source for Civil War history, and have proved more serviceable to later historians than they did to politicians of 1872. The other product was the series of cartoons by Thomas Nast, hero of the Tweed *exposé*. Portraying Greeley as a fool, lampooning him for every act of his life, Nast proved a veritable gad-fly to the harassed Liberal candidate.

Throughout the campaign Grant sat in seeming imperturbability in his cottage at Long Branch. Only occasional trips to Washington to hold routine Cabinet meetings and visits to friends near by broke

[74] Washburne to Chandler, Sept. 6, 1872, Chandler MSS.; N. Y. *Tribune*, Sept. 20, 1872.
[75] New York *Times*, June 13, 1872.
[76] Chandler to Washburne, August 16, 26, 1872, Washburne MSS.
[77] Chandler to Washburne, September 22, Washburne MSS. The Democrats doubtless lost votes by retailing the scandalous story of how the Reverend Cramer, Grant's German born brother-in-law who was minister to Denmark, had been ostracized by Copenhagen society for public drunkenness. New York *Times*, June 15, 1872.
[78] New York *Tribune*, September 19, 1872.
[79] *Ibid.*, August 10, 1872.
[80] Anna Joclyn Gage to Chandler, September 2, 1872, Chandler MSS.
[81] N. Y. *Tribune*, July 15, 1872; Levi Luckey to Washburne, July 21, 1872, Washburne MSS.

the monotony of the summer. Early in the campaign he told Conkling that he would take no part in it. "It has been done, so far as I remember, by but two presidential candidates heretofore, and both of them were public speakers and both were beaten. I am no speaker and I don't want to be beaten!" [82] Relieved from work by this decision, Grant improved in health and looks.[83] While politicians worried, he showed no signs of anxiety over the outcome. Chandler complained that he complacently regarded himself as a man of destiny, and one observer declared the President was "just as easy as tho' he were driving horses on a smooth road with a good cigar in his mouth. He has no doubts and no fears." [84] Such an attitude disgusted Chandler, who complained that Grant should do something to influence the Pennsylvania situation. Lincoln, said Chandler, would have used the full power of his position to carry the State, "but I haven't much hope from an Administration that did nothing in politics for 2½ years, . . . and has only begun to do well in the last six months." [85] Moreover, Chandler resented Grant's ingratitude: "Since I left these rooms four years ago no word of thanks has been uttered to me for my services. I am a fool for going into this campaign, but I love my party." [86]

Not all of Chandler's complaints were justified. Grant received visitors at Long Branch and advised with them on the campaign. He made changes in Federal officials in a number of States on Chandler's advice, and dropped an occasional word to newspaper correspondents in correction of some of Greeley's allegations.[87] But he refused to show the anxiety which he must have secretly felt over the outcome. When the October returns came, Garfield visited the White House with the news that Ohio had given 14,000 for the State Republican ticket. The Liberal Republican movement reminded the President of an experience he had once had with howling coyotes in the West. He had estimated there were a hundred when he heard the noise made by two.[88]

[82] Conkling, *Conkling*, 435.
[83] W. W. Belknap to Washburne, August 28, 1872, Washburne MSS.
[84] Pierrepont to Washburne, October 2, 1872, Washburne MSS.
[85] Chandler to Morgan, July 11, 1872, Chandler MSS.
[86] Chandler to Washburne, July 19, 1872, Washburne MSS.
[87] New York *Tribune*, July 24, 1872.
[88] Garfield MS Diary, October 19, 1872.

In the beginning Greeley planned to follow Grant's course and remain silent during the campaign. But silence ill became such an aggressive fighter, and it was not long before he was making stump speeches to visiting delegations. He appeared in Maine for a series of addresses,[89] and in September toured New Jersey, Pennsylvania, Ohio, and Indiana. At every stop he delivered a different speech, impressing many with his versatility. Yet he would have done better to follow Grant's example, for observers thought his speeches hurt more than they helped. In Indiana he so annoyed the local Democratic managers that they requested him to cut short his visit and return home. After the October elections, he remained at home sadly contemplating his inevitable defeat.[90]

On election day both candidates remained quietly at home. So likewise did many voters. In the cities a strange epidemic, known as the epizoötic, deranged the transportation systems by killing off horses by the thousands; and it seriously hampered party workers in getting voters to the polls. But lack of enthusiasm counted for more. Though the popular vote was lighter than in 1868, Grant's majorities were far greater. In the whole Union, Greeley carried only six Southern States. Georgia, Kentucky, Maryland, Missouri, Tennessee, and Texas—in only two of which the Republicans had made a fight—gave him 66 electoral votes against Grant's 276.

Surveying the wreck of their campaign, Liberals concluded that the wealth of the country "and especially the incorporated wealth, rallied to the support of General Grant, and poured out its millions in his behalf." Manufacturers and bankers were making profits, and considered Greeley unsafe.[91] Many Liberals blamed the Democrats for Greeley's defeat. Republican leaders, on the other hand, felt that a great peril had been avoided. Some hoped that victory would bring about reforms; [92] others were inclined to mingle hope with skepticism. Garfield thought that there were dangers inherent in so overwhelming a victory, and looked for an era of "arrogance and recklessness" which would break the party before Grant's new Administration was

[89] New York *Tribune*, August 16, 1872.
[90] New York *Tribune*, August 13, September 19, 21, 26, 27, 28, 30, October 31, 1872; J. H. Warwick to Chandler, September 26, Chandler MSS.; Smith, *Garfield*, I, 496.
[91] New York *Tribune*, November 6, 1872.
[92] *Ibid.*, November 7, 1872; Wm. Claflin to Chandler, November 7, 1872, Chandler MSS.; Thos. Hood to Fairchild, October 23, 1872, Fairchild MSS.

half over.[93] But through all postmortems and speculations Grant sat as imperturbable as during the campaign. Not even the vindication of the election could make him articulate. In the future as in the past, men must watch his actions to learn what he thought.

[93] Smith, *Garfield*, I, 497.

THE election of 1872 marked the half-way point in Grant's occupancy of the White House. It was his misfortune that he came upon the national scene at a moment when our entire national life was going through a process of transition. The eight years of his presidency marked the transfer of authority from the lords of the manor to the masters of capital. New men and new measures occupied the public attention, and gave a strange character to the era which was just emerging. In politics, the quiet dignity and confidence of the "gentlemen statesmen" who had graced legislative halls in the forties and fifties was rapidly being replaced by the aggressive manners of the practical politician. In economics, the merchant and planter gave way to new men—the war-rich contractors and the often loud-mouthed lords of industry. In the realm of public thought there were equally great changes. One heard little of State Rights, or even the Constitution, but much of the nation. Faith in American progress supplanted the ancient pride in American democracy. On the whole, it was an age of confusion, with its vulgar, crude, or tasteless features frequently looming so large as to conceal its more solid virtues. Historians and romanticists have attempted to characterize the era by a phrase, and the very variety of their labels is suggestive of the confusion of the period. To some, who have seen calamity in the decline of an older mode of life it has been a "Tragic Era," while others, looking at the "Emergence of Modern America," have contended that these hectic years witnessed the "birth of a nation." Others, with eyes largely upon the South, but cognizant of the far-reaching significance of the passing of Southern dominance, have sought to give the term "reconstruction" a larger connotation, and allege that the entire national life was reconstructed during Grant's eight years in the White House. But whatever the name applied, the facts of transition stand out in bold relief. In every field of human endeavor a new and startlingly different society was evolving. When Grant left the White House in 1877 America was as different from the America of 1861 as the cottage in Galena was different from the Executive Mansion.

Nations emerging from such periods of transition are prone to become contemptuous of their adolescent years. Like Queen Victoria, whose name has been perverted to connote all that was deemed stuffy in the days of her reign, Grant has been transformed into the representative figure of an age considered vulgar and ostentatious. "Late General Grant" applies to a stage of architectural design in much the same manner that "Victorian" describes an outmoded system of manners and morals.

Perhaps no better illustration of the cultural confusion of the age of General Grant can be found than the State, War and Navy Department building, adjoining the White House grounds. The ornate character of this rambling structure contrasts as sharply with the Executive Mansion as the period of General Grant contrasts with that of John Adams. The presidential residence, of classic simplicity, was in thorough harmony with the simple dignity of its first occupant. The other public buildings of the earlier years reflected the desire of a new nation for dignity, and if they borrowed heavily from Republican Rome they but illustrated the national ambition to achieve the virtues of the days of Cincinnatus. In contrast, public buildings of the Grant régime show a complete departure from the older days, but bear no evidence that the nation had reached a new plane of culture. The State Department building, frosted outside like a wedding cake, had on the inside labyrinthine passageways, and swinging doors redolent of the corner saloon. The architects, all unknowingly, had captured in marble the vulgar ostentation, "elegance" in ornament, and inner crudity of adolescent America.

The public ceremonies and the official society of the Grant régime reveal how accurately the architecture of the State Department reflected the spirit of the age. Commentators on Washington society were in general agreement that social life in the Capital city was as artificial as the streets themselves. "Washington is the concrete of seediness," exclaimed one dismayed feminine visitor. "It is a poor relation of prosperous cities. It is out at the elbows, shabby at the toes, generally dingy and neglected, while the public buildings shine upon its poverty like pinchbeck jewelry." There were no streets, complained the astounded lady. "There are vast, dreary, uninhabited tracts, destitute of verdure and roamed over by herds of horse cars and hacks." As for society, it was topsy-turvy. To begin with, the new-

MRS. JULIA DENT GRANT

comer made the first calls, and if she were invited to any of the myriad of public receptions, she would be completely lost in the crowd. The weekly routine of calls and receptions never varied, and "through it all is a sense of unrest and undurability." [1] Another visitor found no society, but only one long revel "from the ringing of the Christmas chimes to the tolling of Ash Wednesday bells." It was a "revel into which scamp or courtesan enters without exclusion, the one because she controls a power, the other because he is a power—a revel where the innocent young débutante whirls in the close clasp of some man wrecked soul and body long ago, sits beside a painted woman, . . . and dips her ladle into the punchbowl and tosses off her dram like the best of them. . . ."

This was the opinion of visitors, who observed the apparent meaningless whirl of Washington social life, where "simplicity of satin will over-lay the shortcomings of grammar, clean bank notes disguise foul lives." [2] To those who were part of the society, these external crudities were less patent. General Badeau defended Washington society as " 'good' in the best sense of the word." Rich and poor mingled on a plane of equality, power was more important than money, and great deeds counted more than wealth.[3] Ben: Perley Poore bore similar testimony, and pointed to the Knickerbocker tradition which was kept alive by Hamilton Fish, and the Bostonian simplicity of Boutwell and Hoar.[4]

In truth, both observers and participants were right in their characterization of Washington social life. Washington society, like Washington architecture, and indeed, like American life in this period of transition, contained elements of good and bad. Vulgar ostentation mingled strangely with Doric simplicity, and the contrasts between the façades of the public buildings was not more strange than the contrasts between the dignified household of the Secretary of State and the hectic home of W. W. Belknap, Secretary of War. Anomalous—even artificial—the society may have been, but it was not more so than that in any other city where new capitalists mingled with old families. When men of the private morality of Jim Fisk and Jay Gould could publicly combine in schemes for wholesale corruption it is not to

[1] New York *Tribune,* February 25, 1867.
[2] *Ibid.,* December 30, 1870.
[3] Badeau, *Grant in Peace,* 245–246.
[4] Ben: Perley Poore and O. H. Tiffany, *Life of U. S. Grant,* Part 2, 69.

be wondered that débutantes danced and drank with *roués*. Public taste was passing through the confusion of youth; out of the clashing elements a new society, and a new America, would be born.

Into the midst of this society, the accident of public events had thrown the Grant family. With their advent Washington society re-oriented itself, for the first time since Buchanan, about the White House. Lincoln's wife had disgusted a nation by her extravagance in the midst of war, and had failed in her ambition to be a social leader. The simple Tennessee family which preceded the Grants watched the social whirl, but Mrs. Johnson's invalidism prevented any but the most formal participation. But now the White House again became the center of Washington society.

Although the general was the undismayed hero of a thousand receptions, the Grants fitted a little awkwardly into their social routine. Mrs. Grant customarily asked the wives of Cabinet members, politicians, or army officers to receive with her. Mrs. Fish, of impeccable taste, and Mrs. Borie, of long experience in society, were frequently pressed into service, and their advice taken. Mrs. Logan, too, was often at the First Lady's side. On at least one occasion when Hamilton Fish was preparing to resign, Grant appealed to him to remain because of Mrs. Grant's need for Mrs. Fish. At her own *soirées*, at public dinners, and at the dreaded public levees, the first lady consistently wore black velvet which set off her shoulders and arms. Those who watched her to detect social blunders turned away disappointed. She was, said one observer, "a sunny, sweet woman; too unassuming to be a mark for criticism; too simple and kindly to make the mistakes which invite it." [5] Occasionally some Democratic journal reminded its readers that she had a squint in her eye, or spoke suggestively of her "unfortunately short memory," but even they admitted that she possessed both tact and ability.[6] As time passed and Mrs. Grant became more accustomed to her public station, she became more of an autocrat. Then Mrs. Logan usually displaced Mrs. Fish as her companion. Eventually, Mrs. Grant became so attached to the White House that she welcomed every suggestion for a third term.[7]

In contrast with her growing enjoyment of Washington society,

[5] New York *Tribune*, February 25, 1867.
[6] New York *World*, February 20, 1870.
[7] Badeau, *Grant in Peace*, 242.

Grant never became enamoured of his social duties. Every other Thursday during the social season the President took up his stand in the "Blue Room" and for two hours wore his "fight it out on this line" expression.[8] On such occasions he appeared even more inarticulate than usual. Destitute of small talk and petty social graces, he was as unable to appear at ease in crowds as he was to address an audience. His social genius flowered in the bosom of his family, or when surrounded by close friends.

Behind the formal reception rooms of the White House, little seen by the general public, the family life of the Galena cottage was reproduced. The circle was elastic, varying in size as relatives or close friends joined it for extended visits. Before moving into the executive mansion the Grant ménage comprised Congressman Washburne, members of the General's staff, the father and brother of Mrs. Grant, and Jesse Grant, in addition to Grant's immediate family.[9] In the White House it included Secretaries Badeau, Babcock, and Porter, Chief Usher Fred Dent, "Grandpa" Dent, sons "Buck" and Jesse, and daughter Nellie, while "Grandfather" Jesse Grant was almost a permanent guest. Other members of both the Grant and Dent clans came frequently and stayed long with their high-placed relatives.

Within this circle, Grant laid aside the mask which hid him from the public. His affection for members of his family, though it found some expression in the appointment of relatives to office, was unsuspected by the public. Between "Ulyss" and Julia there existed an almost idyllic attachment, which made them both miserable when separated. During the war Julia had followed the army whenever possible, and had taken up headquarters in Vicksburg and at Fortress Monroe in order to be near her husband. Whenever reunited after a separation, they held hands like lovers. A life of failure had suppressed Grant's emotions, and only in Julia's sympathetic presence was he entirely at ease. Julia alone knew how to deal with him; she alone knew the bolstering effect that her confidence had on him. After Vicksburg she gave him the pet name "Victor," well knowing that such affectionate admiration was manna to his warped and sensitive soul. After his final report as general, she found the New York *Herald* calling him "Cæsar" and adopted that name for her husband.

[8] Poore and Tiffany, *Life of Grant*, 68–70.
[9] Cf. Comstock MS. Diary, December 15, 1865, June 25, 1866.

But the original authorship of the title was distasteful, and there was too much popular odium attached to the word. Seeing it displeased him, she returned to "Victor." Because of her understanding love, no person exerted more influence on Grant than his wife.[10]

Unfortunately, Julia's judgment was not always as strong as her love. Those who knew the family sometimes understood that Grant's favor was to be obtained through her intercession. Politicians flattered her—she was not without social vanity—and her desire for a longer lease on public life was one of the potent influences causing Grant, against his own judgment and inclination, to silently acquiesce in a third term movement. Seldom, however, did she interfere with political affairs.

In dealing with their children both General and Mrs. Grant displayed an indulgence which was uncommon in their day. Neither of the great formative elements in American life—the Puritan inheritance and the frontier—had accorded rights to children, and the rising industrialism, based largely upon the labor of exploited children, contributed nothing to the advance of the younger generation. On farms and in factories child labor was almost the universal rule, and those children whose lot in life allowed them educational opportunities found that the schools were administered with little attention to their basic problems. The accepted rules of child training had crystallized into such axioms as "spare the rod and spoil the child," and "children should be seen and not heard," and there were few to question such precepts.

Among those who were protesting against the old methods of treating children, the Grants were not heard, but in their own practice affection and sympathy replaced the stern parental frown and the disciplinary sessions in the woodshed which characterized the usual American home. Grant's children were to remember with gratitude that their father never whipped nor scolded them for their misdeeds.

When the Grants entered the White House but two of their children were regularly at home. Fred, who had followed his father through the Vicksburg campaign, had been appointed to West Point by Presi-

[10] Cf. Butler, *Correspondence*, IV, 431; Porter, *Campaigning with Grant*, 283–285; Hayes, *Diary and Letters*, IV, 13–14, January 10, 1866; Badeau, *Grant in Peace*, 410–411, and *passim*.

dent Johnson. His cadetship was generally regarded as evidence of
Grant's nepotism, and Democrats found much to criticize in his conduct in connection with the hazing of a Negro cadet. Despite rather
strenuous efforts to attack the President through his son, none of the
newspaper charges could be substantiated.[11] Graduating in 1871
with a standing of 41 in discipline in a class of 41, and with a low ranking in all subjects,[12] Fred became a lieutenant in the Fourth Cavalry.
However, the Democrats soon had good grounds for the charge of
favoritism, for instead of serving with his regiment, Fred was attached
to Sherman's staff, and the fall after his graduation accompanied the
General of the Army on a trip to Europe.[13] In 1873 he was attached to
Sheridan's staff with the pay of lieutenant-colonel, and again the
charges of nepotism rang out.[14]

Ulysses, Jr., universally known as "Buck," entered Harvard as his
father entered the White House. After several years in college, he
began a disastrous career as banker. When he set up in business
in Washington, Grant ordered the Treasury department to send his
salary check to the firm of "Sherman & Grant, Bankers, of this city," [15]
For years the General and Julia regarded Buck as a financial genius,
and trusted him implicitly. Although personally honest, Buck's success
was largely due to his official connections. His judgment was never
sharpened by adversity, and despite his experience he was eventually
the unwitting tool of unscrupulous men who victimized the family.
But at no time did Grant's faith in his second son's abilities waver.
Not even eventual disaster shook his confidence.

With Buck and Fred in school, only Nellie and Jesse were left to
enjoy the notoriety which was inevitable in their station. Young Jesse
was still playing the rôle of family humorist, and his parents and their
guests smiled indulgently at his juvenile wit. Even the Cabinet occasionally set itself to solve Jesse's problems. Once, when a stamp
dealer failed to fill Jesse's order, the Cabinet debated the delinquency
and authorized the White House policeman to write the dilatory
dealer. Jesse's impressions of the public men of the day interested

---

[11] New York *Tribune*, Feb. 7, 15, 1871; Babcock to General E. Upton, Feb. 16, 1871,
Grant Letter Books.
[12] New York *Tribune*, June 14, 1871.
[13] *Ibid.*, November 16, 1871.
[14] *Ibid.*, March 27, 1873; in 1874, Fred Grant married Miss Ida Honore in Chicago.
[15] Grant to D. W. Mahon, May 22, 1875, Grant Letter Books.

his father. The lad liked Bristow and Babcock, and reacted as violently as his father against Sumner.[16]

Realizing the problem which resulted from a boy's residence in the White House, Mrs. Grant attempted to secure a normal outlet for her son by encouraging the formation of a "White House gang." Accordingly, on Christmas Day, 1871, six boys met in a gardener's tool house on the grounds and organized the "K. F. R.,"—a society whose mystic name has been lost in oblivion. Henceforth, the gang solved many of Jesse's psychological problems, though they added nothing to the peace of the Executive Mansion.[17] But Julia Grant's good judgment did not extend to schools for Jesse. In the fall of 1873 he was taken to the Chettenham Academy at Shoemakertown, Pennsylvania. Soon he grew homesick, and began to write home that he was suffering from headaches. Mrs. Grant hastily concluded that he was threatened with typhoid, and the President, who missed the lad, and who was never able to be stern with his children, sent for him to come home. A check was mailed to cover his bill, and henceforth he received whatever educational advantages an occasional private tutor or a short session in a local school might afford.[18]

A casual visitor at the White House, dining with the Grants, found the dinner good and the family circle "very unstiff, chatty and pleasant." In the midst of the conversation, Jesse interrupted to ask, "Papa, what are they fixing up so many war ships for in a hurry—you ain't going to have war with England, are you?" The President replied with the same platitudes he would have used to answer an adult interlocutor: "You know in time of peace we prepare for war, and are always ready for war, but we expect no war with England." [19]

Equally indulgent was the treatment accorded Nellie. From the beginning the President's daughter became a ruling queen of juvenile society, and very soon passed from the children's group into the fast-moving "younger set" of the Capital. Conservative matrons were horrified that she led the cotillion and danced all night—and at an age when she should have been put to bed soon after dark! The criticism was so great that a visitor was surprised to find that "Miss Nellie is a very pretty girl of 16. Behaves just as well as any other

---

[16] Jesse R. Grant, *In the days of my Father*, 69 ff., 117–120.
[17] *Ibid.*, 79 ff.; Roosevelt, *The White House Gang*, 165–166.
[18] Luckey to Rev. Dr. Sam. Clemats, March 2, 1874, Grant Letter Book.
[19] Lucius Fairchild to Sarah F. Deane, March 4, 1872, Fairchild MSS,

NELLIE GRANT

well bred girl would." [20] But the Democrats, whose moral nature was outraged by such laxity, pointed the finger of reproach at the Grants for their failure to give her proper chaperonage. Soon half-grown admirers were paying visits to the White House, and Julia realized that Nellie was becoming too sophisticated for her age.

The solution for Nellie's problem was found in a trip to Europe. The Bories, always intimate friends, were going to England and would be glad to have her with them. In the spring of 1872 Nellie set sail for England. But Julia had counted without the politicians. In England Minister Schenck and Consul-General Badeau proceeded to entertain the child in a manner fit for a princess. Badeau gave a garden party where Nellie could meet the socially élite, and Schenck prepared to have her presented at Court. Mrs. Borie was disgusted: she had planned a quiet trip, and now she must get new dresses in order to dance attendance on the maiden she was chaperoning! But the politicians were not to be denied, and Nellie carried herself with girlish grace through a round of parties and even appeared at ease in the presence of Queen Victoria. Finally, the disgusted Bories cut short their trip and hurried their charge back to the United States.

The final wreck of Julia Grant's well-laid plans came on the homeward trip. While the Bories were confined to their cabin with seasickness, Nellie met Algernon Sartoris, scion of an English country family. By the time the boat landed, Nellie had lost her heart to the youth. Sartoris followed his love to Washington, and one night after dinner at the White House he followed the President into his study to ask for Nellie's hand. Nellie had warned her parents, and Grant gave reluctant consent. In May, 1874, not yet nineteen, she was married in the White House.[21]

The arrangements for her wedding were, according to the newspaper reports, "quiet and unostentatious." The management of details was left to Mrs. Grant, whose simplicity and "quiet taste" came in for fulsome praise. The Marine Band of forty pieces played as the guests gathered in the East Room. Flowers "filled the windows, festooned the walls, wreathed the columns, covered the mantels and tables, hung from chandeliers, and formed arches in the doorways." At the appointed hour Grant led his daughter to an improvised altar where they joined the

[20] Lucius Fairchild to Sarah F. Deane, March 4, 1872, Fairchild MSS.
[21] Badeau, *Grant in Peace*, 412 ff.

pale-faced groom. Dr. Tiffany, of Grant's Methodist Church, read the Episcopal service, while eight bridesmaids waited in the flower banked aisles. After the ceremony the two hundred guests inspected the gifts. Childs had sent a dessert set of eighty-four pieces, Drexel a dinner service valued at $4,500, Hamilton Fish a silver tankard, Creswell an ice cream service. Levi P. Morton of New York gave two rings, an emerald and a diamond, worth $1,000 each. From Robeson came a toilet set and side-pieces of Louis XIV brass, from Babcock a lace fan, from A. T. Stewart a $500 handkerchief, and from the President himself a check for $10,000. All the gifts were arranged by a special agent from Philadelphia, who attractively classified them in accordance with the stores from which they were purchased! [22]

President Grant might well have been pleased that the wedding was so simple. Next month he paid department-store and dressmakers' bills amounting to $3,827.[23]

The wedding with a young Englishman was not popular with the American people, and they were soon willing to listen to rumors that the bride was not happy with her husband. Predictions that she would soon be suing for a divorce were heard.[24] But Marshall Jewell, visiting them in England, found her infatuated with her husband, and Grant never for a moment doubted the felicity of his daughter's marriage.

Toward their parents the Grants were as indulgent as toward their children. "Grandpa" Dent made his home at the White House, where he amused—and sometimes irritated—visitors and staff by declaiming at length on the unconstitutionality of most of the Radical measures.[25] "Grandfather" Jesse Grant was prone to neglect his postoffice at Covington, Ky., to visit the White House. After his first interference in an appointment in Garfield's district he wielded no further influence with his son. Following his accident on inauguration day his health was not good, and in 1873 he died. Grant's mother then moved to New York to make her home with the Corbins. Alone of Grant's relatives she never visited the White House, and, in fact, saw little of her son. Occasionally when Grant went to New York he accompanied her

[22] New York *Tribune,* May 22, 1874.

[23] Letters in Grant Letter Book, June 5–14, 1874. This figure includes only bills paid in New York and Philadelphia.

[24] E. W. Keyes to Fairchild, July 18, 1874, Fairchild MSS.

[25] Comstock MS Diary, June 25, 1866; Poore and Tiffany, *Life of Grant,* 49.

to church; but even after his retirement from the presidency, he saw little of her. In 1880 she wrote a friend that "U. S. Grant paid us a short visent. . . . he Seldom Writes to any of us. . . ." [26]

Grant's daily routine in the White House was simple. Rising at seven, he read the newspapers until breakfast was served at eight-thirty. Then slowly, smoking as he went, he took a short walk, and returned to his office at ten. Callers found him with his secretaries, answering letters, or receiving members of Cabinet and Congress. At three o'clock he closed his office and visited the stables, from which he would go for a drive or a stroll along Pennsylvania avenue. Dinner was served at five, and after dinner, unless social duties interfered, he read the papers and received friends until ten or eleven. The quiet, retiring President preferred such a drab day to those which kept him in the public eye.[27]

The President's tastes were decidedly individual. For art he had no eye, and for music no ear, but a lady in St. Louis was to remember throughout her life the almost feminine enjoyment which he took in her flowers.[28] In food, the suggestion of blood sickened this man of war, whose meat had to be cooked to crispness. In the army, the head-quarters cook "learned that the nearer he came to burning up the meat the better Grant liked it." [29] The President would eat only beef; mutton was taboo, and fowl and game were not allowed on the table. Once, in the army, Grant explained that he would not eat "anything that went on two legs." In addition to meat, the President liked cucumbers, corn, pork and beans, and buckwheat cakes. Many of his foods were indigestible, but he never suffered from digestive disorders.[30] As for drink, coffee was the strongest beverage in which he customarily indulged. Despite Democrats and reformers who constantly raised the accusation of drunkenness against the President, there is not a single reliable witness that Grant drank while President. His letter books of White House days show an occasional note of thanks to a friend for wine, and an occasional order for sherry or port, but the quantities were small, and could barely have sufficed for the White House table.

[26] Hannah Grant to "Sister" King, March 2, 1880, Letter in Library of Congress; New York *Tribune,* February 24, 1885; *National Republican,* July 2, 1773; Grant to Corbin, December 13, 1876, in Grant MSS., Library of Congress.
[27] Poore and Tiffany, *Life of Grant,* 49–50.
[28] Richardson, *Grant,* 169.
[29] Porter, *Campaigning with Grant,* 97.
[30] *Ibid.,* 214–215.

The testimony of every associate shows Grant a temperate man, and it would seem that his last overindulgence was an unfortunate occurrence during Johnson's "Swing around the circle."

Unquestionably Grant's temperance is to be accounted for by the change in his position and environment. In the old army, separated from his family and hopeless of the future, he drank to escape his hardships. At Hardscrabble, with depressing evidences of failure on all sides, he took to drink. Drinking, too, was a means of escape from his embarrassing position as Johnson's companion and the Radical hero in 1866. Grant had ever been a solitary drinker, finding his liquor the escape from himself; now, in the White House, success was his and escape unnecessary. Moreover, by the time he entered the Presidency, Grant had obtained a better perspective and had devised rationalizations which made a resort to drink absurd. When Democrats and reformers criticized, he set down their words as partisanship, and however much his enemies might condemn, his friends were close to sing his praises. Public acclaim and friends were more intoxicating than wine.

For friends, slow in coming when he was a failure, surrounded Grant as President. In their company he lost his reticence and even became loquacious. Unimaginative, and a stickler for verbal accuracy, his friends sometimes thought him "tediously truthful," and occasionally were bored by his habit of stating every detail in a story.[31] His conversation was free from profanity and smut, and he never gossiped. Since he was devoid of small talk, his conversations were likely to be monologues. His information, at the outset, was not extensive, but he showed a remarkable intellectual growth during his presidency. Men were impressed with his simplicity in the beginning; by the end they were impressed by his knowledge and insight. Best of all the general liked to talk of the war; next to that of horses.

Few strangers ever found Grant unguarded, but one, a Frenchman, bearing a letter from Washburne, was permitted an intimate glimpse. Visiting the White House on Thanksgiving day, 1873, he found Grant at church, but Sheridan and Babcock were talking of a forthcoming war with Spain. The *Virginius* had been captured at Santiago, and eight American passengers put to death. The resulting war scare had penetrated the White House. When Grant came in "there was a real

[31] Porter, *Campaigning with Grant*, 340.

council of war," and the admiring guest thought to himself that "these were the men who could wipe out the whole of Spain and Cuba with their butchers without trouble." [32] Even the President might while away a holiday hour with talk of war and thus forget realities, but on the morrow the warrior was a man of peace, supporting the Secretary of State in settling problems by diplomacy.

Partly because he had been long comparatively friendless, and partly because he regarded devotion to friends as one of the cardinal virtues, Grant adhered to his intimates regardless of partisan opposition or factional criticism. Badeau concluded that he took a pride in "not being ignoble" [33] or forgetful; and he was particularly kind to those whose acquaintance dated from before the war. Stories were current in Washington to illustrate this devotion. Once a delegation of Tennesseans, headed by Horace Maynard, called at the White House to urge an appointment to the Nashville postoffice. The rival applicant was a former St. Louis butcher. "Gentlemen," said the President, "when I was a very poor man in St. Louis, just before the war, this German butcher on credit furnished meat to my family, and when I needed the loan of ten or fifteen or twenty dollars he was my banker without security and without charge of interest. Now I intend to appoint this German butcher postmaster of Nashville if it bursts the Republican Party." Another story related how Grant offered an appointment to a St. Louis resident. When the visitor pointed out that he was a Democrat, the President ejaculated: "Oh, damn the politics! Just before the Civil War, when I was standing on a street corner in St. Louis by a wagon loaded with wood, you approached and said: 'Captain, haven't you been able to sell your wood?' I answered: 'No.' Then you said:'I'll buy it; and whenever you haul a load of wood to the city and can't sell it, just take it around to my residence and throw it over the fence, and I'll pay you for it.' I haven't forgotten it." [34]

However apocryphal, such stories are illustrations of Grant's own feeling. To Longstreet he gave a lucrative appointment, to his new-found friends of army days he gave Cabinet posts and foreign missions, and he made Robert Douglas his secretary on the ground that his father had kept him from going over to the Confederacy. Al-

[32] John de la Montaigne to Washburne, November 27, 1873, Washburne MSS.
[33] Badeau, *Grant in Peace*, 402.
[34] Mrs. Archibald Dixon, *True Story of the Missouri Compromise and its Repeal*, 273–274.

though nepotism and perversion of public trust were charged by the Sumner-Schurz faction, Grant's loyalty to his friends struck the popular heart.

Next to this trait his love of horses endeared him to the people. Possibly much of this, too, was a pose. Soon after the election of 1868 he told Sherman that he was adopting horses as his hobby. All men, he explained, had a weakness or vanity and it was "wiser to choose one's own than to leave the newspapers to affix one less acceptable." [35] There was nothing strange in Grant's love of horses, but it was something for the newspapers to dwell upon. At the White House he kept from four to seven horses, the dean of the stable being the war horse "Cincinnati." This horse, presented by citizens of Cincinnati early in the war, was chosen by Grant as the model of the equestrian statue on the front of the Treasury, and lived until 1874, when, a foreleg being broken, Rear-Admiral Ammen had him shot.[36] Another famous horse was "Butcher Boy," so named because the President first noticed his speed and beauty when driven to a delivery wagon. In St. Louis, at the Dent farm, Grant had as many as twenty horses. Democratic journals charged that the seven horses in the White House stables were worth $7,000. Grant sighed and wished they were. Actually, despite the publicity, the presidential equipage was exceptionally modest. Grant himself seldom rode, preferring to drive a light phaëton about the city. Neither horses, harness, nor vehicles were in any way ostentatious.

Aside from horses, Grant was not fond of animals; dogs did not like him, and he never owned one. As a child he had no pets, as President his horses were as definitely a protective device as his childhood horsemanship had been.[37]

In a period when religious emotionalism ran high, Grant was singularly free from religious feeling and attended church irregularly. Methodism claimed him, and when he went to church it was generally a Methodist, but he took little interest in organized religion. A num-

[35] Lewis, *Sherman*, 600.
[36] Daniel Ammen, *The Old Navy and the New*, 515.
[37] On Grant and horses cf. Porter, *Campaigning with Grant*, 165–167; J. R. Grant, *In the days of my Father*, 62; Garfield MS Diary, November 6, 1872, March 15, 1875; J. McDonald, *Secrets of the Great Whiskey Ring*, 95–110; Stevens, *Grant in St. Louis;* New York *Tribune*, November 17, 1865; December 15, 1869; July 19, 1873; New York *Times*, October 7, 1872; *National Republican*, April 25, 1873; New York *World*, July 23, 1869.

ber of Methodist ministers received government appointments at his hands: William A. Pile, an evangelist, was nominated to Brazil, his brother-in-law Cramer served in Copenhagen, and the Rev. J. P. Newman was appointed inspector of consulates in order to give him a trip around the world. He was friendly with Bishops C. Kingsley and Mathew Simpson. Soon after his inauguration he gave $500 to the Washington church which he attended and on whose board of trustees he served, and he contributed to subscriptions for houses for Bishop Simpson and another preacher at Long Branch. These were simply social or political gestures, and Grant at no time manifested any concern over religion. He listened to Moody preach and Sankey sing, but it was not until he lay dying that the Rev. Mr. Newman baptized his unconscious head according to the Methodist rites. Jay Cooke protested to the Republican National Committee in 1868 that Grant worked on Sunday, and feared that "God will not bless us unless our rulers are righteous," but Grant continued to labor on the Sabbath with small respect for Cooke's prejudices. It was not that Grant was irreligious or an agnostic; he merely found no emotional satisfaction in religious activities. On the other hand, he was moral, condemning with his party the excesses of the Mormons; and, as the election of 1876 neared, he announced a support of public education which was generally interpreted as an anti-Catholic speech. In the campaign of 1880 Methodist ministers of the Chicago area called on Grant and endorsed him. Legend has it that he once remarked the presence of three parties in the country—Republicans, Democrats and Methodists. Like his horses, his religion had no deeper significance than political convenience.[38]

More than life in the White House, Grant enjoyed his summer vacations. He made regular trips to attend the graduation exercises at West Point, and it was generally autumn before he settled again in the White House. In 1869 the Grants spent most of the summer in visits to friends. Beginning with a trip to West Point, they journeyed to Boston and New York and returned for a short breathing spell be-

[38] Cramer, *Conversations and Unpublished Letters,* 179; Jay Cooke to Chandler, November 10, 1868, Chandler MSS.; New York *Tribune,* December 24, 1868, March 6, 1869, August 22, 1870, September 19, 1872, December 8, 1875; *National Republican,* March 4, 1869, July 20, 1871; Badeau, *Grant in Peace,* 161; Porter to Cabinet, October 15, 1870, Grant Letter Book; J. N. Davis to Washburne, November 6, 1879, Washburne MSS.

fore visiting Long Branch. In the middle of July they boarded a naval vessel—to the horror of Democrats—and sailed for the famed watering place. For a month they were honored guests at the Stetson House, where dancing, driving, and dress constituted the diversions of the day. Grant then visited friends in New Jersey, his brother-in-law in New York, Hamilton Fish, the Saratoga race track, and, as we have seen, wound up his summer's outing in the mountains of Western Pennsylvania. During this summer Grant adopted the policy, which he followed later, of returning to Washington every two weeks to hold Cabinet meetings and attend to routine business.

Before the second summer of his Administration began there were rumors that he would spend his vacation at Newport and other centers. However, the President early expressed a preference for Long Branch, and real-estate dealers and owners of property in the village took steps to insure the social supremacy of their resort. Soon a list was circulated, subscriptions were made, and Grant was presented with a cottage. Thereafter, there was no doubt where the President would spend his leisure.[39] Compared with the residences of George W. Childs or Thomas Murphy, his cottage was very modest. In architecture it fitted the composite styles of the day, being a "mixture of English villa and Swiss chalet." According to one visitor, it was dingy and unattractive in color.[40] Before the first Administration was over, Grant had built another house on a three-acre plot which he had purchased. This house was more attractive, forty-five feet square, with three stories and basement, and cost $20,000. But he never occupied it. Finding it could be rented for $3,000 for the season he remained in his own more modest dwelling.[41]

To the Long Beach establishment Grant moved his entire household as soon as Congress adjourned in the summer. To it came friends and relatives for visits, and politicians for consultation. Liberal Republicans complained without reason that the public business was neglected and begrudged the President his escape from Washington's heat and humidity. But Grant thoroughly enjoyed life at Long Branch. Although it was still necessary to attend receptions and stand in re-

[39] New York *World*, May 12, 1870.
[40] New York *Tribune*, July 25, 1870.
[41] *Ibid.*, June 12, 1872.

ceiving lines he found time to drive and chat. Borie, Childs, and Murphy played cards with him, and occasionally billiards, and for the moment the President might relax and forget the coyote howlings of his opponents.

AMERICAN political annals reveal no President who was happier in his second Administration than his first. Grant's second term served only to tarnish his reputation, and to wilt the laurels which he had borne from McLean's home to the White House. Beginning in an atmosphere of scandal, the Administration was taken unawares by a financial panic for which it received popular condemnation, and ended with the open corruption of the disputed election of 1876. Contemporaries coined the epithet "Grantism" to connote the moral degradation into which politics had fallen, and historians, aghast at the lack of public virtue revealed in those four years, have labeled them, "The Nadir of National Disgrace." At the end of this term, deserted by all but a small guard of loyal political followers, the victim of intriguing Cabinet members whom he had harbored and betrayed by other members of his intimate circle, the hero of Appomattox might well have surveyed his vanished glories, and cried out with Lear, "I am a man more sinn'd against than sinning."

The opening of Grant's second Administration was not auspicious. The election of 1872 had been little but a personal victory. Although the President's majority was overwhelming, his total vote was lower than in 1868—suggesting that it was disapproval of Greeley rather than approval of Grant that actuated the voters. In contrast with the victory of four years before, the President realized in this his heavy indebtedness to the politicians, and could no longer think himself the "people's President." "Four years ago," he said when formally notified of his election, "there was less regard for party lines. In the last campaign political differences and personal hostilities more clearly defined the lines of party." [1] Now, although he promised to administer the government for all the people, he recognized the necessity for "the approval of the great party which elected me." [2] After Greeley's death, some newspapers proposed that Greeley electors cast their votes for Grant and thus "lift the Administration out of parti-

---

[1] *National Republican,* February 17, 1873.
[2] Cf. New York *Tribune,* November 27, 1872, quoting the *New National Era.*

sanship," [3] but the anti-Grant forces were too embittered to make such a gesture. The Administration began in partisanship, and Grant was definitely a party President.

That the country was far from an era of good feeling was evident when the Forty-Second Congress assembled for its last session. Elected in 1870 when Grant's popularity was at low ebb, the Congress had devoted itself to diligent muckraking in preparation for the presidential campaign. Disappointed with the futility of their scandal-mongering, the Congressmen returned to Washington after the election in a defiant rather than humble mood. Soon they were probing anew the festering sores of public affairs, teaching the country to look with distrustful eyes upon the Administration.

The President's annual message, read to Congressmen as soon as they had resumed their seats, was a remarkably complacent document. Duller and longer than its predecessors, the message was no more than a summary of the departmental reports which accompanied it, with Grant's endorsement of his Cabinet's recommendations. Yet even that was significant of the general's attitude. Peace with foreign powers, the settlement of the Alabama claims, the consistent reduction of the debt—the figures for four years were given—the extension of railroads, the services of the Postoffice and Justice departments, and the progress in agriculture and education, all gave practical proof of the efficiency of the Administration and the prosperity of the country. To the practical President such an array of facts must have seemed a demolition of Democratic and "Liberal" accusations.[4]

The message had been prepared in eight hours,[5] which was more time than Congress gave to its consideration. Interested in sustaining their record for investigations, the Congressmen were soon attracting attention by their inquiry into the infamous Credit Mobilier of America.

By reason of its appearance when Grant's Administration was under fire, the Credit Mobilier has been popularly regarded as one of the series of scandals of "Grantism." Actually, although the investigators uncovered corruption in high places in the Republican Party, neither Grant, his associates, nor his especial champions in Congress were in

[3] New York *Tribune*, December 2, 10, 1872.
[4] Richardson, *Messages*, VII, 184–205.
[5] New York *Tribune*, November 18, 22, 1872.

any way concerned in the investigation. Blaine, Garfield, Dawes, Kelley, Schofield, Bingham, Logan, Brooks, and Patterson were investigated and found guilty of indiscretion or dishonesty in varying degree, but none of these men had been more than a nominal supporter of the President. Vice-Presidents Colfax and Wilson, who were incriminated, were his only political supporters. Moreover, it is usually forgotten that the scandalous acts of Oakes Ames and the Credit Mobilier were all committed before the Grant Administration began.

The Credit Mobilier was a construction company, organized by the larger stockholders of the Union Pacific Railroad to build the road. In their capacity as stockholders they contracted with themselves as members of the Credit Mobilier for construction, and paid themselves in the Union Pacific's first mortgage bonds, its common stock, and whatever cash was obtained by stock sales. During 1868, while the road was being rapidly pushed to completion, the Credit Mobilier declared five separate dividends. Altogether, these dividends amounted to 230% in first mortgage bonds, 515% in Union Pacific stock, and 60% in cash. Estimating bonds and stocks at their lowest market value, the dividends for this year totalled $341.85 on each $100 share.[6] In order to prevent investigation of these enormous profits, Oakes Ames, manufacturer of shovels, director of the Credit Mobilier, and Representative from Massachusetts, proposed to his associates that he be given shares of Credit Mobilier stock to distribute to his congressional colleagues. With shares worth $200, Ames placed 160 shares, at par, among Congressmen where they would "produce most good to us."

From time to time rumors spread concerning the activities of the Credit Mobilier, but it was not until the campaign of 1872 that definite information was published. Then, thanks to a quarrel among the leaders of the construction company, Dana's *Sun* presented a detailed but garbled account of the transactions. Most people discounted the story as one concocted for campaign purposes, but some of the accused Congressmen rushed forth with denials which suspiciously

[6] But, even though their action was possibly legally defensible, the profits made the Credit Mobilier men fearful of any public investigation of their methods. In December, 1867, C. C. Washburne of Wisconsin proposed that Congress regulate freight and passenger rates over the road. By this time, the Union Pacific was not seeking more governmental favors, but they were anxious not to be molested in exploiting what they had already received.

protested too much. On December 2, as soon as the House was organized, Blaine called S. S. Cox to the chair, and took the floor to demand an investigation. Cox appointed a committee, headed by Luke Poland of Vermont, to look into the charges of bribery. In the Senate a committee headed by J. M. Wilson, with G. F. Hoar as secretary, supplemented the House investigation.

Before the public gaze, these committees pilloried Ames and those Congressmen who were shown by his memorandum book to have received Credit Mobilier shares. Evidently he had extended alluring promises of large dividends to his colleagues, and in many instances had held the stock until the rapidly accumulating dividends had paid for it. Some of the purchasers had grown suspicious of their bargain and repudiated their contract, some had paid for and taken their stock, while others had never taken more than an option on the securities.[7]

The witnesses who allegedly took Ames' bribe presented a variety of accounts of their connection. Some frankly admitted their investments, and retorted that they had a right to take advantage of a good offer. These escaped public censure. Others, notably Garfield and Colfax, denied that they had received stock, and said they had rejected the proposition. In a badly muddled story, Colfax sought to explain a $1,200 deposit in his bank account, which coincided in time with an entry in Ames' book, as being a campaign contribution, and got into another scandal as a result. Garfield's elaborate story of a loan from Ames failed to convince the committee of his innocence. In the end, however, the House Committee recommended only that Ames and James Brooks of New York, a director of the Union Pacific, be expelled for accepting bribes. The House modified this to a vote of censure. The Senate Committee recommended the expulsion of J. W. Patterson of New Hampshire, but as his term expired five days after the report, no action was taken.

Ames and Brooks both died within a few months of their disgrace, and Colfax, retiring from the Vice-Presidency, spent the last twelve years of his life under the shadow of bribery. Garfield's political career continued, but the public never forgot his suspicious conduct. The most significant result of the revelations, however, was the stimulation

[7] There is some reason to believe that Ames, as his accusers in the Credit Mobilier alleged, retained some of the stock for himself while crediting it to Congressmen.

of the growing distrust of government and politicians, and especially of the Grant régime. "They tend," lamented a Wisconsin politician, "to create the impression, or perhaps I should say the apprehension, that our whole public life is debased. That our legislation is essentially corrupt and that honesty in official circles is the exception and not the rule." [8]

Thus the Credit Mobilier revelations cast an ugly shadow upon Grant's second Adminstration even before the inauguration. The growing distrust was sedulously encouraged by the anti-Grant press, which continued the sniping tactics that had marked the 1872 campaign. Congressional muddling of financial matters and the final infamy of the "salary grab" filled the public cup to overflowing.

Throughout the campaign, hostile journals and orators had criticized Boutwell's stolid, conservative administration of the Treasury, and even though Grant proudly presented the impressive figures of the declining debt in his annual message, the seeds of doubt had been implanted in the nation's financial centers. Late in December, Boutwell's chances to succeed Vice-President-Elect Henry Wilson in the Senate were discussed in the papers, and widespread fear was expressed that Judge Richardson, Assistant-Secretary of the Treasury, would be promoted to the Cabinet. Some time earlier, Richardson had attempted to relieve a temporary stringency in the money market by reissuing five million dollars' worth of retired greenbacks, and business men were told that he "should not be in a position where he can do such things." [9] Other aspirants named by rumor for the post were Henry Clews of New York and Drexel of Philadelphia—"none of them fit for Cabinet positions." Jay Cooke feared that another Philadelphia banker, closely allied to the rival Drexel & Childs, would be the nominee, and instructed his brother Henry to "bring everything to bear upon General Grant" to defeat the move. "It would be cruel to permit such a party to get into the Treasury," said the financier of the Civil War, and he hoped that "General Grant will certainly not reward our enemies and punish us who have done more than all the rest of the country put together." [10]

In the midst of this uncertainty in financial circles, John Sherman's

[8] Poland Report, *House Documents*, 42nd Congress, 2nd session; Wilson Report, *Senate Documents*, 42nd Congress, 2nd session.

[9] New York *Tribune*, December 31, 1872.

[10] Oberholtzer, *Jay Cooke*, II, 364–365.

committee tried to restore confidence by bringing in a bill for the resumption of specie payments on January 1, 1874. But even this move, though in perfect accord with the alleged desires of Eastern conservatives, was opposed. Sherman's "relations to the President give special significance to his bill," declared the opposition press. "The President's well-known tenacity in pursuing a line of policy once resolved upon should therefore be a timely warning to every business man. Those houses and those enterprises must surely be carried down by the shock of resumption that have large outstanding liabilities to be met hereafter on a gold basis." "Wise business men," said Whitelaw Reid, Greeley's successor on the *Tribune*, "in view of this pronunciamento of . . . the Administration will set their houses in order, will avoid overtrading and will shun debt." [11] The advice was purely partisan for, several days later, when reports stated that Grant was opposed to the bill, the *Tribune* declared that the "faith of the nation" was pledged to resumption, and the bill should pass.[12] But some Eastern members, seeing in the bill too many favors for national banks, joined with inflationists from the West to defeat the measure.[13]

In addition to inaction on specie payment, the Forty-Second Congress closed on a note which furthered the growing disgust with the Administration. Early in the session a proposal to raise the President's salary was discussed in Congress and the newspapers. Opinion was about evenly divided between those who thought the office worth twice as much as Grant was paid and those who alleged that the Chief Executive should live in "republican simplicity." [14] A bill to raise the salaries of President, Vice-President, Cabinet officers, and Supreme Court justices was introduced and discussed, but referred to committees where it would have been buried but for the sudden interest of Ben Butler. From his judiciary Committee, Butler offered a bill to increase the President's salary to $50,000, to raise the Vice-President, Speaker, Cabinet members, and Supreme Court justices to $10,000, and members of Congress to $7,500. With a personal interest in the bill, Congressmen renewed the discussion. To honest men, the bill was outrageous, for the increase for Senators and Representatives applied

11 New York *Tribune,* January 18, 1873.
12 *Ibid.,* January 29, 1873.
13 *Ibid.,* February 6, 1873.
14 *Ibid.,* December 20, 1872.

to members of the Forty-Second Congress. Thanks to Butler's able parliamentary tactics the measure passed, but the indignant public regarded it in no other light than a "salary grab" and a "back pay steal." "Men seem to have lost the faculty of distinguishing between right and wrong," lamented one Senator as he pointed out that the "panic-stricken fugitives" from the Credit Mobilier investigation joined hands with the crowd of members retiring from both houses and "who had no character to lose" to pass the measure. But Grant signed the bill, telling Garfield that if it had not passed he would have had to draw $25,000 from his private property in order to leave town in 1877.[15]

As the session ended, the *Tribune* expressed the general feeling that the "Congress's entire characterization has been that of neglect to public business." Too much time had been devoted to investigations— eight major ones were listed—and too little to legislation. The Senate had been "obstructive, partisan, and unusually corrupt," and the House, while "more resolute" had also been guilty of corruption. That "the country will be relieved of the 42nd Congress" was regarded as a matter for national rejoicing.[16]

Politicians, too, surveying the wreck occasioned by the Credit Mobilier and the salary grab, trembled for the future. "Common sense would suggest that sooner or later corruption will work its own downfall, and a corrupt party no matter what its record must go to the wall," said one commentator, who concluded that men would soon be selected for their character rather than their party record.[17] "There are plenty of patent rights for a new party inventing now-a-days," declared another.[18]

Yet while there was some rejoicing over the adjournment of Congress, there was little acclaim for the new Administration. Four years before, Grant's accession had been hopefully regarded as the end of the quarrel between President and Congress and the harbinger of peace to the South. Despite the solid accomplishments of the Administration in foreign affairs and in reducing the debt, the President had

15 New York *Tribune*, January 9, February 8, 10, 24, 25, March 1, 3, 4, 6, 1873; T. C. Smith, *Garfield*, I, 499–500; Garfield MSS. Diary, March 29, 1873; Senator T. O. Howe to Fairchild, March 23, 1873, Fairchild MSS.
16 New York *Tribune*, March 4, 1873.
17 G. T. Chapman, (Cleveland) to Fairchild, March 7, 1873, Fairchild MSS.
18 E. E. Bryant, (Madison, Wis.) to Fairchild, April 13, 1873, Fairchild MSS.

lost prestige. Instead of a valiant assault on the citadels of the politicians, the Soldier-President had executed political flank movements which confused observers. Lacking understanding of the popular mind, and with none of the demagogue's ability to rally the people to his support, the general had been inarticulate when bold statements of purpose would have served him well. As a result, newspapers could say, that "General Grant's first four years have been the feeblest and most barren in our annals." [19]

Inauguration day dawned cold and bitter. The local committees had planned to introduce the new Administration with high pageantry, but the elements combined to dim the tinselled luster. Flakes of snow fell throughout the day, while a gale from the ice-covered Potomac sent the thermometer to a year's low and forced the celebrants to cling to the shelter of their hotels and boarding-houses. With the wind whipping his words from his mouth, and his breath freezing upon his fresh-cropped beard, Grant took the oath of office and turned to the shivering crowd to read his inaugural address. Slightly longer than his first, this address lacked much of its vigor. His best efforts would be given to enforce the law, but the long essay on the rule of law was lacking. Four years before "the country had not recovered from the effects of a great internal revolution, and . . . it seemed to me wise that no new questions should be raised. . . . Therefore the past four years . . . have been consumed in the effort to restore harmony, public credit, commerce, and all the arts of peace and progress. . . . My efforts in the future will be directed to the restoration of good feeling between the different sections of our common country, to the restoration of our currency to . . . a par with . . . [gold], . . . to the construction of cheap routes of transit throughout the land . . . to the maintenance of friendly relations with all our neighbors and distant nations . . . to the reëstablishment of our commerce . . . to the encouragement of . . . manufacturing industries, . . . [and] to bring the aborigines of the country under the benign influences of education and civilization."

Interspersed in this review of the past and promises for the future were statements reflecting the President's social and political philosophy. Remarkable neither for profundity of thought nor for literary excellence, the succession of platitudes must have convinced the most

[19] New York *World*, March 4, 1873.

conservative skeptic that Grant was "safe." "It is my firm conviction that the civilized world is tending toward republicanism, . . . and that our own great Republic is destined to be the guiding star to all others," sententiously remarked the Chief Executive. "The theory of government changes with general progress," he added in noting that the telegraph and steam engine had brought the States closer together than the original thirteen. "Social equality is not a subject to be legislated upon . . ."; "I believe that our Great Maker is preparing the world, in His own good time, to become one nation, speaking one language, and when armies and navies will be no longer required"; "Wars of extermination . . . are demoralizing and wicked" —these statements completed the creed.

But the most remarkable portion of the inaugural was the last paragraphs. Citing the fact that he had been in the service of his country since the firing upon Sumter, the President declared "I did not ask for place or position. . . . I performed a conscientious duty, without asking promotion or command, and without a revengeful feeling toward any section or individual. Notwithstanding this, throughout the war, and from my candidacy for my present office in 1868 to the close of the last Presidential campaign, I have been the subject of abuse and slander scarcely ever equaled in political history, which today I feel that I can afford to disregard in view of your verdict, which I gratefully accept as my vindication." [20]

On both counts the President was wrong. His vindication, in the light of the earnest work of the party managers and Greeley's unpopularity, rang hollow, but the vituperation to which he had been subjected, though by no means among the worst in history, had evidently cut deeply. It was as a humble man that Grant began his second Administration.

The New York *Tribune* regarded the inaugural address as "the utterance of a man of the best intentions profoundly desirous to govern wisely and justly and profoundly ignorant of the means by which good government is secured." [21] Events seemed to bear out its analysis. With the nation disgusted with the "salary grab," tiring of the endless squabbles over appointments, and regarding the future with a jaundiced eye, the time was ripe for a bold presidential policy. But,

[20] Richardson, *Messages*, VII, 221–223.
[21] New York *Tribune*, March 5, 1873.

unfortunately for his reputation, neither Grant's personality nor his concept of the executive office would permit him to make a strong bid for popular support. Instead, he devoted the first months of his new term to routine, while the general discontent grew stronger. Neither in the conduct of the government nor in the condition of the nation was there anything to inspire confidence in the future. No strength was brought to the Administration by its new Secretary of the Treasury. When the Massachusetts legislature elected Boutwell to the Senate, business interests had speculated on his successor. Despite the disapproval of such powerful journals as the New York *Times* and *Tribune,* Grant selected the First Assistant Secretary, William A. Richardson, for the Treasury post. This appointment, together with the renomination of the rest of the Cabinet, indicated that the second Administration would continue the "same conservative, practical, economical" policies as the first. Richardson's promotion, said ultrapartisans, "means we will have no rash tampering with the public credit, and will go on paying the debt and reducing the burdens of taxation as fast as the commercial interests of the country will permit." In parting company with Boutwell, Grant told him that "your administration . . . has been so admirably conducted as to give the greatest satisfaction to me because . . . it has been satisfactory to the country. The policy pursued . . . by your successor I hope may be as successful as yours has been, and that no departure from it will be made. . . ." When criticisms continued, Richardson sought to stifle them by asserting that he "would not if he could, depart from the well established policies of this Department," and that he regarded Grant's letter as mandatory.[22]

But Richardson's assurances were not highly regarded in financial circles. With the unimaginative conservatism of Boutwell the more daring financiers had found much fault, and the campaign of 1872 had brought out caustic comments on his policy. Moreover, Richardson had once reissued some of the "retired" greenbacks, and this hasty action was forgotten by neither the financiers nor the anti-Grant forces. From the moment he took office, Richardson faced a monetary stringency in New York. The stock market, always a sensitive barom-

[22] New York *Tribune,* January 6, 9, March 13, 17, 18, 1873; New York *Times,* March 12, 18, 1873; *National Republican,* March 13, 14, 17, 18, 20, 1873; W. W. Belknap to Washburne, March 17, 1873, Washburne MSS.

eter of political conditions, fluctuated violently, and a strong group of inflationists urged a further reissue of greenbacks. To prevent Richardson's assurances from having a soothing effect, the *Tribune* gratuitously reminded Wall Street that "One man sits in Washington with absolute power. He holds the key to the industrial, commercial, mechanical, banking . . . interests of the country. . . . Speculation rides rampant on his fickle will. . . . Something should be done to impart an element of certainty to the currency, and take it out of the hands of one man to inflate or contract it at will." [23]

Early in 1873, the financial affairs of the world grew rapidly worse. In Vienna there was panic in the temples of the money changers, which spread rapidly to Berlin and Frankfort. London raised its interest-rates sharply and contracted loans, while in Paris Thiers was over-thrown and the enigmatic Macmahon, whose very presence in the capital seemed to portend a reactionary *coup d'état,* came into power. In New York cautious business men, their fear of inflation increasing, began to hoard gold.[24]

If the business man was alarmed by international affairs, there was nothing in the domestic situation to give him confidence. In every section of the country the turn of events must have convinced financial interests that the era of wartime prosperity had come to an end. "Money is scarce and the financial waves are agitated from the peaceful prairies of the West to the bull-rings and bear-gardens of Wall Street," remarked Wisconsin's patronage boss. "On the whole the thing is anything but encouraging." [25] In the South, racial clashes brought conservative interests to the realization that Radical Reconstruction had gone too far. In the West, the rising tide of Grangerism struck terror to the master manipulators of railroad finance. In Washington and Boston the activities of "Boss" Shepherd and Ben Butler seemed to threaten disaster to honest men. The combination of these and other malign forces meant collapse for Wall Street and political catastrophe for the Grant Administration.

Particularly in the South was the situation inimical to public confidence. In Alabama and in Arkansas, as in Louisiana, the elections of 1872 had resulted in the erection of rival governments, and Federal

23 New York *Tribune,* April 7, 1873.
24 For comments on the international situation cf. New York *Tribune,* May 26, 1873.
25 E. W. Keyes, (Madison) to Fairchild, April 24, 1873, Fairchild MSS.

troops were used to intimidate the Democrats. Grant planned to make a trip in the spring into the South, and many hoped that this journey would result in a moderation of his policy. But the pressure of public business and the burning of the Dent home near St. Louis forced a change of plans. Grant went West instead of South, while the troubles in Arkansas and Louisiana continued to grow. Throughout the summer reports came from Louisiana of bad conditions in the State's finances, of failure to redeem its tax warrants, and of the corruption of the Kellogg government which Grant supported. The plight of Arkansas, with its conflict between two Republican factions headed by Brooks and Baxter, gave confirmatory evidence that Republican policies in the South were leading to violence. While these troubles were simmering, the *Tribune,* not forgetting that Negroes had voted for Grant, published ludicrous descriptions of South Carolina's Negro legislature, and pointed out that bribery and corruption everywhere characterized the States in which Negroes, carpetbaggers and scalawags held control while "men of property and intelligence" were burdened with taxes.[26] Turning his eyes from the South where the "bottom rail" was rising to the top, with attendant corruption and bribery, the frightened Northern business man might survey the situation in the West, where "bottom rails" were seizing political power with the avowed purpose of attacking powerful economic interests. Since 1867 the farmers of the Middle West had been joining "Granges" of the "Patrons of Husbandry," and under the cloak of this secret coöperative society had been launching a vigorous attack upon the economic system which exploited them. The particular *bêtes noire* of the Grangers were the railroads, which, conceived in fraud and born in corruption, lived and grew by extortionate freight and passenger rates. Next to the railroads in the farmer's index of tyrants were the manufacturers and jobbers who sold farm machinery at exorbitant prices. Through the Grange, the farmers hoped to bring pressure on legislatures to regulate railroad rates. Off to a fair start in 1867, the Granger movement grew rapidly in the election year of 1872, and in the first months of Grant's second Administration. In these two years 9,500 "Granges" were established, and the membership, representing all but four States, numbered

[26] The phrase "men of property and intelligence" is borrowed from Rhodes, *History of the United States.* Throughout his descriptions of Reconstruction, Rhodes seems to reflect the change that went on in the minds of the Conservative Northern business men on the subject of the South.

nearly 1,500,000.

In 1867 the embattled farmers forced the Illinois legislature to pass a Warehouse Act which would compel railroads to carry grain to independent grain elevators. In 1870 a Constitutional convention, dominated by the farmers, gave the legislature the right to regulate railroad rates, and the next year the legislature forbade rate discriminations and established a commission to enforce compliance. Other States followed the example of Illinois until the practical operation of the railroads was as much under fire in many legislatures as their financial origins were in Congress. In the summer of 1873 the Illinois Supreme Court declared the regulatory law of 1871 unconstitutional, and the outraged farmers talked of impeaching the Chief Justice. In the State elections the farmers' candidates won, and the threat of even lower rates struck fear into the hearts of railroad magnates. Throughout the West men were preparing for "a great fight with powerful corporations and other monopolies," and predicting a "lively time over the railroad and bank questions." [27] In the East the uprising was watched with interest, and the journals of the railroad and industrial interests constantly reiterated the advice that "until the farmer recognizes that all his tampering with transportation problems will be useless and even mischievous, they are fighting a dangerous and powerful enemy." From California, in the summer of 1873, came the strident voice of Governor Newton Booth castigating the railroads for the Credit Mobilier, for discriminatory rates, for their terrorization of farmers and small merchants, and for their corruption of the elections. That fall Booth was sent to the Senate. In other Western States the movement went on. In Wisconsin, the Republican Convention renominated Governor Washburne on a platform excoriating the salary grab and Credit Mobilier, and demanding cheap transportation. Even in the South the Granger movement was growing stronger, and showing a tendency to bid for Negro votes. In Missouri, for example, veterans of the Mexican war and the "Patrons of Husbandry" held a joint meeting, which, in addition to attacks upon the railroads, condemned carpetbaggers for misleading the blacks.[28] Even in the East men were beginning to ask, "Why could not our War Dept. run our

[27] O. N. Conover to Fairchild, November 2, 1873, Fairchild MSS.
[28] Nevins, *Emergence of Modern America*, 167–177; Solon J. Buck, *The Agrarian Crusade;* New York *Tribune,* June 3, 12, August 15, 28, September 1, 6, 19, 1873.

Rail Roads in the interests of the people as well as the British do the Telegraph?" [29] Everywhere in the summer of 1873, exploited groups, with a program directed against the masters of capital, were threatening the stability of the economic system.

The ease with which the lower economic classes could be rallied to assault the citadels of property was illustrated in the National Capital. The partial paralysis of enterprise which had resulted in the South from the combination of propertyless carpetbaggers and dependent freedmen might appear to Northern voters as simple penance for the sins of the former slaveholders, but in the District of Columbia a similar combination took on more sinister aspects. Granted the suffrage by an excess of Radical zeal during the fight with Johnson, the freedmen of Washington proved their gratitude by voting Republican, but showed little discrimination in the choice of candidates for office. In 1871 Congress created a Territorial government, with a governor, executive council, and elective legislature, for the District. With the avowed purpose of improving the appearance of the capital, the new government was authorized to borrow money to the extent of five per cent of the assessed value of property, and beyond that amount upon the approval of a majority of the voters. To the gubernatorial chair Grant appointed Jay Cooke's brother Henry, but the center of interest in Washington was Alexander R. Shepherd, who had risen from plumber to contractor and headed the Board of Public Works. With Negroes supporting a favorable majority in the legislature, and outvoting the property-holders on new bond issues, Shepherd's board launched an ambitious program. Streets were paved, street levels graded, the stinking Tiber converted into an underground sewer, the Potomac's bordering swamps reclaimed, and parks and squares improved. Statues, mostly of Civil War and Revolutionary generals, were erected to adorn the city. After three years of Shepherd a visitor would not have recognized Washington—and the debt was enormous!

That such improvement could be made without incurring the indignation of local taxpayers was improbable, but "pulling Washington out of the mire" was not solely a local problem. Early in 1873 the District government demanded that Congress pay its share of the costs for improvements about public buildings, and the nation immediately turned its attention to Shepherd and his Board of Public

[29] Geo. B. Lincoln, (Providence) to Fairchild, August 14, 1873, Fairchild MSS.

Works. In New York a Democratic Congressman, Robert B. Roosevelt, compared the Board with Tammany Hall, and the *Tribune* took up the cry, alleging that millions had been spent without authority of law, the funds misused, and the city bankrupted. Shepherd replied to the *Tribune,* while his supporters, pointing to the improvements, declared that real-estate values had been raised twenty-five per cent. Meantime, the opposition in Washington gathered the school teachers and police, whose pay had been momentarily stopped, into mass-meetings to inquire where their money was being spent, and taxpayers' committees reported that the new paving had been poorly laid. Propertied citizens signed petitions to abolish the new government, and Henry Cooke resigned the governorship.

But if Cooke was timorous, the fight had no terrors for a President who had just passed through a campaign of vituperation. Never in his career had Grant deserted a capable subordinate under fire, and the charges of Shepherd's corruption seemed but another partisan attack on the Administration. To the horror of the taxpayers and financial circles generally, the President appointed Shepherd governor of the District!

Immediately the press which had been condemning Shepherd turned upon Grant. He was in league with the Washington ring, he was going to recommend that Congress assume the District's debts, he had misplaced his personal friendship, and had abused the public trust by appointing Shepherd. On every side the President was attacked. "The confidence of the people will not be strengthened" by the appointment, observed the St. Louis *Democrat*.[30]

Neither was the confidence strengthened by what was occurring in conservative centers. In Massachusetts, which had just emphasized its illiberal characteristics by sending Boutwell to the Senate, Ben Butler, the Radical antithesis of the new Senator, announced his candidacy for Governor. Nothing could be more horrifying to Brahmin interests than the prospect of Butler at the head of the State, and the conservative press hastened to the support of Butler's opponent. With the odium of the "salary grab" upon him, Butler was taken as the symbol of Republican degradation. "The trouble with the Republican Party," said the New York *Tribune,* "is that its scum rules it." There-

[30] Blaine, *Twenty Years,* II, 547–549; Dunning, *Reconstruction,* 244–245.

B. H. BRISTOW   W. A. RICHARDSON

JOHN A. RAWLINS   MARSHALL JEWELL

FOUR CABINET MEMBERS

after, this paper kept its far-flung body of readers informed on the progress of the Butler campaign. But the "salary grab" soon became the least of the hated Butler's crimes. On July 4th the candidate announced his program to a temperance meeting in South Farmington. His two main planks were public ownership of railroads and the enforcement of prohibition! Butler, said the *Tribune,* was trying to "make himself governor of Massachusetts by proving his fitness for the penitentiary." Moreover, it was obvious to the *Tribune,* as to Democrats and Conservatives, that Grant was supporting Butler. Butler was "the flower and the fruit of the time," the outcome of the "natural growth of [his] party, and the best illustration of its tendency." "It did not matter to Massachusetts that a Republican government was set up in Louisiana," by Federal patronage, but now the old Bay State was facing the same sort of interference. By implication the *Tribune,* which was not only widely read and quoted, but widely imitated, suggested that the Administration, after sponsoring corruption in Louisiana and fostering attacks on property in Washington, was now supporting both in Massachusetts. In September Butler was defeated, but the *Tribune* would not drop the subject—Butler was still "the best representative of a force in politics which is struggling for the mastery of the government. Mr. Butler is not discouraged; he still is determined to fight, and he will." [31]

Throughout the summer of 1873 the fluctuating stock market reflected the general suspicion with which business men regarded the social and political phenomena of the day. Speculators raised a cry for more greenbacks, and conservative financiers feared that Richardson would hearken to inflationary appeals. Lack of confidence in the Republicans in general, and the Grant Administration in particular, found expression in both anti-Grant and hard money circles. Representing both, the New York *Tribune's* columns are significant. In April, the *Tribune* had stated that the power of inflating the currency rested with Richardson, which was "too much power for one man." [32] In May, the editors looked at the "evergrowing turbulence of the Republican masses" in France, and pointed out that "our people should be warned . . . that inflated values are one great source of our grow-

[31] New York *Tribune,* June to Sept., 1873; cf. especially issues of April 5, June 24, 28, July 5, 7, 11, 26, 28, 31, August 8, 9, 15, 18, 26, 27, 28, September 4, 5, 9, 11, 12, 1873.
[32] *Ibid.* April 7, 1873.

ing political and commercial profligacy. . . ." [33] During the next two
months the *Tribune* called attention to Richardson's alleged favoritism to the syndicate which was handling a new bond issue,[34] and began to question the Secretary's monthly statements of debt reduction.
"Many people believe," it said, "that there are two great stocks of
gold; one in the Treasury, the other in New York banks. This is an
error. Only a few thousand gold coins are in private hands in New
York." [35] "Honest business men," insinuated the editors, wanted "to
know what they can depend upon. The effect of the syndicate operations, combined with what is called 'book-keeping,' has been to falsify
the public debt statements of the coin balances in the Treasury; to
cause the public to believe there are 14 to 15 million dollars in coin
in the Treasury, which there are not. The Secretary of the Treasury
instead of telling the truth has lied and done injury to himself. Let
him go to Congress and be whitewashed." [36] When Richardson's
August report showed a reduction in the debt the *Tribune* branded
it "wholly fictitious." [37]

With evidences of corruption on every hand, with "bottom rails"
on top in West, South, and North, and with the Administration suspected of conspiring with dishonesty in the South, the District of
Columbia, and in New York, public faith in the stability of government was shaken. The card house of the nation's financial structure
tottered violently, and fell. Too much capital had been invested in
railroad stocks of doubtful value, the Government's failure to resume
specie payments had invited speculation, but "diminishing faith in
the management of corporate property in this country; [and] the
uncertainty as to the condition of the government"—a condition due
as much to partisan politics as to actual financial insecurity—played
the major part in precipitating the panic of 1873.

Early in September, following the "wholly fictitious" report of the
Treasury, gold declined on the New York market.[38] During the next
fortnight several large banking houses failed. "Uncle Daniel" Drew,
a partner in Kenyon, Cox & Co., permitted the company to fail be-

[33] New York *Tribune,* May 26, 1873.
[34] *Ibid.,* August 2, September 6, 1873.
[35] *Ibid.,* August 21, 1873.
[36] *Ibid.,* August 23, 1873.
[37] *Ibid.,* September 2, 1873.
[38] *Ibid.,* September 9, 1873.

cause he was "short" on the market.[39] Two days later the Brooklyn Trust Company, having concealed defalcations of a half million for weeks, closed its doors. The Midland Railroad Company went down with the bank.[40] Stocks declined rapidly, and a panic was already upon the city when, on the morning of September 18, news arrived that Jay Cooke & Company had closed its doors.

It was universally agreed that Jay Cooke's failure was due to the heavy commitments of the company in securities of the Northern Pacific Railroad. Cooke's own faith in Northern Pacific was greater than that of his partners, and he attributed the failure to the immediate "stringency of affairs." A few days before the crash the partners had met and "agreed to scramble around and put in some fresh capital." Owing to the failure of other roads, and "the agitation of the farmer's granges," this proved more difficult than was expected. Unable to raise fresh capital, the house closed its doors, but the pious Cooke was a man of great faith. "We have courage," he declared—and added the patriotic note, "The country . . . is just as rich as ever." [41]

In the train of Cooke's failure came a rush of others. "The firm, next to the government, was the most firmly established in public confidence and esteem," [42] and its collapse brought down many more. Fisk & Hatch, the Union Trust Company, the National Bank of the Commonwealth, and the National Trust Company, New York institutions, failed before the end of the week. Large bankers failed in other cities, and by the end of the year 5,183 businesses with a capitalization of $228,499,000 failed.[43]

Astounded by the extent of the catastrophe, the same journals whose partisan sniping had contributed to the collapse took up the note of patriotism and began to minimize the disaster. Two days after Cooke's failure, the *Tribune* was pointing out that "it has been purely a fancy stock crash. . . . Not a mercantile house nor savings bank has been affected. General business in New York is good." But the *Tribune* editors, true to both the Greeley traditions of moral philosophy and to partisanship, found the panic in one breath a blessing in disguise—for it pointed out the dangers of speculation!—and in

[39] New York *Tribune*, September 15, 1873.
[40] *Ibid.*, September 18, 1873.
[41] Jay Cooke to W. E. Chandler, October 6, 1873, Chandler MSS.
[42] *National Republican*, September 19, 1873.
[43] New York *Commercial and Financial Chronicle*, January 24, 1874.

the next exulted that "Experience teaches that no money consisting of paper not convertible on demand into actual gold and silver on its face value can be safe."

While the *Tribune* adorned its tale with pointed morality, those who had been caught with heavy indebtedness and no cash jumped to the equally easy conclusion that there was not enough money in circulation. Runs on savings banks and the hoarding of money—both gold and greenbacks—began as soon as the first failures were known. Since more money would ease the situation, all eyes turned to the government, and a babel of voices arose with conflicting demands for government action. As debtors clamored for money, creditors raised angry shouts that the panic was no concern of the Administration. Hard money men and inflationists sought the ears of Secretary Richardson and President Grant.

THE night before Jay Cooke's failure, Grant was a visitor at "Ogontz," the financier's palatial home. He had arrived to put young Jesse in a neighboring school, and the evening was spent with no mention of the impending disaster. Early on the 18th, urgent messages arrived for Cooke, but, as a perfect host, he breathed no word of his troubles to his distinguished guest, and Grant continued his journey ignorant that he had slept in a doomed house.[1] On the way back to Washington the President's train met with an accident. The engineer and fireman were seriously hurt, and many passengers were bruised. At the moment of the shock the President was smoking and talking. With hardly a break in his conversation, and with a gesture scarcely perceptible, Grant grasped the back of the seat before him. His calm presence of mind saved him from injury.[2] His calmness was to stand him in good stead during the coming days.

Back in Washington, Grant consulted Richardson, and the Secretary announced that his department would purchase $10,000,000 in bonds in order to put money into circulation.[3] On the day after this announcement, Sunday, September 21, Grant and Richardson went to New York to study the situation. In the Fifth Avenue Hotel—a year before the headquarters of the regimented army of victorious Republicanism—President and Secretary heard the crowds of bankers, brokers, capitalists, merchants, manufacturers, and railroad men who besought them to increase the currency, declaring that unless the government came to the rescue nothing could save the country from bankruptcy and ruin.[4] Yet even as these men demanded government action the conservative interests pointed out that "Boutwell's interference with Wall Street a year ago was conspicuously more advantageous to certain 'friends of the Government' among speculators . . . than to men engaged in legitimate business." This "interference" was one of the causes of the panic.[5]

[1] Oberholtzer, *Jay Cooke,* II, 421–422.
[2] New York *Tribune,* September 19, 1873.
[3] *Ibid.,* September 20, 1873.
[4] Foulke, *O. P. Morton,* II, 317–319.
[5] New York *Tribune,* Sept. 20, 1873.

Primarily the demands of Grant's visitors were that the Government should loan the New York banks the $44,000,000 in greenbacks which had been retired by law. These greenbacks, although in the Treasury and uncancelled, were no longer legally a part of the national currency. Smarting under the attacks upon his previous issue of greenbacks for a temporary need, Richardson staunchly refused to inflate the currency. In the conversations the retired greenbacks were referred to as a "reserve," but Grant, while not combating this interpretation, pointed out that, however good the security, there was no constitutional authority for the government to loan its money to any private corporation. The only thing the government would do was to use the $20,000,000 in the New York sub-treasury in the purchase of bonds. Conservative bankers assured the President this would be sufficient for the crisis. It remained for Richardson, however, to sum up the Administration's attitude. "This, gentlemen," he told some particularly insistent bankers, "is not my funeral!" [6]

During the week which followed, Grant had no relief from the pressure of the inflationists, who followed him to Washington or bombarded him with letters of advice.[7] In general, however, the press supported his refusal to take action. The Philadelphia *Press*, the Providence *Journal*, and the Springfield *Republican* lauded the action, and the New Haven *Palladium* observed that "the proverbial obstinacy of General Grant has never found a better field for display. . . ." [8] The St. Louis *Republican* called the proposal for government aid a "lunatic notion." [9] Late in the week, with skies somewhat clearer, Grant wrote H. B. Clafin that the government was doing all in its power to relieve business. Realizing that the restoration of public confidence was the first essential, the President promised to take all *legal* measures possible. "But it is evident the Government's efforts will not avail without the active coöperation of the banks and moneyed corporations of the country. . . . The banks," wrote the President, citing the money the Treasury was paying out for bonds, "are now strong enough to adopt a liberal policy on their part and by a generous system of discounts to sustain the business interests of the country." If the banks would shoulder their portion of the load, the Government

[6] New York *Tribune*, September 22, 1873; *National Republican*, September 22, 1873.
[7] Cf. Babcock to Jno. Hoey, September 26, 1873, Grant Letter Book.
[8] New York *Tribune*, September 24, 1873.
[9] *Ibid.*, September 25, 1873.

would regard the forty-four millions in greenbacks as a reserve "to meet the needs of the public." [10]

Although the public approved of this advice to bankers, the bankers themselves were alarmed by the assumption that the retired legal tenders might be reissued. As revenue fell off rapidly, the Secretary of the Treasury found it necessary to draw upon this "reserve," and early in October it was seen that Richardson would have to issue some eight or nine millions of the greenbacks. Immediately the hard money men denounced the Secretary for his "illegal" and "injurious" exercise of arbitrary power.[11] By the time Congress assembled, Richardson had inflated the currency by $26,000,000.

As the bankers turned upon the President with charges that he was threatening them with inflation, Grant replied with an assurance that he had not meant to threaten but to advise. To one bank president, Grant set forth an interesting theory of the situation. Admitting that bank presidents knew the condition of their banks, and he did not, he informed them that he and his Secretary "know more about the financial ability of the government, [and] its ability to render aid" than did the bankers. His allusion to the reserve was simply to prove that the government could take action. With this, the General turned to an analysis of the panic. "I do not believe that the present panic will work to individuals half the injury it will work general good to the country at large," was his general thesis. The monetary system of the country, thought the President, lacked elasticity, and he had no doubt that Congress would legislate to relieve this want. Again, the panic had brought greenbacks to a par with silver, and Grant entered into a lengthy dissertation on the possibilities of silver replacing paper money as the "hoarding medium" of the country. Hoarding, in a small way, would be in silver. "I confess," said the financier-President, "to a desire to see a limited hoarding of money. It insures a firm foundation in time of need." Silver hoarding would "consume two or three hundred millions in time," and release paper money "to perform the legitimate functions of trade, and will tend to bring us back, where we must come at last, to a specie basis." [12] To A. J. Drexel, Grant repeated that the panic was a blessing, adding that "there is no reason

---

[10] Grant to H. B. Clafin and H. B. Anthony, September 27, 1873, Grant Letter Book.
[11] New York *Tribune*, October 9, 10, 1873.
[12] Grant to Cowdrey, October 6, 1873, Grant Letter Book.

now why silver should not begin to flow out, and when it does I predict that greenbacks will never again fall below par for silver." [13] Evidently, the President did not remember that he had signed the Mint Bill of 1873 which had demonetized the white metal!

A few days after expressing himself on silver, Grant let it be known that he would recommend to Congress two remedies for the situation. The first was that the entire $44,000,000 be reissued, and the second that a Post Office bank, in which everybody would have confidence, and which should pay four per cent interest, be established. "It's a pity," remarked the *Tribune*, "the President's financial ideas are not as good as his intentions." His intentions included a speedy restoration of specie payments, a discouragement of stock speculation, and a reform of banking, but the inflation of the currency and government intervention in business were poor means to a good end.[14] On the other hand, Garfield, whose regard for the President was never high, visited the White House and came away impressed by Grant's "discussion of the financial situation," which "showed more study and reflection than I've ever known him to give" to any other subject.[15]

For the two months between the fall of Jay Cooke's financial pyramid and the assembling of Congress both Grant and the country gave much attention to economic problems. Prominent among the phenomena of the panic was the idea, given much currency in the conservative press, that the time was opportune to resume specie payments.[16] Though Grant stated his belief that the panic would result in resumption, the actions of the Government were in the direction of inflation. As Richardson issued "retired" greenbacks to meet current expenses, conservative journals howled their protest. Late in October, Senator Boutwell entered the lists with a proposal for "free banking" and the warning that resumption could not be accomplished until there was a favorable balance in foreign trade.[17] Since Richardson considered himself the heir to Boutwell's policy as well as his office, the contractionists circulated a rumor that Grant felt his Secretary lacked "the breadth of experience and capacity" for his duties, and would appoint

---

[13] Grant to Drexel, October 10, 1873, Grant Letter Book.
[14] New York *Tribune*, October 13, 1873.
[15] Garfield MSS. Diary, November 18, 1873.
[16] Cf. New York *Tribune*, of October 3, 1873, quoting the Chicago *Tribune*, Hartford *Post*, Providence *Press*, New Haven *Register*, Toledo *Commercial*, and the St. Paul *Pioneer*.
[17] New York *Tribune*, October 23, 1873.

E. E. Morgan, an intimate of the bankers, to the Treasury Department.[18] If this rumor was intended as a suggestion, its subtle force was lost on the direct President. Grant bluntly denied that he intended to change Secretaries, and began to prepare his recommendations to Congress.[19]

As the time for the opening of Congress drew near, the financial outlook became even more muddled. "I look on the coming session," said Garfield, "as the most troublesome and uncertain of any that I [have] ever seen at this distance from it. The great financial panic which has swept and is still sweeping over the country will be the most difficult element to handle. There will be a babel of opinions and remedies laid before the public with great uncertainty as to the outcome. Everything has tended to saturate the public mind with suspicion and unfaith." [20]

On December 1, Grant sent his annual message to Congress. With seeming reluctance to get to finances, he spent more than his wonted space on routine foreign affairs, recommending constitutional amendments permitting the President to veto parts of bills, and limiting special sessions to the subjects mentioned in the call. With these topics out of the way, he turned to affairs in the Treasury. The financial statement of the Government showed an excess of receipts over expenses exceeding $43,000,000. "But it is not probable that this favorable exhibit will be shown for the present fiscal year," said the President as he urged economy on Congress. Specifically, he recommended that appropriations for public buildings authorized but not yet begun, and for harbor facilities where there was no real need, be discontinued. Public works, thought Grant, were not to be used to provide profits— "I would have this work conducted at a time when the revenues of the country would abundantly justify it."

As for the panic, the President reiterated his belief that it would work a benefit to the country. "One long step has been taken toward specie payments," and without this "we can never have permanent prosperity." But a specie basis could not be reached until the balance of foreign trade was favorable. Exports should be increased, but to do this "sufficient currency is required to keep all the industries of our

18 New York *Tribune,* October 31, 1873.
19 *Ibid.,* November 1, 1873.
20 Garfield MS. Diary, Nov. 12, 1873.

country employed." Between these ideas of an inflation to increase exports and yet maintain specie payments, the President found a solution in an elastic currency. "Elasticity to our circulating medium, therefore, and just enough of it to transact the legitimate business of the country and to keep all industries employed, is what is most to be desired." After elasticity, the next desideratum was the prevention of speculation. In order to attain these objects of specie payments, elastic currency, and no speculation, Grant proposed that the Secretary of the Treasury be authorized "to issue at any time to national banks of issue any amount of their own notes below a fixed percentage of their issue (say 40 per cent), upon the banks depositing with the Treasurer of the United States an amount of Government bonds equal to the amount of notes demanded, the banks to forfeit . . . 4 per cent of the interest accruing on the bonds. . . ." In addition, Grant proposed that banking be made free, and asserted that the amount of currency outstanding was not in excess of the needs of the country.[21]

This message was received with a greater divergence of opinion than had been expressed on any of Grant's former literary efforts. The New York *Tribune* was convinced that "the President's views as to finances are not good, and do not show good sense," while the Philadelphia *Press* thought it "sensible, full of strong points." The Chicago *Times* found it "awkward in construction, timorous in spirit, [and] feeble in expression," but the Springfield *Republican,* admitting the clumsiness in expression, headlined it "General Grant's Best." The *Tribune,* inadvertently correct for once, summed up the journalistic response by deciding that none of the opinions was of any value.[22] There was hope for both inflationists and "sound money men" in the President's suggestions. All would depend on the attitude of Congress.

Within a few days of the opening of Congress, more than sixty bills and resolutions were presented in one or the other of the houses. John Sherman, heading the Senate Committee on Finance, was surprised to find measures "expressing every variety of opinion from immediate coin payments to the wildest inflation of irredeemable paper money." [23] Despite the attractive distractions of sniping at the Administration's appointments and raking new corruptions out of the political muck,

21 Richardson, *Messages,* VII, 235–255.
22 Cf. New York *Tribune,* December 3, 1873.
23 Sherman, *Recollections,* 490.

Congress expended much time and oratory on problems of the currency. Subjected to constant clamor for action from newspapers and bankers, debtors and manufacturers, the members were forced to act. Financial knowledge was rare among the nation's legislators; financial wisdom still rarer. In the halls of the Capitol, neither was highly prized. Such conservatives as Sherman, Hoar, and Garfield, with an unreasoned prejudice for specie payment and contraction, were in a minority, while Butler, Logan, and Morton, sponsoring wild and equally reasonless schemes of inflation, carried Western and Southern members with them. "The financial problem," observed Senator Howe of Wisconsin, ". . . would not be so difficult if we were content to do what is right & were not a little ambitious to do something smart." [24] The necessity for retrenchment and higher taxes bore heavily upon the Ways and Means and Appropriations Committees, but members of the House objected to the increased levies which the Secretary of the Treasury recommended. While the debate proceeded, Richardson issued more and more of the greenback "reserve" to meet the declining revenues of the Government. Eventually he had issued $26,000,000 bringing the total of outstanding greenbacks to $382,000,000.

It was shown in January that the inflationists had a clear majority in the House. On a routine question involving the currency, the vote stood 125 for inflation against 98 for hard money.[25] Immediately afterward, a bill was reported from the Ways and Means Committee fixing the amount of greenbacks which could be issued at $400,000,000, and providing for additional issues of national bank notes. Ostensibly designed to legalize Richardson's issue of $26,000,000, the bill set the limit of greenbacks at a figure which would authorize the reissue, if necessary, of the $18,000,000 left in the greenback reserve.[26] Considering the majority for inflation, the President's recent statement that the outstanding currency (in which he included the "reserve") was no more than enough for the needs of the country, and the Administration's obvious intention of using the reserve, the measure, so far as it related to greenbacks, could hardly be called excessive inflation. As for the bank notes, inflationists declared them merely replacements of outstanding issues. But even so, it aroused the conservative East to a

[24] T. O. Howe to Fairchild, March 17, 1874, Fairchild MSS.
[25] New York *Tribune*, January 20, 1874.
[26] *Ibid.*, January 22, 23, 1874. Cf. *Cong. Globe,* 43rd Congress, 1st session, page 3078, for votes in House.

high pitch of indignation. "Congress is stupid and weak, without sense, honesty or character on questions for currency and finance," fumed Gideon Welles in retirement.[27] and in Europe Grant's Minister to Russia grieved that "the condition of affairs at Washington is scandalous. Inflation appears to be the order of the day against the wish and judgment of the entire Eastern and Central States and the better class of the West." [28] Inflation was "simply monstrous," and would lead to greater evils.[29] Even in the West opposition was heard. "This is a triumph of the National Banks and the speculators. . . . It is also a plain violation of the promises of the Republican party," declared a Western business man.[30]

Since the Capitol swarmed with inflationists, devotees of the gold standard looked hopefully to the White House. Rumors that the President was expressing concern over the course of events came from the Executive Mansion, and efforts were made to assure the country that Grant "sympathizes strongly with the business interests." [31] It was even stated that Grant would send a special message to Congress reminding his party of their platform pledges.[32] As the discussion in Congress progressed, the President's disapprobation became more pronounced. Any bill sent to him, he told Congressmen, would be carefully examined in the light of the needs of the people and the amount of inflation involved.[33] George F. Hoar visited the President and urged him to veto the measure which Congress was debating. "Well," replied Grant, "if you send it up to me, make it just as bad as you can." [34]

As the bill passed the Senate, the New York *Tribune* commented ruefully on the "feminine" fickleness of Fortune and "her devotion to the least worthy men." Grant was a case in point; he had trifled with good fortune during the war, but had been successful. Now the same unworthy person was in a position to put himself at the head of the "honest" element in the party. "It remains to be seen whether he has sufficient independence to break away from coarse, strong-willed men. . . ." [35] Yet when the bill passed, fears were general that Grant

[27] Welles to Edgar Welles, February 21, 1874. Welles MSS.
[28] Marshall Jewell to Washburne, March 28, 1874, Washburne MSS.
[29] Jewell to Fairchild, March 21, 1874, Fairchild MSS.
[30] A. M. Conover (Madison, Wis.) to Fairchild, March 22, 1874, Fairchild MSS.
[31] New York *Times,* March 21, 1874.
[32] New York *World,* April 1, 1874.
[33] New York *Tribune,* April 3, 1874.
[34] Hoar, *Seventy Years,* I, 206–208.
[35] New York *Tribune,* April 14, 1874.

would yield to pressure and sign it. A delegation of New York merchants called on Grant to urge a veto, but while they waited for an audience, Ben Butler "rushed in ahead of them and got Grant off in a corner while the committee twirled their hats." Bad as was this omen, it was made worse when Logan, Carpenter, and Senator Ferry of Michigan—inflationists all—came in while the committeemen were making their speeches. The merchants learned that the bill had been discussed in Cabinet, and the Cabinet believed Grant would sign it.[36] Even Administration papers thought that Grant would approve the bill and urge Congress to pass further legislation superseding it.[37]

With the friends of honest money in despair, and the inflationists correspondingly elated, Grant suddenly, on April 22, sent back the bill with a veto. He had tried, he said, to justify signing it, but was unable to find valid reasons. To friends, the President explained that he had intended to sign the bill and had written out a message showing that the moderate inflation involved was not dangerous. But his own arguments were not convincing, and he had torn them up and written a veto message.[38] To Congress he said that he doubted if the bill would practically increase the currency of the country, but that it ostensibly increased the circulation by $90,000,000.[39] "It is a fair inference, therefore, that if in practice the measure should fail to create the abundance of circulation expected of it the friends of the measure, particularly those out of Congress, would clamor for such inflation as would give the expected relief." The theory, said the President, was "a departure from true principles of finance, national interest, national obligations to creditors, Congressional promises, party pledges (on the part of both political parties), and of personal views and promises made by me in every annual message sent to Congress and in each inaugural address."

Grant's alarming figure of $90,000,000 was hardly candid. The provisions of the bill, upon which the President laid so much stress, called for a possible issue of $46,000,000 of national bank notes. But these would be protected by bond deposits and were not considered by either bankers or Congressmen as inflating the currency. This put

[36] New York *Tribune*, April 18, 1874.
[37] New York *Times*, April 21, 1874.
[38] Garfield MSS. Diary, April 23, 1874.
[39] The printed form of the message (cf. Richardson, *Messages*, VII, 269) gives $100,000,000, but Grant corrected this the next day. Cf. Letter of Babcock, April 23, 1874, Grant Letter Book.

the actual figure of inflation at $44,000,000, and it was on this feature of the bill that Congress and country fixed attention. Yet $26,000,000 of this $44,000,000 had already been issued under Grant's authority. This brought the total possible inflation contemplated by the bill to $18,000,000. But even this was, for all practical purposes, already part of the currency. "The forty-four millions," said Grant in his veto message, "have ever been regarded as a reserve, to be used only in case of an emergency, such as has occurred on several occasions, and must occur when from any cause revenues suddenly fall below expenditure. . . ." If this interpretation were true, Grant's veto of the inflation bill amounted to a gesture in favor of hard money. Its validity depended upon the President's contention that it would be the entering wedge for further inflationary concessions. But even this reasoning is hardly valid. The bill was specifically worded to fix a maximum limit of inflation at $400,000,000. Literally at least, the bill was not designed to promote or encourage inflation.

But whatever the practical considerations, the veto was a credit to Grant's political acumen and balanced calm. Unlike excitable Congressmen, the President could remember that in 1868 and in 1872 the Eastern position on the currency had been approved by the voters. Always peculiarly immune to popular clamor, Grant recalled the crucifixion of Pendleton's "Rag Baby" in the Democratic party, and the firm stand of the Republicans since 1868. His gesture was based upon a good memory and a realization that the inflationists' insistence was but a passing cloud. It was a gesture in behalf of the conservative bankers whose support of his Administration had been constant, and constantly successful.

The political consequences of the veto were far-reaching. From conservatives everywhere came pæans of praise. "For twenty years no President has had an opportunity to do the country so much service by a veto message as Grant has, and he has met the issue manfully," declared Garfield,[40] as he hastened to the White House with gratitude and congratulations.[41] "Once more General Grant has deserved well of the country," admitted the New York *Tribune*, as it commended the veto.[42] Joseph Medill added his thanks "to those of all right

[40] Garfield to A. B. Hinsdale, April 23, 1874, Garfield MSS.
[41] Cf. Garfield MSS. Diary, April 23, 1874.
[42] New York *Tribune*, April 23, 1874.

thinking men" for Grant's "wise, courageous executive act" which had "saved the country from a grievous wound on its credit and reputation." [43] Even a Wisconsin Democrat found the veto "very popular . . . among all classes of people." [44] On the other hand, the inflationists were outraged. Logan condemned the President, Morton told his constituents that Grant had vetoed a bill which a Republican Congress had passed on the recommendation of Grant's annual message, and Cameron "scowled," mumbling that Pennsylvania was lost.[45] Westerners and Southerners announced they would keep up the fight,[46] but Garfield noticed that they were "very much toned down" since the veto.[47] During the discussion of prospects, Congress passed an act legalizing Richardson's issue of twenty-six millions of greenbacks. Thereafter, the greenbacks were not to go over $382,000,000. Though this was certainly as much an entering wedge for inflation as the bill setting the figure eighteen millions higher, the political purposes of the veto had been obtained, and the President approved.[48]

Grant's veto of the Inflation Bill was generally considered "as the turning of the corner by the American people, and setting the face of the Government toward specie payment and honest money." [49] Political observers thought that the move had strengthened the Administration with the moneyed interests, but as one remarked, "the fact remains that business South and East is distressingly dull. . . ." In the West, said this commentator, "the political elements are lying around loose and uncertain, and the business situation of the country promises to be very unfavorable to us this fall." [50] W. E. Chandler, most capable political organizer in the party, believed that if the Republican Party could rid itself of some bad men "without tearing too much up," it could win in 1876. Grant, thought Chandler, had improved as a politician.[51] Before the veto Chandler declared, "we were drifting hopelessly on a lea shore," but the veto changed matters. Now all that was necessary was a "vigorous administration of the Treasury by a western hard money man." With this, the congressional elections

[43] Medill to Grant, April 24, 1874, Barrett Collection.
[44] Geo. B. Smith to Fairchild, May 1, 1874, Fairchild MSS.
[45] Foulke, O. P. Morton, 345–347; New York Tribune, April 23, 1874.
[46] New York Tribune, April 25, 1874.
[47] Garfield to Halsey Hall, May 20, 1874, Garfield MSS.
[48] New York Tribune, June 23, 1874.
[49] Hoar, Seventy Years, I, 206.
[50] J. H. Ela to Washburne, May 19, 1874, Washburne MSS.
[51] John Jay to Chandler, April 10, 1874, Chandler MSS.

in the fall could be carried.[52] A Western politician concluded that the "back pay grabbers" would have to be displaced by honest men, but believed "we can clean out the Reformers this fall." [53]

Like Chandler, who was in Washington at the moment, Grant perceived the necessity of a Western hard-money man for the Treasury. Richardson, long anathema to the bankers, had outlived his usefulness and had been retained only because he was under fire. Though Grant's loyalty to his subordinates frequently subjected him to popular criticism, it was appreciated by the officeholders. But Richardson had been too long the *bête noire* of the Eastern financiers, and when a committee reported on the Sanborn contracts, he resigned to escape a vote of censure. Grant was ready to let him go, and in his place turned to Washburne. Fish, Robeson, and Chandler urged the Minister to France to return to Washington. Washburne's political wisdom would have stood the Administration in good stead, but he was enjoying his stay in France too much to return. His health was still bad, and he wrote the President that he could not accept the position.[54] Moreover, he had political ambitions which, in that period of fierce partisanship, would be improved by remaining out of the fray.

With Washburne out, Grant selected Benjamin H. Bristow for the Treasury. A native of Kentucky, Bristow had already attracted the President's attention as Solicitor-General. In his early forties, with an attractive personality and abundant energy, the new Secretary entered Grant's official family with every prospect that he would become as well one of the President's personal friends. To those not of the inner circle the appointment came as a surprise. "Grant can do more unexpected things in the same length of time than any man I know," exclaimed Marshall Jewell, Minister to Russia. "Still," he reasoned, "Grant knows his men pretty well, and I will bet on this being a good appointment." [55] The conservative East, finding Bristow "sound on the main question," cordially acclaimed his selection. The new Secretary promptly went to work cleaning up the Department—"It certainly needed it badly," remarked Grant's private secretary—and established civil service rules for new appointees.[56] Soon he offered $79,000,000

[52] Chandler to Washburne, May 4, 1874, Washburne MSS.
[53] W. W. Field to Fairchild, May 12, 1874, Fairchild MSS.
[54] Washburne to Grant, May 7, 1874, Grant MSS., Chicago Historical Society.
[55] Jewell to Washburne, June 4, 1874, Washburne MSS.
[56] Levi P. Luckey to Washburne, July 3, 1874, Washburne MSS.

in new five per cent bonds, and the bankers with fresh confidence in the Treasury quickly took them. Grant was pleased, and thought that the five per cents would pave the way for four per cents and for specie payment.[57]

The President was right; events of the summer and fall of 1874 brought home to his party the fact that resumption was more to be desired than inflation. The congressional elections turned largely on the depression, and although Democrats with inflationary schemes won many places, the Republicans concluded that sound money and conservative finance offered the inevitable platform of their party. Moreover, leading Republicans were convinced that the government should follow a conservative policy in expanding money. Before Congress met a number of newspapers and some of the more oratorical Congressmen began to advocate large appropriations for public works in order to relieve unemployment. Grant was on the verge of making such a suggestion in his annual message, but Bristow, intent upon gaining political capital for himself from a favorable Treasury report, stayed his hand. Garfield, chairman of the House Appropriation Committee, supported the Secretary. "It is not part of the functions of the national government to find employment for the people," thought Garfield, who believed that "if we were to appropriate a hundred millions for this purpose we should be taxing forty millions of people to keep a few thousand employed. By no such artificial and reckless method can industry and prosperity be restored."[58]

Grant's sixth annual message dealt largely with the financial condition of the country. Beginning by renouncing any intention of speculating on the causes of the panic, the President devoted most of his remarks to showing that the greenbacks in circulation had produced the trouble. Three "essential elements of prosperity"—capital, labor, and natural resources—were plentiful, but speculation had been encouraged by the fluctuating currency. The first step toward restoring prosperity, said the President, "is to secure a currency of fixed stable value." Calling attention to the repeated pledges of preceding Congresses, Grant urged a speedy return to specie payments. Condemning inflation as dishonest and burdensome to the wage-earners, the President declared his belief that "it is in the power of Congress at this session to devise such legislation as will renew confidence, revive all the industries, start us on a career of prosperity to last for many years, and to save the credit of the nation and of the people."

Specifically, Grant recommended free banking as the method by with elasticity might be given to the currency, a readjustment of the tariff for increased revenue, and a subsidy to American steamship lines in the hope of reviving commerce.[59]

Willing though Congressmen might be to repudiate the unpopular President, these financial recommendations presented a situation too urgent to be ignored. The President's consistent record on specie payments was an element of party strength, and the Republicans, finding that Grant had gained by his veto, while Congressmen who had supported the inflation bill were defeated, turned to the task of making amends for their apostasy in the preceding April. Under Sherman's guidance a Senatorial committee set to work to draft a bill which would redeem the party's record. Inflationists and contractionists sat together on the committee, and agreed to ambiguous phrases which would pass Congress. The bill provided for the coinage of subsidiary silver coins to redeem the outstanding fractional currency notes, and for free banking according to Grant's suggestion—with a provision that the Secretary of the Treasury should withdraw $80 in greenbacks for each $100 of bank notes issued. The Secretary was also authorized to sell bonds and use the Treasury surplus to redeem notes. The date for the resumption of specie payments was set at January 1, 1879. By that time, the inflationists thought that the policy would have proved a failure, while hard money men believed that the distant date would give the Secretary time to meet any demands. With both factions concurring, the bill passed the Senate December 22 and the House January 7. On January 14, Grant signed it and, unwilling to let the country forget who was its original sponsor, sent a message to the Senate congratulating it on a measure which "I deem most beneficial legislation on a most vital question to the interests and prosperity of the nation."

Thanks partly to Grant and partly to their defeat in the previous November, the Republican Party had recovered its sanity. The Resumption Act was a peace-offering after its inflationary philandering. Thereafter the party dwelt in connubial felicity with the bankers.

[59] Richardson, *Messages*, VII, 284–305.

ALTHOUGH the financial problems resulting from the panic of 1873 occupied the major portion of men's thoughts in the first part of Grant's second Administration, the problem of the South continued to trouble the ruling party and its President. With the mass of thinking men constantly more critical of Grant's conduct, his course in regard to Southern troubles seemed but to confirm the people in their distrust of the party. Democrats and "Liberals" found themselves in hearty disagreement with the President's measures, and in the end even the Republicans turned against their President. Eventually the Southern whites profited from Grant's declining popularity.

By the election of 1872, the States of Georgia, Tennessee and Texas went into the "redeemed" column, and together with Kentucky, Maryland, and Missouri gave Greeley the only electoral votes he polled in the Grant landslide. In the Carolinas, Virginia, Alabama, Florida, and Mississippi the combination of Federal office-holders, United States troops, and Negro voters kept a majority in line for Grant. The reform elements in the North were not inclined to forget the part which this combination played in their defeat, and lost no opportunity to attack Grant's Southern policy.

In all of the Republican States of the South there was much with which Grant's opponents could quarrel, but after the election of 1872 the situation in Louisiana made such a stench in the national nostrils that other and less putrid spots were generally ignored. The Louisiana muddle was the President's most constant source of embarrassment and anxiety.

The roots of the Louisiana troubles lay deep in the period when military governors aided carpetbaggers and scalawags in using Negro voters to control the State. Fraud and violence had marked the bitter struggle in which the native whites had sought to recapture political control. As in the rest of the South, the carpetbaggers and Negroes had extravagantly increased the State's debt in their haste to bring it abreast of Northern progress. Expenditures for schools and loans or guarantees to nascent railroads increased all debts in the South, and in

Louisiana these were augmented by loans to a private levee company designed to keep the obstreperous Mississippi within its artificial channel. Under the beneficent rule of the carpetbaggers the debt grew from $6,000,000 in 1868 to almost $50,000,000 two years later. Planters of the Creole State had little use for such Yankee notions as public schools and railroads, and were content to leave the maintenance of the levees to abutting property holders. But the planters were seldom considered by the visiting statesmen who were playing fox and geese with the State's finances. The planters only paid the taxes!

Heading the horde of political missionaries in Louisiana was the young Henry Clay Warmoth, who had hurried to Louisiana after an inglorious career in the Federal army. In 1868 he became governor and practical dictator of the State. Soon he was joined by Grant's brother-in-law, James F. Casey, whom the President, in his first lapse into political nepotism, had appointed Collector of the Customs. Like Murphy in the New York Custom House, Casey interpreted his position to involve the control of local politics in the interests of the national Administration.

For a time these two carpetbaggers coöperated in controlling the State, but in 1870 local jealousies caused a split in the Republican ranks and Warmoth refused to support Casey's candidacy for the United States Senate. Thereafter, Casey and his Custom House Gang opposed Warmoth. In alliance with Casey was the United States Marshal, S. B. Packard, who controlled the Federal troops. In August, 1871, the troops excluded Warmoth's supporters from a Republican convention in the Custom House and Warmoth appealed to Grant. But Grant refused to listen to their memorial and declared that he would take no part in local politics. His sympathies were wholly with Casey and the Federal officials.

In January of 1872 Warmoth called a special session of the legislature. Since the supporters of the Federal office-holders were in a minority, Casey and Packard attempted to prevent a session. Packard issued warrants for Warmoth's arrest, and Casey took a number of "Custom House Senators" aboard a revenue cutter and steamed up the river out of reach of sergeants-at-arms who were vainly attempting to muster a quorum. The House of Representatives, controlled by Casey's henchmen, organized and planned to impeach Governor Warmoth. This time both sides appealed for aid to the commander of the

Federal troops, General Emory, who asked permission of his superiors to declare martial law. Grant again refused to help either side, and asked Congress to investigate. The congressional committee, reporting on the eve of the Philadelphia convention, declared that there had been no conspiracy of Federal officials against the State. The situation, however, played into the hands of the Democrats, who went into the campaign of 1872 charging that Grant had interfered in local politics to support his corrupt brother-in-law.[1]

Finding himself unsupported by the Administration, Warmoth began to make overtures to the Louisiana Democrats, went to the Liberal Republican Convention, and supported Greeley in the campaign. The election passed off with only the customary disturbances, but immediately afterwards Warmoth, with no intention of losing control of the State, began to juggle the returning board which had the authority to throw out the vote of any parish or precinct in which corruption was found. By dismissing members of the board, Warmoth secured a majority of 10,000 for the Liberal Republican-Democratic gubernatorial candidate, John McEnery.

To meet this action, Casey and Packard constituted a board of their own and found, on the basis of spurious affidavits and newspaper returns, that their candidate, William P. Kellogg, another carpetbagger, had been elected by 18,000 majority.[2] Since Warmoth had control of the legal returns, the Republicans appealed to Judge Durell of the Federal Circuit Court. Late one evening, in his own home, Durell was visited by leaders of the Republican Party and persuaded to recognize the Kellogg government and to issue an injunction forbidding the Warmoth legislature to assemble in the State House. Packard willingly executed the order, using the Federal troops to expel the Warmoth legislature and seat the Republican lawmakers in their stead. Both sides again appealed to President Grant.

To most Northerners there was little to choose between the contending Louisiana factions, but Grant was thoroughly Republican and wholly in sympathy with the Casey-Packard-Kellogg cohorts. When a committee of citizens of New Orleans, favorable to Warmoth, announced they would carry a petition to Washington, Attorney-General Williams told the press their journey would be futile, as Grant was

[1] Cross, *Grant,* 80–88; N. Y. *Tribune,* August, 1871–May, 1872.
[2] Packard to Chandler, December 4, 1872, Chandler MSS.

determined to recognize the Kellogg government.[3] When the rival governors appealed to him, Grant asked Secretary Belknap to telegraph General Emory "not to be drawn into taking any *side* should there be a conflict. . . . It will be his duty to maintain order should there be a disturbance. But it may be legitimate for the so-called Warmoth State Government to organize to retain a position 'in court.' If so, they should be allowed to peaceably organize but should at the same time be requested to abstain from any act of legislation until the courts have established which of the two bodies is the legal legislature." [4]

With the courts likely to decide in favor of the Louisiana Republicans, Grant was willing to submit the matter to judicial determination. But at the moment that Louisiana was troubling the national scene, the Credit Mobilier was occupying the attention of Congress, and the animosities of the presidential campaign were by no means dead. Congressional leaders were coming to see that Grant's Southern policies boded no good for the country or the party. Accordingly, many were of the opinion that the matter should be left to Congress. In the House a majority opinion condemned Durell's illegal injunction, and Congressmen, talking seriously of their constitutional obligation to insure a republican form of government in the States, declared the Pinchback-Kellogg régime "not much better than a successful conspiracy." [5] In the Senate, the Committee on Privileges and Elections was forced to undertake an investigation when the mulatto Pinchback, elected by the Kellogg legislature, arrived to claim a seat. The fact that the Senate's action would decide the Louisiana dispute, at least inferentially, led to a concentration of attention on the Senatorial investigation.[6]

When the Senate counted the electoral vote it threw out both sets of returns from Louisiana. A few days later the committee reported that the entire election had been unfair and both governments were illegal. The committee recommended a new election to be held under Federal supervision.[7] A minority report by Oliver P. Morton held that since the courts had declared for Kellogg, Pinchback should be seated and Kellogg supported until the next regular election. The President,

---

[3] N. Y. *Tribune*, December 16, 1872.
[4] Grant to Belknap, January 5, 1873, Grant Letter Book.
[5] N. Y. *Tribune*, January 14, 1873.
[6] *Ibid.*, January 25, 1873.
[7] *Ibid.*, February 22, 23, 1873.

said Morton, was obliged to uphold Kellogg unless Congress by its action recognized some other contender.[8]

Like Morton, Grant felt that it was a dangerous precedent to overthrow a State government. Accordingly, he went to the Capitol to urge the Senators to take some definite action on Louisiana. When his personal appeal brought no response, he sent a message explaining his position. "Grave complications," he declared, had grown out of "an organized attempt on the part of those controlling the election officers and returns to defeat . . . the will of a majority of the electors of the State." After this direct assault on Warmoth, the President cited the laws upon which his use of the troops had been based, and declared that the courts had upheld the action of Packard's returning board. However, the Senate investigation had "developed so many frauds and forgeries as to make it doubtful what candidates received a majority of the votes actually cast." With no recommendation to make, Grant announced that he would support the government recognized by the courts unless Congress took action.[9]

That Grant's support of Kellogg was simply the partisan support of a Republican admits of no doubt. Less than two weeks earlier he had interpreted the election of 1872 as drawing the lines of party more distinctly, and he was not willing to abandon a State to the enemy. Rhodes thinks that "of all the alternatives the President chose the worst," and that "substantial justice" would have been done by withdrawing support from Kellogg.[10] But such a retreat, amounting to a betrayal of a loyal group of supporters, was foreign to Grant's nature. Four years later, when Hayes withdrew the Federal troops and allowed Louisiana to fall into Democratic hands, Grant was astounded. "I would have supported Packard or I would not have accepted the electoral votes of Louisiana," he declared.[11] On this principle he acted, nor could he understand any suggestion that he do otherwise.

But once the President had declared himself, the opposition newspapers took up the cudgels in behalf of Warmoth. In December the New York *Tribune* had admitted that Warmoth was doubtless dishonest, but once Grant had taken a stand the paper found the Kellogg government a notorious usurpation, "fraudulently established." [12]

[8] N. Y. *Tribune*, February 24, 1873.
[9] Richardson, *Messages and Papers of the Presidents*, VII, 212–213.
[10] Rhodes, *History of the United States*, VII, 175.
[11] Young, *Around the World with General Grant*, II, 359–362.
[12] N. Y. *Tribune*, December 13, 1872, March 1, 1873.

Despite the fact that party lines were clear, the Senate failed to provide for a new election in Louisiana, and adjourned without any action which would guide the administration. When this result was known in New Orleans, riots took place between the supporters of the two governments, and the opposition press in the North correctly assessed the blame upon a cowardly and partisan Congress. Late in March, Grant reappointed Casey as Collector of Customs, giving further assurance that he would not be turned from his course.[13] A few weeks later there were riots throughout Louisiana, some sixty Republicans, white and black, being murdered in the court-house of Grant Parish. As disorders spread, Kellogg appealed to Grant for troops, and the President on May 22 issued a proclamation declaring that Congress had tacitly recognized Kellogg. He ordered all "turbulent and disorderly persons to disperse" within twenty days.[14] With troops convenient, the Louisiana scene soon became quiet, but the embattled partisans had only begun to trouble the Grant Administration.

The quiet lasted only during the summer. When Congress opened, contestants for the Senatorship appeared again in Washington. A Senate committee reviewed the charges and countercharges of the factions, and came to the conclusion that a new election should be held. But the Kellogg faction employed W. E. Chandler as their lobbyist and lawyer, and Chandler, inspired by a fee which he never collected and by his devotion to his party, wrote pleadingly to Grant to stop the move for resubmitting the contest to the people. "A new election . . . would be absolutely and certainly fatal to the loyal men of the State." It would overthrow Kellogg, and Chandler was certain that "rather than desert Governor Kellogg now it would have been better to have abandoned him a year and a half ago. . . . Will not the President adhere to his well-considered and triumphant position, which has given a State victory to the Republicans of Louisiana who entered the fight in 1872 mainly to secure success in the presidential contest, and who are now entitled to the same consideration and fairness to which they would be if the presidential election depended upon sustaining them?" Kellogg wired Grant to the same effect.[15]

Ominous harbingers of the election of 1876, these letters convinced

13 N. Y. *Tribune,* March 3, 6, 25, 1873.
14 Richardson, *Messages,* VII, 223, 224, 308; N. Y. *Tribune,* April 21 ff. May 23, 1873.
15 Chandler to Grant, January 22, 1874; cf. also correspondence between Kellogg and Chandler in Chandler MSS.

the reluctant President that he should throw his influence into the scales against a new election. Already he had planned a message on Louisiana, but he withheld it and as a result the bill was not pushed. But the President had lost all love for Kellogg, Pinchback, Casey, *et al.*, and privately deplored the political entanglements which bound him to support a set of scoundrels.

At this stage of the Louisiana imbroglio a fine opportunity arose for Grant to demonstrate that he had had a change of heart on the South. Early in 1874 there were contested elections in both Texas and Arkansas, and in each the Republican claimant for the governorship appealed to the White House. But in neither instance would Grant give assistance. Newspapers quoted the President as saying that he did not want a repetition of the Louisiana affair in Texas. In Arkansas, the "Brooks-Baxter war" was settled by a presidential proclamation recognizing the conservative Baxter. Arkansas passed into the hands of the Democrats, and Grant's actions were widely hailed as an abandonment of his former Southern policy.[16]

Unfortunately for this view of the situation, the Republican Party had little chance of carrying either State. Later developments were to show that Grant abandoned the Republican Party in the South only when its cause was hopeless. When, as in Louisiana, the efforts of the Administration would strengthen the local Republicans, Grant gave effective if reluctant assistance.

During the summer of 1874 the Louisiana scene became momentarily quiet and the Administration took some of the troops from New Orleans to send to other parts of the South. But the quiet was merely the lull before a new storm, and the local Democrats, perceiving in the pending congressional campaigns a new opportunity of appealing to Northern sympathies, planned to take action. Inspired by a zeal to do something for the Democratic cause in the rest of the country, D. B. Penn, the McEnery lieutenant-governor, suddenly proclaimed himself governor. Riots broke out in New Orleans, barricades appeared over night in the streets, and the hastily mobilized battalions of the "Conservatives" took possession of the State House while Governor Kellogg found refuge with Casey in the Custom House. From this sanctuary, he hurriedly wired Grant for troops.

If it were Penn's purpose to embarrass Grant, he was eminently suc-

[16] N. Y. *Times, Tribune,* January 13, 1874; Ramsdell, *Reconstruction in Texas,* 316–317.

cessful. Ardent Radicals, seeing an opportunity to vindicate the national power, thought "the Louisiana business was a godsend to the administration," and advised presenting "McEnery and Penn with a suitable momento of gratitude for favors received and expected." [17] But the President, who found the corrupt Kellogg daily becoming more burdensome, was in a quandary and "grew black in the face" with rage over the new development. President and Cabinet agreed that "Kellogg . . . is a first-class cuss, but there's no way of getting rid of him." The Cabinet sought in vain for a means of supporting the Republican government in Louisiana "without backing these worthless reprobates." [18] Its members realized that supporting Kellogg meant the defeat of the party, and some of them proposed martial law, with the announcement that there had been no election in the State, trusting that the people would accept such a solution. But Grant would not listen to such a proposal. He had taken the electoral votes of Louisiana, he had informed Congress he would support Kellogg, and his determination on the subject was fixed. The jewel of consistency never shone brighter or in a less worthy setting than in this decision. He issued a proclamation ordering Penn's rebels to disperse and calmly awaited the consequences.[19]

The Penn forces, their service to the Democrats of the nation accomplished, retired from the scene and Kellogg ventured out of the Custom House. Democrats rejoiced at the turn of events. "General Grant has vanquished the people of Louisiana again," proclaimed the *Tribune*. "He has telegraphed to his generals and his admirals; he has set the army and navy in motion; and the lawful government of Louisiana surrenders." Grant's proclamation was indisputable evidence that the President supported usurpation in Louisiana; it was an "outrage" which stood out "in all its naked deformity"—an unpardonable crime against popular suffrage and the sovereignty of a State. And so it was considered throughout the North, where men were going to the polls to reverse the policy of the national government toward the South.[20]

Thoroughly tired of the Louisiana troubles and smarting under the attacks of the Democrats as well as from the defeat of the elections, Grant laid the Southern situation before Congress in his annual message

[17] J. G. Jenkins (Milwaukee) to Fairchild, September 28, 1874, Fairchild MSS.
[18] The words are Marshall Jewell's to Washburne, September 19, 1874, Washburne MSS.
[19] *Ibid.;* Cf. also Richardson, *Messages,* VII, 276–277; 296–297.
[20] N. Y. *Tribune,* September 18, 1874.

of December, 1874. Explaining conditions in Louisiana, the President reminded Congress that he had called attention to the "fraud and irregularity" in the election of 1872, but that he had expressly, and Congress tacitly, recognized Kellogg. "I must repeat," he said, "that in the event of no action by Congress I must continue to recognize the government heretofore recognized by me." In regard to the other States, Grant mentioned the annual pre-election outbreaks of violence and intimidation "to deprive citizens of the ballot because of their political opinions." White Leagues and military organizations spread terror, while employers threatened to discharge their colored laborers if they exercised their political privileges. The Fifteenth Amendment and the Ku Klux Acts were passed to prevent such intimidation, but there had arisen considerable criticism of executive interference in the affairs of the States. To the people of the North the President turned with a request that instead of magnifying or belittling or justifying the accumulated wrongdoing in the South, they should make an objective survey and rebuke wrongs and aid the authorities. "While I remain Executive," proclaimed the President, "all the laws of Congress and the provisions of the Constitution, including the recent amendments added thereto, will be enforced with rigor, but with regret that they should have added one jot or tittle to the Executive duties or powers."

"Let there be fairness in the discussion of Southern questions," implored the President, "the advocates of both or all political parties giving honest, truthful reports of occurrences, condemning the wrong and upholding the right, and soon all will be well. Under existing conditions the Negro votes the Republican ticket because he knows his friends are of that party. Many a good citizen votes the opposite, not because he agrees with the great principles of state which separate parties, but because, generally, he is opposed to Negro rule. This is a most delusive cry. Treat the Negro as a citizen and a voter, as he is and must remain, and soon parties will be divided not on the color line but on principle. Then we shall have no complaint of sectional interference." [21]

Able and moderate as this message was, Grant's popularity was definitely on the wane, and the turn of events soon gave evidence that the legislators would ignore his plea for moderation. Less than a month after his message, mass meetings to denounce the President were being

[21] Richardson, *Messages*, VII, 284–303.

organized in the principal cities of the North, and wholesale condemna-
tions uttered on the floor of Congress. The cause of the criticism lay
in the use of Federal troops in a fresh disturbance in Louisiana.

The election of 1874 in Louisiana almost duplicated the election of
1872. Democrats apparently polled a majority of the votes and elected
80 members of the 111 in the lower house of the legislature. But the
returning board, still under the control of the Republicans, investigated
the election, found cases of intimidation, and threw out enough returns
to cut the Democrats to 53 seats. Republicans, too, were given 53 seats,
and five cases were referred to the legislature. On January 5, 1875, this
legislature assembled, and 52 Republicans and 50 Democrats answered
to their names. Amid scenes of wild disorder, and in a highly irregular
manner, a Democrat was declared Speaker. Seizing the gavel, the
Speaker hurriedly swore in the members and received a motion to seat
the five contesting Democrats. To break a quorum, Republican members began to withdraw, but hastily appointed sergeants-at-arms herded
them back to their seats. Those Republicans who escaped from the
house assembled in the hallways and fomented disturbances among the
spectators. The Democrats who had organized the house appealed to
General De Trobriand, commander of the Federal troops, for protection.
Upon the general's approach the crowd dispersed. The Democrats had
been saved by the Federal troops.

But the army was not long on the side of the Democrats. Within two
hours De Trobriand was back at the State House with a squad of soldiers. Acting under Governor Kellogg's orders, the general drove from
the Capitol the five Democrats who had no certificates from the returning board. The Republicans, gathering in the wake of De Trobriand's
soldiers, organized the House with a speaker of their own choosing.

In December Grant, anticipating trouble, had requested Sheridan to
go to New Orleans to keep an eye on affairs. On the evening of January
4, after De Trobriand had purged the legislature, the lieutenant-
general took charge of the Federal forces. Advising Grant of this action,
Sheridan gave assurances that he could maintain order. To his mind it
was evident that the disorders were the result of the organized and
armed "White Leagues" of the State. "I think that the terrorism now
existing in Louisiana . . . could be entirely removed and confidence
and fair dealing established by the arrest and trial of the ringleaders
of the armed White Leagues." Congress, thought Sheridan, should de-

clare the Leaguers "banditti" and allow him to try them by military courts.

Sheridan's harsh suggestion offered perhaps the most efficient means of dealing with the Louisiana troubles, but politics rather than practicability dominated the discussion of the situation. So far as Louisiana was concerned, Sheridan's assumption of command served to prevent violence. Louisiana had tasted his hard rule in the days of its military government, and Democrats refrained from violence while he remained in the city. Insult and imprecation dogged his footsteps, and political murders continued, but the general kept his temper during the abuse, and no Democrat dared make an effort to overthrow the Kellogg government. In the country, however, this comparative peace was not appreciated. The electorate had just returned from the polls, where they had voted for Democrats against the Grant forces. Ignoring the Democratic violence in originally organizing the legislature, the people of the North could see in the situation only an effort to use military force to overthrow the will of the people. Sheridan's suggestion that the Democratic leaders of the White Leagues be declared "banditti" was made the subject of countless condemnatory editorials, and Democrats in Congress demanded investigations. When Grant approved Sheridan's course, talk of impeachment filled the air. The Senate asked Grant for information on Sheridan's actions.

On January 13, the President complied with this request in a long message on Louisiana affairs. "Lawlessness, turbulence, and bloodshed have characterized the political affairs of that State since its reorganization," said Grant as he began a review of the election of 1872. This election, he declared, "was a gigantic fraud, and there are no reliable returns of its result." Kellogg had possession of the office, and Grant believed he had more right to it than McEnery. This belief was borne out by a report of the Senate Committee on Privileges and Elections, which had declared that Warmoth had manipulated the returns to change 20,000 votes. From this, Grant passed to a consideration of the many instances of mob violence and political murder which had taken place in the State. Citing the decision of the New Orleans Circuit Court in the case of *United States versus Cruikshank,* Grant quoted a description of the Colfax massacre. "Fierce denunciations ring throughout the country about officeholding and election matters in Louisiana, while every one of the Colfax miscreants goes unwhipped of justice, and no way can be found in this boasted land of civilization and Christianity to punish the perpetrators of this bloody and monstrous crime." The Coushuatta massacre of August, 1874, was summarized by the President with Biblical terseness—"Several Northern young men of capital and enterprise had started the little and flourishing town of Coushatta. Some of them were Republicans and officeholders under Kellogg. They were therefore doomed to death." Yet despite this unpunished massacre, Grant had listened to the representations that there would be no violence if the irritating Federal troops were withdrawn from the State. Only a small garrison was left in New Orleans, and political quiet reigned for a brief moment. "But," continued the President, "the November election was approaching, and it was necessary for party purposes that the flame should be rekindled." Accordingly, there had followed the uprising of the White Leagues at the call of Penn, and the inevitable dispatch of more Federal troops.

As for the intervention of military forces in the organization of the legislature, the President admitted that he had no information. But he pointed out that both sides had called upon the Federal troops, that if Kellogg had used the police force this would have precipitated a riot with the White Leagues, and that the pressure of the Federal troops prevented bloodshed. Moreover, "nobody was disturbed by the military who had a legal right at that time to occupy a seat in the legislature." The Democrats had used fraud and violence, which "were a part of a premeditated plan" to organize the House, reorganize the outlaw "McEnery" Senate, depose Kellogg, "and so revolutionize the State government." As for Kellogg's action in using any available means to defeat "these lawless and revolutionary proceedings," Grant refused to express an opinion, but he called attention to the fact that it had been the Democrats who first began the trouble. "When those who inaugurate disorder and anarchy disavow such proceedings, it will be time enough to condemn those who by such means as they have prevent the success of their lawless and desperate schemes."

To Grant, whose realistic view of the situation was far clearer than that of men whose vision was clouded by partisan sympathies, Sheridan's actions were thoroughly justified. "No party motives nor prejudices" could be imputed to the Lieutenant-General, declared the President. Instead, "honestly convinced by what he has seen and heard there, he has characterized the leaders of the White Leagues in severe terms, and has suggested summary modes of procedure against them, which, though they cannot be adopted, would, if legal, soon put an end to the troubles and disorders in that State." But even if he could not follow Sheridan's suggestions, the President vigorously asserted his determination to prevent Ku Klux Klans, White Leagues, or any such organizations "using arms and violence" from governing any part of the country. He would use his power, within the limits of the law, to prevent "Union men or Republicans" from being "ostracized, persecuted, and murdered on account of their opinions."

Finally, Grant placed the blame squarely upon Congress. He had appealed to the legislative body to take action on Louisiana. "I cannot but think that its inaction has produced great evils." The work of the army, on the other hand, "has been always on the side of preservation of good order, the maintenance of law, and the protection of life." Congress should act to make clear the President's duty in such a situation.[22]

Before this message was sent to the Senate, the whole situation was discussed in the Cabinet. Jewell, the reforming Postmaster-General, was wholly in sympathy with Grant's stand. "The President is hopeful and plucky and serene," he reported in December, "and proposes to protect the colored voter in his rights to the extent of his power under the law, and if we cannot protect them we shall lose most of the fruits of this tremendous war." [23] But newspapers declared that Fish and Bristow had threatened to resign if Grant upheld Sheridan. In Congress, a Republican caucus had violently divided over the issue, but there was a general desire to accept Sheridan's analysis of affairs. In the country there was widespread excitement.[24] Democratic governors of Massachusetts, Tennessee, Ohio, and Missouri demanded that the people of their States arise and rebuke the President and his party.[25] In the newspaper discussions some inkling of the real points at issue were apparent to him who would read between the lines. The *Tribune* remarked on the difficulty which white people of the South experienced in submitting to the "rule of ignorance and dishonesty," [26] and declared that "wealth and intelligence" were on the side of the White Leagues.[27]

[22] Richardson, *Messages*, VII, 305–314.
[23] Jewell to Fairchild, Dec. 28, 1874, Fairchild MSS.
[24] Garfield MS. Diary, January 9, 1875.
[25] N. Y. *Tribune*, January 8, 1875.
[26] *Ibid.*, January 11, 1875.
[27] *Ibid.*, January 7, 1875.

Republicans who were anxious to repudiate Grant's leadership of the party could not regard the Louisiana trouble as an unmixed blessing. The party itself was too closely tied up with the affair for Grant to be deserted. Garfield thought that Louisiana was the millstone about the party's neck,[28] and Democratic papers were diligent in placing the entire blame on Grant and in advising their opponents to rid themselves of their Cæsar. "His heel is on Louisiana, and his thumb is on Congress." [29] To Congressmen who were reluctant in taking this advice, Grant's message came as a relief. It was praised as able and satisfactory by Congressmen,[30] and the Republican press called it "a moderate, strong, and sensible document" which made it unnecessary for "Republicans to cast themselves into the arms of the Democrats in despair of securing a just policy from their own party." [31] Even the opposition press, momentarily convinced by Grant's able discussion, could find no quarrel with his conclusions.[32] The *Tribune,* however, explained that Grant had changed his tone in order to keep his best Cabinet members from resigning, although it had to admit that Senators in general were satisfied with the President's exposition.[33]

The good effects of Grant's message were immediately destroyed by the report of a subcommittee which had been investigating the Louisiana election of 1874. On January 15, this committee, composed of Democrats and "reforming" Republicans, reported that the action of the retiring board had been "arbitrary, unjust, and . . . illegal." There had been innumerable frauds on the part of the Republicans, there had been intimidation of Negroes by Negroes, but there had been neither fraud nor intimidation on the Democratic side. The committee had been present when the legislature had been organized, and when it had been purged. Its members had seen the White Leagues and their arms, yet they had no suspicion that the Democratic action on January 4 had been, as Grant alleged, for the purpose of revolutionizing the State. Although their report dealt only with the election, by implication it cleared the Democratic skirts of all disorderly conduct.[34]

Meanwhile, to further prevent Grant's words from having the weight

[28] Garfield to Hinsdale, Garfield MSS. and in MS. Diary of Jan. 8, 1875.
[29] N. Y. *World,* Jan. 11, 1875; N. Y. *Tribune,* Jan. 13.
[30] Garfield MS. Diary, Jan. 13, 1875.
[31] N. Y. *Times,* Jan. 14, 1875.
[32] N. Y. *World,* Jan. 14, 1875.
[33] N. Y. *Tribune,* Jan. 14, 1875.
[34] House Reports, Number 101, 43rd Congress, 2nd session.

which logic might have given them, the country itself was rising in indignation. On January 11, before Grant had been heard from, and with only Sheridan's "banditti" dispatches to guide them, opponents held a "non-partisan" mass-meeting at Cooper Institute. Democrats spoke, and William Cullen Bryant, a Republican, condemned Grant, Sheridan, and Kellogg. On January 15, in Boston, a similar meeting was held in Faneuil Hall, where General S. M. Quincy and John Quincy Adams took up the cudgels against the unholy triumvirate who were so cruelly oppressing the Democrats of Louisiana. Resolutions denouncing the use of Federal troops and condemning Secretary of War Belknap were adopted.[35] Wendell Phillips, however, came to Grant's defense. On the same night as the Boston meeting, Baltimore citizens listened to Reverdy Johnson and three alleged Republicans declare that Grant was violating the Constitution and destroying the States in his selfish ambition for a third term.[36] Throughout the country similar meetings were held, and Democratic legislatures discussed resolutions instructing their representatives in Congress to hasten the withdrawal of troops.[37] Even in England there was widespread sympathy for the South, and general condemnation of Grant's course.[38]

The result of these meetings was to further demonstrate the necessity for a united party action on Louisiana. Radical leaders in Congress studied the report of their committee and denounced it. Morton believed that the committee were negligent in seeking for facts, and too inclined to accept the hospitality of Kellogg's New Orleans enemies.[39] On his motion, a new sub-committee, headed by George F. Hoar, was appointed to visit New Orleans and repair the damage done by the first visitors. The committee was absent for three weeks and spent its time collecting, with Sheridan's aid, an imposing list of atrocities. But atrocities were not enough to convince the country that Federal interference was justified. In fact, the committee had a serious duty to perform in really settling the Louisiana problem. As a result of their tactful approach an agreement known as the "Wheeler Compromise" was made in Louisiana. William A. Wheeler, a member, brought Louisiana Democrats and Republicans to agree to a truce. By its terms the

[35] N. Y. *Tribune*, January 16, 1875.
[36] *Ibid.*, January 16, 1875.
[37] D. D. Crowley to Logan, January 27, 1875, Logan Mss.
[38] Fairchild, (Liverpool) to Mrs. S. F. Dean, January 9, 1875, Fairchild MSS.
[39] N. Y. *Tribune*, January 18, 1875.

Democrats were given control of the House, the Senate went to the Republicans, and Kellogg was guaranteed possession of his office until the end of his term. With this settlement, quiet once more reigned in Louisiana—a quiet which was not broken until the next election.[40]

The settlement of the Louisiana troubles reflected no credit upon the President. The party had repudiated the report of its "reforming" element, and had arranged for peace in the State, but Grant was ignored in the settlement. As political manœuvres the Hoar Report and the Wheeler Compromise were excellent; they saved the party without saving the President, and yet did not repudiate him. But practical repudiation of the President was already accomplished. While the Hoar committee was in Louisiana, a House committee headed by Luke P. Poland of Vermont reported on conditions in Arkansas. That State, as we have seen, had witnessed a conflict during the previous year over the governorship, and Grant, in May, had recognized the Democratic contender. Following this, a new Constitution, replacing the Reconstruction instrument, had been submitted to the people. In the November elections the Constitution had been adopted, and a new government, fully officered, was inaugurated under it. The Poland Committee approved of this course, and announced that peace and quiet prevailed in the State. But on the day after this report, Grant, answering a request for information, took issue with the House Committee. He submitted to Congress papers which purported to show that he had made a mistake in recognizing the Democratic governor the previous May, that the Republican claimant was entitled to the governorship, and that the new Constitution, adopted by fraud and by the intimidation of voters, was illegal. Contemplating this action, Grant raised the question whether other States might not follow the example of "changing their Constitutions and violating their pledges if this action in Arkansas is acquiesced in?" The President asked Congress to decide "whether a precedent so dangerous to the stability of the State Government, if not of the National Government also, should be recognized by Congress." [41]

Debate followed this presidential message, with Poland battling for a resolution which would recognize the right of Arkansas to change its Constitution at will. The issue whether the Southern States might re-

[40] Cf. N. Y. *Tribune,* Jan. and Feb., 1875; Hoar, *Seventy Years,* I, 208 ff., 243–245.
[41] Richardson, *Messages,* VII, 319; House Report 127, 43rd Congress, 2nd session.

pudiate their previous pledges after receiving congressional representation was ignored. Instead, Poland dwelt at length on the horrors of carpetbag and Negro rascality, and on the violence and corruption which characterized Republican rule. The House hearkened to the appeal of "wealth and intelligence" and accepted the Poland Report. Grant, standing for the permanence of the agreement which had been made with the reconstructed States, was defeated; and ex-Confederates in other parts of the South prepared to follow the Arkansas trail to white control. Constitutional change rather than political intimidation came to be the method by which the old ruling classes of the South resumed their sway.[42]

The defeats for the President in Arkansas and Louisiana were followed by one other. Radicals in Congress, led by Butler, drafted and tried to pass a Force Bill which would give Grant power to suspend the writ of habeas corpus in Alabama, Arkansas, Louisiana, and Mississippi for two years. The obvious political purpose of this bill caused it to be attacked, and a Democratic filibuster delayed action. In the end, it passed the House through Butler's efforts, but failed in the Senate. Republicans, whatever the necessity, could not afford to be counted among those who would continue military rule in the South. The vote, although Grant was not interested in the bill, was counted another defeat for the President. Butler's sponsorship of the measure, since Grant and Butler were popularly supposed to be acting together, was but an additional burden upon the President.[43]

Butler, however, was successful in another measure relating to the South. The Civil Rights Bill, designed as a monument to Charles Sumner, was passed in the last days of Congress under Butler's supervision. Grant had no use for Butler—he had chuckled over a dispatch from Massachusetts in November: "Butler defeated, everything else lost" [44] —and had stated that he would veto the Civil Rights Bill.[45] However, since the measure had lost some of its worst features, he signed it on March 1. The measure was relatively harmless in the South, but it cost him the support which Border State Republicans had hitherto given the party.[46]

---

[42] *Cong. Record*, 43rd Congress, 2nd session, March 2, 1875, pp. 2117.
[43] N. Y. *World*, February 8, 1875; N. Y. *Tribune*, February 11, March 1, 5, 1875.
[44] Jewell to Washburne, December 5, 1874, Washburne MSS.
[45] N. Y. *World*, November 21, 1874.
[46] N. Y. *Tribune*, March 2, April 1, 1875.

As the last session of the Forty-Third Congress closed its work it was evident that popular condemnation had led the Republicans to abandon Grant's leadership. Moreover, foreshadowing the policy of President Hayes, the South was practically turned over to the Southern whites and Democrats. Grant was repudiated; the accumulating scandals of 1875–76 could only complete the work of turning the party from him to some reformer. To old-line Republicans the prospect seemed blue enough. "Seriously," the consul at Nuremburg asked the consul at Liverpool, "is it not too d—d bad that our party should be ruined and have to go to the wall through the careless labor of such cattle as Kellogg, Casey & Co.? I believe," he continued, "Genl Sheridan told the simple truth—but the truth is our people are tired out with this worn out cry of 'Southern outrages'!!! Hard times & heavy taxes make them wish the 'nigger,' 'everlasting nigger,' were in——or Africa. . . . It looks to me as though the game was up for 1876. . . . God help the country if the Democrats once get in power." [47]

[47] T. Wilson to Fairchild, January 17, 1875, Fairchild MSS.

WITH the shadow of the depression hanging over the national government and the ever-recurrent problems of Louisiana and the South troubling his days, Grant's second Administration was predestined for failure. Throughout his first term he had learned much. He had learned that his best-intentioned actions would be misinterpreted by carping critics, that his safety lay in close alliance with the politicians of his party. Also he had learned to disregard all criticism as the howling of prairie wolves. The lesson was acquired too well, for Grant showed little appreciation of the fact that there was a deep-seated popular disgust with the machinations of the politicians. Men who sensed the people's will rode to power as Grant obstinately disregarded an outraged public opinion. Completely ignoring the Civil Service Commission's rules, the President appointed officials "according to political preferences." [1] Although he asked Garfield to put through Congress an appropriation for extra pay for the Commission's clerks,[2] and declared himself anxious to correct abuses, his actions belied his vocal devotion.[3] G. W. Curtis, observing the tide of events, at first concluded that the Cabinet was unfriendly, "but fortunately Grant is tenacious and resolved upon the spirit which should govern appointments." [4] Soon, however, Curtis decided that Grant had abandoned "both the spirit and the letter of the rules," and he resigned his chairmanship of the Civil Service Commission.[5] For his place Grant selected Dorman B. Eaton, one of the most ardent reformers, and continued, at the same time, to make political appointments. Yet in April, when Joseph Medill resigned from the Commission to become Mayor of Chicago, Grant wrote him repeating the words of the inaugural—"The spirit of the rules will be maintained." [6] Inevitably, these two resignations made their contribution toward bringing the President into disrepute.

[1] N. Y. *Tribune*, November 27, 1872, citing *New National Era* and the *National Republican*.
[2] Babcock to Garfield, December 13, 1872, Grant Letter Book.
[3] Grant's notes to his secretary for March 24, 1873, are preserved by Mr. O. R. Barrett of Chicago. Even 20 days after the inauguration Grant was writing about 23 appointments ranging from visitors to West Point, and keepers of light houses to territorial governors.
[4] Cary, *George W. Curtis*, 232.
[5] N. Y. *Tribune*, April 1, 2, 9, 1873.
[6] Grant Letter Book, April 9, 1873.

Two months after the inauguration, popular attention turned to speculation over the Chief Justiceship. Chief Justice Chase died on May 7, 1873, and immediately the friends of various legal luminaries began to urge their merits. Few prominent judges or lawyers escaped mention, but the appointment was expected to be from among Edwards Pierrepont, Senator Howe, Attorney-General Williams, and William M. Evarts. Justice Noah D. Swayne remembered that two years earlier Grant had told him he would appoint the next Chief Justice from the bench, and hastily enlisted Garfield's service in keeping the office in Ohio. Although he preferred Evarts, Garfield, returning to Washington early in November, dogged Grant's footsteps for several days in Swayne's behalf. Throughout the summer there had been much discussion of Conkling as the new Chief Justice, and Garfield found Grant confused in mind as to his course. Republican journals had heralded Conkling's name with praise, but the independent press had opposed the New Yorker on the grounds that he was a politician who had little experience in legal practice and was a "salary grabber." Though Grant kept his own counsel, Garfield decided that the appointment lay between Conkling and Swayne, and that if Swayne were promoted, B. H. Bristow would be given the vacancy.

Garfield's guess was only half right. The selection of a Chief Justice from the bench entered very little into Grant's thoughts, but Conkling seemed to him an excellent appointment. In November, he offered Conkling the place; to his own and the country's astonishment, the Senator refused. Garfield was reminded of the younger Pitt's refusal of any but the first place, and thought Conkling must be actuated by the same ambitions, but Grant, with no time for speculating on historical parallels, hastened to get an appointment ready before Congress met. After Cabinet consultation, he decided to send in the name of Attorney-General Williams! [7]

The first session of the Forty-Third Congress, assembling in December, 1873, was faced primarily by the financial issue. But the members were politicians rather than financiers, and preferred to devote their efforts to activities with which they were familiar. Although discussion of economics was never lacking on the floor of Congress, and the newspapers were constantly lecturing Congressmen on public economy, both

---

[7] N. Y. *Tribune*, May 20, July 23, Oct. 4, 11, 15, Dec. 1, 1873; Garfield MS. Diary, November 13–24, 1873; Garfield to Bristow, November 19, 1873, Garfield MSS.

politicians and press directed their major efforts to the tried and proven subjects of patronage and corruption.

During the summer months, newspapers, massmeetings, and political conventions had given ample warnings to incoming Congressmen that the "salary grab" should be repealed. "The very devil seems to have possessed the last Congress," said one observer as he noted the bitter popular feeling. "No course is left to us as a party except to denounce it." [8] The Democratic caucus, realizing that the continuance of the act worked greater hardships on their opponents than on them, resolved to sustain it [9] but the Republicans, with even Butler approving, voted to abandon the offending measure.[10] Before a month had elapsed, the affrighted majority passed a bill to reduce their own salaries. The pay of executive and judicial departments, however, remained at the increased figure.[11] The Chicago *Tribune* editorially reminded its readers that "the President's salary is a fortune" and was far too much. Lincoln, it said, lived on much less.[12]

With this concession to public demand, Congressmen felt free to resume their wonted policy of quarreling with the Administration over appointments. Along with his annual message, Grant sent the newly organized Senate the nominations of Williams for the Chief Justiceship, Shepherd for Governor of the District of Columbia, and B. H. Bristow for Williams' place in the Cabinet.[13] Better carcasses for the partisan vultures in the Capitol could not have been found.

The discussion of Williams quickly indicated that the Attorney-General was one of the most unpopular men in the country. "The country should be ashamed and disgraced by the nomination of such a man," said the Cincinnati *Commercial*. There was "no act of his life, no merits as a lawyer, no fame as a pleader, no reputation as a jurist," to justify his appointment. The Louisville *Courier-Journal* called him "the worst appointment yet," and other papers echoed the sentiment. There was universal agreement that the appointment was "characteristic of Grant," and the only favorable note was struck by a few papers which thought Williams preferable to Conkling.[14]

[8] C. K. Davis, (St. Paul) to Fairchild, August 24, 1873, Fairchild MSS.
[9] N. Y. *Tribune,* Dec. 2, 1873.
[10] *Ibid.,* December 3, 1873.
[11] *Ibid.,* Dec. 15, 18, 1873, Jan. 12, 1874.
[12] Cf. *Ibid.,* Dec. 15, 1873.
[13] Garfield MS. Diary, December 2, 1873.
[14] N. Y. *Tribune,* December 6, 15, 1873.

On December 11 the Judiciary Committee reported favorably on Williams, but so much opposition developed that the nomination was referred back to the committee, where it remained under discussion until after the Christmas recess. Meanwhile, Senators sought reasons for rejection, and were able to dig up a charge that the Attorney-General had spent $1,600 of Departmental funds on a carriage for his wife, and kept his accounts on the government pay-rolls. With no more serious accusations than these, the Judiciary Committee visited the White House to advise the President to withdraw the nomination. Believing that part of the objection to Williams was caused by preference for some of the associate justices, Grant refused to withdraw his name and told the Senators that he would not promote one of the judges. But this failed to have any effect; it was plain that Williams could not be confirmed. Fish persuaded him to ask for a withdrawal. On January 8, Grant took the nomination from the Senate.[15] Under cover of the agitation over Williams, Shepherd's confirmation slipped through with little opposition.

With Williams out, Grant, for no apparent reason, nominated Caleb Cushing for the Chief Justiceship. Cushing was a lawyer of merit who had recently served as counsel at the Geneva Arbitration, but he was a lifelong Democrat, had presided over the Democratic Convention which nominated Breckenridge for President in 1860, and had not renounced his heresies. Seekers for sinister motives found the devious mind of Ben Butler behind the candidate,[16] but Tom Murphy decided that "the old man got mad" and sent in Cushing's name because "they made such a fuss over . . . Williams." [17]

Whatever the reasons for the nomination, the Senate was determined to have none of Cushing. It made immediate objection because of the Massachusetts lawyer's unsound judgment, and resorted to a hasty scramble for more valid reasons. With far greater speed than had attended the demolition of Williams, Senators found a letter in the Pickett papers of the Library of Congress, from Cushing to Jefferson Davis, recommending a friend for appointment to office in the Confederacy! With this as an excuse, the Republican Caucus asked Grant to withdraw the nomination. Grant immediately complied with the request,

[15] N. Y. *Tribune*, December 8, 9, 15, 17, 18, 19, 22, 23, 1873, January 1, 6, 9, 1874; Levi P. Luckey to Washburne, December 21, 1873, Washburne MSS.

[16] *Ibid.*, January 12, 1874.

[17] Cited in Rhodes, *History of the United States*, VII, 91.

"CHILDREN CRY FOR IT."
U. S. G. "IF YOU CAN STAND IT I CAN."

ADMINISTERING THE CIVIL SERVICE

dropping Cushing with a promptness that delighted the President's enemies. The ghost of Horace Greeley might exult that the Pickett archives, purchased to ruin Greeley's campaign, had "proven a boomerang" to demolish Grant's Chief Justice.[18]

After this fiasco, efforts were made to have Conkling reconsider his decision, but the Senator again refused.[19] Expecting this, Grant had again looked about for a Chief Justice, this time resolving that his appointee should be confirmed. The new nominee, whose name was sent in on January 19, was Morrison R. Waite of Ohio. If this was as unexpected as those which had failed to run the Senate gauntlet, it was less vulnerable to partisan attacks. Essentially mediocre, a lawyer of merit with a reputation in Ohio, Waite was regarded by none as the best man for the place. But "he is an honest man and a fair lawyer, and that," sighed the bored public, "is as much as can reasonably be expected from Grant." [20] Without enthusiasm the Senate gave its approval, and even so disgruntled a commentator as Gideon Welles was thankful that Grant had "done so well." Old Gideon remembered that Waite's father was "a man of solid substantial mind," and rather expected the son would do well.[21]

This muddle settled, Congress turned its attention to an investigation of the ill-savored Sanborn Contracts. Before 1872, informers who reported evasions of Federal taxes were rewarded with a portion of the delinquent collections. Such a system was dangerous to many businesses, whose practices were liable to true or false accusations by disgruntled employees, and in 1872 the Revenue Act repealed the legislation as provocative of blackmail. However, Butler got inserted in the Revenue Act a clause permitting the Treasury to make three contracts with outsiders by which the contractors would receive a percentage of any delinquent taxes which they detected and collected. These contracts were made during Boutwell's incumbency. One, signed by Assistant-Secretary Richardson, authorized John D. Sanborn, one of Butler's Massachusetts henchmen, to retain as commission fifty per cent of any delinquent taxes collected. Although the compensation was higher than was necessary to ferret out tax dodgers, the contract was neither illegal nor dishonest. Corruption, however, almost immediately crept into the

---

[18] N. Y. *Tribune,* January 10–15, 1874; Richardson, *Messages,* VII, 259.
[19] Conkling, *Life of Conkling,* 463–465.
[20] N. Y. *Tribune,* January 20, 1874.
[21] Welles to E. T. Welles, January 22, 1874, Welles MSS.

situation when Sanborn, armed with his contract and a letter from Richardson, entered the Boston office of the collector of internal revenue to ask for a list of delinquents. Obtaining them, he ordered the taxes collected and paid over to him. Deducting his fifty per cent, the amiable collector turned the remainder over to the Treasury. Another interesting method by which Sanborn obtained the names of delinquents was by copying the names of six hundred railroads from a railroad guide, and swearing they were all tax evaders. His average of accuracy was remarkably high, which doubtless accounted for the information of his activities coming before Congress. Investigation revealed that he had not collected one cent which would not have come into the Treasury by the normal processes of collection, but that, for his services, he had received $213,500! Of this, Sanborn told the investigating committee, he had spent $156,000 in looking up cases and employing assistants. The committee suspected that the assistants had been more valuable to Butler's political ambitions than the Treasury, but they were unable to prove any collusion between the collector and the Congressmen. Others suspected that Boutwell had been made Senator through the efforts of Sanborn, but here too they were unable to fix any guilt. The only person who could be caught was Secretary Richardson, and the committee, after three months of investigation, reported in May that he deserved "a severe condemnation." With his Assistant-Secretary, Richardson resigned before a censuring vote could be put through the House.[22]

In the midst of the investigation, the Senate saw another chance of getting at Butler. When the Collector of the Port of Boston resigned, Grant nominated William A. Simmons for the position. Simmons was a supporter of Butler, and a war politician who possessed ability in appealing to the submerged classes against the ruling financiers and "men of property and intelligence" in New England. Butler and Boutwell endorsed the nominee, while Sumner, together with the Hoars and some five "respectable" members of the House, opposed him. The opposition was sufficient to incense Grant, and when a committee of the Senate reported against confirmation, the President refused to yield. His defeat on the Chief Justiceship was too recent to permit of another

[22] House Executive Documents, 43rd Congress, 1st session, No. 132. All newspapers and especially the New York *Tribune,* carried almost daily accounts of the investigation from February to May.

surrender, and his obstinacy gained the confirmation for his appointee.

The furor aroused by this appointment was used to full advantage by the Administration's opponents. Especially timely were the comments of the "independent" press that Butler was running the government. Butler was the new leader of the Republicans, declared the *Tribune,* as it pointed out the "bond between Butler and Grant is the natural one of sympathy in pursuit of vulgar ends by vulgar means." As such remarks filled the newspapers, Butler humorously said to George F. Hoar, "I have a hold over Grant, and he does not dare withdraw Simmons' name." But Hoar was devoid of humor and hastened to the White House to tell the President what Butler was saying The President, too, lacked a sense of humor, but he perceived what Hoar was trying to obtain. Grant was never a person to repel such an approach by argument or explanation. He did not like Butler, but he knew such pressure as Hoar was bringing should be ignored. With temper under perfect control, the President looked coldly at his visitor. Hoar withdrew in confusion, but in explaining the incident to his friends, and later to the world in his *Autobiography,* he implied that Grant's silence was an admission that he feared Butler. No one who knew Grant's habit of silence when displeased would have been deceived by Hoar's story; however, in that manner sprang the long-lived legend that Butler had boasted of a mysterious power over the President and Grant had admitted it! [23]

While attacks on the Administration and on Grant's handling of the patronage were coming from all sides, the President made two gestures which seemed to indicate a wavering from his customary partisan stand. In April he sent a civil service report to the Senate, and in the next two months he called two excellent men to his Cabinet.

The constant pressure to which he was subjected in regard to the patronage caused him to show a renewed interest in civil service reform. Captious critics such as the New York *Tribune* delighted in pointing the finger of shame to any case which might be interpreted as a departure from the adopted rules. The *Tribune* referred to the movement as "the late civil service reform," and declared the President its greatest enemy.[24] In April, Grant sent Congress a report on which the Civil

[23] On Simmons' appointment cf. *Tribune,* February 19, 20, 26, 27, March 2, 3, 4, 1874; For Hoar's story see his *Autobiography,* I, 210, 386, II, 3. Rhodes got the story from Hoar, and gave it currency. Cf. *History of the United States,* VII, 88.
[24] N. Y. *Tribune,* January 26, April 21, 1874.

Service Commission had been working for a year, and took occasion to point out that the rules already adopted were being satisfactorily enforced, while Cabinet members were enthusiastic. However, the rules could not be applied to those officers whose appointment needed Senatorial assent, unless the Senate should accept the regulations.[25] Needless to say, the Senate, already jealous of its powers over appointments and content with the existing system, ignored the suggestion, leaving Grant to worry over the distribution of the spoils. Small wonder that the President eventually decided that civil service reform was mostly cant.[26]

Bristow's appointment to succeed the unpopular Richardson was well received by the financial centers. Late in June, Creswell, last of the original Cabinet, resigned,[27] and in his place Grant selected Marshall Jewell, a native of Connecticut, and for a year, Minister to Russia. Jewell was astounded at his appointment. "I don't know yet why Creswell left or why they want me," he wrote to Washburne while he packed his trunks, "but believing in Grant I propose to go when he calls." [28] Stopping but a week in London in order to see Nellie Grant in her idyllic happiness,[29] Jewell hastened to Washington, where he was soon "going for" claim agents, and cleaning up the postoffices. "I am running the department strictly within the Civil Service rules," he told Washburne at the end of the summer. "I found the President meant business by it, and really wanted it carried out—so we follow the rules strictly, and find they work well—and the more I see of it the more I like it." [30] Certainly in Bristow and Jewell, as always in Fish, Grant had Cabinet officers with whom neither capitalists nor reformers could find fault.

But if Grant escaped censure in these Cabinet selections, the chain of ill-fortune that attended his appointments was not broken. Late in the session of Congress, the plaints of those District of Columbia property owners whose taxes were steadily mounting before "Boss" Shepherd's feats in municipal improvement came to the ears of the Congressmen. Investigation revealed that contracts had been hastily and perhaps corruptly made by the all-powerful Board of Public Works;

[25] Richardson, *Messages*, VII, 263; cf. also Luckey to D. B. Eaton, April 1, 1874, Grant Letter Book.
[26] Young, *Around the World*, II, 265–268.
[27] Grant to Creswell, June 24, 1874, Grant Letter Book.
[28] Jewell to Washburne, July 6, 1874, Washburne MSS.
[29] Jewell to Fairchild, July 28, 1874, Fairchild MSS.
[30] Jewell to Washburne, October 17, 1874, Washburne MSS.

and a House Committee recommended a change in the government of the district and was unsparing in denunciation of the unpopular Shepherd. In the last days of Congress a bill abolishing the territorial government was rushed through the houses. In its place, provision was made for a transitional government to hold District affairs in abeyance until Congressmen could return in the winter to discuss matters at leisure. This was obviously aimed at Shepherd; but the lawmakers felt aghast when Grant, approving their bill, nominated him for a place on the temporary Board of Commissioners. Grant's loyalty to men under criticism, combined with the obvious propriety of putting an informed man on the territorial board, was sufficient explanation of the appointment. But the Senate was outraged, and rejected the erstwhile Governor by an overwhelming vote. Only six Senators had the temerity to support him. When Grant heard the news it was his turn to be outraged, and he stormed about the White House in high dudgeon. But the Senate's action was final, and he was forced to abandon the man who had lifted Washington out of the mire.[31]

With the Sanborn contracts and Shepherd's alleged corruption as political manna for their enemies, the Republicans in Congress returned to the people. It was a bad year for ambitious men of the ruling party. The steady decline of public confidence in the Administration, the disordered state of business, and the long record of investigations boded no good for the men in power. Divided on questions of finance, the shadow of the salary grab still hanging over them, the Republicans faced a campaign in which the odds were heavily in favor of their enemies. The Senate passed some legislation to protect Negro rights, partly as a tribute to Charles Sumner, who died in March, and partly in the hope of finding political capital. But Southern members of the House opposed according social rights to Negroes, and the Representatives ignored the Senate's action. As the congressional campaign began, the Republicans found themselves without a party program, with every likelihood that the campaign would turn on the endorsement of the Administration. The Democrats were delighted to meet on that battleground.

The most interesting phenomenon of the campaign was the discovery by the anti-Grant forces that he was ambitious for a third term.

[31] N. Y. *Tribune*, March 10, May 21, June 24; Jewell to Washburne, June 4, 1874, Washburne MSS.; Dunning, *Reconstruction*, 244.

Soon after the election of 1872, Republican journals, in the exuberance of victory, had proclaimed that he would again lead the party to triumph in 1876.[32] From that time rumors that he would be the candidate were discussed, though little serious attention was given them. But early in 1874 the New York *Herald* took up the matter, and began to berate the Republicans and the President for conspiring to overthrow the government. Grant attempted to spike the rumor by telling a friend that he would not be a candidate under any circumstances, and had run before only at the solicitation of his friends.[33] To stand-pat Republicans who saw in Grant their best chance of controlling the Negro vote, talk of a third term was pleasing. Men close to him noticed that mention of a reëlection "seemed to be disagreeable" to the President. The idea, said Grant, had been formulated by the *Herald*, which had been loudly talking of "Cæsarism," and which was "a journal so utterly devoid of character" that it was not allowed in the White House.[34]

Such was the situation down to the veto of the inflation bill. In the meantime, political observers speculated on the chances of Blaine, Boutwell, Morton, or Conkling for the succession.[35] But the veto message restored Grant's popularity for a moment, and Marshall Jewell believed that "Grant's straightforward, sturdy integrity, and strong horse sense, and the way he has of always meeting a great crisis like a great man will sort of force him into prominence for another term, in spite of friend or foe." Moreover, Jewell noticed that the veto dispelled "the notion that Grant is run by someone, and I am glad to find that bubble broken anyhow, for you and I know quite well," he wrote to Washburne, "that so far from anybody running Grant, he runs himself so entirely that his left hand does not know what name his right hand is going to write." [36]

From the time of the veto to the fall elections no word escaped Grant concerning his ambitions for a third term. Southern Republicans took up the third term cause, and combined it with a promise that Grant would veto the Civil Rights Bill if it should pass. Many Northern Republicans, hopeful that some wind of chance would blow them into the White House, grew restive under Grant's silence but were nevertheless

[32] Cf. New York *Tribune*, November 26, 1872.
[33] *Ibid.*, January 2, 1874.
[34] John M. Francis to Washburne, February 16, 1874, Washburne MSS.
[35] Henry O'Connor, (Washington) to Fairchild, July 25, 1874, Fairchild MSS.
[36] Jewell to Washburne, June 4, 1874, Washburne MSS.

constrained by party loyalties to avoid the issue. In the press, Grant's candidacy was discussed pro and, con, with loyal Republican papers denying that he wanted reëlection. So potent a political weapon was the third term charge, that John A. Dix, Republican nominee for Governer of New York, was forced to come out, late in the campaign, against Grant. But Dix's conversion was too late. Samuel J. Tilden defeated him by 30,000 majority. Dix and Grant had carried the State in 1872 by 53,000, and the shift of 80,000 votes was declared by anti-Grant men to be solely on account of the President's ambitions.[37]

Late in the campaign, after the October States had gone Democratic, Grant discussed the third term talk with his Cabinet. It was, said the President, solely the result of newspaper agitation, and he was not interested.[38] Considerations of party advantage were weighed against the disadvantages of any presidential declaration, and the only result of the discussion was an "inspired" dispatch from Washington which stated that Grant stood where he had in 1872—in the hands of his friends! [39] Evidently there was as much to be lost as gained by any declaration of intentions. Grant was doubtless pleased by the mention of his name, and despite the clamor of his foes, there is no evidence that the third term agitation was more than a minor factor in the Democratic victories of 1874.

As the Democrats tried to make the contest turn on the endorsement of Grant, the Republicans fell back on the Southern issue. As election day approached, violence between the races in the South broke out anew. It was an inevitable concomitant of the social struggle in the South, where neither Democrats nor Republicans were inclined to conduct their campaigns peaceably. The one appealed to the lower-class white voters with stories of Negro insolence and exaggerated stories of the corruption in Negro-ruled commonwealths. The other found in atrocity tales a means of keeping Federal troops in the South, keeping Negro voters in the Radical ranks, and keeping Northerners convinced that only the Republican Party should be in control of the government. Some men among the Northern Democrats vainly urged Southern whites to make allies instead of enemies of the Negroes.

[37] The third term agitation is best followed through the columns of the New York *Tribune,* which garnered press comments from all parts of the country. See also Cortissoz, *Whitelaw Reid,* I, 287–299, for an account of the *Tribune* in the N. Y. campaign.
[38] N. Y. *Tribune,* October 29, 1874.
[39] *Ibid.,* November 2, 1874.

Had the struggle in the South been purely political, this might have been accomplished, but the relations of the races in the South involved questions of social control and economic exploitation which would only be complicated by political alliance.[40] Southern Democrats were unwilling to quell the outbreaks of lynching, mob violence, and political murder which characterized every election, and Republicans, rejoicing in the disorders, sedulously gathered stories of horrors for the delectation of Northern voters.

In previous elections this propaganda had been thoroughly successful, but in the campaigns of 1874 the tested methods proved less efficacious. Northern voters were less susceptible than formerly to tales of outrages in the South, and Southern Republicans found it hard to present credible accounts for their Northern allies.[41]

The difficulties of the Republican Party in the South were clearly brought to light in October when representative Republicans from all the Southern States assembled at Chattanooga to formulate the program of the party's Southern branch. One hundred and fifty delegates assembled in the village which Grant had made famous and which carpetbaggers were rapidly transforming into an industrial city of the "New South," to discuss the situation. Dark-skinned delegates from the Cotton States came to demand that the party indorse the Civil Rights Bill in order that Negro voters might be reassured. White scalawags from the Border States opposed such endorsement, for it would cost them the support of their poor-white allies. Politicians wanted a list of authenticated atrocity stories to spread in the Northern States—thus keeping Republicans in control of the government, and keeping their protectors behind them. But other Northerners, having identified themselves with the industrial development of the South, feared that atrocity stories would frighten investors and immigrants from Southern manufactures. Amid such chaos of aims, the Republicans of the South failed to present a united front. Committees on Resolutions and on Facts and Statistics were appointed, and the conflicting opinions of the delegates were fought out behind closed doors. The Resolutions Committee made no report on Civil Rights, and contented itself with resolving against dishonest officials, and in favor of improving Southern water courses and education.

[40] N. Y. *Tribune,* August 21, 27, 1874.

[41] For an account of atrocities in Alabama, supplied by Congressman Hayes, and disproved by the New York *Tribune,* see *Tribune,* September 1, October 7, 12, 15, 23, 1874; cf. also New York *Times,* October 24, 26, and the *Nation,* October 15, 1874.

The "Outrage" Committee asked for more time in which to compile their statistics of bloodshed. No report was ever made, and the Chattanooga Convention failed to contribute fresh blood for the bloody shirt.[42]

The result of the congressional campaigns of 1874 was an overwhelming defeat for the Republicans. Although the financial situation of the country was largely responsible for the result, the general condemnation of corruption, Grant's Southern policy, and the third term renders it impossible to weigh the various factors. Certainly, in the minds of the people, Democrats and Republicans alike, the election meant the defeat of "Grantism." In the next House the Democrats would have 168 seats, the Independents 14, and the Republicans 108. "We have met the enemy and we are theirs," quoted Postmaster-General Jewell. "We needed a little punishment, but we don't want as much as this." [43] Surveying the wreck of their party, Republicans were uncertain whether the third term, the Civil Rights bill, or Louisiana had caused the catastrophe.[44] Democrats were sure their "day of redemption" was at hand and saw the "wearing out of Republican ascendancy" in the toll of the votes.[45]

Alone in the Republican Party, President Grant remained unperturbed by the defeat. Jewell noticed that Grant was "a very sanguine sort of man, and don't think this is much of a shower anyhow." [46] In the Cabinet, Grant laughed at the idea that the third term talk had been effective, and concluded that the Civil Rights Bill had hurt the party.[47] Pointing to Dix's defeat in New York, he declared that Democrats had won because Dix repudiated the Administration.[48] The defeat in other States had been due to local causes, to bad congressional legislation, and to poor candidates. As for him, he would cling more closely than ever to the principles which had guided him in the past.[49]

The significance of the elections of 1874 might not have been evident to President Grant, but it was obvious to members of the Republican Party. However much the depression had contributed to a desire for

[42] New York *Tribune*, October 14, 15, 21, 23, 1874.
[43] Jewell to Washburne, October 17, 1874, Washburne MSS.
[44] Cf. J. N. Denham to Washburne, November 6, 1874, Washburne MSS.; N. Y. *Tribune*, November 5, 1874; Blaine, *Twenty Years in Congress*, II, 563.
[45] Thomas Hood to Fairchild, October 19, 1874, Fairchild MSS.
[46] Jewell to Washburne, October 17, 1874, Washburne MSS.
[47] N. Y. *Tribune*, November 7, 1874.
[48] *Ibid.*, November 9, 1874.
[49] *Ibid.*, November 13, 1874.

change, the fact remained that the country had expressed its disapproval of the Administration. Perhaps the fundamental cause of the Republican defeat was the reaction from the materialism of the Grant régime. President Grant was no idealist in either politics or war. In both he was a realist, reacting to conditions rather than theories, and gathering about him practical men rather than theorists. In the elections, his main objective was to win victories, and he employed practical men with realistic methods to gain his ends. Yet if there was ever a time in American history when idealism was in order, it was during the depression following the panic of 1873. In religion, Moody and Sankey were calling the faithless back to the fold with sermons full of fire and brimstone and songs which held hope for repenters! In politics somebody should be doing something for the fallen.

The Republican Party had been founded in idealism, and had grown strong in the great national crusade of the Civil War. Its long lease of power had brought corruption in its train, and the maintenance of this power had become important after the party's original objectives had been attained. Grant's Administration came in a period of transition, while the party was passing from its earlier ideal of preserving the Union into the long period when its goal was protection of the economic interests of Big Business. A high tariff, "sound" money, and government aid to but no control of business, were coming to be the aims of a party which had originally embodied the dreams of the common man for free lands dedicated to freedom. Men who joined it in its radical infancy, who adhered to it during the war, found themselves in strange company when, with Grant in the White House, professional politicians ran it to serve the interests of conservative business men.

Although the elements in the Republican Party were diverse, all were impressed by the elections of 1874. To business men, it was evident that the corruption in the party should be ended. That this involved bringing to an end the incongruous alliance between Eastern financiers and the illiterate black voters of the South was apparent to the politicians, if not to the reformers. To the politicians the elections were a warning that the party would have to return to idealism—and a return to idealism clearly meant that Grant would have to be scrapped. The President was too closely identified with the current régime in the popular mind, he had been the victim of too much criticism and he was too blundering to lead the party. Moreover, the constant threat of a third term inclined those who were aspirants for the highest office to welcome any move to displace the President.

In the months after the congressional elections, the movement to undermine and discredit Grant went steadily on. The President's "selfishness," and his lack of principles, were kept constantly before the country by the partisan press,[50] and the politicians began to agree that he had made calamitous mistakes.[51] "Grant had beaten the life out of us," bemoaned one politician. "By adhering to him we have lost the prestige gained by a dozen years of hard work." [52] Jewell, in the Cabinet, thought that Grant was responsible for the defeat, and decided that "if we are going to carry the next presidential election at all it will be because the Republican Party show themselves to be up to the times." [53] Even Jay Gould, trying surreptitiously to get advance information on Grant's financial recommendations, observed: "I don't suppose anything he may say will have much effect here as his voice is less potential than formerly." [54] Vice-President Wilson told Garfield that Grant was "the millstone around the neck of our party that would sink it," and Garfield found Blaine, whose eyes, like those of Wilson, were on the White House, of the same opinion.[55] Garfield felt as if "all the Gods had conspired to destroy the Republican Party." [56] Wisconsin's Senator Howe feared that "unless the Democratic Party comes to our rescue soon . . . there is no salvation for us." [57] The only solution of the party's difficulties, the *Tribune* piously advised, was to "unload" Grant.[58]

Only partly cognizant of the growing unpopularity, Grant determined to hew to the line which he had previously followed. Realizing that retrenchment and reform were the order of the day, he planned to devote himself to good government, conservative legislation, and a return to specie payments.

When Congress met, with 150 of its members smarting from a defeat which they were willing enough to attribute to Grant, the President and Cabinet set themselves to weather "the worst session yet." Schemes

[50] Cf. *Tribune*, November 11, 1874.
[51] Garfield MSS. Diary, November 12, 1874.
[52] William Faxon (Hartford) to Chandler, December 3, 1874, Chandler MSS.
[53] Jewell to Washburne, December 5, 1874, Washburne MSS.
[54] Gould to Chandler, December 4, 1874, Chandler MSS.
[55] Garfield MSS. Diary, January 7, 1875; Smith, *Garfield*, I, 519.
[56] Garfield MSS. Diary, January 8, 1875.
[57] T. O. Howe to Fairchild, June 14, 1875, Fairchild MSS.
[58] N. Y. *Tribune*, February 12, 1875.

to make the Government come to the aid of Jay Cooke's Northern Pacific Railroad, and schemes for refunding the tax collected on Southern cotton after the war, were only two of the many "jobs" which the members were interested in. "A corrupt and violent session" was expected by all, and Grant planned to veto their more excessive measures. The violence did not belie men's fears. Southern problems were passed in bitter review, and Grant was excoriated for his course in Louisiana, Arkansas, and throughout the South. The only blessing that Grant could have found was that it was mercifully short. When it adjourned in March, he had been completely repudiated.

Just after Congress ended its feeble labors, there came another change in the Cabinet. Attorney-General Williams, Grant's "Secretary of State for Southern affairs," retired from his office. His services to the Administration had been well performed, and the reasons for his retirement were not discussed in the press. Fish, writing to Washburne, contented himself with innuendo—quoting: "In our hours of ease, uncertain, coy, and hard to please." In his place, Grant selected Edwards Pierrepont, a man with whom the reformers could find no fault. Pierrepont soon attracted attention with new appointees, which according to the critics of Grant, meant that he was "clearing the house" of the corruption which had marked Williams' tenure of office. But despite the fact that Pierrepont, Bristow, and Jewell raised the caliber of the Cabinet to the highest point, it was too late to save the Administration. Grant had ignored the reforming sentiment too long, had adhered too closely to his partisan advisers, and had made too many mistakes. The next Congress would be Democratic and perhaps the next President would be from that party!

THE elections of 1874 and the succeeding session of Congress completely broke Grant's leadership of his party. Henceforth all but a handful of spoilsmen who were so closely identified with the Administration that they could not answer to the bugle call of reform deserted him and sought new policies and a new leader. Inevitably, the presidential bee buzzed in men's bonnets, and aspirants for the succession lost no occasion to put themselves on record as opposing Grant. Vice-President Wilson, who was not averse to thinking of himself as President, was constantly remarking for publication that the Republican Party had a chance to win new victories if it would adopt "broad, wise, and magnanimous" policies.[1] Wilson was sure that the people of the country were opposed to a third term for any man.[2] John A. Logan, whom Grant had accused of having the presidential "bug" two years before, hoped that some turn of fate would give him the Republican nomination, and, during the summer went to California, where he found the people for him. His policy was to say nothing and do nothing while "things take shape."[3] Throughout the country there was considerable sentiment for Minister Washburne—a man whose reforming zeal, financial ideas, and close connection with the politicians made him popular with all classes, East and West.[4] Washburne's health, however, prevented his making any effort for the nomination. He doubtless expected that the Grant forces among the officeholders—the real organization of the party, would be thrown to him. Hamilton Fish was frequently mentioned. Another potential heir of the Administration was Oliver P. Morton, and in many circles political speculators were willing to wager on Conkling's chances.

Far stronger than any of these aspirants was James G. Blaine, Speaker of the House and a party wheelhorse whose ability to straddle an issue increased his availability with both reforming and regular Republicans. His popularity in the House assured him widespread sup-

[1] New York *Tribune,* January 19, September 13, 1875.
[2] *Ibid.,* June 5, 1875.
[3] Logan to Mrs. Logan, August 7, 1875, Logan MSS.
[4] J. Russell Young to Washburne, September 27, 1875, Washburne MSS.

port, but his closest friends feared that he was too well known and had been prominent far too long. Garfield was afraid that Blaine had been "trying too hard" to be really successful.[5] The Speaker, however, was a shrewd political observer and a sagacious judge of men. A fondness for intrigue, and the fact that he came from the never-doubtful State of Maine were Blaine's most noticeable disadvantages.[6]

The most significant political development in 1874 was the rise of Secretary Bristow as a main contender for the presidency. From the moment of his assumption of the Treasury, Bristow had made a strong bid for the attention of the reform element among the Republicans. His management of the national finances was sufficient to gain for him the commendation of the New York financial interests, and his pronouncements against corruption endeared him to the conservative classes.[7] With these elements sympathetic, the Secretary began to measure the political landscape. Immediately before him lay two obstacles, the third term menace, and the opposition of some of Grant's more potent henchmen. With his vision distorted, or clarified, by his presidential dreams, Bristow concluded that Secretary Delano, "Boss" Shepherd, and General Babcock were intriguing to drive him from the Cabinet. Immediately he set to work to defeat their aims, and began to buttonhole Congressmen who visited his department, carry them into his private office, and discuss the situation with them.[8]

Secretary Delano was not popular with members of Congress, and when Bristow unburdened himself to Garfield, the Ohio Congressman, who had known the Secretary in the politics of his home State, piously hoped that Bristow would not be the one to leave the Cabinet. Delano, however, "could be spared without damage to the country."[9] Soon the newspapers began a vague discussion of an approaching Cabinet crisis,[10] and in April charges against the Secretary were brought before the Cabinet. They were unfounded, and Grant defended him, but some accompanying charges that his son John Delano had used his influence in blackmailing men doing business at the Land Office seemed to be substantiated. The matter was discussed in the Cabinet, and Grant, finding his Administration again attacked, refused to accept the Secre-

---

[5] Garfield MS. Diary, March 16, 1875.
[6] Smith, *Garfield*, I, 584–585.
[7] N. Y. *Tribune*, March 24, 1875.
[8] Garfield MS. Diary, Dec. 19, 1874.
[9] Garfield to Captain Charles E. Henry, December 24, 1874, Garfield MSS.
[10] N. Y. *Tribune*, February 23, 1875.

tary's resignation. Delano himself, not suspecting the source of the accusations against him, told Garfield that the attack was against the Republican Party in general. "It appears to be special in his case," Garfield smirkingly confided to his diary.[11] Late in the summer, when the newspaper criticism had died away, Grant accepted Delano's resignation. In his place, the President appointed ex-Senator Zach Chandler of Michigan, a realistic politician who could carry out reforms without moral cant, and without bidding for the applause of the reformers.[12]

While Delano's problems were before the country, Bristow kept up the alarm over Grant's third term aspirations. To Garfield the Secretary revealed that he had been "reluctantly compelled to come to the conclusion that the President is really meditating a third term." The White House, according to Bristow, was overrun by a disreputable group who planned to continue Grant in office. The Ohio Congressman took up the cry and in Bristow's behalf wrote to friends in Ohio advising them that "we must throw off the third-term nightmare before we can have any party success. . . . We must in plain and unmistakable words for ourselves repudiate the doctrine of a third term." [13] The President, he said, was running the party, and had degraded the position of a Cabinet officer.[14]

It was not Bristow, or Garfield, or the reformers of the party, however, who defeated the third term idea. In the spring elections in Connecticut the Republicans were badly defeated, and again many charged that the President's ambitions were responsible.[15] Fearful lest such a charge, unanswered, might bring further injury to the party, Grant awaited the first favorable opportunity to state his position. Late in May, on the eve of the assembly of a Pennsylvania convention, Grant wrote to the presiding officer repudiating any desire for a third term. "I did not want the first," said the President, as he pointed out that he had left a permanent office with high salary to serve the good of the country. He had appreciated the second nomination and election, but as for a third term, "I do not want it any more than I did the first. I would not write nor utter a word to change the will of the

---

[11] Garfield MSS. Diary, August 2, 1875.
[12] Grant to Delano, July 16, 28, 1875, Grant Letter Book.
[13] Smith, *Garfield*, I, 583–584.
[14] *Ibid.*, I, 585; cf. also, Garfield MSS. Diary, March 9, 16, 1875.
[15] Jewell to Washburne, April 23, 1875, Washburne MSS.

people in expressing and having their choice. . . . I am not, nor have I ever been, a candidate for a renomination. I would not accept a nomination even if it were tendered unless it should come under such circumstances as to make it an imperative duty, circumstances not likely to arise." [16]

An interesting domestic comedy accompanied this renunciation. Like many of their friends who had privileges connected with the White House, Mrs. Grant was pleased by the thought of another term in the Executive Mansion. Knowing that his action would be disagreeable to her, the President gave his letter to the press without her knowledge. When Mrs. Grant read the letter in the newspapers, she scolded Badeau, the only close associate who had known the President's intention, for not having stayed the general's hand. The decision, however, was irrevocable, and Mrs. Grant had to content herself with being an ex-First Lady.[17]

Although Grant had seemed to hedge with his statement about "imperative duty," the politicians were glad to be relieved from the restraints of personal loyalty to the President. Among politicians there was general agreement that his decision had saved the party, and each potential candidate redoubled his efforts. Most active among them was the Secretary of the Treasury.

On May 10, three weeks before Grant's third term letter, Bristow delivered a dramatic stroke against the notorious whiskey rings which had been defrauding the government of millions annually since the days of Andrew Johnson. No important distillery center was without its ring, and few honest distillers were to be found in the country. These conditions had been suspected for years, and newspapers and minority politicians had perennially returned to the theme that governmental circles showed a remarkable reluctance to investigate the charges. Until Bristow entered the Treasury there had been no real effort to apprehend the criminals, and under Boutwell and Richardson their activities in official circles had increased in number and in importance.

The methods of the whiskey rings, although by no means uniform, usually consisted in false reports to the government of the amount of spirits manufactured or rectified, and in the use of duplicate serial

[16] New York *Tribune*, May 31, 1875.
[17] Badeau, *Grant in Peace*, 244.

numbers on forged internal revenue stamps. Gaugers, employed at the distilleries and rectifying houses by the government, being poorly paid, were susceptible to bribery by manufacturers of "crooked whiskey." The alliance of gauger and distiller was supplemented, in some of the internal revenue districts, by higher officials, extending even to the collector of the district himself. But the ramifications of this organized corruption did not stop with the boundaries of a collection district. In the Treasury Department itself, in the Bureau of Internal Revenue, were officials who received money from the rings and rendered a valuable service in informing the thieves of any adverse moves by the highest officials. The investigation of these rings revealed that their influence extended beyond the portals of the White House, and that their agents had ready access to the ears of the President!

Because of these informers in the Department, Bristow's early efforts to catch the whiskey rings met with defeat. Agents secretly sent to the distilleries found everything in good shape and no fraud evident. A few honest agents reported their suspicions to the Secretary, while more venal inspectors, suspecting where they could not prove, used their commissions to blackmail the thoroughly alarmed distillers. Defeated by unknown informers close to his secrets, Bristow sought other means of securing evidence. Shipping records from some of the distilling centers, notably St. Louis, revealed that more whiskey was being shipped than was reported to the government. Fully convinced of corruption, Bristow confided to only one officer in his department. Together the Secretary and his assistant secretly gathered a force of incorruptible agents and sent them to the distilleries. Suddenly, on May 10, these men struck. In Milwaukee, St. Louis, and Chicago they seized sixteen distilleries and a like number of rectifying houses. The offices of the collectors of internal revenue were seized, and the books and papers of both officers and distillers were put under seal until they could be examined by Bristow and Attorney-General Pierrepont.[18]

In Milwaukee the local ring was found to have engaged in widespread political corruption. E. W. Keyes, the State's patronage boss, had drawn heavily from the corrupt coffers of the ring and the raid fell upon him without warning. Matt. Carpenter, whose Senate seat had been lost by too vigorous a defense of the "salary grab," was found to have aided the ring in getting complaisant officials appointed and to

18 New York *Tribune*, May 10, 1875.

have "turned revenue frauds to political account." [19] In Illinois suspicion named every prominent Republican as a participant in illegal distilling.

Most important of these rings, however, both from the amount of its stealings and the extent of its political influence, was that in St. Louis. There, as collector of internal revenue, was General John McDonald, an old friend of the President's, whom Grant had appointed at the time Carl Schurz was carrying the Missouri electorate into opposition to the Administration. McDonald was illiterate, and his moral character, according to the Missouri Congressmen who had protested against his appointment, was such that it would add no strength to the Administration. But as McDonald was an excellent politician, and Grant was not inclined to accept Schurz's judgment concerning the moral character of Administration supporters, he gained the place, and soon began to organize a ring among the distillers and officers. The proceeds, which totaled more than $2,500,000, were originally devoted to the Republican organization, in whose interests a newspaper in St. Louis was purchased, a strong party to resist the local Liberal Republican-Democratic coalition in Missouri was created, and large amounts were contributed to W. E. Chandler's 1872 campaign coffers. In operating his ring, McDonald revealed great acumen. Beginning in a modest way, he blackmailed distillers into partnership by finding them guilty of some minor infraction of the complicated liquor laws, and giving them the choice of prosecution or further corruption. Through his political influence honest officials were forced to turn dishonest or to sacrifice their positions. The business of the ring grew so large that an experienced manager was brought in from outside to collect from the distillers and distribute the ill-gotten proceeds among the ring's official members.

Among the recipients of dividends from the ring were William Avery, chief clerk of the Treasury, and the ubiquitous Colonel Babcock, Secretary to the President, Commissioner of Buildings and Grounds of the National Capitol, brevet Brigadier-General in the United States army, and former conspirator with and very extraordinary ambassador to Santo Domingo's President Baez. A partner of Shepherd in Washington, a friend of speculators in Indian affairs, suspiciously mentioned in connection with "Black Friday" and the Leet-Stocking "general order" business, Babcock seems to have had intimate contacts with

[19] T. O. Howe to Fairchild, June 14, 1875, Fairchild MSS.

most of the corrupt men of a corrupt decade. He fished for gold in
every stinking cesspool, and served more than any other man to blacken
the record of Grant's Administrations. From the St. Louis ring, Babcock's pickings were enormous. Cigar boxes with thousand dollar
bills, letters carrying five hundred dollars at a time, diamonds of great
weight and flawless water, rare liquors, receipted hotel bills, and even
a "sylph's" charms were bestowed on him by McDonald and his thieves.
Altogether, McDonald estimated, $25,000 was given Babcock in cash;
the other gifts, of untold value, were too numerous to count.

That such a man could retain his position as confidential secretary
to the President at the same time that he lined his pockets from all
parts of the country, was at once a tribute to his personality and his
genius for persuading the sensitive Grant that every attack was inspired by the sore-headed "reforming" politicians who were sniping at
the Administration. No better illustration of Grant's complete conversion to the politician's ideology can be found than in the attitude
which he took toward the exposure of the St. Louis whiskey ring. A
realist in politics, sensitive to personal criticism, and fully devoted to
the social order which the Republican Party had come to represent,
Grant could see in the reformers only another and rival political group.
His customary reaction was to draw in his lines, strengthen his position, and fight with all the political forces at his command.[20] Personally
honest, he ascribed honest motives to those who agreed with him, and
suspected his opponents of dishonest cant. Unwilling to believe evil of
his associates, he rationalized all attacks on his party as the product
of evil conspiracies. He had heard the cry of "thief" raised so often
that when thieves came he ignored the clamor. So thoroughly was he
convinced that the reform agitation was all a political trick that he
refused to remove corrupt officers under fire. "I do not feel so well
satisfied as I did that a change should be necessary," he wrote Pierrepont in reference to a judge who was attacked by the press, "and even
if a change should be necessary in the end I do not wish to contribute
to the triumph of the enemies that are assailing the Administration." [21]
Obviously, he had no comprehension of the susceptibility of the American people to moral appeals.

[20] The President, said Postmaster-General Jewell, was "utterly incapable of trim-
ming. . . . He is so honest and outspoken that he lacks as a politician." Jewell to Washburne, December 5, 1874, Washburne MSS.
[21] Grant to Pierrepont July 17, 1875, Grant Letter Book.

His own personal honesty and unwillingness to suspect his friends led Grant into the grievous error of too much association with McDonald. The St. Louis collector made frequent visits to the White House, where he dined with the President or drove with him through the streets of Washington. On these visits McDonald talked of Missouri politics, and Grant, trusting him, left the details of political manipulation in Missouri to him and Babcock. So cleverly did McDonald proceed that he persuaded honest officers in St. Louis that Grant was a member of, and a recipient of money from, the ring.

Ever appreciative of marks of personal devotion, Grant was led into the further error of accepting gifts from McDonald. In October, 1874, the President, accompanied by members of his family and Colonel Babcock, visited the St. Louis fair. Before his arrival, McDonald had got himself appointed a judge of livestock and had pinned a blue ribbon on a colt which Grant had entered from the Dent farm. The colt was so hopelessly outclassed that the award was an obvious piece of sycophancy. "This is an outrage," ejaculated the President, as he hurled his cigar from him in disgust.[22] But, doubtless to spare the managers' embarrassment, the President did not protest, as he should have done, against the undeserved honor.

Despite this crude flattery, Grant accepted the loan of McDonald's team during his visit to St. Louis. As he was leaving, he made McDonald an offer for it. His famed horse Cincinnati had been shot but a few weeks before, and he needed horses. The collector agreed to sell, and several weeks later the horses, in charge of one of the workers on Grant's Missouri farm, arrived at the White House. Accompanying them was a carriage, a set of harness with gold heartplates, and a $25 buggy whip. In December McDonald visited the White House and Grant paid him $1758.50 for the complete outfit. The deal was pure business, but in later years the horses were pointed out as a gift from the corrupt collector to his presidential accomplice.[23]

[22] Stevens, *Grant in St. Louis*, 111–114.

[23] There are two main sources for the Whiskey Ring. The House of Representatives investigated the ring and published their report as House Miscellaneous Document, 44th Congress, 1st Session, Number 186. In 1880, McDonald published, as an anti-Grant campaign document, his *Secrets of the Great Whiskey Ring*. This work is credible in few places. McDonald attempted to prove Grant a member of the ring, but failed to establish his contention. In regard to the horses, the erstwhile collector alleged that he transferred title to the horses to the President for three dollars. Cf. pp. 109. Col. U. S. Grant 3rd possesses the original receipted bill for this sale. McDonald alleged that Grant paid him the nominal sum for a bill of $3,000; but the horses were paid for at full value.

Although a man of more acuteness, or one less conscious of his own rectitude, might have suspected both McDonald and Babcock, Grant continued unconsciously to play into their hands. In December, 1874, Bristow was making an effort to send inspectors into McDonald's district. Babcock blocked the move, and wired his co-conspirators that they could continue their stealing. Remembering the illicit pleasures of his recent visit, the President's secretary signed his telegram "Sylph." Later, Bristow hit upon another scheme. He would change the supervision of the collection districts in order to detect the dishonest ones. Learning of this plan, McDonald hastened to Washington and told Grant that the order removing him to Philadelphia would damage the party organization. Moreover, McDonald pointed out, as was perfectly true, that the removal, ordered for a month later, would give the crooked agents ample opportunity to get their books in order. Persuaded by this reasoning, Grant revoked Bristow's order.[24]

By April, Bristow's obvious determination to stop the revenue frauds had thoroughly alarmed the St. Louis ring. McDonald returned to Washington to try his influence again at the White House. To Grant he complained that Bristow was ruining the party. Grant replied that the move was against the distillers and not against the officers. The collector explained that the connection between them was too close, and that the newspapers would distort the facts to launch a new attack on the Administration. The President, who was prone to listen to the advice of practical politicians, promised to discuss with Bristow the concealment of any evidence damaging to the country. Bristow, however, less anxious than the President about maintaining intact the Republican organization, forced McDonald to admit that collections in St. Louis were not more than two-thirds efficient. Before the interview was over, McDonald had tendered his resignation.[25]

Upon his return to St. Louis, McDonald's associates sent in their resignations. Distillers began to clear up their stocks and to destroy their records, but in the midst of this housecleaning, Bristow's secret police descended upon them. In Washington, Bristow cleaned up his own department by dismissing one Douglass,[26] who had been informing the ring of forthcoming raids. Grant coöperated with orders to dismiss

[24] J. McDonald, *Secrets of the Great Whiskey Ring*, 121–125.
[25] *Ibid.*, 32–50.
[26] New York *Tribune*, May 6, 1875.

the district attorneys at St. Louis and Milwaukee.[27] Early in June, Federal Grand Juries indicted McDonald and in succeeding months found true bills against more than 350 distillers and government officials, chiefly in the three whiskey centers of St. Louis, Milwaukee, and Chicago. Evidently Bristow would make a strong bid for the support of the reformers. Until the trials began in the autumn, both he and Pierrepont labored diligently to furnish information to investigating juries and to prepare cases against the criminals. Pressure was brought on the Secretary to induce him to compromise cases against distillers, but Grant backed Bristow in his refusal to be deflected from his intentions.[28] In the midst of his searches, Bristow found certain suspicious telegrams from Washington warning McDonald of impending visitations of inspectors. The telegrams were signed "Sylph," and Bristow, suspecting his old enemy Babcock, sought for the originals. As he thought, the originals on file in Washington were in Babcock's handwriting.

With this evidence in hand, Bristow and Pierrepont called upon the President at Long Branch. On the back of a letter bringing charges against Babcock, Grant wrote: "Let no guilty man escape. . . . No personal consideration should stand in the way of performing a public duty." To Pierrepont, Grant declared that "if Babcock is guilty, there is no man who wants him so proven guilty as I do, for it is the greatest piece of traitorism to me that a man could possibly practice." [29] Despite the evidence, Grant continued to keep Babcock in his service. Slowly it dawned upon him that Bristow was playing a game of his own. Babcock was a convincing talker and was able to persuade Grant that the whiskey trials were designed for Bristow's advancement. Senator Logan was positive that Bristow's activity in prosecuting the Chicago ring was merely a "raid" upon him; [30] Collector Casey, himself implicated in frauds in New Orleans, also believed in Bristow's perfidy. These, with others of like mind, sought out the President at Long Branch and presented the political aspects of the case. As Grant perceived the implications of Bristow's moves, he gradually became less cordial to the Secretary, and less zealous for reforms. In October, Bristow presented the "Sylph" telegrams in Cabinet meeting, and Grant

[27] Luckey to Pierrepont, May 20, 1875, Grant Letter Book.
[28] New York *Tribune,* July 22, August 14, 1875.
[29] Whiskey Frauds Report, 11, 30, 485.
[30] Logan to Mrs. Logan, August 7, 1875.

called Babcock in to explain them. Babcock explained that he and McDonald had blocked the efforts of a woman called "the Sylph" to blackmail the President, and explained that each of the telegrams related to Missouri politics. The explanations were more satisfactory to Grant than to Bristow and Pierrepont.[31]

Protesting his innocence, Babcock demanded a military court of inquiry to determine his guilt. This suggestion, invoking less likelihood of political reverberations, appealed to the President. But before action was taken, new evidence was produced in the trial of McDonald showing Babcock as an active participant in the ring. Babcock wired protests of his innocence to St. Louis, and openly demanded a trial, but almost immediately his bluster faded, and he turned to the President with a renewed plea for investigation by a military court. Promptly Grant appointed Generals Sheridan, Hancock, and Terry—two of them friends of the Administration—and the Generals called upon the government's attorney in St. Louis for his papers. But the prosecution in St. Louis, unwilling to surrender its evidence to another jurisdiction, had the Grand Jury hastily indict the President's secretary.[32]

Babcock's indictment came two days after Congress assembled, and popular interest centered in a St. Louis courtroom rather than in the Capitol. Good Republicans everywhere soon came to the conclusion that the Administration was being prosecuted. Early in November rumors from St. Louis said that the Grand Jury would indict Orville Grant, the President's brother, Fred Dent, his brother-in-law, Babcock, the Republican National Committeemen of 1872, and Grant himself as receivers of stolen goods.[33] In St. Louis, there was much talk of a "rebel grand jury" "which was trying to indict the whole Administration." [34] In Washington this opinion was so general that even Pierrepont came to believe that Babcock's indictment was designed to injure the President and the Republicans.[35] Among agents of the Treasury Department, working on whiskey cases, there was a definite understanding that Bristow was to be the next President as a result of the investigations.[36]

[31] Whiskey Frauds Report, pp. 2–3, 23.
[32] McDonald, *Secrets,* 212–216, 227 ff.; N. Y. *Tribune,* December 1, 3, 1875; Babcock to Grant, Dec. 2, 1875, Grant Letter Book.
[33] New York *Tribune,* November 6, 1875.
[34] Levi P. Luckey to Washburne, March 8, 1876, Washburne MSS.
[35] J. B. Henderson, Whiskey Frauds Report, 73–74.
[36] William A. Gowette testimony, Whiskey Frauds Report, 375–376, 378, 379.

If there were doubt of the political motivation of the whiskey trials in Grant's mind it was dissipated early in December, when ex-Senator John B. Henderson, addressing one of the trial juries, asked: "Why did Douglass bend the supple hinges of his knee and permit any interference by the President?" Henderson was one of the seven Senators who had deserted his Radical colleagues to vote for the acquittal of Andrew Johnson, and was known to be no friend of Grant. His implication that Grant interfered in the Treasury Department to protect the whiskey ring was immediately resented in Washington. Pierrepont, hurriedly getting Grant's hearty approval, wired to the government council in St. Louis: "Evidence has reached here that in the trial of Avery, Mr. Henderson assailed the President. . . . His efforts in that line will no longer be paid for by this Department." [37]

Meanwhile, Grant had set about to learn what, if any, grain of truth there was in the charges against his private secretary. Predisposed to a favorable judgment, the President allowed Babcock to influence him in a private investigation. One of the St. Louis grand juries, primed by McDonald, went to the White House to tell the President the secrets of the jury room. The nineteen-year-old son of this juror was rewarded with a German consulate.[38] In addition, Grant sent an agent to Pierrepont's department to learn just what evidence there might be against his secretary. The agent, who was in collusion with Babcock, tried to steal incriminating documents from the files of the prosecution.[39]

The fine hand of Babcock shows in every move of the President. No man more thoroughly deceived Grant than did this wily, obsequious, and genial secretary. Thanks to his work, Grant became convinced, on insufficient grounds, of Babcock's innocence. Possibly as a result of Babcock's suggestion, Grant, late in January, 1876, ordered Pierrepont to respect no agreement made by his attorneys to recommend light sentences for whiskey ring members who turned state's evidence. Seeing how helpful this order would be to his case, Babcock stole it and gave it to the press. Doubtless this kept evidence from the court.[40]

Babcock's case was called in February. A battery of skilful lawyers, headed by former Attorney-General Williams, appeared in his behalf.

[37] Pierrepont to D. P. Dyer, December 9, 1875, Grant Letter Book.
[38] Dyer's Report, Whiskey Frauds Report, 40–41; McDonald, Secrets, 216–218.
[39] Bell Testimony, Whiskey Frauds Report.
[40] Pierrepont's Testimony, Ibid.

PROTECTING BABCOCK

Instead of a fair presentation of the case, as might have been their procedure with an innocent client, the defense attorneys took advantage of every trick of their trade to prevent the introduction of evidence. The prosecution, seeking to prove Babcock had received money from the ring, put on a witness who testified that he had seen Joyce, second to McDonald as a leader of the ring, place $500 in an envelope addressed to Babcock at the White House. The witness himself had dropped the letters into a mailbox. But this damaging testimony was combated by the defense. With a magical skill Babcock's lawyers produced a rabbit-like postman who testified that he had taken the letters out of the box and returned them to Joyce—without taking a receipt! Joyce, already convicted, cheerfully testified that he had been merely bluffing—seeking to impress his colleagues in crime with his official influence. With such obvious perjury did the defense combat its opponents.

In the midst of the trial, Grant made a deposition in favor of his secretary. Since Vicksburg Babcock had been associated with him, and had always been a faithful and efficient officer. He had never attempted to influence the President's appointments in St. Louis. Moreover, said the President, he had great confidence in Babcock's integrity. This was sworn to before the Chief Justice, and in the presence of attorneys for the government and Babcock.[41]

This deposition, combined with the tricks of the defense, defeated the government's case against Babcock. Alone of the many indicted in the whiskey ring, Babcock was acquitted. In Washington the news of the result was hailed as a victory for the party. Friends of the Administration quickly started a subscription to raise $30,000 to pay Babcock's legal expenses.[42]

But the enthusiasm of the party leaders was no longer shared by the President. Charges were piling up against the secretary. He was accused of being implicated in "Black Friday," in a safe burglary, and in Shepherd's District Ring. Although Grant still believed in Babcock's innocence, he mistrusted his discretion. With the party in jeopardy, Babcock could no longer remain at the White House. Moreover, during his absence, Fred and "Buck" Grant had served as confidential secretaries to their father. Mrs. Grant wanted to keep her sons about

---

[41] McDonald, *Secrets of the Great Whiskey Ring,* 265–275.
[42] New York *Tribune,* March 4, 1876.

her for the last year in the White House, and Grant, agreeing with her, found a political argument to justify another piece of nepotism. With his own sons as his secretaries, any partisan attack would have to be directed against the President himself. When Babcock returned, he was closeted with the President for an hour. Both men kept the secret of what was said there, but when Babcock emerged he left the White House immediately. Although he continued as director of public works for the District of Columbia, never again was he an intimate member of the President's household.

Before the Babcock trial was over relations between Bristow and Grant became strained. The press was full of rumors that Grant had told Bristow he would hold him personally accountable unless the charges against Babcock were proved true. Even though such rumors were denied, it was evident that neither liked the other's conduct. Bristow offered objections in Cabinet to Grant's going to St. Louis as a witness, and Grant was quoted as saying that he understood perfectly well that certain men, pretending to be friends, were trying to build themselves up at his expense. After Babcock's trial, Grant was ready to dismiss Bristow, but the excitement of the press over the mere rumor stayed his hand. Bristow in the Cabinet might be less dangerous than out of it. Although their personal relations were never friendly, the President held Bristow in the Cabinet until after the Republican Convention had made its selections.

DURING the summer of 1875, while Bristow gathered his evidence against the whiskey corruptionists, preliminary manœuvres for the campaign of 1876 got under way. From the early summer until the campaign was launched men in both political camps, at home and in Congress, girded their loins to do battle for their parties. Every hopeful politician watched developments with an eye to capitalizing the sentiment of the moment and to divining the future.

In the fall of 1875, "off-year" elections were to be held in Ohio, Pennsylvania, and New York, and all eyes were directed to them as omens for 1876. In Ohio the Democrats nominated the aged William Allen, and adopted a platform calling for inflation. Sound money men in the East were thoroughly alarmed, and rejoiced when the Republicans stood firmly for hard money and drafted for their candidate ex-Governor Rutherford B. Hayes, who had a consistent record as a reformer. In Pennsylvania, inflation was the major issue and conservatives feared that the western districts would carry the State for cheap currency. In New York, both Republicans and Democrats stood for reform, sound money, and against a third term.

With clocklike regularity, the Southern problems arose to harass the candidates. This time it was Mississippi where disorders were great enough to attract Northern attention. In 1874 there had been riots in Vicksburg before the elections, and after the campaign Grant had felt compelled to issue a proclamation ordering lawless mobs to disperse.[1] Sheridan had included the White Leagues of Mississippi in his "banditti" dispatches, and Governor Ames had had difficulty in maintaining order. As the approach of another election brought its customary intimidation and acts of mob violence, Ames appealed to Grant for Federal troops.

Grant and the party had learned a lesson from the protests of the preceding January. Although Sheridan and Wheeler had brought peace to Louisiana, renewed interference in the South would have played into the hands of the Democrats. Personally Grant would have preferred

---

[1] Richardson, *Messages*, VII, 322–323, December 31, 1874.

to comply with Ames' request, but a delegation of Ohio politicians arrived on the scene in time to prevent action. Intervention in Mississippi, they declared, would cause Hayes' defeat. Grant yielded to the greater party consideration, and refused to meddle in the Southern question. Unprotected by the troops, the Negroes of Mississippi were afraid to vote, and the home of Jefferson Davis was "redeemed." [2]

With the Democrats monopolizing the reform issue and the Republicans urging undramatic arguments for specie payments and a gold standard, the campaigns passed off quietly. In October Grant went west to visit St. Louis and attend an army reunion at Des Moines. In the latter city he spoke briefly, but with the obvious purpose of injecting a new note into the campaign. Of all the sufferers from the panic of 1873 perhaps none were worse off than the nation's teachers. In the depression years school enrollment fell off, schools were abandoned, and teachers' salaries declined, until observers feared the collapse of the struggling public school system before the onslaughts of distracted taxpayers. Charles W. Eliot, youthful president of Harvard, noticed that a demand for retrenchment in local governmental costs bore hardest on on the schools, and was proclaiming that "the last place to save money is in the education of the children." [3] Realizing that the Republican Party had inherited a devotion to public education, while the Democratic Party, thanks to its Southern conservative wing and its Catholic following in the North, had never been regarded as favoring free public schools, Grant sought to re-align the party in favor of education. That there were a quarter of a million voters among the nation's teachers made his attempt politically wise. To the veterans he pointed out the need for State and Federal aid to education: every State, he said, "should furnish to every child growing up in the land the means of acquiring a good common school education." Beyond the common school, the President thought that every State should do whatever its wealth permitted. [4] Although many Republican leaders felt that the money question "brings in no votes" [5] and welcomed this suggestion, the President was accused of injecting an anti-Catholic issue into the campaign. In Ohio the school issue was raised, but the party was soon

[2] New York *Tribune,* September 9, 10, October 12, 18, 1875.

[3] Reports of the Commissioner of Education, 1878, 1879, 1880; *American Journal of Education,* October 1875; C. W. Eliot, "Wise and Unwise Economy in Schools," *Atlantic Monthly,* June, 1875.

[4] Grant to S. S. Kirkwood, (Iowa City) November 17, 1875, Grant Letter Book.

[5] Jewell to Washburne, n.d., 1875, Washburne MSS.

forced back to money. After the campaign, Blaine spoke on the fact that there was nothing in the Constitution to prevent any state from establishing a state church, and suggested an amendment to ward off the impending danger. "Every politician knows," commented the New York *Tribune,* "that there is no subject on which the average well-to-do citizen in the country districts is so sensitive as upon the possibility of Roman Catholic aggression." But the religious issue was reminiscent of the Know-Nothings, and schools had little appeal to a party of wealthy men. The elections were contested on the original issues.[6]

The vote was decisive on one point: The Republican Party was not dead. Hayes, reform, and sound money won in Ohio; [7] Massachusetts, Pennsylvania, Minnesota, and Wisconsin went for the Republicans; while Democrats could count only New York and Maryland as outstanding victories.[8] Inflation had been defeated, and business men and financiers breathed a sigh of relief. The elections showed, said the *Tribune,* that the Democrats could survive only by sticking to the national honor, and the Republicans could win only by casting overboard Grant and Grantism.[9] As for the politicians, observers agreed the canvass had changed the face of things. Grant and the third term were gone. Blaine had lost his hold on Maine; Allen was dead in Ohio, together with Hendricks, Pendleton, and Morton. Hayes came out of the campaign as a man who might lead the Republicans to victory, while among the Democrats Tilden was the leading figure.[10] Late in November, Vice-President Wilson died,[11] leaving Hayes, Blaine, and Bristow to contest the nomination against a host of favorite sons.

The news of the election was received by Republicans with rejoicings and renewed hopes. In Washington enthusiastic partisans fired a salute of one hundred guns and marched to the White House with the band playing "Hail to the Chief." Smiling, Grant congratulated them on the splendid victories. Although the Republican majorities were not large, he said, they showed that there would be no tampering with the currency; moreover, exulted the President, "I think we have assurance the Republicans will control the government for four more years." [12]

[6] New York *Tribune,* November 9, December 1, 1875.
[7] H. J. Eckenrode, *Rutherford B. Hayes, Statesman of Reunion,* 102–103.
[8] New York *Tribune,* November 3, 1875.
[9] *Ibid.,* November 4, 1875.
[10] *Ibid.,* November 13, 1875.
[11] Richardson, *Messages,* VII, 331.
[12] New York *Tribune,* November 8, 1875.

A month later the President was able to send a hopeful message to the Congress, even though, for the first time since secession, one legislative branch was in the hands of the Democrats. New faces were before the clerk as he read Grant's seventh annual message. Ben Butler was gone, and Confederate generals—the "rebel brigadiers"—were in the seats of the once scornful Radicals. The President recalled that it was the beginning of the "centennial year of our national existence as a free and independent people." From a population of three millions supported by agriculture the country had grown to forty millions, supported largely by manufacturing. "Our liberties remain unimpaired," proclaimed Grant with his customary sententiousness, as he listed the progress of the country "in science, agriculture, commerce, navigation, mining, mechanics, law, medicine" and education. Each of these was passed in review. "From the fall of Adam for his transgression," said the President in one of his rare references to Holy Writ, "to the present day no nation had ever been free from threatened danger to its prosperity and happiness." Greatest of the dangers which the President foresaw was that which arose from ignorance. "We are a republic whereof one man is as good as another before the law. . . . Hence the education of the masses becomes of the first necessity for the preservation of our institutions." Therefore Grant proposed a constitutional amendment requiring each State to "establish and forever maintain free public schools" for all children irrespective of "sex, color, birthplace, or religion." The amendment would forbid the teaching of any religious tenets in these schools, or the granting by legislatures or municipalities of any funds or taxes for schools of a religious denomination.

That Grant was as much actuated by a hostility to churches as by a devotion to education was seen in his next proposal—the taxation of church property. One billion dollars' worth of property was tax free, said the President, and "so vast a sum . . . will not be looked upon acquiescently by those who have to pay the taxes." He proposed that this property be taxed.

The remainder of the message contained a formal review of the work of the Departments throughout the preceding year, with a serious discussion of the importation of Chinese women and a condemnation of polygamy. At the end, Grant recapitulated "the questions which I deem of vital importance which may be legislated upon and settled at this session." These were free public schools, in which "no sectarian tenets shall ever be taught," a literary test for voters after 1890, the end of licensed immorality "such as polygamy and the importation of women for illegitimate purposes," and the enactment of laws which would "insure a speedy return to a sound currency." [13]

As a program for a new century, announced in a centennial year, these suggestions did little credit to Grant's intelligence or statesmanship, but as a program for a Democratic Congress in an election year the message was a good smoke screen for real issues. As such, it indicated how completely Grant had abandoned the high ground of impartial statesmanship for the petty tricks of the politician. A Methodist tract society indorsed him as a candidate for reëlection, while many Protestants as well as Catholics were offended by the anti-religious suggestions.[14] Congress, however, not to be deflected from more profitable reform, did not even pay polite attention to the President's proposals for the coming century.

Instead of following Grant's suggestions for feeble legislation the first session of the Forty-Fourth Congress devoted itself to gathering political ammunition. Although the legislators stayed in session long after the nominees were before the country, neither the Democratic nor Republican Party benefited from their labors. Democrats in the House debated at length on the currency, and finally "harmonized" on a bill "postponing" the date for the resumption of specie payments. A Republican Senate and President made such action impotent, but the Democrats had played into the hands of the Republicans, who were still standing staunchly for "national honesty." Equally hopeless was a Democratic tariff bill. Meanwhile, the Congressmen delayed appropriations until Grant, in disgust, reminded them that they were obliged to carry on the government.[15] The only financial legislation passed was a measure authorizing the Treasury to redeem fractional greenbacks with small silver coin. But the constant discussion in the House increased the distrust with which the financial interests customarily regarded the Democratic Party.

More adept at smelling corruption and in attacking the Republicans than in devising pecuniary panaceas for the country, the Democratic

[13] Richardson, *Messages*, VII, 332–356.
[14] New York *Tribune*, December 8, 10, 1875.
[15] *Ibid.*, December 1875 to August 1876; Richardson, *Messages and Papers*, VII, 368–370, 373–375.

House interested itself in attacking Grant and in conducting penetrating investigations. As soon as Congress organized, it passed resolutions declaring a third term unpatriotic, dangerous, and contrary to the American spirit. Since Grant had long before renounced all intention to succeed himself, the resolution was a gratuitous insult, yet only a handful of Republicans refrained from voting to repudiate their erstwhile leader.[16] Thereafter, the Democrats and their reform allies took especial delight in attacking the President. Their press howled against Grantism [17] and advised the Republicans to "pluck up courage," throw Grant overboard, and "disclaim all responsibility for his acts and appointments, his policies, his associates." Grant, said the *Tribune*, had "kept his party in hot water for three years." He was unfit for his office, and the time had come to "unload." [18] In April Congress passed a bill to reduce the President's salary to $25,000. The obvious purpose of the measure was to show that Grant was the chief benefactor of the old "salary grab," but the President met the issue squarely, returning the bill with an emphatic veto.[19] Hardly was this done when a congressional investigating committee announced that he had used the secret service fund to influence elections. The charge was true. Grant had used $32,000 for detectives who uncovered false Democratic registrations in Northern cities—thus influencing the results! [20] When this move failed to get anywhere, the House asked for information about Grant's long vacations and frequent absences from Washington. What executive acts had he performed when absent from the seat of government? To this Grant replied that he failed to find in the Constitution any authority for the House to ask the Executive for an account of his acts. If the House was gathering information for impeachment, Grant refused to be a witness against himself. He had been absent from the capital, but he had not neglected his duties. Instead of the account which the House asked, Grant sent them a summary of the absences of his predecessors from Washington to Lincoln.[21]

Despite the finesse with which Grant handled this Democratic sniping, it did not cease. Although no charge touched him personally, the

---

[16] New York *Tribune*, December 6, 16, 22, 1875.
[17] *Ibid.*, February 8, 1876.
[18] *Ibid.*, March 4, 1876.
[19] *Ibid.*, April 17, 19, 1876; Richardson, *Messages*, VII, 380–381.
[20] *Tribune*, April 20, 21, 1876; New York *World*, April 21, 1876.
[21] Richardson, *Messages*, VII, 861–866.

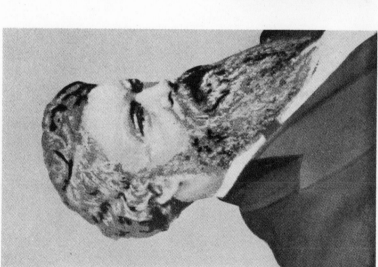

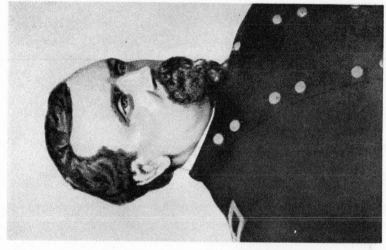

W. W. BELKNAP   ORVILLE E. BABCOCK

CENTRAL FIGURES OF TWO GREAT SCANDALS

congressional muckrakers made sure that his prestige did not rise during the campaign. Discarded by his party, condemned by his associates, betrayed by official and personal friends, he patiently bore the continued fire, which was really a tribute to his influence. Until the election was over, his character had to be besmirched for the ends of both parties. A Jonah had been thrown overboard. Perhaps the storm would cease.

Congress also investigated the officers and acts of the Administration. A House committee inquired into the Whiskey Frauds. Like the "rebel" grand jury in St. Louis, they were unable to bring any indictment against the President, but they had a voluminous report ready by the time the campaign began. Soon after his triumphant return from St. Louis, Babcock was indicted for complicity in a safe robbery, and the delighted Democrats investigated that.

But more important as campaign material was the investigation of the Secretary of War, who had been receiving bribes from a trader at an Indian post. The facts in the case seemed to be that Secretary Belknap's first wife had entered into an agreement with a New Yorker named C. P. Marsh to obtain an appointment for him and to share with him in the profits from a very lucrative post tradership at Fort Sill, Indian Territory. Marsh then made an arrangement with the incumbent at the post by which he received $12,000 annually not to take the position. Half of this money was sent to Mrs. Belknap to enable her to maintain herself in the extravagant society of Washington. Upon the death of Mrs. Belknap, Marsh paid the money to the Secretary of War himself, who used it to support the even more expensive tastes of his second wife, sister of the first.

On the morning of March 2, Bristow, who somehow interested himself in any case of reform which hit close to the Administration, came to the White House while Grant was at breakfast to urge him to give an interview to Lyman K. Bass, Congressman from Buffalo, who had been gathering the information about Belknap. Grant had been so interested in the Babcock trial that this was his first information about the Secretary of War. Making an appointment to see Bass at noon, the President prepared to leave the White House to sit for a portrait painter. Just as he was going, Belknap and Zach. Chandler hurriedly entered. Visibly agitated, Belknap blurted out that he wanted to resign immediately. Chandler interrupted to give a somewhat more coherent account of the situation. Evidently Grant came to the conclusion that the Secretary had become entangled by some illegal act of his wife and wished to resign to protect her. Without going to his office, he sent to have a letter accepting the resignation written. When it came, he signed it and turned it over to Belknap.

As Belknap and Chandler left, Senators Morrill and Morton entered. From them Grant first learned the significance of the resignation which he had just accepted. The Secretary of War had tricked the President into enabling him to avoid an impeachment. Grant had believed that he was protecting a lady, and had helped a criminal to escape. That afternoon the House passed resolutions of impeachment, and presented Belknap before the bar of the Senate. In April the trial opened, and late in May a verdict of acquittal was delivered. The verdict, however, did not stamp Belknap as innocent. A two-thirds majority believed him guilty, but there were enough Senators who doubted the Senate's jurisdiction and therefore voted for acquittal to prevent the punishment he clearly deserved. In Washington social circles there was much sentimental gossip about Belknap's innocence, and Grant's ill-considered act received some silly praise.

Throughout the criticism which attended this case, Grant preserved an even temper. Conscious of right intentions, he showed unruffled calm. On the morning of Belknap's resignation he had kept his appointment with an artist, and when Garfield asked him if the painter found anything strange in his expression, he seemed surprised at the query. He had felt no emotion, he said. Marveling at this imperturbability, Garfield wondered if it sprang from greatness or stupidity. Grant had the Attorney-General investigate the Belknap case to see whether there was ground for criminal prosecution; but despite Belknap's own admissions, Pierrepont found no case against him. For Belknap's place, Grant selected Alphonso Taft of Cincinnati, a judge of more respectability than ability.[22]

Its appetite for corruption thus whetted, Congress discovered other equally unsavory morsels for the delectation of the November voters. Prominent among them was the case of Minister Schenck, who, in addition to introducing the game of poker to English society, had

[22] Garfield MSS. Diary, March 3, 1876; Grant to Hiester Clymer, and Grant to Belknap, March 2, 1876, Grant Letter Book; N. Y. *Tribune*, March 4, 6, 8, 9, 18, May 1, *et sec.* 1876; New York *World*, March 4, 8, 1876; Jesse Grant, *Days of My Father*, 120–127.

attempted to introduce British investors into the intricate mysteries of American corporate finance, another form of gambling. With gross impropriety, Schenck had endorsed—for a consideration—the stock of the Emma Mine, and accepted a paid directorship in the company. When British investors inquired about their promised profits, Schenck found himself in very hot water, and Democrats, scenting scandal, investigated. The mine had been the basis of very shady manipulations, in which Senator Stewart of Nevada had a share; and Schenck had used his inside knowledge of its affairs to unload his stock at high figures while the British public suffered. He came home in disgrace, and resigned his office. A House Committee, under the chairmanship of Abram S. Hewitt, quickly brought in an excoriating report.

Schenck's resignation brought in its train another shift in Grant's kaleidoscopic Cabinet. The President first nominated Richard H. Dana for the vacancy. In 1868, Dana, with more valor than discretion, had invaded Butler's district to contest the Massachusetts dragon's place in Congress. Grant had secretly endorsed this knightly act, and Dana was now belatedly rewarded. But Butler's influence was still great. He was able to bring into play enough force to secure the rejection of the erstwhile St. George. When the Senate rejected Dana, Grant turned to Attorney-General Pierrepont, who was promptly confirmed. To Pierrepont's place the President promoted Secretary of War Taft, and for the vacant War Department chose Simon Cameron's son, Don. Thus both New York and Pennsylvania were strengthened for the coming campaign. Reformers with little appreciation of Grant as a juggler of both the "good" and "bad" elements of his party wondered why the President always followed an acceptable appointment with one that was eminently unfit.[23]

Although Grant was harassed by the unerring congressional marksmanship which picked off first his Secretary of War and then his Minister to England, the Democrats received little reward from the country. Just as the Belknap scandal was at its height, and while Babcock's technical acquittal was still causing nationwide suspicion, spring elections were held in Connecticut and New Hampshire. In both States the Republicans, to everyone's astonishment, carried the day. Republicans took heart at the result, and the Democrats might well have heeded those who told them that positive legislation would catch more

[23] N. Y. *Tribune*, March 7, 8, April 1, 5, 6, 1876.

votes than fishing in the sewers.[24]

But if Democrats could count no votes as a result of their investigations, they at least could enjoy the squabble between the leading Republicans over the succession. Belknap and Babcock, the frauds in internal revenue and in Indian traderships, served further to impress upon the Republicans that Grant's usefulness to his party had come to an end. For the first time since 1860, the Republican Party faced a convention in which the members would have to select a ticket. In 1864, 1868, and 1872 the convention had been given over to the enthusiastic ratification of previously selected nominees. In 1876, no man occupied the place in the party that Lincoln and Grant had filled; instead, there were a host of candidates ranging from such national figures as Blaine, Bristow, Conkling, Morton, and Washburne to favorite sons whose States would give them a preliminary send-off of a few votes and who might hope for some accession of strength in subsequent manoeuvres. Democrats could look forward to seeing a few Republican heads roll in the dust.

Leading the field of Republican aspirants was James G. Blaine, former Speaker of the House, whose adherence to Grant and friendship with Grant's leading critics marked him as a middle-of-the-road man of considerable ability. Early in the congressional session, Blaine seized an opportunity not only to present himself dramatically to the country, but also to change the election issues from Grantism and corruption to the tried program of previous elections—the salvation of the Union by the Republicans.

The occasion was an Amnesty Bill which Democratic House members were pushing to completion in order to win reform and Southern votes. Applying to all veterans of the sectional struggle, the bill would remove the final restrictions from the few ex-Confederates who still remained unpardoned. With an eye to vote-catching, Blaine arose to offer an amendment. He would exclude Jefferson Davis from the terms of the amnesty. The Confederate President was still under indictment, still out on the bail which Horace Greeley and others had executed for him. For his treason Blaine might forgive him. He could not, however, forgive him for his diabolical plot to destroy the luckless prisoners whom the rebel government had held at Andersonville. With oratorical flourishes Blaine tugged upon the heartstrings of the Northern people,

[24] N. Y. *Tribune,* March 16, April 1, 6, 22, 1876; Smith, *Garfield,* I, 598.

and with a cunning born of long experience in debate heckled the Southerners into furious replies. Hill of Georgia replied, and by Blaine's skilful questions was aroused to a fury which threw discretion to the winds. Other Southerners joined him, piling assertion upon absurdity, until in the renewed fires of sectional hate the Republicans saw the possibility of winning another election by waving the "bloody shirt." [25]

So delighted were the Republicans by this new issue that they planned to capitalize its full value. Garfield went for a long walk with the Maine orator, and they talked over the possibilities of winning the nomination and election for Blaine on a Civil War platform. On their return Garfield hastened to the White House to enlist Grant. The President was in a mood for warfare—he had just been reading Sherman's *Memoirs* and the atmosphere of his relatively carefree days in the Wilderness was about him. In this mood he thanked Garfield for his contribution to the amnesty debate—"It had done the country much good"—and mentioned points upon which the neo-Federals should have enlarged. Garfield marveled at Grant's "unusual amount of keen comprehension." To his diary he confided: "My opinion of the President was heightened by this evening's interview." [26]

Senator Morton also saw the possibility of waging the campaign on the old battle-ground. As eager for the presidency as Blaine, he had the advantage of being the oldest champion of the Administration's Southern policy. Mississippi troubles were almost as constant as those in Louisiana, and Morton hobbled onto the Senate floor to recite a story of barbarism, of Ku Kluxism, and of murder in Jefferson Davis' home State. But Morton was not so powerful an orator as his rival in the House, and his story lacked the freshness that Blaine's attack on Davis possessed. The device was too thin, and the Northern people, who might still become indignant over atrocities to prisoners in Andersonville, could no longer be perturbed over the persecution of carpetbaggers by the "men of property and intelligence" in the South.[27]

Despite Morton's efforts, Blaine remained the leading candidate, and as such became the target for Democrats as well as rivals within his own party. His long prominence had raised a host of enemies among

[25] Blaine, *Twenty Years of Congress*, II, 554–555.
[26] Garfield MS. Diary, January 16, 1876.
[27] N. Y. *Tribune*, January 28, 1876. The phrase is again Rhodes'. Northern business men had come to see that their best alliance in the South was with the conservative, property-holding whites rather than with the Negroes and the carpetbaggers.

the Republicans, and objective observers thought that geography would prevail to give the nomination to someone from a doubtful State. Taking the field earlier than other candidates, and approaching the convention with the greatest strength, Blaine bore the brunt of the pre-convention campaign. In American politics, the man who would dominate the pre-convention campaign must be of such personal and political purity as to stand the full light of publicity. Unfortunately for his ambitions, Blaine was not such a man, and rumors were soon circulating that he had been involved in a malodorous railroad deal.

As the rumors persisted, Blaine demanded an investigation. His Democratic colleagues in the House, welcoming the chance, immediately began to pry into his connection with the Little Rock & Fort Smith Railroad. In 1869 he had undertaken to sell first mortgage bonds of this road to friends in Maine. With the bonds there went equal amounts of preferred stock, common stock, and land bonds—a nominal four dollars' value for every dollar invested. Of all these so-called securities, only the land bonds were readily negotiable, and these Blaine retained as his commission. His friends therefore received only preferred and common stock with their first mortgages. Some time later the Little Rock & Fort Smith fell upon hard times, and Blaine's friends began to question their investment. In order to still them, Blaine had to repurchase the bonds. To raise the money, it was now said, he had sold his own almost worthless bonds to the Union Pacific Railroad at a high price.

Inevitably, critics wondered why such a railroad as the Union Pacific, almost wholly dependent on official favor, should have been willing to pay the Speaker full value for depreciated securities? The House Committee heard various witnesses on the issue of the bond sales, but found no absolutely definite evidence against Blaine. However, when one James Mulligan appeared and said that he held Blaine's letters to one of the officers of the Little Rock & Fort Smith, Blaine showed visible signs of alarm. He hastily got the committee to adjourn its hearing, and went to Mulligan's hotel. With tears in his eyes he pleaded for a sight of the letters, and then for permission to reread them. Mulligan consented; Blaine pocketed the letters, consulted his lawyers, and refused to turn them over to the committee or to return them to Mulligan. Public suspicion became intense, and his presidential chances sank rapidly.

It was early in June when Blaine refused to show the incriminating letters; the Republican nominating convention was to meet June 14. If Blaine were to snatch the nomination in the very face of his accusers, instant action was necessary. On June 5, the action came. before a full House and crowded galleries, Blaine stepped into the aisle to speak in his own defense. He had refused, he said, to give up his private correspondence. He had defended this right before the committee. Now, having vindicated his rights, he would show the forty-four millions of his countrymen that he had nothing to hide. He had the letters. He would read them to the House and to the nation.

Amid the applause of the Republicans and the galleries, Blaine read the letters. Interspersed with his comments, doubtless edited as they were read, and with some letters perhaps suppressed entirely, the correspondence appeared innocent enough. Then, the reading finished, Blaine again gave battle to the dead Confederacy. The South was angry with him for his amnesty speech. The Democrats had packed the investigating committee with Southerners. The chairman of the committee—as he said it Blaine strode down the aisle to the seat of Proctor Knott, the accused chairman—the chairman of the committee had withheld a telegram which completely exonerated him. The enthusiasm which followed this dramatic stroke was unbounded. The galleries cheered, and Republicans on the floor echoed. "Uncle Joe" Cannon was a young man then, but in his old age he remembered that he "cheered Blaine that day until my voice frazzled to a squeak and weakness made me inarticulate." [28]

To ardent partisans, like Cannon, the dramatic defense was convincing, but to politicians the thought of carrying Blaine and the Mulligan letters through the campaign was oppressive. On the Sunday following his spectacular defense Blaine collapsed on the steps of his church. It was sunstroke, said his friends; it was mere sham to avoid reappearing before the committee, said his enemies; the hand of the Lord, said the more pious Democrats. His managers in the convention were faced with the dual task of proving that Blaine's physical as well as moral strength was equal to the strain of the presidency.[29]

In the minds of Blaine and his friends there was something suspicious about the sudden attack upon him. The answer seemed to be Bristow.

[28] L. White Busbey, *Uncle Joe Cannon*, 313–315.
[29] Rhodes, VII, 258–270.

Whether Bristow instigated the "raids" upon him or merely rejoiced at them, Blaine could not quite decide. Mrs. Blaine's mind, however, was made up. Recently some criticisms of her had appeared in the papers, and Bristow, she was sure, was at the bottom of it.[30] Whether right or not, the Blaine men went to the convention prepared to do anything to defeat the Secretary of the Treasury.

Bristow's candidacy had progressed steadily. The only man to make political capital out of the Grant Administration, he expected to ride the wave of reform into the White House. In this ambition he could have had the active support of the organized reformers in his party, but for some strange reason he failed to avail himself of their aid. The Liberal Republicans kept up their correspondence with each other, and bent a kindly eye on the rising young reformer in the Treasury Department. "Go in for Bristow with all your energy," Henry Adams told young Henry Cabot Lodge, but added the warning that Bristow had made many enemies and could not be nominated. Through Lodge, Adams and his reforming friends in Boston tried to attach Bristow to their cause. But Bristow would not agree to accept a Liberal Republican nomination if he could not get the regular nomination. He was a "Kentucky Republican and has all the old traditions of party fealty," decided Adams. Yet, since Bristow was the only man who fully met their approval, the reformers clung to the hope that he would be nominated. For Hayes and Washburne, popular with some reformers, the Adams group had little use. Both of these candidates were too acceptable to the professional politicians to be welcomed by radical reformers. "Our object is clear enough," Henry Adams explained. "We want to break down party organizations which are the source of all our worst corruption."[31]

With such a goal the obvious course of these reformers was to nominate Charles Francis Adams, and, ignoring the politicians, appeal to the people on the basis of honesty and integrity in public office. Unfortunately, Adams's name made no appeal to the people. When he was mentioned for the Republican nomination, Blaine wrote Whitelaw Reid that his father and grandfather had killed their parties. The Republican party, said Blaine, could be beaten and still live, "but if it should win with Adams it would never live again."[32] Even Henry

---

[30] Josiah G. Reiff, (N. Y.) to Chandler, June 9, 1876, Chandler MSS.
[31] *Letters of Henry Adams*, 279–285.
[32] Cortissoz, *Life of Whitelaw Reid*, I, 331–333.

Adams realized that there was no dramatic appeal in his father's name. He wrote Lodge: "Lose no opportunity of putting your foot on any revival of the Adams scheme. We are well rid of it. . . . We can do better by other tactics." [33]

The "other tactics" of the reformers were revealed in April when a call went out for a conference of notable men to meet at the Fifth Avenue Hotel to devise means to "protect the honor of the American name." Lodge was secretary of the group issuing the call, and William Cullen Bryant, Horace White, and Carl Schurz were among the signers. On May 15–16 the conference met and solemnly resolved to support no candidate who was not staunchly for reform in every department of the government. Secretly, the meeting agreed to follow Bristow into the convention and nominate him if possible. [34]

With this support Bristow could go into the convention with the avowed friendship of the more irregular hangers-on of the party, and with the avowed or tacit enmity of every favorite son and every candidate who made a pretense of party regularity. All of his reforms in the Treasury Department, all of his punishment of whiskey defaulters, had brought him in the end only the secret endorsement of the most impotent of the insurgent groups. Although he commanded a number of votes, his chances of nomination were nil. Regular Republicans suspected him of secret plots—they called him a "detective"—and were prepared to unite on anyone to defeat him.

Other candidates grew more hopeful as the Blaine and Bristow balloons were slowly deflated. Prominent among them were Roscoe Conkling and Oliver P. Morton, each with the support of his own State. Morton's strength came chiefly from the carpetbaggers and "loyal" men of the South, although he thought that Grant had promised him his personal support. [35] Conkling, too, had some reason to expect assistance from Grant. In January the President assured him that he was not a candidate. Immediately the New York *Tribune* assumed that Grant's influence would be given to Conkling, and raised a protest against presidential interference in the campaign. [36] Although Grant really hoped for Conkling's success, [37] he gave him no active help. Fed-

[33] *Letters of Henry Adams*, 283.
[34] *Annual Cyclopedia*, 1876, pp. 779 ff.
[35] Foulke, *O. P. Morton*, 353; N. Y. *Tribune*, April 13, 1876.
[36] Cortissoz, *Reid*, I, 334; N. Y. *Tribune*, January 25, 29, 1876.
[37] Young, *Around the World With General Grant*, II, 275; New York *Tribune*, April 25, May 24, 1876.

eral appointees in New York had long been under Conkling's control, and these sent an instructed delegation to Cincinnati; but Grant wisely kept out of the mêlée.

Among Americans in Europe, there was general agreement that Washburne was the logical man for the nomination. General Sickles had served as Minister to Spain, and had watched his colleague in Paris handle a delicate situation during the Franco-Prussian war. In Sickles' opinion, Washburne had grown a great deal in Paris, had obtained broader views and had become less provincial. Sickles thought that Washburne's chances in the convention would increase as it was seen that Blaine could not be nominated, for neither Hayes nor Bristow had his ability to attract both reformers and politicians.[38] The little handful who clung without hope to a third term for Grant were willing to take Washburne as second choice; [39] and in general, the supporters of other candidates were willing to consider Washburne as second choice. Grant himself, though regarding Hamilton Fish as the strongest man available, hoped that the convention would nominate Washburne if it could not agree on Conkling or Morton.[40] But Grant's wishes would have little weight with the Republicans who were gathering at Cincinnati.

[38] Sickles to Chandler, March 29, May 26, 27, 1876, W. E. Chandler MSS.
[39] N. Y. *Tribune*, January 7, 1876.
[40] Cf. Cortissoz, *Reid*, I, 336; and J. R. Young, *Around the World with General Grant*, II, 275.

ON June 14, 1876, the Republican convention met in Cincinnati. Bristow reformers, independents, third term advocates, supporters of favorite sons and of national candidates, mingled with carpetbaggers, scalawags, and Negroes from the South. On the second day the platform, calling for resumption, protection of labor and Negroes, non-sectarian schools, and civil-service reform, and endorsing Grant's services in war and peace, was adopted. Immediately the convention turned to the nomination of a candidate. One after another, Morton, Bristow, Blaine, Hayes, Conkling, Hartranft of Pennsylvania, and Marshall Jewell were presented to the convention. For most of these men there was little enthusiasm. Neither Conkling nor Bristow moved the delegates, and the favorite sons inspired no feeling outside of their States. Such applause as the convention had was reserved for Morton, in whose honor the Southern delegates made a demonstration, and for Blaine, whose nomination by Robert G. Ingersoll caused the convention to cheer long minutes for the "plumed knight" who had so recently snatched "the mask of Democracy from the face of rebellion." With enthusiasm for Blaine still running high, the convention was ready to ballot, but darkness interrupted their labors. In the cool of a June evening, pulses which had run high with Ingersoll's oratory resumed their normal pace.

Whether, as the Blaine men charged, Bristow's friends had cut the gas pipes leading to the convention hall so that a delay might be gained, will never be known. But that night the reformers worked diligently, and many were the understandings arrived at before morn. When the balloting recommenced, feeling was tense. On the first ballot, Blaine had 285 votes, Morton 124, Bristow 113, Conkling 99, Hayes 61, Hartranft 58, Jewell 11, and William A. Wheeler of Louisiana-Compromise fame, 3. A vote of 378 was necessary to nominate.

On the five succeeding ballots there was little change. Blaine and Bristow each gained, but the most remarkable increase was shown by Hayes. Michigan swung to the Ohio Governor on the fifth ballot, and his count rose to 104. Morton's vote steadily declined. On the sixth ballot Blaine had 308 votes, and Hayes had risen to 113. Blaine's opponents then suddenly coalesced, and before the seventh ballot was taken the Conkling, Bristow, and Morton forces had gone over to Hayes. The count showed Hayes 384, Blaine 351, and Bristow 21. The nomination was made unanimous, and Wheeler was chosen on the first ballot as Vice-President.[1]

The situation in the Democratic Party was meanwhile clearer than it had been since Buchanan quarreled with Stephen A. Douglas. Thanks to their investigations, they had an issue. With reform inscribed on their banners, and with "Grantism" on the lips of their orators, Democrats might hope for victory in November. Moreover, they were not disturbed over candidates. While the fall of the gods in the Republican Party had permitted a host of hitherto submerged men to assert their pretensions, war and defeat had depleted the ranks of Democratic leaders until few of presidential stature remained. Outstanding among the Democrats of ability was the sixty-year-old Samuel J. Tilden, once a protégé of Van Buren, who had learned the secrets of political manœuvre from the Red Fox. Barnburner, Free-Soiler, and Copperhead as political need commanded, Tilden had managed to keep himself so obscure that his record as a loyal Democrat was unquestioned. According to Blaine, he "professed devotion to the Wilmot Proviso as earnestly as one of the old Abolitionists, and turned from it as if its advocacy had been the amusement of a summer vacation." [2] But in recent years this early obscurity and vacillation had been overshadowed by prominence and even consistency. When the Tweed Ring was brought to bay Tilden leaped into the fight with the zeal of a reformer, and as a reward became Governor of New York in the anti-Grant wave of 1874. As Governor he was in full accord with the reforming spirit of the National Democrats, and signalized his administration by the successful prosecution of the "Canal Ring." To Blaine, who was far from an impartial critic, it seemed that Tilden "understood better than any other man the art of appropriating to himself the credit of events which would have come to pass without his agency, and of reforms already planned by his political opponents." [3]

The Democratic Convention, meeting at St. Louis on June 27, was controlled by Tilden men, and he was nominated on the second ballot.

[1] Blaine, *Twenty Years of Congress*, II, 569–572.
[2] *Ibid.*, 573.
[3] *Ibid.*, 575.

The platform was all that it should be. It denounced Grant, recounted the abuses of the Republicans, and declared for the repeal of the Resumption Act on the ground that it was a hindrance to the resumption of specie payments! Hendricks of Indiana was nominated for Vice-President.[4]

As soon as the balloting in the Republican Convention was over, Grant wired his congratulations to Hayes, and informed the candidate that he felt "the greatest assurance that you will occupy my present position from the fourth of March next." [5] Yet this assurance carried no especial warmth. Hayes had been nominated by a combination of Conkling and Morton votes, it is true, but the Bristow-reform elements in his support were distasteful to the President. Grant's dissatisfaction grew when, on July 8, Hayes wrote a letter of acceptance in which he took advanced ground on civil service and stated that he would not be a candidate in 1880. His position on the finances was sound, but he promised to permit the Southern States to resume local self-government without Federal control. Only on the finances could Grant agree with his party's standard-bearer: on civil service and the South Hayes seemed to be repudiating Grant's policies, while his remarks about a second term were actually insulting. To a visiting Ohioan, Grant declared that Hayes' letter was in bad taste and reflected on the Administration.[6] When Hayes learned of Grant's attitude, he hastened to explain his own. "I was not a prominent candidate," declared the nominee, pointing out that four men were ahead of him in the convention. His remarks were made with that in mind, and were intended to "unite and harmonize their friends." [7] But this explanation was only half accepted, and Grant continued to regard Hayes with suspicion. As Carl Schurz deserted his reform friends, and, inspired by Cabinet aspirations, came out for Hayes, and as such newspapers as the *Nation,* the New York *Tribune,* and the Springfield *Republican*—Greeley journals in 1872—declared for the candidate, Grant concluded that his enemies had at last taken over the party.[8] Yet in spite of this feeling, he lent his efforts to help the Republican campaign. No longer leader of the party, Grant was ignored by the campaign managers in New

---

[4] Blaine, *Twenty Years of Congress,* II, 578–579.
[5] Grant to Hayes, June 16, 1876, Grant Letter Book, Telegram.
[6] New York *Tribune,* July 15, 1876.
[7] Hayes *Letters and Diary,* Vol. III, p. 334, July 14, 1876.
[8] Cortissoz, *Life of Whitelaw Reid,* I, 325, 337 ff.; *Nation,* July 27, 1876; George S. Merriam, *The Life and Times of Samuel Bowles,* II, 280 ff.

York even more than he had been in the elections of 1868 and 1872. Having become too good a party man to sulk in his tent, he acted during the campaign for partisan advantage.

The first action of the President was the selection of a successor to Bristow. On June 17, the day of Hayes' nomination, Bristow sent in his resignation as Secretary of the Treasury. Grant accepted it without commenting on Bristow's work, but with the hope that their personal relations "may continue as heretofore, and that you may find that peace in private life, denied to anyone occupying your present official position." [9] Newspapers suspected that Bristow's resignation was a confession that "after the nomination in Cincinnati he had no further object in remaining in the Treasury." [10] He retired to New York, and remained politically dead for the remainder of his life. During the campaign he played little part, and Hayes ignored him in selecting advisers for the next Administration. The "Bristow reformers," once so enthusiastic for the Kentucky crusader, followed Schurz, and it was the German statesman who received the rewards for bringing the Independents back into the fold. Perhaps the politicians, like Blaine and Grant, could only suspect that Bristow was untrustworthy.[11]

For his place, Grant selected Senator Lot M. Morrill of Maine. Long an advocate of high tariffs and hard money, Morrill was thoroughly acceptable to the financial interests, who, as in past campaigns, were opening their coffers to the Republican National Committee.[12] No reformer, Morrill was both efficient and personally honest. His appointment made room for Blaine in the Senate, and enabled the "plumed knight" to avoid a continuance of the House investigation of his railroad deals.

In other appointments during the summer, Grant did his best to aid the Republican cause. Protests by Republicans led him to withdraw nominations,[13] and he even asked for resignations "in order to comply with the popular will of Republicans." [14] When the two Senators from Illinois called to protest against J. Russell Jones, Grant's personal friend, the President ordered Jones to resign "for the good

[9] Grant to Bristow, June 19, 1876, Grant Letter Book.
[10] New York *Tribune,* June 19, 1876.
[11] *Letters of Henry Adams,* 299.
[12] New York *Tribune,* June 22, 1876.
[13] *Ibid.,* July 11, 1876.
[14] See letter to E. Y. Goldsborough, Marshall in Missouri, August 11, 1876, Grant Letter Book.

of the party." [15] He warned Maryland Republicans to unite if they expected his aid in their campaign,[16] and generally disposed of the offices at the requests of the party managers. Schurz and the reformers, who could see nothing good coming from the White House, alleged that Grant was simply turning Bristow men out of office,[17] and Marshall Jewell, whose early efforts at reform in the postoffices had met Grant's wholehearted approval, resigned in disgust. In his place Grant appointed James N. Tyler, from doubtful Indiana, who would have no scruple about using the postoffice for the party's good.

It was not only in appointments that Grant rendered yeoman service to Hayes' campaign. In the South, where the party needed strengthening, he followed his usual course in dealing with Southern troubles. With Hayes' approbation, Republican orators in the North were "waving the bloody shirt" with all the vigor which had characterized campaigns since 1865, and the South was responding according to custom. In July there was a massacre in South Carolina, and Governor Chamberlain, who had tried in vain to create a conservative and white Republican Party, appealed to Grant. The massacre, said the President, was "cruel, blood-thirsty, wanton, unprovoked and uncalled for," but it was "only a repetition of the course that has been pursued in other Southern States in the past few years." Mississippi and Louisiana were "governed today by officials chosen through fraud and violence such as would scarcely be accredited to savages, much less to a civilized and Christian people." Chamberlain was advised to go on in the honest performance of his duties, "and I'll give every aid for which I can find law or constitutional power." [18]

A leading argument among wavers of the bloody shirt was that Tilden, if elected, would be under the control of the Southerners, who would demand compensation for their losses in the Civil War. Republican orators rang the changes on this theme in an attempt to carry terror into the camp of the capitalists. With all the earmarks of campaign fiction, the charge has been regarded as purely specious by later historians. Yet even intelligent men seriously believed it at the time. Edwards Pierrepont was one of the best lawyers of his day, with a long and honorable record in civil life. Far removed from the scene of

[15] Grant to J. R. Jones, August 13, 1876, Grant Letter Book.
[16] New York *Tribune,* August 18, 1876.
[17] *Ibid.,* July 12, 1876.
[18] Grant to Chamberlain, July 26, 1876, Grant Letter Book.

the campaign as minister at the Court of St. James's, he could have served no partisan purpose by writing Washburne in Paris concerning his real fears of Southern control. The Democratic Party, said Pierrepont, meant to undo the work of the war. The man made President by the votes of the Confederacy would be under Confederate control. "I had much opportunity when in the Cabinet of General Grant to judge of the real sentiment of the South," he explained, "and I assure you it is *one;* and it is that they have been impoverished by the North and that if the chance comes they mean to be paid back what they have lost. It is useless to tell our Northern people this—they turn a deaf ear; do not believe it, and do not heed it any more than they believed the South meant war in 1860." To Pierrepont, there was a "strange fatuity about our Northern people in their reluctance to believe that the South would attempt when restored to power to get pay by some direct or indirect way for their slaves." [19]

If men of Pierrepont's training and opportunities for observation honestly suspected a Southern conspiracy against the treasury, it is not surprising that less able men believed a real danger lay in Democratic victory. Grant's Cabinet entertained no doubt that Southerners were determined to use whatever violence might be necessary to gain control. In South Carolina outrages continued, and as election day approached, "rifle clubs" paraded ostentatiously and made no secret of their intention to "redeem" their State. October 17, Grant decided that action should be taken. Governor Chamberlain called for Federal troops to prevent violence at the polls, and Grant issued a proclamation calling on the rifle clubs to disperse. [20] The Secretary of War sent troops to the State on the same day, and newspapers approved Grant's firmness. [21] But neither troops nor proclamation restrained the Democrats, and in November the election results were in dispute.

The result of Grant's coöperation in the campaign was to restore the President to the good graces of many who had become critics of his Administration. At the beginning the *Tribune* was demanding that the party throw him overboard. Grant's character, his appointments, his associates, and his "selfish and personal" policy, said the *Tribune,* had made possible Tilden's rise as a reformer. [22] When Grant changed office-

---

[19] Pierrepont to Washburne, August 31, 1876. Washburne MSS.
[20] Richardson, *Messages and Papers,* VII, 396–397.
[21] New York *Tribune,* October 18, 1876.
[22] *Ibid.,* July 1, 1876.

holders, the *Tribune* raised the cry that he was turning the Bristow men out to put his own corrupt associates into their places. As the campaign progressed, even the *Tribune* began to see method in Grant's madness. By late August, Whitelaw Reid was praising his "public and patriotic services," and repeating the clauses of the Republican platform with the zeal of a convert telling his rosary—the President's services "in war and peace" were worthy of the Republic's "respect and gratitude." Conkling's plank in the New York platform praising Grant now appeared "fit and proper . . . a piece of good breeding of which nobody will complain." "Unpopular as the later years of his Administration have been, he will . . . go out of office amid general good will." [23] Like the *Tribune*, Garfield, whose nominal regularity had poorly concealed his dislike for the President, changed his mind. "Today," he wrote in his diary, "I was again impressed with the belief that when his presidential term is ended, General Grant will regain his place as one of the foremost of Americans. His power of staying, his imperturbability, has been of incalculable value to the nation, and will be prized more and more as his career recedes." [24]

The value of Grant's increasing popularity and his willingness to coöperate in a campaign in which he was little interested were greater than Garfield realized. In the troublous days from the election in November until the settlement of the election dispute, just before inauguration, it was Grant's character, his popular prestige, and his desire for peace which, as much as any other single factor, saved the Presidency for the defeated Republicans, and prevented armed resistance by the outraged Democrats. The campaign of 1876 was ably managed on both sides. At the head of the Republican Committee, Zachariah Chandler, Secretary of the Interior, managed the Hayes campaign almost as capably as Abram S. Hewitt conducted that of Tilden. Republican officeholders were assessed as diligently and the business interests were bled as efficiently as in former campaigns. Orators with trunks filled with greenbacks were sent to wave the bloody shirt and buy votes in strategic points of the country. Hayes may have received his nomination from the reformers, but the campaign was entrusted to the capable hands of the practical politicians.

While Republicans followed the beaten track in their campaign, the

[23] New York *Tribune*, August 25, 1876.
[24] T. C. Smith, *Garfield*, II, 742, October 18, 1876.

Democrats departed from tradition. The addled management which had encompassed the defeat of Seymour and Greeley gave way to a highly efficient organization which carried the party to popular victory. Hewitt, at the head of this organization, had for many years been the leading American ironmaster, and was now one of the ablest Democrats in Congress. Directing the campaign from New York City, he brought into service the most successful methods of business and politics. Local Democratic officials were assessed, and more than the usual amounts of money collected from business interests whose affection for reform or devotion to low tariff principles made them repel Republican appeals. Tilden lent no little assistance. But unfortunately for Tilden's ambitions, his experience was limited to election technique; when crisis came, he degenerated to a legal quibbler, belying the promise of leadership given by his gubernatorial career and campaign acumen.

The October States bore depressing evidence to Republicans that Tilden might sweep the country. Vermont and Maine, voting in September, had gone Republican according to expectations. Indiana and Ohio were both doubtful, and the October elections did not remove them from the doubtful column. Republicans carried Hayes' State by 6,636, while the Democratic majority in Indiana was but 5,084. In either State a month's campaign and the proper use of money might turn the tide.

Redoubling their activity, both parties looked anxiously forward to November 7. That night men watching the telegraph reports learned that Tilden had carried New York, New Jersey, Connecticut, and Indiana. The South, with a solid block of Democratic votes, would give him the election. His popular majority, it was estimated, would run over a half-million. Everywhere men conceded the Democratic victory, and Hayes put his paper and pencil aside and resigned himself to defeat. In the Fifth Avenue Hotel, Zach. Chandler sank into the sleep of exhaustion, convinced that failure had attended his efforts. Only in the newspaper offices were there signs of activity; the morning papers with the election tabulations were running through the press.

Suddenly there came to the editorial offices of the New York *Times* a request from Democratic State headquarters. Could the paper give the last reports on South Carolina, Florida, and Louisiana? Evidently the Democrats were not sure of those States which the Republicans had conceded them without a thought. Hasty calculations were made. The three States would give Hayes 185 votes—one more than a majority of the electoral college. Without replying to the Democrats, one of the editors rushed hatless to the Republican headquarters. At the hotel door he met W. E. Chandler, committeeman from New Hampshire. No stranger to the dark hallways of intrigue, Chandler immediately perceived the possibility of saving the day, and went with the excited editor to rouse the sleeping Zach. Chandler. Half awake, the chairman gave them leave to do as they pleased.

So instructed, W. E. Chandler began to send telegrams to Republican leaders in the three Southern States. If they could "hold" their States, he told them, Hayes would be elected. Fully acquainted with the desperate characters who dominated the Republican Party in the South, and having served them in good stead in their many calls upon the government for protection, Chandler knew that his appeal would not go unheeded. In the early morning the New York *Times* declared the election in doubt, and in the afternoon Zach. Chandler claimed victory for Hayes.

Without loss of time, W. E. Chandler took the train for Florida, where he could watch the leaders. Preceding him went a telegram to the party chiefs: "The election of Hayes depends on Florida. W. E. Chandler has gone to Florida to see you with full powers to act and make terms. You can put a man in the Cabinet or elsewhere if you choose to demand it. Do so and get a friend where he can help you. Don't be modest. Agree to carry the State through the three counts and you have your own terms in your own hands." [25] Similar promises went to the leaders in the other States. The Republicans were preparing to steal an election!

On the night of November 8, Grant was in the Philadelphia home of George W. Childs. During the evening Cameron and other Republicans came in. All were convinced that Hayes was elected, and all were jubilant over the victory. Suddenly Grant spoke. "Gentlemen," said the President emphatically, "it looks to me as if Mr. Tilden was elected." [26]

Fully convinced that Tilden had been chosen, Grant returned to Washington intent on preserving order. Unlike Hayes, who had been

[25] T. W. Osborne to "Dear Gorn," November 9, 1876, W. E. Chandler MSS.
[26] Burr, *Life and Deeds of General Grant,* 981; G. W. Childs, *Recollections of General Grant,* 10.

speculating on what would happen if there were a contested election, Grant was unprepared to face the emergency. Fully aware of the danger, from November to March Grant's main thought was to preserve the peace. Back in Washington he gave orders to strengthen the military forces at danger-points in the South, and wired to Sherman to take precautions. "Instruct General Augur in Louisiana and General Ruger in Florida," ordered the Commander-in-Chief, "to be vigilant with the force at their command to preserve peace and good order, and to see that the proper and legal boards of canvassers are unmolested in the performance of their duties. Should there be any grounds of suspicion of a fraudulent count on either side it should be reported and denounced at once. No man worthy of the office of President should be willing to hold it if counted in or placed there by fraud. Either party can afford to be disappointed in the result. The country cannot afford to have the result tainted by the suspicion of illegal or false returns." [27]

Eager to avoid both bloodshed and fresh charges of fraud, Grant took steps to secure an honest count of the votes in Louisiana. To a number of Republican politicians, not especially identified with his Administration, Grant sent messages asking them to go to New Orleans and stay until the vote was counted by the returning board. Governor Kellogg, Grant explained to Garfield, had requested the presence of "reliable witnesses" to see that the count was fair.[28] Still others were requested by the Republican National Committee to go to Louisiana,[29] and Hewitt and the Democratic Committee followed suit by sending leading Democrats to watch both the Louisiana Returning Board and the Republicans. As a result, Grant's hopes for an honest count went glimmering.

Scrutiny of the returns in South Carolina left little doubt that Hayes had carried the State. The presence of the troops sent by Grant had emboldened the Negroes, who were an overwhelming majority of the population, to venture to the polls. The Republican majority, however, was less than a thousand.[30] But the situation in Louisiana was very different. The Republicans whom Grant had requested to visit New Orleans were interested in a fair count only if it should be favorable to Hayes. Garfield, who had denounced Governor Kellogg the year before,

[27] Blaine, *Twenty Years,* II, 581–582.
[28] See Smith, *Garfield,* I, 614; Grant to Garfield, November 15, 1876, Garfield MSS.
[29] New York *Tribune,* November 13, 1876.
[30] Governor Chamberlain to "Dear Sir," November 15, 1876, W. E. Chandler MSS.

now dined with him, and wrote in his diary that "my opinion of the Returning Board is far better than it was before I came." [31] Senator John Sherman was equally convinced of the honesty of the Returning Board members. Soon after his arrival in Louisiana, Sherman wrote Hayes that Governor Wells and Colonel Anderson of the returning board were "firm, judicious, and as far as I can judge thoroughly honest and conscientious." [32] This was a good enough story to tell Hayes, who was avoiding any knowledge of corruption, but ten days earlier Sherman had entered into negotiations for the delivery of the Board to the Republicans. In an interview with two leading carpetbaggers, D. A. Weber and James E. Anderson, he had promised to take care of them if the Board should make the proper decisions. Leaving Sherman, the two conspirators determined to get the promise in writing. "Your assurance that we shall be taken care of is scarcely specific enough. In case we pursue the course suggested by you we would be obliged to leave the State." In reply, Sherman piously assured them that "neither Mr. Hayes, myself, the gentlemen who accompany me, or the country at large can ever forget the obligations under which you will have placed us should you stand firm. . . . From a long and intimate acquaintance with Govr Hayes I am justified in assuming responsibility for promises made and will guarantee that you shall be provided for as soon after the Fourth of March as may be practicable, and in such manner as to enable you both to leave Louisiana should you deem it necessary." [33] With such assurances, the Returning Board connived at perjury, ruled arbitrarily on returns from the parishes, and changed a Tilden majority of almost 9,000 to a Hayes majority of over 3,000. In Florida, a Democratic majority of a hundred was turned into a Republican majority of a little less than a thousand.[34]

That the Democrats would calmly acquiesce in these frauds was too much to be expected. As the count proceeded in the South there were threats that on March 4 two Presidents would be inaugurated. Tilden would be recognized by the House, and Hayes by the Republican Senate.[35] Troublesome clouds were rising in the South. In Florida and

[31] Smith, *Garfield*, I, 622.
[32] Sherman, *Recollections*, I, 558–559.
[33] D. A. Weber and James E. Anderson to Sherman, and reply, November 20, 1876, W. E. Chandler MSS. For a fuller statement of promises made in various parts of the South, see a typewritten statement in Chandler MSS., numbers 8689 to 8692.
[34] Paul Leland Haworth, *The Hayes-Tilden Disputed Presidential Election of 1876*, 68, 113–114.
[35] New York *Tribune*, November 21, 1876.

South Carolina the Democrats carried their case to the courts, and in the former got a decision which enabled a newly elected Democratic legislature to order a recount and forward a set of contesting returns to the United States Senate. In South Carolina violence broke out, and armed bands announced their intention of installing General Wade Hampton in the Governor's mansion.[36] Governor Chamberlain appealed again to Grant for Federal aid. Grant ordered the Secretary of War to sustain him with the military and naval force of the country, and to maintain the republican form of government in the State.[37] As the South Carolina legislature assembled, United States troops examined the certificates of election of the members, and permitted those whose papers were regular to take their seats.[38] As in Florida, South Carolina Democrats planned to cast the State's vote for Tilden.

In the midst of this controversy, and before the formal electoral votes were cast, the Forty-Fourth Congress reassembled for its second session. Grant had written a message which spoke volumes for his own calmness. Not a word of it related to the election dispute—the issue was not formally before the Congress. There was a recommendation for legislation to settle disputed presidential elections, but there was hardly an intimation of the chaos and revolution in the South. Instead of a document which would reveal his own secret fears, Grant took occasion to review the eight years which were passing into history. "It was my fortune, or misfortune," he began with a personal note, "to be called to the office of Chief Executive without any previous political training. Under such circumstances it is but reasonable to suppose that errors of judgment must have occurred. Even had they not, differences of opinion between the Executive, bound by an oath to the strict performance of his duties, and writers and debaters must have arisen. It is not necessarily evidence of blunder on the part of the Executive because there are these differences of views. Mistakes have been made, as all can see and I admit, but it seems to me oftener in the selection made of the assistants appointed to aid in carrying out the various duties of administering the Government—in nearly every case selected without a personal acquaintance with the appointee, but upon recommendations of representatives chosen directly by the people." Having

[36] New York *Tribune*, November 27, 1876.
[37] Grant to J. D. Cameron, November 26, 1876, Grant Letter Book.
[38] New York *Tribune*, December 1, 1876.

thus shifted the burden for his errors to the shoulders of Congress, Grant asserted: "I have acted in every instance from a conscientious desire to do what was right, constitutional, within the law, and for the very best interests of the whole people. Failures have been errors of judgment, not of intent."

Turning from an apology for his mistakes, Grant reviewed the accomplishments of his Administration. He had come into office immediately after the "wrangling" between Johnson and Congress over Reconstruction. As Grant saw it, this struggle had been over "whether the control of the government should be thrown immediately into the hands of those who had so recently and persistently tried to destroy it, or whether the victors should continue to have an equal voice with them in this control." This was the meaning of the Reconstruction which had really begun when Grant took office. Moreover, it had been expected that the enfranchisement of the Negroes would mean an addition "to the Union-loving and Union-supporting votes." Reconstruction, thought Grant, was the work of Congress: "My province was wholly in approving their acts." In addition to this, Grant's Administration had seen the ratification of the Fifteenth Amendment, the contraction of the public debt, the reduction of annual interest charges, lowering of taxes, and a shift in the balance of foreign trade from an adverse total of $130,000,000 to a favorable figure of $120,000,000.

Grant's recommendations for further legislation were mostly routine, and the body of his message was a dull summary of departmental reports. However, the President could not forego the opportunity of airing an ancient grievance. As naïve testimony that the wound he had received had cut deep, he reverted to his greatest defeat at the hands of Congress. In the midst of a national crisis, the President dragged forth the dried bones of his only original project—Santo Domingo! "If my views had been concurred in the country would be in a more prosperous condition today, both politically and financially."

With this generalization as an introduction, he began a recitation of familiar phrases—"San Domingo is fertile . . . sugar, coffee, dye-woods. . . . About 75% of the exports of Cuba. . . . Flour shipped from the Mississippi River. . . . The Cuban question would have been settled long ago. . . . Hundreds of American vessels. . . . The soil would soon have fallen into the hands of United States capitalists. . . . Emigration there would have been encouraged. . . . " In fact, all the old arguments, all the grandiose visions, all the appeals to national pride and speculative cupidity which had been used to bolster up Grant's venture into imperialism were paraded again. Part of it was I-told-you-so; but most of it was reverie to escape from recent errors and from the danger of the immediate future.[39]

Congress paid little attention to this farewell address with its combination of apology and nostalgia. Newspapers paid little more—dismissing it, for want of interest, with the trite remark that it was "characteristic" of Grant. "The message," said the *Tribune,* "is that of a man who is weary of public life and tired of political strife." [40] But newspapers, Congress, and the public were interested in the question of Grant's successor. On the day after the annual message, presidential electors assembled in the State capitals to cast their votes. From the three disputed Southern States came two sets of returns, one for Hayes and one for Tilden. From Oregon, too, came two sets of votes, for, although Hayes had carried the State, one of the electors was a postmaster and ineligible for the electoral honor. The Democratic Governor had given a certificate of election to a Democratic elector whose single vote would elect Tilden.

With two sets of returns from the States, the question arose how they were to be counted. The Constitution was woefully inadequate as a guide. It stated that the Vice-President, or President of the Senate, should open the votes in the presence of the two houses of Congress, but the fundamental law then faded into incoherence as to what should thereafter be done. After the President of the Senate had opened the ballots, read the Constitution, "the votes shall then be counted." "By whom?" asked the nation. "By the President of the Senate," answered the Republicans, who were sure that the acting Vice-President, Mr. Ferry, would count the Hayes votes. "By the two Houses of Congress," answered the Democrats, whose control of the lower House would enable them to block Hayes. With the country debating constitutional interpretation, Grant exerted himself to arrange for a fair settlement of the contest. A few days after the electors had voted, Hewitt, who was alarmed lest he seat Hayes by military force, called for an interview at the White House.[41] As Grant saw the situation, Florida and South Carolina had honestly gone for Hayes, but nothing could be done to pre-

[39] Richardson, *Messages and Papers,* VII.
[40] New York *Tribune,* December 6, 1876.
[41] *Ibid.,* December 11, 1876.

vent Louisiana and the presidency going to Tilden. That Grant personally preferred Tilden to Hayes was generally believed,[42] but the President was too good a party man to do anything to help the Democrats. On the other hand, his suspected sympathies and the public confidence in his honesty contributed to the acceptance of any solution which had his approval. Following Hewitt's visit, the Democrats showed willingness to coöperate in devising a method for counting the vote. On December 14 the House appointed a committee of seven to sit with a similar committee of the Senate to draft a law for the emergency. On January 18, the joint committee reported a bill by which the vote from any State sending in but one return could be touched only by joint action of the two houses. If there were more than one return from a State, it should be referred to an electoral commission composed of five members of each house, and five justices of the Supreme Court. The decision of this commission could be overruled only by the joint action of the two houses.

Grant, who had been consulted by the committee, gave his approval to this bill, and urged Conkling to push it in the Senate. January 25 the bill was passed, with Grant approving, and both candidates and the Republican press in opposition. Only Grant's insistence had saved the measure from defeat, and on January 29 he sent a special message approving the law. Industries were arrested, labor unemployed, capital idle, and enterprise paralyzed by the delay, said the President. The bill would bring assurance that the country could avoid Civil War.[43]

Grant's wish for peace was almost the only hopeful sign in the country. Among the Democrats there was much talk of installing Tilden by force. To discourage any effort which might be made, Grant quietly gathered troops in Washington. Although some Democrats suspected that the military force was for the purpose of putting Hayes in office, Hayes tells us that "every honest man knew that the President's intention was to preserve order and to see that the conflict . . . was settled according to law." [44]

Meanwhile, as confidence in Grant grew, the Democrats became disgusted with Tilden. Hewitt had followed an able campaign with a demonstration of efficiency equal to that of the Republican National

---

[42] Oberholtzer, *History of the United States since the Civil War*, III, 292–294, devotes considerable space to showing that Grant preferred Tilden.

[43] Richardson, *Messages*, VII, 422–424.

[44] Blaine, *Twenty Years*, II, 582.

Committee. He too sent "visiting statesmen" to Louisiana and Florida, where they attempted to combat the influence of John Sherman and W. E. Chandler. He had taken measures to appeal to public sentiment. But as the dispute over the count of the vote progressed, Democrats began to lose faith in Tilden. The promise of leadership which he had given in the campaign proved hollow when the crisis came. Instead of action, he spent his time in a compilation of precedents on disputed elections. The result of his researches was a credit to his scholarly ability, and he showed conclusively that it was the function of Congress, and not of the President of the Senate, to count the votes. It was the same conclusion that Grant and the congressional leaders had arrived at by political, rather than historical, technique. Tilden was obviously better qualified for a professorship than for the presidency.[45] Moreover, Democrats began to count the cost of Tilden's election. John Bigelow had helped Tilden with his book on election precedents, and was hanging around the candidate's New York home. Bigelow, Parke Goodwin, and Charles Francis Adams, all "renegades" from Republican ranks, were in line for appointments. If Tilden were to appoint such men the Democratic party would fall to pieces.[46]

On January 31 the Electoral Commission was organized with three Democrats from the House and two from the Senate, three Republicans from the Senate and two from the House, three Supreme Court justices with Republican proclivities, and two with Democratic leanings. According to an original understanding, the members of the Commission from the Supreme Court were to be two Republicans, two Democrats, and one Independent. The fifth member, whom everyone understood was to be Justice David Davis of Illinois, was to be selected by the other justices. But the Illinois legislature, to Davis' intense relief, had just elected him to a seat in the Senate as a Democrat. With Davis removed, the four justices agreed on the mildest remaining justice—a Republican. The fifteen members of the Electoral Commission were therefore divided eight to seven. There were few who expected the justices to arise above partisanship, and when the votes were taken, the count in every case stood eight to seven in favor of Hayes.

[45] Cf. John Bigelow, *Life of Samuel J. Tilden*, (New York, 1895), II, 19; and Bigelow, *Writings and Speeches of Samuel J. Tilden*, II, 385 *passim*.
[46] Badeau to Washburn, December 30, 1876, Washburne MSS.

The scrutiny of the count began on February 1, and continued throughout the month. Not until March 2, two days before Grant's term expired, was the count completed and the results—Hayes 185, Tilden 184—announced. Although there were ample grounds for repudiating the work of the Commission, there was nothing more than grumbling from the Democrats. The Southern leaders had already decided to acquiesce in the result, and had set about getting what they could from the situation. Despairing of Tilden, and with no desire for a new civil war, they approached Hayes' closest friends to make a bargain, and found the reformers ready to negotiate for peace.

In January, Governor Chamberlain in South Carolina and Packard in Louisiana were inaugurated in the face of Democratic opposition. The votes which had given them their offices were the same votes that had been cast—or counted—for Hayes. In both States, the Republicans were immediately forced to appeal to Grant for support. The President gladly gave his support to Chamberlain, but announced that his support of Packard was only temporary. He would support him only until the count was made.[47] As the case stood in either State the simple withdrawal of the Federal troops would bring a revolution which would put Democrats in the Governor's chair. As the Southerners expressed it, "good" government would be insured if the troops were withdrawn. Moreover, the Southerners were willing to promise to treat the Negroes humanely, and to forego any proposals to use force in inaugurating Tilden. Such was the proposal which Southern leaders like L. C. Lamar, Senator Gordon of Georgia, and Henry Watterson of Kentucky presented to John Sherman, Garfield, and other friends of Hayes. On February 26, these men came together in the Wormley Hotel in Washington. On that day Reconstruction ended, for the Hayes men promised that the troops would be withdrawn from the South. In other words, the Republicans surrendered the Negro to the Southern ruling class, and abandoned the idealism of Reconstruction, in return for the peaceable inauguration of their President! [48]

While the electoral vote was occupying the major attention of the

[47] Smith, *Garfield*, I, 628.

[48] Accounts of the disputed election of 1876 are to be found in all works on the period. The best study of the election is Haworth, *The Hayes-Tilden Disputed Presidential Election of 1876*. Good accounts are given in Rhodes, *History of the U. S.*, VII, 291–350; and Oberholtzer, *History of the United States*, III, 281–314.

country, Grant was winding up the affairs of his office. With public business practically suspended, the President waited anxiously for his release.[49] Relatives visited him to spend a night or eat another meal in the White House, and a few political debts were paid in complimentary appointments. John McDonald was released from prison by an executive pardon,[50] and Babcock was ordered back to his regiment in a letter praising his "faithful and efficient service" as private secretary, and giving "the assurance of my confidence in his integrity and great efficiency." [51] He stood by his friends," said the New York *Tribune* in a sarcastic vein of antagonism that was renewed when Grant insisted on the Electoral Count Act.[52]

As February drew to a close, Grant accepted Secretary Fish's invitation to visit him in Washington after vacating the White House. "Buck" Grant, who had served as his father's private secretary after Babcock's troubles, planned to leave for New York to practice law. Fred Grant, on leave from Sherman's staff, would return with his young wife to army headquarters in Chicago. The ex-President and Mrs. Grant were planning a trip to Europe.[53]

March 2, the day the election results were announced, President-elect Hayes arrived in Washington, and went direct to the home of Senator Sherman. The next evening, the successful candidate dined with Grant at the White House. As the following day was Sunday, and the inauguration ceremonies had been postponed to Monday, Grant had become fearful of the resulting interregnum. Even a Sunday afternoon without a President might have disastrous consequences. Just before dinner, Grant led Hayes, the Chief Justice, and a few friends into the "Red Room." There, in secret, Hayes took the oath of office as President of the United States. General Grant's presidency was over! [54]

On Monday, Hayes was publicly sworn into office. Together Grant and he returned to the White House after the ceremonies. Mrs. Grant had supervised the preparation of her last dinner in the White House, and for the last time acted as hostess. After dinner, the Grants left to visit Fish, and Hayes was in possession of the Executive Mansion. Mrs.

[49] New York *Tribune,* February 5, 1877.
[50] McDonald, *Secrets of Whiskey Ring,* 332–3.
[51] Grant to Babcock, March 1, 1877, Grant Letter Book.
[52] N. Y. *Tribune,* Feb. 1, 1877.
[53] *Ibid.,* February 19, 1877.
[54] Badeau, *Grant in Peace,* 252.

Grant had thoughtfully ordered a day's supply of groceries left in the pantry.[55]

As newsboys in the streets insultingly cried "Old Eight to Seven" after the incoming President, and men spoke of Hayes as "His Fraudulency," or "the Boss Thief," Grant's popularity increased in contrast. The popular heart, Whitelaw Reid admitted in the *Tribune,* had always been true to Grant, and even Reid confessed that he had "no disposition to remember his errors and shortcomings." [56] Less grudging was the tribute of James A. Garfield. "No American," wrote the party chieftain, "has carried away greater fame out of the White House than this silent man who leaves it today." [57]

[55] Badeau, *Grant in Peace,* 259.
[56] New York *Tribune,* March 3, 1877.
[57] Smith, *Garfield,* II, 742.

FROM the windows of Fish's Washington home, ex-President Grant watched the first acts of a new Administration. It was an Administration with which he had little sympathy. Eight years before, he had come into office with the confidence of the people behind him. In the first month of his presidency he had been attacked by a combination of "reformers" and Democrats, representing as he thought an insignificant minority of the American people. Taking exception to the President's request for repeal of the Tenure of Office act, Sumner, Schurz, and a handful of partisans raised the cry of reform and defeated Grant's purpose of reforming the public service by wholesale dismissals. Shortly thereafter these men in the much-abused name of Democracy, had defeated the President's single-handed adventure into imperialism. Forced by this opposition to become a partisan, Grant had distributed the Federal patronage to those Congressmen upon whose loyalty he could depend. In 1872, Republican soreheads, "reformers," and "moderates," had deserted the party and formed an incongruous alliance with the Democrats. Defeated in their treasonable acts by the political machine which Grant's use of the patronage had built up, these "Liberal" Republicans had, four years later, secured the nomination of Rutherford B. Hayes. When the election was over, and Hayes had been rejected by a majority of the American voters, the men who had cried aloud for reform had made corrupt bargains, promised offices, and sold the South to the Southern Bourbons in order to place their reforming candidate in the White House. That they were successful was a tribute to the public confidence in Grant's honesty and integrity, but the result could hardly have been satisfactory to the former President.

Grant was glad to be relieved from the cares of the presidency. Behind the imperturbability which had deceived even penetrating observers into thinking that he was unemotional or even stupid was the most sensitive man who was ever President of the United States. The professional politicians, from whose ranks all but three of his predecessors had come, were usually trained in the law, and the courts and hustings had worn their emotions callous. But Grant had had no experience in the give and take of politics. Instead, behind him lay forty years of failure which had cut deep into his soul. Ridiculed in childhood, hazed at West Point as a green lad from the uncouth West, unable to succeed in the army, and a complete failure in every business he tried, he was emotionally unfitted for success. When it came, he was unprepared for it, and met it with the same stolidity with which he had accepted his succession of defeats. With more of his father's conceit, Grant might have talked himself out of the hearts of his countrymen, but he was inarticulate before cheering mobs. The masses concluded that he was a tower of silent strength, and though individuals who saw closer told them it was stupidity, the crowds never got over the illusion. No one saw the truth: that the man who faced them could not quite believe in his own success, but could remember other yelling crowds—crowds of small boys teasing the bewildered son of the most unpopular man in Georgetown! In 1877 a boy who had once changed his name to avoid ridicule, who had found in horses an escape from the cruelty of play-mates, looked on while his enemies vowed to destroy the work which he had accomplished.

Grant had many reasons for disliking the Hayes Administration. The Cabinet, which met an approval denied to Grant's selections eight years before, contained Carl Schurz, whom he hated more than any other besides Sumner. Worse still was the new President's policy in regard to the South. Louisiana was a cesspool of political corruption, and none knew it better than Grant; but when Hayes, by withdrawing the Federal troops from the State, allowed the rotten Packard régime to fall, Grant could see neither justice nor consistency in the action. To his son Jesse he declared, "If I had been in Mr. Hayes's place, I would have insisted upon the Republican Governor being seated, or I would have refused to accept the electoral vote of Louisiana." [1]

Like Grant, faithful Republicans in Congress wondered at the in-consistency of Hayes. "No act of President Hayes did so much to create discontent within the ranks of the Republican Party," Blaine was to remember several years later.[2] Other Republicans of the old "Radical" wing were offended at the appointment of "Greeley sore-heads" to offices. Babcock thought that "Republicans who elected Hayes are not going to step back . . . and when they want a place

---

[1] Jesse Grant, *In the Days of My Father*, 205; Badeau, *Grant in Peace*, 253.
[2] Blaine, *Twenty Years of Congress*, II, 596.

find 'Civil Service' flung in their face." [3] True to Babcock's predictions, the men who had supported Grant soon turned against Hayes. A minority in the party, they began much the same tactics of opposition that the "reformers," now in power, had used against Grant's Administration. The result was that Hayes became increasingly unpopular, while Grant continued a potent factor in American politics. For the quadrennium following his presidency Grant occupied the peculiar position of being, without his willing it, the rallying point for the "stalwart" minority of his party.

At the moment of leaving the White House Grant had no further political ambitions. For sixteen years the cares of public office, in the most critical period in American history, had occupied his mind. For some time he had planned to take a trip around the world. The presidency had left the Grants, thanks to the salary grab, savings of $100,000, most of which was invested in mining stock and railroad bonds. Houses had been given him, Mrs. Grant had real estate in Washington, and money from public subscriptions after the war was invested in government bonds. Grant's income from most of these sources was not large, but "Consolidated Virginia" mining stock was paying well. Babcock, who knew his financial status, did not see how the General could travel in Europe without drawing on his principal, and predicted that the trip would never be made. The ex-President planned to spend $25,000, which he hoped would last two years. There was reason to believe this a gross underestimate, and Grant realized it; but his son "Buck," now in business in California, made investments for his father which gave him an additional $60,000 which he felt free to use in his travels. [4]

Babcock therefore proved a poor prophet. Both General and Mrs. Grant had long dreamed of a European trip, and financial considerations did not deter them. If the mining stock continued to pay, they thought they could afford to take two years to see the wonders of the world. After waiting in Washington until the birth of a grandson— Nellie's child—they left for a visit to Galena. In May, after a round of receptions in Philadelphia, they set sail for England. Of their family, only young Jesse accompanied them.

Scenting news in the travels of a great General and ex-President, the

---

[3] Babcock to Badeau, March 17, 18, 20, 1877, Babcock MSS.
[4] Babcock to Badeau, April 11, 1877, Babcock MSS.; Badeau, *Grant in Peace*, 316.

New York *Herald* sent John Russell Young to report the tour in detail. Young made the most of his opportunities, and carefully cultivated Grant's acquaintance. On shipboard he drew Grant into long reminiscences on the Civil War, and into shorter comments on his political career. Thanks to Young's letters in the *Herald,* the American people were in almost daily contact with the travelers. It was excellent publicity, and Young's letters kept the ex-President alive as a politician.

But it was not as an ex-President that Grant went to Europe. Europeans had little interest in Grant's political career. Statesmen and an occasional student of American politics might have some curiosity as to his administrations, but Europeans in general saw in him only the greatest soldier of his day, the hero of the world's greatest war since the fall of Napoleon. It was "General" Grant that the Europeans welcomed, and Americans, looking through the dispatches of John Russell Young, once more saw the Hero of Appomattox. By the time he returned to the United States, he had almost regained the place in the popular esteem that he had held in the years after Lee's surrender.

Late in May the Grants arrived in Liverpool. For the next month, their time was occupied in attending one state dinner after another. Before Grant arrived in England, Pierrepont, whom Hayes left at his post until after Grant's departure, busied himself with the task of seeing that the distinguished American should be properly welcomed. Van Buren and Fillmore had each visited England after their presidencies, and had received little recognition. Pierrepont determined that Grant should be accorded every possible honor. When Britishers protested that he was without position at home, Pierrepont proposed that he be received as a former sovereign, taking precedence over all but the royal family. This was agreed to, and the Prince of Wales aided the American Minister by having Grant as his special guest at several functions. Henceforth, ignoring titles, the Hero of Appomattox sat near the head of the table.

During June the Grants dined, saw reviews, and visited most of the cities of Great Britain. The Duke of Wellington entertained them at dinner; London and Edinburgh conferred the freedom of the city; at Liverpool, Manchester, and countless other cities crowds of workingmen gathered about Grant and proclaimed him the friend of the common man. To English workers the Civil War had been a phase of the worldwide battle for human freedom, and the cheering crowd little understood that the man who had led Lincoln's armies, and sat in Lincoln's chair, was a friend of the masters of capital rather than the spiritual disciple of the Great Emancipator. But the crowds cheered, and Grant acknowledged his devotion to the laboring man at the same time that he kept his eye on the gathering storm of labor troubles in the United States. As the great railroad strike of 1877 spread, Grant found time amid his receptions to tell Badeau, half hopefully, that he might be called back by the emergency. America, he said, comparing himself with Hayes, needed a strong man.[5]

One incident of the English visit sets in relief the whole social adjustment of the Grant family. Throughout the world the period of Grant's prominence was the age of the *nouveaux riches*. In France the parvenu court of Napoleon III, in the other countries the newly-rich bourgeoisie, and in America the men of Big Business, had all obtained wealth more rapidly than culture. Good taste was at a low ebb in the Victorian age; the Grants were typical of their time, and even more typical of the American tourists who, with wealth acquired in vulgar trade, were to seek a superficial culture in foreign travel. Few of these tourists were to visit royalty in later years, and the episode of Jesse Grant might have contributed to the royal reluctance to entertain wandering notables.

Late in June Queen Victoria invited Grant and his *entourage* to visit her at Windsor Castle. The *entourage* consisted of Consul-General Badeau and young Jesse, who had left college to bask in reflected glory. Arriving at the royal residence, the Grants were received by Her Majesty, after which they retired to their rooms to dress for dinner. In the midst of their preparations, announcement was made that General and Mrs. Grant would dine with the Queen, while Jesse and Badeau would dine with the "Household." Both Jesse and the Consul-General were social climbers, and both had expected to dine with the Queen. At Badeau's suggestion, Jesse protested against being relegated to the "kitchen with the help." Although it was carefully explained that the "Household" were not servants, Jesse and his social mentor insisted that when the Prince of Wales visited America he was accorded no such treatment. After a hectic hour, in which the *attachés* of the Castle buzzed in wonderment at this unprecedented presumption, the Queen, still a lady, asked Jesse to dine with the "family." Dinner that eve-

[5] Badeau, *Grant in Peace*, 315.

ning was coldly formal, for Grant, ever the doting father, had sympathized with Jesse in his tempestuous climb to the Queen's table. The next day, without seeing Her Majesty again, the Grants left Windsor Castle.[6]

While their commander was dining with the Queen, the Army of the Potomac was holding its annual meeting. Inordinately proud of the honor to their chief, the veterans cabled their congratulations "in care of Queen Victoria, Windsor Castle, England," and cartoonists, with humor typically American, portrayed a messenger ringing the Castle's doorbell while Victoria leaned out an upper window. "Who's there," asks the Queen. "Cable for General Grant," replied the messenger. "Is he staying at this house?" In gentle laughter men were forgetting the fierce contests of Grant's presidency. Through such forgetfulness, Grant might once more become a political power.

From England, the Grants departed for the continent. In Belgium, where they stayed but a few days, problems of etiquette were solved by the King visiting the general at his hotel and bidding him welcome to the country. From Belgium Grant went down the Rhine, and into Switzerland. In September he was back in England and Scotland for more receptions, mostly in the mill towns, and in November visited Paris. Italy came next, then Spain, and by March, 1878, the Grants were visiting Constantinople and dining with the King of Greece at Athens. Returning to Italy, the American tourists saw the wonders of Rome and the beauties of Florence in the springtime. In July they were in Copenhagen, visiting brother-in-law Cramer, Minister to Denmark. Russia came next, then Paris again, and the year 1879 began with Grant in Ireland. Unlike other generations of tourists, the Grants did not "do" Europe with system—checking off countries on their fingers—but wandered as fancy prompted.

But wherever they went, they displayed the homely earth of their makeup. Badeau complained that the General was not "over-refined," and remembered that he soon grew weary of museums and mouldy castles. In Berne he refused to be dragged to the Cathedral. He had seen Cologne, Mayence, and Brussels: "Why should we waste our time on any more architecture?" In Rome Grant was quickly bored by

---

[6] Badeau, *Grant in Peace*, 282–285; Badeau dined with the "Household." At a dinner given by the Prince of Wales in London several days later, Grant was seated near the foot of the table. N. Y. *Tribune*, July 5, 1877.

pictures and statuary, and Badeau took him to see the equestrian Marcus Aurelius. "I thought he would like the horse," said Badeau, whose hope of educating Grant was abandoned when the general refused to show interest.[7] The ex-President's realistic remark that Venice would be a pretty city if it were only drained has tickled for threescore years the sense of superiority felt by the disciples of the culture-absorbing Badeau.

But if Grant was not interested in pictures, statuary, architecture or crumbling ruins, he was intensely interested in the evidences of Europe's modern progress. Through his eyes the spirit of America looked at bridges, roads, railroads, mines, and found therein food for its patriotic admiration for American achievements. History, literature, and the fine arts interested him but little; he responded to hotels, steamships, and sewer systems. He was an American of the Golden Age of American Business, not an esthete.

People, too, interested Grant. With Badeau for his companion, he walked the streets and watched the people. In Cophenhagen he was more impressed by the Tivoli Gardens than by the two picture galleries, six museums, thirteen scientific, and thirty charitable institutions which he visited, along with the Royal Library, in six days. He thought all cities ought to have places like the gardens, "where the rich and the poor, the high and the low, may meet on a footing of equality. . . . It would keep the poor people from grumbling, as well as from revolutionary tendencies."[8] Such were the social ideas of the man, who, twenty years before, had pawned his watch for the Christmas holidays!

Leaving Europe after crossing and recrossing it on various trips, during which he had dined with kings and addressed peasants and met the great men from Thiers to Gladstone and Bismarck, Grant set forth early in 1879 for the Orient. Egypt and the Near East had been reviewed, and they went on to India, China, and Japan. As in Europe, the general sought for the "germs of progress," and found them in China's resources, and "wonderfully industrious, ingenious, and frugal people."[9] But it was for Japan that his highest encomiums were reserved. The country was beautiful, every foot was under cultivation, and the people from highest to lowest were kind in heart and clean in person. But the most impressive feature of Japan was the whole-souled

[7] Badeau, *Grant in Peace*, 305 ff.
[8] Cramer, *Conversations and Unpublished Letters*, 11.
[9] Badeau, *Grant in Peace*, 517.

manner in which they were adopting the material civilization of the Americans. To a man who had seen machinery in the process of conquering the American frontier, the spectacle of that same industrialism winning victories over Oriental medievalism was inspiring. After Europe's unwashed and germ-resisting masses, the cleanly Japanese appealed to Americans who had so recently become sanitation-conscious. Impressed with the country, Grant spent August in the island empire, being entertained more lavishly than at any other places on his tour. Everywhere he saw opportunities for American investments, and the beginnings of an Oriental policy formed in his mind. If only he were President—! [10]

Late in September, 1879, he arrived in San Francisco, after twenty-six months' absence from the United States. His return was by no means pleasing to his political friends in the Republican Party. During his absence, his successor had been having even more trouble than is usually the misfortune of the occupant of the White House. Surrounded by reformers, himself pledged to civil service reform, Hayes found arrayed against him a solid Democracy and the steadily increasing bitterness of his fellow Republicans. Conkling, with the figure and bearing of a Greek god, seemed to descend from Olympian heights to hurl sarcastic thunderbolts at the reformers, while regular Republicans cheered him to the echo. From Europe came evidence that Grant had heard—and approved.[11]

As each mistake of the Hayes Administration was recorded, the Grant Administration loomed brighter by contrast. Thanks to Young, Grant was more constantly in the public eye than he had been during the presidency, and the American people, reading Young's letters, could see their hero standing beside the great of the earth, dining with kings, and being received by statesmen. As Young portrayed these meetings, the ex-President compared more than favorably with the princes and potentates. Even Grant's provincialism pleased a people who had been taught to admire material achievements rather than bygone glories. If he would only remain in Europe until near election time—!

[10] The best source for Grant's trip is J. R. Young, *Around the World with General Grant*. Headley, *Life and Travels of General Grant*, was based on Young's dispatches to the New York *Herald* and this pirate book beat Young's to the public. See also Tyler Dennet in *American Historical Review* for Grant's Oriental policy.
[11] Babcock to Badeau, October 7, 1877, Babcock MSS.

Letter after letter from friends and associates begged the general to remain abroad. "They have designs for me which I do not contemplate for myself," he told Badeau.[12] But when he received more money from home he extended his plans for travel. Still, his mind was not made up whether he should permit his friends to push him for office, and, devoid of plans, he wandered, letting events shape their course. Not until Mrs. Grant's nostalgia for home and children forced him to sail homeward did Grant make a move not advised by his friends. When he did, he probably made a mistake. Had he delayed his return for six more months he might have received the Republican nomination in 1880.

During the ex-President's wanderings, the Grant boom was carefully nurtured by Hayes' opponents. A year before the general's return, newspapers were openly yearning for a "man of iron" to take the place of "a man of straw." The Grant movement, said one journal, was "the natural reaction of the Republican Party against the insipidity and imbecility of the present Administration."[13] Former Attorney-General Williams told interviewers that a third term for Grant was not only possible but highly probable,[14] while even Henry Adams could only think of Hayes as a "respectable nullity." In August, 1878, ten thousand people of Illinois attended a meeting where banners waved over them, announcing to the world that they were for "Grant for President in 1880."[15]

Grant's policies were subjected to scrutiny by those who would be glad to see him President. The achievements of the Hayes Administration were claimed for him, and men were eager to testify, in letters to the papers, that Grant had told someone that he would have withdrawn the troops from the South.[16] When, in the fall elections of 1878, the Republicans lost control of the Senate as well as of the House, political prophets were sure that the "election means Grant." Hayes had produced a Solid South which could only be met by a Solid North. And a Solid North could only be obtained for Grant. "You cannot realize," said Babcock to Badeau, "how deep the Grant sentiment has sunk into the minds of the people of the North."[17]

As this sentiment sunk deeper and took root in Northern minds, men

[12] Badeau, *Grant in Peace*, 316.
[13] St. Louis *Globe Democrat* quoted in New York *Tribune*, July 22, 1878.
[14] New York *Tribune*, July 24, 1878.
[15] Mt. Carmel, Ill. See N. Y. *Tribune*, August 10, 1878.
[16] See letter of Horatio N. Powers to N. Y. *Tribune*, August 24, 1878.
[17] Babcock to Badeau, (undated), Babcock MSS.

began to prepare the Grant bandwagon. The city council of Philadelphia wrote to their touring idol asking when he would return to his home city. They were prepared to make the occasion an official holiday! [18] As 1879 began, Republicans made ready to receive their hero with all the paraphernalia of shouting crowds, blaring bands, and military parades.

Deep though the sentiment for Grant might have been in the North, there were some whose memories were long enough to recall the actual conditions when Grant was in the White House. The Boston *Transcript* was convinced that his renomination would be a blunder which would "cast all Democratic errors in the shade." George William Curtis in *Harpers Weekly* was inclined to the belief that the enthusiasm for Grant was partly fictitious, and partly due to a fear of what Democrats would do with power.[19] Even Grant was hesitant. Ever sensitive, he dreaded the criticisms which the new boom would bring upon him. "I dread getting back," he wrote. "The clamor of the partisan and so-called independent press will be such as to make life there unpleasant for a time." [20]

Although the politicians believed his return premature, they made the best of it and gave him a reception unique in the annals of the nation. From the moment of his arrival in San Francisco until his leisurely journey had momentarily ended at Galena, Grant was entertained with banquets, bands, oratory, and parades in every city, town, and hamlet he deigned to visit. Cities invited him to visit them, Union Leagues planned receptions, and veterans of the Civil War turned out in thundering mobs to welcome their chieftain home.

From September, 1879, until the following January, Grant moved across the country in slow triumphal procession. At no time in the course of his reception did he make mention of the possibility of his becoming a candidate. When curious toastmasters introduced him with leading questions and pointed remarks, he evaded the issue. Privately, he told his friends, "I am not a candidate for any office, nor would I hold one that required any manœuvring or sacrifice to obtain." [21] Badeau, who knew him as well as anyone, attributed this unwillingness to declare himself to his obsession that he would fail to secure anything

[18] New York *Tribune*, October 28, 1878.
[19] *Ibid.*, April 30, 1879.
[20] Cramer, *Conversations and Letters,* 163–164.
[21] Badeau, *Grant in Peace,* 318.

that he tried to get. It was evidently not reluctance to hold the office, for Grant consulted the politicians at every train-stop. More than likely Badeau was right; forty years of failure had made indelible marks on Grant's personality. And the formula for success so far had been not to aim at it!

Despite his assertions to his friends, there is no doubt that Grant desired another term in the White House. Part of the reason was doubtless to be found in the inner recesses of his soul, where conflicting forces struggled for mastery. Sensitive to an extreme, he dreaded the criticisms which came with honors; yet pride, which could never forget the long years spent in crushing obscurity, drove him to hope even when he would not reach forth to obtain.

Equally potent as a driving force was the need of money. Some $100,000 in investments, together with houses, and some income from money in trust, constituted his possessions. Were he to live in a style befitting his station, he must have employment. "It must be employment or a country home," he wrote to Badeau. "My means will not admit of a city home without employment to supplement them." [22] At the moment, Admiral Ammen was dangling before his eyes the presidency of the Nicaragua Interoceanic Canal Company, which offered both honor and emolument. Grant was tempted, but the lure of the White House was upon him. He traveled on, met the politicians, heard them make glowing predictions, and, with an indecision which was by no means characteristic, held off Ammen's proposition until he could see if the politicians' dreams might come true. [23]

For a time the politicians who consulted the auspices were persuaded that Grant's nomination was inevitable. From all sections came indications that he alone could save the party. Iowa expressed a demand for him based partly on the uncertain finances, and partly on a desire for a strong leader to save the country from the domination of the Southerners who would control the next Congress. Grant, it was freely admitted, had made mistakes, but he alone could carry the party to victory. [24] From the East came a cry for a man safe on the currency question—free silver was raising its terrifying head in Washington. But it was from the South that the most insistent calls came. Despair-

[22] Badeau, *Grant in Peace*, 318.
[23] For the canal scheme see *Tribune*, August 28, September 10, November 26, 1879.
[24] New York *Tribune*, July 12, 1879.

AND THEY SAY, "HE WANTS A THIRD TERM"

RUMOR OF A THIRD TERM

ing Southern Republicans, abandoned by the Hayes Administration, looked to Grant to save them. "We may not be able to help much in electing a President," said one of them regretfully, but "I feel assured that much may be done toward breaking up a Solid South by the selection of a proper candidate." [25] The rebels, said another, "dread the strength of no one, as a Republican candidate, as they do his." [26]

But even when the Grant tide seemed to be running highest, it began to recede. In December, Grant went East, visiting Philadelphia, and passing on to Washington—which Hayes hastily left— [27] to spend Christmas. The constant round of receptions alarmed Republicans who were desirous of the nomination for themselves. Blaine, John Sherman, and a host of lesser aspirants were disturbed by the evidences of Grant's continued popularity. Soon it became plain that he had returned too soon. Logan, who, together with Washburne, was directing the Grant campaign in Illinois, noticed that local candidates were springing up all over the country, each trying to take some of the Grant strength. Moreover, he feared that the "reception business" was being overdone. "Country people" were objecting to the numerous receptions which Grant had received in Chicago. The general, Logan advised, should stay away from all but the largest demonstrations.[28] At the same time that Logan noticed the reaction of the country people and the local politicians, Washburne found that the Germans had no especial love for Grant. Moreover, he believed that Grant's visit to Washington was a bad move.[29] In addition, Washburne began to receive letters from men who said, "I shall vote the Republican ticket down to the last constable, but I shall *never* vote for Grant electors. . . ." [30] As the new year began, even the newspapers began to criticize Grant's pageant. He came as a politician, seeking office, declared the Philadelphia *Telegraph*, a Republican paper. "The people have had enough of him." [31] As one of Washburne's correspondents summed up the situation, there was an ebb in the Grant tide. "If he really wants to be President he came home too soon, and having come, he lingered in Philadelphia too long." [32] Convinced that Grant had made a mistake

[25] W. H. Gibbs, (Jackson, Miss.) to Washburne, October 18, 1879, Washburne MSS.
[26] Silas Reed, (St. Louis) to Washburne, November 8, 1879, Washburne MSS.
[27] Washburne to Logan, December 29, 1879, Logan MSS.
[28] Logan to Washburne, December 18, 1879, Washburne MSS.
[29] Washburne to Logan, December 29, 1879, Logan MSS.
[30] Caspar Butz, (Chicago) to Washburne, January 6, 1880, Washburne MSS.
[31] Cited in New York *Tribune*, January 8, 1880.
[32] Chas. H. T. Collis, (Philadelphia) to Washburne, January 14, 1880, Washburne MSS.

and that his continued presence in the country would lead to more, the Grant managers hustled him off for a visit to Cuba and Mexico. Perhaps—it was almost a hopeless wish—when he returned he could recapture some of his rapidly fading popularity.

With Grant in Cuba, the political lines rapidly formed. In the East, Blaine angled for the support of anti-Grant factions. In New York, Conkling, long an enemy of the Maine statesman, geared the State's political machine in favor of Grant. In Vermont there was a movement for Edmunds, while in Ohio John Sherman counted upon the state delegation. In other States, Treasury agents and a new "customs' house gang" worked for the Secretary of the Treasury. In Illinois, Sherman and Blaine men "hunted in couples" in a desperate effort to do "anything to beat Grant." Grant clubs vied with "Anti-Third-Term Clubs" for the support of the electorate. From all sections there came scattered voices in favor of Washburne. He could carry the German vote, and Grant men were inclined to name Grant's oldest political friend as second choice. Meantime, the New York *Tribune,* whose hatred of Conkling led it to take an anti-Grant position, began to gather statements from public men to the effect that Grant had no chance. Other ex-Liberal papers followed its lead, yet even the *Tribune* had to admit Grant was the strongest candidate in the field.[33]

While Grant saw Cuba's sights and passed on to Mexico for a month, his managers kept him advised on their progress. At Washburne's advice, he arrived in Galveston just as the delegates for the Texas State Convention were being chosen.[34] Acting through Fred Grant, Washburne advised the general to move rapidly on Illinois, approaching the State through Cairo, and thence by easy stages to Galena. At each stop the general should show himself. After reaching Galena, Grant was to make forays under Washburne's tutelage into neighboring counties.[35] All of this schedule was followed; enroute he visited his old headquarters in Memphis,[36] and prepared to arrive in Arkansas just as the State Convention assembled.[37]

[33] Letters from: W. E. Johnston, January 7; Chas. H. T. Collis, January 14; E. B. Cowdin, January 16; George Wellsmore, January 22; J. D. Platt, January 23; G. B. C., (Knoxville, Tennessee), January 30, 1880, to Washburne in Washburne MSS.
[34] Grant to Washburne, March 23, 1880, Washburne MSS.; N. Y. *Tribune,* March 25, 1880.
[35] Washburne to Logan, April 8, 1880, Logan MSS.
[36] New York *Tribune,* April 14, 1880.
[37] *Ibid.,* April 15, 1880.

As the State Conventions made their choices it was evident that the Grant men were losing ground. More and more the cry was heard that if he were nominated he would lose the election. The *Tribune* studied the votes of the conventions and decided that both parties had grown in strength since early in the year. The Democrats had gotten rid of Tilden, while the Republicans were eliminating Grant. The Democrats, said the *Tribune,* were less afraid of Grant than anyone the Republicans could nominate.[38] Thurlow Weed assured Washburne that Grant was the only man who could lose either New York or Pennsylvania.[39]

Illinois, however, was the critical point. Unless the general could go into the Convention with the almost unanimous vote of his home State he could not carry the election. Washburne was a veteran of a hundred political battles, and laid his plans carefully. When Grant arrived in Chicago, Washburne found him "calm as a summer evening and feeling fully assured of success." Buoyed by Grant's sanguine views, Washburne decided that failure was impossible and predicted a nomination by acclamation.[40]

Safely settled in Galena, Grant began to take an interest in the campaign. With never a word escaping him, he began to count votes, watch the State Conventions, and talk with his advisers.[41] His vigil, however, was not wholly pleasant. State Conventions gave votes to Sherman and Blaine, while anti-Grant conventions to select contesting delegations assembled in St. Louis and New York. By the middle of May the New York *Tribune* printed tables to show that Grant would have 224, Blaine 241, Sherman 91, Edmunds 31, and Washburne 13 votes when the convention opened.[42]

As it became evident that Grant would not have a majority in the convention, his managers hit upon a trick to count votes for their candidate. They would adopt the unit rule of the Democrats and thereby count 378 votes—and the nomination—for the ex-President.[43] Against this scheme all the other candidates united. Sherman instructed his men to coöperate with Blaine,[44] and faced with a unified opposition,

[38] New York *Tribune,* April 6, 9, 1880.
[39] A. J. Perry, April 20, and Thurlow Weed to Washburne, April 30, 1880, Washburne MSS.
[40] Washburne to Logan, April 30, 1880, Logan MSS.
[41] Badeau, *Grant in Peace,* 319 ff.
[42] N. Y. *Tribune,* May 6–10, 19, 20, 21, 1880; Logan to Mrs. Logan, May 9, 1880 and Grant to Logan, May 25, 1880, Logan MSS.
[43] N. Y. *Tribune,* May 11, 24, 25, 26, 1880.
[44] Sherman to General Nelson A. Miles, May 21, 1880, J. Sherman MSS.

Conkling consented to a compromise. The anti-Grant forces might nominate three men from whom Conkling would select the presiding officer. By this arrangement George F. Hoar was made chairman, and the scheme for forcing the unit rule on the convention was defeated.[45]

As the convention opened the unity of the anti-Grant forces became apparent. Several States declared against the unit rule, while defections from Grant were openly announced. Even in the New York delegation eighteen delegates signed a protest against the ex-President.[46] On two successive days Conkling lost on technical points to the anti-Grant men.[47] On the third day he offered a resolution pledging the delegates to support the nominee of the convention. On a vote, three members from West Virginia refused. Conkling then moved that they be expelled. In their defense, Garfield rose to speak, and the vote showed even Grant men in opposition.[48] Conkling recognized in Garfield's action that the Ohio delegate was the "dark horse" of the convention. He must also have recognized that in three days of skirmishing, the Grant forces had steadily lost strength.

On the night of the third day the candidates were presented to the convention. Jay of Michigan made a poor speech nominating Blaine. Then Conkling arose to present Grant:

> "When asked what State he hails from
> Our sole reply shall be—
> 'He hails from Appomattox
> With its famous apple tree.' "

It was wretched doggerel, but to the listening Grant men it seemed sublime poetry! The next election, said the speaker, was the Appomattox of American politics. The issue was whether the country should be Republican or Cossack. A candidate was needed who could carry New York! The oration was superb, and a forty-minute demonstration showed the enthusiasm of Grant's devotees.[49] Then Garfield nominated Sherman, and the convention adjourned until Monday.

Balloting was the first order of the new week. The first vote revealed the relative strength of the candidates. Grant received 304 votes, Blaine 284, Sherman 93, Edmunds 34, and Washburne 30. Three hun-

---

[45] New York *Tribune,* May 28, 29, 30, 31, 1880.
[46] *Ibid.,* June 1, 1880.
[47] Conkling, *Life of Conkling,* 588–589; N. Y. *Tribune,* June 4, 1880.
[48] Conkling, *Life of Conkling,* 591.
[49] N. Y. *Tribune,* June 6, 1880.

dred and seventy votes were necessary to nominate. Throughout the day the voting continued until 28 ballots were taken. Grant's strength varied little, going as low as 302 and as high as 309. Conkling's discipline over his forces was excellent and the lines were never broken. Blaine's strength, too, was steady, but not so certain as Grant's. His opening vote was the highest for the day—except for an extra ballot picked up on the thirteenth—and fell as low as 275 on some of the later ballots. Sherman increased slowly from 93 to 97, and ended with 91. Garfield received one vote on the second, added another on the seventh, and ended the day with two votes.[50]

Tuesday morning the balloting was resumed. The deadlock continued until the thirty-sixth ballot. Throughout the morning Garfield's strength grew. Blaine lost strength on the later ballots, going down to 257 on the thirty-fifth. On that ballot Sherman had 99, Washburne 23, and Garfield 50. At the end of the ballot there were shifts to Garfield, and as the thirty-sixth ballot was taken the Ohioan's strength sharply increased. When the shift had stopped, Blaine had declined to 42 true supporters, and Garfield had 399 and the nomination, while the Grant ranks were unbroken by the stampede. There were 306 delegates still voting for the Hero of Appomattox! Conkling arose to propose that the nomination be made unanimous. That afternoon the Grant forces got what little satisfaction they could from the choice of Chester A. Arthur, a Conkling henchman, for the second place.[51]

From the defeated candidate at Galena there came no indication of his disappointment. His closest friends, who had studied him after his return from Europe, were convinced the party had made a great mistake. In a new Administration, they were persuaded, Grant would avoid the mistakes of the old. Appointments would be made with more scrupulous attention to the moral merits of the appointee, and those close to Grant's mind realized that he had an Oriental policy which he wanted to try. A policy in regard to Mexico was also generating in his mind. If he were President, opportunities for the expansion of American investment would be created. Backed by the power of the nation, our capitalists would be able to develop the resources of the backward nations. "He was never so fit to be President as when his party rejected him," thought Badeau.[52] Yet, largely because the country could not

[50] N. Y. *Tribune,* June 8, 1880.
[51] N. Y. *Tribune,* June 9, 1880; Conkling, *Conkling,* 606; Hoar, *Seventy Years,* I, 278–93.
[52] Badeau, *Grant in Peace,* 319 ff.

believe in their calmer moments that Grant had changed, he was rejected. George F. Hoar, whose refusal to enforce the unit rule had beeñ the primary cause of Grant's defeat in the convention, decided, much later, that it was only Grant's bad appointments which caused him to be rejected. In his favor was "the solid confidence of the business men," the old soldiers, and the Methodist church.[53] What Hoar forgot was that Grant's candidacy ran counter to the ambitions of a growing number of politicians who believed themselves worthy of the nation's highest honor. The long-continued abuse to which the well-meaning President had been subjected had begun again, and the popular mind remembered the fiercest battles of Grant's two Administrations.

Twice elected by the politicians, Grant could little understand how he had been defeated. Logan persuaded him that Washburne had been guilty of a kind of personal treason, and although Washburne had remained steadfast, Grant never forgave him, and never spoke of him again without bitterness.[54] This alienation from his oldest friend is the best evidence of how greatly the general desired a third term. But however deeply he may have felt, no word of disappointment escaped him. Babcock, visiting him in Chicago, found him "quiet and philosophical as usual." [55] To Boutwell, Grant declared "I feel greatly relieved by the action of the Chicago Convention. I feel a great responsibility removed from my shoulders. I feel more indebted to my friends whose gallantry stood by me than if they had succeeded in their endeavors." [56] But this was rationalization; deep in his heart Grant felt no relief. However, he was not personally opposed to Garfield, and after a few weeks of nursing his wounds he began to work for the cause. Newspapers carried assurances that he was in favor of the Republican nominee.[57]

As the campaign progressed it became evident that Grant's statements to newspapers had not convinced his most loyal supporters that they should vote for the party's nominee. Garfield was especially anxious that he should declare himself more dramatically. From the beginning Sherman had doubted Conkling's sincerity,[58] and the nomi-

[53] Hoar, *Seventy Years,* 384 ff.
[54] Badeau, *Grant in Peace,* 322.
[55] Babcock to Badeau, June 27, 1880, Babcock MSS. "Mrs. G. not as tranquil," reported Babcock.
[56] N. Y. *Tribune,* July 2, 1880.
[57] *Ibid.,* June 14, July 4, 20, 1880.
[58] John Sherman to Wm. Dennison, June 9, 1880, Sherman MSS.

nee wanted some definite gesture from all the Grant men. Grant had said to some questioners that he would visit Garfield on his way East, and Garfield suggested to the National Committee that Conkling, Sherman, and Blaine should all meet with Grant and visit the candidate.[59] Not all of this delegation could be gathered, but arrangements were made for Grant and Conkling to come.[60] After a rally at Warren, O., the party journeyed the few miles to Mentor to take tea with the candidate they had assembled to honor. Democrats alleged that a "treaty of Mentor" was made there, but the participants denied any political agreement, and events indicated that whatever "treaty" was drafted between Conkling and Garfield was only a truce for the duration of the campaign.[61]

After his visit to Mentor, Grant became active in the campaign. Early in October he arrived in New York, where he was met by such political notables as Arthur and Tom Murphy, and subjected to a round of banquets and parades.[62] From New York he went to Boston, and then to Hartford. During the last two weeks of the campaign he appeared at meetings in New Jersey, Connecticut, and New York. At Utica he presided over a meeting, and at Syracuse and Rochester appeared in a new rôle. For some time, in fact ever since his European trip began, Grant had been slowly developing into a public speaker. In England he had learned to reply in platitudes to addresses of welcome. Returning to America, he continued to make responses of somewhat greater length than had been his custom. The burden of his public addresses was still that he was unable to make a speech. In fact, the returned tourist became so adept at explaining that he was no orator that he could extend his half-humorous remarks on the subject for a quarter of an hour. But in the campaign, he momentarily forgot his much practiced after-dinner speech and began to expound his position. With no hesitancy about dragging the bloody shirt into the campaign, he declared himself at Utica as being in favor of freedom of opinion in the South. At Syracuse he warned his hearers that the South would control the Democratic Party if it came into power, and "would sweep down with one stroke all your industries and prosperity, all of your banks and your manufactories and your industries of all sorts and

[59] Smith, *Garfield*, II, 1009.
[60] N. Y. *Tribune*, September 3, 1880; Garfield to Logan, Sept. 30, 1880, Logan MSS.
[61] Cf. Caldwell, *James A. Garfield*, 305–306.
[62] New York *Tribune*, October 10–12, 1880.

descriptions." At Rochester he expressed his fears of the "Rebel brigadiers" who would rule the nation. The country, said General Grant, must be governed by the Northern men! [63]

How much effect Grant's activity had on the election cannot be determined, but Chauncey Depew declared that Grant's "generous, unselfish and enthusiastic support" was "the greatest help which Garfield received" and brought into the fold the "whole of the old soldier vote." [64] Grant himself thought he was entitled to some credit for the victory, and immediately after the election proceeded to advise the President-elect on the proper course of the Republican Party. For his own part, he wanted no reward—he had received many favors at the hand of the people—but he would give advice.[65]

Not only did the ex-President advise the President-elect on policy, but also on appointments. After the election Grant was deluged by officeseekers beseeching his aid. Most of their letters he consigned to the waste-paper basket, but some were of such moment that he referred them to Garfield with his endorsement. Remembering his own attitude toward his Cabinet, Grant told Garfield: "Now of all places within the gift of the President the last one where unsolicited advice should be given is in regard to who [sic] should occupy so delicate a position as that of constitutional advisor to the Executive." [66] As for minor offices, the ex-President had no hesitancy in suggesting names. In December he gave unsolicited advice on the appointment of Southern men. In his opinion it was "wrong to Union men, North and South, to select men for such powers who were against us in the war and who have shown no sign of change since." But if one-time rebels had changed their minds, "I would not make their former opposition a barrier to their recognition now." [67]

All this gratuitous advice was not especially liked by Garfield, but he was too good a politician to ignore Grant entirely. On several appointments, he asked for the ex-President's advice and suggestions.[68]

[63] New York *Tribune*, October 22–30, 1880.

[64] Depew, *Memories,* 111. There is little room for doubt that Grant and Conkling together carried the day. Conkling, armed with money, went into doubtful Indiana and saved it by methods best understood by practical politicians. Grant devoted a month to the campaign.

[65] Grant to Garfield, Nov. 11, 1880, Garfield MSS. The letter has been extracted from the Garfield papers, and a note summarizing its contents substituted.

[66] Grant to Garfield, Nov. 19, 1880, Garfield MSS.

[67] *Ibid.,* Dec. 21, 1880.

[68] *Ibid.,* Dec. 29, 1880.

The Postmaster-General was chosen at the solicitation of Grant and Conkling, and, at the urgent suggestion of Grant and Logan, Robert Lincoln was made Secretary of War.[69] Grant did not attend the inauguration, explaining to Logan that "if I was there I would be obliged to dine at the White House on the 3rd to meet Garfield and all the Hayes Cabinet. I should like very much to meet Garfield and his wife, but I have no fancy for hobnobbing with John Sherman or Schurtz [sic]."[70] But a week later, Grant visited and was entertained at the White House.

Unfortunately, good relations did not last. Garfield ignored Grant's request that Badeau be left in the London consul-generalship, and soon Grant took Conkling's side in a quarrel with the President over the appointment of Collector of the Port of New York. The ex-President wrote vigorously to the White House, and gave his letter to the press. The letter, said the *Tribune*, "was written from as low a level of personal and factional politics as that occupied by Mr. Conkling himself and is nothing better than a hasty bungling plea in defense of the old spoils theory.—The letter will effectually destroy the belief which grew out of General Grant's wise and apparently unselfish conduct in the last campaign, that he holds himself above the contests of factions and the ambitions and animosities of place-hunters and patronage mongers."[71] Garfield tried vainly to mollify his predecessor, and suggested to his Cabinet that he call on Grant. The Cabinet disapproved, but some time later Grant spoke to the President and attended a reception in his honor.[72] Garfield was pleased, but hard feeling continued until Garfield's death. "Garfield," said Grant to Badeau, "has shown that he is not possessed of the backbone of an angleworm."[73]

This quarrel did much to terminate Grant's connection with politics. The *Tribune* thought he was but making "a hasty bungling plea in defense of the old spoils system." But even it was willing to admit that he was now impotent. The people, said the editor, had learned to turn from Grant's "occasional political mistakes" with a "Nevertheless."

---

[69] Smith, *Garfield*, II, 1072–1074, Jan. 28, 1881; Grant to Logan, Feb. 28, 1881, Garfield to Logan, Jan. 31, 1881, Logan MSS.
[70] Grant to Logan, Feb. 28, 1881, Logan MSS.
[71] N. Y. *Tribune*, May 20, 1881.
[72] Badeau, *Grant in Peace*, 328–331; Smith, *Garfield*, II, 1132–1134, 1174–1176.
[73] Badeau, *Grant in Peace*, 534.

FROM the time that the loyal 306 went down in defeat at Chicago, Grant's political career was closed. When an assassin, proclaiming himself a Stalwart, murdered Garfield, the bullet pierced the heart of the Grant and Conkling wing of the Republican Party. With Arthur, whom he had once appointed to the most lucrative job under the government, Grant's relations were strained. The President ignored the general's recommendations and followed the policy of conciliating the discordant factions while Grant looked on in uncomprehending disgust. "He seems more afraid of his enemies," said the general, ". . . than guided either by his judgment, personal feelings, or friendly influences." The remark throws considerable light on Grant's own Presidency.[1]

Removed from politics, Grant turned his attention to a search for employment. With all of his children married and well established in life,[2] Grant could look forward to a pleasant old age in the companionship of his devoted Julia, and, so long as he refrained from politics, the admiration and the devotion of the nation. However, as he wrote Badeau, "one thing is certain; I must do something to supplement my income, or continue to live in Galena or on a farm. I have not got the means to live in a city." [3] With no desire to spend his days in Galena, the general kept an eye open for business opportunities and showed, in his travels, a constant interest in factories, banks, and the stock market.[4]

Opportunities for employment were supplied by corporations which hoped to profit from the use of Grant's name. A gold mining company in New Mexico elected him its president; [5] and he was offered the presidency of the "New York World's Fair Commission." [6] But these enterprises were speculative and promised little emolument. Instead, he accepted the presidency of a Mexican railroad company, one of Jay

---

[1] Badeau, *Grant in Peace*, 334–339.
[2] Fred was in the army, attached to Sherman's staff. Both Jesse and "Buck" married during the campaign of 1880.
[3] Badeau, *Grant in Peace*, 350.
[4] Cf. N. Y. *Tribune*, Dec. 20, 1879.
[5] *Ibid.*, July 25, 1880.
[6] New York *Tribune*, January 7, 1880.

Gould's projects. During his visit to Mexico the previous winter Grant had become interested in the transportation system of the neighboring Republic. This was the "Mexican policy" which he was formulating while he was hoping for the Republican nomination. His decision to head an American company for building a line from Mexico City to the Pacific throws a light upon his Dominican and Oriental policies. He was a whole-souled believer in the expansion of American capital—a devotee of material progress. The presidency of such an enterprise appealed to his imagination. It identified him with the spirit of the age.

In April, 1881, accompanied by Mrs. Grant, his son "Buck" and his bride, and Senor Romero, ex-Minister to the United States, Grant again visited Mexico. In Mexico City Romero lobbied in the Government offices, and the Grant were entertained not only as distinguished guests but as visiting capitalists, Schemes were revolving in the minds of Romero and Grant to extend the Mexican Southern Railroad's lines northward to the American border.[7] The mission was successful; a contract with the Government was signed, Romero proceeded to obtain congressional approval, and the Grants returned to America.[8]

In the winter of 1882, President Arthur appointed Grant as American Commissioner to draw up a treaty of commerce with Mexico. Grant had devoted much of his time, since his return, to showing the business men of New York the necessity for developing commerce with the Mexicans. To the same Commission the Mexican Government appointed Senor Romero. The two friends found little difficulty in agreeing on a treaty, but suspicion was immediately aroused. Political enemies in Mexico City and Washington were not slow to point out the suspicious circumstance of partners agreeing, and were able to find in the treaties confirmation of their suspicions. Though both Grant and Romero denied collusion, the Senates of both countries rejected the treaty.[9]

Shortly after returning from Mexico, Grant became interested in the phenomenal success which his "Buck" was making in the banking business. He was in partnership with two other youths, James D. Fish and Ferdinand Ward. Ward was reputed a genius of finance, and after a meteoric rise as banker had agreed to take the young Grant into partnership. In a short time, "Buck" found that he had accumulated a

[7] New York *Tribune*, April 4, May 4, 1881.
[8] Badeau, *Grant in Peace*, 330–341; cf. Grenville M. Dodge, *Personal Recollections of President Abraham Lincoln, General Ulysses S. Grant, and William T. Sherman*, 883.
[9] Badeau, *Grant in Peace*, 396, 351–354; N. Y. *Tribune*, January 4, 24, 1883.

fortune of $400,000. He thereupon proposed to let his father into the business. With implicit faith in his son's ability, Grant invested $100,-000, all his liquid capital. Following him, Jesse put his savings, $10,000, into the firm. Mrs. Grant, Mrs. Corbin, and other members of the family also invested their money.

That Grant's capacity for business had not increased since the days when he failed as a rent-collector in St. Louis and let a stranger ride off on his brother's horse was demonstrated by his failure to study his new venture. Evidently Ward was running a business on pyramided borrowings, but Grant knew so little of the technique of finance that he could not ascertain its fragile character. When he invested, he demanded only that no money should be loaned to men with government contracts. Ward promised, and hastened to assure his creditors that there was collusion between Grant and Arthur by which the bank had a favored position, and was obtaining fabulous profits from contracting with the government.

It was a fool's paradise in which Grant was living. The man who as President had been considered "safe," who had vetoed the inflation bill and led the nation from the "rag-baby" to the Resumption Act, the friend of financiers who had sought a third term that he might further the overseas expansion of American capital, was demonstrating how money might be made in a land of opportunity—demonstrating it without knowing how his paper profits were obtained. Moreover, he spoke of it boastfully, telling friends of his mounting wealth. Badeau listened with suspicion and told General Porter. The latter, who knew something of banking and more about bankers, said that such profits could not be made honestly and went to warn his chief. But while they were talking, young Ward came in; Porter watched the warmth with which Grant welcomed the author of his fortunes and departed without saying anything. Porter knew too well Grant's attitude toward all who criticized his friends. Mrs. Grant had suspicions, but she believed in her husband, even more in her son, and held her tongue. Conservative bankers, friends of the general, knew Ward was dishonest, and kept silent out of respect for the man who had served them so well. Grant estimated his wealth at $1,500,000, and there was no one with courage to tell him that he was losing all he had.

The dream house could not long stand, but preceding the financial failure came physical misfortune. On Christmas Day, 1883, Grant was returning home from a round of social calls. As he turned to pay his cabman, he slipped on the icy street, rupturing a muscle in his thigh. In January, while still unable to walk, he suffered an attack of pleurisy which confined him to his bed for several weeks. Hardly had he regained sufficient strength to hobble about on crutches when financial disaster came.

On the night of May 5, 1884, Ward came to Grant to borrow money. Checks were outstanding which were not covered. He needed $150,000 for an immediate but temporary emergency. Listening to Ward's explanation, Grant offered to visit his friend W. H. Vanderbilt and ask for a loan. Vanderbilt bluntly told the general that he would not loan to Grant & Ward. He would, however, loan Grant anything he needed. Pledging his own faith, Grant carried Vanderbilt's check to Ward.

The next day the general went to his office. There he was met by his white-faced son, who broke the news that the bank had failed and Ward was gone. Unable to speak, Grant stumbled into his railroad office and slumped into a chair.

When he was able to go home he and the ever-faithful Julia went over their assets. He had $80 in cash in his pocket. Mrs. Garfield had $130 in the house—all that was left of their supposed fortune. Immediately he began to take stock. To Vanderbilt he consigned his New York house and his war trophies. Vanderbilt gallantly offered to turn them back to Mrs. Grant, but to save them from creditors the offer was refused. Vanderbilt deeded them to the Government. There were homes in Washington—Mrs. Grant offered them for sale, and they were taken. There was also a trust fund of $250,000—raised by subscription at the end of the war—but it was bearing no interest and was tied up in the estate of the executor. So far as the future was concerned the Grants were not poverty-stricken; but until something could be realized on their assets, they were destitute.

The public responded to the failure of Grant and Ward with complete sympathy for the ruined general. Outside of politics, Grant's hold on the people was as great as ever and no word of criticism was raised. No partisan questioned the wisdom or judgment of a man who would put all his eggs in one basket; no one made observations about Grant's inability to judge men. His connection with the firm was assumed to be "nominal," and the *Tribune* voiced a general sentiment by remarking "he has never had any aptitude for the kind of business in which the firm was engaged." Friends called to offer aid—and all were refused. But the Grants were especially grateful for two gifts. A letter came from Charles Wood of Lansingburg, N. Y., containing a check for $1,000— "On account of my share for services ending April, 1865." The other was from Romero, who called. When he left, Grant found a check for $1,000 on the table. Both loans were repaid with the first money Grant earned.[10]

One result of Grant's business failure was the production of his *Personal Memoirs.* Impoverished and in debt, the general devoted the last days of his life to writing an account of his war experiences. More and more as time passed, Grant forgot the unpleasant memories of his presidency and turned to the days of his success. In Europe he had been received as a great commander and most of his conversations there had been on the war. Everywhere in America men were willing to forget the partisan bitterness of his eight years in the White House and remember, instead, his days in the Wilderness. More friendly with soldiers than with politicians and financiers, Grant loved nothing better than to gather his one-time military associates about him and live again in the memories of a campaign. As a teller of war stories he had a volubility which never appeared on other subjects. Psychologically, the President was overshadowed by the general; with financial failure added to the bitter memories of his presidency, avenues of escape became even more necessary.

Some time before, while the general was still a master of finance, the Century Company asked him to prepare some papers for their projected series of "Battles and Leaders of the Civil War." At that time Grant felt no interest in the project, and replied that he had nothing to add to Badeau's *Military History of General Grant.* Somewhat later he tentatively agreed to give an interview on some of his battles, but this had not been done before the failure of Grant & Ward. After that failure the Century Company approached Grant, this time through Badeau, suggesting that the General might welcome a "diversion" "from his present troubles." Soon after, Grant wrote the publishers that he would write for the series, and an agent called at Long Branch, where the Grants were spending the summer. Agreements were made for four articles at $500 each.

[10] Badeau, *Grant in Peace,* 404–406, 418–419, 439; N. Y. *Tribune,* May 6–28, 1884; Cramer, *Conversations,* 172; Robert U. Johnson, *Remembered Yesterdays,* 211–213.

Grant immediately set to work, and within a few weeks had prepared a "dry official report" of the battle of Shiloh. The publishers were unable to use it, and an agent again called at Long Branch. Soon Grant was describing the battle with gusto and vividness, and the agent subtly suggested that it was such a description his company wished. Under the skilful tutelage of the Century agent, Grant rewrote the account. Soon thereafter, suddenly enamoured of his literary activity, he completed an article on Vicksburg. When he began writing on the Wilderness the general asked for and got one thousand dollars for the article.

The publication of these articles met with immediate success, and from all sides there came a demand for a book by General Grant. Pleased with his success, Grant announced that he would write his *Memoirs*. Immediately publishers swarmed to Long Branch. The Century Company expected the contract, but Mark Twain, of the Webster Company offered a far more liberal contract. Realizing the rich possibilities in the volume, the company offered the author seventy-five per cent on all domestic and eighty-five per cent on all foreign sales.[11]

But even this success could not be enjoyed. As cold weather approached, the general, now sixty-two, began to complain of pains in his throat. His family physician advised a specialist, who diagnosed the malady as cancer. By December, the general, working on his *Memoirs*, was suffering acutely from pains in his mouth.[12] In January he improved, and throughout February the writing went rapidly ahead. In March, however, he had a relapse, and in April had sunk so low that brandy was injected into his veins. Pain was constant, and for months Grant was unable to lie down. Sleep would not come, and through the long nights the sufferer remembered how well he had rested during the battles in the Wilderness. By day the general, with an obstinacy which showed that he had not changed since the war, drove himself to record his memories of his battles. To provide for his ruined family he bore his pain and raced with death to finish the book.

With the end inevitable, the *Memoirs* went rapidly forward. Badeau was employed to assist, and Fred Grant, who had resigned from the army before the failure of Grant & Ward and had gone down in the

[11] New York *Tribune*, July 27, 1885; *Letters of Richard Watson Gilder*, 123; Johnson, *Remembered Yesterdays*, 211–219.
[12] Badeau, *Grant in Peace*, 416, 426–427; Cramer, *Conversations*, 175–176.

crash, acted as amanuensis. Much of the book Grant dictated, but a large portion was written by his own hand when his illness made talking impossible. On May 23, 1885, the *Personal Memoirs*, dedicated to the "American Soldier and Sailor," were ready for the press.

The two large volumes produced by the dying commander constitute the ablest personal account of the Civil War. Beginning with his boyhood, the general told briefly of his days at West Point, in the army, and in the Mexican War. Then in detail he related his services from the first war meeting in Galena to Appomattox. For wealth and accuracy of detail the book was unique among war memoirs. Part of the accuracy was due to the guiding hand of Badeau, whose own writings had been facilitated by access to the War Department records, and whose notes were available to Grant. In telling the real truth about the war, the book fell far short of finality. It constituted, in fact, Grant's own rationalization of the struggle, based upon his reports of battles shortly after they were fought. In his hands these reports fitted into a well-rounded story of military strategy, carefully thought out and efficiently executed. Yet the story as told by Grant has been little modified by later writers. In part this is due to the peculiar merits of the book. Its style is simple yet dramatic; it shows a complete absence of personal bitterness. Sherman and Sheridan were praised immoderately and Ben Butler was allowed to escape without a phrase of criticism. When published, the *Memoirs* sprang immediately into the ranks of the "best sellers" and set a record for sales still unsurpassed in American publishing history. The liberal royalties restored the fortunes of the Grant family, and laid the foundations for Mark Twain's wealth and failure.

In his illness and his heroic struggle to provide for his family, Grant's full measure of popularity returned. The acclaim that came to Lincoln only after his assassination came to Grant as he sat tortured with death in his throat. When the general grew weaker crowds waited before his house; the attending physicians issued bulletins to the people, and newspapers carried daily accounts.

Popular sympathy for the dying leader was given tangible expression by Congress. From time to time since his retirement from the White House proposals had been made to restore him to his rank in the army, with the pay of a retired officer. Each time the movement failed, until at the close of the last session of Congress during Arthur's Administration it came up again. Finally, just as the Congress was ending its labors, the measure reached the calendar, having made its laborious way through Senate and committees. The bill bore the name of Samuel J. Randall, Democratic floor leader. Just before it on the calendar was an election contest. As the House was preparing to receive Cleveland, minutes before the end of the session, Randall moved to suspend rules and pass the Grant Relief Bill. The member in charge of the election case demanded that it be first considered. Deadlock faced the House when "Tama Jim" Wilson, whose seat was contested but who had sat throughout the session, sprang to the top of his desk and waved his arms for attention. He was willing, said "Tama Jim," to be sacrificed if the Grant Bill could go through. Inspired by this renunciation, the House impulsively passed it just as the galleries were filling with specta-tors for the inaugural ceremonies. Arthur, as the last act of his Ad-ministration, signed the bill; Cleveland, as the first act of his, appointed Grant to his former position. Democrat and Republican joined at last in honoring the nation's leading citizen— "The piercing rebel yell mingled with the applause of the Northern men," said "Uncle Joe" Cannon.[13]

The Grant family was delighted. Grant was very low when the news was brought to him by his wife. "Hooray," she cried, "we have our old General back again!" The honor was like a tonic to the dying soldier. The money was badly needed; the honor was a help in the long, sleepless nights when reproachful memories crept through the shadows.

If other evidence of popular good feeling were needed, it could be found in the host of visitors who came to the house in New York or sought the cottage on Mt. McGregor to which Grant was removed late in June. Soldier and politician, layman and cleric, Republican and Democrat, Confederate and Federal, called to pay their respect. For-rest, of Tennessee; Longstreet and Hancock; Conkling and Bristow; friend and foe came to express their sympathy and to bury their griev-ances. Those whom the general saw received renewed evidence of his friendship or his forgiveness for their past misunderstandings. Nothing warmed his heart more than the presence of Confederates among his visitors. In their coming he saw again the vision of a reunited nation.

During these trying days the Grant household was crowded. Nellie returned from England to be with her father, Jessie and "Buck" and

[13] Busbey, *Uncle Joe Cannon*, 303–306.

Fred with their families stayed at the bedside. The Rev. Dr. Newman of the Methodist Church attached himself to the household to give spiritual solace to the sorrowing families. Physicians were in constant attendance. As the general sank lower and lower one afternoon the doctors were barely able to detect the faint beatings of his heart. While medical experts injected brandy into Grant's veins, Newman seized a bowl of water and baptized the unconscious man according to the rites of the Methodist Church. As the patient revived, the cleric exclaimed: "It is Providence. It is Providence." "No," replied the scientist, "it was the brandy."

As July came, Grant was noticeably weaker, but there were periods when he was able, in his wheel chair, to go out of the house. On July 21 he went out, but a relapse followed. The next day was marked by a fit of hiccoughing which necessitated the injection of morphine. Under the drug the sufferer sank into a stupor. Once he rallied to mutter "water," and sank back again. At eight o'clock on the morning of July 23 relief came at last.[14]

In his death a nation mourned its loss. From Ohio, California, Missouri, and Illinois, from Vicksburg, Chattanooga, and Richmond, from Philadelphia, Washington, and New York, came sorrowing tribute. The mistakes of the politician were forgotten in the glories of the soldier and the heroism of the man. Not without significance, men carved above his tomb the words of his first political manifesto—"Let Us Have Peace."

---

[14] John Bach McMaster, *The Life and Memoirs . . . of General Grant;* Horace Green, "General Grant's Last Stand," *Harpers Magazine,* April, 1935, 532–540.

Bibliography

Abbott, John S. C., *The Life of General Ulysses S. Grant* . . . , Boston, 1868.

Adams, Charles Francis, *Lee at Appomattox and other papers*, Boston, 1902.

Adams, Charles Francis, *Chapters of Erie*, Boston, 1886.

Adams, Henry, *Letters of Henry Adams*, W. C. Ford Ed. New York, 1930.

Alexander, Augustus W., *Grant as a soldier*, St. Louis, 1887.

Allen, Walter, *Ulysses S. Grant*, Boston, 1901.

"An Old Army Officer," *Life and memoirs of General Ulysses S. Grant*, New York, 1885.

Ames, Mary C., *Ten Years in Washington* . . . , San Francisco, 1874.

Ammen, Daniel, *The old navy and the new*, Philadelphia, 1891.

"An American Citizen," *The great American empire, or General Ulysses S. Grant, emperor of North America*, St. Louis, 1879.

Appleton's annual cyclopaedie and register of important events, 1868–1880.

Babcock, Orville E., Manuscripts. Fifteen letters to Adam Badeau in Library of Congress.

Badeau, Adam, *Grant in Peace. From Appomattox to Mount McGreagor*, Hartford, 1867.

Balch, William Rawlston, *Life and public services of General Grant* . . . , Philadelphia, 1885.

Balch, T. W., *The Alabama arbitration*, Philadelphia, 1900.

Barnes, Wm. Henry L., *Grant, a study*, San Francisco, Calif., 1896 (a pamphlet.)

Barnes, Wm. Horatio, *Lives of General Ulysses S. Grant and Hon. Henry Wilson* . . . , New York, 1872.

Bard, Samuel, *A Letter from Governor Samuel Bard to President Grant on the political situation in Georgia and the South*, Atlanta, Dec., 1870.

Barrett, O. R., Private manuscript collection.

Beale, H. K., *The critical year, a study of Andrew Johnson and reconstruction*, New York, 1930.

Battles and Leaders of the Civil War. 4 vols., New York, 1887.

Beatty, John, "Ulysses S. Grant, a characterization sketch," *Ohio Archeological and Historical Society Publications*, XI, Columbus, 1903.

Bigelow, John, *Retrospections of an Active Life*, 5 vols., New York, 1909 to 1913.

Bigelow, John, *Life of Samuel J. Tilden*, 2 vols., New York, 1895.

Bigelow, John, *Letters and Literary Memorials of Samuel J. Tilden*, 2 vols., New York, 1885.

Belknap, W. W., Manuscripts, two papers in Library of Congress.

Black, Jeremiah Sullivan, Manuscripts, 1813–1904. 73 vols. Library of Congress.

Blaine, James Gillispie, *Twenty years of Congress* . . . , 2 vols., Norwich, Conn., 1884.

Bort, Ph. von, *Grant and the Jews*, New York, 1868.

Boutwell, George S., *Reminismences of sixty years in public affairs*, 2 vols., New York, 1902.

Boutwell, George S., *The lawyer, the statesman, and the soldier*, New York, 1887.

Boyd, James P., *Military and civil life of Gen. Ulysses S. Grant*, Philadelphia, 1885.

Boynton, H. V., "Whiskey Ring," *North American Review*, October, 1876.

Brisbin, James S., *The Campaign lives of Ulysses S. Grant and Schuyler Colfax*, Cincinnati, 1868.

Brinkerhoff, Racliff, *Recollections of a lifetime*, Cincinnati, Ohio, 1900.

Brockett, Linus Pierpont, *Grant and Colfax; their lives and services*, New York, 1868.

Brockett, Linus Pierpont, *Our great captains, Grant, Sherman, Thomas, Sheridan, and Farragut*, New York, 1865.

Brooks, Elbridge S., *The true story of U. S. Grant, the American soldier*, Boston, 1897.

Brown, E. E., *Life of Ulysses Simpson Grant*, Boston, 1885.

Brosius, Marriot, *In memoriam, Ulysses S. Grant*, Washington, 1900.

"Burleigh," *Caesarism, General Grant for a third Term*, New York, 1873.

Burr, Frank A., *A new original and authentic record of the life and deeds of General U. S. Grant* . . . , Philadelphia, 1885.

Burton, Alma Holman, *The story of Ulysses S. Grant* . . . , Chicago, 1898.

Busbey, L. White, *Uncle Joe Cannon*, New York, 1927.

Butler, Benjamin F., *Private and official Correspondence . . . during the period of the Civil War*, 5 vols., Norwood, Mass., 1917.

Butler, Benjamin F., *Autobiography and personal reminiscences . . . Butler's book*, Boston, 1892.

Butler, Benjamin F., Manuscripts, c. 50,000 letters in Library of Congress.

Bowers, Claude G., *The tragic era*, New York, 1929.

Caldwell, Robert J., *James A. Garfield: party chieftain*, New York, 1931.

Cannon, John, *History of Grant's campaign for the capture of Richmond*, London, 1869.

Campbell, Helen M., *Famous Presidents*, New York, 1903.

Carlton, Mabel Mason, *Ulysses Simpson Grant*, Boston, 1923.

Cary, Edward, *George William Curtis*, New York, 1894.

Chamberlain, D. H., *Charles Sumner and the treaty of Washington*, Boston, 1901.

Chandler, William E., Manuscripts. Library of Congress.

Childs, George W., *Recollections of General Grant*, Philadelphia, 1885.

Church, William Conant, *Ulysses S. Grant and the period of national preservation and reconstruction*, New York, 1897.

Coleman, Charles H., *The election of 1868*, New York, 1933.

Conkling, Alfred Ronald, *Life and letters of Roscoe Conkling, orator, statesman, advocate*, New York, 1889.

Coolidge, Louis A., *Ulysses S. Grant*, Boston, 1917.

Colfax, Schuyler, Manuscripts, two items, Library of Congress.

Comstock, C. B., Manuscript diary, 1863–1867, Library of Congress.

Conger, A. L., *The rise of U. S. Grant*, New York, 1931.

Coppée, Henry, *Life and services of General U. S. Grant*, New York, 1868.

Coppée, Henry, *Grant and his campaigns—A military biography*, New York, 1866.

Cortambert, L., and F. de Tranaltos, *Le général Grant*, New York, 1868.

Cortissoz, Royal, *The life of Whitelaw Reid*, 2 vols., New York, 1921.

Cox, Samuel S., *Union—disunion—reunion. Three decades of federal legislation, 1855–1885 . . .*, Providence, 1885.

Cox, J. D., "How Judge Hoar ceased to be attorney-general," *Atlantic Monthly*, August, 1895, vol. XXVI.

Crafts, William A., *Life of Ulysses S. Grant*, Boston, 1868.

Cramer, M. J., *Ulysses S. Grant, conversations and unpublished letters*, New York, 1897.

Cramer, Jesse Grant, *Letters of Ulysses S. Grant to his father and his youngest sister, 1857–1878*, New York, 1912.

Cross, Nelson, *Life of General Grant: his political record*, New York, 1872.

Crummer, Wilbur F., *With Grant at Fort Donelson, Shiloh, and Vicksburg, and an appreciation of General U. S. Grant*, Oak Park, Ill., 1915.

Cudmore, P., *President Grant and political rings. A Satire*, New York, 1878.

Cullom, Shelby M., *U. S. Grant*, Springfield, Ill., 1885.

Curtis, Geo. William, *The correspondence of John Lothrop Motley*, 2 vols., New York, 1889.

Cushing, Caleb, *The treaty of Washington*, New York, 1873.

Dana, Charles A., *Life of U. S. Grant, general of the armies of the United States*, Springfield, 1868.

Dana, C. A., *Recollections of the Civil War*, New York, 1898.

Davis, J. C. Bancroft, Manuscripts, 1856–1902, 54 vols., Library of Congress.

Davis, J. C. B., *Mr. Fish and the Alabama claims*, Boston, 1893.

Davis, William Watson, *Civil war and reconstruction in Florida,* New York, 1913.

Deming, Henry C., *Life of Ulysses S. Grant*, Hartford, 1868.

Denison, Charles Wheeler, *The tanner boy,* Boston, 1864.

Dennett, Tyler, *John Hay,* New York, 1933.

Depew, Chauncey M., *My memories of eighty years,* New York, 1922.

Dodge, Grenville M., *Personal recollections of President Abraham Lincoln, General Ulysses S. Grant, and William T. Sherman,* Council Bluff, Ia., 1914.

Dunning, William Archibald, *Reconstruction, political and economic,* New York, 1907.

Dunning, William Archibald, *Essays in the civil war and reconstruction and related topics,* New York, 1904.

Doolittle, James, Manuscripts. Wisconsin State Historical Society Library.

Edmonds, Franklin Spencer, *Ulysses S. Grant,* Philadelphia, 1915.

Elson, Henry W., *The story of a great general, Ulysses S. Grant,* Philadelphia, 1899.

Eckenrode, Hamilton J., *Rutherford B. Hayes, statesman of reunion,* New York, 1930.

Eckenrode, Hamilton J., *The Political history of Virginia during reconstruction,* Baltimore, 1904.

Fairchild, Lucius C., Manuscripts. State Historical Society of Wisconsin Library, Madison.

Ford, Worthington Chauncey, *Letters of Henry Adams (1858–1891),* Boston, 1930.

Fleming, Walter L., *Civil war and reconstruction in Alabama,* New York, 1905.

Fleming, Walter L., *Documentary history of reconstruction . . . ,* Cleveland, 1906.

Foulke, William Dudley, *Life of Oliver P. Morton.* 2 vols., Indianapolis, 1899.

Fuller, J. F. C., *The generalship of Ulysses S. Grant,* New York, 1929.

Garfield, James A., Manuscripts (including Manuscript Diary). 244 vols. Library of Congress.

Garland, Hamlin, *Ulysses S. Grant: his life and character,* New York, 1898.

Garner, James Wilford, *Reconstruction in Mississippi,* New York, 1901.

Grant, Jesse Root, *In the days of my father, General Grant,* New York, 1925.

Grant, Ulysses S., Manuscripts. 4 volumes of "letters sent" and about 20 scattered items in Library of Congress.

　　Manuscripts. Chicago Historical Society.

　　Manuscripts. Missouri Historical Society, St. Louis.

Grant, Ulysses S., *Personal Memoirs of U. S. Grant,* 2 vols., New York, 1885. (Also manuscript in Library of Congress.)

Grant, Ulysses S., *Speeches of General U. S. Grant,* Washington, 1868. (Campaign collection)

Grant, Ulysses S., *General Grant's letters to a friend, 1861–1880*, New York, 1897.

Grant, Hannah, Manuscript. One letter in Library of Congress.

Green, Horace, "General Grant's Last Stand," *Harpers Magazine*, April, 1935.

Henkels, Stan V. Jr., *Autograph catalogs*, Philadelphia, v. d.

Hamilton, J. G. De Roulhac, *Reconstruction in North Carolina*, New York, 1914.

Hart, Albert Bushnell, *Salmon Portland Chase*, New York, 1899.

Hart, B. H. Lidell, *Sherman: soldier, realist, American*, New York, 1929.

Hayes, Rutherford B., *Diary and Letters of*, Ed. Charles R. Williams, Columbus, Ohio, 1924.

Haworth, Paul Leland, *The Hayes-Tilden disputed presidential election of 1876*, Cleveland, 1906.

Headley, J. T., *The life and travels of General Grant*, Philadelphia, 1879.

Headley, P. C., and George Lowell Austin, *Life and deeds of General U. S. Grant*, Boston, 1885.

Hesseltine, William Best, *Civil war prisons—A study in war psychology*, Columbus, O., 1930.

Hoar, George F., *Autobiography of seventy years*, 2 vols., New York, 1903.

Holt, Joseph, Manuscripts. Library of Congress.

Harris, Wilmer C., *Public life of Zachariah Chandler*, Lansing, Mich., 1917.

Johnson, Robert Underwood, *Remembered yesterdays*, Boston, 1923.

Lee, Robert E. Jr., *Recollections and letters of General Robert E. Lee*, New York, 1904.

Lives of Grant and Colfax, Cincinnati, 1868.

Logan, John A., Manuscripts. Library of Congress.

Long, Mordenn, "Sir John Rose and the informal beginnings of the Canadian high commissionership," *Canadian Historical Review*, March 1931, XII, pp. 23–43.

Lynch, John R., *The Facts of Reconstruction*, New York, 1913.

Madigan, Thomas F., *Catalog of Autographs* and *A Catalog of Lincolniniana*, New York, v.d.

McClellan, George B., Manuscripts, 1863–1874, 94 vols., Library of Congress.

McCulloch, Hugh, *Men and measures of half a century*, New York, 1888.

McDonald, John, *Secrets of the great whiskey ring*, St. Louis, 1880.

McMaster, John Bach, *The life and memoirs, military career and death of General U. S. Grant . . .* , Philadelphia, 1884.

McPherson, Edward, *The political history of the United States during the period of reconstruction*, Washington, 1871.

Merriam, George S., *The life and times of Samuel Bowles*, New York, 1885.

Meade, George, *Life and letters of George Gordon Meade, Major General United States Army*, 2 vols., New York, 1913.

Moore, W. G., Manuscript diary. Library of Congress.

Motley, J. L., *The correspondence of John Lothrop Motley*, 2 vols., Ed. G. W. Curtis, New York, 1889.

Moore, John Bassett, *History and digest of international arbitrations to which the United States has been a party, etc.*, Washington, 1898.

Milton, George Fort, *The age of hate*, New York, 1930.

Milton, George Fort, *The eve of conflict—Stephen A. Douglas and the needless war*, Boston, 1934.

Mende, Elsie and Henry Greenleaf Pearson, *An American soldier and diplomat, Horace Porter*, New York, 1927.

Nevins, Allan, *The emergence of modern America*, New York, 1927.

Nicolay, John C. and John Hay, eds., *Abraham Lincoln, complete works*, New York, 1894.

Norton, Sarah, and M. A. De Wolfe Howe, *Letters of Charles Eliot Norton*, 2 vols., New York, 1913.

Oberholtzer, Ellis Paxson, *Jay Cooke, financier of the Civil War*, 2 vols., Philadelphia, 1907.

Oberholtzer, E. P., *A History of the United States since the Civil War*, 4 vols., New York, 1916.

Pearce, Haywood J., *Benjamin H. Hill: secession and reconstruction*, Chicago, 1928.

Pierce, Edward L., *Memoir and letters of Charles Sumner*, 4 vols., Boston, 1894.

Porter, Horace, *Campaigning with Grant*, New York, 1906.

Poore, Ben Perley and O. H. Tiffany, *Life of U. S. Grant*, New York, 1885.

Poore, Ben Perley, *Perley's reminiscences of sixty years in the national metropolis*, Philadelphia, 1886.

Richardson, Albert D., *A personal history of Ulysses S. Grant*, Hartford, 1868.

Ramsdell, Charles William, *Reconstruction in Texas*, New York, 1910.

Reid, Whitelaw, *After the war; a southern tour, May 1, 1865 to May 1, 1866*, New York, 1910.

Rhodes, James Ford, *History of the United States from the compromise of 1850 . . .*, 7 vols., New York, 1910–1919.

Richardson, James D., *Messages and papers of the Presidents*, vols. VI and VII, Washington, 1898.

Romero, Matias, *Speech of Senor Don Matias Romero, April 25, 1887, on the 65th Anniversary of the birth of Ulysses S. Grant*, Washington, 1887.

Schafer, Joseph, *Intimate letters of Carl Schurz, 1841–1868*, Madison, 1928.

Schofield, John M., *Forty-six years in the army*, New York, 1897.

Schouler, James, *History of the United States under the Constitution*, 7 vols., New York, 1913.

Schurz, Carl, *Reminiscences*, New York, 1907.

Scott, Hugh Lenox, *Some memories of a soldier*, New York, 1928.

Sherman, John, *Recollections of forty years in the House, Senate and Cabinet*, 2 vols., New York, 1895.

Sherman, John, Manuscripts; 80 volumes, Library of Congress.

Sherman, W. T., *Home letters of General Sherman*, (Ed.) M. A. De Wolfe Howe, New York, 1909.

Sherman, W. T. and John, *The Sherman letters, correspondence between General and Senator Sherman from 1837 to 1891.* (Edited by Rachel Sherman Thorndyke) New York, 1894.

Sherman, W. T., *Personal Memoirs*, New York, 1875.

Simkins, Francis Butler and Robert Hilliard Woody, *South Carolina during reconstruction*, Chapel Hill, 1934.

Smith, Theodore Clark, *The Life and letters of James Abram Garfield*, 2 vols., New Haven, 1925.

Smith, Nicholas, *Grant, the man of mystery*, Milwaukee, 1909.

Smith, W. F., *From Chattanooga to Petersburg under Generals Grant and Butler*, Boston, 1893.

Staples, Thomas S., *Reconstruction in Arkansas, 1862–1874*, New York, 1923.

Stevens, Walter Barlow, *Grant in St. Louis*, St. Louis, 1916.

Sumner, Charles, *The Works of Charles Sumner*, 10 vols., Boston, 1875.

Taylor, Alrutheus Ambush, *The negro in the reconstruction of Virginia*, Washington, 1926.

Taylor, Alrutheus Ambush, *The negro in South Carolina during the reconstruction*, Washington, 1924.

Taylor, Richard, *Destruction and reconstruction: personal experiences of the late war*, New York, 1879.

Thayer, William Roscoe, *The life and letters of John Hay*, 2 vols., New York, 1915.

Thompson, Charles Willis, *The fiery epoch, 1830–1877*, Indianapolis, 1931.

Thompson, Clara Mildred, *Reconstruction in Georgia, economic, social, political, 1865–1872*, New York, 1915.

Truman, Benjamin C., "Anecdotes of Andrew Johnson," *Century Magazine*, 1913, vol XXXXV.

Trumbull, Lyman, Manuscripts, 1855–1872, 77 vols., Library of Congress.

Warmoth, Henry Clay, *War, politics, and reconstruction; stormy days in Louisiana*, New York, 1930.

Washburne, E. B., Manuscripts, 89 vols., Library of Congress.

Weed, Thurlow, *Autobiography*. (Edited by his daughter, Harriet A. Weed) Boston, 1884.

White, A. D., *Autobiography*, New York, 1905.

White, Horace, *Life of Lyman Trumbull*, Boston, 1913.

Wilson, J. H. and Charles A. Dana, *Life of U. S. Grant*, Springfield, 1868.

Wilson, J. H., *Under the old flag, recollections of military operations, etc.*, New York, 1912.

Wilson, J. H., *Life of Charles A. Dana*, New York, 1907.

Wilson, James Grant, *Great Commanders, General Grant*, New York, 1897.

Wing, Henry E., "Stories of a war correspondent," *Christian Advocate*, Feb. 6, 1913.

Welles, Gideon, *Diary of Gideon Welles*, 3 vols., Boston, 1911.

Welles, Gideon, Manuscripts (including Ms. of Diary) Library of Congress.

Welles, Gideon, "Lincoln and Johnson," *Galaxy*, VIII, 1872.

Welles, Sumner, *Naboth's vineyard, the Dominican Republic, 1844–1924*, 2 vols., New York, 1928.

Young, John Russell, *Around the world with General Grant*, New York, 1879.

Index

461